New South Wales

Ryan Ver Berkmoes, Sally O'Brien, Miriam Raphael, Paul Smitz,
Rick Starey, Justine Vaisutis, Lucas Vidgen, David Millar

Contents

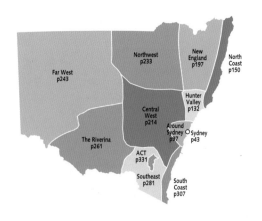

Destination: New South Wales

Given Australia's vast distances, New South Wales (NSW) is a very manageable place to visit, combining everything you could love – beaches, bush and a vibrant urban centre – in the one state.

Sydney, Australia's premier city, is reason enough to make the trek to NSW. Fast, bold and spectacular, the best things in Sydney are free: beaches, surf, mountains and the much-loved harbour. A few hours away, you'll find the historic towns and remote bushwalks of the Blue Mountains, while nestled in the temperate valleys further north are the wineries of NSW's wonderful Hunter Valley, worth every bit of its reputation for verdant charm seasoned with historical towns.

All-round, this state offers great variety. At the top of the Great Dividing Range, the misty rainforests of Washpool National Park are a World Heritage–listed site. Down south, the Australian Capital Territory (ACT) has some modern charms, including the museums of Canberra. If action is more your thing, the tallest peak in Australia, Mt Kosciuszko, lures skiers, climbers and hikers. NSW's legendary beaches start with Sydney's Bondi, and stretch hundreds of kilometres both ways. Want a beach with a vibrant scene? Head to Byron Bay. A beach that's a natural paradise? Eden, of course.

Inland, you'll find red-soil country and limitless horizons without having to travel to central Australia. Bourke is the legendary gateway to the outback, while remote yet refreshing Broken Hill combines iconic Aussie outback charm with a thriving Australian arts scene.

There's all you could want and more in the state with a bit of every part of Australia in it.

From the bright lights and sybaritic thrills of Sydney to the rustic beauty of the outback, New South Wales offers experiences for every taste and mood. Wineries, whales and walking trails are just some of the joys found in Australia's most populous and diverse state.

Cruise Sydney Harbour (p47)

RICHARD I'ANSON

GLENN BEANLAND

Browse for a bargain at Sydney's weekend markets (p93)

Look along George Street in The Rocks (p47) to the Sydney Harbour Bridge

GREG

PAUL BEINSSEN

Stretch out on the sand, soak up the sun and show off at Manly Beach (p56)

Take in spectacular views at the Bridal Veil Falls (p115) in the Blue Mountains

ROSS BARNETT

WAYNE WALTON

Mind the Gap (p54); stunning coastal cliffs at Sydney's eastern suburbs

RICHARD I'

Bathe in the first sunlight to touch the land, at the peak of Mt Warning (p194)

Make waves at The Pass (p181), one of the best surf spots in Byron Bay

JOHN BORTHWICK

Walk a straight line along the vines (if you can) in the Hunter Valley's marvellous wineries (p132)

OLIVER STREWE

WAYNE WALTON

Regain paradise in Eden (p328)

Fish and dive off the wharf at Merimbula (p326)

DAVID BRYANT

MATT ALEXANDER

Stumble on a rock formation at the Kosciuszko National Park (p290)

ROSS BARNETT

Wander the Garden of Australian Dreams at the National Museum of Australia (p338), Canberra

Sticker 'nother beer in the fridge at St Patrick's Race Day (p257), Broken Hill

Mine for opals at White Cliffs (p251)

Join the action at the annual Ute Muster (p278) in Deniliquin

Seek out the Walls of China (p259) at Mungo National Park

Getting Started

New South Wales (NSW) is – like much of Australia – a traveller-friendly, tourism-conscious place that provides options for travellers on all budgets. Combining many aspects of the country, it can be a good place to experience Australia in a relatively more compact form.

WHEN TO GO

Truth be told, any time is a good time to be *somewhere* in NSW. But remember, Australia's seasons are the antithesis of those in Europe and the USA. Summer starts in December (when the weather and longer daylight hours are perfect for swimming and other outdoor activities), autumn in March, winter in June and spring in September. The climate in NSW varies depending on the location, but the rule of thumb is that the further north you go the warmer and more humid it'll be. It's also hotter and drier the further west you go.

Sydney is lovely for much of the year. The temperature rarely falls below 10°C except overnight in winter, and although temperatures can hit 40°C during summer, the average summer maximum is a pleasant 25°C. The average monthly rainfall ranges from 75mm to 130mm. Much the same can be said for the climate on the coast, although the swimming season starts earlier by a month or more towards Byron Bay.

Canberra is cold in winter and scorching in summer, so spring and autumn are the best times to visit the Australian Capital Territory (ACT).

Inland, it gets hot soon after winter and just keeps getting hotter the further you get from the more temperate coast and highlands. The outback regularly stays above 40°C.

See Climate (p359) for more information.

Unless you want to compete with hordes of grimly determined local holiday-makers in 'Are we there yet?' mode – for road space, seats on all forms of transport, hotel rooms and camp sites, restaurant tables and the better vantage points for every major attraction – avoid the state's prime destinations during school and public holidays. See Holidays (p366) for more information. During these times, you're also likely to encounter mysterious, spontaneous rises in the price of everything from accommodation to petrol.

COSTS

The often-malnourished Australian dollar has made the country a fairly economical destination, which remains true even if the Aussie dollar becomes more robust. Manufactured goods tend to be relatively expensive, but daily living costs such as food and accommodation are relatively cheap.

DON'T LEAVE HOME WITHOUT...

- Double-checking the visa situation (p370)
- Sunscreen, sunglasses and a hat to deflect ultrafierce UV rays (p390)
- A sense of direction to stay oriented through the many traffic roundabouts
- Extra-strength insect repellent to fend off merciless flies and mosquitoes (p361)
- A willingness to call absolutely everyone 'mate', whether you know or like them, or not
- Good maps if you are heading west to the outback (p243)
- Your favourite hangover cure, especially if spending lots of time in Sydney (p86)

How much you should budget for depends on what kind of traveller you are and how you'll be occupying yourself. Seeing the sights, having a good time, staying in decent places and enjoying the often wonderful food will cost you $100 to $150 per person per day. But you can easily spend much more. Travellers with a demanding brood in tow will find there are many ways to keep kids inexpensively satisfied, including beach and park visits, camping grounds and motels equipped with pools and

TOP FIVES
MUST-SEE MOVIES

One of the best places to do your essential trip preparation (ie daydreaming) is on a comfy couch with a bowl of popcorn in one hand, the remote in the other and your eyeballs pleasurably glued to the small screen. Head down to your local video store to pick up these Australian flicks with a New South Wales bent. See p25 for reviews of some of these and other locally produced films.

- *Two Hands* (1999)
  Director: Gregor Jordan
- *The Dish* (2000)
  Director: Rob Sitch
- *The Year My Voice Broke* (1987)
  Director: John Duigan
- *Sirens* (1994)
  Director: John Duigan
- *Puberty Blues* (1981)
  Director: Bruce Beresford

TOP READS

They may literally be full of fiction, or invention, but when it comes to a good novel, even the most imaginative and unreal story will speak of truths that exist beyond the page. The following page-turners have won critical acclaim in Australia and abroad, not least because they have something to reveal to the reader about contemporary NSW issues, culture and relationships. See the Culture chapter (p26) for reviews of some of these, and other, books.

- *True History of the Kelly Gang*
  Peter Carey
- *The Idea of Perfection*
  Kate Grenville
- *The Showgirl & the Brumby*
  Lucy Lehman
- *Eucalyptus*
  Murray Bail
- *The Harp in the South*
  Ruth Park

FESTIVALS & EVENTS

Australians will seize on just about any excuse for a celebration – due as much to good-humoured exuberance, an enjoyment of the arts and an (often highly vocal) appreciation of sport as it is to an excuse to consume the output of its many fine vineyards and breweries. These are our top five reasons to get festive – other events are listed on p364, and throughout this book.

- Sydney to Hobart Yacht Race (p365)
  December to January
- Country Music Festival, Tamworth (p200)
  January
- Sydney Gay & Lesbian Mardi Gras (p61)
  February
- Surfest, Newcastle (p137)
  March
- Mudgee Wine Festival (p219)
  September

games rooms, junior-sized restaurant meals and youth/family concessions for attractions. For more information on travelling with children see p359.

TRAVEL LITERATURE

Considering Australia's enormous size and its social extremes – from cityscapes to isolation, yuppies to nomads – it's perhaps surprising that relatively little in the way of travel literature has appeared on this continental subject. That said, some inspiring, thought-provoking and just plain entertaining books have been written about this country – and NSW gets its fair share of attention.

Author Ruth Park scores with the eponymous *Ruth Park's Sydney*, an account which combines her lyrical prose with obvious affection and deep knowledge of the city.

There's nothing romantic about *Leviathan: The Unauthorised Biography of Sydney* by John Birmingham. The book looks at every seamy aspect of the town imaginable.

Noted novelist Peter Carey gives his own account of his home town in *30 Days in Sydney*. It's quirky, goofy and highly readable.

The Pilliga Scrub in the Northwest (p237) is the focus of *A Million Wild Acres* by Eric Rolls. The book looks at how settlers, failed farms and dead koalas combined to propagate the vast forest of today.

The River, by Patrice Newell, is a fascinating account of the Pages River (a branch of the Hunter River); political, environmental, and historical aspects of NSW flow through the book.

For comfortably predictable reading, pick up a copy of Bill Bryson's *Down Under*, in which the humorist takes his usual well-rehearsed potshots at a large target.

Finally, *The Fatal Shore* by Robert Hughes endures as a richly detailed and engrossing tale of England's convicts washing ashore in NSW.

INTERNET RESOURCES

Lonely Planet (www.lonelyplanet.com) Get started with summaries, links to related sites and travellers trading information on the Thorn Tree.

NSW National Parks & Wildlife Service (www.nationalparks.nsw.gov.au) Official site with reams of information on nearly 200 parks.

Sydney Morning Herald (www.smh.com.au) Site for Sydney's best paper, with plenty of news about what's happening in Sydney and NSW.

Tourism New South Wales (www.visitnsw.com.au) The state's tourism site has vast amounts of information on accommodation, activities and much more.

LONELY PLANET INDEX

One litre of petrol (city price) 80c to $1

One litre of bottled water $2 to $3

Glass of beer (Toohey's) $2.50

Souvenir T-shirt $20

Street treat (meat pie) $2 to $2.50

Itineraries

CLASSIC ROUTES

THE NORTH

Two weeks / Sydney–Byron Bay–Port Stephens

Wineries, country music, rainforests and stunning coast await north of Sydney. You'll find country markets tugging at your purse strings and beautiful beaches tugging at your drawstrings. It takes at least two weeks to cover this 1700km round trip.

Escape **Sydney** (p43) to the north and head straight for **Brisbane Water National Park** (p129), where walking among the springtime wild flowers will shake the city out of your system. It will also prepare you for a different kind of ramble through the Hunter Valley (p132): once you hit **Cessnock** (p140), prepare to settle in and make the rounds of the wineries.

For a change of pace, follow the New England Hwy northeast to **Tamworth** (p200) where beer is the drink, and country the music of choice. The music festival in January is a major draw. Keep north to **Glen Innes** (p207), where a jaunt west on the Gwydir Hwy will put you in **Washpool National Park** (p209). The World Heritage–listed park has craggy peaks, tall trees and rushing water that are otherworldly. Continue west to **Grafton** (p174) and head north on the Summerland Way. The far north coast hinterland is speckled with delightful little towns like **Nimbin** (p191), and all sorts of craft and food markets operate on weekends.

Make your way to the ocean in fun-filled **Byron Bay** (p180). From here you head south to Sydney along one of the most beautiful coasts in the world. Stops should include **Port Macquarie** (p157) and the coastal towns that make up **Port Stephens** (p152). On the way back, you can also stop at **Newcastle** (p135) for its surprisingly pleasant beaches.

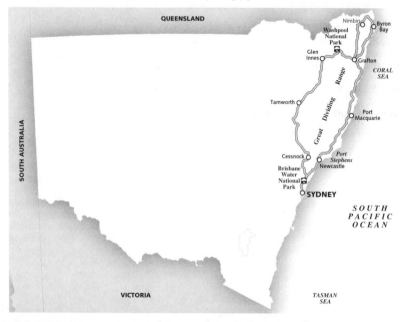

THE SOUTH

Two weeks / Sydney–Eden–Bathurst–
Blue Mountains National Park

From **Sydney** (p43), head south to enjoy the beaches, letting your fancy tell you when to stop to enjoy one; the clear waters at **Jervis Bay** (p313) and **Merimbula** (p326) – perfect for diving, snorkelling and swimming – will demand your attention. Continue south and catch the whales in the waters off the aptly named **Eden** (p328).

Then bid the azure seas farewell and head inland for the heights of **Kosciuszko National Park** (p290), using **Khancoban** (p298) or **Jindabyne** (p288) as bases for exploring the area. If it's winter, enjoy the ski resorts around **Mt Kosciuszko** (p290); otherwise, go for an alpine ramble.

From here, it's a short hop to the Australian Capital Territory (ACT) and **Canberra** (p336), where you can check out museums, galleries and either take a guided tour, or self-navigate your way, around Parliament House.

To really warm up, drive north into the Central West and stop at one of the many wineries scattered along the Olympic Hwy from **Young** (p231) northeast to **Cowra** (p229). The terrain here is anything but flat, with rivers carving deep canyons in places – Cowra clings to the side of a steep hill above the Lachlan River.

From Cowra, make for the Victorian streetscapes of history-soaked **Bathurst** (p216). Now turn east and climb along the Great Western Hwy into the **Blue Mountains** (p108); these hills abound with nature reserves like Blue Mountains and Wollemi National Parks. In summer people flock here to escape the heat in Sydney – avoid the crowds with some quiet bushwalking. Your legs comfortably stretched, continue east to Sydney.

This trip combines the wonderful coast with the urban charms of Canberra and the lofty heights of Mt Kosciuszko. Complete the trip with visits to a few wineries, and a ramble in the Blue Mountains. Covering all 1400km will take at least two weeks.

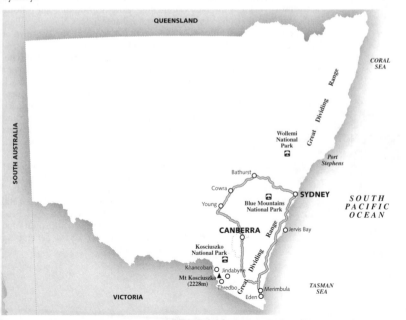

TAILORED TRIPS

DELIGHTS AROUND SYDNEY

In Sydney, head for the water at **Manly** (p56) and then north to the spectacular **Whale** and **Bilgola** (p57) beaches. Cross Broken Bay and take in the pleasures of **Bouddi National Park** (p130). Enjoy the coast to the north and head inland at Budgewoi to the Lower Hunter Valley. The wineries around **Cessnock** (p140) are superb.

Loop north from the valley and take Putty Rd south along **Wollemi National Park** (p108), NSW's largest forested area, to **Windsor** (p106), which is due west along the **Bells Line of Rd** (p118), the most scenic way through the Blue Mountains. Check out the **Mt Tomah Botanic Garden** (p118) along the way. Lithgow is a good place to turn east again and take the Great Western Hwy back into the mountains. Stop in **Katoomba** (p111) and sample tasty treats at its Art Deco cafés. Work off the cake with walks along the many remote trails in the **Blue Mountain National Park** (p108). You can spend days ambling about here – and you may as well, because the return trip to Sydney will take only a couple of hours.

GREAT WESTERN TOWNS

This trip begins fittingly enough on the Great Western Hwy. Enjoy **Katoomba** (p111) and the Blue Mountains before moving through historic **Bathurst** (p216), then on to sample the wines at **Orange** (p222). Now it's rolling, wild flower–bedecked hillsides till you get to **Dubbo** (p225), the last town of any size you'll see on this trip. Stock up at the many stores there.

Nyngan (p250) is a classic rural NSW town near the centre of the state. Continue on the Mitchell Hwy to **Bourke** (p245), a lovely respite on your

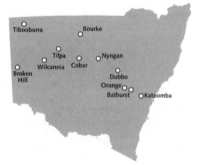

trip and the legendary gateway to the outback (the 'back of Bourke'). Your options from here are many: take the tracks west into the outback and **Tibooburra** (p249), or follow the Darling River southwest through **Tilpa** (p248) to **Wilcannia** (p251) – but note that this course is unsealed and impassable after rain. The easiest road is the one south from Bourke to semi-arid **Cobar** (p250); you'll see plenty of emus and kangaroos on this typically lonely route.

From Cobar it's 445km west to **Broken Hill** (p254) on the Barrier Hwy. A literal oasis, Broken Hill rewards the traveller with traditional rural tough-living culture and a developing Aboriginal arts scene.

The Authors

RYAN VER BERKMOES — Coordinating Author & Northwest

Ryan Ver Berkmoes has spent more time Down Under than in his native San Francisco in the past few years. In fact he's come to expect summer in December. From banging his head on the ceilings of caves in Lightning Ridge to splashing about in the surf near Byron Bay, he's explored no end of NSW delights. But he always finds time for yet another stay in Sydney where he takes pleasure in discovering yet another atmospheric pub on some side street. When not ordering yet another James Squire, Ryan works as a travel journalist.

My New South Wales

I keep checking the property prices in the far north hinterlands near Byron Bay (p188). The town itself is a perfect beach town with incredible sand, a laid-back vibe and great local walks. The little places to stay, well south of the centre, often make me wish to check in for a lifetime.

Inland, the oddball little towns like Nimbin (p191) are endlessly beguiling. I could easily spend day after day in the little weekend markets that dot the region. Who can resist farmhouse cheeses made by former hippies with a passion for organic food? Really the best thing to do is to get a nice little house with a big porch near the perfectly named Nightcap National Park (p191). You know, maybe I will.

SALLY O'BRIEN — Sydney

Sally has flitted back and forth between Sydney and other cities from a young age. One memorable stint in the harbour city lasted 25 years, but despite attending schools close to the eastern beaches, she didn't cut class, only learned to surf when she moved to Victoria and didn't appreciate beer gardens until she realised Melbourne's weather conspired against them. Now, on trips home, it's all part of her 'research'.

MIRIAM RAPHAEL — Central West, Far West & The Riverina

Miriam ate her way through the Far and Central West and the Riverina. Before this she tried hard to stay out of trouble but often fell by the wayside – dodging mafia men in Calabria, bullets in Nablus and aggro coastguards in Cyprus. She has worked as a radio producer, karaoke hostess and wilderness koala, none of which taught her anything about reverse angle parking, small-town cops or the absurd humour of outback Australia.

PAUL SMITZ
Australian Capital Territory

Paul lives in Melbourne but spent his (de)formative years grappling with the deceptive homogeneity of Canberra. He enjoyed revisiting the city to take a fresh look around its slow-paced environs, and to reacquaint himself with the natural beauty that lies within the Australian capital's territorial boundaries. Paul has also written about the ACT for Lonely Planet's *Australia* guidebook.

RICK STAREY
Hunter Valley, North Coast & New England

Rick updated the North Coast, Hunter Valley and New England chapters. This was his fifth road trip up the coast, and what better way than this to indulge his ongoing passion for fine wine, sandy beaches and the *real* Australia. Add in the rich history of all three areas and the great people who inhabit them, and you have a dream research project.

JUSTINE VAISUTIS
Around Sydney

Justine first became addicted to the nomadic lifestyle when she lived in South Africa and South Korea as a little tacker. Mostly, though, she grew up in Canberra, exploiting the Australian lifestyle every summer on the south coast of New South Wales. After completing an arts degree in Third World development studies, she decided it was more enjoyable to save the world by writing about it, and embarked on the noble career of travel writer.

LUCAS VIDGEN
Southeast & South Coast

Lucas first travelled to New South Wales in the back of an HQ Holden at the age of four. It must have made an impression because he's been travelling through, to and around there ever since. These days Lucas rarely asks 'Are we there yet?', but has been known to insist that his sister stay on her side of the back seat.

CONTRIBUTING AUTHORS

Dr Tim Flannery contributed the Environmental Challenges boxed text (p28) to the Environment chapter. Dr Flannery is a naturalist, explorer and writer. He is the author of a number of award-winning books, including *The Future Eaters* and *Throwim Way Leg* (an account of his adventures as a biologist working in New Guinea) and the landmark ecological history of North America, *The Eternal Frontier*. He lives in Adelaide where he is director of the South Australian Museum and a professor at the University of Adelaide.

Dr David Millar wrote the Health chapter (p386). Dr Millar is a travel medicine specialist, diving doctor and lecturer in wilderness medicine who graduated in Hobart, Tasmania. He has worked as an expedition doctor with the Maritime Museum of Western Australia, accompanying a variety of expeditions around Australia. Dr Millar is currently a Medical Director with the Travel Doctor in Auckland.

Snapshot

The burning issue in New South Wales continues to be bushfires. Although these conflagrations have been occurring with regularity for centuries, if not longer, it is the impact of growth that has made them the vital issue they are today.

The ever-escalating property prices in and around Sydney, coupled with population growth, has fuelled development in once-rural areas prone to bushfires. Each year the chance for huge loss of property and life increases.

In fact, even in areas of the coast where fires are less of a concern, growth is an important issue. Residents of a once-remote spot such as Nimbin voice concern about being priced out of their homes. Along the coast, one almost gets the sense that the hordes are due any day now. A quick visit to some of the developed horrors of the Gold Coast is enough to fuel any nightmare.

Conversely, a spot like Newcastle, once considered an industrial nightmare, is enjoying a renaissance thanks to the pressures of growth from the south, which forces companies and people to find more affordable areas. Once people push past the ring of factories, they find a town that can rival beach-side cities anywhere.

Meanwhile, in the relatively unpopulated interior (see p24), no one is worried about the crowds coming; rather, the main concern is the few left leaving. Populations in country towns are shrinking and farmers now have real reason to despair of having a generation to bequeath their lands to. Agricultural products are uncertain and many export products face gluts in world markets. Those who live in rural areas can only look on as the two-thirds of NSW's population who live in the Sydney region seem to get all the attention and services.

But despite the uncertainty and harsh conditions, NSW's country dwellers love their land and work hard to shore up their diminishing communities. And since wheat isn't the guaranteed livelihood it once was, farmers are having to diversify and try new crops in order to find a profitable market. A good example of agricultural success can be found in the ever-expanding wine-growing regions, which have been successful at marketing NSW wine to the world. Seeing how many travellers will happily trot off to see grapes growing on vines has led to the introduction of crops, such as olives and pecans, around Moree in the hope of luring consumption-minded travellers anxious to see their favourite foods in the wild.

One unifying conversational force throughout the pubs of NSW is – as always – politics. In a state where the Australian Labor Party (ALP) is serving its third term (p22) the policies of Prime Minster John Howard and the Liberal Party government are viewed with greater circumspection than in a more conservative place, such as Queensland. Premier Bob Carr has enjoyed a good run in NSW and, especially in political circles in Canberra, people wonder when, or if, he might make a play for the big time. And if Howard and company are cosy with the American administration, it's a warmth that's not universal. Although American travellers will encounter nothing but warmth, a Bush going for a ramble might find things rather chilly.

But these are mere quibbles, really. More often than not talk will centre on the latest reality-TV intrigue, and Australia's need to produce another major celebrity fast so that Nicole Kidman can be given a rest.

FAST FACTS

Population: 6.8 million

People: 94% European descent, 4% Asian, 1.8% Aboriginal

Sheep shorn: 34.4 million in NSW in 2003 – one-third of Australia's total

Average annual population growth rate: 1% for NSW, compared with 1.2% for Australia

Wine grapes harvested: 296,000 tonnes in 2003

Number of wineries in NSW: 367 in 2003

Average annual population growth rate: 1.3% in Sydney, -2.5% in the Far West

Median age of NSW brides and grooms: 28.3 years and 30.3 years respectively

Flag of New South Wales: a British Blue Ensign that sports the state badge. The flag was adopted in response to British Admiralty criticisms that the previous flag was too similar to that of Victoria.

History

ABORIGINAL AUSTRALIA

Aboriginal (which literally means 'indigenous') society in Australia has the longest continuous cultural history in the world, with origins dating to the last ice age. Although mystery shrouds many aspects of Australian prehistory, it seems almost certain that the first humans came here across the sea from Southeast Asia around 70,000 years ago.

They were the first people in the world to manufacture polished edge-ground stone tools, cremate their dead, and engrave and paint representations of themselves and the animals they hunted.

When Europeans arrived in New South Wales (NSW) in the late 18th century there were some 750,000 Aborigines in Australia, speaking a total of 250 regional languages – many of these languages as distinct from each other as English is from Chinese.

Aboriginal society, based on family groups rather than large political units, couldn't present a united front to the European colonisers, and in the crude realpolitik of the late 18th century, the British assumed that a people that didn't defend its land had no right to that land. Some Aborigines were driven away by force and thousands succumbed to disease.

Stuart Macintyre's *A Concise History of Australia* (1999) is easily the most readable account of the national past, while *Sydney's Aboriginal Past* by Val Attenbrow & Phillipe Erlanger (2002) is a detailed study of NSW Aboriginal history.

THE FOUNDING OF NEW SOUTH WALES

The inhospitable north and west coasts of Australia had been charted in the 1640s by Dutch explorer Abel Tasman, who had named the continent New Holland. It was not until 1770 that Captain James Cook, the British explorer, sailed up the fertile east coast, landing at Botany Bay and naming the area New South Wales.

Following the American Revolution, Britain was no longer able to transport convicts to North America. In 1786, with jails and prison hulks already overcrowded, it was decided that NSW would be a fine site for a colony of thieves.

In January 1788 the First Fleet sailed into Botany Bay (p99) under the command of Captain Arthur Phillip, who was to be the colony's first governor. Looking for greener pastures, the fleet with its 750 male and female convicts, 400 sailors, four companies of marines and enough livestock and supplies for two years, moved on to Sydney Cove.

The early settlement did it hard. The soils proved poor and the tools were worse. No relief came from England for 2½ years.

For the convicts, NSW was a harsh and horrible place. The reasons for transportation were often minor, and the sentences, of no less than seven years with hard labour, were tantamount to life sentences as there was little hope of returning home.

Hunger to the point of weakness afflicted most of the convicts. A farm was established at Parramatta (p103; today's Parramatta Rd basically follows the old cart track), where the soil was more fertile, and gradually the situation improved.

As crops began to yield, NSW became less dependent on Britain for food. However, there were huge social gulfs in the fledgling colony. Officers ran

DID YOU KNOW?

The New South Wales government's official website is a storehouse of facts and details about the state and has lots of news as well: www.nsw.gov.au.

TIMELINE	60,000–35,000 BC	1788
	The exact date is debatable, but Aborigines settle in Australia	The First Fleet arrives in Sydney Harbour with its cargo of convicts

the show and soldiers, free settlers and even emancipated convicts were beginning to eke out a living; yet the majority of the population was in chains, regarded as the dregs of humanity and living in squalor.

An effort to spur economic development led to land grants for non-convicts. The principal beneficiaries of the grants were the ruling officers now known as the NSW Corps. With money, land and cheap labour at their disposal, the officers became exploitative, making huge profits at the expense of everyone else.

RUM & REBELLIONS

To encourage the convicts to work, the officers paid them in rum. The officers quickly prospered and were soon able to buy shiploads of goods and resell them at huge profits as NSW became an important trade centre. Now known as the Rum Corps, the officers met little resistance and grew richer and more arrogant.

A new and ultimately infamous governor, William Bligh, was appointed to restore order, but the bad temper that had resulted in a mutiny on the *Bounty* again proved his ruin. He was arrested by the Rum Corps in an upheaval that gained a rather prosaic name: the Rum Rebellion. This proved the final straw for the British government, which in 1809 dispatched Lieutenant Colonel Lachlan Macquarie with his own regiment and orders for the return to London of the NSW Corps.

Now-governor Macquarie, having broken the stranglehold of the Rum Corps, set about putting the colony to rights. He instituted a building programme, employing talented convict architect Francis Greenway, several of whose buildings remain today (see Macquarie St, p51, and Windsor, p106). Macquarie encouraged explorers to find a route across the Blue Mountains and, when they did, had a road completed in just six months, then established the town of Bathurst (p216) on the plains beyond.

But all was not well. The gentry of Sydney Cove wanted nothing to do with ex-cons, while others – no doubt nostalgic for the anything-goes days of the Rum Corps – carped about the cost of Macquarie's public works and their employment of much of the local cheap labour. Macquarie returned to England under a cloud in 1821, but his reign had been a watershed for the colony. When he arrived it was a struggling penal settlement; when he left there was little doubt that a permanent and potentially wealthy colony had been established.

EXPLORATION & EXPANSION

While Sydney was consumed by various intrigues, bands of hardy explorers were busy exploring the continent that lay beyond the growing farms of Parramatta.

In 1819 a route to Bathurst from Cow Pastures (around Camden) was found, thereby opening up the southern highlands to graziers, and James Meehan explored a route from the southern highlands to the coast near Jervis Bay, finding still more fertile land.

In 1824 the explorers Hamilton Hume and William Hovell, starting from near present-day Canberra, made the first overland journey south-wards, reaching the western shores of Port Phillip Bay. On the way they

1824	1848
Hume and Hovell make the first overland trip from Sydney to Port Phillip Bay	The last boatload of convicts arrives in Sydney

discovered a large river and named it after Hume, although it was later renamed the Murray.

By the mid-1830s the general layout of present-day NSW was understood, and settlers eagerly followed the explorers' routes. The settlers often pushed into territory that was outside the defined 'limits of settlement', but the government inevitably expanded those limits.

In Sydney the growing wealthy class did its best to echo what it perceived as British culture. Buildings began to flaunt the colony's wealth, notably 1839's Elizabeth Bay House (p54).

The increasing number of large landholders began to debate whether convicts (cheap but unreliable) or the free-born (good workers but uppity and expensive) made better farm labourers. A growing minority wanted an end to transportation altogether. This view eventually prevailed and the last ship bringing convicts to NSW arrived in 1848.

Meanwhile NSW shrank. In the early 1800s, NSW comprised about half of the continent. The mainland colonies were progressively carved from NSW – South Australia (SA; 1834), Victoria (1850) and Queensland (1859). From *being* Australia, NSW became one of several Australian colonies.

The backbone of any sheep station in NSW is the Kelpie breed of sheep dog. Read all about these hard-working Aussie-bred pooches at www.australiankelpie.com.

GOLD, GLOOM & GROWTH

The discovery of gold in the 1850s brought about the most significant changes in the social and economic structure of the colony.

The large quantities of gold found at Ophir (near Orange, p222) in 1851 caused a rush of hopeful miners from Sydney, and for the rest of the century there were rushes throughout NSW and much of Australia. Certainly, without gold, it's hard to imagine how places like Broken Hill (p254) would ever have reached the size they did.

Although few people made their fortunes on the goldfields, many stayed to settle the country, as farmers, workers and shopkeepers. At the same time, the Industrial Revolution in Britain produced a strong demand for raw materials. With the agricultural and mineral resources of such a vast country, Australia's economic base became secure.

During the 1890s, calls for the separate colonies to federate became increasingly strident. A sense of an Australian identity, spurred by painters and writers, had grown and there were economic considerations as well.

With Federation on 1 January 1901, NSW became a state of the new Australian nation. But Australia's loyalties and many of its legal ties to Britain remained. When WWI broke out in Europe, Australian troops were sent to fight in the trenches of France and in the Middle East, including at Gallipoli in Turkey.

The site for Canberra (p334), the new national capital, was chosen in 1908 (after much bickering between Sydney and Melbourne), and the Australian Capital Territory (ACT) was created in 1911.

There was great economic expansion in the 1920s, but all this came to a halt with the Great Depression, which hit Australia hard. In 1931 almost a third of breadwinners were unemployed and poverty was widespread.

By 1932 the economy was starting to recover as a result of rises in wool prices and a rapid revival of manufacturing. With the opening of the Harbour Bridge (p48) in that same year, Sydney's building industry picked up again.

DID YOU KNOW?

Until the late '90s, bars in Canberra could be open 24 hours. Many still resent having to close from 5am to 8am.

1901	1932
The colonies of Australia unite to become a federation and NSW becomes a state, Sydney's population is 500,000	Sydney Harbour Bridge opens

ABORIGINAL ISSUES

By the early 1900s, legislation designed to segregate and 'protect' Aboriginal people imposed restrictions on Aborigines' rights to own property and to seek employment. The Aboriginals Ordinance of 1918 authorised the state to remove children from Aboriginal mothers and place them in foster homes or institutional care if it was suspected that the father was non-Aboriginal. This practice continued until the 1960s, resulting in bitterness that persists to this day, especially among those who have come to be known as the 'Stolen Generation'.

After WWII, 'assimilation' of Aboriginal people became the stated aim of the government. To this end, the rights of Aboriginal people were subjugated even further – the government had control over everything, from where Aborigines could live to whom they could marry.

In the 1960s this policy came under scrutiny, and non-Aboriginal Australians became aware of the inequities. In 1967 non-Aboriginal Australians voted to give Aborigines and Torres Strait Islanders the status of citizens, including the right to vote, and gave the federal government power to legislate for them in all states.

The years since have seen an ongoing coming to terms with the outrages of the past. Aboriginal land claims are a hot topic and where 'assimilation' was once the phrase in play, now it is 'reconciliation'. As legal and governmental decisions have come down in favour of Aboriginal rights, a large part of the populace publicly demonstrated their break with the policies of the past. National Sorry Day is just that, a day (now really a week) in late May when Australians show their contriteness over the past. A mass march over the Sydney Harbour Bridge in 2000 drew hundreds of thousands of participants from across NSW.

WWII & POSTWAR NSW

When WWII broke out, Australian troops again fought beside the British in Europe, but after the Japanese bombed Pearl Harbor Australia's own national security took priority. The Japanese advance was stopped by Australian and US forces in Papua New Guinea, and ultimately it was the USA, not Britain, that helped protect Australia from the Japanese.

In the postwar years, construction boomed again in Sydney and the city rapidly spread west. New immigration programmes brought growth, prosperity and lots of new Australians from Europe and Asia.

In NSW, long years of conservative rule ended in 1976 with the election of the Australian Labor Party (ALP). Ten years later the conservatives (who, unhelpfully for non-Australians, call themselves the Liberal Party) returned to power. Their goals were cleaning up the budget and landing the year 2000 Olympic Games. On the latter, at least, they won. In 1995 the ALP was elected under the leadership of Bob Carr. The ALP increased its margin in 1999 and did so yet again in 2003. Much credit for this goes to the party's relatively centrist policies and its ability to outspend the Liberals in key elections.

The last several years have seen Sydney – and to a much lesser extent the rest of NSW – boom. The 2000 Olympics helped ensure the city retains its swagger on the international stage. Development has run up against the Blue Mountains and many a hapless commuter makes two crossings daily of the hills. Up and down the coast, many seaside towns have shared the same property boom that has both vexed and beguiled Sydney residents. Inland, however, all is not so go-go in the 65% of NSW used as farmland. In some towns it might as well still be the 1950s, and globally depressed farm prices are a constant worry.

DID YOU KNOW?

White males in NSW were given the vote in 1857; women in 1902. Aborigines won the right to vote in 1967.

Recent politics takes centre (centrist?) stage in Andrew West's *Bob Carr – A Self-Made Man* (2003).

1967	2000
Aborigines are finally given the status of citizens	Sydney hosts the Summer Olympics to international acclaim (and Australia wins 16 gold medals)

The Culture

REGIONAL IDENTITY

Australia's national identity is rooted in its past. The seminal times of the colony of New South Wales were characterised by extreme hardship, resentment at being sent so far with so little, and an incalculable sense of loss of loved ones and homes left behind. To cope with this struggle against nature and tyranny, Australians forged a culture based on the principles of a 'fair go' and back slaps for challenges to authority, and told stories of the Aussie 'battler' that were passed down through generations.

The Eureka Stockade conflict (1854), one of Australia's first anti-authoritarian struggles, saw miners, or 'diggers', rising up against what they saw as unjust gold-mining licences. Ultimately the miners won out, but not before great loss of life. Although staged in Victoria, this event had a national impact. Some chose to see this battle as an age-old clash between the poor Irish Catholics and the ruling English Protestants, this time on foreign soil where the Irish had come to start life afresh and had no intention of returning to the status quo of old Britain.

The next major challenge to the Brits came with Gallipoli, fought on Turkish soil during WWI. The Australian and New Zealander contingent, the Anzacs, lost their bloodied conflict and blamed the Brits for sending them to fight a battle that could not be won. The Anzacs were revered as heroic battlers, remembered as those who showed the British and Europeans that Australians weren't just parochial colonials, but tough Aussies fighting with courage, honour and tenacity.

Ned Kelly is another of Australia's beloved heroes. Was Ned a thief and murderer, or a poor Irish hero, railing against a society diseased with injustice and poverty? Most Australians prefer to believe the latter account, of Ned as a true-blue Aussie battler, striving for equality and justice – and handsome to boot.

Immigration has had a huge effect on the influence of the early white settlers on Australian culture. Newcomers have brought their own stories, cultures and myths to meld with those of the colonial 'battler'. Many migrants have come with a huge sense of hope and expectancy, to start life afresh. Colonial history has been revisited through art, literature and cinema, and as a result, the iconic 'battler' has become less relevant. And there's a long-overdue acknowledgment that the original Aboriginal inhabitants of this country are fundamental to a true definition of Australian culture today. The immense prosperity the landscape has given has forged the title 'lucky country', the land of opportunity, and for most Australians this rings true. Australians enjoy a sophisticated, modern society with immense variety, a global focus, if not a regional one, and a sense of optimism, if tempered by world events.

Although there's some truth in the stereotypes that Australians are open-minded, down-to-earth, big-hearted, laconic, larrikin-minded, egalitarian and honest, these definitions are largely one-dimensional. Australian culture is much richer for its indigenous heritage and multicultural mix. So while on your travels in Australia you may hear 'g'day' from an Akubra-wearing, laconic, whiskery, bush larrikin, his voice will be but one among many. This exciting time of redefinition for multicultural Australia will throw unexpected people and experiences in your path. It's a young culture melding with the oldest culture in the world; and the incredibly rich opportunities are only starting to be realised.

True History of the Kelly Gang (Peter Carey) This Booker Prize–winning interpretation of Ned Kelly's trials brings him to life in language and spirit, with Carey's take depicting him as ultimate victim of an unjust system. Beautifully told and paced – you won't be able to put it down.

LIFESTYLE

Australians have been sold to the world as outdoorsy, sporty, big-drinking, croc-wrestling, thigh-slapping country folk. But despite the stereotypes, you could count the number of Australians that wrestle crocodiles on one hand, most Australians can barely swim a lap and many wouldn't be seen dead in an Akubra hat. Peek into the Australian lounge room and you may be surprised with what you find (although that's not to underplay the sporting life that infects parts of Sydney, especially its beachside communities).

The 'Australian Dream' has long been to own an overgrown house on a quarter-acre block, so sprawling suburbia is endemic in Australian towns and cities. Inside the average middle-class suburban home, you'll probably find a married heterosexual couple, though it is becoming increasingly likely they will be de facto, or in their second marriage. Gay marriage is not sanctioned by law in Australia, but most Australians are open-minded about homosexuality, especially in the gay mecca, Sydney.

Our 'Dad and Mum' couple will have an average of 1.4 children, probably called Joshua and Chloe, Australia's names of the moment (and yes, Kylie is still popular). The average gross wage of either parent is probably around $899 per week (compared to the UK's average of $1160).

Our typical family drags a caravan off to the beach every holiday, and on weekends they probably watch sport, go to the movies or head to the shops. And our couple likes a few quiet ones up the pub, though despite the long-held reputation that Australians are boozers, recent figures show they drink less than Brits. Today wine is the number-one drink of choice.

DID YOU KNOW?

Australia's state funding of professional sports is among the highest proportionally in the world.

POPULATION

Australia has been strongly influenced by immigration, and its multicultural mix is among the most diverse in the world. At the last census (2001) around 23% of the population were foreign-born, compared with an estimated 11.5% in the US. Many foreign-born Australians came from Italy and Greece after WWII, but recent immigrants are mostly from New Zealand and the UK, and from China, Vietnam, Africa and India among many other places. Some 2.2% of the population identify as being of Aboriginal origin.

Almost half of Australia's recent population growth is due to immigration, with NSW attracting the majority (38%) of newcomers. This helps account for the state's population growth of almost 1% a year. Like the rest of Australia, two-thirds of NSW's 6.8 million residents live in cities, primarily in Sydney (population just over four million) and its surrounds, with large concentrations up and down the coast. Inland, the small towns – many with little or negative growth – contribute to a population density that is the lowest in the world, with an average of 2.5 people per square km.

The autobiography *Cathy Freeman* gives great insight into the national and Aboriginal icon who was a gold-medal runner at the Sydney Olympics in 2000.

SPORT

In NSW, National Rugby League (NRL) games (www.nrl.com.au) are the spectator sport of choice. NRL players represent their states (NSW or Qld) in the annual State of Origin series. To see one of these games is to acquire a terrifying appreciation of Newton's law of motion: a force travelling in one direction can only be stopped with the application of an equal and opposite force. There are also international games, although they might as well be called 'Australia versus North England', or 'Australia versus New Zealanders who can't play union'.

Historically, rugby union was an amateur sport played by 'our sort of people, old chap' and its century-long rivalry with professional rugby league was the closest thing sport had to a clash of ideologies. In 1995, however, rugby turned professional and after years of 'defections' to league, the trend reversed with league stars such as Wendall Sailor and Lote Tuqiri crossing the fence to union.

The Wallabies is the national team. Apart from the World Cup (which everyone is trying to forget after 2003's loss to England), Bledisloe Cup matches against New Zealand are the most anticipated fixtures and form part of the Tri-Nations tournament that also includes South Africa.

At the time of writing, Australian cricket teams are the best in the world at both Test and one-day cricket. The men have not lost the Ashes to England since 1987. You will see cricket grounds throughout NSW, attracting local clubs of varying skills and professionalism.

Former Australian cricket captain Steve Waugh's *Never Say Die: The Inspiration Behind an Epic Hundred* is the autobiographical account of his amazing performance in the fifth Ashes Test in Sydney in 2003 at a time when critics said he should have retired.

ARTS

New South Wales has a thriving arts scene anchored by the big money of Sydney. Towns up and down the coast and in the mountains also attract their share of artists and as you explore the state you'll encounter many fine galleries and studios.

Sydney, by virtue of its population and stature, has a thriving music scene. Much of the action is around rock and pop. Local performers of note include long-time favourites the Whitlams, whose Sydney-centric material has managed to translate into popularity Australia-wide, and the rowdy punk energy of Frenzal Rhomb, whose live appeal to thrashing teenagers has to be seen to be believed. Other acts are the hard-to-define Machine Gun Fellatio; the pop band Waikiki; the talented Gelbison; Bondi-based noise-merchants Cog; and the most-hyped local act of the new millennium, the Vines. You can pretty much find any other musical genre you can imagine in and around the city.

Elsewhere in NSW, you'll likely here a lot of traditional rock with a lot of country and western as well (local popularity of the latter is inverse to the dryness of the landscape). Each year Tamworth's festival draws hundreds of thousands. Aboriginal artists often merge their traditional music with rock, hip-hop and other styles. Look for Yothu Yindi or Christine Anu.

Look for the CD *All You Mob*, a compilation of indigenous sounds assembled in Sydney. Notable is the song 'Down River' in which young Aborigines rap about their lives.

Cinema

Most people need little introduction to Australia's vibrant movie industry, one of the first established in the world and playground for screen greats Errol Flynn, local-lass-turned-world-celebrity Nicole Kidman and come-hither-eyed Russell Crowe (born in New Zealand, but who's trifling over details?). Construction of Fox Studios Australia in Sydney cemented the already healthy industry, which in addition to producing its own films has become a location of choice for many American productions drawn by Sydney's talent pool and – depending on exchange rates – relatively low costs. Big-budget extravaganzas, financed with overseas money and made for the overseas market, include *The Matrix* (featuring numerous Sydney skyscrapers) and *Mission Impossible 2*. Sydneysider Baz Luhrmann's *Moulin Rouge* was also made there, and starred 'our' Nicole.

Films from the 1990s such as *Strictly Ballroom*, *Muriel's Wedding*, and *The Adventures of Priscilla, Queen of the Desert* consolidated Australia's reputation as a producer of quirky comedies about local misfits. Actors who got their cinematic start around this period include Russell Crowe, Cate Blanchett, Heath Ledger, Toni Collette and Rachel Griffiths.

In the last few years most films made for an Australian audience have abandoned the worn-out ocker stereotypes and started to explore the country's diversity. Indigenous stories have found a mainstream voice on the big screen, with films such as *The Tracker, Beneath Clouds* and *Rabbit Proof Fence* illustrations of a nation starting to come to terms with its racist past and present. Cultural and gender stereotypes continue to erode in a genre of intimate dramas exploring the human dimension, such as *Lantana,* and *Head On*, the latter featuring a gay Greek-Australian as the lead character. By staying relevant to contemporary Australians, the industry continues to survive and thrive.

A few notable Australian films:

Bliss (1985, director Ray Lawrence) Kooky, sexual romp through the life of Harry Joy, Sydney advertising exec and spineless twit, and his appalling family.

Lantana (2001, director Ray Lawrence) Touted as a 'mystery for grown-ups', this is an extraordinary ensemble piece and deeply moving meditation on life, love, truth and grief.

Looking for Alibrandi (2000, director Kate Woods) A charming story of what it's like to grow up Italian in modern Sydney.

Muriel's Wedding (1994, director PJ Hogan) Life in suburban NSW is less than dull for Muriel. Things pick up after a tropical vacation, a name change and more.

Puberty Blues (1981, director Bruce Beresford) Southern Sydney's 1970s surf culture at its most 'perf'.

Sirens (1994, director John Duigan) Set at the home of writer and artist Norman Lindsay at Springwood in the Blue Mountains; when an English preacher drops by and models shed their clothes all sorts of fun ensues.

The Dish (2000, director Rob Sitch) Australia's role in the *Apollo 11* moon mission is explored in this warm-hearted film set at the satellite station at Parkes (p228).

The Year My Voice Broke (1987, director John Duigan) Classic look at NSW country life in 1962 Braidwood (p284). A coming-of-age story based on the triangular relationship of three adolescents learning to deal with the perceptions and prejudices of their townsfolk.

Two Hands (1999, director Gregor Jordan) A humorous look at Sydney's surprisingly daggy criminal underworld.

Literature

In the late 19th century, an Australian literary flavour began to develop through the Bulletin School (named after the magazine of the same name that is still available in Sydney), with authors such as Henry Lawson (1867–1922), AB 'Banjo' Patterson (1864–1941) and Miles Franklin (1879–1954), whose novel *My Brilliant Career* (1901) caused a sensation, especially when it was revealed that Miles was a woman.

The aftereffects of the Bulletin School's romantic vernacular tradition lasted many years, and it wasn't until the 1970s (a time of renewed interest in Australian writing) that images of the bush, Australian ideas of mateship and the chauvinism of Australian culture were fully questioned by readers and writers and a new voice began to make itself heard. This voice was more urban, and reflected the concerns of an increasingly confident Australia. Questions about the past were asked and assumed literary styles were found wanting; a uniquely Australian voice began to emerge. A rather quirky strain of 'magic realism' can be found in many recent Australian novels – an interesting quality, given the reputation of Australians for straightforwardness.

Australian writers of international stature include: Patrick White (winner of the Nobel Prize in Literature 1973), Thomas Keneally (Booker Prize–winner 1982), Peter Carey (Booker Prize–winner 1988 and 2001), David Malouf (International Impac Dublin Literary Award 1996), Murray Bail (Commonwealth Writers Prize 1999) and Kate Grenville (Orange Prize 2001).

DID YOU KNOW?

All the recent *Star Wars* prequels were largely shot at Fox Studios in Sydney.

The annual NSW Premier's Awards recognise the best local literary works in a number of categories. Winners are announced each May as part of the Sydney Writers' Festival (p60).
www.arts.nsw.gov.au /awards/LiteraryAwards /litawards.htm

Here are just a few excellent books with NSW settings:

Eucalyptus (Murray Bail) A fairy tale set among the iconic gum trees of remote NSW. A father sets high standards for his daughter's suitors, but she has other ideas.

The Harp in the South (Ruth Park) Accounts of an impoverished family's life in Surry Hills when the suburb was a crowded slum. In the 1980s this book was turned into a popular television miniseries.

The Idea of Perfection (Kate Grenville) Ideas and cultures clash when a Sydney museum curator goes to rural NSW to save an old bridge and meets a reticent engineer charged with destroying it.

The Showgirl & the Brumby (Lucy Lehman) Modern-day rural life in NSW is the focus of this novel about two girls and dreams lived and refused. Perfect context for your drives through fields of cotton and sheep.

Voss (Patrick White) Written in 1957, this novel contrasts the harsh and unforgiving outback with colonial life in Sydney. In the 1980s *Voss* was transformed into an opera, with a libretto by David Malouf.

Environment

THE LAND

There are four main geographical areas of NSW.

The strip of land between the sea and the Great Dividing Range runs from Tweed Heads on the Queensland border to Cape Howe on the Victorian border. The coast is lined with superb beaches and there are many bays, lakes and meandering estuaries.

The Great Dividing Range runs like a spine along the length of Australia's east coast. In the south of NSW the range rears up to form the Snowy Mountains, with Australia's highest peak, Mt Kosciuszko (2228m). The enormous Kosciuszko National Park (p290) protects much of the 'Snowies'. The eastern side of the range tends to form a steep escarpment and is mostly heavily forested. Most of the ancient range's peaks have been worn down to a series of plateaus or tablelands, the largest ones being the New England tableland, the Blue Mountains, the Southern Highlands and the Monaro tableland. Short, swift and bountiful rivers rise in the Great Dividing Range and flow east to the sea. In the north of the state these eastward-flowing rivers have large coastal deltas and are mighty watercourses.

The western side of the Great Dividing Range is less steep than the eastern and dwindles into a series of foothills and valleys, which provide some of the most fertile farmland in the country. Also rising in the Great Dividing Range, but meandering westward across the dry plains to reach the sea in SA, are the Darling and the Murray Rivers, and their significant tributaries such as the Lachlan and the Murrumbidgee. These rivers have often changed their sluggish courses, and the Murray-Darling basin takes in nearly all of the state west of the Great Dividing Range. The plains are riddled with creeks, swamps and lakes.

The western plains begin about 300km inland, and from here westward the state is almost entirely flat. On the western edge of NSW, Broken Hill (p254) sits at the end of a long, low range that juts into the state from South Australia (SA) and is rich with minerals. North of the Darling River, which cuts diagonally across the plains, the country takes on the red soil of the outback.

WILDLIFE

Most of Australia's many unusual types of wildlife can be abundant in NSW. The one real notable missing star is the deadly box jellyfish – so no loss there. Native animals you're most likely to see in the wild are wallabies and kangaroos, possums and koalas. However, there's a huge range of small, mainly nocturnal, animals going about their business unobserved.

Australia's most distinctive fauna are the marsupials and monotremes. Marsupials such as kangaroos and koalas give birth to partially developed young, which they suckle in a pouch. Monotremes – platypuses and echidnas – lay eggs but also suckle their young.

Animals

BIRDS

The only bird larger than the Australian emu is the African ostrich, also flightless. The emu is a shaggy-feathered bird with an often curious nature. After the female emu lays the eggs, the male hatches them and raises the young. Emus are common in the Riverina (p275) and the far west (p243).

Tim Flannery's *The Future Eaters* is a 'big picture' overview of evolution in Australasia, covering the last 120 million years of history, with thoughts on how the environment has shaped Australasia's human cultures.

DID YOU KNOW?

NSW has three UN World Heritage Sites: the Central Eastern Rainforest Reserves (p188), the Blue Mountains (p108) and Willandra Lakes (p259). whc.unesco.org /heritage.htm

There's an amazing variety of parrots and cockatoos. The common pink and grey galahs are noisy, although the sulphur-crested cockatoos are even louder. Rainbow lorikeets have brilliant colour schemes and in some parks accept a free feed from visitors.

A member of the kingfisher family, the kookaburra is heard as much as it is seen – you can't miss its loud, cackling laugh, usually at dawn and sunset. Kookaburras are common near the coast, particularly in the southeast.

The lyrebird, found in moist forest areas, is famous for its vocal abilities and its beauty. Lyrebirds are highly skilled mimics that copy segments of other birds' songs to create unique hybrid compositions. During the courting season, with his colourful fern-like tail feathers spread like a fan, the male puts on a sensational song-and-dance routine to impress potential partners.

The black-and-white magpie (no relation to the European bird of the same name) has a distinctive and beautiful warbling call.

Pizzey and Knight's *Field Guide to Birds of Australia* is an indispensable guide for bird-watchers, and anyone else even peripherally interested in Australia's feathered tribes. Knight's illustrations are both beautiful and helpful in identification.

DINGOES

Australia's native dog, the dingo is thought to have arrived in Australia around 6000 years ago. It was domesticated by the Aborigines, but after the Europeans arrived and Aborigines could no longer hunt freely, the dingo again became 'wild'. By preying on sheep (but mainly rabbits, rats and mice) dingoes earned the wrath of graziers. These sensitive, intelligent dogs are legally considered to be vermin. Some are still found in the high country.

KANGAROOS

The extraordinary breeding cycle of the kangaroo is well adapted to Australia's harsh, unpredictable environment.

The young kangaroo, or joey, just millimetres long at birth, claws its way unaided to the mother's pouch where it attaches itself to a nipple that expands inside its mouth. A day or two later the mother mates again, but the new embryo doesn't begin to develop until the first joey has left the pouch permanently.

At this point the mother produces two types of milk – one formula to feed the joey at heel, the other for the baby in her pouch. If environmental conditions are right, the mother then mates again. If food or water is scarce, however, the breeding cycle is interrupted until conditions improve.

As well as many species of wallabies (some endangered), there are two main species of kangaroos in NSW: the grey kangaroo and the majestic red kangaroo, which is common in the far west and can stand 2m tall. The no-nonsense reds have been known to disembowel dogs that bother them.

Kangaroos have an affinity for golf courses. You can spot them in more natural settings in national parks such as Murramarang National Park (p316) and Blue Mountains National Park (p108).

DID YOU KNOW?

The wedge-tailed eagle is found in NSW's open wooded areas. Its wingspan of 2.5m makes it the largest bird of prey in Australia.

KOALAS

Distantly related to the wombat, koalas are found along the eastern seaboard and inland in places like Gunnedah (p238). Their cuddly appearance belies an irritable nature, and they'll scratch and bite if sufficiently provoked. However, most of the time they resemble an inert fur bag asleep in high branches of trees.

Koalas initially carry their babies in pouches, but later the larger young cling to their mothers' backs. They feed only on the leaves of certain types of eucalypt (found mainly in the forests of the Great Dividing Range) and are particularly sensitive to changes to their habitat. The Macquarie Marshes (p240) is a good place to see the little fellas.

PLATYPUSES & ECHIDNAS

Despite anything an Australian tells you about koalas (aka dropbears), there is no risk of one falling onto your head (deliberately or not) as you walk beneath their trees.

The platypus and the echidna are the only living representatives of the monotremes, the most primitive group of mammals. Both lay eggs, as reptiles do, but have mammary glands and suckle their young.

The amphibious platypus has a duck-like bill, webbed feet and a beaver-like body. Males have poisonous spurs on their hind feet. The platypus is able to sense electric currents in the water and uses this ability to track its prey. Platypuses are shy creatures, but they occur in many rivers. Bombala, in the state's southeast, is a good place for platypus-spotting.

The echidna is a spiny anteater that hides from predators by digging vertically into the ground and covering itself with dirt, or by rolling itself into a ball and raising its sharp quills.

POSSUMS

There's a wide range of possums – they seem to have adapted to all sorts of conditions, including those of the city, where you'll find them in parks, especially around dusk. Some large species are found in suburban roofs; they eat cultivated plants and food scraps.

REPTILES

There are many species of snake in NSW, all protected. Many are poisonous, some deadly, but few are aggressive and they'll usually get out of your way before you realise that they're there. See Dangers & Annoyances (p361) for ways of avoiding being bitten and what to do in the unlikely event that you are.

There's a wide variety of lizards, from tiny skinks to prehistoric-looking goannas which can grow up to 2.5m long, although most species in NSW are much smaller. Goannas can run very fast and when threatened use their big claws to climb the nearest tree – or perhaps the nearest leg!

Bluetongue lizards are slow-moving and stumpy. Their even slower and stumpier relations, shinglebacks, are common in the outback.

WOMBATS

DID YOU KNOW?
Over 700 species of plants and animals are listed as endangered under the NSW Threatened Species Conservation Act.

The wombat is a slow, solid, powerfully built marsupial with a broad head and short, stumpy legs. These fairly placid, easily tamed creatures are legally killed by farmers, who object to the damage done to paddocks by wombats digging large burrows and tunnelling under fences. Like other nocturnal animals, they tend to lumber across roads at night and are difficult to see.

ENDANGERED SPECIES

The yellow-footed rock wallaby was thought to be extinct until a group was found in western NSW in the 1960s. National parks were created to protect them and local farmers agreed to protect them on their properties. But the wallabies can't compete with feral goats for food and shelter and their numbers are decreasing. They can still be seen in Mutawintji National Park (p253) northeast of Broken Hill.

INTRODUCED SPECIES

The Acclimatisation Society was a bunch of do-gooders in the Victorian era devoted to 'improving' the countries of the British Empire by introducing plants and animals. On the whole, their work was disastrous.

Exotic animals thriving in NSW include rabbits, cats (big, bad feral versions of the domestic moggie), pigs (now bristly black razorbacks with long tusks) and goats. In the Snowy Mountains and towards the Queensland border you might see wild horses (brumbies). These have all been disastrous for native animals, as predators and as competitors for food and water.

Probably the biggest change to the ecosystem has been caused by sheep. To make room for sheep the bush was cleared and the plains planted with exotic grasses. Many small marsupials became extinct.

Plants

Australia has a huge diversity of plant species – more than Europe and Asia combined.

The eucalyptus – often called the gum tree – is everywhere except in the deepest rainforests and the most arid regions. Of the 700 species of the genus *Eucalyptus,* 95% occur naturally in Australia.

Gum trees vary in form and height. Species commonly found in NSW include the tall, straight river red gum; the stunted, twisted snow gum with its colourful trunk striations; the spotted gum common on the coast; and the scribbly gum, which has scribbly insect tracks on its bark. Eucalyptus oil is distilled from certain types of gum trees and used for pharmaceutical and perfumed products.

Around 600 species of wattle are found in Australia. Most species flower during late winter and spring, when the country is ablaze with the bright yellow flowers and the reason for the choice of green and gold as the national colours is obvious. The golden wattle is Australia's floral emblem.

INTRODUCED SPECIES

The majestic Norfolk Island pine, naturally enough a native of Norfolk Island, lines the foreshores of many coastal towns in NSW. There are many other introduced species – most, such as oaks and willows, brought in by homesick settlers to replicate their homeland. One of the most outstanding introduced trees in NSW is the jacaranda. In spring and summer, its vivid mauve or blue flowers bring a splash of colour to many towns around the coast and the ranges.

Some introduced plants have also caused major problems by choking out native flora and pastures. Noxious weeds such as Paterson's curse (viper's bugloss) can be found growing wild in many parts of the state.

NATIONAL PARKS

There are close to 200 national parks and protected areas in NSW, covering about four million hectares and protecting environments as diverse as the peaks of the Snowy Mountains, the subtropical rainforest of the Border Ranges and the vast arid plains of the outback. Some parks include designated wilderness areas that offer outstanding remote-area walking.

The **National Parks & Wildlife Service** (NPWS; ☎ 1300 361 967; www.nationalparks .nsw.gov.au) does a good job, and many national parks have visitors centres where you can learn about the area, as well as camp sites and often walking tracks. Where there isn't a visitors centre, visit the nearest NPWS office for information. Bush camping (ie heading into the bush and camping where you please) is allowed in many national parks, but not all – check before you go.

There are car entry fees for 44 of the more popular national parks: generally around $3 to $10 per car ($15 per car per day for Kosciuszko National

The Australian Conservation Foundation (ACF) is the largest nongovernment organisation involved in protecting the environment.
www.acfonline.org.au

DID YOU KNOW?

If you're going to visit a lot of national parks in NSW, consider an annual pass to cover the cost of entering the 44 parks that charge daily vehicle entry fees. There are four options ranging from $20 for any one designated park (excluding Kosciuszko National Park) to $80 for access to all parks.

ENVIRONMENTAL CHALLENGES *Tim Flannery*

The European colonisation of Australia, commencing in 1788, heralded a period of catastrophic environmental upheaval, with the result that Australians today are struggling with some of the most severe environmental problems to be found anywhere. It may seem strange that a population of just 20 million, living in a continent the size of the USA minus Alaska, could inflict such damage on its environment, but Australia's long isolation, its fragile soils and difficult climate have made it particularly vulnerable to human-induced change.

Damage to Australia's environment has been inflicted in several ways, the most important being the introduction of pest species, destruction of forests, overstocking rangelands, inappropriate agriculture and interference with water flows. Beginning with the escape of domestic cats into the Australian bush shortly after 1788, a plethora of vermin – from foxes to wild camels and cane toads – has run wild in Australia, causing extinctions in the native fauna. One out of every 10 native mammals living in Australia prior to European colonisation is now extinct, and many more are highly endangered. Extinctions have also affected native plants, birds and amphibians.

The destruction of forests has also had a profound effect. Most of Australia's rainforests have suffered clearing, while conservationists fight with loggers over the fate of the last unprotected stands of 'old growth'. Many Australian rangelands have been chronically overstocked for more than a century, the result being extreme vulnerability of both soils and rural economies to Australia's drought and flood cycle, as well as extinction of many native species. The development of agriculture has involved land clearance and the provision of irrigation, and here again the effect has been profound. Clearing of the diverse and spectacular plant communities of the Western Australian wheatbelt began just a century ago, yet today up to one-third of that country is degraded by salination of the soils. Between 70kg and 120kg of salt lies below every square metre of the region, and clearing of native vegetation has allowed water to penetrate deep into the soil, dissolving the salt crystals and carrying brine towards the surface.

In terms of financial value, just 1.5% of Australia's land surface provides over 95% of agricultural yield, and much of this land lies in the irrigated regions of the Murray-Darling Basin. This is Australia's agricultural heartland, yet it too is under severe threat from salting of soils and rivers. Irrigation water penetrates into the sediments laid down in an ancient sea, carrying salt into the catchments and fields. If nothing is done, the lower Murray River will become too salty to drink in a decade or two, threatening the water supply of Adelaide, a city of over a million people.

Despite the enormity of Australia's biological crisis, governments and the community have been slow to respond. It was in the 1980s that coordinated action began to take place, but not until the '90s that major steps were taken. The establishment of Landcare (an organisation enabling people to effectively address local environmental issues; www.landcareaustralia.com.au) and the expenditure of $2.5 billion through the National Heritage Trust Fund have been important national initiatives. Yet so difficult are some of the issues the nation faces that, as yet, little has been achieved in terms of halting the destructive processes. Individuals are also banding together to help. Groups such as the Australian Bush Heritage Fund (www.bushheritage.asn.au) and the Australian Wildlife Conservancy (AWC; www.australianwildlife.org) allow people to donate funds and time to the conservation of native species. Some such groups have been spectacularly successful; the AWC, for example, already manages many endangered species over its 1.3 million acre holdings.

So severe are Australia's problems that it will take a revolution before they can be overcome, for sustainable practices need to be implemented in every arena of life – from farms to suburbs and city centres. Renewable energy, sustainable agriculture and water use lie at the heart of these changes, and Australians are only now developing the road-map to sustainability that they so desperately need if they are to have a long-term future on the continent.

Tim Flannery is a naturalist, explorer and writer. He is the author of a number of award-winning books. Tim lives in Adelaide where he is director of the South Australian Museum and a professor at the University of Adelaide.

Park, p290). Camping fees are about \$2 to \$9 per person, and sometimes free for bush camping with limited facilities.

The NPWS is also responsible for some other reserves. State recreation areas often contain bushland, but the quality of the forest might not be as good as in national parks. Many are centred on lakes or large dams where water sports are popular, so they can be crowded in summer. There's often commercial accommodation (usually a caravan park), and bush camping is usually not permitted. There are exceptions to this, however.

Nature reserves are generally smaller reserves, usually with day-use facilities, protecting specific ecosystems.

Historic sites protect areas of historical significance, such as the ghost town of Hill End (p219) near Bathurst and Aboriginal rock-art sites.

STATE FORESTS

State forests, used for timber harvesting, conservation purposes and public recreation, cover around three million hectares. Bush camping (free) is allowed in most state forests, as are trail bikes, 4WDs, horses and pets. Often there are designated walking trails.

Brochures and maps are available from the **State Forests Information Centre** (☎ 02 9980 4100; www.forest.nsw.gov.au). These forests are administered by State Forests of NSW, which has regional offices and forest centres around the state.

DID YOU KNOW?

Almost two million hectares of park land is protected wilderness areas, close to 2% of NSW. Such areas are considered largely untouched by modern human activity.

44

New South Wales Outdoors

Although New South Wales (NSW) provides plenty of excuses to sit back and do little more than roll your eyes across some fine land and seascapes, those same 'scapes lend themselves very well to any number of energetic pursuits, whether it's on the rocks, wilderness trails, and mountains of dry land, or on the offshore swells and reefs.

There's world-class surfing in NSW, and the beaches themselves are justifiably famous – from those radiating glitz to ones where it will be only you, the sand and the surf. On land, cycling, bushwalking and skiing are popular; the many national parks in the state offer lots of good places to explore.

NSW's varied terrain and climate mean that you can probably find a place with just the right features and conditions for just about any activity you wish to pursue.

Local professionals can set you up with equipment and training. Climbing Australia has excellent info on rock climbing in NSW. www.climbing.com.au

ABSEILING & ROCK CLIMBING

Fantastic sites for rock climbing and abseiling include the Blue Mountains, especially around Katoomba (p111) and Warrumbungle National Park (p237). Climbing Bald Rock (p210), the largest granite rock in the southern hemisphere, is a challenge that rewards with great views.

BIRD-WATCHING

NSW is a twitchers' haven, with a wide variety of habitats and birdlife, particularly water birds. **Birds Australia** (☎ 02-9436 0388; www.birdsaustralia.com.au; PO Box 1322, Crows Nest, NSW 1585) runs feathered-friend observatories and nonprofit reserves in NSW and is an excellent source of information.

Lonely Planet's *Walking in Australia* provides detailed information about bushwalking.

BUSHWALKING

Opportunities for bushwalking abound in NSW, with a huge variety of standards, lengths and terrains available. Almost every national park has marked walking trails or offers wilderness walking.

In Sydney, try the jaw-droppingly beautiful Bondi to Coogee Walk (p58) or the wonderful 9km-long Manly Scenic Walkway (p56). The walkway also has a 2km-long wheelchair-accessible path. Near Sydney there are popular walks in the Blue Mountains (p108) and Royal National

PUBLIC LIABILITY

Huge increases in the cost of public liability insurance around Australia in the past few years have forced the closure or scaling back of numerous tours and organised outdoor activities such as horse riding and rock climbing, and threatened the viability of many small businesses. Also at risk are volunteer-run community events that have been unable to get affordable insurance.

The exorbitant insurance costs faced by small businesses and volunteer organisations have been blamed on a vast range of issues: the relatively recent collapse of several major Australian insurance companies; insurance industry greed; some ridiculously high legal pay outs awarded to people for minor incidents; a growing culture of litigation; low safety standards; and ambulance-chasing lawyers seeking the biggest pay out possible.

Federal, state and territory representatives have met several times to discuss the problem and at the time of writing appeared to have agreed on measures to reform negligence law. But these are yet to be fully implemented and, in the meantime, more businesses may go to the wall by the time you read this book.

CONSIDERATIONS FOR RESPONSIBLE BUSHWALKING

Please consider the following when hiking, to help preserve the ecology and beauty of Australia.

■ Do not urinate or defecate within 100m (320ft) of any water sources. Doing so can lead to the transmission of serious diseases and pollutes precious water supplies.

■ Use biodegradable detergents and wash at least 50m (160ft) from any water sources.

■ Avoid cutting wood for fires in popular bushwalking areas as this can cause rapid deforestation. Use a stove that runs on kerosene, methylated spirits or some other liquid fuel, rather than stoves powered by disposable butane gas canisters.

■ Hillsides and mountain slopes are prone to erosion; it's important to stick to existing tracks.

Parks (p101), with the wilderness areas of Wollemi National Park (p108) not far away.

In fact, for a good walk, you can't go wrong in most national parks. The hiking and walking in and around Barrington Tops National Park (p148), a world heritage site in the Hunter Valley, is superb. In the Southeast's Kosciuszko National Park (p290), you can walk to the summit of Australia's highest peak, Mt Kosciuszko, and branch off onto a number of other alpine trails.

In the northwest, there are many good walks around Warrumbungle National Park (p237).

Far west in the outback, you can enjoy being taken on a guided bushwalk in Mutawintji National Park (p253) by the land's traditional owners.

Longer routes include the three-day Six Foot Track (p117) to the Jenolan Caves. The Great North Walk (p129) from Sydney to Newcastle can be walked in sections, or covered in a two-week trek.

The eponymous Hume & Hovell Walking Track (p301), from Yass to near Albury, follows the route of two early explorers, and passes through some beautiful high country. It can be walked in sections, or done in a trek of up to 25 days.

Outdoor stockists are good sources of bushwalking information. Alternatively, the Confederation of Bushwalking Clubs NSW maintains a large website with lots of useful information. www.bushwalking.org.au

CANOEING & KAYAKING

A good place to have your initial kayaking adventure is right in Sydney Harbour (p57) – although it is busy and can be challenging for a novice.

Many of NSW's waterways are suitable for canoeing, with adventurous runs on the short, swift rivers flowing to the coast and inland from the Great Dividing Range, and long, lazy treks on the meandering inland rivers.

There's good white-water rafting on the Upper Murray River. Another exciting place to run the rapids is the Nymboida River (p209) in New England.

CYCLING

Those who cycle for fun have access to great cycling routes and touring country for day, weekend or even multiweek trips, while very experienced pedallers can consider trips through the outback or a tour of the coast. Sydney (p57) has a recreational bike-path system and an abundance of bike-hire places. Canberra (p342) is another good place for cycling, with a large network of bike paths.

Longer-distance rides in NSW are limited only by your endurance and imagination. The coast is an obvious choice with parks, beaches and little towns constantly providing reasons to dismount. The Hunter Valley (p132) and Blue Mountains (p108) can provide good challenges and, again, offer much beyond just the open road.

Contact the New South Wales Canoeing Association (☎ 02-9660 4597) for information on canoe and kayak courses and hire. www.nswcanoe.org.au

Conversely, the northwest and west to the outback are notable for their open roads. In the more moderate months, you can enjoy long-distance rural rides on roads relatively untravelled, without running the risk of becoming summer-scorched roadkill. Some good cycling organisations:

Bicycle New South Wales (☎ 02-9281 4099; www.bicyclensw.org.au; Level 5, 822 George St, Sydney; 9am-5.30pm Mon-Fri) Excellent organisation; a stop by the office for advice, maps and books is worthwhile. Publishes the mighty fine *Cycling Around Sydney*, which details routes and cycle paths in Sydney, the Blue Mountains, Illawarra and the Central Coast. It publishes other booklets on cycling in the state.

Bicycles Network Australia (www.bicycles.net.au) Excellent omnibus website.

Pedal Power ACT (☎ 02-6248 7995; www.pedalpower.org.au)

> See Lonely Planet's *Cycling Australia* for other useful contacts and details of popular routes.

DIVING

Sydney has many good spots for shore dives (p57), including the Gordons Bay Underwater Nature Trail, north of Coogee; Shark Point, Clovelly; and Ship Rock, Cronulla. Popular boat dive sites are Wedding Cake Island, off Coogee; around the Sydney Heads and off Royal National Park. Elsewhere in NSW, the waters around Jervis Bay (p314), Ulladulla (p315), Narooma (p320) and Merimbula (p326) are among the more popular. Diving outfits typically offer four-day Professional Association of Diving Instructors (PADI; www.padi.com) dive courses from around $350.

SAILING

Sydney Harbour is one of the world's great – and most photogenic – sailing locations. If you're in the city, you might as well feel the wind at your back and the spray in your face. There are plenty of sailing schools in Sydney (p58). Even if you don't want to become a master diver, an introductory lesson can be a fun way of getting out on the harbour.

Elsewhere in NSW, you'll find little marinas littering the coast like high-priced flotsam. At most you'll find an opportunity to take lessons or just pitch in and help crew a yacht. The best places for information are the local sailing clubs.

SKIING & SNOWBOARDING

Australia has an enthusiastic skiing industry, with snowfields straddling the NSW–Victoria border. But the season is relatively short, running from about mid-June to early September, and snowfalls can be unpredictable. Nor are the mountains ideal for downhill skiing – their gently rounded shapes mean most long runs are relatively easy, and the harder runs short and sharp. Worse, short seasons mean operators have to get their returns quickly, so costs are high.

> The Skiing Australia website has links to major resorts and race clubs. www.skiingaustralia.org.au

The good news is that when there's snow and the sun is shining, the skiing can be superb. At the resorts, you'll find lively nightlife, decent restaurants, fine scenery and slopes to keep you interested. And families are well catered for with most resorts offering programs and lessons for children, plus there are usually a few tubing hills for the youngest snow bunnies. The aptly named Snowy Mountains (p292) in and around Kosciuszko National Park hold the top places to ski: resorts such as Charlotte Pass, Perisher Blue, Selwyn and Thredbo, which tend to get crowded on weekends. Note, during winter heavy penalties apply if drivers don't carry snow chains – even if there's no snow.

Cross-country skiing is popular and most resorts offer lessons and hire out equipment. Kosciuszko National Park includes some of the country's best trails, and often old cattle-herders' huts are the only form of accommodation, apart from your tent.

SURFING

It was summer, 1915. Hawaiian waterman Duke Kahanamoku demonstrated the art of surfboard riding before a packed grandstand of Australians. He'd carved a board from local timbers before taking to the ocean at Freshwater, on Sydney's north shore.

For more information, news, surf cams and photos, look up www.coastalwatch.com.

Today, compared to Australian surfing's humble beginnings, the scene is rip and gouge. Aussies flock to the coast in record numbers searching out the next new swell. But given Australia's vast coastline and relatively small population, there are still days when you, like the Duke, could be the only one out.

Australia boasts several world champions and many world-class breaks. Name practically any coastal town in NSW and there will be good surf nearby.

Sydney's beaches (p54 and p57) are well known for their good surf too; check out www.realsurf.com for surf reports. Manly, Dee Why, Narrabeen and Avalon are the most popular northern beaches. To the east of Sydney check out the areas around Bondi, including Tamarama, Coogee and Maroubra, and to the south, past Botany Bay, there's good surf around Cronulla.

For daily reports call the Surf & Snow Line on (☎ 1900 911 525).

On the far north coast are Byron Bay (p180), Lennox Head (p179) and Angourie (p177), while on the mid-north coast are Coffs Harbour (p168) and Nambucca Heads (p164). On the lower north coast are the beaches off Newcastle. Down on the South Coast, try the beaches off Wollongong (p124), Jervis Bay (p313), Ulladulla (p315), Merimbula (p326) and Pambula (p327).

Combining a holiday with learning to surf is an increasingly popular pursuit. Two good operators in Sydney:

Learn to Surf (☎ 1800 851 101; www.wavessurfschool.com.au; lessons from $65)
Let's Go Surfing (Map p84; ☎ 02-9365 1800; www.letsgosurfing.com.au; 128a Ramsgate Ave, Bondi; lessons from $55)

Elsewhere in NSW, surf shops offering lessons can be found in most popular surfing spots.

TOP 10 BEACHES

You see the images adorning the walls from the moment you step off the plane at Sydney Airport: beaches. NSW has scores of beaches and visiting one (or more) has to be near the top of almost every traveller's itinerary.

One thing you will be spoilt for is choice: there are hundreds, from hidden gems in the south to the famed silica of Bondi.

Here are 10 of our favourites:

Bondi Beach (p54) Captivating, stylish, crowded and more.
Byron Bay (p181) There's a month's worth of beaches here. Start right in the town centre.
Crescent Head (p162) Longboard capital of NSW – affords fine views of surfers.
Jervis Bay (p313) On the South Coast, there's a bunch of lovely little beaches with bright white sand and crystal-clear water.
Maroubra Beach (p55) A bigger, quieter and less-fabled beach south of Coogee.
One Mile Beach (p152) An almost-deserted haven near Port Stephens.
Pearl Beach (p129) On the Central Coast, this historic beach is set in bushland.
Pebbly Beach (p316) In Murramarang National Park, this secluded beach features native creatures like kangaroos.
Reef Beach (p47) On the stunning Manly Scenic Walkway, this beach is not nudist, despite what you may have heard.
Yuraygir National Park beaches (p172) Compared to nearby resorts, the beaches here are untrammelled.

SWIMMING & OTHER WATER SPORTS

A visit to NSW will involve swimming at a beach sooner or later – because not only are there so many, it's a state obsession. There are also many lakes and rivers where you can cool off. Most towns have an Olympic-sized pool with regular public hours. These range from big pools in small towns in the west to the grand Sydney Aquatic Centre (p58), which was used for the 2000 Olympics. At any of the pools, you'll see plenty of Australians dreaming of winning their own gold medal.

If you want to do something more daring than the breast stroke, most major beach resorts will rent out windsurfing gear and there are outfits offering parasailing (behind a speedboat) and jet-boating.

WHALE- & DOLPHIN-WATCHING

Migrating southern right and humpback whales pass close to Australia's southern coast between the Antarctic and warmer waters, and whale-watching cruises allow you to get close to these magnificent creatures. Good spots are Eden (p328) in southern NSW and along the mid-north coast of NSW.

Dolphins can be seen year-round at many places along the coast, such as Jervis Bay (p313), Port Stephens (p152) and Byron Bay (p180).

Food & Drink

Born in convict poverty and raised on a diet heavily influenced by Great Britain, Australian cuisine has come a long way. This is now one of the most dynamic places in the world to have a meal, thanks to immigration and a dining public willing to give anything new, and better, a go. Sydney can claim to be a dining destination worthy of touring gourmands from New York to Paris. More importantly real people, including travellers, will feel the effects of New South Wales' (NSW) ever-blossoming food culture.

The influx of immigrants (and their cuisine) has found locals trying (and liking) everything from lassi to laksa. This passionate minority has led to a rise in dining standards, better availability of produce and a frenetic buzz about food in general. It's no wonder Australian chefs, cookbooks and food writers are so sought-after overseas.

We've coined our own phrase, Modern Australian (Mod Oz), to describe our cuisine. If it's a melange of East and West, it's Modern Australian. If it's not authentically French or Italian, it's Modern Australian. Mod Oz is our attempt to classify the unclassifiable.

Dishes aren't usually too fussy; the flavours are often bold and interesting. Spicing ranges from gentle to extreme, coffee is great (it reaches its greatest heights in the cities), and meats are tender, full-flavoured and usually bargain-priced.

STAPLES & SPECIALITIES

Australia's best food comes from the sea. Nothing compares to this continent's seafood, harnessed from some of the purest waters you'll find anywhere, and usually cooked with care.

Connoisseurs prize Sydney rock oysters (a species living along the NSW coast). Rock lobsters are fantastic and fantastically expensive, and mud crabs, despite the name, are a sweet delicacy. Another odd-sounding delicacy are 'bugs' – like shovel-nosed lobsters without a lobster's price tag. Yabbies (freshwater crayfish) can be found throughout the region.

Prawns are incredible, particularly sweet school prawns or the eastern king (Yamba) prawns found along northern NSW. Add to that countless wild fish species and you've got one of the greatest bounties on earth.

Almost everything grown from the land (as opposed to the sea) was introduced to Australia. The fact that the country is huge (similar in size to continental USA) and varies so much in climate, from the tropical north to the temperate south, means that there's an enormous variety of produce on offer in NSW.

Australians' taste for the unusual usually kicks in only at dinner. Most people still eat cereal for breakfast, or perhaps eggs and bacon on weekends. They devour sandwiches for lunch with nearly the same verve as they do in the UK, and then eat anything and everything in the evening. *Yum cha* (the classic southern Chinese dumpling feast), however, has found huge popularity with urban locals in recent years, particularly for lunch on weekends.

DRINKS

You're in the right country if you're after a drink. Once a nation of tea-and-beer-swillers, Oz is now turning its attention to coffee and wine. In fact, you're probably not far from a wine region right now.

The closest region to Sydney, the Hunter Valley, first had vines planted in the 1830s, and does a lively unwooded Sémillon that is best aged. Further inland, there are vineyards at Canberra, Cowra, Orange and Mudgee.

An annual publication with lots of useful information on many readily available wines is the *Penguin Good Australian Wine Guide*, by Huon Hooke and Ralph Kyte-Powell.

Plenty of good wine comes from big producers with economies of scale on their side, but the most interesting wines are usually made by small vignerons where you pay a premium – but the gamble means the payoff, in terms of flavour, is often greater. Much of the cost of wine (nearly 42%) is due to a high taxing program courtesy of the Australian government.

Beer, for years, has been of the bland, chilled-so-you-can-barely-taste-it variety. Now microbrewers and boutique breweries are filtering through. Keep an eye out for James Squire amber ale from Sydney.

In terms of coffee, Australia is leaping ahead, with Italian-style espresso machines in virtually every café, boutique roasters are all the rage and, in urban areas, the qualified *barista* (coffee maker) is virtually the norm.

CELEBRATIONS

Celebrating in the Australian manner often includes equal amounts of food and alcohol. A birthday could well be a barbecue (barbie) of steak (or prawns), washed down with a beverage or two. Weddings are usually big slap-up dinners, though the food is often far from memorable.

Many regions of NSW are now holding food festivals. There are harvest festivals in wine regions, and various communities, such as the town of Orange (p223) hold annual events. Look for weekly markets in places like Nimbin (p192) where a variety of producers – many organic – sell an array of interesting produce and foods.

For many an event, especially in the warmer months, many Australians fill the car with an Esky (a portable, insulated ice chest to keep everything cool), tables, chairs, a cricket set or a footy, and head off for a barbie by the lake/river/beach. If there's a 'total fire ban' (which, increasingly, occurs each summer), the food is precooked and the barbie becomes more of a picnic, but the essence remains the same.

WHERE TO EAT & DRINK

Typically, a restaurant meal in Australia is a relaxed affair. It may take 15 minutes to order, another 15 before the first course arrives, and maybe half an hour between entrées and mains. The upside of this is that any table you've booked in a restaurant is yours for the night, unless you're told otherwise. So sit, linger and live life in the slow lane.

DID YOU KNOW?

North Americans are constantly flummoxed by the local nomenclature in which the opening dish in a three-course meal is called the entrée, and the second course (the North American entrée) is called the main course.

A competitively priced place to eat is in a club or pub that offers a counter meal. This is where you order your meal (usually staples such as a fisherman's basket, steak or Vienna schnitzel) at the kitchen, take a number, and wait until it's called out over the counter or intercom.

Solo diners find that cafés and noodle bars are welcoming, good fine-dining restaurants often treat you like a star, but sadly, some mid-range places may still make you feel a little ill at ease.

One of the most interesting features of the dining scene is the Bring Your Own (BYO), a restaurant that allows you to bring your own alcohol. If the restaurant also sells alcohol, the BYO bit is usually limited to bottled wine only and a corkage charge is added to your bill. The cost is either per person, or per bottle, and ranges from nothing to $15 per bottle in fancy places. Be warned, however, that BYO is a dying custom, so ask when you book.

Most restaurants open at noon for lunch and from 6pm or 7pm for dinner. Locals usually eat lunch shortly after noon, and dinner bookings are usually made for 7.30pm or 8pm, though in the major cities some restaurants stay open past 10pm.

Quick Eats

There's not a huge culture of street vending in NSW, though you may find a pie or coffee cart in some places. Most quick eats traditionally come from a milk bar, which serves traditional hamburgers (with bacon, egg, pineapple and beetroot if you want) and other takeaway foods. Fish and chips is still hugely popular, most often eaten at the beach on a Friday night.

American-style fast food has taken over in recent times – though many Aussies still love a meat pie, often from a milk bar, but also from bakeries, kiosks and some cafés.

Pizza has become one of the most popular fast foods; most home-delivered pizzas are American-style (thick and with lots of toppings) rather than Italian-style. That said, wood-fired, thin Neapolitan-style *pizze* are often available, even in country towns. In Sydney, Roman-style *pizze* (buy it by the slice) is becoming more popular, but you can't usually buy American-style pizza in anything but whole rounds.

> **DID YOU KNOW?**
>
> Australia's first espresso cafés opened in the 1950s – Bar Coluzzi (p87) in Sydney is still in business.

VEGETARIANS & VEGANS

In NSW's cities vegetarians will be well catered-for. Cafés seem to always have vegetarian options, and even the best restaurants may have complete vegetarian menus. Take care with risotto and soups, though, as meat stock is often used. Vegans will find the going much tougher, but there are usually dishes that are vegan-adaptable at restaurants. The Australian Vegetarian Society's useful website (www.veg-soc.org) lists vegetarian-friendly places to eat throughout NSW.

> The *Sydney Morning Herald* puts out an annual restaurant guide, the *Good Food Guide*, that rates over 400 restaurants in NSW.

WHINING & DINING

Dining with children in NSW is relatively easy. Avoid the flashiest places and children are generally welcomed, particularly at Chinese, Greek or Italian restaurants. Kids are usually more than welcome at cafés; bistros and clubs often see families dining early. Many fine-dining restaurants don't welcome small children. Most places that do welcome children don't have separate kids menus, and those that do usually offer everything straight from the deep fryer – such as crumbed chicken and chips. It is better to find something on the menu (say a pasta or salad) and have the kitchen adapt it slightly to your children's needs.

The best news for travelling families, weather permitting, is that there are plenty of free or coin-operated barbecues in parks. Beware of weekends

---

BILLS & TIPPING

The total at the bottom of a restaurant bill is all you really need to pay. It should include Goods and Services Tax (GST), as should menu prices, and there is no 'optional' service charge added. Waiters are paid a reasonable salary, so they don't rely on tips to survive. Often, though, especially in cities, people tip a little in a café, while the tip for excellent service can go as high as 15% in whiz-bang establishments.

---

and public holidays when fierce battles can erupt over who is next in line for the barbie. For more on travelling with children, see p359.

HABITS & CUSTOMS

At the table, it's good manners to use British knife and fork skills, keeping the fork in the left hand, tines down, and the knife in the right, though Americans may be forgiven for using their fork like a shovel. Talking with your mouth full is considered uncouth, and fingers should only be used for food that can't be tackled any other way.

DID YOU KNOW?

A Tim Tam Shooter is where the two diagonally opposite corners of this rectangular chocolate biscuit are nibbled off, and a hot drink (tea is the true aficionado's favourite) is sucked through the fast-melting biscuit as if through a straw.

If you're lucky enough to be invited over for dinner at someone's house, always take a gift such as a bottle of wine, flowers or a box of chocolates.

'Shouting' is a revered custom where people rotate paying for a round of drinks. Just don't leave before it's your turn to buy! At a toast, everyone should touch glasses.

Australians like to linger a bit over coffee. They like to linger a really long time while drinking beer. And they tend to take quite a bit of time if they're out to dinner.

In NSW, smoking is banned in restaurants, cafés and other eateries where food is consumed indoors, so sit outside if you love to puff.

COOKING COURSES

Many good cooking classes are run by food stores such as **Simon Johnson** (☎ 02-9319 6122) in Sydney. Others are run by markets, such as the **Sydney Seafood School** (☎ 02-9004 1111). Some longer courses for the inspired:

Elise Pascoe Cooking School (☎ 02-4236 1666; www.cookingschool.com.au; Jamboree Valley) Food writer and renowned cook Elise Pascoe runs mostly weekend cooking classes in a stunning setting two hours south of Sydney.

Le Cordon Bleu (☎ 1 800 064 802; Sydney) The original must-do French cooking course is available thanks to a joint venture down under. Courses run from 10 weeks to five years (part-time).

EAT YOUR WORDS

Australians love to shorten everything, including peoples' names, so expect many other words to be abbreviated. Some words you might hear in NSW:

barbie – a barbecue, where (traditionally) smoke and overcooked meat are matched with lashings of coleslaw, potato salad and beer

Esky – a portable, insulated ice chest to hold your tinnies, before you pop them in your tinny holder. May be carried onto your *tinny*, too.

Bill's Food, by Bill Granger, is a cookbook that will make you want to hop out of bed and fire up the stove. Granger is the undisputed king of breakfast in Sydney.

middy – a mid-sized glass of beer

pav – pavlova; the meringue dessert topped with cream, passionfruit and kiwifruit or other fresh fruit

sanger/sando – a sandwich

schooner – a big glass of beer; but not as big as a pint

snags – (aka surprise bags); sausages

Tim Tam – a commercial chocolate biscuit that lies close to the heart of most Australians

tinny – usually refers to a can of beer; also a small boat you go fishing in

tinny holder – insulating material used to keep the tinny ice-cold

Sydney

CONTENTS

Sydney is the queen bee, the top dog, the cat's pyjamas and just plain 'it' when it comes to New South Wales (NSW) – and doesn't she know it? The place where it all started not only for the state, but also Australia, Sydney is the country's oldest (and best-located) city and buzzes with a can-do, buoyant energy that may leave locals and visitors breathless. The city has come a long way from its convict beginnings, but it still has a rough-and-ready energy that makes it an exciting place to visit. It offers an invigorating blend of the old and the new, the raw and the refined.

The Sydney experience can be so many different things: the smell of tropical flowers on a balmy night, catching a bus from the CBD to a world-famous beach just because you can, eating food from all round the world in one suburb or on one street, or sharing a cold beer with vocal crowds at feverish sporting events. Even just being reminded that the best things in life – namely the climate and the great outdoors – are free.

A potpourri of ethnic groups contributes to the city's cultural life. Sydney attracts the majority of Australia's immigrants, and the local mixture of pragmatic egalitarianism and natural indifference has made it a beacon of pluralism; it is one of the world's most tolerant and diverse societies. In addition, evidence of the region's original inhabitants survives in the Aboriginal stencils that can be found in coastal caves, and in the indigenous names of many streets and suburbs.

HIGHLIGHTS

- Get out and get filled – Sydney's **eating** (p80) options are the best in the country and easy to enjoy

- Bring out your inner water baby at the magnificent **Sydney Harbour National Park** (p47)

- Check out **historic beauties** (p54) like Elizabeth Bay House or Vaucluse House

- Shop till you drop at one of Sydney's fabulous **weekend markets** (p92)

- Take the jaw-droppingly beautiful **Bondi to Coogee Walk** (p58)

- Savour the sights, sounds and smells of **Chinatown** (p81)

- Drink in one of **The Rocks**' (p87) many watering holes

- Scale the **Sydney Harbour Bridge** (p48) for the best views

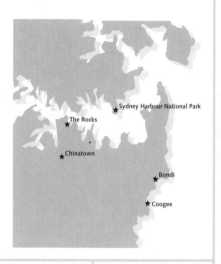

Sydney Harbour National Park

The Rocks

Chinatown

Bondi

Coogee

- TELEPHONE CODE: ☎ 02 | - POPULATION: 4,041,400 | - AREA: 12,407 SQ KM

HISTORY

It was at Sydney Cove, where the ferries run from Circular Quay today, that the first European settlement was established in 1788 – so it's not surprising that Sydney has a strong sense of history. The city is built on land once occupied by the Eora tribe, whose presence lingers in the place names of some suburbs and whose artistic legacy can be seen at various Aboriginal engraving sites around the city (p54). Many ascribe Sydney's raffish spirit to the fact that the military was essentially in charge of things in the late 18th and early 19th century. Paying for labour and local products in rum (hence the name, the Rum Corps), the soldiers upset, defied and outmanoeuvred three of the colony's early governors, including one William Bligh, of *Bounty* mutiny fame.

ORIENTATION

The harbour divides Sydney into northern and southern halves, with the Sydney Harbour Bridge and the Harbour Tunnel joining the two shores. The city centre and most places of interest are south of the harbour. The city centre is long and narrow, stretching from The Rocks and Circular Quay in the north to Central Station in the south. It is bounded by Darling Harbour to the west and a string of pleasant parks to the east.

East of the city centre are the inner-city suburbs of Darlinghurst, Kings Cross and Paddington. Further east again are exclusive suburbs like Double Bay and Vaucluse. To the southeast of these are the ocean-beach suburbs of Bondi and Coogee. Sydney's Kingsford Smith Airport is in Mascot, 10km south of the city centre, jutting into Botany Bay.

West of the centre are the previously working-class but now gentrified suburbs of Pyrmont, Glebe and Balmain. The inner west includes Newtown and Leichhardt.

Suburbs stretch a good 20km north and south of the centre, their extent limited by national parks.

The suburbs north of the bridge are known collectively as the North Shore. The western suburbs sprawl for 50km to the foothills of the Blue Mountains, encompassing the once separate settlements of Parramatta and Penrith.

Maps

Just about every brochure includes a map of the city centre, but Lonely Planet's *Sydney City Map* ($7.80) has good coverage of the city centre and also covers the Blue Mountains. If you intend to drive around the city, the *Sydney UBD* street directory ($35) is invaluable. For topographic maps, visit the **Department of Land & Water Conservation** (DLWC; Map pp68-70; ☎ 9228 6111; 23-33 Bridge St, Sydney).

INFORMATION
Bookshops

Ariel (Map pp72-3; ☎ 9332 4581; 42 Oxford St, Paddington; ☺ 9am-midnight) Good for art and design titles.
Dymocks Books (Map pp68-70; ☎ 9235 0155; 424-430 George St, Sydney; ☺ 9am-6.30pm Mon-Wed & Fri, 9am-9pm Thu, 9am-6pm Sat, 10am-5pm Sun) Over 250,000 titles over three floors.
Gleebooks (Map p74; ☎ 9660 2333; 49 Glebe Point Rd, Glebe; ☺ 8am-9pm) Frequent winner of 'bookshop of the year' awards.
Lesley McKay's (Map pp66-7; ☎ 9327 1354; 346 New South Head Rd, Double Bay; ☺ 9am-10pm Mon-Sat, 10am-10pm Sun) Extremely helpful, well-informed staff.
Travel Bookshop (Map pp68-70; ☎ 9261 8200; 175 Liverpool St, Sydney; ☺ 9am-6pm Mon-Fri, 10am-5pm Sat) Crammed with, you guessed it, travel books.

Emergency

Lifeline (☎ 13 11 14) Over-the-phone counselling services, including suicide prevention.
NRMA (Map pp68-70; ☎ 13 21 32; 74 King St, Sydney) For automobile insurance and roadside service.
Police Stations (Map pp68-70; ☎ 000; 132 George St, The Rocks; 570 George St, Sydney)
Rape Crisis Centre (☎ 1800 424 017, 9819 6565)
Wayside Chapel (Map p71; ☎ 9358 6577; 29 Hughes St, Potts Point) 24-hour crisis centre in the heart of Kings Cross.

Internet Access

Global Gossip Kings Cross (Map p71; ☎ 9326 9777; 111 Darlinghurst Rd, Kings Cross; ☺ 8am-midnight); Bondi (☎ 9365 4811; 37 Hall St, Bondi) Central Station (☎ 9212 1466; Shop 3, 770 George St, Sydney) City Centre (☎ 9281 6890; 415 Pitt St, Sydney)
Travellers Contact Point (Map pp68-70; ☎ 9221 8744; Level 7, 428 George St, Sydney) Free for first 30 minutes, though it's email only.

Medical Services

Kings Cross Travellers Clinic (Map p71; ☎ 9358 3066; 13 Springfield Ave, Kings Cross; ☺ 10am-1pm & 2-6pm Mon-Fri, 9am-noon Sat) Bookings advised for morning-after pill scripts and dive medicals.

SYDNEY IN...

Two Days

Start your day in Sydney with a walk around the historic Rocks area before heading to the **Sydney Opera House** (p48) and the **Royal Botanic Gardens** (p52). Walk to the **Art Gallery of New South Wales** (p51) before scooting off for a spot of lunch in **Bondi** (p54), then enjoying a dip in Sydney's most famous beach. That night, catch a performance at the Opera House, before or after dining at one of Sydney's city restaurants.

Your next day should start with a ferry or JetCat trip to **Manly** (p56), where a cruisy open-air breakfast awaits, followed by a swim or long walk along the Manly Scenic Walkway. That night, head to **Surry Hills** (p82) for dinner and drinks.

Four Days

Scale the **Sydney Harbour Bridge** (p48) by joining a Bridgeclimb tour. You'll need some serious sustenance after that, so lunch (preferably *yum cha*) in **Chinatown** (p81) is looking good. That night, take in the bright lights and trashy good times available at **Kings Cross** (p86).

On the fourth day, get out of town by taking the train to the majestic **Blue Mountains** (p109), and join in the sighing as you gaze upon the **Three Sisters** (p111). Have lunch in **Katoomba** (p111) before heading back to Sydney or staying the night in one of the mountain villages.

One Week

All of the above beckon, plus a trip to the 'insular peninsula' known as the **Northern Beaches** (p57), where you can frolic amongst the moneyed sets of **Palm Beach**. If that doesn't appeal, a trip to the **Hunter Valley** (p132) will make you an expert on fine red wine in no time.

The next day take a tour of one of **Sydney Harbour National Park's** (p47) attractions, before a ferry ride to **Watsons Bay** (p54) transports you to beer-garden heaven at the Watsons Bay Hotel.

Shop till you drop on your last day in Sydney, loading up on fashion in Sydney's **Paddington** (p53) and then goodies for the folks back home in **The Rocks** (p47) or at one of Sydney's many markets. Dinner with a view is a must on your final night.

Sydney Hospital (Map pp68-70; ☎ 9382 7111; 8 Macquarie St, Sydney) This central city hospital has a 24-hour emergency ward.

Travellers Medical & Vaccination Centre (Map pp68-70; ☎ 9221 7133; Level 7, 428 George St, Sydney; ⏰ 9am-5.30pm Mon, Wed & Fri, 8am-5.30pm Tue, 9am-7.30pm Thu, 9am-1pm Sat) The best place to get your shots and medical advice related to travel.

Money

There are plenty of ATMs throughout Sydney. Both **American Express** (see p368) and **Travelex/Thomas Cook** (p368) have branches throughout Sydney.

Seven-day exchange bureaus include one in the coach terminal at **Central Station** (Map pp68-70; ⏰ 8am-8pm), another opposite Wharf 6 at **Circular Quay** (Map pp68-70; ⏰ 8am-10pm) and one at the pedestrian juncture of Springfield Ave and Darlinghurst Rd in **Kings Cross** (Map p71; ⏰ 8am-midnight).

Post

The original **general post office** (GPO; Map pp68-70; 1 Martin Place, Sydney; ⏰ 8.15am-5.30pm Mon-Fri, 10am-2pm Sat) is central, and there's another **post office** (Map pp68-70; 130 Pitt St, Sydney) with counter service. The **poste restante service** (Map pp68-70; 310 George St, Sydney; ⏰ 8.15am-5.30pm Mon-Fri, 10am-2pm Sat) has computer terminals that enable you to check if mail is waiting for you. You'll need identification.

Tourist Information

City Host Information Kiosks (Map pp68-70; ⏰ 9am-5pm winter, 10am-6pm summer) Circular Quay (cnr Pitt & Alfred Sts); Martin Place (btwn Elizabeth & Castlereagh Sts); Town Hall (cnr Druitt & George Sts)

Sydney Coach Terminal (Map pp68-70; ☎ 9281 9366; Eddy Ave, Central Station; ⏰ 6am-10.30pm) Bus and hotel bookings, plus luggage storage.

Sydney Visitors Centre (☎ 9667 6050; Sydney International Airport; ⏰ 6am-midnight) Can book discounted hotel rooms, tours and entertainment tickets.

Sydney Visitors Centre (Map pp68-70; ☎ 9240 8786; 106 George St, The Rocks; ⏰ 9am-6pm)

Visitors Centre (Map pp68-70; ☎ 9281 0788; Darling Harbour; ⏰ 10am-6pm) Next to the Imax Theatre.

SIGHTS

Sydney wasn't a planned city and its layout is further complicated by its hills and by the numerous inlets of the harbour. The harbour divides Sydney into northern and southern halves, which are connected visibly by the iconic Sydney Harbour Bridge and not-so-visibly by the Harbour Tunnel. Central Sydney and most sites of interest lie south of the harbour, embedded in the bustling inner-city suburbs like Darlinghurst, East Sydney, Surry Hills and Kings Cross. Popular beachside suburbs to visit include Bondi and Coogee in the southeast, and Manly on the north side.

Sydney Harbour

Sydney's stunning harbour (**Port Jackson**) is both a major port and the city's playground. It stretches some 20km inland to join the mouth of the Parramatta River. The headlands at the entrance are known as North Head and South Head. The most scenic part of the harbour is between the Heads and the Harbour Bridge, 8km inland. **Middle Harbour** is a large inlet that heads northwest a couple of kilometres inside the Heads.

Sydney's **harbour beaches** are generally sheltered, calm coves with little of the frenetic activity of the ocean beaches. On the south shore, they include **Lady Bay** (nude beach), **Camp Cove** and **Nielsen Park**. On the North Shore there are harbour beaches at **Manly Cove**, **Reef Beach**, **Clontarf**, **Chinamans Beach** and **Balmoral**.

SYDNEY HARBOUR NATIONAL PARK

This park protects the scattered pockets of bushland around the harbour and includes several small islands. It offers some great walking tracks, scenic lookouts, Aboriginal carvings and a handful of historic sites. On the south shore it incorporates South Head and Nielsen Park; on the North Shore it includes North Head, Dobroyd Head, Middle Head and Ashton Park. Fort Denison, Goat, Clarke, Rodd and Shark Islands are also part of the park. Pick up information at **Sydney Harbour National Parks Information Centre** (Map pp68-70; ☎ 9247 5033; Park Office, Cadmans Cottage, 110 George St, The Rocks; ☼ 9am-5pm Mon-Fri, 9.30am-4.30pm Sat & Sun), which is housed inside historic Cadmans Cottage.

Previously known as Pinchgut, **Fort Denison** is a small, fortified island off Mrs Macquaries Point, originally used to isolate troublesome convicts. The fort was built during the Crimean War amid fears of a Russian invasion (seriously!). Tours of Fort Denison can be booked at, and depart from, Cadmans Cottage. Take your pick of the heritage tour

(adult/child/family $22/18/75) or the brunch tour (adult/child $50/45).

There are tours of **Goat Island**, just west of the Harbour Bridge, which has been a shipyard, quarantine station and gunpowder depot. Take a heritage tour (adult/child/family $20/16/65) or a Gruesome Tales tour ($25). Again, tours are booked at, and depart from, Cadmans Cottage. **Clarke Island** off Darling Point, **Rodd Island** at Iron Cove near Birkenhead Point, and **Shark Island** off Rose Bay, make great picnic getaways, but you'll need to hire a water taxi or have access to a boat to reach them. To visit these islands you need a permit from Cadmans Cottage. Landing fees are $3 per person. These three islands are open from 9am to sunset daily.

The Rocks   Map pp68-70

Sydney's first European settlement was established on the rocky spur of land on the western side of Sydney Cove, from which the Harbour Bridge now crosses to the North Shore. It was a squalid, raucous and notoriously dangerous place full of convicts, whalers, prostitutes and street gangs, though in the 1820s the nouveaux riches built three-storey houses on the ridges overlooking the slums – starting the city's obsession with prime real estate, which continues today.

It later became an area of warehouses and maritime commerce and then slumped into decline as modern shipping and storage facilities moved away from Circular Quay. An outbreak of bubonic plague in the early 20th century led to whole streets being razed, and then the construction of the Harbour Bridge resulted in further demolition.

Since the 1970s redevelopment has turned much of The Rocks into a sanitised, historical tourist precinct, full of narrow cobbled lanes, fine colonial buildings, converted warehouses, tearooms and Australiana. If you ignore the kitsch, it's a delightful place to stroll around, especially in the poky back-streets and in the less-developed, tight-knit community of Millers Point.

Cadmans Cottage (☎ 9247 5033; 110 George St, The Rocks; ☼ 9.30am-4.30pm Mon-Fri, 10am-4.30pm Sat & Sun) is the oldest house in Sydney (1816) and the former home of the last government coxswain, John Cadman; it's now home to the Sydney Harbour National Parks Information Centre.

Despite the entire helpful tourist infrastructure, the beauty of The Rocks is that it's as much fun to wander around aimlessly as it is to visit particular attractions. Soak up the atmosphere, sample the frequent entertainment in the **Rocks Square** on Playfair St, browse the stores for gifts, grab a beer at one of the pubs, admire the views of Circular Quay and Campbells Cove, and join the melee at the weekend **Rocks Market** (George St).

A short walk west along Argyle St through the awe-inspiring convict-excavated **Argyle Cut** takes you to the other side of the peninsula and **Millers Point**, a delightful district of early colonial homes with a quintessentially English village green. Nearby is the 1848 **Garrison Church** and the more secular delights of the **Lord Nelson Hotel** and the **Hero of Waterloo Hotel**, which tussle over the title of Sydney's oldest pub.

Sydney Observatory (☎ 9217 0485; Watson Rd, Observatory Hill; admission free; ☒ 10am-5pm) has a commanding, copper dome–bedecked position atop Observatory Park overlooking Millers Point and the harbour. Nightly sky-watching visits (adult/child/family $10/ 5/25) are possible, but must be booked in advance. In the old military hospital building close by, the **SH Ervin Gallery** (☎ 9258 0123; Watson Rd, Observatory Hill; adult/child $6/4; ☒ 11am-5pm Tue-Fri, noon-5pm Sat & Sun), in the National Trust Centre, has temporary exhibitions on Australian art that invariably prove popular. It's also the home of the annual Salon des Refuses show, for rejected Archibald Prize contenders.

At Dawes Point, on Walsh Bay, just west of the Harbour Bridge, are several renovated wharves. **Pier One** now houses a luxury hotel; **Pier Four** is beautifully utilised as the home of the prestigious Sydney Theatre, Bangarra Dance Theatre, Sydney Dance Company and Australian Theatre for Young People (ATYP). Others appear to be getting the 'luxury waterfront apartments' treatment.

Sydney Harbour Bridge

The much-loved 'old coat hanger' crosses the harbour at one of its narrowest points, linking the southern and northern shores and joining central Sydney with the satellite business district in North Sydney. The **bridge** (Map pp68-70) was completed in 1932 at a cost of $20 million and has always been a favourite icon, partly because of its sheer size, partly because of its function in uniting the city and partly because it boosted employment during the Depression.

You can climb inside the southeastern stone pylon, which houses the **Pylon Lookout** (Map pp68-70; ☎ 9247 3408; adult/concession $8.50/3; ☒ 10am-5pm), or you can join a climbing group and scale the bridge itself (see p58).

Cars, trains, cyclists, joggers and pedestrians use the bridge. The cycle-way is on the western side and the pedestrian walkway on the eastern; stair access is from Cumberland St in The Rocks and near Milsons Point Station on the North Shore.

The best way to experience the bridge is undoubtedly on foot; don't expect much of a view crossing by car or train. Driving south (only) there's a $3 toll.

Sydney Opera House

Australia's most recognisable icon and Sydney's premier must-see sight sits dramatically on Bennelong Point on the eastern headland of Circular Quay. The postcard-perfect, soaring shell-like roofs (made up of an incredible 1,056,000 Swedish tiles) were actually inspired by palm fronds, but look more like white yacht spinnakers or a 'nun's scrum' (a common nickname). Construction commenced in 1959 and the **Sydney Opera House** (Map pp68-70; ☎ 9250 7111; www.sydneyoperaho use.com; Bennelong Point) was officially opened in 1973 after an operatic series of personality clashes, technical difficulties and delays.

It's truly memorable to see a performance here, visit the **Sunday market** (selling Australian-made arts and crafts) or sit outdoors and watch harbour life go by. The Opera House itself looks fine from any angle, but the view from a ferry coming into Circular Quay is one of the best.

The Opera House has four main auditoriums, and stages dance, theatre, concerts and films, as well as opera. There's also a venue called the **Studio**, which stages contemporary arts events, including comedy, cabaret, rock and roll, and even the odd bit of tongue-in-cheek karaoke. Over 2000 events are staged at the Opera House every year.

A variety of worthwhile **tours** (☎ 9250 7250; tours $17-28; ☒ 8.30am-5pm) of the Opera House buildings can take you from the 'front of house' to backstage. Not all tours can visit all theatres because of rehearsals, but you're more likely to see everything if you take an early tour. Let them know in advance if you will need wheelchair access.

The bimonthly *Opera House Diary* details forthcoming performances and is available free inside. Kids at the House is the Opera House's pint-sized entertainment program, with music, dance and drama on offer, including the delightful Babies' Proms series.

Disabled access is good for the most part, although some areas of the building still require staff assistance. Subtitles are a feature of opera performances and guide dogs are welcome throughout the building or at performances. There's a car park directly under the building (day rate from $14 to $32).

Circular Quay
Map pp68-70

Circular Quay, built around Sydney Cove, is one of the city's major focal points. The first European settlement grew around the Tank Stream, which now runs underground into the harbour near Wharf 6. For many years this was the shipping centre of Sydney, but it's now both a commuting hub and a recreational space, combining ferry quays, a train station and the **Overseas Passenger Terminal**, with harbour walkways, parks, restaurants, buskers and fisher-folk.

The **Museum of Contemporary Art** (MCA; ☎ 9241 5892; 140 George St, The Rocks; admission free; ☼ 10am-5pm) fronts Circular Quay West and is set in a stately Art Deco building. It has a fine collection of modern art from Australia and around the world (including sculpture, painting, installations and the moving image) and temporary exhibitions on a variety of themes (prices vary). The MCA store has a good range of postcards and gifts, and the café serves classy food.

Macquarie Place & Surrounds
Map pp68-70

Narrow lanes lead south from Circular Quay towards the centre of the city. At the corner of Loftus and Bridge Sts, under the shady Moreton Bay figs in Macquarie Place, are a cannon and anchor from the First Fleet flagship, HMS *Sirius*, and an **obelisk**, erected in 1818, indicating road distances to various points in the nascent colony. The square has a couple of pleasant outdoor cafés and is overlooked by the rear façade of the imposing 19th-century **Lands Department Building** (DLWC Building; Map pp68-70) on Bridge St.

The excellent **Museum of Sydney** (☎ 9251 5988; 37 Phillip St; adult/child/family $7/3/17; ☼ 9.30am-5pm) is east of here, on the site of the first and infamously fetid government house built in 1788. Sydney's early history (including pre-1788) comes to life here in whisper, argument, gossip and artefacts. There's also a worthy café on the premises and a damn fine shop.

The 1856 **Justice & Police Museum** (☎ 9252 1144; 8 Phillip St; adult/child/family $7/3/17; ☼ 10am-5pm Sat & Sun), in the old water-police court and station on the corner of Phillip and Albert Sts, has fascinating exhibitions on crime and policing, with a Sydney focus. It has wheelchair access to the ground floor only; Braille and audio guides are available.

City Centre
Map pp68-70

Central Sydney stretches from Circular Quay in the north to Central Station in the south. The business hub is towards the northern end, but most redevelopment is occurring at the southern end and this is gradually shifting the focus of the city.

Sydney lacks a true civic centre, but **Martin Place** lays claim to the honour, if only by default. This grand, revamped pedestrian mall extends from Macquarie St to George St and is impressively lined by the monumental buildings of financial institutions and the colonnaded Victorian post office at No 1. There's plenty of public seating, a **cenotaph** commemorating Australia's war dead and an amphitheatre where lunchtime entertainment is sometimes staged.

The **Town Hall**, a few blocks south of here on the corner of George and Druitt Sts, was built in 1874. The elaborate chamber room and concert hall inside matches its outrageously ornate exterior. Next door, the Anglican **St Andrew's Cathedral**, built around the same time, is the oldest cathedral in Australia.

The city's most sumptuous shopping complex, the Byzantine-style **Queen Victoria Building** (QVB), is next to the town hall and takes up an entire city block bordered by George, Druitt, York and Market Sts. Another lovingly restored shopping centre is the **Strand Arcade**, on Pitt St Mall and George St.

There are 45-minute tours of the splendidly over-the-top **State Theatre** (☎ 9373 6652; 49 Market St; adult/child $12/8; ☯ 11.30am-3pm Mon-Fri), which was built in 1929.

To the southwest are the **Spanish Quarter** and **Chinatown**, dynamic areas spreading and breathing life into the city's lacklustre southeastern zone, where Central Station lies isolated on the southern periphery.

Darling Harbour   Map pp68-70

This huge waterfront leisure park on the city centre's western edge, once a thriving dockland area, was reinvigorated in the 1980s by a combination of vision, politicking and big money. The supposed centrepiece is the **Harbourside** centre, which has struggled to shrug off its 'white elephant' tag ever since it was built, despite extensive refurbishment in the last few years. It houses shops and restaurants. The real attractions are the stunning aquarium, excellent museums and Chinese Garden.

Until recently, the emphasis here was on tacky tourist 'entertainment', but the snazzy new wining and dining precincts of **Cockle Bay Wharf**, built opposite Harbourside, and **King St Wharf** have lent the area a bit more kudos with Sydneysiders and visitors alike.

Looking for subdued good taste and muted colour schemes? Dream on, at the mammoth temple of mammon that is **Star City Casino** (☎ 9777 9000; 80 Pyrmont St, Pyrmont; ☯ 24hr). Star City includes two **theatres**, a lurid volcano, as well as the inevitable try-hard nightclub, hotel and retail outlets.

The monorail and metrail link Darling Harbour to the city centre. Ferries leave from Circular Quay's Wharf 5 and stop at Darling Harbour's Aquarium and Pyrmont Bay wharves ($4.50). The Sydney Explorer bus (p59) stops at four points around Darling Harbour every 20 minutes.

The main pedestrian approaches are across footbridges from Market and Liverpool Sts. The one from Market St leads to **Pyrmont Bridge**, now a route for pedestrian and monorail only, but once famous as the world's first electrically operated swing-span bridge.

The **visitors centre** (☎ 9281 0788; ☯ 10am-6pm) is under the highway, next to Imax.

SYDNEY AQUARIUM

Near the eastern end of Pyrmont Bridge, this magnificent **aquarium** (☎ 9262 2300; Aquarium Pier, Darling Harbour; adult/child/family $23/11/50; ☯ 9am-10pm) displays the richness of Australian marine life. Three 'oceanariums' are moored in the harbour with sharks, rays and big fish in one, and Sydney Harbour marine life and seals in the others. There are also informative and well-presented exhibits of freshwater fish and coral gardens. The transparent underwater tunnels are eerily spectacular.

AUSTRALIAN NATIONAL MARITIME MUSEUM

This wonderful thematic **museum** (☎ 9298 3777; 2 Murray St; adult/concession/family $10/6/25; ☯ 9.30am-5pm) tells the story of Australia's relationship with the sea, from Aboriginal canoes and the First Fleet to surf culture and the America's Cup. Even the building, with its sail-like roof and wavelike lines, harkens to the sea. The museum is near the western end of Pyrmont Bridge, and has good disabled access. Regular guided tours are available too.

POWERHOUSE MUSEUM

Sydney's hippest **museum** (☎ 9217 0100; 500 Harris St, Ultimo; adult/concession/family $10/3/23, under-5s & seniors free; ☯ 10am-5pm) covers the decorative arts, social history, and science and technology, with eclectic exhibitions ranging from costume jewellery and modern music to space capsules. The collections are superbly displayed and the emphasis is on hands-on interaction and education via enjoyment. Find it behind the Sydney Exhibition Centre – it's in a former power station for Sydney's now-defunct trams.

CHINESE GARDEN OF FRIENDSHIP

The tranquil **Chinese Garden** (☎ 9281 6863; adult/child/family $4.50/2/10; ☯ 9.30am-5.30pm), in the southeastern corner of Darling Harbour, was designed by landscape architects from Guangdong. It is an oasis of lush serenity – enter through the Courtyard of Welcoming

Fragrance, circle the Lake of Brightness and finish with tea and cake in the **Chinese teahouse** (☺ 10am-4.30pm), or by having your photo taken in a Chinese opera costume (hey, Liv Tyler did).

SYDNEY FISH MARKET

With over 15 million kilograms of seafood sold here annually, this enormous **fish market** (Map p74; ☎ 9004 1100; cnr Pyrmont Bridge Rd & Bank St, Pyrmont; ☺ 7am-4pm) is the place to get on first-name terms with a bewildering array of still-thrashing piscatorial pals. You can see fish auctions (early mornings), eat sushi, attend seafood cooking classes (call for details) and wonder if you'll ever get the stink out of your nostrils. It's west of Darling Harbour, on Blackwattle Bay. The metrail is the best way to get here (the stop's called Fish Market).

Macquarie Street   Map pp68-70

Sydney's greatest concentration of early public buildings grace Macquarie St, which runs along the eastern edge of the city from Hyde Park to the Opera House. Many of the buildings were commissioned by Lachlan Macquarie, the first governor to have a vision of the city beyond it being a convict colony. He enlisted convict forger Francis Greenway as an architect to realise his plans.

Two Greenway gems on Queens Square, at the northern end of Hyde Park, are **St James Church** (1819–24) and the Georgian style **Hyde Park Barracks Museum** (☎ 9223 8922; Queens Square, Macquarie St; adult/child/family $7/3/17; ☺ 9.30am-5pm) built in 1819. The barracks were built originally as convict quarters, then became an immigration depot, and later a court. The museum details the history of the building and provides an interesting perspective on Sydney's social history, with the best use of rats (see for yourself) we've ever seen in a display. Next door is the lovely **Mint Building** (☎ 9217 0311; Macquarie St), which was originally the southern wing of the infamous Rum Hospital built by two Sydney merchants in 1816 in return for a monopoly on the rum trade. It became a branch of the Royal Mint in 1854. There's a café on the premises, but nothing else is open to the public.

The Mint's twin is **Parliament House** (☎ 9230 2047; Macquarie St; admission free; ☺ 9.30am-4pm Mon-Fri), which was originally the northern wing of the Rum Hospital. This simple, proud building has been home to the NSW Parliament since 1829. The public gallery is open on days when parliament is sitting. Wheelchair access is excellent.

Next to Parliament House is the **State Library of NSW** (☎ 9273 1414; Macquarie St; ☺ 9am-5pm Mon-Fri, 11am-5pm Sat & Sun), which is more of a cultural centre than a traditional library. It holds over five million tomes, the smallest being a tablet-sized *Lord's Prayer*, and hosts innovative temporary exhibitions in its **galleries** (☺ 9am-5pm Mon-Fri, 10am-5pm Sat & Sun). The library's modern wing (easy to spot) also has a great bookshop, filled with Australian titles. Disabled access is excellent.

The **Sydney Conservatorium of Music** (☎ 9351 1222; Macquarie St) was built by Greenway as the stables and servants' quarters of Macquarie's planned government house. Macquarie was replaced as governor before the house could be finished, partly because of the project's extravagance. See p89 for details on music recitals held here.

Built between 1837 and 1845, **Government House** (☎ 9931 5222; Macquarie St; admission free; ☺ grounds 10am-4pm daily, house 10am-3pm Fri-Sun) dominates the western headland of Farm Cove and, until early 1996, was the official residence of the governor of NSW. It's a marvellous example of the Gothic Revival style. Tours of the house depart every half-hour from 10.30am.

Art Gallery of New South Wales

The **art gallery** (AGNSW; Map pp68-70; ☎ 9225 1744; Art Gallery Rd; admission free; ☺ 10am-5pm) has an excellent permanent display of 19th- and 20th-century Australian art, Aboriginal and Torres Strait Islander art, 15th- to 19th-century European and Asian art, and some inspired temporary exhibits. It's in the Domain, east of Macquarie St. Free guided tours are held at 1pm. There's a free Aboriginal dance performance at noon Tuesday to Saturday. There's usually a charge for some temporary exhibitions. The often controversial, much-discussed Archibald Prize exhibition is held here annually, with portraits of the famous and not-so-famous bringing out the art critic in almost every Sydneysider. Wheelchair access is good.

Australian Museum

This natural history **museum** (Map pp68-70; ☎ 9320 6000; www.amonline.net.au; 6 College St; adult/child/family $8/3/19; ⏰ 9.30am-5pm) has an excellent Australian wildlife collection and a gallery tracing Aboriginal history and the Dreamtime. It's on the eastern flank of Hyde Park, on the corner of College and William Sts. There's an indigenous performance at noon and 2pm every Sunday, and a range of kids' activities in the holidays. It's also wheelchair accessible.

Royal Botanic Gardens

The city's favourite picnic spot, jogging route and place to stroll is the enchanting **Royal Botanic Gardens** (Map pp68-70; ☎ 9231 8111; Mrs Macquaries Rd; admission free; ⏰ 7am-sunset, visitors centre 9.30am-5pm) which borders Farm Cove, east of the Opera House. The gardens were established in 1816 and feature plants from the South Pacific. These include the site of the colony's first paltry vegetable patch, which has been preserved as the First Farm exhibit.

There's a fabulous **Sydney Tropical Centre** (Map pp68-70; adult/child $2.20/1.10; ⏰ 10am-4pm) housed in the interconnecting Arc and Pyramid glasshouses. It's a great place to visit on a cool, grey day. The multistorey Arc has a collection of rampant climbers and trailers from the world's rainforests, while the Pyramid houses the Australian collection, including monsoonal, woodland and tropical rainforest plants. Other attractions in the gardens include the Fernery, the Succulent Garden and the Rose Garden.

Free guided tours depart at 10.30am daily from the information booth at the Gardens Shop. As far as wildlife goes, you can't fail to notice the gardens' resident colony of grey-headed flying foxes (Pteropus poliocephalus), who spend their days hanging around (literally) and their nights in flight.

The park's paths are, for the most part, wheelchair accessible, although there are some flights of stairs scattered about.

Other Parks & Gardens

The **Domain** (Map pp68-70) is a pleasant grassy area east of Macquarie St that was set aside by Governor Phillip for public recreation. Today it's used by city workers as a place to escape the city hubbub, and on Sunday afternoon it's the favoured gathering place for soapbox speakers who do their best to engage or enrage their listeners.

On the eastern edge of the city centre is the formal **Hyde Park** (Map pp68-70), once the colony's first racetrack and cricket pitch. It has a grand avenue of trees, delightful fountains, and a giant public chessboard. It contains the dignified **Anzac Memorial** (Map pp68-70), which has a free exhibition on the ground floor covering the 10 overseas conflicts in which Australians have fought. **St Mary's Cathedral** (Map pp68-70; ☎ 9220 0400; cnr College St & St Mary's Rd; ⏰ 6.30am-6pm), with its new copper spires, overlooks the park from the east, and the 1878 **Great Synagogue** (Map pp68-70; ☎ 9267 2477; 187a Elizabeth St) from the west. Free tours of the synagogue take place at noon Tuesday and Thursday (entry at 166 Castlereagh St).

Sydney's biggest park is **Centennial Park** (Map pp72-3), which has running, cycling, skating and horse-riding tracks, duck ponds, barbecue sites and sports pitches. It's 5km from the centre, just southeast of Paddington.

Moore Park (Map pp72-3) abuts the western flank of Centennial Park and contains sports pitches, a golf course, an equestrian centre, the Fox film studio and entertainment complex, the Aussie Stadium and the Sydney Cricket Ground (SCG). **Sportspace Tours** (☎ 9380 0383; adult/child/family $20/13/52; ⏰ 10am & 1pm Mon-Fri) offers behind-the-scenes guided tours (1½ hours) of the SCG and Aussie Stadium.

Kings Cross

The Cross is a cocktail of strip joints, prostitution, crime, and drugs shaken and stirred; with a handful of great restaurants, smart cafés, upmarket hotels and backpacker hostels. It attracts an odd mix of highlife, lowlife, sailors, tourists and suburbanites looking for a big night out.

The Cross has always been lovably raffish, from its early days as a centre of bohemianism to the Vietnam War era, when it became the vice centre of Australia. It appeals to the larrikin spirit, which always enjoys a bit of devil-may-care and 24-hour drinking. Many travellers begin and end their Australian adventures in the Cross, and it's a good place to swap information, meet up with friends, find work, browse notice boards and buy/sell a car.

Darlinghurst Rd is the trashy main drag. This doglegs into Macleay St, which continues into salubrious Potts Point. Most hostels are on Victoria St, which diverges from Darlinghurst Rd just north of William St, near the iconic Coca-Cola sign. The thistlelike **El Alamein Fountain** (Map p71), in the Fitzroy Gardens, has a small market here every Sunday.

In the dip between the Cross and the city is **Woolloomooloo**, one of Sydney's oldest areas, and an interesting place to stroll around. The **Finger Wharf** (Map pp68-70) houses apartments, restaurants and a hotel. **Harry's Café de Wheels** (Map pp68-70), next to the wharf, must be one of the few pie carts in the world that is a tourist attraction. It opened in 1945, stays open 18 hours a day and is the place to go for a late-night fill-up.

The easiest way to get to the Cross from the city is by train (adult/concession $2.20/ $1.10). It's the first stop outside the city loop on the line to Bondi Junction. Bus Nos 324, 325 and 327 from Circular Quay pass through the Cross. You can stroll from Hyde Park along William St in 15 minutes. A longer, more interesting route involves crossing the Domain, traversing the pedestrian bridge behind the AGNSW, walking past Woolloomooloo's wharf and climbing McElhone Stairs from Cowper Wharf Rd, ending up at the northern end of Victoria St.

Inner East

The backbone of Darlinghurst, Surry Hills and Paddington, **Oxford Street** is one of the more happening places for late-night action. It's a strip of shops, cafés, bars and nightclubs whose flamboyance and spirit can be largely attributed to the vibrant and vocal gay community. The route of the Sydney Gay & Lesbian Mardi Gras parade passes this way.

The main drag of Oxford St runs from the southeastern corner of Hyde Park to the northwestern corner of Centennial Park, though it continues in name to Bondi Junction. Taylor Square is the main hub. (An orientation warning: Oxford St's street numbers recommence on the Darlinghurst-Paddington border, west of the junction with South Dowling and Victoria Sts.) Bus Nos 380 and 382 from Circular Quay, and No 378 from Railway Square, run the length of the street.

Darlinghurst is a vital area of urban cool, full of bright young things. There's no better

---

BEST VIEWS IN TOWN...

Sydney is an ostentatious city that offers visitors a dramatic spectacle. You can see the complete panorama by whooshing to the top of **Sydney Tower** (Map pp68-70; ☎ 9223 0933; www.sydneyskytour.com.au; cnr Market & Castlereagh Sts; adult/child/concession/family $22/ 13.20/15.85/55; ☼ 9am-10.30pm, 9am-11.30pm Sat), a needle-like column with an observation deck and revolving restaurants set 250m above the ground. The views extend west to the Blue Mountains and east to the ocean, as well as to the streets of inner Sydney below. Skytour is a virtual reality ride through Australia's history and landscape, and is included in the admission price. To get to the tower, enter Centrepoint from Market St and take the lift to the podium level where you buy your ticket.

The **Harbour Bridge** is another obvious vantage point: try the **Pylon Lookout** (Map pp68-70) or a **Bridgeclimb tour** (p58).

There are impressive ground-level views of the city and harbour from **Mrs Macquaries Point**, and from **Observatory Hill** in Millers Point. **Blues Point Reserve** and **Bradleys Head** are the best vantage points on the North Shore.

The most enjoyable and atmospheric way to view Sydney is by boat. If you can't persuade someone to take you sailing, jump aboard a ferry at Circular Quay. The Manly ferry offers an unforgettable cruise down the length of the harbour east of the bridge for a mere $5.80.

If you're in the vicinity of Kings Cross, the northern end of Victoria St in **Potts Point** is an excellent vantage point to take in the cityscape and its best-known icons, especially at night.

---

way to soak up its studied ambience than to loiter in a few outdoor cafés and do as the others do. Darlinghurst is wedged between Oxford and William Sts, and encompasses the vibrant 'Little Italy' of Stanley St in East Sydney. The **Sydney Jewish Museum** (Map p71; ☎ 9360 7999; 148 Darlinghurst Rd; adult/child/family $10/6/22; ☼ 10am-4pm Sun-Thu, 10am-2pm Fri, closed Jewish holidays), on the corner of Darlinghurst Rd and Burton St, has evocative and powerful exhibits on Australian Jewish history and the Holocaust.

South of Darlinghurst is Surry Hills, home to a mishmash of inner-city residents and a swag of good pubs. Once the undisputed centre of Sydney's rag trade and print media, many of its warehouses have been converted to flash apartments. The **Brett Whiteley Studio** (Map pp72-3; ☎ 9225 1744; 2 Raper St; adult/concession $7/5; ✆ 10am-4pm Sat & Sun) is in the artist's old studio. You'll be able to identify it by the two large matches (one burnt, one intact) at the door. Surry Hills is a short (uphill) walk east of Central Station or south from Oxford St. Catch bus No 301, 302 or 303 from Circular Quay.

Next door to Surry Hills, Paddington is an attractive residential area of leafy streets, tightly packed Victorian terrace houses and numerous small art galleries. It was built for aspiring artisans, but during the lemming-like rush to the outer suburbs after WWII the area became a slum. A renewed interest in Victorian architecture and the pleasures of inner-city life led to its restoration during the 1960s and today many terraces swap hands for a million dollars.

Most facilities, shops, cafés and bars are on Oxford St but the suburb doesn't really have a geographic centre. Most of its streets cascade northwards down the hill towards Edgecliff and Double Bay. It's always a lovely place to wander around, but the best time to visit is on Saturday when the **Paddington Markets** are in full swing (p92).

At **Moore Park**, much of the former RAS Showgrounds has been converted into **Fox Studios** (Map pp72-3; ☎ 9383 4333; Lang Rd, Moore Park; ✆ 10am-midnight) film and entertainment complex. As well as the film studio, the complex includes cinemas, a bowling alley and a shopping/dining precinct.

Eastern Suburbs

A short walk northeast of the Cross is the harbourside suburb of **Elizabeth Bay**. **Elizabeth Bay House** (Map pp68-70; ☎ 9356 3022; 7 Onslow Ave; adult/child/family $7/3/17; ✆ 10am-4.30pm Tue-Sun), by architect John Verge, is one of Sydney's finest colonial homes and dates from 1839.

Beautiful **Rushcutters Bay** is the next bay east. Its handsome harbourside park is just a five-minute walk from the Cross and a great spot for cooped-up travellers to stretch their legs.

Further east is ritzy **Double Bay**, a suburb well endowed with old-fashioned cafés and exclusive stores. The views from the harbour-hugging New South Head Rd as it leaves Double Bay, passes Rose Bay and climbs east towards wealthy Vaucluse are stupendous.

Vaucluse House (Map pp66-8; ☎ 9388 7922; Wentworth Rd, Vaucluse; adult/child/family $7/3/17; ✆ 10am-4.30pm Tue-Sun), in Vaucluse Park, is a beautifully preserved colonial mansion dating from 1827. The Bondi Explorer bus (p59) stops here.

At the entrance to the harbour is **Watsons Bay**, a snug community with restored fisherman's cottages, a palm-lined park and a couple of nautical churches. If you want to forget you're in the middle of a large city, it's handy. Nearby **Camp Cove** is one of Sydney's best harbour beaches, and there's a nude beach (mostly male) near South Head at **Lady Bay**. South Head has great views across the harbour entrance to North Head and Middle Head. **The Gap** is a dramatic cliff-top lookout on the ocean side, which has a reputation for suicides.

Bus Nos 324 and 325 from Circular Quay service the eastern suburbs via Kings Cross. Sit on the left side heading east to make the most of the views.

Eastern Beaches

Bondi lords it over every other beach in the city, despite not being the best one for a swim, surf or, damn it, a place to park. The suburb itself has a unique atmosphere due to its mix of old Jewish and other European communities, dyed-in-the-wool Aussies, New Zealanders who never went home, working travellers and the *seriously* good-looking.

Bondi has shed much of its previously seedy façade – a lick of paint, some landscaping and flash cafés set it up to be 'rediscovered' by the world and his wife in the early 1990s, and it hasn't quietened down since.

The ocean road is Campbell Pde, home to most of the commerce. There are **Aboriginal rock engravings** (Map p84) on the golf course in North Bondi – look for the large chimney on the hill.

Catch bus No 380, 382, L82 or 389 from the city to get to the beach or, if you're in a hurry, catch a train to Bondi Junction and pick up one of these buses as they pass through the Bondi Junction bus station.

Just south of Bondi is **Tamarama**, a lovely cove with strong rips. Get off the bus as it kinks off Bondi Rd onto Fletcher St, just before it reaches Bondi Beach. Tamarama is a five-minute walk down the hill.

There's a superb beach hemmed in by a bowl-shaped park and sandstone headlands at **Bronte**, south of Tamarama. The cafés with outdoor tables on the edge of the park make it a great chill-out destination. Catch bus No 378 from Railway Square or catch a train to Bondi Junction and pick the bus up there; sit on the left side for a breathtaking view as the bus descends Macpherson St. You can walk to Bronte along the wonderful cliff-top footpath from Bondi Beach or from Coogee via Gordon's Bay, Clovelly and the sun-bleached Waverley Cemetery.

Clovelly Bay is a narrow scooped-out beach to the south. As well as the saltwater baths here, there's a wheelchair-access boardwalk so the chair-bound can take a sea dip.

Something of a poor cousin to Bondi, **Coogee** has spruced itself up in recent years. It has a relaxed air, a good sweep of sand and a couple of established hostels and hotels. You can reach Coogee by catching bus No 372 from Railway Square or No 373 from Circular Quay. Alternatively, take a train to Bondi Junction and pick up bus No 314 or 315 from there.

Bondi too busy? Coogee too crazy? Head a little further south to **Maroubra** and you'll certainly get the feeling that this beach hasn't been overtaken by outsiders. In fact, it's avowedly local – punch-ups have been known to occur when visitors 'drop in' on waves earmarked for locals, and it seems that every wave is earmarked for a local. Those wanting a simple swim or beachside stroll will have no hassles though.

Inner West

West of the centre is the higgledy-piggledy peninsula suburb of **Balmain**. It was once a notoriously rough neighbourhood of dockyard workers but has been turned into an arty, middle-class area of restored Victoriana flush with pubs and cafés. It's a great place for a stroll or for its wonderful Saturday **market** (p92). Catch a ferry from Circular Quay or bus No 442 from the QVB.

Cosy, bohemian **Glebe** is southwest of the centre, bordering the northern edge of the University of Sydney. It has a large student population, a cruisy café-lined main street, a tranquil Buddhist temple, aromatherapy and crystals galore, and several decent places to stay. A **market** is held at Glebe Public School, on Glebe Point Rd, on Saturday. It's a 10-minute walk from Central Station along smoggy Broadway or you can walk from the city centre across Darling Harbour's Pyrmont Bridge and along Pyrmont Bridge Rd (20 minutes). Bus Nos 431 to 434 from Millers Point run via George St along Glebe Point Rd. The Metro Light Rail also travels through Glebe.

Bordering the southern flank of the university is **Newtown**, a melting pot of social and sexual subcultures, students and home renovators. King St, its relentlessly urban main drag, is full of funky clothes stores, bookshops and cafés. While it's definitely moving upmarket, Newtown comes with a healthy dose of grunge, and harbours a decent live-music scene. The best way to get there is by train, but bus Nos 422, 423, 426 and 428 from the city all run along King St.

Predominantly Italian **Leichhardt**, southwest of Glebe, is becoming increasingly popular with students, lesbians and young professionals. Its Italian eateries on Norton St have a citywide reputation. Bus Nos 436 to 440 run from the city to Leichhardt.

North Shore   Map p76

On the northern side of the Harbour Bridge is **North Sydney**, a high-rise office centre with little to tempt the traveller.

McMahons Point is a lovely, forgotten suburb wedged between the two business districts, on the western side of the bridge. There's a line of pleasant alfresco cafés on Blues Point Rd, which runs down to Blues Point Reserve on the western headland of Lavender Bay. The reserve has fine city views.

Luna Park, on the eastern shore of Lavender Bay, is currently closed, but the big mouth is a highly visible landmark. At the end of Kirribilli Point, just east of the bridge, stand **Admiralty House** and **Kirribilli House**, the Sydney residences of the governor general and the prime minister respectively. (Admiralty House is the one nearer the bridge.)

East of here are the upmarket suburbs of **Neutral Bay**, **Cremorne** and **Mosman**, all with pleasant coves and harbourside parks perfect for picnics. Ferries go to all these suburbs from Circular Quay.

On the northern side of Mosman is the pretty beach suburb of **Balmoral**, which faces

Manly across Middle Harbour. There are picnic areas, a promenade and three beaches.

Taronga Zoo

In a superb harbourside setting, **Taronga Zoo** (Map pp66-7; ☎ 9969 2777; Bradleys Head Rd, Mosman; adult/child/family $23/13/57; ⏱ 9am-5pm) has more than 2000 critters (from seals to tigers, koalas to giraffes, gorillas to platypuses) all (thankfully) well cared for. Ferries to the zoo depart from Circular Quay's Wharf 2, half-hourly from 7.15am on weekdays, 8.45am Saturday and 9am Sunday. The zoo is on a steep hillside and it makes sense to work your way down if you plan to depart by ferry. If you can't be bothered to climb to the top entrance, take the bus or the Sky Safari cable car. A **ZooPass** (adult/child $32/16), sold at Circular Quay and elsewhere, includes return ferry rides, the Sky Safari and zoo admission.

Manly   Map p56

The jewel of the North Shore, Manly is on a narrow peninsula that ends at the dramatic cliffs of North Head. It boasts harbour and ocean beaches, a ferry wharf, all the trappings of a full-scale holiday resort and a great sense of community. It's a sun-soaked place not afraid to show a bit of tack and brashness to attract visitors, and makes a refreshing change from the prim upper-middle-class harbour enclaves nearby.

The **Manly Visitors Information Centre** (☎ 9977 1088; Manly Wharf; ⏱ 9am-5pm Mon-Fri, 10am-4pm Sat & Sun), just outside the ferry wharf, has free pamphlets on the 10km Manly Scenic Walkway and bus information. Ferries and JetCat catamarans operate between Circular Quay and Manly. JetCats seem to traverse the harbour before you get a chance to blink, while the ferries do the trip in a cool 30 minutes and offer fantastic views.

The ferry wharf is on the Manly Cove foreshore. A short walk along Manly's pedestrian mall, The Corso, brings you to the ocean beach lined with towering Norfolk pines. North and South Steyne are the roads running along the foreshore. A footpath follows the shoreline from South Steyne around the small headland to tiny **Fairy Bower Beach** and the picturesque cove of **Shelly Beach**.

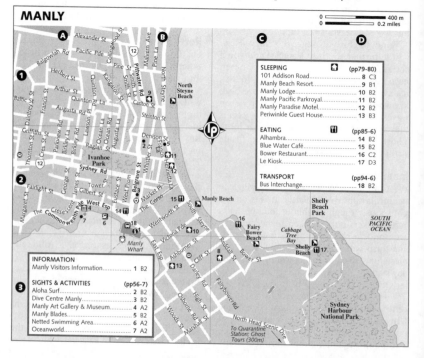

MANLY

0 — 400 m
0 — 0.2 miles

The **Manly Art Gallery & Museum** (☎ 9949 2435; West Esplanade Reserve; adult/child/concession $3.50/free/1.10; ☺ 10am-5pm Tue-Sun), on the Manly Cove foreshore, focuses on the suburb's special relationship with the beach.

Oceanworld (☎ 9949 2644; West Esplanade; adult/child/family $16/8/25; ☺ 10am-5.30pm) is next door. The big drawcards are the sharks and stingrays. Check to see what times you can view divers feeding the sharks. An underwater perspex tunnel offers dramatic (but dry) close encounters with the fish, plus there's some wheelchair and pram access.

Behind the gallery, starts the wonderful 9km-long **Manly Scenic Walkway**. It has has a 2km-long wheelchair-accessible path.

North Head, at the entrance to Sydney Harbour, is about 3km south of Manly. Most of the dramatic headland is in Sydney Harbour National Park. The **Manly Quarantine Station** represents an interesting slice of Sydney's social history; it housed suspected disease carriers from 1832 right up until 1984. To visit the station, book a **guided tour** (☎ 9247 5033; adult/child $11/7.70; ☺ 1.15pm daily except Tue & Thu). The station is reputedly haunted and there are spooky three-hour ghost tours (adults only) at night from Friday to Sunday ($22 to $28).

Northern Beaches

A string of ocean-front suburbs sweeps 30km north from Manly, ending at beautiful, well-heeled **Palm Beach** and the spectacular Barrenjoey Heads at the entrance to **Broken Bay**. Beaches along the way include **Freshwater**, **Curl Curl**, **Dee Why**, **Collaroy** and **Narrabeen**. The most spectacular are **Whale Beach** and **Bilgola** (near Palm Beach), both with dramatic, steep headlands. Several of the northernmost beach suburbs also back onto **Pittwater**, a lovely inlet, and favoured sailing spot, off Broken Bay.

Bus Nos 136 and 139 run from Manly to Curl Curl and Freshwater respectively. Bus No L90 from Wynyard Park bus interchange in the city runs to Newport and then north to Palm Beach.

ACTIVITIES
Canoeing & Kayaking

The obvious choice for a kayaking experience in Sydney is Sydney Harbour – although you might want to bear in mind that the harbour is both big and busy, especially if you're a novice. Contact the **New South Wales Canoeing Association** (☎ 9660 4597; www.nswcanoe.org.au; Wentworth Park Complex, Wattle St, Ultimo) for information on canoe courses and hire.

Natural Wanders (☎ 9899 1001; www.kayaksydney.com) has exhilarating kayak tours of the harbour which pass under the bridge and stop in secluded bays ($90 for a half-day tour).

Cycling

Sydney's geography, humidity and drivers can all lead to frustration for the cyclist – the best spot to get some spoke action is Centennial Park. **Bicycle NSW** (Map pp72-3; ☎ 9281 4099; www.bicyclensw.org.au; Level 5, 822 George St, Sydney) publishes a handy book *Cycling Around Sydney*, which details routes and cycle paths.

CYCLE HIRE

Many cycle-hire shops require a hefty deposit (about $500) or a credit card.

Cheeky Monkey (Map pp68-70; ☎ 9212 4460; 456 Pitt St, Sydney; per day/week $25/100; ☺ 8.30am-6.30pm Mon-Sat) Very cheap and basic – extras will cost you.

Inner City Cycles (Map p74; ☎ 9660 6605; 151 Glebe Point Rd, Glebe; per day/week $33/90; ☺ 9.30am-6pm Mon-Wed & Fri, to 8pm Thu; to 4pm Sat, 11am-3pm Sun)

Wooly's Wheels (Map pp72-3; ☎ 9331 2671; 82 Oxford St, Paddington; per day/week $33/180; ☺ 9am-6pm Mon-Wed & Fri, to 8pm Thu, to 4pm Sat, 11am-4pm Sun) Across from the Victoria Barracks and very handy to Centennial Park.

Diving

The best shore dives in Sydney are at the Gordons Bay Underwater Nature Trail, north of Coogee; Shark Point, Clovelly; and Ship Rock, Cronulla. Popular boat dive sites are Wedding Cake Island, off Coogee; around the Sydney Heads; and off the Royal National Park.

Dive Centre Bondi (Map p84; ☎ 9369 3855; 192 Bondi Rd, Bondi)

Dive Centre Manly (Map p56; ☎ 9977 4355; 10 Belgrave St, Manly) The two branches of this dive outfit have courses starting from $350 and a good reputation.

In-line Skating

The beach promenades at Bondi and Manly and the paths of Centennial Park are the most favoured spots for skating.

Manly Blades (Map p56; ☎ 9976 3833; 49 North Steyne, Manly) Hires blades (from $12), scooters (from $7) and baby joggers (from $12) from their handily located premises, which will let you whizz around Manly in no time.

Total Skate (Map pp72-3; ☎ 9380 6356; 36 Oxford St, Woollahra; first hr $10, per hr thereafter $5) Perfectly positioned near Centennial Park and includes protective gear such as helmets and kneepads in the in-line skate hire fee.

Sailing

There are plenty of sailing schools in Sydney and even if you're not serious about learning the ropes, an introductory lesson can be a fun way of getting out on the harbour.

Eastsail Sailing School (Map pp68-70; ☎ 9327 1166; www.eastsail.com.au; d'Albora Marina, New Beach Rd, Rushcutters Bay) A sociable outfit with a lot of boats. They run a range of courses from introductory ($470) to racing level.

Sydney by Sail (Map pp68-70; ☎ 9280 1110; www.sydneybysail.com) Departs daily from the Australian National Maritime Museum in Darling Harbour and offers a comprehensive introductory sailing course ($450) that takes place over a whole weekend. A wide range of other sailing packages are also available.

Surfing

South of the Heads, the best spots are Bondi, Tamarama, Coogee and Maroubra. Cronulla, south of Botany Bay, is also a serious surfing spot. On the North Shore, there are a dozen surf beaches between Manly and Palm Beach; the best are Manly, Curl Curl, Dee Why, North Narrabeen, Mona Vale, Newport Reef, North Avalon and Palm Beach itself.

Aloha Surf (Map p56; ☎ 9977 3777, 44 Pittwater Rd, Manly; half/full day board hire $25/50) Hire surfing equipment and try your luck on Manly Beach.

Learn to Surf (☎ 1800 851 101; www.wavessurfschool.com.au; lessons from $69) Positive feedback and trips to the Royal National Park (p101) and Byron Bay (p180).

Let's Go Surfing (Map p84; ☎ 9365 1800; www.letsgosurfing.com.au; 128a Ramsgate Ave, Bondi; lessons from $59) You can learn to surf on Bondi Beach with this outfit.

Swimming

Sydney's harbour beaches offer sheltered swimming spots. But if you just want to frolic, nothing beats being knocked around in the waves that pound the ocean beaches, where swimming is safe if you follow instructions and swim within the flagged areas patrolled by lifeguards. There are some notorious but clearly signposted rips, even at Sydney's most popular beaches, so don't underestimate the surf just because it looks safe.

Outdoor pools in the city:

Andrew 'Boy' Charlton Pool (Map pp68-70; ☎ 9358 6686; Mrs Macquaries Rd, The Domain; adult/child $4.50/3.50; 6.30am-8pm) Saltwater, smack bang on the

harbour and popular with gays, this is Sydney's best pool. It's more for serious lap-swimmers than those wishing to splash around, but the five-star change rooms will soon psych you into it.

North Sydney Olympic Pool (Map p76; ☎ 9955 2309; Alfred St South, Milsons Point; adult/child $4.20/2; 5.30am-9pm Mon-Fri, 7am-7pm Sat & Sun) Just near the entrance to Luna Park, this is a nice outdoor pool (there's an undercover 25m one too) on the North Shore.

Sydney Aquatic Centre (map p66-7; ☎ 9752 3699; Olympic Blvd, Sydney Olympic Park, Homebush Bay; adult/child $5.80/4.60; 5am-8.45pm Mon-Fri, 6am-6.45pm Sat & Sun) State-of-the-art facilities as used in the Sydney 2000 Olympic Games, where many world records were smashed, thus proving its reputation as a 'fast pool'.

WALKING TOUR
Bondi to Coogee Coastal Walk

This beautiful coastal walk leads south from North Bondi, along Bondi Beach to the beaches of Clovelly and Coogee, via Tamarama and Bronte. It combines panoramic views, swimming opportunities and loads of chances for a cup of coffee or a freshly squeezed juice at a beachside café.

Begin at the **Bondi Golf Course (1)** to see the **Aboriginal rock engravings (2)**. Follow Military Rd south and turn left into Ramsgate Ave to get to mind-blowing views of Bondi Beach. The walking path from here leads to the beach. After a quick dip (even if it's just your toes), you may want to visit the **Bondi markets (3**; p92) for cool clothes or retro furnishings. Otherwise, pop your head into the **Bondi Pavilion (4)** to see if there's an art show or musical performance in progress.

Walk to **Campbell Pde** and the surrounding little streets for a snack or to purchase an itsy-bitsy bikini, or continue up the beach promenade to Notts Ave to the lavishly refurbished **Bondi Icebergs (5)**. It has one of Sydney's hottest restaurants and a dramatic, icy, seaside swimming pool. Get your camera ready: the walking path, with its impressive cliff and ocean views, starts here (keep an eye out for surfers, and maybe, just maybe, a dolphin or whale). The track leads to pretty **Tamarama Beach (6)** and on to **Bronte Beach (7)**, which has a host of wonderful cafés to sustain you.

Continue past the **Bronte Baths (8)**, and head south past the atmospheric sun-bleached **Waverley Cemetery (9)**. When you reach the **Clovelly Bowling Club (10)**, you might be tempted to pop in for a beer or a game

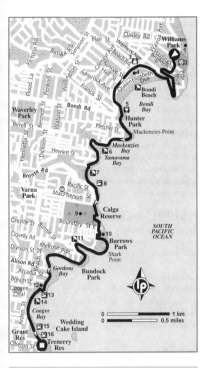

WALK FACTS

Start: bus No 380 or 389 North Bondi
Finish: bus No 314, 372-4 Coogee Beach
Distance: 5km
Time: 2-2½ hours

of bowls (the club has to-die-for ocean views). From here, cut through Burrows Park and Bundock Park, to reach **Clovelly Beach (11**; p54**)**, where you can also grab a coffee should the mood take you, or make a toilet stop.

Follow the footpath up through the car park, then head along Cliffbrook Pde and down the steps to small Gordons Bay. The parkland continues from here all the way to **Dunningham Reserve (12)** and the charming **Giles Baths rockpool (13)**. A hop, skip and a jump down some steps puts you smack-bang on glorious **Coogee Beach (14)**. If you walk the length of the beach, you'll reach the historic seabaths of **Wylie's Baths (15)** and **McIver's Baths (16)**, both in Grant Reserve.

SYDNEY FOR CHILDREN

Sydney offers children a wealth of options. A good publication to look out for is the free *Sydney's Child* magazine. Many attractions, such as galleries and museums, have school-holiday programs, and a few sights are aimed solely at kids.

Kids' ghost tours (Map p56; ☎ 9247 5033; Quarantine Station, North Head Scenic Dr, Manly; admission $14; ☾ 5.45pm Fri) are given at the Quarantine Station and should get them revved up for a night of squeals. Bookings are essential.

A dinky **People Mover** (☎ 0408-290 515; adult/child $3.50/2.50) snakes around Darling Harbour's attractions every day, relieving tired little legs.

TOURS
Harbour Cruises

There's a wide range of cruises on the harbour, from ferry boats and cruisers to paddle-steamers and sailing ships.

Harboursights Cruises (☎ 13 15 00; adult/child/family from $15/7.50/38) Run by the State Transit Authority (STA), these excellent short cruises allow you to take in the sights, sounds and, sometimes, smells of the harbour. Take your pick from the Morning Cruise (one hour), the Afternoon Cruise (2½ hours) or the Evening Harbour Lights Cruise (1½ hours). Tickets can be bought at ferry ticket offices in Circular Quay.

Magistic Cruises (☎ 8296 7222; www.magisticcruis es.com.au; King St Wharf 5, Darling Harbour or Wharf 6, Circular Quay; adult/child/family $20/15/55) With regular departures daily and all the Sydney Harbour icons on the itinerary, the fancy boats of Magistic are a good way to see the sights (with a free beer) in an hour.

Matilda Rocket Express (☎ 9264 7377; www.matilda .com.au; Pier 26, Aquarium Wharf, Darling Harbour; adult/ child/family $21/11/50) A good option for those wanting to savour it quickly, these cruises will take you to Darling Harbour, Watsons Bay, Sydney Aquarium, Taronga Zoo, The Rocks, the Opera House and the Royal Botanic Gardens. The best bit is that you can start your cruise at one of five locations. Commentary, tea, coffee and biscuits all provided.

City Bus Tours

The best bus tours are operated by the STA.

Bondi Explorer (☎ 13 15 00; adult/child/family $30/ 15/75; ☾ 8.45am-4.15pm) Operates along similar lines, running a much larger circuit from Circular Quay to Kings Cross, Double Bay, Rose Bay, Vaucluse, Watsons Bay, the Gap, Bondi Beach and Coogee, returning to the city along Oxford St. Just riding around the circuit takes two hours, so if you want to get off at many of the 19 places of interest along the way, start early. Buses depart every 30 minutes or so, and tickets can be purchased on board or at STA offices.

Sydney Explorer (☎ 13 15 00; adult/child/family $30/15/75; ☼ 8.40am-5.20pm) Red STA tourist buses navigate the inner city on a route designed to pass most central attractions. A bus departs from Circular Quay every 20 minutes but you can board at any of the 26 clearly marked, red bus stops on the route. Tickets are sold on board and at STA offices, and entitle you to get on and off the bus as often as you like. There's commentary, and sights include the Opera House, the AGNSW, Kings Cross and the Powerhouse Museum, among others.

Walking Tours

Bridgeclimb (Map pp68-70; ☎ 8274 7777; www .bridgeclimb.com; 5 Cumberland St, The Rocks; adult $145-175, child $100-125) Once, it was only daredevils and bridge painters who scaled the heights and saw the breathtaking views from the Harbour Bridge. Now everyone (who's not afraid of heights) can do it. The 3½-hour tour (day or night), for which you're thoroughly well prepared by enthusiastic staff, is worth every uphill step. Go to the toilet *before* you start the climb.

Maureen Fry (☎ 9660 7157; www.ozemail.com.au /~mpfry; 15 Arcadia Rd, Glebe) Maureen caters mainly for groups, but she can take individuals or perhaps fit you in with a group. A two-hour guided walk costs $16 per person, with a minimum of 10 people. Options include Sydney and its suburbs, or lesser-known destinations within a few hours' reach of Sydney.

Sydney Aboriginal Discoveries (☎ 9599 1693; www .sydneyaustour.com.au/abordiscover.html; tours $90-180) Offers a variety of interesting tours focused on indigenous culture and history. Options include a harbour cruise, an enjoyable walkabout tour, a feast of native Australian foods, and a Dreamtime cruise. We've had good feedback about these tours.

Sydney Architecture Walks (Map pp68-70; ☎ 0403-888 390; Level 4, Customs House, 31 Alfred St, Circular Quay; adult/child $20/15) These enthusiastic building buffs will open your eyes to Sydney's architecture, both old and new. Those into the Opera House will love the Utzon walk. Strolls last two hours, and depart from Customs House in Alfred St, Sydney.

The Rocks Walking Tours (Map pp68-70; ☎ 9247 6678; Shop 4, Kendall Lane, The Rocks; adult/child $17.50/ 10.50) With regular 90-minute tours of this historic area, this outfit is the best qualified to entertain and exercise you. There are tours thrice daily on weekdays and twice daily on weekends and public holidays.

Other Tours

Bikescape (Map pp71; ☎ 9356 2453; www.bikescape .com.au; 191 William St, East Sydney; tours $95-395) Bikescape is a thoroughly trustworthy source of motorcycles for hire for a wind-in-your-hair (well, if you didn't have to wear a helmet) pillion ride. It can be as simple as a whirl round town, or a day in a national park or winery country.

Sydney by Seaplane (Map pp66-7; ☎ 1300 656 787; www.sydneybyseaplane.com; Imperial Peking Restaurant Jetty, Lyne Park, Rose Bay; adult $85-585, child $45-220) If you think Sydney looks beautiful from the ground or sea, a scenic flight will knock your socks off. This organisation has a variety of scenic flights (from 15 to 90 minutes) and charter flights/packages that allow you to view areas such as Bondi Beach, Sydney Harbour, Palm Beach and the Hawkesbury River from on high.

Sydney Jet (Map pp68-70; ☎ 9982 4000; Cockle Bay Wharf, Darling Harbour; adult/child/family from $50/35/135) Strap on a life jacket and cop a face full of sea spray with this fishtailing, fast-turning speed boat. Who knows if you'll actually manage to see anything in all that excitement, but it sounds like fun.

FESTIVALS & EVENTS

Sydney has plenty of festivals and special goings-on year-round. Visitors centres can advise you what's on when you're in town.

January

Sydney Festival This massive event floods the city with art in January, including free outdoor concerts in the Domain.

Australia Day (26 January) Australia's birthday is celebrated with BBQs, picnics and fireworks on the harbour.

February

Chinese New Year Celebrated in Chinatown with fireworks in late January or early February.

Tropfest This home-grown short-film festival ensures its flicks are fresh with the inclusion of compulsory props (announced just before the competition). Big-name stars are often the judges (eg Keanu Reeves, Nicole Kidman, Russell Crowe).

Sydney Gay & Lesbian Mardi Gras The highlight of this world-famous festival is the colourful, sequined parade along Oxford St, culminating in a bacchanalian party at the Fox Studios, in Moore Park, in late February.

March/April

Royal Easter Show This 12-day event is an agricultural show and funfair held at Homebush Bay. Bring the kids and pet the baby animals.

May

Sydney Writers' Festival Celebrates the literary in Sydney, with guest authors, talks and forums.

June

Sydney Film Festival A 14-day orgy of cinema held at the State Theatre and other cinemas.

Sydney Biennale An international art festival held in even-numbered years at the AGNSW, the Powerhouse Museum and other venues.

GAY & LESBIAN SYDNEY

In Sydney, one could be forgiven for thinking that gay is the new straight – gay and lesbian culture forms a vocal and vital part of Sydney's social fabric.

The colourful Sydney Gay & Lesbian Mardi Gras is Australia's biggest annual tourist event, and the joyful-hedonism-meets-political-protest Oxford St parade is watched by over half a million people. The Sleaze Ball (a Mardi Gras fundraiser) takes place in October, with leather taking the place of Lycra. Tickets are restricted to Mardi Gras members. Gay and lesbian international visitors wishing to attend the parties should contact the **Mardi Gras office** (☎ 9549 2100; www.mardigras .org.au) well in advance – tickets sell fast.

The Taylor Square region of Oxford St is the hub of gay life in Sydney, although there are 'pockets' in suburbs such as Paddington, Newtown, Alexandria and Leichhardt. Gay beach life is focussed on Lady Bay (nude) and Tamarama (also known as Glamarama). You may also want to check out Red Leaf Pool, on New South Head Rd just past Double Bay, or Andrew 'Boy' Charlton pool (p58). For men, tans and heavy pecs are a 'classic' look. The scene for women is a bit more inclusive.

However, there's still a homophobic side to some 'true blue' Aussies, and violence against homosexuals isn't unheard of, particularly during holidays. (For the record, in New South Wales the age of consent for homosexual sex is 16 for both men and women.)

The Sydney Gay & Lesbian Mardi Gras has established an online travel service, **Mardi Gras Travel** (www.mardigras.org.au), to assist gay and lesbian travellers coming to Australia. The free gay press includes the *Sydney Star Observer* and *Lesbians on the Loose*. These can be found in shops and cafés in the inner east and west, and have excellent listings of gay and lesbian organisations, services and events. **Gay & Lesbian Tourism Australia** (GALTA; www.galta.com.au; PO Box 208, Darlinghurst NSW 2010) can provide a wealth of information about gay and lesbian travel in Oz.

If you're keen to take part in Sydney's gay nightlife scene you can find plenty of listings in the local gay press. The following represent a mix of old favourites and newer club nights that cover both low-key and 'out-there' bases.

ARQ (☎ 9380 8700; 16 Flinders St, Darlinghurst) This excellent, large club has a 24-hour licence and very flattering lighting, which should be compulsory in more places. Good DJs are often heard here, and it's a popular place to 'recover' on Sundays.

Colombian (Map pp72-3; ☎ 9360 2151; cnr Oxford & Crown Sts, Darlinghurst) The newest kid on the gay block and kitted out like an interior decorator's dream. It's a good mix of handlebar moustaches, good music, ventilation, buff bods, plenty of space and quite a few women.

Imperial Hotel (Map pp66-7; ☎ 9519 9899; 35 Erskineville Rd, Erskineville) The film *Priscilla – Queen of the Desert* was inspired by the nightly drag here, and it's world-class. For the ladies, there's Go Girl on Thursday.

Lansdowne Hotel (Map p74; ☎ 9211 2325; 2 City Rd, Chippendale) Upstairs at the Lansdowne Hotel there's a brilliant Saturday nighter called Red Room. It's mostly for lesbians, but the atmosphere is pretty inclusive.

Lord Roberts Hotel (Map pp68-70; ☎ 9331 1326; 64 Stanley St, Sydney; ⏲ 5pm-midnight Sun) Sunday nights should probably see this place change its name to Lady Roberts, thanks to its deservedly popular (especially with lesbians) night 'Better House & Beer Garden', with lots of raucous competition at the pool table and great DJs.

Midnight Shift (Map pp72-3; ☎ 9360 4463; 85 Oxford St, Darlinghurst) It's hard to believe that a gay scene existed before this place (also nicknamed the Midnight Shirtlift). The ground floor is quite publike, but upstairs it's a licence to booze and cruise with less conversation. We like the fact that you can find a range of men here – not all of them are clones.

Newtown Hotel (Map p74; ☎ 9557 1329; 174 King St, Newtown) In Sydney's other gay enclave, the Newtown does a roaring trade with gay folk who just want to go to the local and have a good time. The drag acts are pretty good too.

Oxford Hotel (☎ 9331 3467; 134 Oxford St, Darlinghurst) With an industrial hardcore theme going on at ground level and the luxe ambience of the Gilligans and Gingers cocktail bars upstairs, this place covers the bases on Taylor Square.

Stonewall (☎ 9360 1963; 175 Oxford St, Darlinghurst) Nicknamed 'Stonehenge' by those who find it a little too ancient for their liking, this place is usually pumping and pumped-up.

July
Yulefest Christmas comes early, and is as close to white as Australia gets in this popular Blue Mountains celebration.

August
City to Surf Run This 14km-long fun run takes place on the second Sunday in August and attracts a mighty 40,000 entrants who run from Hyde Park to Bondi Beach.

September
Carnivale There's plenty of colour at this multicultural arts festival held in early spring.
Royal Botanic Gardens Spring Festival Spring into spring, with concerts, flower displays and plenty of pollen.

October
Rugby League Grand Final The two best teams left standing in the National Rugby League (NRL) meet to decide who's best.
Manly Jazz Festival Held over the Labour Day long weekend in early October and featuring lots of jazz performances, mostly free.
Kings Cross Carnival Taking place in late October or early November, this street fair includes a bed race.

November
Sculpture by the Sea Held in mid-November, the Bondi-to-Bronte walk is transformed into an outdoor sculpture gallery.

December
Christmas Day (25 December) Thousands of backpackers descend on Bondi Beach on Christmas Day, much to the consternation of the civil authorities and the overworked lifesavers.
Boxing Day (26 December) Sydney Harbour is a fantastic sight as hundreds of boats farewell the competitors in the gruelling Sydney to Hobart Yacht Race.
New Year's Eve (31 December) The Rocks, Kings Cross and Bondi Beach are traditional gathering places for alcohol-sodden celebrations on New Year's Eve, although alcohol-free zones and a massive police presence are aimed to quell the rowdier elements.

SLEEPING
As Australia's largest city, Sydney has a huge variety of accommodation – from a large selection of travellers' hostels, to deluxe hotels with harbour views and a high staff-to-guest ratio. In between, there are cosy B&Bs, comfortable motels and authentic Aussie pubs.

The city proper has a wide range of options. The largest concentration of hostels is in Kings Cross, but there are clusters (some might say ghettoes) in other areas, including Glebe, Manly, Bondi and Coogee. In these suburbs you'll also find stylish boutique hotels. The North Shore has less in the way of sleeping (apart from Manly), but rewards its guests with a tad more serenity.

Budget facilities vary from small dorms with a bathroom, TV, fridge and cooking facilities to just a plain room with a couple of bunks. Some hostels have set hours for checking in and out, although all have 24-hour access once you've paid.

In this chapter, mid-range accommodation sits in the $81 to $165 price range for a double with bathroom, unless otherwise specified. Top-end hotels and serviced apartments charging from $165 a double abound in Sydney, but since many cater to business people their rates may be lower on weekends. Serviced apartments sometimes sleep more than two people and, with lower weekly rates, they can be an inexpensive option if shared by a group.

City Centre, The Rocks & Circular Quay
BUDGET
Budget Hotels
Y on the Park (Map pp68-70; ☎ 9264 2451; www.ywca-sydney.com.au; 5-11 Wentworth Ave, Sydney; s $70-120, d & tw $100-140; 🔀) This child-friendly YWCA (that allows men to stay too) has Hyde Park across the road and the city centre and Oxford St a short walk away. The standard is high, with spotless, well-furnished rooms, some well-appointed business rooms and very comfortable, secure dorms.

Hostels
Sydney Central YHA (☎ 9281 9111; sydcentral@yhansw.org.au; 11 Rawson Pl, Sydney; dm $25-30, d/tw $75/85; 🅿 🖳) This huge heritage-listed building on the corner of Pitt St and Rawson Pl is very close to Central Station. It has wonderful kitchens, wheelchair access, a barbecue, sauna, 24-hour security access, a **travel desk** (☎ 9281 9444) and its own bar and supermarket. Some twin rooms are set up for disabled travellers, but these should be booked in advance. Call ahead and reserve your place.

Wanderers on Kent (Map pp68-70; ☎ 9267 7718; www.wanderersonkent.com.au; 477 Kent St; dm $24-33; s & d $85; 🔀 🖳) This has good, wheelchair accessible rooms and provides great access to central Sydney. Security is a strong point, and there are electronic lockers, plus a solarium, so you can get that sun-damaged look that's so popular in Oz.

MID-RANGE
Motels
Pentura Hotel (Map pp68-70; ☎ 9283 8088; 300 Pitt St; d & tw $140; ⬛) Many travellers recommend this place, and with good reason. Its location is close to both the north of the city and the area around Chinatown and Central Station, plus the rooms are in very good condition. Staff are helpful.

Quality Hotel SC Sydney (Map pp68-70; ☎ 9282 0987; www.qualitysydney.com.au; 111 Goulburn St; d $145; ⬛ ⬛ ⬛) Once known as the Southern Cross, and after refurbishment, it certainly deserves its new moniker. Rooms are very comfortable, well appointed and wheelchair friendly. It's handy to both the CBD and Darling Harbour.

RG Hotel (Map pp68-70; ☎ 9281 6999; www.rghotel .com.au; 431 Pitt St; d $125-145; ⬛ ⬛ ⬛ ⬛) Handily located near Sydney's Capitol Theatre, Chinatown, Darling Harbour and Central Station, the courteous RG has serviceable rooms and a handy business centre, plus a rooftop pool if you feel like escaping the city's bustle.

Hyde Park Inn (Map pp68-70; ☎ 9264 6001; www.hydeparkinn.com.au; 271 Elizabeth St; s $145, d & tw $160, tr $180; ⬛ ⬛) It's easy to miss this well-situated hotel, as it's nothing much to look at from the outside. Hyde Park Inn has some great views over Hyde Park and perfectly suitable 'standard' rooms with kitchenette (deluxe ones cost around $15 more). The Hyde Park Inn also has some good two-room apartments for families or larger groups.

Pubs
Australian Hotel (Map pp68-70; ☎ 9247 2229; www.au stralianheritagehotel.com; 100 Cumberland St; d $125) Despite the fact that it has shared bathrooms, we like this place for the pub downstairs and the extremely cosy communal rooms. Bedrooms are just as attractive, and the terrace area allows you to inhale Sydney Harbour.

Lord Nelson Brewery Hotel (Map pp68-70; ☎ 9251 4044; www.lordnelson.com.au; 19 Kent St; d $120; ⬛) This swish boutique pub has its own brewery and is in a historic sandstone building in the less-obviously touristy part of The Rocks. All rooms (with lovely dormer windows) have fax machines and data port facilities. The ones with bathrooms cost 50% more.

Palisade Hotel (Map pp68-70; ☎ 9247 2272; www.palisadehotel.com; 35 Bettington St; d/tw $115/125) Standing sentinel-like at Millers Point, the Palisade Hotel has nine solidly furnished rooms, some with breathtaking views of the harbour and bridge. It's a lovely old heritage building (although the shared bathrooms reflect its age), and it's in a part of The Rocks that has thankfully avoided that twee, 'ye olde worlde' tourist-trap feel.

Grand Hotel (Map pp68-70; ☎ 9232 3755; 30 Hunter St; s/d/tr; $80/100/110) The heritage-listed Grand Hotel is a pretty good city pub. Rooms are quite modest (bathrooms are shared), sizes vary and all have TV, fridge and tea- and coffee-making facilities. But the real selling point is the location, which puts you within spitting distance of the harbour.

Mercantile Hotel (Map pp68-70; ☎ 9247 3570; merc@tpg.com.au; 25 George St; d $140) This green-tiled hotel is a restored pub with a strong Irish connection. It's right near the bridge and the rooms are good. Breakfast is included in the price and there are some rooms without private bathrooms for $110. Be warned, St Patrick's Day is a madhouse here.

TOP END
Hotels
Establishment Hotel (Map pp68-70; ☎ 9240 3100; info@establishmenthotel.com; 5 Bridge Lane; d from $290; ⬛) Slicker than grease and smooth as silk, this 31-room hotel plays host to the likes of low-key moguls and secretive stars. Every (stylish) mod con is provided and eating and drinking options are literally at your feet in the same building.

Four Seasons (Map pp68-70; ☎ 9238 0000; www.four seasons.com; 199 George St; d from $360; ⬛ ⬛ ⬛ ⬛) Easily one of the main contenders for the title of 'best hotel in Sydney', the Four Seasons features luxurious rooms, extraordinarily professional staff and knockout views (city, Opera House, or harbour – take your pick) from over half its rooms. Packages are available and no request is too tricky – particularly for business travellers. Wheelchair friendly.

Park Hyatt (Map pp68-70; ☎ 9241 1234; www.sydney .hyatt.com; 7 Hickson Rd; d from $700; ⬛ ⬛ ⬛ ⬛) The super-luxurious Park Hyatt has one of the best locations in Sydney – snaking along the waterfront at the edge of Campbells Cove, almost at the Harbour Bridge and facing the Opera House. Watch out for reduced-price weekend packages that can offer substantial discounts. If you need a 24-hour butler service, this is the hotel for you.

Bed & Breakfast Sydney Harbour (Map pp68-70; ☎ 9247 1130; 142 Cumberland St; s/d from $215/230; ⊠) This charming B&B gets rave reviews from guests and has a marvellous location. We love the fact that it captures an authentically Australian flavour without succumbing to Australiana overload. A few small rooms with share bathrooms are also available at mid-range rates.

Russell (Map pp68-70; ☎ 9241 3543; www.therussell .com.au; 143a George St; s/d from $220/235; ⊠) This superbly located hotel is small and friendly, with rooms straight out of a Laura Ashley catalogue, pleasant lounge areas and a sunny roof garden. A smattering of cheaper rooms with share bathrooms is also available. Mind the perilously steep stairs, though!

Chinatown & Darling Harbour
MID-RANGE
Motels
Vulcan Hotel (Map pp72-3; ☎ 9211 3283; vulcanho @ozemail.com.au; 500 Wattle St; d & tw from $100; P ⊠ ☐) Another good option that keeps you close to the city centre is the Vulcan, a newish place with very appealing rooms in a charming heritage-listed building.

Aaron's Hotel (Map pp72-3; ☎ 9281 5555; res@ aaronshotel.com.au; 37 Ultimo Rd; d from $100; ⊠) Right in the heart of Chinatown and very close to Darling Harbour, this hotel has plainly decorated, clean, light-filled rooms with sparkling bathrooms. Popular with group bookings.

Hotel Ibis (Map pp68-70; ☎ 9563 0888; www.accor hotels.com.au; 70 Murray St; d $160; P ⊠ ☐) One of those places that sprouted up around Darling Harbour in the development-mad 1990s – staffed by the young and enthusiastic, perfectly acceptable and colourless. Still, some of the views of Darling Harbour are appealing.

Capitol Square Hotel (☎ 9211 8633; www.gold spear.com.au; cnr George & Campbell Sts; d $165; P ⊠) A very convenient place to stay near Chinatown and Darling Harbour, especially given that extremely good deals are often available. Rooms go for a 'plush' feel. Wheelchair access is available too.

Wake Up! (Map pp72-3; ☎ 9288 7888; www.wakeup .com.au; 509 Pitt St; d & tw $90) This newish place has plenty of dorm beds, and very presentable double and twin rooms with bathrooms. It's just on Railway Square, making public transport a breeze. It's enthusiastically run (and recommended).

Pubs
Glasgow Arms Hotel (Map pp68-70; ☎ 9211 2354; admin@glasgowarmshotel.com.au; 527 Harris St; s/d $110/125; ⊠) Just across the road from the excellent Powerhouse Museum, this award-winning hotel has traditionally decorated rooms and access to many of Chinatown's and Darling Harbour's attractions, plus a verdant courtyard.

Kings Cross Area
BUDGET
Guesthouses & Budget Hotels
Maisonette Hotel (Map pp68-70; ☎ 9357 3878; maisonettehotel@bigpond.com; 31 Challis Ave; s & d $90, tr $115) This friendly place represents excellent value, with small, bright rooms and spotless bathrooms. There are also single rooms with share bathrooms, and good weekly rates for longer stays.

Royal Sovereign Hotel (Map p71; ☎ 9331 3672; royalsov@solotel.com.au; cnr Liverpool St & Darlinghurst Rd; d from $80) Located directly above one of our favourite drinking dens, the small but nifty rooms here put you in the thick of it at a bargain price. The communal bathrooms are immaculate, and some of the rooms have air-conditioning (bring your own earplugs if you're a light sleeper).

Highfield Private Hotel (Map p71; ☎ 9326 9539; www.highfieldhotel.com; 166 Victoria St; s/d $55/70) A clean and welcoming hotel owned by a Swedish family (and therefore popular with Swedish guests), this place has good security, simple rooms (shared bathrooms) and 24-hour access.

Hostels
Original Backpackers (Map p71; ☎ 9356 3232; www .originalbackpackers.com.au; 160-162 Victoria St; dm/s/d $22/45/65) A hostel for over 20 years, this really is the original backpackers. A big 176-bed place in two historic houses, it has friendly staff, good security, safety and facilities (laundry, kitchen etc), plus Blinky the dog. It's open 24 hours and all rooms have fridge and TV.

Eva's Backpackers (Map p71; ☎ 9358 2185; www.evasbackpackers.com.au; 6-8 Orwell St; dm $24, d & tw $60) Eva's is a perennial favourite with many travellers, particularly Germans. It's family owned and operated, and is clean and well-managed. There's a good rooftop barbecue area and a sociable kitchen/dining room. It's often full, so book ahead.

Jolly Swagman Backpackers (Map p71; ☎ 9358 6400; www.jollyswagman.com.au; 27 Orwell St; dm $23, d & tw $60) This 134-bed hostel has 24-hour security and a social life that gets the thumbs up from more than a few travellers. The rooms are modern and have lockers, fridges, reading lamps, fans and TV (no TV in dorms). Safety standards are high, and the staff are friendly and helpful with information.

Pubs

O'Malley's Hotel (Map p71; ☎ 9357 2211; www.omalleyshotel.com.au; 228 William St; s/d/tr $70/80/90) This is a friendly Irish pub that has traditionally decorated, well-furnished rooms with bathrooms. It's also surprisingly quiet, given its location.

MID-RANGE
Motels

Victoria Court Hotel (Map p71; ☎ 9357 3200; info@victoriacourt.com.au; 122 Victoria St; d $135-165; P) This is a sweetly run hotel with old-fashioned service and comfortable rooms in a lovely pair of Victorian houses. There's security parking, and a pleasant courtyard.

Hotel 59 (Map p71; ☎ 9360 5900; hotel59@myoffice.net.au; 59 Bayswater Rd; s/d from $100/125) This small, friendly hotel in the quiet stretch of Bayswater Rd has charming rooms and friendly staff who go out of their way to make your stay a happy one. There's also a small café, which turns out great cooked breakfasts. Reservations are a good idea.

Crest Hotel (Map p71; ☎ 9358 2755; www.cresthotel.com.au; 111 Darlinghurst Rd; d $110-130; P) With the quintessential Kings Cross location, the Crest has built a reputation for catering to business types, visiting Koreans (there's the wonderful Ginseng Bathhouse on the premises) and boys' nights out that last for days. The rooms are comfy and could be anywhere in the world if you don't have a harbour view.

Macleay (Map pp68-70; ☎ 9357 7755; www.themacleay.com; 28 Macleay St, Potts Point; d & tw/tr $115-135/130-150; P) This complex of serviced apartments with equipped kitchenettes and en suites has a pleasant surprise in the form of pretty decent views of the harbour (from rooms at the top end of the price scale). Other rooms look out onto the neighbourhood, which is in the throes of gentrification.

Oaks Crescent on Bayswater (Map p71; ☎ 9357 7266; www.theoaksrhm.com.au; 33 Bayswater Rd; d $134-152; P) This hotel, in a huge brick building, is close to everything and includes breakfast. For light sleepers, you'll be pleased to know it has double-glazing on the windows. Rack rates are higher than we've quoted, but there are always specials on, so ask.

Cross Court Tourist Hotel (Map p71; ☎ 9368 1822; www.crosscourthotel.com.au; 203 Brougham St; s/d/tr $75/85/95) A friendly, well-run place with 20 rooms and some great views (a deluxe room with private bathroom costs $105), this is one of the better small, simple hotels in the area.

Bernly Private Hotel (Map p71; ☎ 9358 3122; www.bernlyprivatehotel.com.au; 15 Springfield Ave; s/d/t $85/95/135) This larger-than-it-looks hotel has simple rooms with fairly old décor, reliable and courteous 24-hour reception and a rooftop garden. There are also numerous rooms without private bathrooms and some dorms. Its backstreet location may make some nervous late at night, although the greatest risk probably comes from dodging dog poo.

TOP END

W Hotel Sydney (Map pp68-70; ☎ 9331 9000; www.whotels.com; 6 Cowper Wharf Roadway, Woolloomooloo; d from $400; P 🐾 🖥) This is a lavish interpretation of minimalist chic, with some splendid views available and the great temptation of the Water Bar on the premises. Business travellers will be mighty pleased with the slick technology available in the rooms, and the lofts are full of spacious freedom.

Simpsons of Potts Point (Map pp68-70; ☎ 9356 2199; www.simpsonspottspoint.com.au; 8 Challis Ave, Potts Point; s/d from $145/165; P 🐾) The former grand residence of a member of parliament, this charming B&B offers extremely comfortable rooms and plush communal areas, including a delightful conservatory for breakfast. It's a popular honeymoon choice.

Regents Court (Map p71; ☎ 9358 1533; regcourt@iname.com; 18 Springfield Ave, Potts Point; d $220-255; P 🐾 🖥) One of Potts Point's smartest options, this is a swanky, modernist haven of discretion, with natty black-and-white bathrooms, a well-equipped kitchenette for each room and a wonderful rooftop garden.

(Continued on page 77)

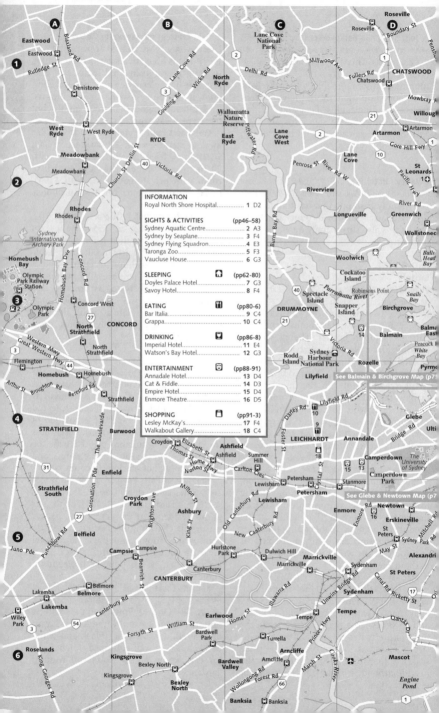

INFORMATION
Royal North Shore Hospital.............. 1 D2

SIGHTS & ACTIVITIES   (pp46–58)
Sydney Aquatic Centre................... 2 A3
Sydney by Seaplane....................... 3 F4
Sydney Flying Squadron................. 4 E3
Taronga Zoo................................. 5 F3
Vaucluse House............................. 6 G3

SLEEPING 🏠   (pp62–80)
Doyles Palace Hotel....................... 7 G3
Savoy Hotel.................................. 8 F4

EATING 🍽   (pp80–6)
Bar Italia..................................... 9 C4
Grappa....................................... 10 C4

DRINKING 🍷   (pp86–8)
Imperial Hotel............................. 11 E4
Watson's Bay Hotel...................... 12 G3

ENTERTAINMENT 😃   (pp88–91)
Annandale Hotel.......................... 13 D4
Cat & Fiddle............................... 14 D3
Empire Hotel............................... 15 D4
Enmore Theatre........................... 16 D5

SHOPPING 🛍   (pp91–3)
Lesley McKay's............................ 17 F4
Walkabout Gallery........................ 18 C4

0 ——— 2 km
0 ——— 1.0 miles

E   **F**   **G**   **H**

To Beachouse
YHA (8km)

See Manly Map (p56)

Cabbage
Tree
Bay

1

Middle
Cove
Crag
Cove
Castlecrag

Middle
Harbour
Frenchs Forest Rd
Seaforth
Balgowlah

Manly
Cove

MANLY

Blue
Fish
Point

Northbridge

Clontarf

Smedleys
Point   Manly   Little
North   Point Manly Point
Harbour

2

Cammeray

Cremorne

The
Spit

Balmoral

Hunters
Bay
Balmoral
Beach

Grotto
Point

Middle
Head

Dobroyd
Head

Cannae
Point

Sydney
Harbour
National
Park

Port Jackson
(Sydney
Harbour)

South
Pacific
Ocean

North Head

Crows
Nest
orth
dney
Neutral
Bay

Mosman

Military Rd

Gerard St

South
Head
Lady
Bay
Camp
Cove

Hornby
Island

Watsons
Bay

3

Neutral
Bay
Lavender
Bay
Milsons
Point
Kirribilli

Chowder
Bay

Taylors
Bay

Little
Sirius Point
Robertsons
Point

Georges
Head
Chowder Head

Shark
Bay

Bradleys
Head

Laings Point

Vaucluse
Point
Steel
Point
Hermit
Point

Watsons
Bay
Parsley
Bay
Vaucluse
Bay

Village Point

Gap
Bluff
The
Gap

Dunbar
Head

Outer
South Head

The
Rocks
SYDNEY

Potts Point

See Central Sydney Map (pp68–70)

Shark
Island

Clarke
Island
Point
Piper
Felix
Bay

Vaucluse

Diamond
Bay

4

See Kings Cross &
Darlinghurst Map (p71)

Woolloomooloo

Darlinghurst

Rushcutters
Bay
Darling
Point

Point
Piper
Woollahra
Point
Double
Bay

Rose
Bay

New South Head Rd

Double
Bay

Rose
Bay

Sydney
Royal Golf
Course

Dover
Heights

Edgecliff

Paddington

Oxford St
Moore Park Rd

Surry
Hills
Redfern

Cleveland St

Moore
Park

Fox
Studios

Cooper
Park

Woollahra

Bellevue
Hill

North
Bondi

Bondi Beach
Public
School

Bondi Beach

Bondi
Golf
Club

5

Zetland
Kensington

See Surry Hills, Paddington
& Woollahra Map (p72)

Queens
Park

Waverley

RANDWICK

Willis
Playground
Randwick
Racecourse

Alison
Park

St
Judes
Cemetery

Writtle
Park

BONDI
Junction

Bondi
Beach

Bondi Rd

Tamarama

Bronte

Clovelly

BONDI

Ben Buckler

Mackenzies Point

Mackenzies
Bay
Tamarama
Bay

Waverley
Cemetery

Bondi
Bay

SOUTH
PACIFIC
OCEAN

Roseberry
Kensington
Park

Australian
Golf
Club

Eastlakes

Pagewood

Lachlan
Swamps

Southern
Gardeners Rd

Kingsford

South
Coogee

Coogee Bay Rd
Gordons
Bay
Coogee
Oval
Coogee

Coogee
Bay

Shark
Point

See Eastern Beaches Map (p84)

6

Maroubra

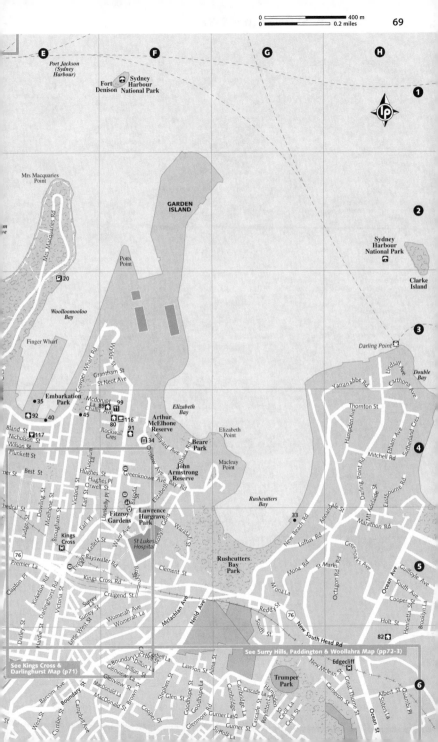

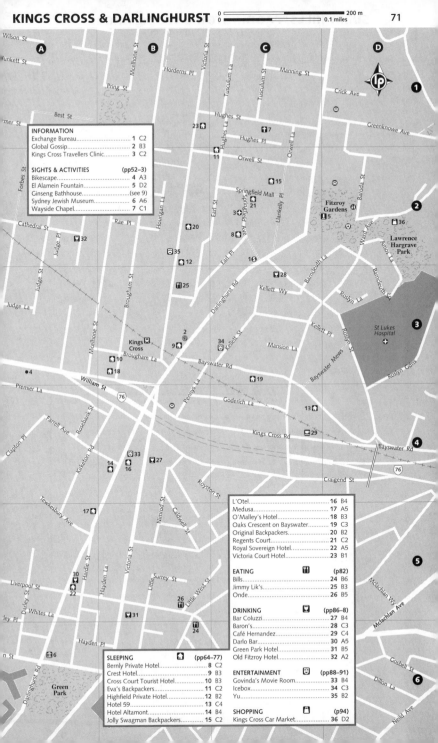

INFORMATION

Exchange Bureau	1 C2
Global Gossip	2 B3
Kings Cross Travellers Clinic	3 C2

SIGHTS & ACTIVITIES (pp52–3)

Bikescape	4 A3
El Alamein Fountain	5 D2
Ginseng Bathhouse	(see 9)
Sydney Jewish Museum	6 A6
Wayside Chapel	7 C1

SLEEPING (pp64–77)

Bernly Private Hotel	8 C2
Crest Hotel	9 B3
Cross Court Tourist Hotel	10 B3
Eva's Backpackers	11 C2
Highfield Private Hotel	12 B2
Hotel 59	13 C4
Hotel Altamont	14 B4
Jolly Swagman Backpackers	15 C2
L'Otel	16 B4
Medusa	17 A5
O'Malley's Hotel	18 B3
Oaks Crescent on Bayswater	19 C3
Original Backpackers	20 B2
Regents Court	21 C2
Royal Sovereign Hotel	22 A5
Victoria Court Hotel	23 B1

EATING (p82)

Bills	24 B6
Jimmy Lik's	25 B3
Onde	26 B5

DRINKING (pp86–8)

Bar Coluzzi	27 B4
Baron's	28 C3
Café Hernandez	29 C4
Darlo Bar	30 A5
Green Park Hotel	31 B5
Old Fitzroy Hotel	32 A2

ENTERTAINMENT (pp88–91)

Govinda's Movie Room	33 B4
Icebox	34 C3
Yu	35 B2

SHOPPING (p94)

Kings Cross Car Market	36 D2

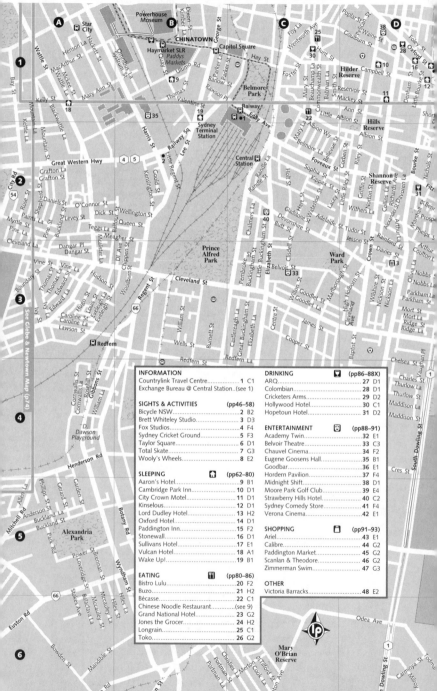

INFORMATION
Countrylink Travel Centre....................1 C1
Exchange Bureau @ Central Station..(see 1)

SIGHTS & ACTIVITIES (pp46–58)
Bicycle NSW...2 B2
Brett Whiteley Studio..........................3 D3
Fox Studios...4 F4
Sydney Cricket Ground.........................5 F3
Taylor Square.......................................6 D1
Total Skate...7 G3
Wooly's Wheels....................................8 E2

SLEEPING (pp62–80)
Aaron's Hotel.......................................9 B1
Cambridge Park Inn............................10 D1
City Crown Motel................................11 D1
Kinselous...12 D1
Lord Dudley Hotel...............................13 H2
Oxford Hotel.......................................14 D1
Paddington Inn....................................15 F2
Stonewall..16 D1
Sullivans Hotel.....................................17 E1
Vulcan Hotel..18 A1
Wake Up!...19 B1

EATING (pp80–86)
Bistro Lulu...20 F2
Buzo..21 H2
Bécasse...22 C1
Chinese Noodle Restaurant............(see 9)
Grand National Hotel...........................23 G2
Jones the Grocer.................................24 H2
Longrain..25 C1
Toko..26 G2

DRINKING (pp86–88X)
ARQ...27 D1
Colombian...28 D1
Cricketers Arms...................................29 D2
Hollywood Hotel..................................30 C1
Hopetoun Hotel...................................31 D2

ENTERTAINMENT (pp88–91)
Academy Twin.....................................32 E1
Belvoir Theatre....................................33 C3
Chauvel Cinema..................................34 F2
Eugene Goosens Hall...........................35 B1
Goodbar..36 E1
Hordern Pavilion.................................37 F4
Midnight Shift......................................38 D1
Moore Park Golf Club..........................39 E4
Strawberry Hills Hotel..........................40 C2
Sydney Comedy Store..........................41 F4
Verona Cinema....................................42 E1

SHOPPING (pp91–93)
Ariel..43 E1
Calibre...44 G2
Paddington Market..............................45 G2
Scanlan & Theodore............................46 G2
Zimmerman Swim................................47 G3

OTHER
Victoria Barracks..................................48 E2

0   500 m
0   0.3 miles

E Green Park
Liverpool St
West St
ton St

See Kings Cross & Darlinghurst Map (p71)

F

Lawson St
Stephen St
Glen St
Hoddle St
Goodhope St
Cambridge St
Cascade St

G
Glenmore Rd
Alma St
Cambridge La
Hampden St
Cecil St

Trumper Park

New McLean St
Edgecliff
Cameron St
Great Thorne St

H
Albert St
Quamби Pl
Sisters La

1

Barcom Ave
Boundary St
MacDonald La
MacDonald St
Brown St
Cooper St
Gurner La
Gurner St
Sutherland St
Cascade St

See Central Sydney Map (pp68-70)

Trelawney St
Fullerton St

Comber St
Campbell Ave
Hopewell La
Mary St
Gipps St

Olive St
Broughton St
Stafford St
Stafford La
Heeley St
Heeley St
Union St
Norfolk St
Norfolk La
Sutherland St
Harris St
Hargrave La
Hargrave St

Tara St
13

Ocean St

32
36 **43**
42 **17**

Napier St
8

Young La
Begg La
Ormond St
Heeley St

Hopetoun St
Hopetoun La
Dudley St
Windsor St
Windsor La
Paddington La
Taylor St

Holdsworth St
Spicer St

2

Albion Ave
Selwyn St
urch St
Greens Rd
Iris St
Josephson St

34
Walter Reid Gardens
Belmore
Oxford St
20
William St
15
Victoria St
Queen St
Underwood St
Elizabeth St
Caledonia St
Point Piper La

Morrell St
Alton St

Rush St

Chiswick La
Kanimbla St

Little Dowling St

48

Oatley Rd
Alexander St
Renny St
Renny La
Walter St
Martin St
Regent St
26
23
Paddington La
21

Dalley St
Barnett La
Bowden St
Wallis St

Moore Park Rd

Stewart St
Gordon St
Leinster St

44
45
George St
46
Jersey Rd
47
7
Smith St
James St
Halsted Ave
Victoria Ave
Queen St
Dwyer La
Montour St

John St
Oxford St

3

es St
Anzac Pde

Moore Park

Kippax Lagoon

Driver Ave
Gregory Ave

Aussie Stadium

Poate La
Poate Rd
Furber Rd
Furber La
Mitchell St
Centennial La

Carrington Dve
Hamilton Dve
Grand Dve

4

Loch Ave

Sydney Boys & Girls High Schools

70

5

37

Cook Rd
Darvall St

Lang Rd

41
4

Dickens Dve

Centennial Park

Grand Dve

39

Grand Dve

Robertson Rd
Oxley La
Martin Rd
Dibbs St

Busby's Pond

Parkes Dve

Lily Pond

5

Moore Park Golf Club

acey Ave

Sydney Athletic Field

Abbotford La
Abbotford St

Kensington Pond

70
Carlton
Carlton St

Alison Rd

Randwick Pond

Duck Pond

Dairy Rd

Huddart La
Evans St
White St
Dangar La

Govett St
Mort St
Mort La

6

ompton Rd
Salisbury Rd
eigh rk

Boronia St
Balfour Rd
Balfour La
Anzac Pde
Goodwood St
Doncaster Ave
Eleanor St

John St
King St
Prince La

Randwick Racecourse

William St

Tramway La

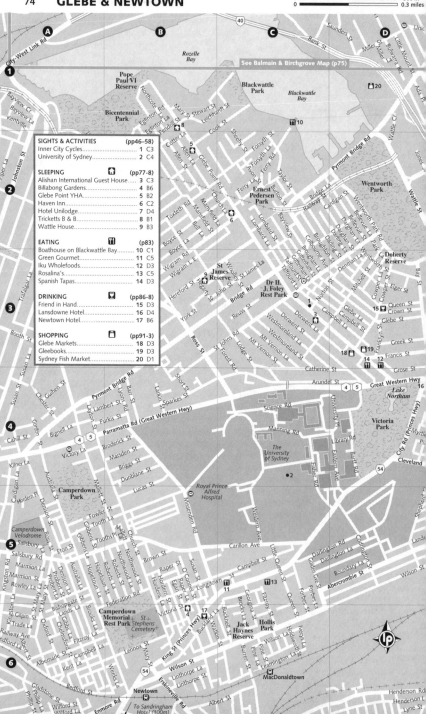

0 _____ 500 m
0 _____ 0.3 miles

See Balmain & Birchgrove Map (p75)

SIGHTS & ACTIVITIES	(pp46–58)
Inner City Cycles	1 C3
University of Sydney	2 C4

SLEEPING	(pp77–8)
Alishan International Guest House	3 C3
Billabong Gardens	4 B6
Glebe Point YHA	5 B2
Haven Inn	6 C2
Hotel Unilodge	7 D4
Tricketts B & B	8 B1
Wattle House	9 B3

EATING	(p83)
Boathouse on Blackwattle Bay	10 C1
Green Gourmet	11 C5
Iku Wholefoods	12 D3
Rosalina's	13 C5
Spanish Tapas	14 D3

DRINKING	(pp86–8)
Friend in Hand	15 D3
Lansdowne Hotel	16 D4
Newtown Hotel	17 B6

SHOPPING	(pp91–3)
Glebe Markets	18 D3
Gleebooks	19 D3
Sydney Fish Market	20 D1

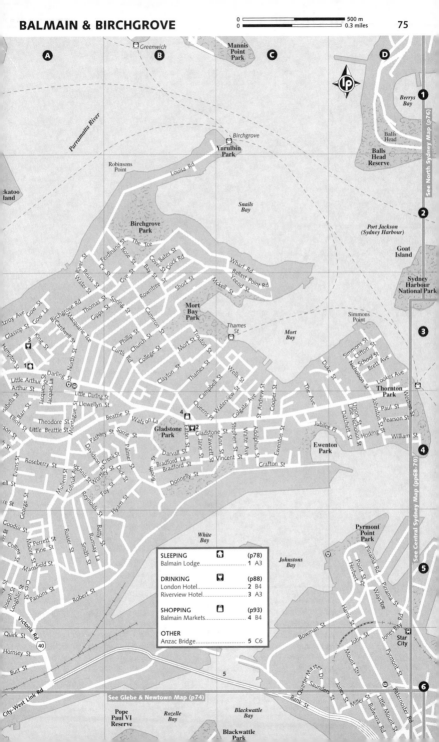

SLEEPING   (p78)
Balmain Lodge..................... 1 A3

DRINKING   (p88)
London Hotel........................ 2 B4
Riverview Hotel.................... 3 A3

SHOPPING   (p93)
Balmain Markets................... 4 B4

OTHER
Anzac Bridge........................ 5 C6

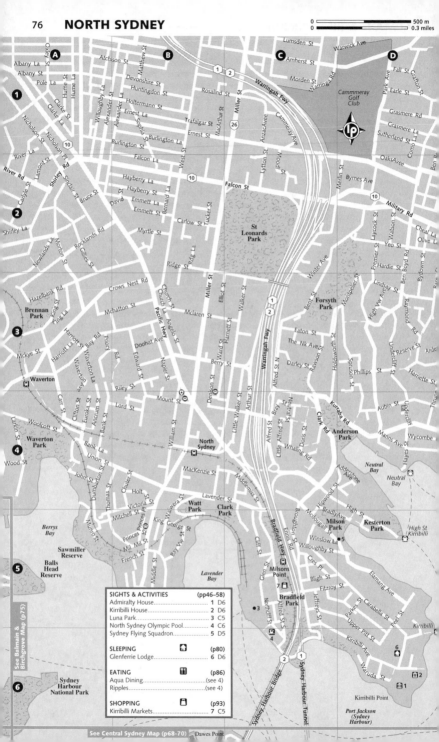

0 — 500 m
0 — 0.3 miles

SIGHTS & ACTIVITIES (pp46–58)
Admiralty House.............................1 D6
Kirribilli House.............................2 D6
Luna Park.............................3 C5
North Sydney Olympic Pool.............4 C6
Sydney Flying Squadron.............5 D5

SLEEPING (p80)
Glenferrie Lodge.............................6 D6

EATING (p86)
Aqua Dining.............................(see 4)
Ripples.............................(see 4)

SHOPPING (p93)
Kirribilli Markets.............................7 C5

See Balmain &
Birchgrove Map (p75)

See Central Sydney Map (p68-70)   Dawes Point

(Continued from page 65)

Darlinghurst & Surry Hills
MID-RANGE
Motels

Hotel Altamont (Map p71; ☎ 9360 6000; hotel altamont@yahoo.com; 207 Darlinghurst Rd; d $130; 🐾) This is quite a find, with its smart-looking rooms with bathroom. Communal areas are welcoming (especially the terrace) and it's mighty handy for the Cross and the area surrounding it. There are also discounts for longer stays.

L'Otel (Map p71; ☎ 9360 6868; hotel@lotel.com.au; 114 Darlinghurst Rd; d from $150; 🐾) This hip, stylish 16-room place is friendly and very well appointed, thanks to designers *du jour* Burley Katon Halliday, who've gone for a blindingly white look. Rooms have phone, fax and data port connections and a general air of subdued smartness.

Cambridge Park Inn (Map pp72-3; ☎ 9212 1111; www.parkplaza.com; 212 Riley St; d $142-164; 🐾 🕴) Over the years, we've had very positive feedback for this place, which offers solid standards and is nice and close to some of Surry Hills' most pleasurable eating options. It's not an attractive building – but it has a heated pool, spa, sauna and gym, some good views, plus multilingual staff.

City Crown Motel (Map pp72-3; ☎ 9331 2433; www .citycrownmotel.com.au; 289 Crown St; d $85; 🐾 💻) With clean, simple rooms (none particularly spacious), this is a popular place during Mardi Gras, when prices increase by 50%.

TOP END
Hotels

Medusa (Map p71; ☎ 9331 1000; www.medusa.com.au; 267 Darlinghurst Rd, Darlinghurst; d from $270; 🅿 🐾 💻) This 18-room hotel is pure Sydney – glamorous, well-situated, a little bit flashy, a lot sexy, professional and decadent. You could lose yourself (or any number of people) in the beds here, and when you suss out the luxury gadgets, gizmos and features of each room, you'll never want to leave. It's popular with affluent gay travellers and design buffs.

Paddington
MID-RANGE
Motels

Sullivans Hotel (Map pp72-3; ☎ 9361 0211; www .sullivans.com.au; 21 Oxford St; d $130-145; 🅿 🐾 🕴) Situated in an area often referred to as 'Paddinghurst', this well-managed 64-room motel has simple but smart rooms and a charming courtyard area. It's popular with gay travellers.

Eastern Suburbs
MID-RANGE
Motels

Doyles Palace Hotel (Map pp66-7; ☎ 9337 5444; www.doyles.com.au; Military Rd, Watsons Bay; d $145-370; 🅿 🐾) In one of the most beautiful spots in all Sydney, this is really a top-end hotel, but there are some delightful mid-range rooms available. Reservations are strongly advised.

Savoy Hotel (Map pp66-7; ☎ 9326 1411; www .savoyhotel.com.au; 41 Knox St, Double Bay; d $120-150; 🅿 🐾) This lies smack bang in Double Bay's coffee-lounge belt, which is just off busy New South Head Rd, and has nicely decorated rooms and a few suites that cost a little more. It's a quiet spot, popular with those who like their social life relaxed.

Metro Inn (Map pp68-700; ☎ 9328 7977; www .metroinns.com.au; 230 New South Head Rd, Edgecliff; d $160; 🐾) Like many creatures of a certain age in this neighbourhood, the Metro Inn has been getting some work done over the years. Some rooms (all neat and shiny) have great views of the harbour, and it's close to Edgecliff train station. If you book on the Internet, there are some fearsome discounts.

Glebe
BUDGET
Hostels

Glebe Point YHA (Map p74; ☎ 9692 8418; glebe@ yhansw.org.au; 262-264 Glebe Point Rd; dm $23-27, d & tw $64; 💻) This large, friendly hostel offers good facilities – a kitchen, TV lounge, laundry and clean linen. The rooms are simple but clean, as are the bathrooms, and credit-card reservations are accepted.

MID-RANGE
Bed & Breakfasts

Wattle House (Map p74; ☎ 9552 4997; stay@wattle house.com.au; 44 Hereford St; d $80; ✂) A lovely Victorian house accommodating 26 people, this place is excellent – super-tidy, friendly and efficient. It's nonsmoking, alcohol-free and reservations are advised. It has a minimum stay of three nights, although this can be negotiated. Bathrooms are shared.

Alishan International Guest House (Map p74; ☎ 9566 4048; kevin@alishan.com.au; 100 Glebe Point Rd, Glebe; s/d $100/115) In a big, quiet old house in the centre of Glebe, the Alishan is clean, quiet and well run (multilingual staff), with good communal areas and a room that can accommodate disabled travellers. There are also a few dorm beds ($27 to $33) available.

Motels

Hotel Unilodge (Map p74; ☎ 9338 5000; www .unilodge.com.au; cnr Broadway & Bay St; s/d & tw/tr $120/170/195; P ⚊) This swanky-looking joint offers good value for its larger rooms, and has impressive facilities and amenities, such as a business centre and an indoor lap pool. It's the kind of place that gets pretty popular for conferences and the like at nearby Sydney University.

Haven Inn (Map p74; ☎ 9660 6655; www.havenin nsydney.com.au; 196 Glebe Point Rd, Glebe; d $150-195; P ⚊) When we popped into this inn on the corner of Wigram Rd, renovations were in progress, and things were looking promising. Rooms are comfortable and well appointed, plus there's a heated swimming pool. Avoid the overpriced continental breakfasts though, and head down Glebe Point Rd on a café crawl instead.

TOP END

Tricketts Bed & Breakfast (Map p74; ☎ 9552 1141; trickettsbandb@hotmail.com.au; 270 Glebe Point Rd, Glebe; s $150, d $180-200; P ⚊) The lovely Liz Trickett has lovingly restored this magnificent 19th-century mansion, and her attention to detail is evident throughout. Rooms are downright sumptuous, and all have bathrooms. Reservations are advised.

Newtown

MID-RANGE
Motels

Billabong Gardens (Map p74; ☎ 9550 3236; book@ billabonggardens.com.au; 5-11 Egan St; d $90; P ⚊) This quality, long-standing motel/hostel is clean and quiet and has received good word-of-mouth reviews from many travellers. There is a small solar-heated pool and good kitchen. There are also budget rooms with shared bathrooms, as well as some dorm rooms that come with bathrooms. Guests can be picked up at the airport by prior arrangement.

Balmain

BUDGET
Guesthouses & Budget Hotels

Balmain Lodge (Map p75; ☎ 9810 3700, fax 9810 1500; 415 Darling St; s/d $65/80; P) Located on Balmain's backbone, Darling St, this is a handy place with capable management and spartan, clean rooms. Wheelchair access is available, as is parking, making this a convenient option for less mobile travellers. Bathrooms are shared.

Bondi

BUDGET
Hostels

Bondi Beachouse (Map p84; ☎ 9365 2088; bondi@ intercoast.com.au; 63 Fletcher St; dm $26, s $60, d & tw $70; ⚇ ⚊) The staff here are as clued-up as you'd expect from a YHA joint, and there are excellent communal areas to be enjoyed, plus some delightful rooftop views over Tamarama Beach from the spa. Catch bus No 380 and alight at the Fletcher St stop.

Indy's (Map p84; ☎ 9365 4900, fax 9365 4994; 35a Hall St; dm $30; ⚊) With a relaxed, easy-going vibe, this hostel is a socially gregarious backpacking option. Facilities are well-used but OK, and it's security-conscious. There's a kitchen, courtyard and Internet access.

MID-RANGE
Bed & Breakfasts

Bondi Beach Homestay (Map p84; ☎ 9300 0800; 10 Forest Knoll Ave; bondibnb@bigpond.net.au; s/d $80/125; P) In a charmingly decorated home with friendly owners, this is one of Bondi's hidden gems. Bathrooms are shared, but you could probably eat off the floors. Breakfast on the terrace is a must in summer.

Bondi Beach B&B (Map p84; ☎ 9365 6522; info@bondibeach-bnb.com.au; 110 Roscoe St; s $100, d & tw $150, tr $190; P) Owners Nadia and Michael go all out to make this place feel like your own home (only cleaner). You're close to all the good stuff in Bondi, but you can also find a park. It's a small place, so be sure to make reservations, and ask about discounts for the low season.

Motels

Bondi Sands (Map p84; ☎ 1800 026 634; www.bondi sands.com; 252 Campbell Pde; d & tw $90-120) The Bondi Sands caters for those after double and twin rooms. They're simple, clean affairs with shared bathrooms, but a few have stunning views (ask for No 7, 8, 17 or 18). If you miss out on those, there's always the wonderful rooftop area. Low-season reductions are both generous and negotiable.

Beach Road Hotel (Map p84; ☎ 9130 7247; 71 Beach Rd; s/d $75/90; ☒) This chipper hotel is a large, box-like pub two blocks back from the beach. Heavy on the beach-themed décor, it has several bars, a couple of eateries and a nightclub. Rooms are clean and bright and come with TV and decent bathrooms. The whole feel of the place is very low-key and casual.

Pubs
Hotel Bondi (Map p84; ☎ 9130 3271; hotelbondi@ ozemail.com.au; 178 Campbell Pde; s $75, d & tw $110, tr $130) Hotel Bondi is the peach-coloured layer-cake on the beachfront. The rooms are small and tidy, but be warned – the Bondi Hotel below is a very popular nightspot with young, drunk travellers. Still, if you have a view of the beach you'll be laughing.

TOP END
Hotels
Ravesi's (Map p84; ☎ 9365 4422; www.ravesis.com.au; cnr Campbell Pde & Hall St; d $120-275, ste $245-450; ☒) With only 16 rooms, Ravesi's is popular and it is easy to see why. Rooms were freshly renovated when we visited, with the minimalist look that Sydney loves so much right now. It's right on the beach and the views are straight from heaven. A popular drinking spot attached to the hotel is your entrance.

Coogee
BUDGET
Guesthouses & Budget Hotels
Grand Pacific Private Hotel (Map p84; ☎ 9665 6301; cnr Beach & Carr Sts; s/d $35/45) In *no* way is it grand, but rather charming in a dilapidated, down-at-heel way, and the beachside location is great. Grab that person you're having a dirty affair with (having bumped off their spouse) and hole up for a seedy seaside weekend straight from a true-crime novel.

Hostels
Coogee Beachside Accommodation (Map p84; ☎ 9315 8511; www.sydneybeachside.com.au; 178 Coogee Bay Rd; d & tw $75, f $95) This is a good option for budget travellers looking for simple but clean double and twin rooms in a converted house with kitchen facilities and tidy shared bathrooms.

Wizard of Oz Backpackers (Map p84; ☎ 9315 7876; www.wizardofoz.com.au; 172 Coogee Bay Rd; dm $27) Smack bang on Coogee Bay Rd in a refurbished California bungalow, this place is laid-back and run by the same people from Coogee Beachside Accommodation (free airport pick-up available for both). Dorms sleep from four to 14 people, and communal rooms are in good working order. Both of these places open their offices between about 8am and noon and from 5pm to 8pm.

MID-RANGE
Motels
Dive Hotel (Map p84; ☎ 9665 5538; www.divehotel .com.au; 234 Arden St; d & tw $150-165) This delightful, small boutique hotel has been beautifully decorated in a modern style that retains interesting original tilework and a sense of beach-house space. There are more expensive rooms with views available, and each room has a kitchenette and groovy bathroom.

Pubs
Coogee Bay Boutique Hotel (Map p84; ☎ 9665 0000; 9 Vicar St; d $100; ℙ ☒) Right in the centre of Coogee, this heritage hotel with a casual feel has rooms available in its original Coogee Bay Hotel building as well as in the newer, fancier and quieter wing (these are top-end prices though). Enter from Vicar St, parallel to Arden St. Rooms have fridge, TV and telephone – and you can hear many of the bands playing downstairs if you're trying to sleep in the pub rooms.

Manly
MID-RANGE
Bed & Breakfasts
Periwinkle Guest House (Map p56; ☎ 9977 4668; periwinkle.manly@bigpond.com; 18-19 East Esplanade; s/d $135/165; ℙ) This is a beautifully restored Victorian house facing the harbour beach at Manly Cove. Rooms are elegant and well appointed, and there's a stylish but cosy kitchen. Laundry facilities are available, and so are some cheaper rooms with share bathrooms.

101 Addison Road (Map p56; ☎ 9977 6216, fax 9976 6352; 101 Addison Rd; s/d $100/140) A sweet-looking four-star B&B with lovely rooms and very cosy communal areas. If you fancy tickling the ivories of a grand piano, Jill, the owner, is happy to oblige. There are only a couple of rooms, so book ahead.

Motels

Manly Lodge (Map p56; ☎ 9977 8655; enquiries@manly lodge.com.au; 22 Victoria Pde; d & tw $145-160; 🐾) This is a quaint guesthouse with a vaguely Spanish appearance. Rooms have bathroom, TV, video and fridge; some have spas. There's also a communal sauna, spa and gym, and a pleasant outdoor area, plus larger suites and family rooms. Rates rise in summer.

Manly Paradise Motel (Map p56; ☎ 9977 5799; www.manlyparadise.com.au; 54 North Steyne; d $110-165; 🅿 🐾 🛆) Catering to families and business travellers for many years, this efficient and thoughtful place can provide cots if required, plus there's an elevator and rooftop pool. Rooms are very 1980s, but spacious and well cared-for. There are some more expensive rooms available (to $190), which have sea views.

Manly Beach Resort (Map p56; ☎ 9977 4188; manlybch@ozemail.com.au; 6 Carlton St; s $115, d & tw $140, tr $150; 🅿) This is a reasonable 1970s-era motel (breakfast included) with good security and car parking. There are also family rooms available and one studio, plus a separate backpackers' section. The sign says 'affordable and friendly', but it's really only affordable as far as we can tell.

TOP END

Manly Pacific Parkroyal (Map p56; ☎ 9977 7666; 55 North Steyne, Manly; d from $250; 🅿 🐾 🖳 🛆) This big hotel has full-frontal views of the beach and is easily Manly's fanciest place to stay. There's a gym, heated rooftop pool, spa, sauna and undercover parking, plus a real sense of seaside swank.

North Shore

BUDGET

Guesthouses & Budget Hotels

Glenferrie Lodge (Map p76; ☎ 9955 1685; www.glen ferrielodge.com; 12a Carabella St, Kirribilli; s $60, d & tw $75; 🖳) This is in a large, beautiful old house with a ridiculous sculpture out the front. It has clean rooms with fridge, and helpful, friendly management. Shared bathrooms are in good nick. Prices for simpler rooms are cheaper, with reductions for longer stays on all rooms. Accessible from Milsons Point train station or Kirribilli wharf by ferry.

Hostels

Sydney Beachhouse YHA (☎ 9981 1177; mail@sydne ybeachouse.com.au; 4 Collaroy St, Collaroy; dm $20-25, d & tw $60, f $105) This clean, airy place gets some great reviews from travellers (it's wheelchair and child friendly) and is close to some of Sydney's best beaches. If you really want to feel like an extra from *Home & Away*, then this is probably your best bet. Catch bus Nos L90 or L88 from Railway Square, Town Hall or Wynyard train stations.

Camping

Lakeside Caravan Park (☎ 9913 7845; info@sydney lakeside.com.au; Lake Park Rd, Narrabeen; camp/caravan site $25/32; 🅿) This camping area is 26km north of Sydney, in the prime real estate area of the northern beaches. If caravanning doesn't appeal, there are good cabins and lakeside 'villas'.

Lane Cove River Caravan Park (☎ 9888 9133; www.lanecoveriver.com; Plassey Rd, North Ryde; camp/caravan site $23/26; 🅿) This cheery place is 14km north of the city and has good facilities (including over 150 caravan sites, plus cabins). You can cool off in the pool too, when temperatures swelter in this part of the city.

EATING

With great local produce, innovative chefs and BYO licensing laws, eating out is one of the great delights of Sydney. The two f-words are the key to dining here – freshness and flavour.

You can find yourself greeting the day with a heart-starting espresso and a serve of ricotta hot cakes in the inner city, then chowing down on the freshest catch of the day at a waterfront restaurant or on the beach. You can stave off the afternoon hunger pangs with tapas, gobble a pie and sauce at a footy game or after a night on the tiles, rise above it all with a glittering harbour view and the boldest and most beautiful top-end cuisine, or spend the wee hours revelling in a post-midnight supper in one of Chinatown's chandelier-and-laminex eating dens.

There are thousands of fast-food options for the choosing in Sydney. You will find them on the main streets and near train stations in most suburbs. Go for the great Aussie fish and chips option, preferably by the beach.

City Centre, The Rocks & Circular Quay

Buena Vista Café Bar (Map pp68-70; ☎ 9230 8221; Level 14, Supreme Law Courts Bldg, St James Square; mains $8-20; ☺ breakfast & lunch Mon-Fri) This is not the best food you'll have in Sydney (although it's perfectly decent for pasta). The reason people come here is a breathtaking view – over the Botanic Gardens, the harbour and the inner eastern suburbs. Legal eagles in legal gowns and Old-Age Pensioners (OAPs) in their city best flock here for the sort of views that usually cost an arm and a leg.

Rockpool (Map pp68-70; ☎ 9252 1888; 107 George St, The Rocks; mains $49-60; ☺ lunch & dinner Mon-Fri, dinner Sat) This place is always featured in the 'best of' lists, and with good reason – it's one of the most famous and most highly regarded restaurants in Sydney, and its influence is considerable. Chef Neil Perry is still churning out some of the most beautiful (in all senses) dishes in Sydney – and it's a particularly good place to sample Sydney's best seafood. Go for the southern rock lobster tajine with roast apricots and couscous for two and thank them (and us) profusely. Reservations essential.

Guillaume at Bennelong (Map pp68-70; ☎ 9250 7548, Sydney Opera House; mains $35; ☺ lunch Thu & Fri, dinner Mon-Sat) In the Sydney Opera House, and maximising the building's stunning architecture, this restaurant is supremely chic. There's no better place to turn that old cliché of 'dinner and a show' into something more meaningful. Award-winning chef Guillaume Brahmini's masterful style is evident in every dish, and the wine list is aptly show-stopping. Reservations advised.

Sailor's Thai (Map pp68-70; ☎ 9251 2466; 106 George St; mains $15.50-26; ☺ lunch-8pm) Sit at the long, communal stainless steel table and feast on some of the best Thai eating this side of Bangkok. A power crowd of arts bureaucrats and politicians mingles with the young and lively, all to good effect. Save superlatives for the food though.

Bodhi (Map pp68-70; ☎ 9360 2523; Cook & Phillip Park; yum cha $4-9; ☺ lunch & dinner) The animal lovers at Bodhi offer tasty, healthy vegetarian yum cha in flash-looking surrounds. It's got a nice (albeit sometimes windy) outdoor seating area and fast service. Avoid the 'mock meat' delicacies and dive right into the straight-up vegie fare. Simple, almost ascetic eating was never this stylish.

Casa Asturiana (Map pp68-70; ☎ 9264 1010; 77 Liverpool St; tapas $4-10; ☺ lunch & dinner) This restaurant specialises in northern Spanish cooking (hence the name), and reputedly has the best tapas in Sydney. It's an ideal spot for a quick lunch or a dinner that's big on grazing, chatting, drinking and grinning.

Mother Chu's Vegetarian Kitchen (Map pp68-70; ☎ 9283 2828; 367 Pitt St; mains $8-15; ☺ lunch & dinner Mon-Sat) Mother Chu's blends vegetarian Taiwanese, Japanese and Chinese influences to ensure the perfect tofu or claypot hit. It's a serviceable sort of place, with not much going on in terms of ambience, but the gluten lovers don't seem to notice.

Chinatown & Darling Harbour

BBQ King (Map pp68-70; ☎ 9267 2586; 18-20 Goulburn St; mains $10-30; ☺ lunch & dinner) As the name suggests, you come here for barbecued food, and a lot of people would agree that this place is king. It's an old-school Chinese eatery, with bustling service, huge pots of tea and a scant regard for the niceties of fancy décor. There may be a queue, but it won't last long, and the great roast duck and pork are worth the wait. It's popular as a post-cinema haunt, as it stays open till about 2.30am.

Golden Century Seafood Restaurant (Map pp68-70; ☎ 9212 3901; 393-399 Sussex St, Haymarket; ☺ lunch & dinner) Open to 4am, with lots of fish tanks displaying your nervous-looking dinner, this place is a favourite late-night eating spot for many of Sydney's chefs and hotel workers. The flavours are exotic and engaging, the service fast and slick.

Dragon Star Restaurant (Map pp68-70; ☎ 9211 8988; Level 3, Market Sydney, 9 Hay St, Haymarket; mains $11-market price; ☺ lunch & dinner) This enormous place can seat about 800 people, and regularly gets filled to capacity for its yum cha sessions. Ask the waiter to recommend dishes and you'll be duly rewarded with succulent offerings. As you'd expect, seafood is the speciality.

Zaaffran (Map pp68-70; ☎ 9211 8900, Level 2, 345 Harbourside, Darling Harbour; mains $17-26; ☺ lunch Tue-Sun, dinner daily) In a city with a million cheap Indian joints, this place stands out. The food is expertly cooked, and Zaaffran makes good use of its location in Darling Harbour (generally populated by quite ordinary restaurants). Their take on beef vindaloo ($25) reminds you that well-known dishes need not be ordinary or bland. And vegetarians will thank their lucky stars for the choices on offer.

Chinese Noodle Restaurant (Map pp72-3; ☎ 9281 9051; Shop 7, Prince Centre, 8 Quay St; mains $5-9; ☺ lunch & dinner) At this intimate, busy eatery decorated with grapes and Persian rugs, the noodles are handmade in the traditional northern Chinese style by the expert Cin – and the crowds are glad of it. Small, sweet and the perfect quick noodle fix for lunch or dinner.

Chinta Ria... Temple of Love (Map pp68-70; ☎ 9264 3211; Level 2, Cockle Bay Wharf, 201 Sussex St; mains $15-26; ☺ lunch & dinner) Right on a leafy rooftop at the northern end of Cockle Bay Wharf, this Malaysian-hawker food-inspired temple serves tasty, reasonably priced meals in colourful style – the enormous Buddha will put you in a jolly mood from the moment you enter. The laksa ($14.80) is definitely worth getting excited about.

Darlinghurst & Surry Hills

Bécasse (Map pp72-3; ☎ 9280 3202; 48 Albion St; mains $28; ☺ dinner Wed-Sun) There's nothing flashy or garish about Bécasse, but it will stand out as one of the most memorable dining experiences of your trip. The muted, elegant décor is the perfect complement to the superbly created dishes. The Degustation Menu ($70) is seven courses of gustatory heaven, with salmon, venison, barramundi, suckling lamb and some delightful sweet morsel competing for the title of our favourite dish. Reservations essential.

Longrain (Map pp72-3; ☎ 9280 2888; 85 Commonwealth St; mains $25-38; ☺ lunch Mon-Fri, dinner Mon-Sat) There are no reservations here, and it seems that all of Sydney's beautiful set are as keen to graze on the superb Asian-inspired offerings as you are. Good thing there's an excellent bar on the beautifully kitted-out premises, with cocktails so fine that even a hypoglycaemic can stand the wait. Any of the fish dishes deserve their own church.

Onde (Map p71; ☎ 9331 8749; 346 Liverpool St, Darlinghurst; mains $17.50-23; ☺ dinner) Onde has risen from the ashes of a past kitchen fire and is still offering wonderful French food at hard-to-believe prices – go for the duck confit with mesclun, caramelised apple and walnut ($22) and try to argue with us. It's a smart, sparse-looking place, and mighty popular (no reservations).

Uchi Lounge (Map pp68-70; ☎ 9261 3524; 15 Brisbane St; mains $13.50-16.50; ☺ dinner) Patronised (and staffed) by creative types who aren't about to let a wallet crisis get in the way of dressing to impress, Uchi Lounge resembles a final-year art school installation. The blissful Japanese food takes centre stage; the wasabi mussels ($9), accompanied by an ice-cold Asahi beer, are fabulous. The groovy little ground-floor bar is the perfect place to wait for a table (and wait you will – no reservations).

Pizza Mario (Map pp68-70; ☎ 9332 3633; 50 Burton St, East Sydney; mains $12-22; ☺ dinner) The best pizza you'll find in Sydney is also the most authentic. In fact, Pizza Mario is a certified Neapolitan pizzeria, and the wafer-thin crusts, sparse but tasty toppings and 'no variations' rule on the menu will make you swear you're in Naples. Get in early and beat the hordes, as this place really is special. To find it, go to the 'piazza' area that's part of the Republic apartment complex (Palmer St).

Bills (Map p71; ☎ 9360 9631; 433 Liverpool St, Darlinghurst; mains $18.50-25; ☺ lunch & dinner Mon-Sat) This place has a large communal table and a great selection of glossy magazines for its glossy clientele (who tend to work for glossy magazines). Bill himself is something of a glossy legend in Sydney – after all, when you make the best scrambled eggs in town, you deserve respect.

Kings Cross Area

Fratelli Paradiso (Map pp68-70; ☎ 9357 1744; 12 Challis Ave, Potts Point; mains $11-20; ☺ breakfast, lunch & dinner) You can have lunch here, and it's great, but what keeps us getting out of bed in the morning is the idea of breakfast here. The eggs are magnificent, the rice pudding superb, the coffee from God. Service is friendly, sometimes cheeky, and always brisk – just like in Italy.

Jimmy Lik's (Map p71; ☎ 8354 1400; 186 Victoria St, Potts Point; mains $17-28; ☺ dinner) Long on bench space and its cocktail list, Jimmy Lik's also serves excellent Thai food to the movers and shakers of Sydney's inner eastern suburbs. Generally, there's a bit of a wait for restaurant seating, but with heavenly bar snacks beckoning (the oysters *nam jim* are divine), who's in a hurry to score a table?

Paddington & Woollahra

Bistro Lulu (Map pp72-3; ☎ 9380 6888; 257 Oxford St; mains $26; ☺ lunch Thu-Sat, dinner daily) The subdued lighting, dark wood, snappy service and wonderful bistro food will make you swear you're in Paris. Vegetarians are actually given a choice of dishes that invites debate, and for the carnivores, it's hard to beat the steak with fritts (chips!), thanks to chef Joe Pavlovich. A small but functional wine list makes for a very enjoyable experience.

Buzo (Map pp72-3; ☎ 9328 1600; 152 Jersey Rd, Woollahra; mains $19-25; ⓨ dinner Mon-Sat) Buzo is an intimate, charming restaurant that feels like a neighbourhood secret. Homely Italian and French dishes pepper the straightforward menu (with a smattering of good wines) – we had a great Sicilian roast leg of lamb ($25). Nab a window seat if you can and admire the red-and-white checked tablecloths, hanging garlic and honest victuals.

Toko (Map pp72-3; ☎ 9380 7001; 362 Oxford St, Paddington; sushi from $2.50; ⓨ lunch Mon, lunch & dinner Tue-Sat) Our favourite sushi train in Sydney is right here. Start with a bowl of great miso soup, then do a hit-and-run on the tasty morsels that are rolling by. It gets crazy at lunchtimes when the nearby markets are on, filling up with pretty young things and buff young studs.

Jones the Grocer (Map pp72-3; ☎ 9362 1222; 68 Moncur St, Woollahra; mains $8-16; ⓨ breakfast & lunch) With the lovely food on display it's easy to see why this is one of Sydney's favourite places to stock up on fancy deli goods. The mixed platter at lunchtime is a good refuelling option. But it's also nice for the old coffee-and-cake break.

Grand National Hotel (Map pp72-3; ☎ 9363 4557; 161 Underwood St, Paddington; mains $22.50-28.50; ⓨ lunch & dinner Tue-Sun) Chef Craig Edmond cooks pub grub with a difference – it's inventive and consistently stylish. With well-chosen wine recommendations adding even more punch to the experience, this place is easily first past the post in the Paddo pub stakes. The crispy salmon with borlotti beans and stuffed tempura zucchini flowers ($24.50) had crunch in all the right places.

Glebe

The Boathouse Blackwattle Bay (Map p74; ☎ 9518 9011; Ferry Rd, Glebe; mains $28-42; ⓨ lunch & dinner Tue-Sun) Not only the best restaurant in Glebe, but one of the best restaurants in Sydney. From oysters so fresh you'd think you shucked them yourself to a snapper pie that will have you placing it at the top of your fave dish list. And yep, there's a view

of the bridge – only this time it's the Anzac Bridge. Reservations essential.

Iku Wholefoods (Map p74; ☎ 9692 8720; 25a Glebe Point Rd; mains $2.50-9; ⓨ lunch & dinner) This stalwart of healthy eating offers wonderful vegan and vegetarian food in a relaxed, small setting (takeaway is a good idea) at bargain prices. It's a handy spot for either dinner or lunch, and while other branches are scattered throughout the city, this one remains a favourite of ours.

Spanish Tapas (Map p74; ☎ 9571 9005; 28 Glebe Point Rd; tapas $7.50-14; ⓨ dinner) There's quite a party vibe here, with average to great tapas dishes, low lights, music and a convivial bunch of diners. Grab a jug of sangria ($16) and throw yourself into the festive spirit.

Newtown

Rosalina's (Map p74; ☎ 9516 1429; 30 King St; mains $14-16; ⓨ dinner Tue-Sun) Cuter than cute, Rosalina's is like a clichéd 'little Italian place' from central casting, complete with dodgy mural. Charming service, home-made vino and great pasta make it very popular on weekends, so book ahead. Those hankering for a classic steak Dianne ($16) will be in heaven.

Green Gourmet (Map p74; ☎ 9519 5330; 115 King St; mains $13-15; ⓨ lunch & dinner) Spotlessly clean and kind to animals, Green Gourmet offers great Chinese-Malaysian vegetarian lunch and dinner at good prices. On weekends, grab a few morsels of cruelty-free yum cha and wash it all down with one of the excellent teas on offer. There's no smoking, of course, and no drinking either.

Leichhardt

Bar Italia (Map p66-7; ☎ 9560 9981; 169-171 Norton St; mains $8.50-16; ⓨ breakfast, lunch & dinner Mon-Sat) This enormously popular restaurant, café and gelateria offers pasta mains and bar snacks, but one of its biggest drawcards is its famous *gelato*, which is a must-have accessory for any Norton St *passegiata* (stroll). The outdoor courtyard, good honest food and a little red wine make for a very enjoyable meal. Don't expect much in the way of Italian design from your surroundings – all the pleasure is in the eating.

Grappa (Map p66-7; ☎ 9560 6090; Shop 1, 267-77 Norton St, Leichhardt; mains $28-36; ⓨ dinner Mon, lunch & dinner Tue-Fri, dinner Sat & Sun) You'll enter Grappa via a less-than-attractive garage,

SYDNEY

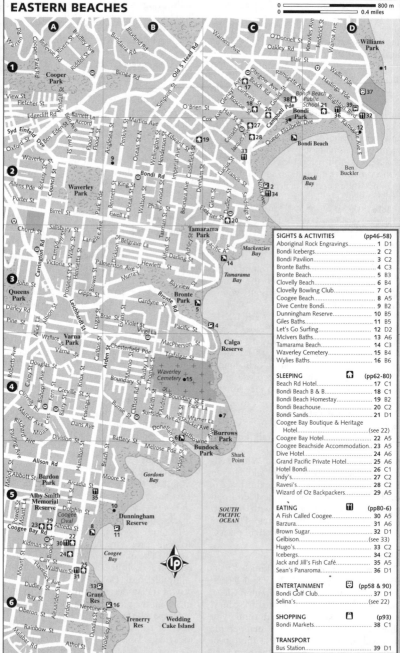

EASTERN BEACHES

0 ———————— 800 m
0 ———————— 0.4 miles

SIGHTS & ACTIVITIES	(pp46–58)
Aboriginal Rock Engravings	**1** D1
Bondi Icebergs	**2** C2
Bondi Pavilion	**3** C2
Bronte Baths	**4** C3
Bronte Beach	**5** B3
Clovelly Beach	**6** B4
Clovelly Bowling Club	**7** C4
Coogee Beach	**8** A5
Dive Centre Bondi	**9** B2
Dunningham Reserve	**10** B5
Giles Baths	**11** B5
Let's Go Surfing	**12** D2
McIvers Baths	**13** A6
Tamarama Beach	**14** C3
Waverley Cemetery	**15** B4
Wylies Baths	**16** B6

SLEEPING	(pp62–80)
Beach Rd Hotel	**17** C1
Bondi Beach B & B	**18** C1
Bondi Beach Homestay	**19** B2
Bondi Beachouse	**20** C2
Bondi Sands	**21** D1
Coogee Bay Boutique & Heritage Hotel	(see 22)
Coogee Bay Hotel	**22** A5
Coogee Beachside Accommodation	**23** A5
Dive Hotel	**24** A6
Grand Pacific Private Hotel	**25** A6
Hotel Bondi	**26** C1
Indy's	**27** C2
Ravesi's	**28** C2
Wizard of Oz Backpackers	**29** A5

EATING	(pp80–6)
A Fish Called Coogee	**30** A5
Barzura	**31** A6
Brown Sugar	**32** D1
Gelbison	(see 33)
Hugo's	**33** C2
Icebergs	**34** C2
Jack and Jill's Fish Café	**35** B5
Sean's Panorama	**36** D1

ENTERTAINMENT	(pp58 & 90)
Bondi Golf Club	**37** D1
Selina's	(see 22)

SHOPPING	(p93)
Bondi Markets	**38** C1

TRANSPORT	
Bus Station	**39** D1

and ascend to a spacious eatery with an open kitchen, snazzy bar and elegant décor – perfect for a swanky yet relaxed dining experience. There's a good range of dishes (the grilled seafood plate is a gem at $29), and an impressive list of grappa, hence the name.

Bondi

Icebergs (Map p84; ☎ 9130 3120; 1 Notts Ave; mains $32-46; ⏰ lunch & dinner Tue-Sun) So damn hot we get scorch marks just walking past, this new venture dares to charge a cancellation fee to errant diners. Why anyone would fail to show (reservations essential, and hard to come by) we've no idea – the décor is 21st-century cool-meets-warm, the views over Bondi to die for, the food fantastic. One bite of the warm salad of Moreton Bay Bugs with kipfler potatoes, tarragon and fresh peas will make you glad you came.

Sean's Panaroma (Map p84; ☎ 9365 4924; 2/270 Campbell Pde; mains $24-35; ⏰ dinner Wed-Fri, lunch & dinner Sat, lunch Sun) Sean and his team have never let us down when we're looking for excellent food in intimate surrounds. It attracts a good-looking crowd, but don't let that put you off – the food is straight from heaven. For starters, grab someone special and share an ox heart tomato salad ($18) before delving into more substantial territory and a judicious wine list. One of Sydney's more romantic dinner spots.

Gelbison (Map p84; ☎ 9130 4042; 10 Lamrock Ave; mains $9.50-19; ⏰ dinner) An old favourite with many beach bums, film industry types (including Mel Gibson) and assorted gluttons looking for great Italian staples, Gelbison never seems to change, and in Bondi that's a rare thing. The pizza and pasta inspire such devotion that a local band took the step of naming themselves after the beloved joint.

Brown Sugar (Map p84; ☎ 9365 6262; 100 Brighton Blvd; mains $7.50-13; ⏰ breakfast & lunch) This cramped space really churns out brekky to the smooth set on weekends – and one bite of their black-stone eggs ($9.50) will tell you why. It's much less frantic on weekdays, and the lunch dishes and salads are truly tasty.

Hugo's (Map p84; ☎ 9300 0900; 70 Campbell Pde; mains $30-42; ⏰ dinner Mon-Fri, breakfast, lunch & dinner Sat & Sun) Hugo's is well known among Bondi dwellers as a good place to have a better-than-average-meal in swish 'look at me' surrounds. It can seem a bit intimidating, but once you've tried some of the food and

had one of the daiquiris, you won't care. Staff are disconcertingly attractive, so if this makes you nervous, put on some sparkle.

Coogee

A Fish Called Coogee (Map p84; ☎ 9664 7700; 229 Coogee Bay Rd; mains $8-16; ⏰ lunch & dinner) This great little fishmonger sells fresh fish and seafood cooked many different ways. Grab some takeaway fish and chips ($8) and sit on the beach – because the tables here are often full, and anyway, it's more Australian that way.

Barzura (Map p84; ☎ 9665 5546; 62 Carr St; mains $15-22; ⏰ breakfast, lunch & dinner) An all-day possibility, Barzura gets packed, thanks to a mix of location (there are outdoor tables with beach views) and good honest eating (the pasta is always popular). On a sunny day, get in early or forget about eating alfresco.

Jack & Jill's Fish Café (Map p84; ☎ 9665 8429; 98 Beach St; mains $12-17; ⏰ dinner Tue-Sat, lunch Sun) This homy, simple place serves good seafood dishes at reasonable prices. It's away from the crowds, but close to the northern end of Coogee Beach. We recommend the Cajun-spiced barramundi with rice ($16.50).

Manly

Bower Restaurant (Map p56; ☎ 9977 5451; 7 Marine Pde; mains $23-29; ⏰ breakfast & lunch) Follow the foreshore path east from the main ocean beach to reach this small restaurant, within spray's breath of tiny Fairy Bower beach. It has wonderful breakfasts, delicious main courses and it's BYO too. Heaven!

Le Kiosk (Map p56; ☎ 9977 4122; 1 Marine Pde; mains $25-32; ⏰ lunch & dinner) Love is in the air at this romantic restaurant; a sandstone cottage rich with history, gentle lighting, an open fireplace and the sounds of the softly lapping water. The food too proves a worthy paramour; the sautéed chilli lime king prawns with pappadum, melon carpaccio and pea leaf salad are swoon-worthy. There are good options for vegetarians too.

Blue Water Café (Map p56; ☎ 9976 2051; 28 South Steyne; mains $14-25; ⏰ breakfast, lunch & dinner) With huge portions, an entrée should be enough for most at this bustling, popular café in a prime position. The whopping great chicken burger with all the trimmings ($13.50) will really satisfy a post-surf hunger, although all the boards on the wall will make you keen to get back out there into the foam.

Alhambra (Map p56; ☎ 9976 2975; 54a The Esplanade; mains $23; ⊙ lunch & dinner) We love coming to Manly, because it means we can be distracted by the heavenly smells wafting from Alhambra, and then we decide it's time to make sure they've maintained their standards. The Spanish-inspired dishes are excellent, and are nicely matched by the Moorish décor. Grab some mates, a few beers and graze on tapas to your heart's (and belly's) content.

North Shore

Aqua Dining (Map p76; ☎ 9964 9998; cnr Paul & Northcliff Sts, Milsons Point; mains $33-36; ⊙ lunch Mon-Fri & Sun, dinner daily) The fit-out was accomplished by Soma design, and while its muted mushroom tones and clean lines are admirable, it never really competes with the view of the Bridge and the harbour. Service here is sterling – that rare mix of courteous, knowledgeable (the wine list beggars belief) and amiable. Put your hand up for the saddle of lamb ($35) and don't even think about a post-prandial swim in the Olympic swimming pool that you're overlooking!

Ripples (Map p76; ☎ 9929 7722; Olympic Dr, Milson's Point; mains $20-25; ⊙ breakfast, lunch & dinner) Ripples was a new arrival when we popped in, and was being touted by all and sundry. Go for breakfast or lunch and be rewarded with fine food, tasty views and the smug sense of being in the thick of Sydney's most attractive geography. It's diagonally across from Aqua Dining at North Sydney's Olympic Pool.

DRINKING

Pubs are an extremely important part of Sydney's social scene. They vary from the traditional (elaborate 19th-century affairs with pressed tin ceilings, or cavernous Art Deco joints with tiled walls), to the modern and minimalist. Bars have a more stylish feel to them, although not all can be classified as swanky. There may well be a door policy with a dress code (smart casual) and the odd bit of entertainment.

There are some nice, old pubs in The Rocks, but determining just how old they are seems to be a less-than-exact science. There are also plenty of notorious boozers, which attract rowdy crowds, especially on weekends and St Patrick's Day (March 17). The main drag, George St, is where

the hubbub is, but try Lower Fort St or Cumberland St too. For infinitely more stylish surrounds and long cocktail lists, Circular Quay is the go. It's popular with a smart after-work crowd, particularly on Friday night.

Twenty-four-hour party people head to Oxford St Darlinghurst or Kings Cross – its trashy main drag, Darlinghurst Rd, has plenty of drinking, and stripping, options – although there are some very stylish spots to imbibe here too. Fashionable types can find popular pubs (even in the daytime) in neighbouring suburbs like Paddington (Oxford St) and Surry Hills. The inner west is great for a low-key schooner, with suburbs like Balmain featuring plenty of pubs along Darling St alone.

Established caffeine strips include Darlinghurst Rd and surrounding streets in Darlinghurst, plus parts of Surry Hills.

Bars
CITY CENTRE

Tank Stream Bar (Map pp68-70; ☎ 9240 3109; 1 Tank Stream Way; ⊠) Tucked away behind the swanky Establishment, this convivial bar, capably run by the charming Sonia, is a great place to unwind after a hard working day. It's subtly decorated with an interesting blend of original features and new flourishes, with plenty of ventilation and nary a TV screen in sight.

Bar Europa (Map pp68-70; ☎ 9232 3377; Basement, 82 Elizabeth St; ⊠) The basement location, flattering lighting and sexy screens separating its three rooms all combine to create a charming drinking den for legal eagles and those who've just shopped till they dropped.

Establishment (Map pp68-70; ☎ 9240 3000; 252 George St; ⊠) Cashed-up and convinced it's still the '80s, the smartly suited crowd here appreciates the fine art of a smart cocktail after a hard day's stockbroking, and so do the designer-dudded types who love 'em. Noise levels approach a dull roar, what with all that marble going on.

KINGS CROSS & DARLINGHURST

Baron's (Map p71; ☎ 9358 6131; Level 1, 5 Roslyn St, Kings Cross) God bless Baron's! Everything looks like it's in a state of decay here – sticky carpet, shabby chairs, yellowing walls – but where else are you going to find a quiet, really late-night drink and a game of backgammon?

Chicane (Map pp68–70; ☎ 9380 2121; 1a Burton St, Darlinghurst; 🔀) You'll feel all grown up once you step into Chicane's up-to-the-minute design, comfortable seating, good wines and luscious cocktails, low ceilings, a fireplace and smooth service. Even the bathrooms are groovy.

Kinselas (☎ 9331 3299; 383 Bourke St, Darlinghurst; 🔀) In what used to be a funeral parlour, this place has come back from the dead more times than we can recall. The downstairs part is poker machines and bad carpet, but the bar upstairs is stylish, modern and incredibly popular with the bright young things. The cocktails are very good too. On hot summer nights, hanging on the miniscule balcony is *de rigueur.*

SURRY HILLS

Mars Lounge (Map pp68–70; ☎ 9267 6440; 16 Wentworth Ave; 🔀) A handful of futuristic-looking booths serves as the perfect spot to sip a cocktail and marvel at the fact that the staff here all look as though they're auditioning to be Michael Jackson's backing dancers.

Cafés

Café Hernandez (Map pp68–70; ☎ 9331 2343; 69 Kings Cross Rd; snacks $5-9) With a delightful old-world atmosphere and some of the best coffee in Sydney, Hernandez has been attracting everyone from taxi drivers to arty students for years. At times you'll think you're in Madrid, especially when it's 3am and this joint's jumping (open 24 hours). Be warned though, there's no bathroom.

Bar Coluzzi (Map p71; ☎ 9380 5420; 322 Victoria St, Darlinghurst) You come here for coffee, not food, and it's almost a meal in itself, so robust is the flavour. Coluzzi has achieved legendary status, and if you have to have coffee in Darlinghurst, this is the place.

Spring Espresso (Map pp68–70; ☎ 9331 0190; 65 Macleay St, Potts Point; mains $7.50-12) For life-changing coffee and good snacks, try this diminutive and bustling café; entry is via Challis Ave and you may have a bit of a wait on your hands during the morning rush, when it seems that half of Potts Point needs a heart-starter.

Pubs

THE ROCKS

Lord Nelson Brewery Hotel (Map pp68–70; ☎ 9251 4044; 19 Kent St, The Rocks) The Lord Nelson is an atmospheric old (1842) pub that claims to be the 'oldest pub' in town (although others do too!) and brews its own beers (Quayle Ale, Trafalgar Pale Ale, Victory Bitter, Three Sheets, Old Admiral, Nelsons Blood and The Lord's Water). It might not be wise to sample them all in one sitting.

Australian Hotel (Map pp68–70; ☎ 9247 2229; 100 Cumberland St, The Rocks) On the corner of Gloucester and Cumberland Sts, this laid-back, friendly hotel has renowned local brews on tap, and it's also a nice sleeping option (p63).

KINGS CROSS AREA

Old Fitzroy Hotel (Map p71; ☎ 9356 6848; 129 Dowling St, Woolloomooloo) Is it a pub? A theatre? A bistro? Actually it's all three. Grab a bowl of laksa, see the acting stars of tomorrow and wash it all down with a beer, for about $30. The little balcony is unbeatable on a hot, steamy night.

Tilbury Hotel (Map pp68–70; ☎ 9368 1955; cnr Forbes & Nicholson Sts, Woolloomooloo) A fab renovation has restored this former cabaret stalwart to (almost) its former glory. Comfy armchairs, plenty of space and a friendly crowd make it a good escape from the crazy scenes up the road.

DARLINGHURST & SURRY HILLS

Hollywood Hotel (Map pp72–3; ☎ 9281 2765; 2 Foster St, Surry Hills) This Art Deco pub looks non-descript from the outside, but the inside reveals one of Sydney's most appealing Friday night drinking dens. A mixed (dare we say, bohemian) crowd crams in and gets down to the business of starting the weekend with gusto.

Darlo Bar (Map p71; ☎ 9331 3672; cnr Liverpool St & Darlinghurst Rd, Darlinghurst) Occupying its own tiny block, this is surely the narrowest pub in Sydney. It's pretty much a neighbour-hood pub, but it's a very interesting neighbourhood. The service is friendly and the furniture is retro mix-and-match, with a boisterous scene on weekend evenings.

Green Park Hotel (Map p71; ☎ 9380 5311; 360 Victoria St, Darlinghurst) The good old Green Park has tiled walls and a bar; it's a popular local watering hole and a cool hang-out for pool-shooters. The last dose of renovations provided much-needed drinking space and better toilets. Punters regularly go back and forth between this place and the Darlo Bar.

Burdekin Hotel (☎ 9331 2066; 2 Oxford St, Darlinghurst) The Burdekin is one of a number of busy drinking options along Oxford St. It has a wonderfully stylish cocktail bar called the **Dug Out**, which you'll find at the back entrance, down a short flight of stairs. Grab a lethal martini and chill out with the good-looking crowd.

Cricketers Arms (Map pp72-3; ☎ 9331 3301; 106 Fitzroy St, Surry Hills) A cruisy, cosy vibe fills this Art Nouveau pub with arty locals and those appreciative of good DJ skills displayed from Thursday to Sunday. There are open fireplaces too.

PADDINGTON & WOOLLAHRA

Paddington Inn Hotel (☎ 9380 5277; 338 Oxford St) This sociable pub is very popular on weekend nights and during the day on Saturday, but it's pretty large and there's room for everyone if you practise your elbow work. The exterior makes good use of peeling paint – the interior is surprisingly swanky.

Lord Dudley Hotel (☎ 9327 5399; 236 Jersey Rd, Woollahra) The Lord Dudley is as close as Sydney really gets to an English pub atmosphere, with dark walls and wood and good beer in pint glasses. It's the sort of place that gets packed with Rugby Union types and their shoulders.

BALMAIN & GLEBE

London Hotel (Map p75; ☎ 9555 1377; 234 Darling St, Balmain) This is a good place for a cleansing ale, especially after a trawl through the nearby Saturday market at St Andrew's.

Riverview Hotel (Map p75; ☎ 9555 8337; 29 Birchgrove Rd, Balmain) This avowedly local pub was once owned by Australian swimming legend Dawn Fraser (a Balmain icon if ever there was one). It's quiet, low-key and a bit of a treasure.

At the unique bric-a-brac–filled **Friend in Hand Hotel** (Map p74; ☎ 9660 2326; 58 Cowper St, Glebe), you can enjoy trivia nights on Tuesday, crab racing on Wednesday, or just beer any day.

BONDI

Bondi Icebergs (Map p84; ☎ 9130 3120; 1 Notts Ave) Getting its name from the members' habit of swimming in winter with blocks of ice in the pool, this is one of Sydney's best-located drinking spots. If you're not into winter swimming, go for a beer in the newly renovated 'Bergs (live bands play frequently during January and February). There's also one of Sydney's most 'it' restaurants on the premises (p85).

Beach Road Hotel (Map p84 ☎ 9130 7247; 71 Beach Rd, Nth Bondi) Weekends here resemble a boisterous multilevel alcoholiday, with Bondi types (think bronzed, buff and brooding) and jolly out-of-towners playing pool, drinking beer and dancing to the regular bands and DJs.

EASTERN SUBURBS

Watsons Bay Hotel (Map pp66-7; ☎ 9337 4299; 10 Marine Pde, Watsons Bay) Surrounded by two overpriced seafood restaurants (both called Doyles) and home to a lovely boutique pub-stay (called Doyles), you'll be pleased to know that you can have the Doyles experience simply by buying a jug of beer, sitting down in the beer garden and enjoying the superlative view of Sydney Harbour. A time-honoured tradition, but avoid weekends, when it's packed to the gills.

ENTERTAINMENT

The *Sydney Morning Herald* 'Metro' lift-out is published on Friday and lists events in town for the coming week. Free newspapers, such as *Drum Media*, *Revolver* and *3D World* also have useful listings and are available from bookshops, bars, cafés and record stores.

Ticketek (☎ 9266 4800; www.ticketek.com.au; 195 Elizabeth St; ⏰ 9am-7pm Mon-Fri, 9am-4pm Sat) is the city's main booking agency for theatre, concerts, sports and other events. Phone bookings can be made and it also has agencies around town.

Halftix (Map pp68-70; ☎ 9279 0855; www.halftix .com.au; 91 York St, Sydney; ⏰ daily except Sun) also has a booth at the upper end of Martin Place and sells half-price seats for shows. Tickets are only available for shows that night, and they can't tell you where you'll be sitting.

Cinemas

Generally, cinema tickets cost between $12 and $15 for adults. Populist theatre chains such as Hoyts, Village and Greater Union also have numerous suburban theatres. Movie listings can be found in Sydney's daily newspapers.

Bondi beach (p54), Sydney

Chinatown (p81), Sydney

Bridgeclimb view (p53), Sydney Harbour Bridge

CITYRAIL'S SYDNEY SUBURBAN NETWORK

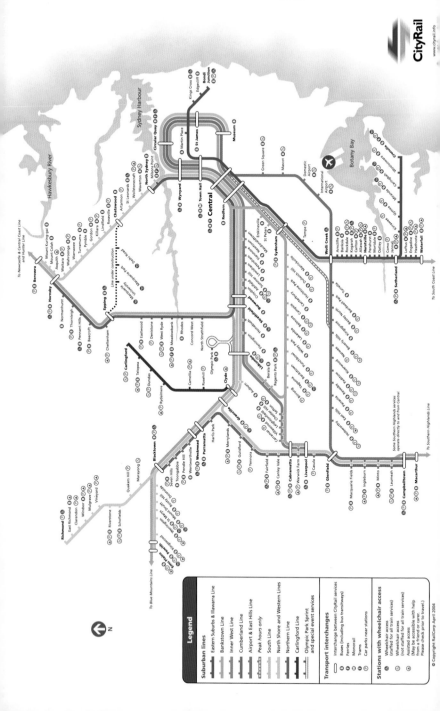

CityRail

Legend

Suburban lines
- Eastern Suburbs & Illawarra Line
- Bankstown Line
- Inner West Line
- Cumberland Line
- Airport & East Hills Line
- Peak hours only
- South Line
- North Shore and Western Lines
- Northern Line
- Carlingford Line
- Olympic Park Sprint and special event services

Transport interchanges
- Interchange between CityRail services
- Buses (including bus transitways)
- Ferries
- Monorail
- Trams
- Car parks near stations

Stations with wheelchair access
- Wheelchair access (staffed for all train services)
- Wheelchair access (not staffed for all train services)
- Assisted access (May be accessible with help from a friend or carer. Please check prior to travel.)

© Copyright RailCorp April 2004

www.cityrail.info

George St Cinemas (☎ 9273 7431; 505 George St, Sydney; ✖) This monster-sized movie palace combines the Hoyts, Village and Greater Union chains in an orgy of popcorn-fuelled mainstream entertainment. They've got more screens than you've had hot dinners.

Dendy Opera Quays (☎ 9252 8879; Shop 9, 2 Circular Quay East; ✖) Right near the Opera House, this is a lavish new cinema with a great bar. The **original branch** (Map pp68-70; ☎ 9233 8166, 19 Martin Pl, Sydney) also has a good bar and well-chosen first-run art house movies.

Chauvel Cinema (Map pp72-3; ☎ 9361 5398; cnr Oxford St & Oatley Rd, Paddington; ✖) This cinema, with its association with the Australian Film Institute (AFI), plays quality releases new and old (with a liberal dose of the quirky and out-there), and also has themed festivals (Jewish, Queer etc).

Verona Cinema (Map pp72-3; ☎ 9360 6099; Level 1, 17 Oxford St, Paddington; ✖) This cinema also has a café and bar, so you can discuss the good (invariably nonmainstream) flick you've just seen.

Academy Twin Cinema (Map pp72-3; ☎ 9361 4453; 3a Oxford St, Paddington; ✖) Just down the street from Verona, this is a smaller cinema that was fitted out in the 1970s. Has art house and independent offerings.

IMAX (Map pp68-70; ☎ 9281 3300; Southern Promenade, Cockle Bay; adult/child $17/12; ✖) This is the world's biggest movie screen. If you're into being wowed by massive images, some in 3D, then IMAX is for you. Movies shown tend to be either thrill-fests or nature docos.

Govinda's Movie Room (Map p71; ☎ 9380 5155; 112 Darlinghurst Rd; dinner & movie $16; ☺ 6-10.30pm) The Hare Krishna Govinda's is an all-you-can-gobble vegetarian smorgasbord, which also gives you admission to the cinema upstairs.

Nightclubs

Sydney's dance club scene is alive and kicking, with local and international DJs making thousands of people wave their hands in the air every weekend. Some places have strict door policies and a lot of attitude; others are great places to catch up with all sorts of people.

Home (Map pp68-70; ☎ 9266 0600; Cockle Bay Wharf, 101 Wheat Rd, Darling Harbour; cover charge $25) A monster-sized pleasure dome sprawling over three levels, this club has a sound system that makes other clubs sound like they're plugged

into transistor radios. Even with a capacity of 2000 people, this place gets packed, especially for club night Sublime (Friday). Some gay nights happen here too.

Slipp Inn (Map pp68-70; ☎ 9299 4777; 111 Sussex St, Sydney; cover charge $15-20) Warren-like and full of different rooms for different moods, this place is full of cool kids and those who love a bit of turntable-inspired dancing – with funk, techno and house breaks on the menu.

Yu (Map p71; ☎ 9358 6511; 171 Victoria St, Potts Point; cover charge $10-20) Yu wants you to get down to the best of house and funk, played by some of Sydney's most venerable DJs. We love After Ours, which solves the dilemma of what to do on a Sunday night. The club itself is slick-looking and full of slick-looking clubbers.

Icebox (Map p71; ☎ 9331 0058; 2 Kellett St, Kings Cross; cover charge $5-15) If you're hankering for those 'Summer of Love' sounds of the late '80s and early '90s, Icebox has Stun on Wednesday nights. Progressive and hard house can be heard Thursday to Sunday, for those who like to party hard until the wee hours.

Q Bar (Map pp68-70; ☎ 9360 1375; Level 2, 44 Oxford St; Fri & Sat cover charge $20) With more reincarnations than Cleopatra over the years, this stayer has DJs playing every night of the week. We like Thursday night's Prom Night, when there's an 'anything goes' musical vibe in the air. On weekends, it might seem that this place should be named Queue Bar.

GoodBar (Map pp72-3; ☎ 9360 6759; 11a Oxford St, Paddington; cover charge $5-10) This hanky-sized club is still attracting gorgeous young fly-girls and B-boys who get past the face control at the door. Its Thursday night groove-fest, Step Forward, is easily its best night, with reggae, funk and hip-hop on the musical menu.

Live Music

Sydney doesn't have as dynamic a music scene as Melbourne, but you can still find live music most nights of the week. For detailed listings of venues and acts, see the listings in the papers mentioned on p88.

CLASSICAL

Sydney Opera House (Map pp68-70; ☎ 9250 7777; www.sydneyoperahouse.com; Bennelong Point, Circular Quay East; **P** ✖) This is the ground zero for performance in Australia, and its Concert Hall and Opera Hall (holding 2500 and 1500 people respectively) are a must for anyone wishing to really experience the nun's scrum (an Opera House nickname). Everything is performed here – theatre, comedy, music, dance and opera – but it's this last art form that really should be sampled while you're here. The box office opens from 9am to 8.30pm Monday to Saturday and 2½ hours before a Sunday performance.

City Recital Hall (Map pp68-70; ☎ 8256 2222; www .cityrecitalhall.com; 2 Angel Pl, Sydney; 😢) This is a purpose-built 1200-seat venue with wonderful acoustics that hosts live music performances. Its architecture is based on the 19th-century European blueprint, and it's an excellent place to hear the Australian Brandenburg Orchestra, among others.

Eugene Goosens Hall (Map pp72-3; ☎ 9333 1500; 700 Harris St, Ultimo; 😢) The Australian Broadcasting Association's (ABC) intimate Eugene Goosens Hall often has good classical recitals that are broadcast live. Don't even think about attending one if you've got a cough!

Sydney Conservatorium of Music (Map pp68-70; ☎ 9351 1222; www.usyd.edu.au/su/conmusic; Macquarie St, Sydney; 😢) A few years and $145 million later, this historic music venue is back in the business of showcasing the talents of its students and their teachers. Choral, jazz, operatic and chamber recitals are held here from March to July, plus a range of free lunch-time recitals and lectures. Visit the website for more information.

JAZZ & BLUES

Sydney has a healthy and innovative jazz and blues circuit, with quite a few venues worth a swing.

Basement (Map pp68-70; ☎ 9251 2797; www.the basement.com.au; 29 Reiby Pl, Circular Quay; 😢) This place has decent food, good music (plus the odd spoken word and comedy gig) and some big international names dropping by to spread the jazz and blues gospel.

Empire Hotel (Map p66-7; ☎ 9557 1701; cnr Parramatta Rd & Johnston St, Annandale) Blues buffs should look no further than the well-run Empire for live acts (aided and abetted by a very good sound system) Tuesday to Sunday nights.

Soup Plus (Map pp68-70; ☎ 9299 7728; 383 George St, Sydney) Soup Plus has live jazz at lunch and

dinner time, as well as cheap food and a casual atmosphere. It's the mainstream end of jazz for the most part, so don't expect any radical tonal experimentation.

Strawberry Hills Hotel (Map pp72-3; ☎ 9698 2997; 453 Elizabeth St, Surry Hills; 😢) This refurbished pub features live jazz in the forms of the Eclipse Alley Five from 4pm to 7pm on Saturday, and Bill Dudley and the New Orleanians from 5pm to 8pm on Sunday.

Wine Banc (Map pp68-70; ☎ 9233 5399; 53 Martin Place, Sydney; 😢) Hands down, this is the sexiest place to hear live jazz in Sydney. The whole place looks like it was carved out of an architect's bunker dreams, and the table service is flawless. A brilliant wine list only adds to the appeal.

ROCK & POP

There's sometimes no charge to see young local bands, while between $5 and $20 is charged for well-known local acts, and at least $60 for international performers. There are a number of venues worth considering.

Annandale Hotel (Map pp66-7; ☎ 9550 1078; 17 Parramatta Rd, Annandale) Thankfully, this place was rescued from the live-music graveyard a few years ago, and it's back to doing what it does best – playing host to a sometimes eclectic assortment of local and international alternative music acts.

Cat & Fiddle (Map pp66-7; ☎ 9810 7931; 456 Darling St, Balmain) In an heroic move, the Cat & Fiddle ripped out its pokies and brought back nightly live music. There's even a small theatre on the premises (about 30 seats).

Enmore Theatre (☎ 9550 3666; 130 Enmore Rd, Newtown) The Enmore hosts major Australian and overseas acts. The Rolling Stones played a brilliant 'intimate' concert here in early 2003.

Hordern Pavilion (Map pp72-3; ☎ 9383 4000; Driver Ave, Moore Park) Not in use as much as it once was, but the Hordern regularly hosts international acts, such as Moby.

Metro Theatre (Map pp68-70; ☎ 9287 2000; 624 George St, Sydney; 😢) This is easily the best place to see well-chosen local and alternative international acts (plus the odd DJ) in well-ventilated comfort.

Selina's (Map p84; ☎ 9665 0000; Coogee Bay Hotel, cnr Coogee Bay Rd & Arden St, Coogee) Selina's, a veritable 'rawk' institution, often has top Australian and international rock bands, resulting in much sticky carpet and tinnitus.

Hopetoun Hotel (Map pp72-3; ☎ 9361 5257; 416 Bourke St, Surry Hills) This great little venue offers flexibility for artists and patrons alike and features modern musical styles from folk to rap to DJs and local bands getting their first taste of life on the road.

Sandringham Hotel (☎ 9557 1254; 387 King St, Newtown) We were nervous that renovations at the Sando would mean the end of live music there, but thankfully, you can still pay a minimal amount of money (say, $5) and get your earwax blasted out from Thursday to Sunday. Quieter acts will merely coax it out.

Sydney Entertainment Centre (Map pp68-70; ☎ 9266 4800; Harbour St, Haymarket; 🔀) This big concrete box is for the Elton Johns and Kylie Minogues of this world. It seats just over 12,000, and despite being purpose-built for these bigger gigs, the sound quality is only adequate at best.

Sport

Spend a day or two in Sydney and you'll notice a little something about its inhabitants. They're shiny, they're hard, they're psyched – and they get (and stay) this way through exercise. Sydney's sunshine, parks, beaches and love of showing off all conspire to make this a delightful city for staying fit or watching sport. If you like to watch, have a credit card handy and book tickets to a variety of sporting events, big and small. If you're the one being sporty, it can be as simple as putting your feet in some jogging shoes or putting in some laps at a beachside pool, or as tricky as getting a golf game on a sunny weekend.

Sydney is one of rugby league's world capitals. The major competition is the National Rugby League's (NRL; www.nrl .com.au) Telstra Premiership, with games played at various grounds around Sydney (around $22 a ticket from Ticketek). Sell-out finals can either be seen at the Superdome (Sydney Olympic Park) or at Aussie Stadium (in Moore Park) in September. The season starts in March.

The **Sydney Cricket Ground** (SCG; Map pp72-3), also in Moore Park, is the venue for sparsely attended state cricket matches, packed five-day Test matches and sell-out one-day World Series cricket matches. Moore Park also has a golf course.

The (at times) high-flying Sydney Swans, this state's contribution to the Australian Football League (AFL), play matches between March and September. Their home ground is the SCG.

Sydney's oldest and largest 18-footer yacht club is the **Sydney Flying Squadron** (Map pp66-7; ☎ 9955 8350; 76 McDougall St, Milsons Point). You can catch a ferry from there to watch skiff racing from 2pm to 4pm on Saturdays between October and April (adult/child $14/10).

Theatre & Comedy

Wharf Theatre (Map pp68-70; ☎ 9250 1700; Pier 4, Hickson Rd, Walsh Bay; 🔀) The Sydney Theatre Company (STC), the city's top theatre company, has its own venue here. It's also the home of the Australian Theatre for Young People (ATYP), Bangarra Dance Theatre, Sydney Philharmonia Choirs and the Sydney Dance Company. A restaurant on the premises (called The Wharf) delivers much better than average pre- and post-show fare.

Capitol Theatre (Map pp68-70; ☎ 9320 5000; 17 Campbell St, Haymarket; 🔀) Lavishly restored after being saved from demolition, this big theatre is home to big-name concerts and long-running musicals.

Lyric Theatre (Map pp68-70; ☎ 9657 9657; Star City, Darling Harbour; Ⓟ 🔀) The large Lyric Theatre stages flashy musical extravaganzas and has good acoustics. We suspect it owes its existence to a placatory gesture to those who didn't want a mother-lovin' big casino in town.

Belvoir St Theatre (Map pp72-3; ☎ 9699 3444; 25 Belvoir St, Surry Hills) Something of a home for original and often experimental Australian theatre, its excellent resident production company is known as Company B, which gets actors like Geoffrey Rush to say 'no' to Hollywood in return for a meaty stage role.

Sydney Comedy Store (Map pp72-3; ☎ 9357 1419; www.comedystore.com.au; Fox Studios, Moore Park; tickets $15-27.50; Ⓟ 🔀) In its purpose-built home in the Fox Studios, this comedy venue has improv, stand-up and open-mike nights.

SHOPPING

The hub of city shopping is **Pitt St Mall**, with department stores, shopping centres and numerous shops all within arm's reach. It's much more relaxing to shop for fashion on popular inner-city strips such as Oxford St, Paddington; for furnishings and antiques on Queen St, Woollahra; for music, DJing and retro fashion needs around Crown St, Surry Hills; for outdoor gear around the corner of Kent and Bathurst Streets in town; or at Sydney's popular markets. The Rocks is where you'll generally find what's known as 'Australiana' (ie souvenirs).

Late-night shopping is on Thursday night, when most stores stay open until 9pm.

Aboriginal Art

Aboriginal & Tribal Art Centre (Map pp68-70; ☎ 9247 9625; 117 George St, The Rocks) Opposite the MCA, this gallery has a broad art and artefact range for sale, plus exhibitions. Overseas packing and shipping can also be arranged, with United Parcel Service (UPS).

Gavala Aboriginal Art (Map pp68-70; ☎ 9212 7232; Harbourside Shopping Centre, Darling Harbour) Proclaiming itself as Sydney's only Aboriginal-owned retail centre and gallery, this is a great place to source everything from a T-shirt to a bark painting, or an Aboriginal flag. Check out the giant boomerang hanging from the ceiling.

Aboriginal Art Shop (Map pp68-70; ☎ 9247 4344; Sydney Opera House) Shoppers make some truly tragic efforts on the didgeridoo here – but the sales assistant doesn't wince. She deserves a medal for patience. Tea towels, didgeridoos, paintings and whatever else takes your fancy can be shipped worldwide.

Walkabout Gallery (Map pp66-7; ☎ 9550 9964; 70 Norton St, Leichhardt) This friendly gallery is part of the World Vision Indigenous Programs, which means you can be sure that Aboriginal artists are getting properly paid, and that the Aboriginal community Australia-wide is benefiting from the sales here.

Australiana

RM Williams (Map pp68-70; ☎ 9262 2228; 389 George St, Sydney) This is a long-established manufacturer and distributor of Aussie outdoor gear, such as Driza-Bones (oilskin riding coats), the classic elastic-sided riding boot beloved by almost every Aussie, and moleskin trousers.

Australian Wine Centre (Map pp68-70; ☎ 9247 2755; Goldfields House, 1 Alfred St, Circular Quay) Downstairs in the building, behind Circular Quay, this centre has wines from every Australian wine-growing region. It will package and send wine overseas, and of course you're welcome to sample a few drops.

Strand Hatters (Map pp68-70; ☎ 9231 6884; Shop 8, Strand Arcade, Pitt St Mall) Wearing a hat to protect oneself from the sun is a good idea in Australia – wearing an authentic rabbit-felt Akubra from this place will ensure you'll never look anything but local – maybe.

Gowings (Map pp68-70; ☎ 9264 6321; cnr George & Market Sts, Sydney) 'Walk Through, No-one Asked to Buy' proclaims the sign. Five floors of staples for every type of Australian (though it mostly deals in men's gear). Get your thongs (that's flip-flops for you Americans and Brits), your flannelette shirt and a damn cheap haircut to boot.

Flame Opals (Map pp68-70; ☎ 9247 3446; 119 George St, The Rocks) If you've been seduced by the colourful opal, this is a good place to get one. Prices range from about $20 to 'if you have to ask, you can't afford it', and the staff are more than happy to help with any questions. It's also tax-free for overseas customers.

Clothing

Scanlan & Theodore (Map pp72-3; ☎ 9361 6722; 433 Oxford St, Paddington) Regularly topping the lists of the favourite designers of with-it gals, Scanlan & Theodore excel in beautifully made pieces for the evening or the office, with fabrics you just can't help but fondle.

Calibre (Map pp72-3; ☎ 9380 5993; 416 Oxford St, Paddington) Smart suiting and hip weekend wardrobe supplies for men are the speciality here. Even if you're a complete fashion misfit, the staff here will sort you out with tact and diplomacy.

Zimmerman Swim (Map pp72-3; ☎ 9360 5769; 24 Oxford St, Woollahra) Half the boobs and bums on Bondi are covered by this wonderful swimwear label, because the Zimmerman sisters understand that Sydneysiders spend a lot of time in their cossies, while still wanting to look sexy.

Country Road (Map pp68-70; ☎ 9394 1823; 142 Pitt St, Sydney) At the more conservative end of Australian fashion, but plenty popular for their comfy jumpers, pants, dresses and suits. It seems that almost everyone (male *and* female) has had a Country Road something in their wardrobe at some point.

Markets

Paddington Markets (Map pp72-3; ☎ 9331 2646; St John's Church, 395 Oxford St, Paddington; ◷ Sat) One of Sydney's most popular markets, it offers everything from vintage clothing and funky designer fashions, to jewellery, food, massage and holistic treatments. More unusual wares include temporary henna tattoos, butterflies under glass, and hammocks. Don't even think about finding a place to park – this is one for public transport.

Paddy's Markets (Map pp68-70; ☎ 1300 361 589; cnr Hay & Thomas Sts, Haymarket; ☺ Sat & Sun) There are two Paddy's Markets. The one on the corner of Hay and Thomas Sts in Haymarket, in the heart of Chinatown, is a Sydney institution where you'll find the usual market fare at rock-bottom prices alongside less-predictable wares like wigs, board games, cheap cosmetics, mobile phones and live budgies. There's also a good selection of fresh fruit, veg and seafood. Paddy's Market in Flemington, on Parramatta Rd near Sydney Olympic Park, operates (along with a huge fruit and veg market) on Friday and Sunday.

Rocks Market (Map pp68-70; ☎ 9255 1717; George St, The Rocks; ☺ Sat & Sun) Held at the top end of George St, under the bridge, this market is closed to traffic. It's a little on the touristy 'Australiana' side, but is still good for a browse – wares include jewellery, antiques, souvenirs, fossils, gems, crystals, retro postcards, musical instruments and a good selection of juggling paraphernalia.

Balmain Markets (Map p71; ☎ 0418-765 736; St Andrew's Congregational Church, 223 Darling St, Balmain; ☺ Sat) This is a really good local market, with crafty stuff like handmade candles, kids' clothing and essential oils. It's also a great spot to hunt down fashion accessories and tasty snacks in the church hall itself.

Glebe Markets (Map p74; ☎ 4237 7499; Glebe Public School, cnr Glebe Point Rd & Derby Pl; ☺ Sat) This market has an assortment of books, clothing, ceramics, glassware, leather goods, herbal teas, oddities and curios. The crowds can be pretty heavy.

Bondi Markets (Map p84; ☎ 9315 8988; Bondi Beach Public School, cnr Campbell Pde & Warners Ave; ☺ Sun) At the northern end of Campbell Pde, this market is good for hip clothing, swimwear, jewellery, furniture, knick-knacks and beautiful-people watching.

Kirribilli Markets (Map p76; ☎ 9922 4428; Bradfield Park North, Milsons Point; ☺ 4th Sat every month) This popular monthly market has new and old bits and pieces for sale and a nice atmosphere. It's a popular haunt with the fashion mag set, when they're in the mood to rediscover vintage clothes.

Shopping Centres & Department Stores

Queen Victoria Building (QVB; Map pp68-70; ☎ 9264 1955; 455 George St, Sydney) The magnificent QVB takes up a whole block with its late 19th-century Romanesque grandeur, and has almost 200 shops on four levels. It is the city's most beautiful shopping centre, bar none. You will find plenty of nice fashion outlets, and plenty of places to buy gifts for those not familiar with Australian knick-knacks. The lower level, which connects to Town Hall Station, also has food bars, shoe repair shops, dry-cleaners and newsagents to service the daily parade of rushing commuters.

Skygarden Arcade (Map pp68-70; ☎ 9231 1811; 77 Castlereagh St, Sydney) This large, modern complex has a range of fashion shops and some food outlets, plus a monster-sized branch of Borders for books and music.

Strand Arcade (Map pp68-70; ☎ 9232 4199; Pitt St Mall, Sydney) Several leading Australian fashion designers and craftspeople have shops at the thoughtfully restored Strand Arcade, between Pitt St Mall and George St. Designer boutiques nestle amid old-fashioned coffee shops, artisans and hairdressing salons.

Market City (Map pp68-70; ☎ 9212 1388; Quay St, Haymarket) This mammoth shopping centre houses Paddy's Markets, a slew of restaurants, cinemas and heaps of retail outlets (mostly the end-of-season variety).

Centrepoint (Map pp68-70; ☎ 9231 1000; cnr Pitt & Market Sts, Sydney) This shopping centre, beside the Imperial Arcade and beneath Sydney Tower, has four storeys of fashion and jewellery shops. You can shortcut Pitt St to Castlereagh St through here, and there are also connecting above-ground walkways with David Jones and Grace Bros.

David Jones (Map pp68-70; ☎ 9266 5544; cnr Elizabeth & Market Sts, Sydney) Considered the city's premier department store, with two locations on Market St, it's a good place to look for top-quality goods. The interior itself, which harkens back to Sydney's golden age of city shopping, is worth a visit even if you don't want to buy anything.

Grace Bros (Map pp68-70; ☎ 9238 9111, 436 George St, Sydney) The seven-level Grace Bros is one of Sydney's largest stores; it's had extensive refurbishments in the last few years. You'll find everything from cafés to cosmetics and everything in between.

GETTING THERE & AWAY
Air
Sydney's Kingsford Smith Airport is Australia's busiest, so don't be surprised if there are delays. It's only 10km south of the city centre, making access easy, but this also means that flights cease between 11pm and 5am due to noise regulations.

You can fly into Sydney from all the usual international points and from all over Australia. Both **Qantas** (☎ 13 13 13) and **Virgin** (☎ 13 67 89) have frequent flights to other capital cities. Smaller airlines, linked to Qantas, fly within Australia.

Boat
There's a new ferry service operating between Sydney and Devonport (Tasmania). **TT Lines** (☎ 13 20 10; www.spiritoftasmania.com.au) runs the Spirit of Tasmania III (from $230 per person, 20½ hours) departing from Sydney 3pm Tuesday, Friday and Sunday, arriving around 11.30am the next day.

Bus
The private bus operators are competitive and service is efficient. Make sure you shop around for discounts if you hold a VIP or YHA card. The government's CountryLink rail network is complemented by coaches. Major operators include **McCafferty's/Greyhound** (☎ 9212 3433; www.mccaffertys.com.au; Shop 4-7, Eddy Avenue, Central Station) and **Murrays** (☎ 13 22 51; www.murrays.com.au).

All interstate and principal regional train and bus services operate to and from Central Station. Note that tickets must be booked in advance.

The **Sydney coach terminal** (Map pp68-70; ☎ 9281 9366; cnr Eddy Ave & Pitt St, Sydney) deals with all the companies and can advise you on the best prices. It's on the corner of Pitt St and Eddy Ave, outside Central Station. Coach operators have offices either in the terminal or nearby. Most buses stop in the suburbs on the way in and out of cities.

Train
Always compare private operator prices for buses to the government's **CountryLink** (Map pp72-3; ☎ 13 22 32; www.countrylink.info) network of trains, which has discounts of up to 40% on economy fares. The state's rail network is an extensive one, with train travel comfortable for the most part.

GETTING AROUND
For information on buses, ferries and trains, phone ☎ 13 15 00 between 6am and 10pm daily.

To/From the Airport
Sydney airport is 10km south of the city centre. The international and domestic terminals are a 4km bus trip apart on either side of the runway.

Airport Link (☎ 13 15 00; www.airportlink.com.au) is a train line that runs from city train stations to the airport terminals (domestic and international) and vice versa. Trains run from approximately 5am to 12.45am daily. A one-way fare from Central Station costs adult/concession $11/7.60.

A taxi from the airport to Circular Quay should cost between $20 and $30.

Bus
Sydney's bus network extends to most suburbs. Fares depend upon the number of 'sections' you pass through. As a rough guide, short jaunts cost $1.60, and most other fares in the inner suburbs are $2.70. Regular buses run between 5am and midnight, when Nightrider buses take over.

The major starting points for bus routes are Circular Quay, Argyle St in Millers Point, Wynyard Park and the Queen Victoria Building on York St, and Railway Square. Most buses head out of the city on George or Castlereagh Sts, and take George or Elizabeth Sts coming in. Pay the driver as you enter, or dunk your prepaid ticket in the green ticket machines by the door.

The bus information kiosk on the corner of Alfred and Pitt Sts at Circular Quay is open daily. There are other information offices on Carrington St and in the Queen Victoria Building on York St.

Car & Motorcycle
BUYING/SELLING A CAR
Sydney is the capital of car sales for travellers. Parramatta Rd is lined with used-car lots. The **Kings Cross Car Market** (Map p71; ☎ 1800 808 188; www.carmarket.com.au; cnr Ward Ave & Elizabeth Bay Rd, Kings Cross) gets mixed reports, but it seems popular with travellers. Always read the fine print on anything you sign with regards to buying or selling a car. Several dealers will sell you a car with an undertaking to buy it back at an agreed price – don't accept any

verbal guarantees, get it in writing. The *Trading Post*, a weekly rag available from all newsagents, is also a good place to look for second-hand vehicles.

Before you buy any vehicle, regardless of the seller, we strongly recommend that you have it thoroughly checked by a competent mechanic. The **NRMA** (Map pp68-70; ☎ 13 11 22; www.nrma.com.au; 74 King St, Sydney; ☺ 9am-5pm Mon-Fri) can organise this. We've heard some real horror stories from readers who've failed to get their vehicles checked.

The **Register of Encumbered Vehicles** (REVS; ☎ 9633 6333) is a government organisation that can check to ensure the car you're buying is fully paid-up and owned by the seller.

RENTAL

Avis (☎ 13 63 33), **Budget** (☎ 13 27 27), **Delta Europcar** (☎ 1300 131 390), **Hertz** (☎ 13 30 90) and **Thrifty** (☎ 1300 367 227) all have desks at the airport. Their rates sometimes include insurance and unlimited kilometres. Some require you to be over 25 years old. Avis and Hertz also provide hand-controlled cars for disabled travellers. The *Yellow Pages* lists many other car-hire companies, some specialising in renting near-wrecks at rock-bottom prices – always read the fine print on your rental agreement carefully if you decide on this option.

Bikescape (Map p71; ☎ 9356 2453; www.bikescape .com.au; 191 William St, East Sydney; per day from $95) is a thoroughly trustworthy source of motor-cycles for hire – think well-serviced, low mileage and well-informed staff, who can also organise excellent tours.

TOLL ROADS

The Harbour Tunnel shoulders some of the Harbour Bridge's workload. It begins about half-a-kilometre south of the Opera House, crosses under the harbour just to the east of the bridge, and rejoins the highway on the northern side. There's a southbound (only) toll of $3 for both. If you're heading from the North Shore to the eastern suburbs, it's much easier to use the tunnel. The Eastern Distributor imposes a northbound toll (from $3.50 to $7.50).

Fare Deals

The SydneyPass offers three, five or seven days unlimited travel over a seven-day period on all STA buses and ferries as well as the red TravelPass zone (inner suburbs) of the rail network. The passes cover the Airport Express, the Explorers, the JetCats, RiverCats and three STA-operated har-bour cruises. They cost adult/child/family $90/45/225 (three days), $120/60/300 (five days) and $140/70/350 (seven days). Passes can be obtained from STA offices, train stations, and from Airport Express and Explorer bus drivers.

TravelPasses are designed for commuters and offer cheap weekly travel. There are various colour-coded grades offering com-binations of distance and service. A Red TravelPass (Rail, Bus & Ferry, for unlimited seven-day use) costs $32. TravelPasses are sold at train stations, STA offices and major newsagents.

If you're just catching buses, get a TravelTen ticket, which gives a big discount on 10 bus trips. There are various colour codes for distances so check which is the most appropriate for you. A red TravelTen (available from newsagents and STA of-fices) costs $24.50 and can be used to reach most places mentioned in this chapter.

FerryTen tickets are similar and cost from $28.50 for 10 inner-harbour (ie short) ferry trips, or $42.90 including the Manly ferry. They can be purchased at the Circular Quay ferry ticket office. Several transport-plus-entry tickets are available, which work out cheaper than catching a ferry and paying entry separately. They include the ZooPass and the AquariumPass.

Ferry

Sydney's ferries provide the most enjoy-able way to get around. Many people use ferries to commute, so there are frequent connecting bus services. Some ferries oper-ate between 6am and midnight, although ferries servicing tourist attractions operate much shorter hours. Popular places acces-sible by ferry include Darling Harbour, Balmain, Hunters Hill and Parramatta to the west; McMahons Point, Kirribilli, Neutral Bay, Cremorne, Mosman, Taronga Zoo and Manly on the North Shore; and Double Bay, Rose Bay and Watsons Bay in the eastern suburbs.

There are three kinds of ferry: regular STA ferries, fast JetCats that go to Manly ($7.50, no concession fares) and RiverCats that traverse the Parramatta River to Parramatta (adult/child $7/3.50). All ferries depart from Circular Quay. At Wharf 4 you'll find the **ferry information office** (☎ 9207 3170; 7am-5.45pm Mon-Sat, 8am-5.45pm Sun) next to the ticket booths. Most regular harbour ferries cost $4.50, although the longer trip to Manly costs $5.80. On weekdays at lunchtime, you can catch Doyle's own water taxi to Watsons Bay from the Harbourmaster's Steps on the western side of Circular Quay. The taxi costs $10 per person return, and services run daily between 11.15am and 3.45pm.

Metro Light Rail & Monorail

The privately operated **Monorail** and **Metro Light Rail** (MLR; ☎ 8584 5288, www.metrolightrail.com .au) are of limited use for Sydney residents but are slightly more useful for tourists. The MLR operates 24 hours a day between Central Station and Pyrmont via Darling Harbour and Chinatown. The service runs to Lilyfield via the Sydney Fish Market, Wentworth Park, Glebe, Jubilee Park and Rozelle Bay from 6am to 11pm Sunday to Thursday (to midnight Friday and Saturday). Tickets cost $2.80 to $5.20 per adult, $1.50 to $3.70 per concession fare and adult/concession/family $8.40/6.30/20 for a day pass. Tickets can be purchased on board.

The Monorail circles Darling Harbour and links it to the city centre. There's a monorail every three to five minutes, and the full loop takes about 14 minutes. A single trip costs adult/concession $4/2.20, but with the day pass ($9) or family pass ($22) you can ride as often as you like for a full day. The monorail operates from 7am to 10pm Monday to Thursday, to midnight on Friday and Saturday and from 8am to 10pm Sunday.

Note that neither of these services – run by the notorious operator Connex – are part of the SydneyPass. Conductors will cheerfully demand full payment while you fruitlessly wave your pass.

Taxi

There are heaps of taxis in Sydney. Flag fall is $2.55, and the metered fair is $1.45 per kilometre or 62.2c per minute waiting time. There are extra charges for fares between 10pm and 6am, for heavy luggage (optional), Harbour Bridge and Tunnel tolls, and a radio booking fee.

The four big taxi companies offer a reliable service:

Legion (☎ 13 14 51)
Premier Cabs (☎ 13 10 17)
RSL Cabs (☎ 13 22 11)
Taxis Combined (☎ 8332 8888)

Train

Sydney has a vast suburban rail network and frequent services, making trains much quicker than buses. The underground City Circle comprises seven city-centre stations. Lines radiate from the City Circle, but do not extend to the northern and southern beaches, Balmain or Glebe. All suburban trains stop at Central Station, and usually one or more of the other City Circle stations as well (a ticket to the city will take you to any station on the City Circle). Trains run from around 5am to midnight.

After 9am on weekdays and at any time on weekends, you can buy an off-peak return ticket, valid until 4am the next day, for not much more than a standard one-way fare.

Staffed ticket booths are supplemented by automatic ticket machines at stations. If you have to change trains, it's cheaper to buy a ticket to your ultimate destination – but do not depart from an intermediary station en route to your destination or your ticket will be invalid.

For train information, visit www.cityrail .info, call the **Transport Infoline** (☎ 12 15 00) or ask at the information centres at Central, Town Hall or Circular Quay stations.

Around Sydney

CONTENTS

Sydney's surrounding landscape sprawls over a coastal plain, enclosed by rugged country on three sides and the South Pacific Ocean on the other. Although the city is at the centre of the largest population concentration in Australia, the urban density diminishes as the kilometres stretch. Fortunately the beautiful aesthetics don't. There is a smorgasbord of small towns, stunning waterways, uncrowded beaches, superb national parks and dense native forests. The diversity of cultures to be found here is as much a lure as are the landscapes themselves.

The proximity of Sydney means that public transport is often good, enabling you to see a lot of the area on day trips even without your own vehicle. To the west, the slopes and forests of the Great Dividing Range are dominated by the awesome Blue Mountains, with their humbling beauty and Art Deco villages. To the south, the secluded beaches, lush rainforests and staggering cliffs of the Royal National Park are met by the superb surf beaches of the Illawarra coast. Inland, there's a glut of historic towns and rich farming land in the Southern Highlands.

Dense woodland and sandstone cut by vibrant waterways in Ku-ring-gai Chase National Park occupy a vast section of Sydney's north. Climbing further, the mighty Hawkesbury River, with its verdant banks and forests, dominates the landscape. Beyond here are the vast inland lakes and beautiful coastline of the Central Coast.

Snaking their way through all of these regions are bush-walking tracks, cycling paths, scenic train routes and roads of all grades.

HIGHLIGHTS

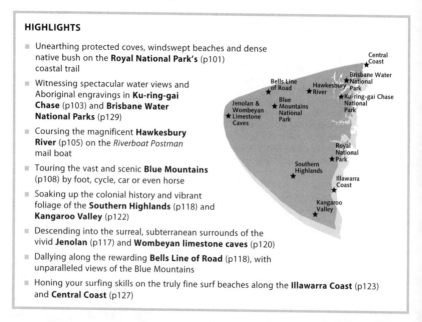

- Unearthing protected coves, windswept beaches and dense native bush on the **Royal National Park's** (p101) coastal trail

- Witnessing spectacular water views and Aboriginal engravings in **Ku-ring-gai Chase** (p103) and **Brisbane Water National Parks** (p129)

- Coursing the magnificent **Hawkesbury River** (p105) on the *Riverboat Postman* mail boat

- Touring the vast and scenic **Blue Mountains** (p108) by foot, cycle, car or even horse

- Soaking up the colonial history and vibrant foliage of the **Southern Highlands** (p118) and **Kangaroo Valley** (p122)

- Descending into the surreal, subterranean surrounds of the vivid **Jenolan** (p117) and **Wombeyan limestone caves** (p120)

- Dallying along the rewarding **Bells Line of Road** (p118), with unparalleled views of the Blue Mountains

- Honing your surfing skills on the truly fine surf beaches along the **Illawarra Coast** (p123) and **Central Coast** (p127)

GREATER SYDNEY

Sydney's teeming metropolis is tempered with a decent dose of natural beauty on its perimeter. Although the Great Western Hwy (M4) leaves a growing trail of development in its wake out west, the expansive Ku-ring-gai Chase and Royal National Parks have stemmed the suburban meld along the coast. Theirs are corridors of native bush and coastline. The wide-open space further afield is devoid of frenetic activity but rich in history, with a scattering of small towns in both directions.

BOTANY BAY

It's a common misconception among first-time visitors to Sydney that the city is built on the shores of Botany Bay. Sydney is actually built around the harbour of Port Jackson, some 10km to 15km north of Botany Bay. The sandy white beaches and rugged landscape dressed in thick native bush that confronted Captain James Cook when he first stepped ashore here still dominate the coastal boundary, but scratching beyond this exposes a fairly industrial pocket of southern Sydney. Despite this, Botany Bay has pretty stretches and holds a special place in Australian history. It was named by Joseph Banks, the naturalist who accompanied Cook, because of the many botanical specimens he found here.

The **Botany Bay National Park** (www.nationalparks .nsw.gov.au; cars $6; ☺ 7am-7.30pm), encompassing both headlands of the bay, is 458 hectares of bushland and coastal walking tracks, picnic areas and an 8km cycle track. Cook's landing place, marked by monuments, is on the Kurnell side of the park. The **Discovery Centre** (☎ 02-9668 9111; kurnell@npws.nsw.gov.au; Cape Solander Dr, Kurnell; ☺ 11am-3pm Mon-Fri, 10am-4.30pm Sat & Sun) conveys the impact of European arrival, and has information on the surrounding wetlands. There's also material relating to Cook's life and expeditions. Entry fees for cars only apply in the southern headland, but pedestrian access is free and as most of the walking tracks are close to the entrance, you may as well park outside. From Cronulla train station (10km away), take **Kurnell Bus Company** (☎ 02-9523 4047) No 987 (adult/child $3.90/2).

La Perouse is on the northern side of the bay entrance, at the spot where the French explorer of that name arrived in 1788, just six days after the arrival of Cook's First Fleet. He gave mother England a good scare as he turned up quite a bit sooner than

---

WILDLIFE PARKS

Several parks on Sydney's fringes enable you to get personal with some cuddly Australian wildlife and to finally rid yourself of that fear of all things fast.

Koala Park Sanctuary

Set inside 4.5 hectares of serene rainforest, **Koala Park Sanctuary** (☎ 02-9484 3141; www.koalaparks anctuary.com.au; 84 Castle Hill Rd, West Pennant Hills; adult/child $17/8; ☺ 9am-5pm) is as much a sanctuary for visitors as it is for the little grey tourist-pullers. Feeding takes place at 10:20am, 11:45am, 2pm and 3pm, during which you can cuddle, cajole and capture (…on film) these adorable creatures. The park is also home to kangaroos, wombats, echidnas, dingoes and a host of native birds. To get here by public transport, take a train to Pennant Hills station and then catch the Glenorie Bus Company's bus Nos 631, 632 or 633 (adult/child $1.20/60c, 10 minutes).

Featherdale Wildlife Park

One of the largest private collections of Australian animals resides at **Featherdale Wildlife Park** (☎ 02-9622 1644; www.featherdale.com.au; 217-29 Kildare Rd, Doonside; adult/child/family $17/8/45; ☺ 9am-5pm) and because they come and go as they please, you don't have to ooh and aah behind a set of bars. You can cuddle a koala here too, but feeding a joey, patting a wallaby or walking with a wombat is just as adorable. Aside from fuzzy marsupials, there's also a diversity of native birds and an impressive crocodile exhibit. Via public transport, take a train to Blacktown, then Busways bus No 725 (adult/child $1.80/90c, 10 minutes).

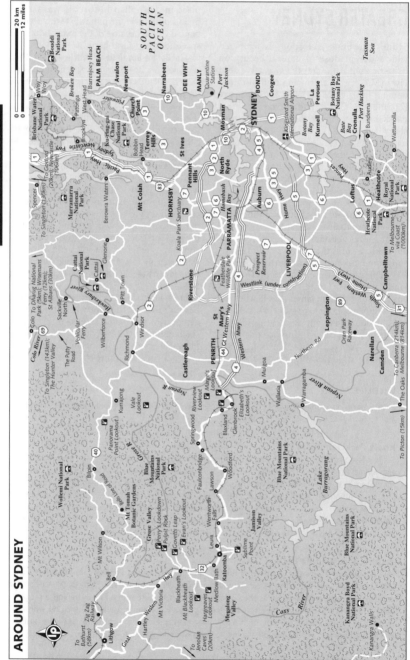

AROUND SYDNEY

0 ____ 20 km
0 ____ 12 miles

expected. La Perouse and his men camped at Botany Bay for a few weeks, then sailed off into the Pacific and were never seen again. It was not until many years later that the wrecks of their ships were discovered on a reef near Vanuatu. There's a monument at La Perouse, built in 1828 by French sailors, to commemorate the explorer. You can also visit the fabulous **La Perouse Museum & Visitors Centre** (☎ 02-9311 3379; Cable Station, Anzac Pde, La Perouse; adult/child/family $5.50/3.50/13.20; ☽ 10am-4pm Tue-Sun) housed inside the old (1882) cable station. The centre has relics from La Perouse's fateful expedition as well as an excellent Aboriginal gallery, with exhibits on local indigenous history.

Just offshore on the northern side of the park is **Bare Island** (☎ 02-9247 5033; adult/concession/family $7.70/5.50/22), a decaying concrete fort built in 1885 to discourage a feared Russian invasion. You must take a guided tour to see the island (one hour, 12.30pm and 2.30pm Saturday and Sunday). To get here by bus take No 394 from Circular Quay, No 393 from Railway Square or No 987 from Cronulla Station.

ROYAL NATIONAL PARK

This 15,080-hectare coastal **park** (car $10, pedestrians & cyclists free) of dramatic cliffs, secluded beaches, scrub and lush rainforest is the oldest gazetted national park in the world. It begins at Port Hacking, 30km south of Sydney, and stretches 20km further south. Several roads run through the park, detouring to the small township of **Bundeena** on Port Hacking, the beautiful beach at Wattamolla and the more windswept Garie Beach. Among the park's many walks is the spectacular 26km coastal trail, which skirts the eastern boundary and is one of the state's great walks.

The sandstone plateau at the northern end of the park is a sea of low scrub. The abundance of small gum trees has actually fuelled three major bushfires in the last decade. The most serious one, in 1994, destroyed up to 95% of the park, but more diligent prevention has been implemented since.

You have to descend into the river valleys to find tall forest, or go to the park's southern boundary on the edge of the Illawarra Escarpment. In late winter and early spring the park is carpeted with wild flowers.

Garie, Era, South Era and **Burning Palms** are popular surf beaches, but **Marley Beach** can be rough (Little Marley is safer). Garie Beach has a surf-lifesaving club and **Wattamolla Beach** has a picnic area and a lagoon for gentle swimming. You can swim in Kangaroo Creek, but not the Hacking River.

All coastal walks require a (free) permit, which you can obtain by calling the visitors centre. The road through the park and the offshoot to Bundeena are always open, but the detours to the beaches are closed at sunset.

The **visitors centre** (☎ 02-9542 0648; www.nationalparks.nsw.gov.au; Audley; ☽ 8.30am-4.30pm) can assist with camping permits, maps and bushwalking details. You can hire exercise paraphernalia at the **Audley Boat Shed** (☎ 9545 4967; Farnell Rd), including rowboats, canoes and kayaks ($16/30 per hour/day), aqua bikes ($12 per 30 minutes) and bicycles ($14/30 per hour/day).

Sleeping

Cronulla Beachouse YHA (☎ 02-9527 7772; enquiries@cronullabeachyha.com; Level 1, 40 Kingsway, Cronulla; s $25-27, d & tw $60-66; Ⓟ) This comfy hostel is run by two gregarious brothers who know the area well. Their cheerful vibe applies itself to visitors and it's a great place to either hone your surfing skills or hook up with others trekking the coastal walk. Catch the train to Cronulla and keep walking until you reach Kingsway. This hostel is also wheelchair accessible.

Garie Beach YHA (☎ 02-9261 1111; Garie Beach, Royal National Park; dm $10) There's no phone or electricity in this basic hostel and you need to bring your own food, but it's close to one of the best surf beaches in NSW and utterly secluded. Bookings are mandatory with the **YHA Membership & Travel Centre** (☎ 9261 1111; 422 Kent St, Sydney) or the Cronulla Beachouse. The nearest store for supplies is 10km away.

Beachhaven Bed & Breakfast (☎ 02-9544 1333; www.beachhavenbnb.com.au; 13 Bundeena Dr, Bundeena; d incl breakfast $200-250; ⊠ ⌨) Smack bang on heavenly Hordens Beach, this lavish place has two extremely comfortable suites, with a healthy splash of antique furniture and electrical luxuries. There's also a beautiful deck, begging for time-wastage, right in front of the beach.

The **camp site** (adult/child $7.50/4) at Bonnie Vale, near Bundeena is accessible by car.

Bush camping is allowed in several areas – one of the best places is Providential Head, after the coastal walk – but you must obtain a permit ($3) from the visitors centre.

Getting There & Away

From Sydney, take the Princes Hwy and turn off south of Loftus to reach the northern end of the park.

From Wollongong the coast road north offers spectacular views of the Illawarra escarpment and the coast from Bald Hill Lookout, just north of Stanwell Park, on the southern boundary of the park.

Enter the park at Otford. There is another entrance at Waterfall, which is just off the Princes Hwy.

The most convenient station in terms of park access is Loftus, 4km from the park entrance and another 2km from the visitors centre. Bringing a bike is a good idea because there's a 10km ride through forest on a vehicle-free track about half an hour's ride from Sutherland station.

The stations of Engadine, Heathcote, Waterfall and Otford are on the park boundary and have walking trails from them into the park.

A scenic way to reach the park is to take a train from Sydney to Cronulla (changing at Sutherland on the way), then the **Cronulla National Park Ferries** (☎ 02-9523 2990; adult/child $3.30/1.60) boat to Bundeena in the northeastern corner of the park. Ferries depart

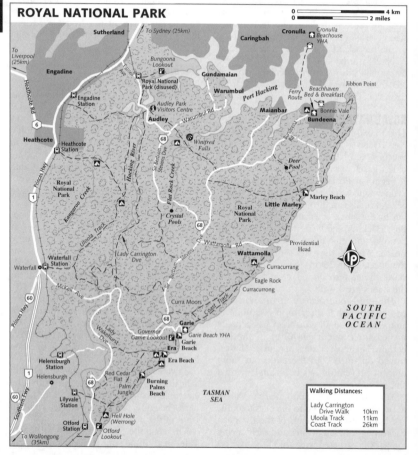

ROYAL NATIONAL PARK

Walking Distances:	
Lady Carrington Drive Walk	10km
Uloola Track	11km
Coast Track	26km

from the Cronulla wharf, just below the train station. Cronulla National Park Ferries also operate daily Hacking River cruises in summer (adult/child/family $15/10/40), with reduced services in winter.

PARRAMATTA

☎ 02 / pop 145,000

Years ago, when Sydneysiders didn't know better, Parramatta bore the label of a daggy metropolis out west. Perhaps the sea of commercial developments and acid wash–clad inhabitants augmented this perception, but with the '80s well and truly over, Parramatta has got on with the task of establishing itself as Sydney's second CBD, injecting a healthy dose of culture and a nascent style of its own.

Modernity aside, Parramatta was the second European settlement in Australia and several colonial buildings remain. The helpful **Parramatta Heritage & Visitor Information Centre** (☎ 8839 3300; www.parracity.nsw.gov.au; 346A Church St; ✆ 10am-5pm Mon-Fri, to 4pm Sat & Sun) can steer you to all the area's attractions.

Sights

Parramatta Park was the site of the area's first farm and here you'll find **Old Government House** (☎ 9635 8149; adult/concession/family $7/5/17; ✆ 10am-4pm). Dating from 1799, this elegant property was built as a country retreat for the early governors of New South Wales; it now houses an interesting museum. **St John's Cemetery** (☎ 9686 6861; O'Connell St; ✆ daylight hr) is one of Australia's oldest cemeteries and the resting place for many first settlers.

East of the city centre, **Elizabeth Farm** (☎ 9635 9488; 70 Alice St, Rosehill; adult/child/family $7/3/17; ✆ 10am-5pm) is the oldest surviving European home in the country. Built in 1793 by the founders of Australia's wool industry, John and Elizabeth Macarthur, the beautiful homestead has a sweeping veranda and is furnished with reproduced period furniture. It's wheelchair accessible.

The beautiful **Experiment Farm Cottage** (☎ 9635 5655; 9 Ruse St, Harris Park; adult/child/family $5.50/4/14; ✆ 10.30am-3.30pm Tue-Fri, 11.30am-3.30pm Sat & Sun) is a fine example of an 1880s colonial bungalow, furnished with exquisite period furniture. The farm itself was originally an experiment; Governor Phillip had the former convict James Ruse cultivate the site to see what would happen. Subsequently Ruse became Australia's first private farmer and his life is illustrated in the cellar museum.

Getting There & Around

By car, follow Parramatta Rd west from the city centre and detour onto the Western Motorway tollway ($2.20) at Strathfield.

CityRail trains run from Sydney's Central station to Parramatta (adult/child $4/2, 30 minutes, frequently). You can also get here from Circular Quay on the *RiverCat* ($6.40, 50 minutes).

From the train station and RiverCat terminal, you can catch the hop-on hop-off **Parramatta Explorer Bus** (☎ 13 15 00; adult/child $10/5; ✆ 10am-4pm), which does a continuous loop, stopping at 11 sights.

KU-RING-GAI CHASE NATIONAL PARK

This 15,000 hectare **national park** (per car $10), 24km north of the city centre, borders the southern edge of Broken Bay and the western shore of Pittwater. It has that classic Sydney mixture of sandstone, bushland and water vistas, plus walking tracks, horse-riding trails, picnic areas, Aboriginal rock engravings and spectacular views of Broken Bay, particularly from West Head at the park's northeastern tip. The park has over 100km of shoreline. There are several roads through the park and four entrances.

The **Kalkari Visitors Centre** (☎ 02-9457 9853; Ku-ring-gai Chase Rd; ✆ 9am-5pm), staffed by friendly volunteers, is about 2.5km into the park from the Mt Colah entrance. The road continues its descent from the visitors centre to the **Bobbin Head picnic area** on Cowan Creek, then to the Turramurra entrance. **Halvorsen** (☎ 02-9457 9011; Bobbin Head) rents out rowboats ($25/60 per hour/day) and eight-seater motorboats ($60/130 per hour/day).

The America Bay Trail, Gibberagong and Sphinx tracks are all recommended for walking and the best places to see **Aboriginal engravings** are on The Basin Track and Garigal Aboriginal Heritage Walk at West Head. There's also a mangrove boardwalk at Bobbin Head.

Swimming in Broken Bay is unwise due to sharks, but there are safe, netted swimming areas at Illawong Bay in the centre of the park and at The Basin, on the western side of Pittwater.

West Head lookout is wheelchair accessible and provides fantastic views across Pittwater to Barrenjoey Head at the end of Palm Beach. You might see **lyrebirds** at West Head during their mating period (May to July).

Sleeping

Pittwater YHA Hostel (☎ 02-9999 5748; pittwater@ hansw.org.au; Ku-ring-gai National Park, via Church Point Rd; dm $22, d & tw $60) Boasting spectacular views over Pittwater and an idyllic location, this hostel has friendly staff and friendlier wildlife. Its isolation and bush setting make it a must for wilderness fanatics, who won't mind the basic but comfy facilities. Book in advance and bring all your food. To get to the Pittwater, take the ferry from Church

Point to Halls Wharf, then trek 10 minutes up the hill.

Basin campsites (☎ 02-9974 1011; adult/child $9/4.50) Camping is allowed only at The Basin, which is a 2.5km walk from West Head Rd, or a ferry or water-taxi ride from Palm Beach. Advance bookings are mandatory.

Getting There & Away

There are four road entrances to the park: Mt Colah, on the Pacific Hwy; Turramurra, in the southwest; and Terrey Hills and Church Point, in the southeast. **Shorelink Buses** (☎ 02-9457 8888) No 577 runs from Turramurra Station to the park entrance ($3.50, 30 minutes, half-hourly) sometimes continuing to Bobbin Head.

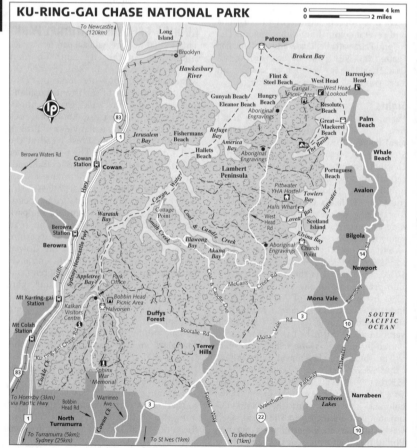

KU-RING-GAI CHASE NATIONAL PARK

From Wynyard Park take **Sydney Buses** (☎ 13 15 00) No 185, which travels along McCarrs Creek Rd in the park. Alternatively, you can take No 190 or L90 to Mona Vale, No 175 to Warringah Mall or L88 to Dee Why where you change to bus No 156 to Church Point. Ask for a ticket for the entire journey ($4.80).

Palm Beach Ferry Service (☎ 02-9918 2747) runs ferries from Palm Beach to The Basin (adult/concession $8/4, eight to 12 daily). **Palm Beach & Hawkesbury River Cruises** (☎ 02-9997 4815; www.sydneysceniccruises.com) operates a ferry from Palm Beach to Bobbin Head, via Patonga (adult/child $16/8, one Monday to Friday, three Saturday and Sunday). **Church Point Water Taxis** (☎ 0428-238 190) operates services on demand between Church Point and Palm Beach ($39 for up to six people).

HAWKESBURY RIVER

The mighty Hawkesbury River begins as a sliver, west of Richmond, from where it ribbons and swells its way around a series of small settlements and dense native bush. By the time it enters the sea, 30km north of Sydney at Broken Bay, its beautiful bulk dominates the landscape, which is dotted with coves, beaches, picnic spots and some fine riverside restaurants. The final 20km or so expands into bays and inlets like Berowra Creek, Cowan Water and Pittwater to the south, and Brisbane Water to the north before it enters the ocean. The river flows between Marramarra and Kuring-gai Chase National Parks in the south and Dharug, Brisbane Water and Bouddi National Parks to the north.

Brooklyn & Berowra Waters

The small town of **Brooklyn** sits on the Hawkesbury as it departs the open space of the estuary and begins to encounter thick bush. Life here, which centres on boats and fishing, picks up significantly on weekends during summer.

The **Riverboat Postman** (☎ 02-9985 7566; Brooklyn Wharf, Brooklyn; adult/child/family $35/20/80; ⊙ departs Brooklyn 9.30am, returns 1.15pm Mon-Fri) is Australia's last operating mail boat and an excellent way to get a feel for the river. It chugs its way up the Hawkesbury for 40km as far as Marlow, near Spencer. In summer it operates additional 'coffee cruises' and you can combine the two for an all-day

---

> ### HOUSEBOATIN' THE HAWKESBURY
>
> The best way to lose yourself on the Hawkesbury is on a houseboat. The **Hawkesbury River Tourist Accommodation Centre** (☎ 02-9985 7611; 2/5 Bridge St, Brooklyn) can assist with bookings and although it gets pricey, most outfits offer affordable low-season, midweek and longer rental specials. As a guide, a two-/four-/six-berth boat for four nights costs from $680/750/1100 between May and September.
>
> Three recommended companies are **Holidays Afloat** (☎ 02-9985 7368; www.holidaysafloat.com.au; 65 Brooklyn Rd, Brooklyn), **Able Hawkesbury River Houseboats** (☎ 1800 024 979; www.hawkesburyhouseboats.com.au; 3008 River Rd, Wiseman's Ferry) and **Ripples Houseboats** (☎ 02-9985 5534; www.ripples.com.au; 87 Brooklyn Rd, Brooklyn).

cruise (adult/child/family $55/35/140); call for days and bookings. The 8.16am train from Sydney's Central Station gets you to Brooklyn's Hawkesbury River station in time to meet the morning boat. You may have to change at Hornsby.

Further upstream, a narrow forested waterway diverts from the Hawkesbury and peters down to the quaint community of **Berowra Waters**. A handful of businesses and residences are clustered around a free, 24-hour winch ferry that crosses Berowra Creek, or you can hire an outboard boat from the marina for about $55 per half-day.

The distinguished **Berowra Waters Inn** (☎ 02-9456 1027; www.berowrawatersinn.com; Kirkpatrick Way, Berowra Waters; mains $30-45; ⊙ lunch & dinner Thu-Sun) is a secluded restaurant that has spectacular views of the surrounding bush and water and an exquisite menu, littered with double-smoked, oven-roasted, pepper berry–glazed delicacies. Bookings are essential as you must arrange a ferry pick-up. There are also several cafés overlooking the water.

Berowra Waters is 5km west of the Sydney–Newcastle Fwy; take the Berowra turn-off. The Brooklyn turn-off is further north, right before the freeway crosses the Hawkesbury. A scenic route to Berowra Waters is to take the road through the Galston Gorge north of Hornsby in Sydney's northeast. CityRail trains run from Sydney's Central Station to Berowra (adult/child $5.20/2.60, 45 minutes, roughly hourly) and onto Brooklyn's Hawkesbury River station (adult/child $6/3, one hour). Berowra station is a good 6km hike from the ferry.

Wisemans Ferry & Around

The tranquil settlement of Wisemans Ferry spills down a hill on a scenic bend of the Hawkesbury River as it heads southward to Windsor. Wisemans Ferry is accessible from the south by taking the direct Old Northern Rd. However, the more scenic route is from the north, via Old Wisemans Ferry Rd, which is wedged in between Dharug National Park and the river. Free 24-hour winch car ferries connect the two banks at Wisemans Ferry.

Note that it may be unwise to swim in the Hawkesbury River between Windsor and Wisemans Ferry during summer due to blue-green algae. Call the **Environment Protection Authority** (EPA; ☎ 02-9325 5555) pollution line for information.

The historic **Wisemans Ferry Inn** (☎ 02-4566 4301; Old Northern Rd, Wisemans Ferry; d & tw $60, f $72) has a few basic rooms with beds, bathrooms and a smudge of '70s décor to dress them up. The main attraction here is the pub, which constantly buzzes with singers, lingerie waitresses and everything in-between. If this type of revelry isn't your thing, the **Del Rio Riverside Resort** (☎ 02-4566 4330; visit@delrioresort.com.au; Chaseling Rd, Webbs Creek, Wisemans Ferry; powered/unpowered sites from $21/19, cabins $83-140; 🖳) is a sizable caravan park on the opposite side of the river, with excellent facilities, and roomy sites and cabins ranging from run-of-the-mill to home-away-from-home. There are signs from the ferry crossing.

Unsealed roads on both sides of the river run north from Wisemans Ferry to tiny, delightful **St Albans**. It's a pretty drive, with bush on one side and the serene flats of the McDonald River on the other. On a tree-lined bend in St Albans, the beautiful old **Settlers Arms Inn** (☎ 02-4568 2111; settlersarms@hotmail.com; 1 Wharf St, St Albans; d $110) is a sandstone slab of a pub dating back to 1836. The authentic **bar** (mains $10-20; 🕒 lunch & dinner) cooks up great pies, steak sandwiches and antipastos, which you can consume lazily at the timber tables out the front.

This place is an excellent day's excursion, but you can stretch it out by staying in one of the comfortable timber cottages.

National Parks

The **Dharug National Park** is a 14,834-hectare wilderness noted for its Aboriginal rock carvings dating back nearly 10,000 years. Forming the western boundary of the park is the dilapidated **Old Great North Road**, built by convicts in the 1820s to link Sydney and Newcastle. There's camping in the park at Mill Creek and Ten Mile Hollow.

On the south side of the Hawkesbury is **Marramarra National Park** (11,760 hectares), with vehicle access from the Old Northern Rd south of Wisemans Ferry. You can bush-camp here. Contact the **NPWS office** (☎ 02-9457 9322) in Ku-ring-gai Chase National Park for more information.

MACQUARIE TOWNS AREA

The river flats of the upper Hawkesbury River, under the lee of the Blue Mountains, offered the young colony of NSW rich agricultural land for much-needed food. It was here that Governor Lachlan Macquarie established the five 'Macquarie Towns' – Pitt Town, Castlereagh, Windsor, Richmond and Wilberforce. Today the latter three form a pleasant meandering triangle, particularly en route to the Blue Mountains on the Bells Line of Road (see p118).

Windsor

☎ 02
Windsor, founded in 1810 on the banks of the Hawkesbury River, was the main Macquarie Town and has many fine colonial buildings. The **Hawkesbury Museum & Tourist Centre** (☎ 4577 2310; 7 Thompson Square; adult/child $3/1; 🕒 10am-4pm), in the 1843 Daniel O'Connell Inn, has a good collection of exhibits portraying pioneering life in the region. There's also a room devoted to Royal Australian Air Force (RAAF) activities and memorabilia, and plenty of tourist information.

Other old buildings include the convict-built **St Matthew's Church** (Moss St), erected in 1820 and designed by convict architect Francis Greenway, as was the 1822 **Old Windsor Courthouse** (cnr Court and Pitt Sts). The **Macquarie Arms Hotel** (George St) is reckoned to be the oldest pub in Australia, though there are a few 'oldest pubs' around. This one was built in 1815. Happily, its history hasn't gone to its head and it's still very much a small-town pub. On Sunday you can satiate all your Australiana cravings at the **Windsor Mall Craft Markets** (Windsor Mall, George St).

Windsor Cruises (☎ 9217 7095; www.windsorcruises.com.au; per person $550) runs two-day cruises up the Hawkesbury from Windsor.

From Sydney, the easiest route to Windsor is on Windsor Rd (Route 40), the northwestern continuation of Parramatta's Church St (you'll have to wind around the Church St mall). West of Parramatta, the Northern Rd climbs its way north from the Great Western Hwy. CityRail trains run from Sydney's Central station to Windsor (adult/child $6/3, one hour 20 minutes, roughly hourly); you might need to change at Blacktown.

Wilberforce & Around

Wee Wilberforce, 6km north of Windsor, is on the edge of the river-flat farmland. Picnickers will enjoy the **Butterfly Farm** (☎ 02-4575 1955; Wilberforce Rd; adult/child $5.50/2.50; ☼ 10am-5pm), where you can BBQ your hamper contents and then work it all off in the swimming pools. There are river beaches here, popular with water-skiers, and a museum featuring insect exhibits and Aboriginal artefacts. Next door at the **Indy 800 Kart Track** (☎ 02-4575 1265; Wilberforce Rd; 30 min/1 hr $52/95; ☼ 9am-5pm Sun, Mon, Thu & Fri, 10am-10pm Sat) you can burn off all your pent-up road rage on the 800m go-kart track. **Westbus** (☎ 02-9890 0000) No 668 or 669 runs (infrequently) from Windsor to Wilberforce.

The pretty 1809 **Ebenezer Church** (Coromandel Rd), 5km north of Wilberforce (turn right off Singleton Rd), is said to be the oldest church in Australia still used as a place of worship. The church's cemetery is littered with pioneer graves and you can continue your reflection at the teahouse in the **Schoolmaster's House** (☎ 02-4579 9350; Coromandel Rd; ☼ 10am-3.30pm).

The old **Tizzana Winery** (☎ 02-4579 1150; www.tizzana.com.au; 518 Tizzana Rd, near Ebenezer, r with breakfast $175-220; ☼ noon-6pm Sat & Sun) has cellar sales and, if you over-indulge on the tastings, you can enjoy the five-star accommodation. One of the rooms here has its own veranda and courtyard; particularly pleasant for knocking off the rest of the red.

About 15km north of Wilberforce there's a long descent to the lovely **Colo River**, a picturesque spot popular for swimming, canoeing and picnicking.

Richmond

☎ 02

Dating from 1810, Richmond has some fine Georgian and Victorian buildings. These include the **courthouse** and **police station** on Windsor St and, around the corner on Market St, **St Andrew's Church** (1845). The similarly historic **St Peter's Church** (Windsor St), built in 1841, has beautiful cedar pews inside and pioneer tombstones in the cemetery, the oldest of which dates back to 1809.

The **Hawkesbury Visitors Centre** (☎ 4588 5895; www.hawkesburyweb.com.au; Bicentennial Park, Ham Common, Windsor Rd, Clarendon), near the RAAF base, is the main information centre for the Hawkesbury region. There's also a **NPWS office** (☎ 4588 5247; Bowmans Cottage, 370 Windsor St; ☼ 9am-12.30pm & 1.30-5pm Mon-Fri), which provides information and any relevant permits for national parks and facilities in the area.

CityRail trains run from Sydney's Central Station to Richmond (adult/child $6.60/3.30, 1½ hours, roughly hourly), you may need to change at Blacktown.

MACARTHUR COUNTRY

The Hume Hwy (South Western Motorway) heads southwest from Sydney, with the rugged Blue Mountains National Park to the west and the coastal escarpment on the east, following a rising corridor. This cleared and rolling sheep country contains some of the state's oldest towns, although many have been consumed by Sydney's ever-expanding suburban girth. You can still savour the rural vistas by avoiding the motorway and taking the Northern Rd between Penrith and Narellan (just north of Camden).

Camden

☎ 02

Camden is a large country town on Sydney's urban fringe, about 50km southwest of the city. It remains distinct from the encroaching package houses and retains its rural flavour with a decent allotment of gardens and historical sites. In the 1830s John and Elizabeth Macarthur conducted sheep-breeding experiments here, a practice that laid the foundations for Australia's wool industry.

John Oxley Cottage (☎ 4658 1370; Camden Valley Way, Elderslie; ☙ 10am-3pm), on the northern outskirts, was built in the 1890s as a work-man's cottage. It now houses the Camden visitors centre and stocks plenty of infor-mation. If you're on foot, pick up a copy of the *Walking Tour of Camden Township* pamphlet, which documents the town's historic sites.

The **Camden Historical Museum** (John St; admission free; ☙ 11am-4pm Thu-Sun), behind the library, has a collection of objects and dis-plays depicting Camden's growth and the region's history.

East of Camden, off Narellan Rd, the **Mount Annan Botanic Garden** (☎ 4648 2477; Mt Annan Dr, Mt Annan; adult/child/family $4.40/2.20/8.80; ☙ 10am-6pm Oct-Mar, to 4pm Apr-Sep) is the largest botanic garden in Australia and the native plant garden of Sydney's Royal Botanic Gardens. Over 4000 species are arranged in 'theme gardens' and making your way through this 400-hectare backyard is a beautiful way to acquaint yourself with Australian flora.

For a comprehensive inspection of Cam-den's scenic surrounds, **Balloon Aloft** (☎ 1800 028 568; www.balloonaloft.com; flight $270) has hour-long hot-air balloon flights that depart from Camden airport. Balloons take off before sunrise.

If you're driving, take tourist drive 18, off the F5 Fwy, if not take a train to Campbelltown ($6) and a Busways bus No 895 or 896 (adult/child $4.80/2.40, 25 minutes) from there.

BLUE MOUNTAINS

For over a century the Blue Mountains have been drawing Sydneysiders and visitors from further afield with truly fantastic scenery, excellent bushwalks and all the gorges, gum trees and cliffs you could ask for. The foot-hills begin 65km inland from Sydney and rise to 1100m, but the mountains are really a sandstone plateau riddled with spectacular gorges formed over millennia by erosion. The blue haze that gives the mountains their name is a result of the fine mist of volatile oil given off by eucalyptus trees.

Three national parks dominate the area's scenery. The most popular and accessible is the **Blue Mountains National Park**, protect-ing large areas to the north and south of the Great Western Hwy. It's littered with breathtaking scenery, which you can enjoy while bushwalking or from numerous look-outs. Southwest of this park is **Kanangra Boyd National Park**, accessible from Oberon or Je-nolan Caves. It has bushwalking, limestone caves and the spectacular Kanangra Walls Plateau, which is surrounded by sheer cliffs. **Wollemi National Park**, north of Bells Line of Road, is the state's largest forested wilderness area (nearly 500,000 hectares). It offers good rugged bushwalking and has lots of wildlife.

Entry to these national parks is free un-less you enter the Blue Mountains National Park at Bruce Rd, Glenbrook, where it costs $5 per car (walkers free).

GLENBROOK TO WENTWORTH FALLS

From Marge's Lookout and Elizabeth's Lookout, near Glenbrook, there are good views back to Sydney. The section of the

---

CLIMATIC CONFUSION

Be prepared for the climatic difference between the Blue Mountains and the coast – you can swelter in Sydney but shiver in Katoomba. However, even in winter the days are often clear and down in the valleys it can be warm.

Although the Blue Mountains are promoted as a cool-climate attraction, they're worth visiting at any time of year. With none of the summer haze, winter can be the best time for bushwalks, but beware of sudden changes in weather and come prepared for freezing conditions. Autumn's mists and drizzle can make bushwalking less attractive, but Katoomba in a thick mist is an at-mospheric place.

It sometimes snows between June and August, and this is usually confined to the upper Blue Mountains.

BLUE MOUNTAINS

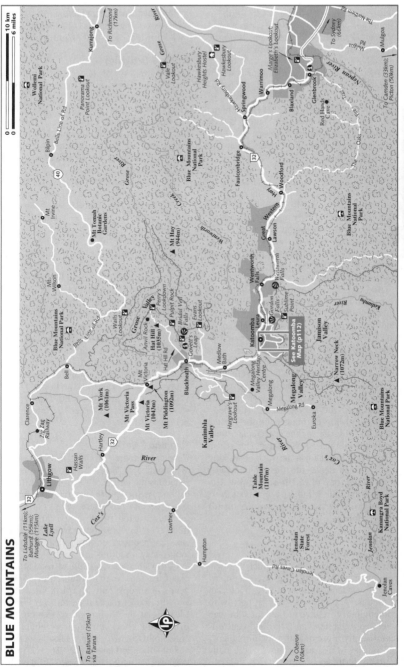

0   10 km
0   6 miles

Blue Mountains National Park south of Glenbrook contains **Red Hands Cave**, an old Aboriginal shelter with hand stencils on the walls. It's an easy, 7km return walk southwest of the NPWS centre.

The celebrated artist and author Norman Lindsay, renowned for articulating his exceptional artistic talent via cheerfully erotic art, lived in Springwood from 1912 until his death in 1969. His home and studio is now the **Norman Lindsay Gallery & Museum** (☎ 02-4751 1067; www.hermes.net.au/nlg; 14 Norman Lindsay Cres, Faulconbridge; adult/child $8/4; ☒ 10am-4pm), with a significant collection of his paintings, water-colours, drawings, and sculptures. The grounds are also perfect picnic material.

Planted in the middle of the bush about 8km northeast of Springwood, the eco-friendly **Hawkesbury Heights Hostel** (☎ 02-4754 5621; www.yha.com.au; 840 Hawkesbury Rd, Hawkesbury Heights; adult/child $19/10) has solar power, wood stoves and even a green toilet. The interior, supported by a beautiful skeleton of unadulterated tree trunks, contains comfortable rooms and facilities including a BBQ and open fireplace. It only sleeps 12 in twins or doubles and reservations are essential. Unless you have your own wheels, be prepared to trek from Springwood.

As you head towards the small town of Wentworth Falls, you'll get your first nibble of the Blue Mountains' gorgeous fare – that is, if the sun has won its daily dispute with the hazy horizon. The views to the south are dominated by the **Jamison Valley** and you can see the spectacular 300m **Wentworth Falls** from **Falls Reserve**. This is also the starting point for a network of walking tracks, which delve into the sublime **Valley of the Waters**: one of the most beautiful sections of the Blue Mountains National Park, encompassing waterfalls, gorges, woodlands and rainforests.

LEURA

☎ 02 / pop 3900

For the most part, Leura is a gracious town, fashioned with undulating streets, unparalleled gardens and sweeping Victorian verandas. Art Deco houses mingle with contemporary architecture and the suburban streets ooze style. The tree-lined centre is significantly more quaint, providing plenty of country stores and cafés for the daily tourist pilgrimage.

Blue Mountains & Leura Tourism (☎ 4784 1404; www.bluemountainstourism.org.au; 121 The Mall) is run by a knowledgeable and helpful staff.

Sights & Activities

Leuralla (☎ 4784 1169; 36 Olympian Pde; adult/child $10/5; ☒ 10am-5pm) is an Art Deco mansion set in five hectares of handsome English garden. The house is a memorial to HV 'Doc' Evatt, a former Australian Labor Party leader and first president of the United Nations. It's also home to a fine collection of 19th-century Australian art, as well as a toy and model-railway museum.

The nearby **Everglades Gardens** (☎ 4784 1938; www.bluemountainsgardener.com.au/bmg_everglades .asp; 37 Everglades Ave; adult/child $6/2; ☒ 10am-5pm Sep-Feb, to 4pm Mar-Aug) is a National Trust property and Leura's horticultural pride and joy – given the surrounding competition, it's a must for green thumbs. The vibrant gardens were designed in the 1930s by famous Dutch landscaper Paul Sorensen. There's also a museum and art gallery well worth perusing and a teashop.

Sublime Point is a dramatic cliff-top lookout south of Leura. On sunny days the clouds put on a good show, shadow-dancing across the vast blue valley below, upstaging the surrounding escarpments. Further north is **Gordon Falls Reserve**, a popular picnic spot from where you can trek the Prince Henry Cliff Walk or take the Cliff Drive, 4km west past Leura Cascades to Katoomba's Echo Point.

Sleeping & Eating

Woodford of Leura (☎ 4784 2240; www.leura.com; 48 Woodford St; d from $135) Right from the Hobbitesque entrance down to the fittings in the pristine bathrooms, this stylish B&B is genteel all over. There's plenty of period furniture, a log fire and spa, and everything is set in a stunning garden. There are standard rooms and more stylish suites and longer-stay discounts are available.

Camp sites are accessible by road at Euroka Clearing (vehicle/adult/child $5/3/6) near Glenbrook and Murphys Glen near Woodford. Get relevant permits for Euroka Clearing at the Richmond **NWPS office** (see p107) and check for updates about the accessibility of areas and tracks.

Post Office Restaurant (☎ 4784 3976; 146 The Mall; mains $15-30; ☒ lunch & dinner) By day this ambient and relaxed restaurant serves fresh café fare. By night the cuisine is positively cultivated and even fussy palates will melt over the fresh pastas and smoked, braised and glazed meat and fish dishes. Excellent service and moody music top it off.

Other recommendations:

Leura House (☎ 4784 2035; www.leurahouse.com.au; 7 Britain St; s $75-194, d $150-388) Grand Victorian home with indulgent rooms and facilities for disabled access.

Loaves & the Dishes (☎ 4784 3600; 180a The Mall; dishes $10; ✆ breakfast & lunch) Gluttonous deli goodies.

Getting There & Around

CityRail runs frequent services from Sydney's Central Station to Leura (adult/child $11.40/5.70, two hours, half-hourly to hourly). **Pearce Mountainlink** (☎ 4782 3333) operates frequent services around Katoomba and Leura. You can hire a car from **RediCAR** (☎ 4784 3443; www.redicar.com.au; 80 Megalong St, Leura) from around $65 per day.

KATOOMBA

☎ 02 / pop 17,900

Thick, tempestuous mists, wide, climbing streets saturated with Art Deco buildings, magnificent views and a healthy miscellany of dining and accommodation options – all make Katoomba the jewel in the Blue Mountains' tourism crown. It's not just the visitors who soak up these features though; Katoomba has a distinctly bohemian feel to it imbued by the local population, which embraces everything from acid-wash jeans to drag-show sequins.

Orientation

Katoomba is set up in a grid pattern, hurdling the Great Western Highway. Bathurst Rd (also known as Main St) runs adjacent to the highway, becoming Gang Gang St as it veers away after Katoomba St. Almost everything visitors will need or want lies south of the highway and Katoomba St, starting at the train station and running south, constitutes the main strip. Echo Point and the Three Sisters lie at the southern end of town, where a dramatic plummet into the Jamison Valley interrupts the soft urban sprawl.

Information

INTERNET ACCESS

Katoomba Book Exchange (☎ 4782 9997; 32 Katoomba St; per 30 min/1 hr $5/8; ✆ 10am-6pm Tue-Sat, noon-6pm

Sun & Mon) Quick access and the first 15 minutes are free if you order a coffee!

MEDICAL SERVICES

Blue Mountains District Hospital (☎ 4784 6500; Great Western Hwy)
Katoomba Medical Centre (☎ 4782 2222; 143 Katoomba St; ✆ 8.30am-6pm Mon-Fri, to noon Sat)

MONEY & POST

There are numerous banks with ATMs on Katoomba St, between Waratah and Gang Gang Sts. The post office is behind the shopping centre, between Katoomba and Park Sts.

TOURIST INFORMATION

Blue Mountains Accommodation Booking Service (☎ 4782 2857; info@bmbookings.com.au; 157 Lurline St) Free accommodation booking service.
Blue Mountains Heritage Centre (☎ 1300 653 408; www.bluemountainstourism.org.au; Echo Point) Sizable centre with knowledgeable staff.

Sights

At the southern end of town, Katoomba's magnificent, scenic drawcard, **Echo Point**, offers spectacular views of the Jamison Valley and the striking **Three Sisters** rock formation. The story goes that the three sisters were turned to stone by a sorcerer to protect them from the unwanted advances of three young men, but the sorcerer died before he could turn them back into humans. Floodlit at night, the rocks are an awesome sight. A walking track follows the road and goes even closer to the edge of the escarpment. A vast vantage point at the lookout allows you to soak up the views without playing elbow hockey.

The **Scenic Railway**, **Skyway** and **Sceniscender** (☎ 4782 2699; www.scenicworld.com.au; cnr Violet St & Cliff Dr; railway & sceniscender adult/child return $12/6, skyway return $10/5; ✆ 9am-5pm) are three excellent ways to experience the Blue Mountains a little differently. The railway, which was built in the 1880s to transport coal miners, has a 52-degree incline and its 200m descent into the thick of the Jamison Valley is quite spectacular. Up above, the Skyway is a cable car that threads its way 200m above Katoomba Falls Gorge. Aside from a motion-picture view of the Three Sisters, the Skyway also takes in good views of Mt Solitary and Orphan Rock. The Sceniscender, Australia's

KATOOMBA

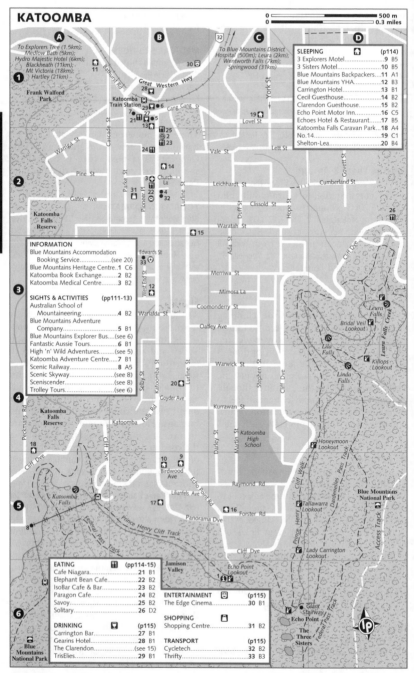

To Explorers Tree (1.5km);
Medlow Bath (5km);
Hydro Majestic Hotel (6km);
Blackheath (11km);
Mt Victoria (18km);
Hartley (21km)

Frank Walford Park

Katoomba Train Station

Great Western Hwy

Gang Gang St

To Blue Mountains District
Hospital (500m); Leura (2km);
Wentworth Falls (7km);
Springwood (31km)

SLEEPING   (p114)
3 Explorers Motel.....................9 B5
3 Sisters Motel.......................10 B5
Blue Mountains Backpackers...11 A1
Blue Mountains YHA..............12 B3
Carrington Hotel....................13 B1
Cecil Guesthouse...................14 B2
Clarendon Guesthouse...........15 B2
Echo Point Motor Inn.............16 C5
Echoes Hotel & Restaurant.....17 B5
Katoomba Falls Caravan Park..18 A4
No.14.................................19 C1
Shelton-Lea..........................20 B4

Bathurst Rd
Cascade St
Warriga St
Pine St
Parke St
Gates Ave

Katoomba Falls Reserve

Lovel St
Vale St
Lett St
Leichhardt St
Cumberland St
Govett St
Diff St
Clissold St
Hope St
Waratah St
Cliff Dve

Church La
Pioneer Pl
Lurline St
Ada St

INFORMATION
Blue Mountains Accommodation
  Booking Service....................(see 20)
Blue Mountains Heritage Centre..1 C6
Katoomba Book Exchange........2 B2
Katoomba Medical Centre.........3 B2

SIGHTS & ACTIVITIES   (pp111-13)
Australian School of
  Mountaineering.....................4 B2
Blue Mountains Adventure
  Company...............................5 B1
Blue Mountains Explorer Bus....(see 6)
Fantastic Aussie Tours..............6 B1
High 'n' Wild Adventures........(see 5)
Katoomba Adventure Centre....7 B1
Scenic Railway........................8 A5
Scenic Skyway......................(see 8)
Sceniscender.........................(see 8)
Trolley Tours.........................(see 6)

Edwards St
Merriwa St
Mimosa La
Coomonderry St
Oatley Ave
Warlalda St
West End St
Selby St
Katoomba St
Warwick St
Lurline St
Stephen St
Katoomba Falls Rd
Coyder Ave
Kurrawan St

Leura Falls
Leura Falls Creek
Bridal Veil Lookout
Lila Falls
Killops Lookout
Linda Falls

Katoomba Falls Reserve

Peckmans Rd
Cliff Dve
Katoomba Falls
Federal Pass Track
Prince Henry Cliff Track

Birdwood Ave
Echo Point Rd
Lilianfels Ave
Panorama Dve
Dudley St
Martin St
Raymond Rd
Forster Rd
Cliff Dve

Katoomba High School

Honeymoon Lookout
Tallawarra Lookout

Blue Mountains National Park

Dardenelles Pass Track
Cliff Walk
Prince Henry Cliff Walk
Access Track

Lady Carrington Lookout

EATING   (pp114-15)
Cafe Niagara........................21 B1
Elephant Bean Cafe...............22 B2
IsoBar Cafe & Bar.................23 B2
Paragon Cafe.......................24 B2
Savoy.................................25 B2
Solitary..............................26 D2

DRINKING   (p115)
Carrington Bar.....................27 B1
Gearins Hotel.......................28 B2
The Clarendon....................(see 15)
TrisElies..............................29 B1

Jamison Valley
Echo Point Lookout

ENTERTAINMENT   (p115)
The Edge Cinema..................30 B1

SHOPPING
Shopping Centre...................31 B2

TRANSPORT   (p115)
Cycletech...........................32 B2
Thrifty...............................33 B3

Giant Stairway
Echo Point
The Three Sisters
Federal Pass Track

Blue Mountains National Park

0   500 m
0   0.3 miles

steepest aerial cable car, is an enclosed, wheelchair-accessible car that delves into the Jamison Valley's rainforest.

The **Explorers Tree**, just west of Katoomba near the Great Western Hwy, was marked by Blaxland, Wentworth and Lawson in their crossing of the mountains in 1813.

Activities

ABSEILING, CANYONING & ROCK CLIMBING

The Blue Mountains are divinely designed for climbing, falling, trekking, scrambling and cycling and several companies offer the lot. Prices below indicate easy or beginner grades. More advanced activities are more expensive.

Australian School of Mountaineering (☎ 4782 2014; www.asmguides.com; 166 Katoomba St; ✆ 9am-4.30pm) Offers full-day abseiling or canyoning ($135) and rock climbing ($165) and two-day bush survival courses ($325). YHA and Australian Geographic members receive discounts.

Blue Mountains Adventure Company (☎ 4782 1271; www.bmac.com.au; 84a Bathurst Rd; ✆ 9am-5pm) Right near the corner of Katoomba St, this place organises abseiling (from $119), canyoning (from $145) and rock climbing (from $155).

High'n'Wild Mountain Adventures (☎ 4782 6224; www.high-n-wild.com.au; 3/5 Katoomba St; ✆ 9am-5pm) Offers half-/full-day abseiling ($79/125), climbing ($99/149) and full-day canyoning ($135). YHA members receive a discount.

Katoomba Adventure Centre (☎ 1800 624 226; www.kacadventures.com; 1 Katoomba St; ✆ 9am-5pm) Offers half-/full-day abseiling ($75/129), canyoning ($99/139) and full-day rock climbing ($139).

BUSHWALKING

Unless the weather is utterly inclement, a bushwalk here is mandatory. The two most popular areas are Jamison Valley, south of Katoomba, and Grose Valley, northeast of Katoomba and east of Blackheath. The area south of Glenbrook is also good.

The **Blue Mountains Heritage Centre** (see p111) has information on short and day walks and the **NPWS office** in Blackheath (see p116) will be able to provide details about longer walks. It's very rugged country and even experienced walkers get lost, so get reliable information, walk with at least one other person and tell someone where you're headed. Take plenty of water or boil or treat what you gather; many of the waterways are polluted. Most importantly, remember that the mountains have their own tempera-

mental weather system so take clothing for all climates.

Guided bushwalking or bush-craft tours can be arranged through several of the activity companies listed above (see Activities this page). Rates range from $39 to $129 per day, depending on the difficulty.

Tours

Wonderbus (☎ 9555 9800; www.wonderbus.com) runs backpacker-friendly tours to the Blue Mountains. Day trips ($70 to $100) take in the Scenic Railway but tickets aren't included in the price. Their overnight tours ($215) incorporate dorm accommodation at the YHA and entry to the Jenolan Caves. Another option raved about by readers is **Oztrails** (☎ 9387 8390; www.oztrails.com.au; day tours $85). Their tours steer into lesser-known pockets of the Blue Mountains and are peppered with insightful and witty commentary (which can be done in English, Italian, German or French).

Fantastic Aussie Tours (☎ 1300 300 915; www.fantastic-aussie-tours.com.au; 283 Main St; adult/child from $85/45; ✆ 9.30am-5.30pm) operates coach tours to the Jenolan Caves. This outfit also operates the double-decker **Blue Mountains Explorer Bus** (☎ 4782 4807; www.explorerbus.com.au; adult/child $25/12.50; ✆ 9.30am-5.15pm), a hop-on hop-off service that does an hourly loop around the Katoomba/Leura area, stopping at 27 attractions. The easiest place to start is Katoomba and tickets last all day. Another hop-on hop-off service taking in the same sights is **Trolley Tours** (☎ 1800 801 577; www.trolleytours.com.au; 285 Main St; tours $12; ✆ 9.15am-5pm). This quaint bus-that-looks-like-a-trolley service is excellent value and a running commentary is included. They also have tours to Jenolan Caves (from $45).

Tread Lightly Eco Tours (☎ 4788 1229; www.treadlightly.com.au; 100 Great Western Hwy, Medlow Bath; 2-hr/day tours $30/165) offers guided bushwalks and 4WD tours, which are better than your average point-and-click opportunities to scrutinise the environmental and cultural aspects of the area.

Festivals & Events

Every year between June and August the area revels in **Yulefest**, when Christmas is celebrated in July. Festivities peak at the **Winter Magic Festival** in Katoomba, when a street parade, market stalls and plenty of frivolity welcomes the winter solstice.

Sleeping

BUDGET

Blue Mountains YHA (☎ 4782 1416; www.yha.com.au; 207 Katoomba St; dm/d/f $19/65/100; 🔀 🖳) The renovated Art Deco exterior of this excellent hostel belies its cavernous, atrium-like interior. The dorms and family rooms are spotless and the bright, expansive common area has more couches and beanbags than bums. Facilities include outdoor seating, pool tables, open fires, central heating, BBQs and a laundry. An older annexe on Lurline St accommodates any overflow.

No 14 (☎ 4782 7104; www.bluemts.com.au/no14; 14 Lovel St; dm $22, d with/without bathroom $65/60) On a much smaller scale, this relaxed hostel has the air of a happy share-house. There's still plenty of nooks and crannies to find some breathing space if you need it, though, and the facilities are good. All dorms have three beds and the attic-style doubles upstairs are classy and private.

Other recommendations:

Blue Mountains Backpackers (☎ 1800 624 226; www.kacadventures.com; 190 Bathurst St; dm/d $19/54) Small, laid-back hostel with cheerful staff.

Katoomba Falls Caravan Park (☎ 4782 1835; Katoomba Falls Rd; camp/powered sites $11/15, cabins from $75) Plenty of surrounding bush but tent sites are a little bald.

MID-RANGE

Clarendon Guesthouse (☎ 4782 1322; www.clarendon guesthouse.com.au; 68 Lurline St; s with/without bathroom from $65/45, d from $130/90; 🐾) This rambling old hotel is light on ceremony and heavy on character. The original rooms (those with shared bathroom) are charming and quaint, while the new additions are modern and accommodating. A consistent stream of convivial vibes snake their way up from the atmospheric bar downstairs.

Shelton-Lea (☎ 4782 9883; www.sheltonlea.com; 159 Lurline St; r with bathroom incl breakfast $95-150) A decent splash of Art Deco style and great facilities make this B&B a very comfortable option. Each of the three rooms here has its own sitting area and classy touches like old wirelesses and period light fittings. Romantic weekenders will appreciate this place, but it's accommodating regardless of your marital status.

Cecil Guesthouse (☎ 4782 1411; cecilguesthouse@ ourguest.com.au; 108 Katoomba St; s with/without bathroom from $65/55, d from $85/75) Stylishly run down in a Fawlty Towers kind of way, this traditional guesthouse has creaky floorboards, unrenovated walls and quirky lounge rooms. Think character before flash and you won't be disappointed. The staff is friendly and there are log fires, a games room and fairly dilapidated tennis court.

There are three practical and affordable options close to Echo Point. Their décor is functional and generic, and their rates are reasonable. All have TVs and tea and coffee making facilities.

Echo Point Motor Inn (☎ 4782 2088, 1800 024 879; www.echopointmotel.com; 18 Echo Point Rd; s/d from $80/90)

3 Sisters Motel (☎ 4782 2911; 348 Katoomba St; s $65-95, d $85-115)

3 Explorers Motel (☎ 4782 1733; 190 Lurline St; r from $90) NRMA, RAC and AAA members get a discount here.

TOP END

Carrington Hotel (☎ 4782 1111; www.thecarrington .com.au; 15-47 Katoomba St; d incl breakfast $170-465; 🔀) The glamour puss of Katoomba's landmarks has been operating since 1880 and although every inch has been refurbished, the Carrington's historical character remains intact. The rooms here are truly indulgent and the dining room, ballroom and cocktail bar are opulent. Special packages are often up for grabs.

Echoes Hotel & Restaurant (☎ 4782 1966; www.echoeshotel.com.au; 3 Lilianfels Ave; s/d from $275/ 335; 🔀) The glorious views, exceptional architecture and superbly furnished rooms at this boutique hotel are all outstanding features. As if that weren't enough, nothing is a stretch for the accommodating staff and breakfast is served with the best views in Katoomba.

Eating

Solitary (☎ 4782 1164; 90 Cliff Dr, Leura Falls; mains $25-35; 🕙 lunch Sat & Sun, dinner Wed-Sun) The sublime views and food at this romantic restaurant are outstanding. With dishes such as venison and juniper sausages and North African tajines, the menu is eclectic and inventive and the desserts are downright sexy. The service is also excellent, and it's wheelchair accessible. Reservations are essential.

Elephant Bean Café (☎ 4782 4620; 159 Katoomba St; mains $9-12, 3-course dinner $25; 🕙 breakfast & lunch Wed-Mon, dinner Sat & Sun) Positively snug but smacking of great food, this petite café serves gargantuan breakfasts and gourmet sandwiches. The tables by the window are great for scrutinising the paper and the multicultural dinner menu boasts Mexican, Middle Eastern, Australian and Italian dishes.

Café Niagara (☎ 4782 4001; 92 Main St; mains $14-17; ◔ lunch & dinner Wed-Mon) High ceilings with ornate cornices, oversized tiles under foot and large wooden booths embellish this overtly gay-friendly eatery. The food is fab too: burgers, pastas and salads with a twist during the day and scrumptious steaks and fish at night.

Savoy (☎ 4782 5050; 26-8 Katoomba St; mains $18-24; ◔ lunch & dinner) The pastel-hued, leopard-printed, Art Deco Savoy dishes up good pastas, focaccias and salads during the day. At night the lights are lowered and the menu lifted with an infusion of flavours such as pan-seared barramundi, baked trout and stir-fried Indonesian beef.

IsoBar Café & Bar (☎ 4782 4063; 40 Katoomba St; mains $12-18; ◔ breakfast, lunch & dinner) Humming with chilled vibes, ambient tunes and mood lighting, this funky injection into Katoomba's main strip serves tasty staples including Turkish toasties, burgers, stir-fries and salads.

Paragon Café (☎ 4782 2928; 65 Katoomba St; mains $15-22; ◔ breakfast, lunch & dinner) This heritage-listed café is Katoomba's undisputed Art Deco masterpiece and sampling the good coffee and fine chocolates in the gorgeous surrounds is a compulsory Katoomba activity.

Entertainment

Café Niagara (☎ 4782 4001; 92 Main St) Once a month, Café Niagara has a cabaret and drag show, featuring the most divine Miss Pastie De Klyne (aka Katoomba's fourth sister). The two-course dinner and show costs $35 and bookings are strongly recommended.

Clarendon (☎ 4782 1322; www.clarendonguesthouse .com.au; 68 Lurline St) When Australia's finest musicians are in town (which is often enough) they strut their vocal stuff at the Clarendon. There's music here most weekends.

Gearins Hotel (☎ 4782 4395; 273 Great Western Hwy) This is Katoomba's best watering hole. The Art Deco fittings are fancy and the amicable locals inject a smoky, unadulterated dose of mountain hospitality. Their 'chocolate draught' is well worth a go on the palate.

For more drinking and dancing:

Carrington Bar (☎ 4782 1111; 10-16 Katoomba St) Shooters, schooners, pool and plenty of Guns n' Roses.
TrisElies (☎ 4782 4026; 287 Bathurst Rd) Good DJs and live music from 10pm Thursday to Saturday.

Katoomba's **Edge Cinema** (☎ 4782 8900; www .edgecinema.com.au; 225 Great Western Hwy; adult/child $11.50/8.50) shows current releases as well as a 40-minute Blue Mountains documentary called *The Edge* on a giant screen (adult/child $13.50/8.50). Tuesday is bargain day for normal features.

Getting There & Around

The quickest way to drive to Katoomba from Sydney is via Parramatta Rd, detouring onto the Great Western Motorway (M4) at Strathfield. The motorway has a toll of $2.20.

Pearce Mountain Link (☎ 4782 3333, 1800 801 577) runs a bus service between Echo Point and Gordon Falls (adult/child $3/1.50, four to nine daily), via Katoomba St and Leura Mall. Buses leave from the top of Katoomba St. The Blue Mountains Explorer Bus (see p113) and Trolley Tours (see p113) also operate circuitous routes through Katoomba and Leura.

Cycletech (☎ 4782 2800; cycletech@pnc.com.au; 182 Katoomba St; half-/full-day $28/50; ◔ 9am-5.30pm Mon-Fri, 9am-4.30pm Sat) rents out 24-speed mountain bikes suitable for negotiating all types of terrain.

Thrifty (☎ 4782 9488; www.thrifty.com.au; 2/19 Edward St) leases cars from $65 per day.

BLACKHEATH & AROUND

The crowds and commercial frenzy fizzle considerably 10km north of Katoomba in neat and petite Blackheath. This small town still measures up in the accommodation and scenery stakes, though, and it's a great base to visit the Grose and Megalong Valleys.

East of town are superb lookouts of **Govett's Leap**, **Bridal Veil Falls** (the highest in the Blue Mountains) and **Evans Lookout**. The Fairfax Heritage Walk is a wheelchair-accessible track leading to Govett's Leap Lookout. To the northeast, via Hat Hill Rd, are **Pulpit Rock**, **Perry's Lookdown** and **Anvil Rock**. There are steep walks into the Grose Valley from Govett's Leap, and Perry's Lookdown is the start of the shortest route (a full day's walk) to the beautiful **Blue Gum Forest**.

To the west and southwest lie the Kanim-bla and Megalong Valleys, with yet more spectacular views from places like **Hargrave's Lookout**. Get details on walks and trail conditions from the **NPWS Heritage Centre** (☎ 02-4787 8877; Govett's Leap Rd).

Pearce Mountainlink operates buses to Hat Hill Rd and Govett's Leap Rd, which lead to Perry's Lookdown and Govett's Leap respectively. Buses will take you to within about 1km of Govett's Leap, but for Perry's Lookdown you will have to walk about 6km from the last stop.

Sleeping & Eating

Jemby-Rinjah Eco Lodge (☎ 02-4787 7622; www .jembyrinjahlodge.com.au; 336 Evans Lookout Rd; standard/ deluxe cabins from $150/199) In an isolated bush setting, these eco-cabins are lodged so thickly in the bush you'll have to run into one to find it. The one- and two-bedroom cabins are extremely comfortable and the deluxe model has a Japanese hot tub, TV, video and stereo.

Gardners Inn (☎ 02-4787 8347; 255 Great Western Hwy; s/d incl breakfast $45/80) This is the oldest hotel (1831) in the Blue Mountains and the rooms here are basic in an authentic kind of way. The swishy **bistro** (mains $10-15, ☺ breakfast Sat & Sun, lunch & dinner daily) downstairs serves good pub nosh on the gourmet side and has a fabulous deck for outdoor dining.

Blackheath Caravan Park (☎ 02-4787 8101; Prince Edward St; camp/powered sites per person $10/14, cabins from $45) Perched next to a dense pocket of bush, this small park has great, isolated camp sites, with the benefit of good facilities. Their cabins are also great value.

There are camp sites located at Perry's Lookdown, which has a car park and is a convenient base for walks into the Grose Valley, and Acacia Flat, near the Blue Gum Forest in the Grose Valley. It's a steep walk down from Govett's Leap or Perry's Lookdown.

Café Memento (☎ 0421-582 509; 36 Govett's Leap Rd; mains $12-17; ☺ breakfast & lunch Wed-Sun) If you have time to plant yourself, Café Memento serves organic breakfasts, wraps, soups, cakes and a social conscience. Political inclinations aside, the food is great and there's a pleasant patio to enjoy the sunshine.

Vulcan's (☎ 02-4787 6899; 33 Govett's Leap Rd; mains $25; ☺ lunch & dinner Fri-Sun) One of the finest places to eat in the Blue Mountains, this cosmopolitan restaurant serves exceptional food, much of it slow-cooked in a wood-fired oven. Bookings are essential.

Other recommendations:

Parklands (☎ 02-4787 7771; www.parklands-cgl.com.au; Govett's Leap Rd; r with bathroom incl breakfast from $225; ☒) Spectacular retreat, extravagant gardens and luxury rooms.

Lakeview Holiday Park (☎ 02-4787 8534; 63 Prince Edward St; cabins from $65) Good self-contained cabins.

Altitude Delicatessen (☎ 02-4787 6199; 20 Govett's Leap Rd; lunches $5-12; ☺ breakfast & lunch) Tasty deli sandwiches, filos and antipastos.

MEGALONG VALLEY

Unless you walk or take Katoomba's Scenic Railway, the only chance you'll get to see what the gorges of the Blue Mountains look like from below is via the Megalong Valley. It feels like rural Australia here, a big change from the quasisuburbs strung out along the ridge tops. The road down from Blackheath passes through pockets of **rainforest**; you can taste the Blue Mountains' beauty by following the 600m Coachwood Glen Nature Trail, 2km before you reach the small settlement of Werribee.

Megalong Valley Heritage Centre (☎ 02-4787 8188; www.bluemts.com.au/megalong; Megalong Rd; adult/ child/family $4.50/3.50/12, dm $35, s/d incl breakfast $80/ 16, 4-bed cottage $140; ☺ 9am-5pm) is agriheaven for little tackers. It's a display farm where visitors can feed and pet a host of farm animals, including ducks, sheep, ponies and alpacas to name a few. Shows and activities are put on during school holidays (entry fees rise accordingly) and accommodation options incorporate basic dormitory beds, B&B rooms in the guesthouse and a fully equipped cottage.

Werriberri Trail Rides (☎ 02-4787 9171; www .bluemts.com.au/werriberri; Megalong Rd; rides from $28) offers horse-riding packages to suit everyone, enabling you to see the area pioneer-style.

MT VICTORIA

☎ 02 / pop 870

More than any other spot along this pass, the National Trust–classified town of Mt Victoria has the atmosphere of a remote, unadulterated mountain village. It's actually the highest town in the mountains, and aside from the crisp air, solitude and towering foliage, the village is littered with historic buildings.

Everything is an easy walk from the train station, where the **Mt Victoria Museum** (☎ 4787 1190; Mt Victoria Railway Station; adult/child $3/50c; 2-5pm Sat & Sun) is teeming with quirky snippets of Australiana. Despite its garden shed–like disposition, it's surprisingly easy to spend a couple of hours gawking at the exhibits, which cover everything from leg irons to stuffed birds. Interesting buildings include the **Victoria & Albert Guesthouse** (see below), 1849 **Tollkeeper's Cottage** and 1870s **church**.

The charming **Mt Vic Flicks** (☎ 4787 1577; www.bluemts.com.au/mountvic; Hartley Ave; adult/child $8/7; Thu-Sun) is a cinema of the old school, with 'usherettes', a piano player and door prizes. It screens a good mix of mainstream and arthouse releases and Thursday mornings all tickets cost only six bucks!

Off the highway, at **Mt York**, is a memorial to the European explorers who first crossed the Blue Mountains. A short stretch of the original road crosses the mountains here.

Countrylink (☎ 13 2232) operates services from Mt Victoria to Oberon ($9.90, one hour, twice on Tuesday and Friday, once on Sunday).

Sleeping & Eating

Hotel Imperial (☎ 4787 1878; www.bluemts.com.au/ hotelimperial; 1 Station St; s with/without bathroom incl breakfast from $105/75, d from $150/90, mains $15-20; lunch & dinner) This grand old dame of the mountains is the best pub in the area by a mountain mile. Downstairs, rooms are budget and basic, upstairs they're grand and gracious and have their own veranda access. The bar's log fire is a great spot to toast the tush, there's a fantastic beer garden to lap up the mountain sun and the brasserie cooks up good pub nosh.

Manor House (☎ 4781 1369; www.themanorhouse.com .au; Montgomery St; r incl breakfast $155-230, mains $25; dinner by arrangement) Another vintage guesthouse, each room in this mountain mansion is distinguished by its own dash of heritage; whether it's a Victorian wardrobe, Art Deco fittings or veranda access. The restaurant has a small but inventive menu consisting of the best food in town; try the confit of duck or pesto and asparagus lasagne.

On the cheaper side **Victoria & Albert Guesthouse** (☎ 4787 1241; www.ourguest.com.au/victoria .albert.html; 19 Station St; r with/without bath incl breakfast from $120/110, mains $15-20; lunch & dinner) has a splendid façade but generic ambience.

HARTLEY HISTORIC SITE

In the 1830s, after the Victoria Pass route made it easier to travel inland from the coast, increasing numbers of travellers crossed the Blue Mountains. However, the discomforts of the old road via Mt York were soon replaced by the discomforts of being bailed up by bushrangers. To counter the problem, a police post was established at Hartley, 11km northwest of Mt Victoria, and the village flourished until the railway bypassed it in 1887. Now deserted, this tiny, sandstone ghost town still has several buildings of historic interest, notably the **Greek Revival courthouse** (1837).

The **NPWS visitors centre** (☎ 02-6355 2117; 10am-1pm & 2-4.30pm) is in the Farmer's Inn (1845). You can wander around the village for free but to enter the **courthouse** (adult $4.40; tours hourly 10am-3pm) you have to take a guided tour.

Collits Inn (☎ 6355 2117; www.collitsinn.com.au; Hartley Vale Rd; d from $180) is a beautifully renovated 1823 inn with elegant rooms and cottages. If you're not stopping overnight, it's worth a visit just to dine on the magnificent French-influenced food. Reservations are essential.

JENOLAN CAVES

Southwest of Katoomba on the western fringe of Kanangra Boyd National Park, the awesome **Jenolan Caves** (☎ 02-6359 3311; www .jenolancaves.org.au; adult/child/family $15/10/39, adventure tour $55; tours 10am-4.30pm Mon-Fri, 9.30am-5pm Sat & Sun, ghost tour 7.30pm Sat, adventure tour 1.15pm daily) are one of the most extensive and complex cave systems in the world. Named *Binoomea* or 'Dark Places' by the Aboriginals, the caves were formed over 400 million years ago and are Australia's best-known limestone caves.

General tours traverse the warren of vivid and surreal stalactites and stalagmites in nine of the caves, but there are also more comprehensive tours on offer, including a ghost tour and a two-hour adventure tour, which includes abseiling. During holidays book ahead, as tours can sell out by 10am. See p113 for details about tours from Sydney and Katoomba.

There's a network of walking trails through the bush surrounding the Jenolan Caves and the 42km **Six Foot Track** from Katoomba to the Jenolan Caves is a fairly

---

DETOUR: BELLS LINE OF ROAD

The Great Western Hwy is the most direct route to the Blue Mountains, but if you have time (and wheels) the spectacular **Bells Line of Road** is far more rewarding. This northern approach was constructed by convicts in 1841, and navigates a pass between Richmond and Lithgow. It's far less congested than the highway and offers fine views towards the coast from Kurrajong Heights on the eastern slopes of the range, clusters of orchards around Bilpin and magnificent sandstone cliff scenery all the way to Lithgow.

To reach the Bells Line of Road, head northwest from Sydney on the Windsor Rd. Once here take the Richmond Rd west, which becomes the Bells Line of Road after Richmond.

Between Bilpin and Bell, **Mt Tomah Botanic Gardens** (☎ 02-4567 2154; adult/child/family $4.40/2.20/8.80; ☼ 10am-4pm Mar-Sep, to 5pm Oct-Feb) is a cool-climate annexe of Sydney's Royal Botanic Gardens. There are native plants and exotic species including a magnificent display of rhododendrons. Parts of the park are wheelchair accessible.

Mt Wilson is 8km north of Bells Line of Road. Like Katoomba, this town was settled by people with a penchant for things English, but unlike Katoomba, with its guesthouses and Art Deco cafés, Mt Wilson is a spacious village of hedgerows, lines of European trees and houses with big gardens. About 1km from the village centre is the **Cathedral of Ferns**, a lovely remnant of rainforest thick with tree ferns.

---

easy three-day walk (it can be done in two days if you are energetic). **Great Australian Walks** (☎ 02-9555 7580) has guided walks along the Six Foot Track with accommodation for $480. They carry everything for you.

Accommodation options in the area include **Jenolan Caves Cottages** (☎ 02-6359 3311; www.jenolancaves.org.au; Jenolan Caves; cottages for 6-8 people $90-125, Bellbird Cottage $145-180). This collection of comfortable, self-contained cottages and the beautifully renovated 1930s Bellbird Cottage is about 8km north of the caves. All have superb views of the surrounding 2416-hectare reserve. Alternatively, **Jenolan Caves Resort** (☎ 02-6359 3322;

www.jenolancaves.com; GateHouse $90-120, Mountain Lodge units $210-480, Caves House $165-490) caters to all wallets and tastes. The stately GateHouse has a series of floors containing rooms that sleep up to six, the Mountain Lodge units are modern and the lavish Caves House is a restored Victorian guesthouse with traditional, opulent rooms.

SOUTHERN HIGHLANDS

The lush Southern Highlands was one of the first inland areas settled by Europeans, who quickly cleared the unruly native foliage to make way for agriculture and English-style villages. This development was early enough in Australia's history for the settlers to regard themselves as English landed gentry rather than Australian farmers, and their unease at being so far from home can be understood amid this landscape of bare hills, brooding pines and stone buildings.

Progress has since made its mark but the appealing towns that coil themselves down the Hume Hwy still have a distinctly gentrified air, accented by beautiful English gardens, antique shops and historic buildings. In between are vast areas of farmland and essentially this region is a daytripper's delight.

MITTAGONG & BOWRAL

☎ 02 / pop 16,670

These two towns form the municipal epicentre of the Southern Highlands, a fact that will be cemented by their steady bleed into one another. Fortunately their pervading charm well and truly overwhelms the threat of generic urban sprawl. Each is dominated by an appealing main street and magnificent foliage, which bursts into colour in April and spring. Both are a good base to explore the area.

If you're driving between Bowral and Mittagong, take the scenic route over **Mt Gibraltar**, which gives good views down the valley.

Information

The **Southern Highlands visitors centre** (☎ 4871 2888; 1300 657 559; www.southern-highlands.com.au; 62-70 Main St, Mittagong) is a sizable information centre with helpful staff and a free accommodation booking service.

THE DON

Sir Donald Bradman is the greatest batsman cricket has ever seen, and is an Australian sporting legend and national treasure. Born in Cootamundra (see p268) in central west New South Wales in 1908, the young Bradman practised for his illustrious cricketing career by hitting a golf ball against a corrugated metal tank using a cricket stump as a bat. By doing this he developed his footwork and his quick eye.

Bradman took the cricket world by storm, humbling England with his batting prowess during the 1930 test series. In fact he was so indomitable, the English captain, Douglas Jardine, devised a method of play specifically to impede Bradman. Known as Bodyline, the method was to condense fielders around the 'legside' of the wicket, and then deliver fast and short balls, or 'bouncers', which would invariably meet with the batsman's head. The batsmen were forced to protect themselves with their bat, and were inevitably caught out. It was a desperate, if not vicious and effective, method and during the 1932–33 Ashes test series several Australian batsmen incurred serious injuries.

After one day's play, during which a ball struck Australian captain Bill Woodford on the chest, he uttered his famous words 'There are two sides out there. One is trying to play cricket, the other is not. The game is too good to be spoilt. It is time some people got out of it'. Ultimately England won the Ashes, but no fans. Bradman's batting average was reduced to 56.57, a stark difference to his Sheffield Shield average of 150. Bodyline was eventually outlawed.

Overall, Bradman got his own back, scoring 19 centuries in Test matches against England between 1928 and 1948. Known to Australians as 'The Don' or simply 'Our Don Bradman', he was instrumental in lifting the spirit of an entire nation after WWII. He captained the 1948 Test team, still regarded as Australia's best-ever side. He retired the same year with a Test batting average of 99.9! The average would have been over 100 had Sir Donald not been dismissed for a duck (0) in his last innings, and it's a mark of the man's character that he didn't play another match to boost the average.

Craigie's Visitors Map of the Southern Highlands ($5.50) covers the area in detail. *The Southern Highlands Visitors Guide* (free) has street maps with indexes of the main towns in the area.

Sights

Sir Donald Bradman began his cricketing career in Bowral and fans can pay homage to the legend at the **Bradman Museum** (☎ 4862 1247; St Jude St, Bowral; adult/child $7.50/3.50; ☻ 10am-5pm). Cricket fans of all persuasions will appreciate the considerable collection of memorabilia and even the layperson will find the history of the Ashes engaging. The museum is several blocks east of the main street, next to…the Bradman Oval.

Festivals & Events

For two weeks over September and October, Bowral's vivid hues are magnified during the **Bowral Tulip Time Festival**. Rich soil and a cool climate ensure this floral extravaganza is always a success and the glut of colour can be found in the Corbett Gardens, off Merrigang St. The festival also showcases jazz bands, folk dancing and cultural activities,

and there's plenty of fine food and wine from the region to enhance it all.

Sleeping

Bowral Cottage Inn (☎ 4861 4157; www.bowralcottage inn.com.au; 22 Bundaroo St, Bowral; r with bathroom incl breakfast $140-250) There's plenty of lace, frills and porcelain inside this B&B, but with a decent balance of antiques, it's stylish rather than gratuitous. Best for adults or couples, it's also in an excellent location, close to Bowral's main street and the Bradman Museum.

Moss Vale Village Caravan Park (☎ 4868 1099; www.mossvalevillagecaravanpark.com.au; Willow Dr, Moss Vale; powered/unpowered sites $18/14, caravans/cabins from $35/65) About 11km south of Bowral, just past Moss Vale, this spacious caravan park has plenty of trees and lawn to park a tent. The cabins are spotless and facilities include BBQs and a children's playground. This is a good spot for families.

Best Western Grand Country Lodge Motel (☎ 4871 3277, 1800 815 923; www.highlandsnsw.com.au; Old Hume Hwy, Mittagong; r $95-150; ☒) Next to Southern Highlands Tourism, this motel has the customary criterion of a good overnighter – smart and open rooms with

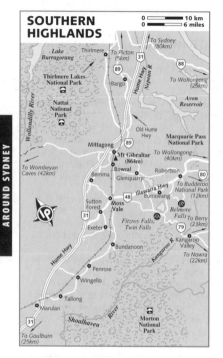

SOUTHERN HIGHLANDS

0   10 km
0   6 miles

couches, cable television, minibars and spotless bathrooms. The décor is plain, the accommodation comfortable and the staff friendly.

Ranelagh House (☎ 4885 1111; www.ranelagh -house.com.au; Illawarra Hwy, Robertson; s incl dinner & breakfast $105-135, d $210-270) Polished, secluded and distinguished, this commanding English manor (1924) has lavish rooms and extensive grounds, populated by deer and peacocks. The views follow the escarpment all the way down to the coast and the Devonshire teas are reputedly the best in the region. Their excellent weekend packages ($250 per person) include all meals.

Other recommendations:

PortOCall Motor Inn (☎ 4861 1779; cnr Bundaroo & Bong Bong Sts, Bowral; r $69-99) Functional, good for groups or families.

Mittagong Hotel (☎ 4872 2255; Old Hume Hwy, Mittagong; s/d from $40/50) '70s décor, facilities and prices.

Getting There & Around

The Hume Hwy runs past Mittagong, which is 1½ hours from Sydney, and Bowral. The Illawarra Hwy links the area with the coast and runs through Moss Vale. Long-distance buses travelling on the Hume Hwy call in at the visitor information centre in Mittagong if someone has booked a ticket. Companies that operate services from Sydney:

Greyhound Pioneer (adult/child $32/25) Two hours, one daily.

McCafferty's (☎ 1800 076 211; adult/child $59/24) 2½ hours, one daily, two Friday and Sunday.

Ferns (☎ 1800 029 918; adult/child $24/19) Two hours, one daily.

Berrima Coaches (☎ 4871 3211; www.berrimabuslines .com.au) runs services between Mittagong and Bowral (adult/child $3/1.50, 15 minutes, frequently weekdays, nine Saturday and Sunday.

Countrylink has buses between Wollongong and Moss Vale (adult/child $9.90/5.50, 1½ hours, three daily) some running via Bundanoon.

CityRail trains run from Sydney's Central Station to Mittagong and Bowral (adult/ child $13/6.50, two hours, roughly hourly).

WOMBEYAN CAVES

These interesting limestone **caves** (☎ 02-4843 5976; www.jenolancaves.org.au; Wombeyan Caves Rd; adult/child/family $12/6/30; ⌚ 8.30am-5pm), 65km northwest of Mittagong, are reached by an even more interesting mountain road. The caves are in a pretty little valley with mown lawns shaded by poplars and pines. The surrounding bushland is a nature reserve with some walking trails and plenty of wildlife. You can walk to a swimming hole at **Limestone Canyon**. The best way to see the caves is on a guided **tour** (adult/child/ family incl entry $15/8/39); these operate twice on weekdays and frequently on weekends and public holidays.

You can pitch a tent next to the caves at the **Wombeyan camping reserve** (☎ 02-4843 5976; camp sites per person $6.50, cabins $68-90), where there's also a kiosk and a well-equipped communal kitchen for campers.

From either Canberra or Melbourne, the Goulburn–Taralga route is quickest and involves only 4km of narrow, winding road. From Sydney, take the road running west from Mittagong. This route is direct but involves about 45km of narrow, steep and winding mountain road – very scenic but slow. It's popular so watch out for oncoming cars, especially on weekends.

Hanging Rock, Blue Mountains
National Park (p108)

RICHARD I'ANSON

SIMON BRACKEN

Camp Cove beach (p47), Sydney

Greaves Creek, Blue Mountains National Park (p108)

ROSS BARNETT

OLIVER

Surfing at Garie Beach (p101), Royal National Park

Blue Gum Forest (p115), Grose Valley,
Blue Mountains National Park

CHRIS BELL

Rock formations at Jibbon beach, Bundeena
(p101), Royal National Park

MANFRED GOTTSCHALK

BERRIMA

☎ 02 / pop 880

When Berrima was founded in 1829 it blossomed as a stopover en route to the wide lands west of the mountains. Unfortunately the road soon became a favourite with bushrangers and eventually the railway bypassed the town.

Dominated by a swathe of towering pine trees, Berrima is now heritage-classified, and a good collection of historical buildings and the ubiquitous tourist-trap stores make it a popular lunch stop. Gluttons for fine food and wine will inevitably turn this into an overnight stop as Berrima has several first-rate offerings.

The best of its old buildings is the neoclassical **Berrima Courthouse**, built in 1838. The court now houses an excellent **Museum & Information Centre** (☎ 4877 1505; cnr Wilshire & Argyle Sts; adult/child/family $6/4/15; ☺ 10am-4pm), where you can see a 15-minute slide show of the brutal justice meted out during early 19th-century trials. There's also an interesting timeline room depicting global versus Berrima events between 1830 and 1839, and a mock-up, complete with mannequins and soundtrack, of the first trial by jury in the courtroom itself.

Berrima Historical Museum (☎ 4877 1130; Market Place; adult/child $3/1; ☺ 10am-4pm Sat, Sun, school & public holidays) houses a local history collection, the highlight of which is a fascinating collection of black-and-white photos from a WWI German internment camp that was established near the town. The nearby **Surveyor General Inn** claims to be Australia's oldest continuously operating hotel (ho-hum). The first owner of the pub built himself a large house – **Harper's Mansion** (☎ 4861 2402; Wilkinson St; ☺ 11am-4pm Sat, Sun, school & public holidays). Recently rejuvenated by the National Trust after a period of disrepair, this beautiful Georgian building is well worth a potter.

Three kilometres north of Berrima, **Berkelouw's Book Barn & Café** (☎ 4877 1370; www.berkelouw.com.au; Old Hume Hwy; ☺ 9.30am-4.30pm Mon-Fri, 9.30am-5pm Sat & Sun) stocks enough second-hand and antiquated tomes to swallow a bookworm for hours. Everything from pug dogs to politics is covered in this two-story extravaganza. Best of all, absorbing your selection on a couch by the wood stove is thoroughly encouraged.

Sleeping & Eating

White Horse Inn (☎ 4877 1204; www.whitehorseinn .com.au; Market Place; s $70-135, d $80-135, mains $25; ☺ lunch & dinner) This beautiful sandstone pub has four tasteful B&B rooms (read cushions, dressers and fluffy towels), but people really come here for the restaurant. Aside from exquisite food with heavy French overtones, there are several private dining rooms, each with their own magnificent table, open fireplace, fine china and restored antique furniture.

Surveyor General Inn (☎ 4877 1226; Old Hume Hwy; r without bathroom $60-80, mains $12-17; ☺ lunch & dinner) There's a real sense of authenticity without tack in this friendly local, and entering the rooms upstairs almost makes you feel like you've just stepped off the Cobb & Co. The bistro is definitely 21st century, dishing up modern, inventive pub fare – no prawn cocktails, but great Thai fish cakes – there's also a fancy BBQ, the kind you can just about drive, where you can choose and cook your own sirloin, rump or T-Bone to perfection.

BUNDANOON & AROUND

☎ 02 / pop 1950

Bundanoon's main attraction is its proximity to the northern escarpments of **Morton National Park**, and there are a number of lookouts and walking trails within reach of the town. Once the guesthouse capital of the area, the trees now outnumber the bipeds and this village remains one of the prettiest and most secluded settlements in the region.

Next to the post office, **Ye Olde Bicycle Shoppe** (☎ 4883 6043; Church St; mains $15; ☺ breakfast & lunch) imbues a good dose of the Med into Bundanoon. The Greek sausages are particularly good and word is obviously out as it's often full on weekends. It also rents out bicycles (half-/full-day $16.50/25).

Bundanoon YHA Hostel (☎ 4883 6010; www .yha.com.au; 115 Railway Ave; dm $21-24, d $50-60, f $65-75) is a beautifully restored Edwardian guesthouse, complete with sweeping veranda, commodious country kitchen and gallons of gingham. This is a great choice if you're sporting kids – the family rooms are accommodating and there's oodles of room outside.

Tree Tops Country Guesthouse (☎ 4883 6372; www.treetopsguesthouse.com.au; 101 Railway Ave; r incl breakfast $145-365), at the other end of the

AROUND SYDNEY

budget, is utterly indulgent. The property is laden with stained-glass windows, four-poster beds, open fireplaces and a splendid dining room (most rates also include dinner). The obliging hosts often hold murder mystery weekends – call for details.

Countrylink operates two services daily between Wollongong and Bundanoon, ($14, two hours, 7.20am and 5.20pm); the earlier one utilises a train connection from Moss Vale. CityRail trains run from Sydney's Central Station to Bundanoon (adult/child $15/7.50, 2½ hours, about six daily); you may need to change at Macarthur.

NATIONAL PARKS

Morton National Park is a vast wilderness area in the Budawang Range. It covers 162,386 hectares and has magnificent sandstone cliffs and waterfalls that fall to the forests deep in the valleys below. It is, however, a very rugged area and you should seek advice and record your proposed walk with the **NPWS visitors centre** (☎ 02-4887 7270; Nowra Rd, Fitzroy Falls), near the park entrance. You can also pick up an entry permit ($6 per vehicle), camping permit ($5) and pamphlets ($5) listing short walks in the park here. For longer bushwalks you'll need specific topographical maps. The closest road access to the park is around Bundanoon and Fitzroy Falls and on the road from near Kangaroo Valley to Tallowa Dam on the Shoalhaven River. There's also the road that runs to Sassafras (surrounded by the park) from either Nowra or Braidwood.

The spectacular **Fitzroy Falls** have an 82m drop and the less well-known **Twin Falls** are about 1km from here along the eastern track. **Glow-Worm Glen**, best visited at night, is a half-hour walk from the end of William St in Bundanoon. In the south of the park is the **Pigeon House**, a curiously shaped mountain. See Ulladulla p315 for information on climbing it.

There's a **camp site** (per person $5) with facilities at the entrance near Bundanoon.

To get to Morton National Park take Bus No 813 from Moss Vale to Bundanoon (adult/child $3.90/2, 20 minutes, four Monday to Friday).

On the northeast edge of Morton National Park is the smaller **Budderoo National Park**, with more waterfalls, lookouts and walking trails. On the west side of the park is the **Minnamurra Rainforest Area** (see p310 for more information). Access to both is from Robertson to the north or from Jamberoo near Kiama.

KANGAROO VALLEY

☎ 02 / pop 340

Heading south from Fitzroy Falls the road winds its way down the steep escarpment to arrive in the lovely town of Kangaroo Valley. Pegged in by a fortress of rainforest escarpments, this town has the lion's share of natural beauty and a healthy dose of candy shoppes and wood galleries. Even when the coaches roll in though, there's still plenty of space and atmosphere.

You enter the valley through the castellated **Hamden Bridge** (1897), a few kilometres north of the township. Near the bridge is the **Pioneer Farm Museum** (☎ 4465 1306; Moss Vale Rd; adult/child $3.50/2.50; ⏰ 10am-4pm Fri-Mon Oct-Easter, 11am-3pm Easter-Sep). This walkabout museum provides a great visual encounter of rural life in the late 19th century. The collection of historical buildings includes an 1860s homestead, blacksmiths forge and reconstructed dairy.

Canoeing, mountain biking and **bushwalking** are popular in and around the Shoalhaven and Kangaroo Rivers. **Kangaroo Valley Escapes** (☎ 1300 730 190; www.kangaroovalleyescapes.com.au; Moss Vale Rd; half-/full-day tours $60-120/from $150) offers environmentally conscious guided tours, which you can design yourself using a combination of activities. They also hire out canoes ($25/50) and mountain bikes (half-/full-day $30/50). **Kangaroo Valley Safaris** (☎ 4465 1502; www.kangaroovalleycanoes.com.au; off Hampden Bridge; full day $30-55) rents out one- to three-person canoes and will organise transport to/from a specified point.

Sleeping & Eating

Glenmack Park (☎ 4465 1372; www.glenmack.com.au; Main Rd; camp sites $16, cabins with/without bathroom $65/55) This sprawling property has good cabins and masses of lush green lawn to pitch a tent. The abundance of trees and ducks enhances the impression of camping out wild, but there's an undercover BBQ in case it gets too rough.

Friendly Inn Hotel (☎ 4465 1355; fihotel@iprimus .com.au; 159 Moss Vale Road; mains $12-20) By night, life converges at this big country pub, which has been ever-so-subtly renovated to retain its local character. The original drinking nooks are still intact and there's a delightful lack of plastic inside. The styled-up pub nosh here includes steaks of spectacular proportions and a sleuth of vegie, fish and chicken dishes.

ILLAWARRA COAST

Illawarra is a strip of coastal towns at the base of the spectacular sandstone escarpment that runs from Royal National Park south past the cities of Wollongong and Port Kembla.

The region was explored by Europeans in the early 19th century, but apart from timber cutting and dairy farming there was little development until the escarpment's coalfields attracted miners. By the turn of the 20th century Wollongong was a major coal port. Steelworks were developed in the 1920s and today the region is one of the country's major industrial centres.

Despite the industry, there is spectacular natural scenery and some great beaches. This beauty can be visually exploited from **Bulli Lookout**, high on the escarpment off the Princes Hwy, with enormous views down to the coastal strip and out to sea. Nearby, **Sublime Point** and **Bald Hill Lookout** in Stanwell Tops are similarly breathtaking. **Mt Keira Summit Park**, Queen Elizabeth Dr on Mt Keira, offers an even higher viewpoint.

WOLLONGONG & AROUND

Wollongong (population 228,850), 80km south of Sydney, is the state's third-largest city and sprawls south to the biggest steelworks in Australia at Port Kembla. There are some excellent surf beaches, especially north of the centre where the Illawarra Escarpment draws closer to the coast. The hills behind provide a fine backdrop, good walks and great views over the city and coast.

Wollongong's surf ethos is a happy spouse to its blue-collar grit, and the result is genuine locals and a laid-back lifestyle. The city's culture and cuisine measure up to that of any major city, though, and Wollongong is an excellent base to explore the area.

Orientation & Information

Crown St is the main commercial street, and between Kembla and Keira Sts is a two-

WOLLONGONG & THE ILLAWARRA COAST

block pedestrian mall. Keira St is part of the Princes Hwy. Through-traffic bypasses the city on the Southern Fwy.

There's a post office and banks with ATMs on Crown St Mall. The **Wollongong visitors centre** (☎ 02-4227 5545, 1800 240 737; www.tourism wollongong.com; 93 Crown St) is well organised and will book Wollongong accommodation for you. There's a **NPWS office** (☎ 02-4225 1455; 4/55 Kembla St; ◷ 8.30am-4.30pm Mon-Fri) and you can jump online at **Network Café** (☎ 02-4228 8686; upstairs shop 4 & 5, 157 Crown St; per hr $6; ◷ 10am-6pm Mon-Wed, to 9pm Thu, to midnight Fri & Sat, to 5pm Sun).

Sights & Activities

Wollongong's fishing fleet is based at the southern end of the harbour, **Belmore Basin**, which was cut from solid rock in 1868. There's a fishing cooperative here (with a fish market, café and the Harbour Front Café Bar Restaurant, see p126) and an 1872 lighthouse on the point. Nearby, on the headland, is the newer **Breakwater Lighthouse**.

North Beach generally has better surf than the south **Wollongong City Beach**. The harbour itself has beaches that are good for children. Other beaches run north up the coast.

The excellent **Wollongong City Gallery** (☎ 02-4228 7500; www.wcg.1earth.net; cnr Kembla & Burrelli Sts; admission free; ◷ 10am-5pm Tue-Fri, 12-4pm Sat & Sun) displays a permanent collection of Australian, indigenous and Asian art and a diversity of temporary exhibits, ranging from contemporary photography to political histories and jewellery.

Quizzical kids of all ages can indulge their senses at the **Science Centre & Planetarium** (☎ 02-4283 6665; www.uow.edu.au/science_centre; Squires Way, Fairy Meadow; adult/child $9.50/6; ◷ 10am-4pm daily). Operated by the University of Wollongong, this two-storey, interactive science extravaganza covers everything from the dinosaur to the electrical age. There are also planetarium shows and the regular Friday night laser show (8pm to 10pm).

The serene **Wollongong Botanic Gardens**, (☎ 02-4225 2636; 61 Northfields Ave, Keiraville; admission free; ◷ 7am-4.45pm Mon-Fri, 10am-4pm Sat & Sun Apr-Sep, to 6.45pm Oct-Mar) is a beautiful spot to wind down with a picnic lunch. The multicultural gardens represent a range of habitats including tropical, temporal, woodland and very-English-garden (well there's a beautiful rose bed). During summer outdoor movies are often played here.

Just south of the city is the Buddhist **Nan Tien Buddhist Temple** (☎ 02-4272 0600; http://members .ozemail.com.au/~nantien; Berkeley Rd, Berkeley; ◷ 9am-5pm Tue-Sun) is the largest temple in the Southern Hemisphere. The custodians of this stunning and ornate complex encourage visitors to participate in meditations and cultural activities, and regardless of your religious inclination, there's more than a hint of divinity to be found strolling the exquisite grounds.

NORTH OF THE CITY

Wollongong sprawls north, nearly to the edge of Royal National Park, but the beachside suburbs are almost individual towns. **Bulli** and **Thirroul** (where DH Lawrence lived during his time in Australia; the cottage where he wrote *Kangaroo* still stands) are both popular. At **Coalcliff** (appropriately named – coal was mined near this cliff for most of the 19th century), the road heads up the escarpment. A short way along, near **Stanwell Park**, it enters thick forest and you drive through the Royal National Park.

Up the coast there are several excellent beaches. Those with good surf include **Sandon Point**, **Austinmer**, **Headlands** (only for experienced surfers) and **Sharkies**.

On the road to the village of **Otford** and Royal National Park, the **Lawrence Hargrave Lookout** at Bald Hill above Stanwell Park is a superb cliff-top viewing point. Hargrave, a pioneer aviator, made his first attempts at flying in the area early in the 20th century. His art has since been picked up by avid hang-gliders and if this sounds like your gig **HangglideOz** (☎ 0417 939 200; www.hangglideoz.com.au) and **Sydney Hang Gliding Centre** (☎ 02-4294 4294; www.hanggliding.com.au) offer tandem flights from $180.

Symbio Wildlife Gardens (☎ 02-4294 1244; 7-11 Lawrence Hargrave Dr, Stanwell Tops; adult/child $15/8; ◷ 9.30am-5pm) has over 1000 cute and furry critters. Some are native, some are exotic and some are...farm animals – but these guys are cute too. This place is great fun for families and there's plenty of opportunity to bond with the inhabitants.

Two outfits in the area cater to horse-riding fans (per hour $35):
Darkes Forest Riding Ranch (☎ 02-4294 3441; www .horseriding.au.com; 84 Darkes Forest Rd, Darkes Forest)
Otford Farm Trail Rides (☎ 02-4294 1296; otford@speednet.com.au; Lloyd Place, Otford)

SOUTH OF THE CITY

Southwest of Wollongong, the **Illawarra Escarpment** is a state recreation area (SRA), which takes in land donated by the Broken Hill Proprietary (BHP) company. There is no vehicle access but the spot is good for

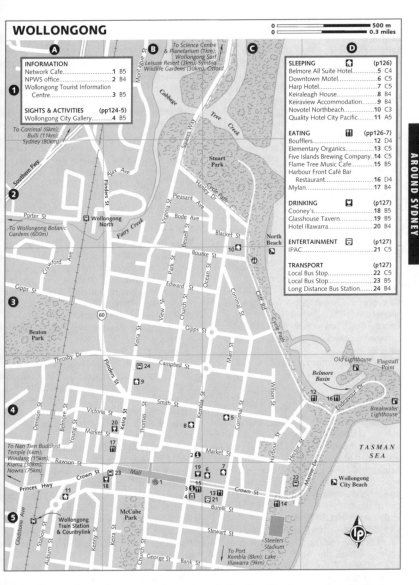

WOLLONGONG

0 _____ 500 m
0 _____ 0.3 miles

AROUND SYDNEY

bushwalking. The park is a number of separate sections from Bulli Pass to Bong Bong; it isn't very large but the country is spectacular. Contact the Wollongong NPWS office (opposite) for information on bush camping.

Just south of Wollongong, **Lake Illawarra** is very popular for water sports including windsurfing. Further south is **Shellharbour**, a popular holiday resort, and one of the oldest towns along the coast. Its name comes from the number of shell middens (remnants of Aboriginal feasts) that the early Europeans found here. There are good beaches on the Windang Peninsula north of the town.

Sleeping

BUDGET

Keiraleagh House (☎ 02-4228 6765; backpack@ primus.com.au; 60 Kembla St; dm/s/tw $18/30/50) This rambling, heritage house is clogged with atmosphere. Towering palm trees out the front shade a coat of peeling wooden shingles and inside there are slightly faded, but comfortable, rooms and a large kitchen. The basic dorms are out the back, along with a sizable patio, bench seating and a BBQ.

Keiraview Accommodation (☎ 02-4229 1132; bookings@keiraviewacco.com.au; 75-79 Keira St; dm/d/f $29/100/110; P 🖵) Brand-new and clinically clean, this complex contains the YHA, which caters to students and backpackers in tidy four-bed dorms. The excellent double and family rooms are a bargain and a step up in style, with verandas and kitchenettes.

There are several beachside caravan parks outside of Wollongong city:

Wollongong Surf Leisure Resort (☎ 02-4283 6999; www.wslr.com.au; Pioneer Rd, Fairy Meadow; unpowered/ powered sites $17/20, cabins from $75)

Corrimal Beach Tourist Park (☎ 02-4285 5688; corrimaltp@wollongong.nsw.gov.au; Lake Pde, Corrimal; cabins $66-164)

Windang Beach Tourist Park (☎ 02-4297 3166; windangtp@wollongong.nsw.gov.au; Fern St, Windang; cabins $40-166)

MID-RANGE

Harp Hotel (☎ 02-4229 1333; theglasshouse@optusnet .com.au; 124 Corrimal St; d $85-95; P 🗶) Close to the hum of Crown St, this hotel is good for an overnighter, with tight, modern rooms, bright and busy décor and compact bathrooms. During the week it's fairly quiet, but you'll need earplugs or oblivion to deal with the downstairs din on weekends.

Downtown Motel (☎ 02-4229 8344; 76 Crown St; s/d $100/120; P) Motel by name and nature, this friendly option has clean, functional rooms with all the motel usuals – TVs, tea and coffee facilities, and fridges. It's also in a very convenient spot.

Another recommendation is the **Belmore All Suite Hotel** (☎ 02-4229 1860; reservations@bel more.net; 39 Smith St; d $115-170 P 🗶), which has self-contained units with disabled access.

TOP END

Quality Hotel City Pacific (☎ 02-4229 7444; www.city pacifichotel.com.au; 112 Burelli St; d $175-200, f $200; P 🗶 🖳) Catering to a largely corporate clientele, this hotel has the air of a stylish, modern office complex – abundant glass, contemporary furniture and soft, block colours. Some rooms have city and water views, and if you can't make it to the beach there's a saltwater pool to cool off in.

Novotel Northbeach (☎ 02-4226 3555; www .novotel.com.au; 2-14 Cliff Rd; r incl breakfast $230-450; P 🗶 🖳) Wollongong's flashiest joint is all style and class and most rooms have views of the ocean or escarpment. The surplus of facilities include a gym, sauna, roof-top tennis court, kids club, hairdresser, bar and restaurant. You'll be so busy exploiting them all you may forget to visit the beach.

Eating

Flame Tree Music Café (☎ 02-4225 7409; 89 Crown St; mains $9; 🕑 breakfast & lunch) You could come here for the great coffee and tasty toasted Turkish sandwiches, but these come second to the hippy-cum-bohemian-cum-affable vibes. Even if you don't burn incense, chilling out on a couch in the timberladen, stained-glass surrounds is decidedly agreeable.

Mylan (☎ 02-4228 1588; 198 Keira St; mains $10-20; 🕑 lunch & dinner Mon-Sat) This perennially popular restaurant serves excellent Vietnamese food in cosmopolitan café surrounds. The seafood is particularly good and the spicy, salty king prawns are a zinger on the tastebuds. It's often packed so reservations are recommended.

Harbour Front Café Bar Restaurant (☎ 02-4227 2999; 2 Endeavour Dr; mains $30; 🕑 lunch & dinner) Fine wine, fabulous views and fresh fish: the Harbour Restaurant is a classy way for seafood gluttons to get their fix. The menu boasts both traditional and inventive dishes, all of which are exquisite. Downstairs the **café** (mains $10-20; 🕑 lunch & dinner) dishes up less-fancy fare, but it's just as fresh and the views aren't shabby either.

Five Islands Brewing Company (☎ 02-4220 2854; www.fiveislandsbrewery.com; WIN Entertainment Centre, cnr Crown & Harbour Sts; mains $25-30; 🕑 lunch & dinner) If modern Australian cuisine means seared seafood, grilled steaks and classy BBQs, then this place fits the bill. Close to the water, with plenty of outdoor seating, this is coastal alfresco at its best. It's also a (brilliant!) brewery so the intimate Saturday night dinner is out.

Other recommendations:

Elementary Organics (☎ 02-4226 6300; 2/47 Crown St; mains $5-15; ⊙ breakfast & lunch) Delectable smells and fresh organic food.

Boufflers (☎ 02-4227 2989; cnr Harbour St & Cliff Rd; mains $5-15; ⊙ 11am-7.30pm Mon-Thu, 11am-8.30pm Fri-Sun) Takeaway seafood at its best.

Drinking

Glasshouse Tavern (☎ 02-4226 4305; 90 Crown St) All blond wood and chrome, this bar-cum-nightclub is a hit with the young and trendy, and if you're looking to make a mate or two, the crowd gets large and happy on Friday and Saturday nights. During the week it's much quieter.

Five Islands Brewing Company (☎ 02-4220 2854; www.fiveislandsbrewery.com; WIN Entertainment Centre, cnr Crown & Harbour Sts) With no less than nine draughts brewed on the premises, plus one kickin' ginger beer, this place is heaven for…well, beer drinkers. There's plenty of mingling space both inside and out, and it heaves on weekends.

Cooney's (☎ 02-4229 1911; 234 Keira St) This dark and nooky bar has dim lighting, booth seating, pool tables and constant tunes. There's also a beer garden out the back if you need to resurface but the convivial vibes should keep you inside for hours. There's often live music here, including DJs.

More drinking and frivolity:

Hotel Illawarra (☎ 02-4229 5411; cnr Keira & Market Sts) Plenty of room and plenty of dancing on weekends.

Harp Hotel (☎ 02-4229 1333; theglasshouse@optus net.com.au; 124 Corrimal St) Devoted karaoke fans create a healthy din Thursday to Saturday nights.

Entertainment

Illawarra Performing Arts Centre (IPAC; ☎ 02-4229 4233; www.ipac.org.au; 32 Burelli St) Wollongong's culture fix presents an excellent and continuous stream of theatre, dance and music. Many performances staged at the Opera House head here and between big gigs, the local contingent struts its talented stuff.

Getting There & Away

BUS

All long-distance buses leave from the **bus station** (☎ 02-4226 1022; cnr Keira & Campbell Sts). The helpful staff will make all necessary bookings for you. Premier Motors operate buses to and from Sydney ($13, two hours, three weekdays, twice weekends) and to

Eden (adult/child $55/34, 7½ hours, twice daily). Murray's travel to Canberra (adult/child $31/19, three hours, one daily). Countrylink runs buses to Moss Vale (adult/child $9.90/5.50, 1½ hours, three daily) from outside the train station.

CAR & MOTORCYCLE

The Princes Hwy (a freeway near Wollongong) runs north to Sydney, or you can follow the coast road north through Otford and the Royal National Park, rejoining the highway near Sutherland. The highway also runs south to Kiama, the south coast and eventually Melbourne.

The Illawarra Hwy runs up the escarpment to the Southern Highlands.

TRAIN

CityRail runs from Sydney's Central station to Wollongong (adult/child $8.80/4.40, 1¾ hours, frequent), continuing south to Kiama, Gerringong and Bomaderry (Nowra).

The **Cockatoo Run** (☎ 1300 653 801; www.3801 limited.com.au; adult/child/family $40/30/110; ⊙ Wed & Sun) is a heritage tourist train that travels inland across the Southern Highlands, from Port Kembla to Robertson. The route traverses the escarpment, coursing through dense rainforest along the way.

Getting Around

Two local bus companies service the area: **Pioneer Motor Services** (☎ 13 34 10) and **Dions** (☎ 02-4228 9855). The main stops are on Marine Dr, and the corner of Crown and Keira Sts. You can reach most beaches by rail and trains are fairly frequent. Bringing a bike on the train from Sydney is a great way to get around; a cycle path runs from the city centre north to Bulli and south to Port Kembla.

CENTRAL COAST

The Central Coast, hemmed in by the Pacific Highway to the west and by the South Pacific ocean to the east, is a tumbling, turning, twisting smattering of coastal Australiana. Starting at Gosford, this series of small towns is connected by a network of scenic roads, swerving their way amid national parks, beautiful saltwater lakes, dense native bush and truly fine surf beaches.

Populated by folk living the quintessential Australian lifestyle – surf and sun – the loose suburban sprawl can appear skeletal during winter months, but come summer it transforms into a teeming menagerie, when city slickers converge here. You're unlikely to visit without spotting the other permanent residents – pelicans. These huge birds paddle around everywhere in search of a meal or glide overhead, looking about as manageable as jumbo jets.

GOSFORD & AROUND

Gosford (population 154,000), the largest town in the area, is dominated by a beautiful esplanade curving its way around Brisbane

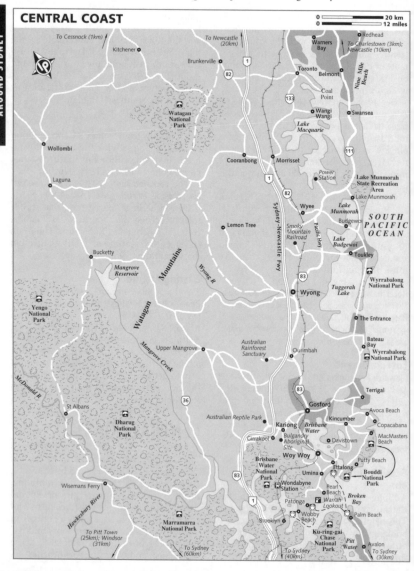

CENTRAL COAST

0   20 km
0   12 miles

GREAT NORTH WALK

There are plenty of transport options for getting from Sydney to Newcastle – planes, trains and automobiles, for starters. But have you ever considered going by foot along the Great North Walk?

This 250km track begins from the centre of Sydney and, after a short ferry ride, follows natural bushland almost the entire way to the city of Newcastle. While not strictly a wilderness walk, it has much to offer visitors and can be done in any season. It has been sited to pass through almost every type of environment found close to Sydney.

The best information on this track comes from the well-researched guide *The Great North Walk*, by Garry McDougall and Leigh Shearer-Heriot, the walk's originators. Maps to the entire route are produced in brochure form ($11) by the **Department of Lands** (☎ 02-9228 6360).

Water and an abundance of greenery in the form of urban parks. Evidence of suburbia is kept at bay by waves of dense bush curling over the surrounding hills and the appealing main strip has a relaxed and ambient feel to it. Gosford is lovely for a day potter but for accommodation you're better off heading to Terrigal (see p130).

Orientation & Information

Mann St, an extension of the Pacific Hwy, is the main strip and host to the post office, banks, hospital and police station The **Gosford visitors centre** (☎ 02-4323 2353, 1300 132 975; www.cctourism.com.au; 200 Mann St) is run by helpful staff and the **NPWS office** (☎ 02-4320 4200; Suite 36, 207 Albany St North) provides relevant permits for national parks in the area.

Sights & Activities

Thirteen kilometres west of Gosford, just off the Pacific Hwy, you can get acquainted with the natives at the **Australian Reptile Park** (☎ 02-4340 1146; www.reptilepark.com.au; Wisemans Ferry Rd, Somersby; adult/child/family $18/9/46; ⏲ 9am-5pm). Tucked inside a bush oasis, the park specialises in spiders, lizards, snakes and crocodiles of all magnitude, as well more tactile locals including koalas, platypuses and kangaroos. It's great fun and the staff are passionate about the inhabitants.

More cute and furries can be found at the **Australian Rainforest Sanctuary** (☎ 02-4362 1855; www.australianrainforest.com.au; Ourimbah Creek Rd, Ourimbah; adult/child/concession/family $12/6/10/30; ⏲ 10am-5pm Wed-Sun, also 6-9.30pm Wed-Sun Nov-Jan). This private rainforest reserve is home to wallabies, wallaroos and a teeming population of over 100 bird species. It makes for pleasant bushwalking and there are picnic and BBQ areas.

South of the Brisbane Water National Park, there are great views over Broken Bay at **Warrah Lookout**. Not far away, but screened from the housing estates of Umina and Woy Woy by a steep road over Mt Ettalong, is **Pearl Beach**, a lovely National Trust hamlet on the eastern edge of the national park.

BRISBANE WATER NATIONAL PARK

On the north side of the Hawkesbury River, 9km southwest of Gosford, **Brisbane Water National Park** extends from the Pacific Hwy in the west to Brisbane Water in the east. Despite its name, the park has only a short frontage onto that body of water.

This park, which is rugged sandstone country, is known for its wild flowers in early spring and for the history and culture etched into it by the Gurringai Aborigines in the form of stone engravings. The most impressive example is the **Bulgandry Aboriginal Engraving Site**, which can be found 2.7km south of the township of Kariong.

Rock climbing, bushwalking and abseiling courses are provided by **Central Coast Bushworks** (☎ 02-4363 2028; www.trak.to/bushworks; Gosford; 2/3-hr abseiling per person $55/75, half-day bushwalking $75). There's generally a minimum requirement of ten people and the larger the group, the lower the rate.

The main road access is at Girrakool; travel west from Gosford or exit the Sydney–Newcastle Fwy at the Calga interchange. Wondabyne train station, on the Sydney–Newcastle line, is inside the park near several walking trails (including part of the Great North Walk). You must tell the guard if you want to get off at Wondabyne and travel in the rear carriage. Ferries from Palm Beach run to Patonga. **Dangar Island Ferry Service** (☎ 02-9985 7566, 0415-274 020) operates ferries (adult/child $8.80/4.40, 15 minutes, six to nine daily) from Brooklyn to Wobby Beach on a peninsula south of the park near some walking trails.

BOUDDI NATIONAL PARK

Bouddi National Park, 19km southeast of Gosford, extends south from MacMasters Beach to the north head of Broken Bay. It also stretches out to sea in a marine reserve; fishing is prohibited in much of the park. Vehicle access is limited but there are walking trails leading to the various beaches. The park is in two sections on either side of Putty Beach, which has vehicular access. The **Maitland Bay Centre** (cnr Maitland Bay Dr & The Scenic Rd; 🕙 11am-3pm Sat & Sun) has information on the park and there's camping (adult/child $7.40/4) at Little, Putty and Tallow Beaches, but you must book through the NPWS office in Gosford (see p129).

Tours

The historic **MV Lady Kendall** (☎ 4323 1655; www .starshipcruises.com.au; adult/child/concession $21/8/15; 🕙 departs Gosford Public Wharf 10.15am & 1pm, Woy Woy Public Wharf 10.40am & 12.10pm Sat-Wed, daily school holidays) has 2½-hour cruises of Brisbane Water. They also operate less-frequent wine-tasting cruises, bush tucker–tasting cruises and Four Island cruises, some of which include lunch.

Getting There & Away

Gosford is quite easily accessible from the Sydney–Newcastle Fwy. You can rent a car here from **Budget** (☎ 4325 0636; www.budget.com.au; cnr York & Melbourne Sts; 🕙 7am-6pm Mon-Fri, 7am-3pm Sat & Sun) or **Hertz** (☎ 4324 9859; www.hertz.com.au; 346 Mann St; 🕙 7.30am-5pm Mon-Fri, 8am-12pm Sat-Sun) from $65 per day.

CityRail trains running between Sydney's Central Station and Newcastle stop at Gosford (adult/child $8/4, 1½ hours, at least hourly).

TERRIGAL & AROUND

The coastal town of Terrigal is an exquisite infusion of beach culture, alternative lifestyle and cosmopolitan café society. It manages to be trendy but not pretentious and there's a constant mingled buzz of locals and visitors all exploiting the tasty views and chilled atmosphere. The beach and surrounding bush are the main attractions here and Terrigal is a great place to bunk for a night. **Terrigal visitors centre** (☎ 02-4385 4430, 1300 132 975; www.cctourism.com.au; Rotary Park, Terrigal Dr) has plenty of information on the surrounding area and helpful staff.

Sleeping

Crowne Plaza (☎ 02-4384 9111; www.terrigal.crowne plaza.com; Pine Tree Lane; d $249-460; 🅿 🖭) Despite several reincarnations, this flashy resort has always been *the* place to stay. Every room has a balcony or courtyard and is subsequently bright and breezy – the best views are on level four and up. Room facilities also include a safe, hair dryer, cable TV and voicemail.

Terrigal Beach Backpackers (☎ 02-4385 3330; www.yha.com.au; 12 Campbell Cres; 4-/8-bed dm $30/25, f $99; 🖳) This large house is so close to Terrigal's main strip you can just about stumble to the beach on the cappuccino scents. It's also home to a commodious

---

WATERTAINMENT

A surplus of surf beaches and inland lakes offers plenty in the activities stakes. The following outfits enable you to do just about anything without any preparation.

Central Coast Charters (☎ 02-4369 6218; http://members.ozemail.com.au/~cccharters; 38 Mirreen Ave, Davistown; half-/full-day charters per person $77/99) offers fishing charters every morning and afternoon charters between September and May. **Hardys Bay Yacht Charters** (☎ 02-4360 1442; www.hbyc .com.au; Killcare; 3hr twilight cruise per person $55, half-/full-day charter per boat $495/695) offers yacht charters including a skipper. **Wandering The Lake Cruises** (☎ 02-4393 6246; www.wanderingcruises.com.au; The Entrance Jetty, The Entrance; 2.5hr cruises adult/senior/child $21/18.50/13) offers sausage sizzle–lunch cruises on the Wyong River, departing from The Entrance wharf.

For those who want to get a little closer to the water, **Ocean Planet** (☎ 02-4342 2222; www .oceanplanet.com.au; 25 Broken Bay Road, Ettalong, adult/child $95/50) has a range of sea- and river-kayaking day trips to suit all enthusiasts. **Terry McDermott Surf Coaching** (☎ 02-4399 3388; www.surfcoaching.com.au; 24 Kailua Ave, Budgewoi; 2hr $45) provides expert surfing tutelage for novices and wannabes. For an even closer inspection, **Pro Dive** (☎ 02-4334 1559; 96 The Entrance Rd, The Entrance; 4-day courses $425) provides PADI dive courses.

lounge littered with couches, accommodating kitchen, laundry and spick-and-span dorms. The staff are downright gracious and there's plenty of information on the area's activities.

Chalet Terrigal (☎ 0407-434 969; younglinda@oz email.com.au; 84 Riviera Ave; d $100-220) Perched in a lofty backstreet, this three-bedroom, self-contained timber lodge is an utter haven. Sheltered from the surrounding mansions by a dense bush garden, The Chalet has spectacular views that you can enjoy while barbecuing on the balcony, and a stylish interior equipped with funky furnishings, a modern kitchen and everything electrical.

THE ENTRANCE & NORTH

The decorous spread of civilisation making its way up the coast turns abruptly into an urban jungle at The Entrance. This town is a dense cluster of relentlessly cheerful cream brick, introduced palm trees, plastic chairs on footpaths and, in summer, hordes of beer-bellied parents and their spirited children. They all come to revel on the supremely beautiful lake and superb surf beach.

The **Entrance visitors centre** (☎ 02-4385 4430; www.cctourism.com.au; Marine Pde) has a wealth of information and Internet access ($2 per 15 minutes). On the beachfront nearby, the resident (voracious!) pelicans are fed daily at 3.30pm. The **Entrance Boatshed** (☎ 02-4332 2652; The Entrance Rd), beside the bridge, rents out aqua-bikes ($20 per hour), canoes ($15 per hour), rowboats ($20 per hour) and motorboats (from $30 per hour).

Entrance Hotel (☎ 02-4332 2001; 87 The Entrance Rd; s/d incl breakfast $40/80) is a genuine pub, sitting defiantly unrenovated at the end of the patioed, fancied-up foreshore. Most of the cosy rooms here have bathrooms and views, but they're popular so book ahead. The **bistro** (mains $10-16; ☉ lunch & dinner) has a sizable courtyard and serves steaks, seafood, and the odd exotic curry.

Paradise Park (☎ 02-4334 5555; cnr Pacific St & Tuggerah Pde; cabins $60-115, villas $85-150) has timber cabins and villas with polished interiors and mod cons, some even with spas. This place is in a quiet spot in front of Tuggerah Lake and there's a good walking path following the shore right outside.

Hunter Valley

CONTENTS

Wine making and horse breeding combine to give the Hunter Valley an ambience of romance and excitement, and are the ingredients that make the valley a playground for the rich and famous. These pursuits, together with the area's long-standing mining industry, make the Hunter Valley a benchmark in measuring the success of modern Australian agricultural pursuits. There is much that is concentrated into this small region: endless vineyards and magnificent wineries, million-dollar foals at imposing horse studs, elite golf courses, long stretches of white-sand beachfront, and rugged bushland filled with interesting walking trails and equally intriguing wildlife.

The Lower Hunter wineries are a hugely enjoyable and accessible weekend trip (not to mention popular!) – prices nose-dive on weekdays so mid-week trips are especially beneficial to the body, soul and wallet. If you prefer a little more breathing space, head for Upper Hunter, or why not put the hiking boots on and explore some of the prime walking tracks in the Barrington Tops National Park. Newcastle, the region's major city, is an absolute surprise and delight; reaping the rewards of an urban renewal programme, it's become downright pretty, with surf beaches that have some of the best breaks on the coast.

Perhaps the secret to the Hunter's appeal is its universal appeal, with excellent activities on offer for families, an abundance of romantic escapes for couples, and a feast of hidden gems for the wandering traveller.

HUNTER VALLEY

HIGHLIGHTS

- Catching a wave at one of Newcastle's spectacular **surf beaches** (p135)
- Watching ships sail by from Newcastle's **Queens Wharf Complex** (p138)
- Taking a stroll out past the lighthouse at **Nobbys Head** (p135), for a view of Newcastle's industrial heritage and modern charm
- Indulging your palate at the **Lower Hunter Wineries** (p141)
- Driving down Segenhoe Rd near **Scone** (p145), looking at future thoroughbred champions
- Enjoying beach days and city nights in **Newcastle** (p135)
- Strolling through the endless **Hunter Valley Gardens** (p141)
- Camping and kayaking at the Steps on the edge of the **Barrington Tops Ranges** (p148)

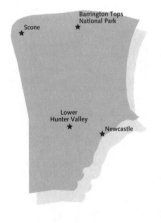

HUNTER VALLEY

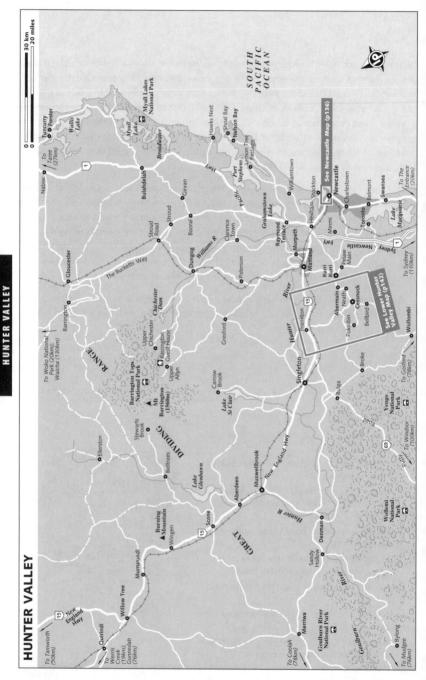

NEWCASTLE

☎ 02 / pop 279,970

Newcastle has battled for most of its life with a perception by Sydneysiders that it is an 'industrial nightmare'. Luckily for visitors to Newcastle, that is no longer the case. Industrial pursuits have given way to a relaxed, artistic surf culture that breeds lazy days on the beach together with a groovy café culture and a happening nightlife. Since BHP ceased its steelworks operation in 1999, the town has undergone a facelift, taking on a stylish, fashionable image.

Home to some magnificent surf beaches, historic architecture and a live-music scene that sends tingles along your backbone, this is an ideal place to soak up the coastal way of life. Newcastle also has one of the greatest concentrations of international students in Australia.

History

Originally named Coal River, Newcastle was founded in 1804 as a place for the most disruptive of Sydney's convicts and was rightly regarded as 'the hell of New South Wales'. Newcastle's convict origins are present in many of its iconic landmarks. The breakwater out to Nobbys Head, and its lighthouse, were built by convicts, as was Bogey Hole, a swimming pool cut into the rock on the ocean's edge below the immaculate King Edward Park. It is still a great place for a dip. The park was built for Major Morriset, an early commander and strict disciplinarian.

In recent times Newcastle has had its share of tragedy. In 1989 it suffered Australia's most destructive earthquake, with 12 people killed and a lot of property damaged.

Orientation

Central Newcastle sits on the end of a peninsula that separates the Hunter River from the sea and tapers down to a long sand spit heading east to Nobbys Head and the lighthouse. Hunter St is the 3km-long east–west main street decorated with classical Victorian architecture.

North of the railway lines (there's a footbridge beginning in Hunter Mall) is the waterfront and Queens Wharf Complex. The swimming and surf beaches are on the unprotected side of the peninsula, a five-minute walk from the city centre in the opposite direction.

Across the Hunter River to the north of Queens Wharf Complex is Stockton, a modest town with exciting beaches and striking views of Newcastle.

Information

The visitors centre (☎ 4974 2999; www.visitnewcastle .com.au; 363 Hunter St) is a solid starting point.

To get onto the web, head to the **Newcastle Region Library** (☎ 4974 5300; Laman St; ⊗ 9.30am-8pm Mon-Fri, to 2pm Sat), or drop by **Nomads Backpackers by the Beach** (☎ 4926 3472; 34 Hunter St), which has a number of computers down in the bunker.

Sights

Newcastle's Famous Tram (☎ 4963 7954; Newcastle train station, Hunter St; adult/child $10/6; ⊗ 10am & 2pm) provides a good overview of the city and an opportunity to view 18 interesting sites.

Take to the city on foot by following the **Bathers Way**, a 5km coastal walk stretching from the lighthouse at Nobbys Head, with great views over Newcastle, to Glenrock Reserve. Another option is the **Newcastle East Heritage Walk**, a 3km walk that includes the Convict Lumber Yard and Fort Scratchley. Maps for both walks are available from the visitors centre.

BEACHES

Surf beaches are a major attraction. Newcastle's favourite surfing son is former world champ Mark Richards, and many surfers come here to seek out the breaks where Richards cut his teeth. The main beach, **Newcastle Beach**, is just a couple of minutes' walk from the city centre. It has an ocean pool and good surf. Just north of here is **Nobbys Beach**, which is more sheltered. At the northern end of Nobbys Beach is a fast left-hander known as the **Wedge**. The most popular surfing break is about 2km south at **Bar Beach**, which is floodlit at night in summer. Nearby **Merewether Beach** has two huge pools. Bus No 207 runs to Merewether Beach ($2, every 30 minutes) via Bar Beach – catch it at the train-station bus stop.

MUSEUMS & GALLERIES

The innovative **Newcastle Regional Museum** (☎ 4974 1400; 787 Hunter St; admission free; ⊗ 10am-5pm Tue-Sun) features an interesting display on the 1989 earthquake, and a Supernova hands-on science display. The building itself

HUNTER VALLEY

HUNTER VALLEY

NEWCASTLE

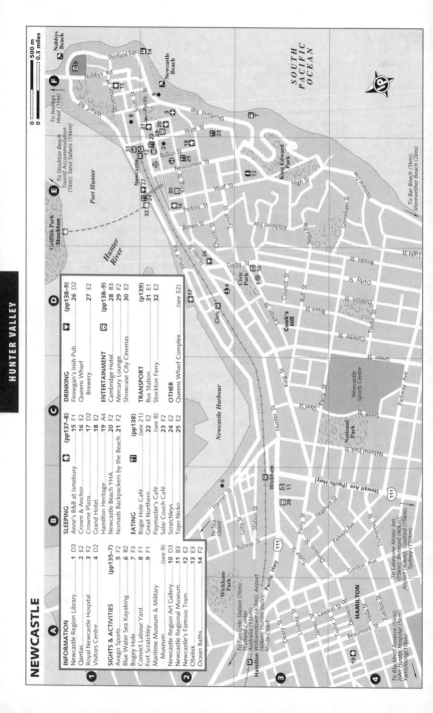

INFORMATION	
Newcastle Region Library............	1 D3
Qantas..	2 F2
Royal Newcastle Hospital............	3 F2
Visitors Centre...........................	4 D2

SIGHTS & ACTIVITIES	(pp135–7)
Avago Sports..............................	5 F2
Blue Water Sea Kayaking............	6 B2
Bogey Hole.................................	7 F3
Convict Labour Yard....................	8 F3
Fort Scratchley...........................	9 F1
Maritime Museum & Military	
Museum.................................	(see 9)
Newcastle Region Art Gallery......	10 D3
Newcastle Regional Museum........	11 B3
Newcastle's Famous Tram............	12 E2
Obelisk.......................................	13 E3
Ocean Baths...............................	14 F2

SLEEPING	(pp137–8)
Anne's B&B at Ismebury..............	15 F1
Crown & Anchor.........................	16 E2
Crowne Plaza..............................	17 D2
Grand Hotel................................	18 E2
Hamilton Heritage.......................	19 A4
Newcastle Beach YHA..................	20 F2
Nomads Backpackers by the Beach.	21 F2

EATING	(pp138)
Bogie Hole Café..........................	(see 21)
Great Northern............................	22 E2
Paymaster's Café.........................	(see 8)
Salar Couch Café.........................	23 F2
Scratchleys.................................	24 E2
Topo Nicko..................................	25 E2

DRINKING	(pp138–9)
Finnegan's Irish Pub....................	26 D2
Queens Wharf	
Brewery.................................	27 E2

ENTERTAINMENT	(pp138–9)
Cambridge Hotel.........................	28 B3
Mercury Lounge..........................	29 F2
Showcase City Cinemas...............	30 E2

TRANSPORT	(p139)
Bus Station.................................	31 E1
Pacific St....................................	32 E2

OTHER	
Queens Wharf Complex...............	(see 32)

is of historical interest, as it was once a buzzing brewery.

Fort Scratchley Maritime & Military Museum (☎ 4929 3066; Nobbys Rd; admission free, tunnels $1.50; ☼ tunnels noon-4pm Fri-Sun) overlooks the Pacific Ocean and was originally built as a deterrent to the Russians. You can wander the tunnels underneath, which are said to run all the way to King Edward Park.

The **Newcastle Region Art Gallery** (☎ 4974 5100; 1 Laman St; admission free; ☼ 10am-5pm Tue-Sun) houses a collection of over 3000 works of art, providing a thorough insight into the history of Australian art, dating back to colonial times. The display of Japanese ceramics provides an interesting contrast.

Ask at the visitors centre about the numerous private galleries throughout town.

CONVICT LUMBERYARD

On the east side of town, the area off Scott Street was once a convict lumberyard enclosed by massive log walls. Now filled with excellent interpretive sculptures, the prominent historic buildings, such as the paymaster's cottage (now a café; see p138), provide the earliest surviving example of a convict industrial workplace.

Activities

Wetlands Centre Australia (☎ 4951 6466; www.wetlands.org.au; Sandgate Rd, Sandgate; adult/child $4.50/2, ☼ 9am-5pm) is a good, low-cost outing where you can walk the boardwalk or hire a canoe and view water dragons, skinks and the like. The centre is a short walk from Sandgate train station.

Set in native bushland about 10km south of Newcastle, **Blackbutt Reserve** (☎ 4952 1449; www.ncc.nsw.gov.au; Carnley Ave, New Lambton Heights; admission free; ☼ 9am-5pm) is a great way to view native wildlife: all the usual suspects, from koalas to kangaroos, emus, wallabies and wombats. Bus Nos 232 and 363 run past the upper entrance, and Nos 216 and 217 past the lower entrance.

Head to **Yamuloong** (☎ 4943 6877; www.yamuloong.com.au; Prospect Rd; 30-min self-guided tours $5, guided tours $20; ☼ 8.30am-4.30pm Mon-Fri) for the chance to taste traditional foods (a plate of croc, roo and emu morsels will set you back $30), learn to dot paint, and listen to the didgeridoo and Dreamtime stories. This is a rather pricey affair, but educational nonetheless.

For those with a sense of adventure, eco-friendly **Sand Safaris** (☎ 4965 0215; www.sandsafaris.com.au; Nelsons Bay Rd, Williamtown; 2hr trips $110; ☼ 8.30am-4.30pm) provides a great outing on the sand dunes with quad bikes.

With harbour tours an option, **Blue Water Sea Kayaking** (☎ 0409-408 618; www.seakayaking.com.au; Newcastle Cruising Yacht Club Marina, Hannell St, Wickham; per hr $15, harbour tours $40) provides a fantastic way to see the city from the ocean (and get in a bit of exercise).

Avago Sports (☎ 0402-278 072; Newcastle Beach; surf board & wet suit per day $40) delivers bicycles, surfboards and other sporting equipment to your door; there is no shortage of ways to enjoy the beaches.

Sea Quest (☎ 4971 3301; Newcastle Harbour; trips $77) is a deep-sea fishing outfit that goes in search of the big bites and has whale watching during the season.

Tours

For coverage of the Lower Hunter wineries, dolphin watching and the history of Wollombi, jump on a bus tour with **Shadows** (☎ 4990 7002; ☼ 9.30am-4.30pm; Hunter tour $40, incl lunch $60) or **Hades** (☎ 4967 5969; www.huntertourism.com.au\html\hades.html; ☼ 9.30am-4.30pm; Hunter tour incl lunch $90). Hades is a little more expensive, but the itinerary is more expansive than Shadows, venturing up to Barrington Tops National Park and Port Stephens. Both companies offer pick-up anywhere.

Festivals & Events

This town knows how to throw a festival and there are a large number throughout the year, so ask the visitors centre about their events calendar.

Maritime Festival (☎ 4929 2588) During the peak of summer, focuses on harbour and foreshore activities, including an organised swim across the harbour.

Jazz & Arts Festival (☎ 4969 1515) In March, injects a certain vibrancy to the city.

Surfest (☎ 0412-127 525) The longest-running professional surfing competition in Australia, held at Newcastle beach every March.

Sleeping

Hand in hand with Newcastle's recent facelift has come an increase in both the type and amount of accommodation on offer. It is still wise to book ahead for weekends, as the demand far outweighs the supply at peak times.

HUNTER VALLEY

BUDGET

Nomads Backpackers by the Beach (☎ 4926 3472; 34 Hunter St; dm/d $20/48; ▣) Modern hostel that has a fresh, funky feel to it with clean rooms; it also holds a prime central position.

Newcastle Beach Youth Hostel Australia (YHA; ☎ 4925 3544; 30 Pacific St; dm/d $25/65; ▣) Matches its rival in value, with a ballroom-turned-common-room that will turn heads: billiard table, open fireplace, French doors.

Stockton Beach Tourist Accommodation (☎ 4928 4333; 68 Mitchell St; dm/d $25/63; ℗) The next step up from the backpackers market, the Stockton is located across the river. The top deck roof offers stunning views back to Newcastle, and the courtyard has a BBQ, great for those balmy summer nights. Catch the ferry from the Queens Wharf Complex ferry terminal to Stockton (two-minute ride), and walk 250m down Mitchell Street.

Crown & Anchor (☎ 4929 1027; cnr Hunter & Perkins Sts; dm $20) Offers satisfactory dorm accommodation in the heart of town.

MID-RANGE

Noahs on the Beach (☎ 1800 023 663; cnr Shortland Esp & Zaara St; s & d $130) This hotel is great for those who want to roll out of bed and onto the beach. Rooms are clean and spacious and some have ocean views.

Hamilton Heritage (☎ 4961 1242; 178 Denison St; s/d $90/110; ℗) A great B&B that has charm, elegance and a price to match. Hamilton is situated on Cameron Hill, 5km northwest of town.

Anne's B&B at Ismebury (☎ 4929 5376; 3 Stevenson Pl; s/d $100/150; ℗) A Federation terrace house that is both charming and homely.

Grand Hotel (☎ 4929 3489; cnr Bolton & Church Sts; d $65) An establishment that offers pleasant open rooms with inviting hosts.

There's a string of cheapish motels along the Pacific Hwy at Belmont, about 15km south of town, such as the **Lake View Motor Inn** (☎ 1800 678 154; 749 Pacific Hwy; r $85; ℗ 🍴 🍷).

TOP END

Crowne Plaza (☎ 4907 5000; Wharf Rd; r from $180; ℗ 🍴 🍷) This freshly built hotel boasts indulgent rooms overlooking the Hunter River, rich in comfort and plush in service.

Eating

For something multicultural, wander down to **Beaumont St**, or for a trendy, cosmopolitan outing, head to **Darby St**. Both streets have an abundance of eateries and your best bet is just to follow your nose. The following are some good options in the east end.

Salar Couch Café (☎ 4927 5329; 54 Watt St; mains $8) Illustrates just how the culture of the town is changing, serving a menu predominantly based around organic goods in a stylish setting.

Bogie Hole Café (☎ 4929 1790; cnr Hunter & Pacific Sts; mains $13-22) An excellent array of simple meals in a lively atmosphere makes this place hard to top.

Paymaster's Café (☎ 4925 2600; 18 Bond St; mains $15-30) In the Convict Lumber Yard, this place has a mouth-watering menu, including wok-fried seafood, and did I mention the magnificent views?

Queens Wharf Brewery (☎ 4929 5792; www.qwb .com.au; 150 Wharf Rd; mains $25) Stunning views over the waterfront, a tasty modern Australian menu and a nice bottle of local wine make this place very desirable.

Topo Nicko (☎ 4929 5148; King St; mains $10-18) Great little BYO restaurant that has some good early-in-the-week pasta deals in a relaxed environment.

Scratchleys (☎ 4929 1111; www.scratchleys.com.au; 200 Wharf Rd; mains $25-40) Renowned for its fresh seafood with a sea breeze. Don't overlook this gem located on the waterfront.

Great Northern (☎ 4927 5728; cnr Scott & Watt Sts; mains $12) Generous pub servings in a spacious environment. Wednesday and Thursday $5 specials are offered on selected mains.

Drinking & Entertainment

World-famous bands Silverchair and the Screaming Jets are both Newcastle exports, and both started their illustrious path to world fame in these live music–mad pubs.

Cambridge Hotel (☎ 4962 2459; 789 Hunter St) Historically where bands have made their mark, it gets a lot of rising stars and many established heavyweights through the door; definitely worth your ear and a beer.

Finnegan's Irish Pub (☎ 4926 4777; 21-23 Darby St) An Irish pub that has found a niche market, Celts nightclub out the back gets going and is good for a boogie when the pints kick in.

Queens Wharf Brewery (☎ 4929 6333; 150 Wharf Rd) is a great place to start the evening; enjoy a couple of beers and watch the ships roll by. Stumble on up to the **Great Northern**

(cnr Scott & Watt St) for a few more of the best (see p138), and then, if you've still got the energy, there's plenty of fun to be had at the **Mercury Lounge** (☎ 4926 1119; 23 Watt St) with its three levels of outrageous tunes.

Showcase City Cinemas (☎ 4929 5019; 31 Wolf St; tickets $11) shows all the latest releases and throws in a few wild cards along the way.

Getting There & Away

AIR

The airport is 40 minutes from Newcastle train/bus station by bus; they run half-hourly to hourly depending on the time of day. Virgin Blue flies to Melbourne ($95), Adelaide ($149, 1½ hours) and Hobart ($169, three hours). Qantas Link flies to Melbourne ($158, 1¼ hours), Brisbane ($176, one hour) and Sydney ($88, 25 minutes).

BUS

All local and long-distance buses leave from Newcastle station. McCafferty's/Greyhound has plenty of buses heading north to Port Macquarie ($41, two hours), Coffs Harbour ($50, five hours), Byron Bay ($63, eight hours) and Brisbane ($67, 10 hours), west to Tamworth ($47, five hours) and south to Sydney ($30, 80 minutes).

Port Stephens Coaches (☎ 4982 2940; www.ps coaches.com.au) runs up the coast to all towns in Port Stephens ($10.40, 45 minutes, 11 departures daily). This fare is the same regardless of what stop you get off at.

Premier Motor Service (☎ 13 34 10; www.prem ierms.com.au) travels up the east coast daily, stopping at all popular destinations.

Busways (☎ 4997 4788, 1800 043 163) runs buses down to Bulahdelah ($19, one hour) and Forster ($36, 1¼ hours).

Rover Coaches (☎ 4990 1699; www.rovercoaches .com.au; 231-233 Vincent St, Cessnock) has return services from Cessnock to Newcastle ($11.20, 80 minutes, four times daily), Sydney ($30, 2½ hours, once daily) and Maitland ($8, 50 minutes, hourly).

Sid Fogg's (☎ 4928 1088; www.sidfoggs.com.au) runs across to Dubbo (Monday, Wednesday and Friday), stopping at all major towns.

CAR

As well as all of the regular car-hire companies, you can hire cars from budget joints such as **Cheep Heep** (☎ 4961 3144; 141 Maitland Rd, Islington; per day $70).

TRAIN

All Countrylink trains stop at Broadmeadow, just west of town, and run up and down the coast and head inland to Tamworth ($47.30, 5½ hours, daily). Coffs Harbour ($69.30, seven hours) and Byron Bay ($94.60, 25½ hours, daily) are both popular destinations.

There are plenty of Cityrail trains heading to Sydney (80 minutes), and daily trains to Maitland, Dungog ($12.10, 1½ hours, daily), Singleton, Muswellbrook and Scone daily.

Getting Around

Port Stephens Coaches (☎ 4982 2940; www.pscoaches .com.au) runs to and from the airport ($5.90, 35 minutes, 11 departures daily Monday to Friday, five departures daily Saturday and Sunday).

Newcastle Buses & Ferries (☎ 131 500; www.new castle.sta.nsw.gov.au; per hr $2.60, day tickets incl ferry $7.80) covers Newcastle and the eastern side of Lake Macquarie. Either grab a map from the visitors centre or check out the maps at the hundreds of bus stops around town. Jump on the Stockton ferry at Queens Wharf Complex (five minutes, every 30 minutes 6am to midnight) and catch a view of Newcastle from a different angle.

Newcastle Taxis (☎ 4979 3000) has depots at the train stations.

MAITLAND

☎ 02 / pop 53,470

Old money, old buildings and early origins make Maitland a true town of the Victorian era. Once seen as a more desirable address than Newcastle, the town had brief dreams of rivalling Sydney as the colony's headquarters. Oh, how times have changed, and this city now feeds off yesteryear with an abundance of classic Victoriana buildings and a vibe to match. Strangely enough, Maitland's most celebrated resident is not one of the old firm but a boxer turned national hero, Les Darcy, who was killed under suspicious circumstances in the USA in 1917.

Orientation & Information

Maitland's main street is High St, which follows the original trail through town. Part of the street is now Heritage Mall, where Victoriana is very much the flavour of the day. The **visitors centre** (☎ 4931 2800; www.hunterrivercountry.com.au; cnr New England Hwy &

High St) is off the New England Hwy on the eastern side of town.

Sights & Activities

The city's 19th-century wealth is reflected in the elaborate Georgian and Victorian buildings that remain. The extraordinary **Masonic Lodge** on Victoria St and the **Courthouse** (1895) at the western end of High St are a couple of the more interesting old buildings on display in Maitland.

Maitland Gaol (☎ 4936 6610; John St; tours $9; ☒ 10am-2pm) is a great place to visit for an insight into the way convicts lived. You can organise a sleepover in the gaol on weekends; inquire within.

Walka Water Works Complex (☎ 4932 0522; Sempill St; admission per car $3; ☒ 7am-8pm) opened in 1887 and provided the rapidly developing region with clean water. It is now a recreation site with marvellous picnic areas surrounded by historic monuments.

A little historic town called **Morpeth** lies 5km to the northeast of Maitland. It was the second port established (after Sydney) and once a hectic regional centre. Nowadays it's home to the most incredible array of specialist old-world knick-knack and craft shops, including the famous Miss Lilly's Lollies that offers free tastings. The grand old bridge over the Hunter River creaks with character.

Festivals & Events

Steamfest A congregation of the last centuries' steam trains attracts 70,000 people each April.
Morpeth Jazz Festival September sees the sleepy town (see p140) play host.

Sleeping

Imperial Hotel (☎ 4933 6566; 458 High St; s/d $65/75) Respectable pub rooms and a friendly bar downstairs for a few cheeky ones.

Molly Morgan Motor Inn (☎ 4933 5422; New England Hwy; s/d $70/75; P ⊠) One of the better motels in Maitland, all rooms are spacious and there is a good à la carte restaurant.

Country Comfort Monte Inn (☎ 4932 5288; New England Hwy, Rutherford; s/d $110/120; P ⊠ ⊠) West of town, it is set in a historic building and the facilities are of resort standard.

Hunter River Retreat (☎ 4930 1114; www.hunter riverretreat.com.au; 1090 Maitland Vale Rd, Rosebrook; d from $100, 2-person cottages for 2 nights $375; P ⊠) Romantic, secluded mountainside cottages.

Eating

Anoushka's Café (☎ 4936 6867; 9 Day St, East Maitland; mains $12; ☒ 9am-4.30pm Thu-Mon, dinner Sat) With an array of modern Australian cuisine on offer, its menu is both original and surprising – food for thought.

Place One Restaurant (☎ 4933 9968; 135 Lawes St; mains $13; ☒ closed Tue) Serves all the regular Chinese dishes; a solid option for vegetarians.

Maneeya (☎ 4933 1717; 473 High St; mains $15; ☒ lunch Mon-Fri, dinner Sat & Sun, closed Tue) Provides remarkably fresh Thai food in a light, inviting atmosphere.

Old George & Dragon Restaurant (☎ 4933 7272; 48 Melbourne St, East Maitland; 2/3 courses $53/65 Sun-Fri, $56/68 Sat) In a restored pub dating from the 1830s, owner and chef Ian Morphy's Anglo-French food attracts well-deserved critical acclaim.

Getting There & Away

The train station is in the city centre on the New England Hwy, which is also known as Les Darcy Drive.

Rover Coaches (☎ 4990 1699; 231-233 Vincent St; www.rovercoaches.com.au) has multiple bus services to Cessnock. Buses leave from the post office and the train station.

Countrylink runs trains to Broadmeadow ($5.50, 30 minutes) or west to Singleton ($5.50, 30 minutes) and Scone ($19.80, 1½ hours). Stops north include Dungog ($5.50, 30 minutes), Gloucester ($14.30, 1¾ hours), Coffs Harbour ($66, six hours) and Byron Bay ($90.20, nine hours).

Cityrail has plenty of trains going into Newcastle and a few heading west to Scone, stopping at all major towns.

CESSNOCK

☎ 02 / pop 17,830

Cessnock is on the southeast edge of the Lower Hunter wineries and basing yourself here is a cute way of cutting the cost of this pricey region. Once a buzzing mining centre, the town is – in a move not uncommon in these parts – gearing itself towards the tourist market, with trendy cafés appearing where seedy pubs once lay.

Sleeping

There are no hostels, but the pubs are good value. The **Cessnock Hotel** (☎ 4990 1002; www.huntervalleyhotels.com.au; Wollombi Rd; s/d Mon-Thu $35/70, Fri-Sun $50/100) is freshly renovated and spacious throughout. The cocktail bar downstairs would appear more at home in the Harbour City, with its glitzy array of cosmopolitan delights. Just up the road is the **Wentworth Hotel** (☎ 4990 7254; 36 Vincent St; s/d Mon-Thu $50/70, Fri-Sun $75/95), a 1920s-style hotel with similar offerings.

Cessnock has five motels. The **Cessnock Motel** (☎ 4990 2699; 13 Allandale Rd; s/d Sun-Thu $60/70, Fri $70/79, s/d $99/110) is a mid-range, recently expanded operation on the right side of town. Over the road, the **Hunter Valley Motel** (☎ 4990 1722; 30 Allandale Rd; d Sun-Thu/Sat $85/125; 🔀) is a little older but just as friendly.

Valley Vineyard Tourist Park (☎ 4990 2573; Mt View Rd; camp site per adult/child $10/5, d cabin $60) presents value for money while still within striking distance of the vineyards.

Eating

Oak Brasserie (☎ 4990 2366; 221 Vincent Street; mains $10-15) This place at the Royal Oak has a good relationship with quality à la carte food.

Kurrajong Restaurant (☎ 4991 4414; Wollombi Rd) For a step up in class, the Kurrajong at the Cessnock Hotel (p140) is extremely popular and the surf & turf dish is a favourite with locals.

Getting There & Away

Cessnock is definitely the cheapest base for visiting the Lower Hunter Valley. For transport information, see p144.

LOWER HUNTER WINERIES

Budding wine experts and happy-go-lucky visitors alike adore this mass concentration of wineries. It is a playground with a little of everything, from mass-producing, commercialised wineries to hidden boutique establishments. Consequently, the valley has many charms and a unique feel. It is an absolute joy to drive, ride or balloon your way around the Lower Hunter.

Before you embark on a palate-enriching tour of the region, try first to decide what you want to achieve as it is almost too easy to lose direction somewhere among the 140 wineries scattered around the valley.

Some aspects of the commercialisation of the Lower Hunter are positive in nature. They come in the form of the Hunter Valley Gardens (see p141), attracting the non-drinkers, and the Greg Norman–designed Vintage Golf Course.

A NEW DIMENSION

Officially opened in 2003, the **Hunter Valley Gardens** (☎ 4998 7600; www.hvg.com.au; Broke Rd, Pokolbin; adult/child $15/8) are part of an $80-million complex that is welcoming a new breed of tourist to the valley. Many (20% of visitors to the region) are making the pilgrimage to the 25 hectares of immaculately manicured themed gardens. From the ever-popular Children's Story Book Garden to a Mosaic Tea Garden, you're unlikely to find an array quite like it anywhere in the world. These are just two of 12 themed gardens on 8km of pathways that will take you past many an exquisite topiary and exotic plant. Absolutely magnificent and well worth investing at least half a day.

As well as garden appreciation, you can play aqua golf, mini golf or just have a barbecue on the sweeping lawns. Harrigan's Irish Pub can mix up your liquid diet with a pint or two of Guinness in an unassuming atmosphere. The four-star hotel is plush and inviting.

Orientation

At the centre of the wineries, the Hunter Valley Gardens (also still referred to as Pokolbin Village) is a great place to stock up on picnic necessities and the like to bring the valley back to budget. From here you can head in any direction for the joy of tasting fermented grapes.

Information

It is utterly imperative to pick up a copy of the *Hunter Valley Wine Country Visitor Guide* before you set out; it will be your bible, providing unparalleled insight into the area and a great map, readily available at all visitors centres statewide.

The **Hunter Valley Wine Country Tourism Centre** (☎ 4991 7396; www.winecountry.com.au; Main Rd, Pokolbin) is just north of Cessnock and can organise accommodation bookings and tours to suit all types.

Sights & Activities
WINERIES

It would be rude to start proceedings without a glass of bubbly, so conveniently positioned near the visitors centre is

LOWER HUNTER VALLEY

0 —————— 5 km
0 —————— 3 miles

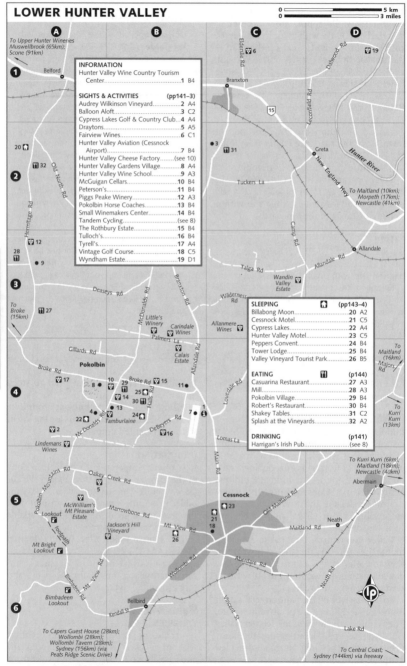

INFORMATION
Hunter Valley Wine Country Tourism
  Center...**1** B4

SIGHTS & ACTIVITIES   (pp141–3)
Audrey Wilkinson Vineyard.............**2** A4
Balloon Aloft....................................**3** C2
Cypress Lakes Golf & Country Club...**4** A4
Draytons...**5** A5
Fairview Wines.................................**6** C1
Hunter Valley Aviation (Cessnock
  Airport)...**7** B4
Hunter Valley Cheese Factory........(see 10)
Hunter Valley Gardens Village.........**8** A4
Hunter Valley Wine School.............**9** A3
McGuigan Cellars............................**10** B4
Peterson's..**11** B4
Piggs Peake Winery.........................**12** A3
Pokolbin Horse Coaches..................**13** B4
Small Winemakers Center................**14** B4
Tandem Cycling...............................(see 8)
The Rothbury Estate........................**15** B4
Tulloch's..**16** B4
Tyrell's...**17** A4
Vintage Golf Course........................**18** C5
Wyndham Estate.............................**19** D1

SLEEPING   (pp143–4)
Billabong Moon...............................**20** A2
Cessnock Motel...............................**21** C5
Cypress Lakes..................................**22** A4
Hunter Valley Motel.........................**23** C5
Peppers Convent..............................**24** B4
Tower Lodge....................................**25** B4
Valley Vineyard Tourist Park............**26** B5

EATING   (p144)
Casuarina Restaurant.......................**27** A3
Mill..**28** A3
Pokolbin Village..............................**29** B4
Robert's Restaurant.........................**30** B4
Shakey Tables..................................**31** C2
Splash at the Vineyards...................**32** A2

DRINKING   (p141)
Harrigan's Irish Pub.........................(see 8)

To Upper Hunter Wineries
Muswellbrook (65km);
Scone (91km)

Belford

Branxton

To Maitland (10km);
Morpeth (17km);
Newcastle (41km)

Creta

Hunter River

Eldersie Rd

Dalwood Rd

Leconfield Rd

New England Hwy

Tuckers La

Allandale

Camp Rd

Allandale Rd

Talga Rd

Wandin
Valley
Estate

Old North Rd

Hermitage Rd

Deaseys Rd

Branxton Rd

McDonalds Rd

Wilderness
Rd

Little's
Winery

Carindale
Wines

Allanmere
Wines

To
Broke
(15km)

Gillards Rd

Palmers La

Calais
Estate

Allandale Rd

Pokolbin

Broke Rd

Broke Rd

Halls Rd

Lovedale Rd

To
Maitland
(16km)

To
Majors
Rd

To
Kurri
Kurri
(13km)

Tamburlaine

DeBeyers Rd

Lomas La

Lindemans
Wines

Mt Donalds Rd

Main Rd

To Kurri Kurri (6km);
Maitland (18km);
Newcastle (40km)

Pokolbin Mountains Rd

Oakey Creek Rd

McWilliam's
Mt Pleasant
Estate

Marrowbone Rd

Jackson's Hill
Vineyard

Mt View Rd

Cessnock

Old Maitland Rd

Abermain

Neath

Maitland Rd

Lookout

Mt Bright
Lookout

Bimbadeen Mt View Rd

Aberdare Rd

Neath Rd

Bimbadeen
Lookout

Bellbird

Kendall St

Vincent St

Lake Rd

To Capers Guest House (28km);
Wollombi (28km);
Wollombi Tavern (28km);
Sydney (156km) (via
Peats Ridge Scenic Drive)

To Central Coast;
Sydney (144km) via freeway

HUNTER VALLEY

Peterson's Champagne House (☎ 4998 7881; www .petersonhouse.com.au; cnr Broke & Branxton Rds, Pokolbin; ⏰ 9am-5pm). From there the valley is your oyster. The elder statesman of the valley is **Tyrrell's** (☎ 4993 7000; www.tyrrells.com.au; Broke Rd, Pokolbin), which has been producing wine for over 140 years. **Piggs Peake Winery** (☎ 6574 7000; 679 Hermitage Rd) is ugly by name but ever so sweet by taste. **Draytons** (☎ 4998 7513; www.draytonswines.com.au; Oakey Creek Rd, Pokolbin) dates back to 1860 and is still owned by the original family. Just like the immortal race-horse, **Tulloch's** (☎ 4998 7580; De Beyers Rd, Pokolbin) Shiraz has a legendary reputation, definitely worth the visit. Small, intimate and ensuring fine attention to detail, **Fairview Wines** (☎ 4938 1116; www.fairviewwines.com.au; 422 Elderslie Rd, Branxton) steers clear of chemicals, resulting in a crisp, natural flavour for its wines. Another first-class establishment is **McGuigan Cellars** (☎ 4998 7402; www.mcguiganwines.com.au; McDonalds Rd, Pokol-bin), which has some magnificent handmade cheese to go with the quality plonk. Visually spectacular and architecturally sound, **Audrey Wilkinson Vineyard** (☎ 4998 7411; De Beyers Rd, Pokol-bin) is regarded as the valley's benchmark for position and historic importance.

GOLF

'The Shark' (aka Greg Norman) has designed the acclaimed **Vintage Golf Course** (☎ 4998 6789; www.thevintage.com.au; Vintage Dr, Rothbury; ⏰ daily), and once the trees grow into the course it will be vintage. To play 18 holes costs $85 Monday to Friday, $110 on weekends.

Like good wine, golf courses improve with age, and the well-established **Cypress Lakes Golf & Country Club** (☎ 4993 1800; cnr McDonalds & Thompsons Rds; green fees for 18 holes Mon-Fri $80, Sat & Sun $100) is rightly regarded by many as the best in the region.

Tours

Hunter Vineyard Tours (☎ 4991 1659; tours@hunter vineyardtours.com.au; day tours $45, with lunch $65) An established operator that caters for individuals and groups; bookings are essential.
Tumbleweed Trike Tours (☎ 4938 1245; 1st hr $100, thereafter $50) With a delivery service to your door, chauffeur-driven three-wheeled bikes are a pricey yet utterly gracious way to explore the boutique wineries.
Wine & Cheese Tasting Tour (☎ 4938 5031; day tours $90) You can request a route or let experienced guides whisk you around a proven track, a good option for a well-rounded adventure.

TOP FIVE ACTIVITIES

■ Get up in the air for sunrise with **Balloon Aloft** (☎ 1800 028 568, 4938 1955; www.balloonaloft.com; Lot 1, Branxton Rd, North Rothbury; flights adult/child 8-12 $270/170), or take a joy flight with **Hunter Valley Aviation** (☎ 4991 6500; www.huntervalleyaviation.com; Main Rd, Cessnock Airport; 20-min flights $50).

■ **Hunter Valley Cheese Factory** (☎ 4998 7744; McDonalds Rd, Pokolbin) A chance to soak up the wine while viewing and sampling award-winning cheeses.

■ **Pokolbin Horse Coaches** (☎ 4998 7305; McDonalds Rd, Pokolbin; half-day tours $44, with picnic lunch $55) Old-fashioned and old-world, this is a romantic clip clop along the valley.

■ **Tandem Cycling** (☎ 4998 6633; Broke Rd, Pokolbin; 4hr $40, day $60) Let your better half do all the work while you handle and drink the precious cargo. Bikes can be delivered to your doorstep.

■ **Hunter Valley Wine School** (☎ 4998 7777; Hermitage Rd, Hunter Resort) Become an instant wine connoisseur and get some tips on the best buys in the val-ley. The two-hour Hard Hat Tour ($25 per person) is all about wine-making procedures; the winery tour ($5 per per-son) is a tour of a working winery.

Festivals & Events

Celebrating the wine-making process, the **Hunter Valley Harvest Festival** (www.hunterharvest festival.com.au) runs from late February to April. October is the month the valley swings to the sound of jazz and resounds with opera:
Jazz in the Vines (☎ 02-4993 7000; Tyrells Vineyards, Broke Rd, Pokolbin)
Opera in the Vineyards (Wyndham Estate, 700 Dalwood Rd, Dalwood)

Call the tourism centre (p141) for more information.

Sleeping

There are some 1700 beds in the region and quality is not hard to come by. The **Hunter Valley Wine Country Tourism Centre** (☎ 4991 7396; www.winecountry.com.au; Main Rd, Pokolbin) has a sensational booking service and plenty of good deals. On the weekend you will find it hard to get a bed in the valley (especially for one-night bookings), so prebooking is essential. For budget or mid-range accommodations you are best basing yourself at Cessnock; see p140 for details.

TOP END

Extravagant, excessive and utterly delightful, the following top-end B&Bs are the best in the business.

Tower Lodge (☎ 4998 7022; www.towerlodge .com.au; Halls Rd, Pokolbin; s/d Sun-Thu $460/510; d Sat & Sun $1020) Luxury, elegance and rooms with individual charm on a property with rare tranquillity. Note that you have to book for minimum two nights on weekends.

Billabong Moon (☎ 65747290; www.billabongmoon .com.au; 393 Hermitage Rd; cottages/studios $170/495) On a billabong and simply gorgeous, Waltzing Matilda's rich relative incorporates everything indulgent and oozes romance.

Peppers Convent (☎ 4998 7764; www.peppers.com .au; Halls Rd; d Mon-Thu/Fri-Sun $360/880) A repositioned convent from Coonamble (600km away) is indicative of the effort this place goes to in providing an experience rarely matched. Note that you have to book for minimum two nights Friday and Saturday.

Cypress Lakes (☎ 4993 1400; www.cypresslakes .com.au; cnr McDonalds & Thompsons Rds; d Sun-Thu/Fri & Sat $360/720) Part of Cypress Lakes Resort, this is your opportunity to savour the rewards of serious pampering, as ancient therapies, cleansing treatments and classic spas rejuvenate the soul and unwind the body.

Capers Guest House (☎ 4998 3211; www.capers guesthouse.com.au; Wollombi Rd; garden ste/verandah ste

for 2 nights $500/600) Originally a sandstone building in Sydney, this house has been moved to a spot high on a hillside. The views are to die for, complemented by elegant rooms and indulgent service.

Eating

The choice is astronomical and the food is divine. Almost all big wineries have a restaurant in their vineyards but if you're looking for some direction, drop past these to indulge.

Robert's Restaurant (☎ 4998 7330; Halls Rd; mains $35) Atmospheric, memorable and affordable, Roberts has great food to complement the valley's best wines.

Shakey Tables (☎ 4938 1744; Branxton Rd; mains $35) Funky, stylish food with an interesting, arty ambience.

Splash at the Vineyards (☎ 6574 7229; www .thevineyardsestate.com.au; 555 Hermitage Rd; mains $25) Oysters, lobster and the latest catch; the seafood is of unquestionable quality and the wine isn't too bad either.

Mill (☎ 4998 7266; www.tuscanywineestate.com.au; cnr Hermitage Rd & Mistletoe Lane; mains $30) Modern Australian cuisine that is highly regarded within the valley; a popular haunt for returnees.

Casuarina Restaurant (☎ 4998 7888; www .casuarinainn.com.au; Hermitage Rd; mains $35) Inundated with awards, this place will do everything and anything to impress, with its Mediter-Asian menu that satisfies all those highbrow foodies.

Getting There & Away

BUS

The bus station in Cessnock is on Vincent St at the southern end of town.

DETOUR: SINGLETON & MUSWELLBROOK

If your driving from the Lower Hunter Wineries up into the valley, a few hours at Singleton can break up the drive nicely. Four kilometres south of the town is the **Royal Australian Army Infantry Corps Museum** (☎ 6570 3257; Singleton Army Camp, New England Hwy; ☾ 9am-4pm Wed-Sun) which hosts the largest collection of small arms in Australia. There's also a comprehensive history of the Royal Australian Regiment that covers campaigns from Korea through to current day peace keeping operations. Singleton boasts the largest sundial in the southern hemisphere, located in the park in town. Continue your drive up the valley to Muswellbrook, a town heavily affected by the coal-mining industry. It also has the distinction of being the breeding place of that great Australian working dog, the Blue Heeler. The breed is a cross of the dingo and the Northumberland Drover dog. Drop in at one of the town's many pubs for a drink that comes in a schooner rather than a glass. The drive will take about half a day including a stop at the museum.

Kean's Travel (☎ 1800 625 587, 4990 5000; 1A Cooper St, Cessnock) has daily buses to Muswellbrook ($19), Scone ($24.50) and Sydney ($30). A service leaves for Sydney at 7.15am from Monday to Saturday.

Rover Coaches (☎ 1800 801 012; www.rover coaches.com.au; 231-233 Vincent St, Cessnock) runs coaches to and from Sydney ($30, 2½ hours, once daily) with drop-offs in Cessnock and throughout the Hunter Valley wine country. It also has multiple daily services to Maitland ($8, 40 minutes, half-hourly) and Newcastle ($11.20, 1¼ hours, four times daily). Buses leave from the main street and from the tourism centre.

CAR

If you're coming from Sydney, jump on the National Hwy 1 for 100km, then follow signs to Cessnock; the famous vineyards lie just beyond. If approaching from the north or Newcastle, drive east out to Maitland and follow signs to Cessnock.

UPPER HUNTER WINERIES

With far fewer wineries, the Upper Hunter is less visited than the Lower, but the country is pretty and the wineries are well worth seeing. Most Upper Hunter wineries are close to the small town of Denman, such as the well-established **Rosemount Estate** (☎ 6549 6450; Rosemount Rd, Denman; ☼ 10am-4pm), or the equally impressive **James Estate** (☎ 6547 5168; Bylong Valley Way), tucked away in a beautiful valley near the hamlet of Sandy Hollow. It also nurtures some small, boutique wineries like **Horseshoe Vineyard** (☎ 6547 3528; Horseshoe Rd, Horseshoe Valley, Denman; ☼ 10am-4pm Sat, Sun & public holidays).

DENMAN

☎ 02 / pop 1410

Denman is an ideal place to have a bite to eat before heading out into the surrounding district to see what wineries tickle your tastebuds. There is no official visitors centre but the **NRMA** (☎ 6547 2308; Olgilvie St; ☼ 9am-5pm) does have a number of pamphlets and is well prepared to answer most queries.

The recently renovated **Denman Hotel** (☎ 6547 2207; 3 Olgilvie St; s/d $20/40) has a good old feel about it. The **Royal Hotel** (☎ 6547 2226; s/d $20/33) is visually spacious and holds a prominent position within the town, as well as being a great place for a meal.

AUSTRALIAN STOCK HORSES

Although it wasn't formally defined as a breed until 1971, the Australian stock horse has participated in many of the major wars of European-Australian history. Originally called Walers (from New South Wales), the breed served as cavalry horses in India, South Africa and during WWI. They carried the 4th Australian Light Horse Regiment in the world's last cavalry charge at the taking of Beersheba in 1916.

The **Australian Stock Horse Society** (☎ 6545 1122; 48 Guernsey St) headquarters is based in Scone.

On the B&B front the options are endless, so inquire at the NRMA, but **Kerrabee Homestead** (☎ 6547 5155; Bylong Valley Way; per person $125-135) is fast developing a brilliant reputation.

Denman Van Village (☎ 6547 2590; 10 McCauley St; camp sites/cabins $15/40) is your only park option.

Sid Fogg's (☎ 4928 1088) buses run both ways Monday, Wednesday, Friday between Dubbo and Newcastle stopping at Denman ($59, six hours), Newman and Denman ($31, two hours) and Dubbo and Denman ($42, four hours).

Osbourne Bus Company (☎ 6543 1271) does the trip to Muswellbrook ($6.80) twice daily.

SCONE

☎ 02 / pop 4560

Scone, in the upper reaches of the Hunter Valley, is Australia's premier horse region. It lives, breathes and revolves around thoroughbreds, and the culture is so horse-dominated that it would not be surprising to stumble across *My Friend Flicka* roaming the ranges. The land is rich in both colour and financial prosperity.

Orientation & Information

Kelly St (New England Hwy) is the main shopping street. Liverpool St runs off Kelly St and becomes the road to Merriwa.

The **visitors centre** (☎ 6545 1526; cnr Kelly & Swan Sts) is on the north side of the town centre, near the famous *Mare & Foal* statue. The **National Parks & Wildlife Service area headquarters** (NPWS; ☎ 6540 2300; 137 Kelly St) is in Scone, servicing Barrington Tops National Park (p148) and Burning Mountain (p146).

HUNTER VALLEY

Sights & Activities

A scenic drive down Segenhoe Rd will take you past many of the multimillion-dollar operations that dominate Australian thoroughbred racing. **Vinery Horse Stud** is immaculately kept and just driving past illustrates how much money is pumped into these future champions.

The **visitors centre** can arrange visits to some of the area's horse studs outside the August/September foaling season. The **Scone Racing Track** is the best country racetrack in the world, well worth a visit for its facilities and visual impact.

BURNING MOUNTAIN

Coal seams beneath **Burning Mountain** were on fire when the first Europeans arrived in the area (they thought it was an active volcano), and calculations based on the burning rate of a metre per year suggest that the fire started as long as 6000 years ago. The mountain is a nature reserve, and a 3km round-trip walking track leads through some diverse terrain up to the smoking vents. The turn-off from the New England Hwy to Burning Mountain is about 20km north of Scone.

Festivals & Events

Not surprisingly all about horses, **Horse Week** sees racing, equestrian and polo matches dominating the stage in mid-May.

Sleeping

Scone YHA Hostel (☎ 6545 2072; 1151 Segenhoe Rd; dm/d $19/43) This rural hostel just east of town occupies the old school campus and has a good country feel about it, overlooking the fine fillies of Arrowfield Thoroughbred Stud.

Airlie House Motor Inn (☎ 6545 1488; www.airliehouse.com.au; 229 New England Hwy; s/d $75/85, historic ste from $100) Centrally positioned and well managed.

Middlebrook Station (☎ 6545 0389; Middlebrook Rd; d/f $88/120) At the foot of the valley 10km north of Scone and on your way to Toowari National Park, Middlebrook Station has modern lodges, picturesque surrounds and attracts live animals in their droves. There's a bush golf course and a building called 'Dawn' (after Dawn Fraser) which has been relocated from the Sydney 2000 Olympics.

Belltrees Country House (☎ 6545 1668; Gundy Rd, Gundy; Whites Cottage per person $110, Mountain Retreat per person $200) Situated on a stunning property, Belltrees is an experience rarely matched. Play polo while the family of Patrick White (the Noble Prize–winning novelist) play host.

Highway (☎ 6545 1078; New England Hwy; camp sites/cabins $17/55) On the southern end of town, this is a neat operation that is compact and a touch noisy.

Eating

Kerv Café (☎ 6545 3111; 108 Liverpool St; mains $10) A modern Art-Deco café with an antique shop within the premises, it excels in gourmet lunches and great coffee.

Scone Bakery & Stabledoor Eatery (☎ 6545 1862; 132 Kelly St; mains $8) Of the same genre as Kerv, it provides scrumptious pies and rich coffee.

Asser House Café (☎ 6545 3571; Kelly St; mains $8) Another appealing café in a lovely historic building.

Getting There & Away

McCafferty's/Greyhound buses has daily services to Sydney ($58, five hours), Newcastle ($39, three hours) and Tamworth ($34, three hours).

Kean's Travel (☎ 1800 625 587) buses leave daily for Cessnock ($24.50), Singleton ($20) and Sydney ($46.50).

Countrylink has train services to Armidale ($41.80, five hours), Muswellbrook ($5.50, 20 minutes) and down to Broadmeadow ($26.40, 2¾ hours).

Cityrail trains run east through the valley, terminating at Newcastle.

MERRIWA

☎ 02 / pop 990

Merriwa is not wine, horses or mining. In fact, Merriwa is surprisingly unaffected by the mass industries of the Hunter. So much so that is has a unique, 'small-town' feel about it. That said, there is not much on offer for the visitor but it can prove a good base from which to enter Goulburn River National Park (p147).

The **visitors centre** (☎ 6548 2607; cnr Bettington & Bow Sts) has history on its side, built in 1847 and home to the Old Colonial Cottage, which takes you right back to the town's origins.

The pleasant **Good Life Café** (☎ 6548 2676; 90 Bettington St; coffee $3) is renowned far and wide for its coffee.

GOULBURN RIVER NATIONAL PARK

Goulburn River National Park, 35km south-west of Merriwa, protects the upper reaches of the Goulburn River (which flows into the Hunter River east of Denman). The park follows the river as it cuts its way through some spectacular **sandstone gorges**. This was the route used by Aborigines travelling from the plains to the sea, and the area is rich in **rock art**. You can camp here during dry weather. No fees apply. Some sites have pit toilets and barbecues but you need to bring your own water. Fires are permitted. Access is from the road running south to Wollar and Bylong; all roads in the park are dry-weather roads only. The Mudgee **NPWS office** (☎ 6372 7199; Shop 1/160 Church Street, Mudgee) has more information.

THE BUCKETTS WAY

This old road is an engaging alternative to the Pacific Hwy as a route north of Newcastle, branching off the highway about 15km north of Raymond Terrace and rejoining it just south of Taree. The road is longer and narrower than the highway but it carries much less traffic and passes through some interesting country. It has a touch of the English Cotswolds countryside about it, and is just as elegant if slightly less historic.

Stroud

☎ 02 / pop 670

Stroud is a small, pleasant village and a pleasurable place in which to invest a few hours. The town's layout is extremely user-friendly, with all sites and stores laid out in a neat, logical fashion. The town's newsagent doubles as the **visitors centre** (☎ 4994 5117; The Bucketts Way), not that you will need it.

Perhaps the reason behind such an efficient layout rests in its founders, the Australian Agricultural Company, which came here in 1826. Several convict-built buildings are still standing, such as **Quambi** (☎ 4994 5400; The Bucketts Way; admission $2; ☺ 10am-2pm Sun & by appointment), the original school. The **Anglican church** stands alongside it; here the infamous bushranger Captain Thunderbolt was married in 1860. The church's **graveyard** has some interesting old headstones, including one that pronounces, rather ominously, 'Vengeance is Mine, Saith the Lord'. The **courthouse** (☎ 4994 5400; The Bucketts Way; admission $2; ☺ 10am-2pm Wed & by appointment) creaks out a few good yarns and is well worth the gold coin.

Just up the hill lies **Silo Hill** (open all hours), home to eight underground silos, one of which you can climb down into – a lot of fun (for those without claustrophobic tendencies) and a genuine reminder of Australia's early agricultural days.

Since 1961 Stroud has exported bricks to its international counterparts, Stroud in the USA, England and Canada, and every July a **brick-throwing competition** is held in unison – a world championship of sorts.

The **Stroud Central Hotel** (☎ 4994 5197; The Bucketts Way; s/d $20/40) is the town's pulse and is centrally located and inviting. Tents can be erected at the showground just north of town.

The **Girvan YHA Hostel** (☎ 4997 6639; 36 Greys Lane; members/nonmembers $10/13) is 15km out of town towards the coast. The hostel is not accessible via public transport and there is no pick-up.

There are no trains to Stroud; you need to take a Countrylink bus to Dungog train station ($7.70) and join up with the coastal trains there.

Gloucester

☎ 02 / pop 2470

This productive country town is nestled on the banks of the Gloucester River. The 'tops' to the left as you are driving into town are a series of monolithic hills known as 'bucketts', a corruption of an Aboriginal word meaning 'big rock' (hence the road called The Bucketts Way).

The town acts as a base camp for any venture into the northern side of Barrington Tops National Park.

INFORMATION

The **visitors centre** (☎ 6558 1408; www.gloucester .org.au; 27 Denison St) can educate you on the surrounding area's activities. For all national park inquiries, head to the **NPWS office** (☎ 6538 5300; 59 Church St).

SIGHTS & ACTIVITIES

Mograni Lookout, 5km east on The Bucketts Way, overlooks the town with rewarding views. In town, the **Belbourie Aboriginal Art Centre** (☎ 6558 2660; 2 Hume St; admission free;

HUNTER VALLEY

8am-4pm Mon-Wed) is worth the visit just to see the *Hands of Friendship* mural that runs down the adjacent shop wall, an artwork that won the local Aboriginal people an Australia Day award.

As well as other adventure sports such as mountain biking, **Barrington Outdoor Adventure Centre** (☎ 6558 2093; www.boac.com.au; 126 Thunderbolts Way; 1-day mountain-bike tour $120, 1-/2-day canoe & kayak $120/330, 2-day combined mountain-bike & kayak tour $330) runs a range of mountain-bike, kayaking and white-water rafting adventures suitable for both adventure seekers and families. Prices include meals and accommodation and the minimum recommended age is 12.

Camp Cobark Trail Rides (☎ 6558 5524; 2457 Scone Rd; per person $40) operates two-hour mountain horse rides that take in stream crossings and unmatched panoramic views.

Operating from a private airstrip off Bucketts Way, **Sky Diving Centre Gloucester** (☎ 1300 135 867; Gloucester Aerodrome, Jack's Rd; tandem jumps $300, solo jumps $400) give passengers a tour of the 'bucketts' from the air.

SLEEPING

Gloucester Hotel/Motel (☎ 6558 1816; Church St; s/d $35/46) A basic motel that fails to excite but holds a handy position at an affordable rate.

Gloucester Country Lodge Motel (☎ 6558 1812; The Bucketts Way; s/d $75/90) An upmarket motel that is well laid out with comfy rooms.

Steps (☎ 6558 3048; www.thesteps.com.au; 535 Manchester Rd, Barrington; camp sites per adult/child $6/3, dm $19, 8-person house $120) A hidden oasis 20 minutes towards Barrington Tops National Park; make the effort for the amazing scenery. The property fronts on 600m of rapids, has prime riverside camping, a backpacker lodge and a couple of shacks for families. You can check out, but the experience never leaves you.

GETTING THERE & AWAY

Countrylink trains travel south to Dungog ($7.70) and Sydney ($44) and north to places like Kempsey ($31.90), Coffs Harbour ($47.30) and Byron Bay ($83.60).

The Bucketts Way runs south to Stroud and beyond, and winds east to the Pacific Hwy just south of Taree. From near Barrington, you can head north on a partly sealed road to Walcha or branch off to

Terrible Billy (great name), from where a sealed road runs to Tamworth. If you keep heading west from Barrington, you'll be on a spectacular unsealed road that winds past Barrington Tops National Park, eventually reaching the New England Hwy near Scone.

BARRINGTON TOPS NATIONAL PARK

Barrington Tops National Park is a World Heritage–listed wilderness area centred on the rugged Barrington Plateau, which rises to almost 1600m around Mt Barrington and Carey's Peak. The park at 73,884 hectares also takes in the Gloucester Tops just to the north. Vegetation in the park ranges from subtropical rainforest in the lower reaches of the park to snow-gum country on the exposed peaks. The slopes in between are dominated by ancient, moss-covered Antarctic beech forest.

There are good walking trails but be prepared for snow in winter and cold snaps at any time. Drinking water must be boiled. **Thunderbolts Lookout Track** is a flat 400m return walk taking in stunning views over the escarpment. There's disabled access on the 400m paved **Devils Hole Lookout** walk, which ends at a great viewing platform. For longer treks, try the 16km **Rocky Crossing Track** which takes you through magical tropical rainforest. The **NPWS office** (☎ 6538 5300; 59 Church St, Gloucester) has more information.

The Steps (see this page) offers whitewater canoeing, kayaking and rafting, and offers courses for those wanting to get qualified as a guide.

Forty-three kilometres from Dungog, on the southern edge of the park, **Barrington Guest House** (☎ 4995 3212; www.barringtonguesthouse.com.au; 2940 Salisbury Rd, Salisbury via Dungog; r with/without bathroom $99/69, cottages per person $129) has a spectacular setting beneath the plateau escarpment. Packages with all meals included are available, as well as trail rides for $15 an hour.

Gloucester River Camping Area (camp site per adult/child $5/3; Gloucester Tops Rd), 31 km from the Gloucester–Stroud road, is the main camp site within the park. Access is via car on unpaved roads. There are flush toilets, and electric or gas BBQs. Call Gloucester NPWS for information.

The park can be reached from the towns of Dungog, Gloucester and Scone.

WOKO NATIONAL PARK

Smaller than nearby Barrington Tops National Park, Woko (80,000 hectares) is similarly undeveloped and rugged, with rainforests and other vegetation. Access is from Gloucester, about 30km to the southeast; head for Rookhurst and take the left fork shortly after. The **Manning River camp site** (camp site per adult/child $5/3), near the park entrance, is the only camping area in Woko National Park. You can get to the camp site by car and caravan via unsealed roads. There's an honesty box at the gate for fees. Facilities include pit toilets, picnic tables and wood BBQs, but bring your own water. There are some good swimming holes nearby. Contact the **NPWS office** (☎ 6538 5300; 59 Church St, Gloucester) for more information.

DUNGOG

☎ 02 / pop 2120

Dungog is a sleepy town on the southern edge of Barrington Tops National Park. Established in the 1830s as a military post with the task of eradicating bushrangers (a task in which it failed), it has succeeded in producing a world-class cricketer in Doug Walters. Today it's more of a service centre for the area's farms. The staff at the **visitors centre** (☎ 4992 2212; cnr Dowling & Brown Sts) are helpful.

The only motel in Dungog is **Tall Timbers** (☎ 4992 1547; 167 Dowling St; s/d $60/80), a homely operation in the centre of town. For a quick bite, head to **Crazy Chairs Café** (☎ 4992 3272; 205 Darling St; mains $10), or **Snack Inn** (☎ 4992 1801; 262 Dowling St; burgers $5) is an efficient, cheap option.

Countrylink services travel to Maitland ($5.50, 40 minutes, daily), Gloucester ($7.70, 40 minutes, daily), Byron Bay ($90.20, eight hours, daily) and Coffs Harbour ($59.40, five hours, daily).

Cityrail trains head down to Maitland and Newcastle and out west to Singleton, Muswellbrook and Scone.

HUNTER VALLEY

North Coast

The relentless pursuit of sandy horizons, coastal havens and good times has transformed this stretch of coast into one of the most well-trodden tourist routes in Australia. Surprisingly, though, many people have stuck to the bright lights of Byron Bay and much of the coastline remains untouched by large-scale tourism.

The New South Wales (NSW) north coast stretches up from the bay of Port Stephens to the Queensland (QLD) border at Tweed Heads. Most places north of Coffs Harbour are tourist meccas, but it's worth taking your time on a trip north from Sydney to explore the excellent beaches and the diverse bushland – you'll see rolling green hills, rainforest, wilderness and everything in between. But that said, the coastal way can turn into a haze of sandy beaches and rugged bushland, and a venture inland can prove both refreshing and rewarding, strange as this may sound.

If you're in search of an eco-friendly family orientated hideaway, the bay of Port Stephens gives a gentle feel that epitomises the North Coast. But for those craving an activity-packed extravaganza Coffs Harbour is the ticket, with enough adrenaline to send you troppo. Behind this adventure heaven lies the tranquil Dorrigo National Park with its dense rainforests.

Due to this coastline's popularity – especially in the far north – prices skyrocket during peak times (Christmas, January, Easter and school holidays). Be warned and book ahead.

HIGHLIGHTS

- Soaking up music at the Global Carnival in **Bellingen** (p166)
- Visiting the wildlife at **Whian Whian State Forest** (p194)
- Spending lazy days, big nights at **Byron Bay** (p180)
- Getting back to nature at **Seal Rocks** (p155)
- Treating the family to year-round fun at **Port Stephens** (p152)
- Experiencing an unforgettable sunrise from **Mt Warning** (p166)
- Marvelling at the plethora of jacaranda in spring in **Grafton** (p174)
- Shopping at the Hinterland's bustling **weekend markets** (p188)

NORTH COAST

LOWER NORTH COAST

It all starts at Port Stephens, a bay that is bigger than Sydney Harbour and home to scores of dolphins and millions of oysters. From there the Lower North Coast sweeps up to the undeveloped Seal Rocks and on to the palm-treed city of Port Macquarie. This stretch of coast is a stone's throw from Sydney and outrageously popular with families.

PORT STEPHENS

☎ 02 / pop 8040

The bay of Port Stephens, just an hour north of Newcastle, incorporates a string of coastal towns, 32km of beach line and a true family feel. The bay is also popular with 160 resident dolphins and the odd passing whale.

The area is pleasantly underdeveloped and the bay's crystal clarity looks set to continue; the community is ecologically driven and many businesses proudly display 'eco-accredited' certificates.

History

Captain James Cook sighted the entrance to Port Stephens in 1770, but the colony of NSW was seven years old before the first official survey of the area was made in 1795. By then, escaped convicts had been up here for five years and were living with local Aborigines – in what must have seemed like heaven after their captivity in Sydney.

Orientation & Information

Nelson Bay (population 7000), located near the south head, is the unofficial capital of Port Stephens. Here you will find the **visitors centre** (☎ 4981 1579; www.portstephens.org.au; Victoria Pde). Shoal Bay, on the point, is the next town along, although the two towns have virtually merged in recent years. The area's most scenic beaches – Zenith, Wreck and Box Beach – back onto Shoal Bay.

Over the Tomaree National Park and down the peninsula is Anna Bay, another small town that has both surf and bay beaches. At the northern end of town is One Mile Beach, and if you have an inclination for a nudist beach, just keep walking. On the southern side of town is the beginning of Stocken Beach, which runs all the way

back to Newcastle. The rolling dunes look strikingly similar to the Sahara Desert, so if you are driving a 4WD, grab a pass from the visitors centre and put it to the test.

Sights & Activities

The restored 1872 **Inner Lighthouse** at Little Beach has displays on the area's history. There's also a **café** with impressive views.

There are a number of outfits that will take you to the dolphins. **Moonshadow** (☎ 4984 9388; 3/35 Stockton St; 1½-hr trip $18) is the most established, with three modern vessels. **Imagine Cruises** (☎ 4984 9000; www.portstephens .org.au/imagine; 123 Stockton St; 4-hr whale-watch tour adult/child $50/25) uses a catamaran and is highly regarded. But both companies can show you the whales that drop by during winter (June and July) and dolphins year round.

If jet boats are more your style, then **Aqua Action** (☎ 4984 7433; Anchorage Marina; 30 min $85) is your port of call. To have a look at the bottom of the ocean, **Dive One Nelson Bay** (☎ 4984 2092; Sprowle St; per dive $55) decks quali-fied divers out with equipment and guides them into a coral wonderland. **Blue Water Sea Kayaking** (☎ 4981 5177; www.seakayaking.com.au; 40 Victoria Pde; 3-hr trip adult/child $45/25) can take you out on idyllic journeys.

If staying on dry sand appeals, **Sahara Trails** (☎ 4981 9077; Port Stephens Dr; 2-hr beach ride $70) can get you galloping down an endless beach into paradise.

If you mix an eccentric German guide, rolling sand dunes and a Bushmobile you get a frightfully entertaining time hurtling down dunes on boards and an equally entertaining bus ride with **Port Stephens Dune Adventure** (☎ 0500-550 066; James Patterson St; tour adult/child $35/25).

Sleeping

The place fills up rapidly and prices rise substantially when the sun is shining, so book ahead on weekends and during holidays.

Sahara Trails Homestead (☎ 4981 9077; Port Stephens Dr; cabins per person $25) This is a great deal, with fully self-contained cabins sur-rounded by neighbours of the neighing variety.

Samurai Beach Bungalows (☎ 4982 1921; cnr Frost Rd & Robert Connel Close; d $66) These offer a good backpacking experience out bush.

Melaleuca Surfside Cabins (☎ 4981 9422; 33 Eucalyptus Dr; dm $25; cabins $100) Clean rooms and picturesque surrounds.

Birubi Beach Caravan Park (☎ 4982 1263; 37 James Patterson St; camp sites/cabins $15/50) On the fringe of the dunes, this has undergone recent renovations.

Renting apartments is a good, affordable option for groups and families. **KD Winning Real Estate** (☎ 4981 1999; www.kdwinning.com.au; 19 Stockton St) is one agency with a number of listings.

Eating

Sandy Foot Café (☎ 4981 1555; Shoal Bay Rd; mains $18) Offers a relaxed eating experience with fresh, casual food. It's part of the Shoal Bay Resort and Spa.

Bubs (☎ 4984 3330; Teramby Rd, Nelson Bay; basket $5) Look here for high-quality fried seafood.

Holbert's Oyster Farm (☎ 4982 7234; Lot 52 Diemars Rd, Salamander Bay; 24 oysters $9.50) Why not grab a nice bottle of wine, some fresh oysters, find a nice spot and enjoy the finer things in life? Incredible value.

Rock Lobster (☎ 4981 1813; d'Albora Marina, Nelson Bay; mains $35) This place is perfect for families, with a beach for the little ones to play on while you enjoy the sunset and stunning views.

Port of Call (☎ 4984 4488; 61a Dowling St, Nelson Bay; mains $24) Take in great views here as you enjoy fresh local produce and a Mod Oz menu that does justice to the term.

Getting There & Around

Port Stephens is an area, not a town, so when driving follow the signs for Nelson Bay.

Port Stephens Coaches (☎ 4982 2940; www.ps coaches.com.au) runs daily from all towns of Port Stephens to Sydney ($31), and services the coast to Newcastle ($10.40).

Port Stephens Ferry Service (☎ 4981 3798) operates between Nelson Bay and Tea Gardens at 8.30am and 3.30pm daily (adult/child $15/8).

If you decide to drive to Tea Gardens, it'll be a long trip as you'll need to double back to Raymond Terrace.

It's worth hiring a bike to get around, as there is a good network of bike paths in the area. **Nelson Bay Sports** (☎ 4981 2333), opposite the tourist office, has a good selection, plus in-line skates, if they're your preferred mode of transport.

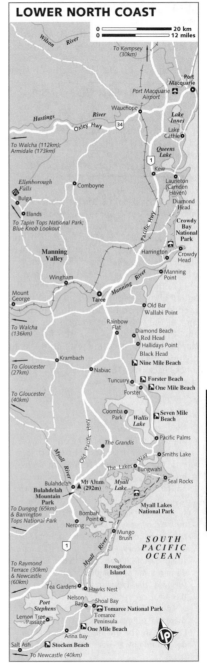

LOWER NORTH COAST

NORTH COAST

BULAHDELAH & AROUND

☎ 02 / pop 1160

Bulahdelah, perched on the **Myall River**, is of interest to the traveller for its surroundings – its contents leave a lot to be desired. You exit the Pacific Hwy here for **Myall Lake** and just north of town for a scenic drive along **The Lakes Way**, which leaves the highway at Bulahdelah and rejoins it about 20km south of Taree. Along its way, it nears the coastal haven of **Seal Rocks** (see p155) and runs through the twin towns of **Forster-Tuncurry** (see p155).

The **visitors centre** (☎ 4997 4981; cnr Pacific Hwy & Crawford St; ☒ 10am-4pm) is just opposite the road to Myall Lake.

The **National Parks & Wildlife Service** office (NPWS; ☎ 6591 0300; www.nationalparks.nsw.gov.au; The Ruins Camping Ground, Booti Booti National Park, The Lakes Way, Pacific Palms; ☒ 8.30am-4pm, Mon-Fri) is on the way to Forster. You can find out there about visiting the many local national parks, as well as nature and conservation.

Looming over the town is **Mt Alum**, the largest aboveground deposit of alum (a salt used in dyeing, medicine and manufacturing) in the world. The mining has ceased and the mountain is now the **Bulahdelah Mountain Park**, with some walking tracks to historic sites. The entrance is a couple of blocks back from the highway, on the same street as the police station.

THE GRANDEST TREE

The mists that circle Mt Alum drift through the surrounding area, and the combination of warmth and moisture is ideal for lush forests. The tallest tree in New South Wales, the Grandis, towers over dense rainforest not far from Bulahdelah. This 400-year-old flooded gum, *Eucalyptus grandis*, is an awesome sight. On a humid, misty day, with the strange calls of whipbirds echoing off palm trees and tall timber, the atmosphere is almost primeval. With its immensely tall, straight trunk it's amazing that the Grandis and some of its slightly shorter cousins survived the logging that continues in this area.

To get here, take The Lakes Way and then the signposted turn-off 12km from Bulahdelah. The Grandis is 6km further on, down a bumpy all-weather road.

Sleeping

Luxury Houseboat Hire (☎ 4997 4380; www.luxuryhouseboat.com.au; Myall Marina; 5 nights incl petrol $1000) To experience the lakes in unforgettable style, stop by here.

Bulahdelah Motor Lodge (☎ 4997 4520; Pacific Hwy; s/d $60/70) Of a number of motels along the Pacific Hwy, this is a decent, relaxing place to stay.

Plough Inn Hotel (☎ 4997 4285; 77 Stroud St; s/d $30/45) A good option if you're backpacking.

If you are planning on camping, it would be better to kick on to Seal Rocks or the Myall Lakes National Park.

Getting There & Away

McCafferty's/Greyhound (☎ 13 20 30) runs daily services to Forster ($24), Port Macquarie ($37), Sydney ($52) and Brisbane ($64).

Premier Motor Service (☎ 13 34 10) does the Melbourne to Cairns east-coast run on a daily basis, stopping frequently.

Busways (☎ 4997 4788, 1800 043 163) runs down to Newcastle ($19) and up to Forster ($30).

Countrylink (☎ 13 22 32) can bus you down to Newcastle, then onto a train to Sydney ($41.80). To go north you have to backtrack to Broadmeadow (Newcastle) and then jump on a northbound train or bus.

MYALL LAKES NATIONAL PARK

Home to the largest natural freshwater (albeit brackish) system in NSW, the lakes are adored by tourists and locals. Water sports are popular, with canoes, sailboards and runabouts available at **Bombah Point**. The southern end of the park has some amazing rainforest walks, while the top end around **Seal Rocks** has great surf and a number of whales. The **Great Lakes Information Centre** (☎ 02-4997 0111; Little St, Forster) looks after the park.

Around Bombah Point, **Myall Shores** (☎ 02-4997 4495; Bombah Point; camp sites/dm/cabins $13/42/63) is a commercial camping ground that has a restaurant, shop and facilities. There are a number of **NPWS camp sites** around and they hold great positions, although restrictions apply to fires and facilities are not as appealing.

In the south, there are motels and caravan parks in **Tea Gardens** and **Hawks Nest**. **Hawk's Nest Beach Caravan Park** (☎ 02-4997 0239; camp sites/cabins $20/42) is conveniently positioned near a good surf beach.

There is road access to the park from Tea Gardens via Bulahdelah on the Pacific Hwy. It means driving from Tea Gardens to Bulahdelah via the **Bombah Point Ferry** (per car $3, every 30 minutes, 8am to 6pm).

There is a track from Bombah Point to Seal Rocks, but it's testing, even with a 4WD, and the park rangers are rather unsympathetic to over-ambitious drivers.

SEAL ROCKS

The news seems to be spreading about this little slice of heaven and it is not surprising. Surrounded by national parks and the ocean – and boasting the odd whale – the undeveloped town has great surf and good camping grounds. Its **historic lighthouse** is well worth the walk to witness the rocks that have claimed many ships over the last 150 years. It is the second–most easterly point on the Australian mainland after Byron Bay.

The town is 11km down a partly sealed road from The Lakes Way, and it is advisable to stock up on food and necessities before embarking on your trip.

The **Seal Rocks Camping Reserve** (☎ 02-4997 6164; Seal Rocks Rd; camp sites/cabins $16/55) is just down the hill from the general store and fronts onto Seal Rocks, a nice right-hand break for the surf-minded.

Turn right at the general store for **Treachery Camp** (☎ 02-4997 6138; 166 Thomas Rd; camp sites/cabins $7.50/72), which has unmarked camp sites and is now attracting the Oz Experience buses, hence a number of backpackers and a vibe to match.

FORSTER-TUNCURRY

☎ 02 / pop 18,000

Perched on either side of Wallis Lake, Forster and Tuncurry have developed into busy twin towns aimed at Aussie family holiday-makers. Summer sees the lakes come alive with water sports, screaming kiddies and sunburnt adults. Visually, it's well on its way to becoming just another sky-rise nightmare, but that doesn't appear to be deterring anyone.

Orientation & Information

Forster (*fos*-ter), on the southern side of the entrance, is the big brother of the pair with the majority of shops, attractions and beaches. The Lakes Way leads into town from the south, first becoming MacIntosh St then turning sharply left into Head St, which runs east to a large roundabout that marks the town centre. The helpful **visitors centre** (☎ 6554 8799; Little St), just beside the lake, comes complete with knowledgeable staff.

Tuncurry, over the long bridge, has more of the same, but in smaller proportions.

Sights & Activities

Whether it's dolphin cruises, water slides or learning to surf, you won't get bored in this activity haven.

Dolphin Watch (☎ 6554 7478; Fisherman's Wharf; cruise adult/child $30/20, swim with dolphins $50) allows you the opportunity of jumping in the water with these precious mammals.

Amaroo Cruises (☎ 0419-333 445; lakeside, opposite post office; 2-hr cruise $32) has the latest in catamaran cruisers and runs a professional regime that includes shark and sea-turtle spotting.

Water-skiing is great on the calm lake with **Summer Ski Rides** (☎ 6554 3454; Aquatic Rd; all equipment per hr $90) taking you the distance. **No 1 Boatshed** (☎ 6554 7733; 1 Little St, Forster; canoe per 30 min $7) has many water activities.

Beaches are of the highest quality in this area, with **Nine Mile Beach** the pick of surrounding surf beaches, **Forster Beach** a good family option with its swimming **pools**, and **One Mile Beach** also popular.

If you want to indulge in museums, **Tobwabba Art** (☎ 6554 5755; 10 Breckenridge St; admission free; ⏰ 10am-4.30pm Mon-Fri) is home to some fascinating pieces. For local history and a look at a classroom of yesteryear, visit the **Great Lakes Historical Museum** (☎ 6554 3012; Capel St; adult/child $2/50c; ⏰ 10am-2pm Wed, 1-4pm Sun).

Kids love a good adventure park and Forster-Tuncurry has two, the **Big Buzz Fun Park** (☎ 6553 6000; The Lakes Way; 1/3hr $8/12; ⏰ 10am-4pm Sat & Sun) is big on water slides, while **Ton O Fun** (☎ 6554 3090; Ton O Fun Rd, adult/child $30/19; ⏰ 10am-4pm Sat & Sun) has quad bikes and water slides.

Festivals & Events

On the second Sunday of each month, the bridge end of Head St buzzes with **market** activity. The **Oyster Festival** is an annual celebration of the local delicacy – early October.

Sleeping & Eating

Motels are everywhere, cheap and basic in Tuncurry, and rising in price and quality in Forster. Campers are blessed with a number of choices. Advance bookings are essential if you are visiting around school holidays. Check with the visitors centre about further accommodation.

Dolphin Lodge (☎ 6555 8155; 43 Head St; s/d $38/54) In a central location, this gets a nice fresh sea breeze.

Stacey's Lakeside Retreat (☎ 6557 6433; 162 Little St; per cabin $75) Fully self-contained units face Wallis Lake. Great for families, with nice open living areas.

Fiesta Motor Inn (☎ 6554 6177; 23-25 Head St, Forster; s/d $55/65; ☒ ☲) This place has spacious rooms.

Forster Palms Motel (☎ 6555 6255; 60 Macintosh St, Forster; per room $78; ☒ ☲) Four stars – a comfortable option, with saltwater pool. It's close to bars, shops and beaches.

Tuncurry Beach Caravan Park (☎ 6554 6440; Beach St; camp sites/cabins $20/55) One of the best camping options, this has ocean and lake frontage, and there's great fishing in the lake.

Sandbar & Bushland Caravan Park (☎ 6554 4095; 3434 The Lakes Way; camp sites/cabins $20/70) Superb facilities and good position, a little south of the town.

For renting, there are options aplenty with **Andrews & Partners** (☎ 6554 5011; www.andrews fn.com.au; 25 Manning St) and **Forster Tuncurry Property Management** (☎ 6555 2000; www.forster property.com.au; 65-67 Wharf St).

If you're after a bite to eat:

Danny's Family Buffet (☎ 6554 6155; Strand St; mains $16; ☽ dinner) Capturing the vibe of the town, 'Danny' provides affordable quality and big servings.

Forster Sunset Grill (☎ 6555 2660; 6 Head St; mains $26; ☽ dinner Tue-Sat) A versatile and tasty menu in a relaxing environment.

Also recommended:

Forster Bowling Club (☎ 6554 6155; Strand St; lunch $5) You'll get a good cheap lunch overlooking the lake here.

Paradise Marina (☎ 6554 7017; 51 Little St; mains $10; ☽ breakfast & lunch) Another great lunch option.

Getting There & Away

The visitors centre (see p155) acts as a booking agent.

Busways (☎ 4997 4788, 1800 043 163) Runs down to Bulahdelah ($30), Newcastle ($36) and Sydney ($47).

Countrylink (☎ 13 22 32) Runs buses out of Tuncurry south to Sydney ($54). To go north you have to double back to Broadmeadow (Newcastle) ($27).

Forster Bus Service (☎ 6554 6431) Has services around the twin towns and south to Pacific Palms.

Premier Motor Service (☎ 13 34 10) Stops daily at Taree on the north and south east-coast runs.

Forster-Tuncurry is off the Pacific Hwy (1) along The Lakes Way, a glorious drive up from Bulahdelah.

THE MANNING VALLEY

This valley extends west from the Manning River delta (between Old Bar and Harrington) through farmland to Taree and Wingham, then north through forests to the plateau containing Bulga and Comboyne. There are better coastal options to the north and south, but the rainforests and national parks are rewarding to investigate.

Taree

☎ 02 / pop 16,660

Although it's the largest town in the Manning Valley, Taree offers little to the visitor and with the **Big Oyster**, its coveted landmark, retired to car-sales duties, the town should be used as little more than a reference point.

The **visitors centre** (☎ 6552 1900; www.manning valley.info; Manning River Dr), on the north side of town, is overflowing with info on the nearby attractions.

Motels are out in force along the Old Pacific Hwy and you're sure to pick up a cheap deal during the week.

Wingham

☎ 02 / pop 4670

This is the oldest town in the area and its English influence is reflected in a large, central green square that now features the **Log**

DETOUR: WINGHAM TO COMBOYNE

If you want to taste the dense, tropical flavour of the surrounding national parks, drive through Wingham and up to **Tapin Tops National Park**, stopping at Dingo Tops rest area. Then continue along the plateau to **Blue Knob Lookout** and follow the road around to the 160m-high **Ellenborough Falls**. It will take you a couple of hours and you can continue through Comboyne and rejoin the Pacific Hwy at Wauchope.

(a 16-metre, 19-tonne log representing the town's timber-felling origins) and a replica **Vampire fighter jet** commemorating the 50th anniversary of the RAAF.

Down by the riverside lies **Wingham Brush**, a subtropical floodplain rainforest where you can take to the boardwalk and see flying foxes.

THE COASTAL WAY

The first section consists of **Black Head**, **Red Head** and **Diamond Beach**. There are some decent surf beaches.

The next offering comes at **Old Bar**, which has a long surf beach and a handy accommodation option in **Old Bar Beachfront Holiday Park** (☎ 02-6553 7274; Old Bar; camp sites/cabins $15/50). Just south of Old Bar is **Walabi Point**, where there's a lagoon for swimming. **Manning Point**, a hamlet serving the oyster farms along the river, is 12km up the coast.

Just across the river – but a hefty drive because there is no bridge shortcut – is **Harrington**, with another lagoon and respectable surf beaches nearby.

Crowdy Head is the pick of the bunch, with glorious sweeping views from the 1878 lighthouse out to sea and overlooking the Crowdy Head National Park.

You can take the unsealed but well-maintained road to **Diamond Head** through the **rainforest** and, if you desire, pitch a tent at one of the two camp sites ($6; honesty system), but bring your own water.

Coming out at the end of the park is **Camden Haven**, which constitutes Laurieton, North Haven and Dunbogan villages – quaint, plain little towns typical of these parts – clustering around the wide sea entrance of **Queens Lake**.

Your final march up the coastline will take you past the biggest town, **Lake Cathie** (*cat*-eye), on a lake with safe beaches ideal for youngsters. The road then enters the sprawling outer suburbs of Port Macquarie.

PORT MACQUARIE

☎ 02 / pop 37,980

Port, as it's affectionately known, boasts the entrance to the subtropical coast. Its palm tree-lined city centre, rolling parklands and beach coves make it the most up-and-coming destination in NSW. Only 10km off the Pacific Hwy, it has escaped a heavy bombardment from backpackers, who only radar in on the town to see the immoderately famous koala population (see this page).

Port is now starting to enjoy the attention that was bound to happen, ever since its spectacular beauty was first discovered.

History

Port Macquarie was the third town to be established on the Australian mainland following Oxley's 1818 visit. Named in honour of Governor Lachlan Macquarie, it was founded in 1821 as a penal colony for those audacious convicts who found life in the harbour city too easy.

Orientation & Information

The city centre corners on the mouth of Hastings River. A string of magnificent beaches rolls south and a spread of suburbs follows. The **visitors centre** (☎ 6581 8000, 1800 303 155; www.portmacquarieinfo.com.au; Clarence St) will rapidly sort out your queries. There is also a **NPWS office** (☎ 6584 2203; 152 Horton St).

You'll find Internet access at **Port Surf Hub** (☎ 6584 4744; 57 Clarence St; per hr $6).

Sights

Convict labour has produced some striking architecture throughout the town. **St Thomas' Church**, circa 1828, (currently being restored) is on top of the hill; and down in town the 1869 **old courthouse** (☎ 6584 1818; www.portmacquarieinfo.com.au/historiccourthouse; cnr Clarence & Hay Sts; adult/child $2/50c; ⊙ 10am-4pm Mon-Sat) and 1835 **garrison** (cnr Clarence & Hay Sts) are time warriors. Part of the **Port Macquarie Historical Society Museum** (☎ 6583 1108; 22 Clarence St; adult/child $5/2; ⊙ 9.30am-4.30pm Mon-Sat, from 1.30pm Sun) dates back to 1836 and is worth a look just for the Victorian-era frocks. Up on the point, the old pilot's cottage (1882) houses the **Maritime Museum** (☎ 6584 1818; 6 William St; adult/child $2/1; 11am-3pm Mon-Sat).

For those looking for answers beyond the horizon of the Pacific Ocean, sneak a peek through the telescope at the **observatory** (☎ 6583 1933; near Town Beach; admission $5; ⊙ nights Wed & Sun).

WILDLIFE

Port Macquarie shares its beautiful gum trees with one of Australia's icons, the koala. Unfortunately, people's housing needs have seen the little fellas' land rights diminish and with that, their own homes.

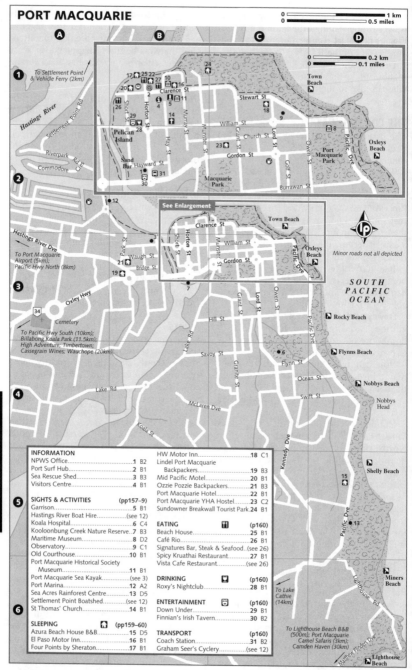

PORT MACQUARIE

NORTH COAST

So as they go searching for their lost oasis, dogs and cars often bring them undone. It's then that they end up at the **Koala Hospital** (☎ 6584 1522; www.midcoast.com.au/~koalahos; Lord St; admission by donation; ☒ feeding time 8am & 3pm). Well-wishers can give these little battlers a cheer-up (no flash photography) and wish them a speedy recovery.

If hand-feeding fighting-fit koalas, kangaroos and the odd emu appeals, **Billabong Koala Park** (☎ 6585 1060; 61 Billabong Dr; adult/child $9.50/6; ☒ 9am-5pm) is a wonderful family experience. Patting times are at 10.30am, 1.30pm and 3.30pm.

NATURE RESERVES

The **Kooloonbung Creek Nature Reserve** (admission free), just south of the town centre, is great for bird-watching. It's also worth finding the **cemetery** (Gordon St), right opposite the end of Horton St, which is testimony to the region's early origins.

For an appreciation of what this landscape has had on offer from times long gone, **Sea Acres Rainforest Centre** (☎ 6582 3355; Pacific Dr; adult/child $10/6; ☒ 9am-4.30pm) is a 70-hectare flora and fauna reserve with a 1.3km elevated wheelchair-friendly boardwalk.

Activities

Anything you can do in water, you can do in Port Macquarie – from surfing, swimming or just wading on the beaches to jet-skiing, open-water canoeing and dolphin-watching.

To hire a boat or canoe, drop by **Port Marina** and grab your fibreglass of choice from **Hastings River Boat Hire** (☎ 6583 8811; Park St, Port Marina; per hour $10). For a guided canoe trip into the upper reaches of the Hastings River, **Port Macquarie Sea Kayak** (☎ 6584 1039; Sea Rescue Shed, Buller St; 2-hr trip $30).

Aspiring divers can complete their PADI certificate with **Rick's Dive School** (☎ 0422-063 528; PADI course $170), the cheapest on the coast, and dive with Port Jackson sharks and turtles at Delicate Nobby.

If you want to swap the water for the desert, camel rides are available south of the town with **Port Macquarie Camel Safaris** (☎ 6583 7650; Matthew Flinders Dr; 30 min $20).

For dramatic landscapes and a good injection of adrenaline into the body, **High Adventure** (☎ 1800 063 648; www.highadventure .au; tandem flight $200) delivers the shot in the form of hang-gliding.

Timbertown (☎ 6585 2322; Oxley Hwy, Wauchope) is a heritage theme park that is well suited to families, with old dust-swept streets, intimate shops and the old (working) steam train all adding to its yesteryear charm. While admission is free, you pay for rides.

Of the four wineries in the region, **Cassegrain Wines** (☎ 6583 7777; 764 Fernbank Creek Rd; ☒ 10am-4pm), 20km out of town, is the closest. Its reputation is growing as the wine is starting to age for the better. It hosts concerts as well as daily cellar door tastings and meals at its restaurant.

Tours

Port Macquarie Cruise Adventures (☎ 6583 8483, 1300 555 890; www.cruiseadventures.com.au; Short St, Town Wharf; 3½ hrs from $20) A number of dolphin cruises will take you to oyster farms, navigate canals and show you the rich timber history that surrounds the town.
Port Venture (☎ 6583 3058; 74 Clarence St; 2-hr cruise $20) For a view of the city from the water.

Sleeping

Ongoing development equates to an abundance of options; the visitors centre has the inside word. Hostels are of consistent quality and are meeting the growing market demand in style. If you have the luxury of planning ahead, you can rent a beautiful apartment in a prime location at a reasonable rate. Get in touch with **Laing & Simmons** (☎ 6583 7733; www.portrealestate.net; 62 Clarence St).

BUDGET

Port Macquarie Hotel (☎ 6580 7888; Clarence St; s/d $35/55) This is the only viable hotel – it's high on quality and perfectly situated near the river.

Ozzie Pozzie Backpackers (☎ 6583 8133; 36 Waugh St; dm/d $20/48) Not only immaculately kept, this also offers free bike and bodyboard hire, as well as bright rooms.

Lindel Port Macquarie Backpackers (☎ 6583 1792, 1800 688 882; cnr Oxley Hwy & Hastings River Dr; dm/d $20/44) Easily identified by the globe out the front, this heritage-listed house has pressed-tin walls, comfy bunks and a friendly atmosphere to bring journeymen together.

Port Macquarie YHA Hostel (☎ 6583 5512; 40 Church St; dm/d $23/65) A neat, compact hostel with fresh owners close to Town Beach.

For campers, **Sundowner Breakwall Tourist Park** (☎ 6583 2755; 1 Munster St; camp sites/cabins $20/70), with brilliant facilities and a roomy feel, is right by the river mouth. Other parks are located by the river and Flynns Beach.

MID-RANGE

This is motel country and you get all makes and models, the cheapest furthest from the beaches along Hastings River Drive and the pricier lining the strip of sand.

HW Escape (☎ 6583 1200; www.hwescape.com.au; 1 Stuart St; per room $150; 🖳 🖳) Recently renovated on the original site of the Port Macquarie Gaol, it has great views (without the iron bars) and is a stone's throw from the water.

Azura Beach B&B (☎ 6582 2700; www.azura.com .au; 109 Pacific Dr; s/d from $100/115) Offers four-star modern luxury overlooking Shelly Beach.

Lighthouse Beach B&B (☎ 6582 5149; 91 Matthew Flinders Dr; s/d $80/90) You can wake up practically on the beach. The particular emphasis here is on relaxation.

El Paso Motor Inn (☎ 6583 1944; 29 Clarence St; s/d $105/119; 🖳) A classic 1960s motel, centrally positioned.

Mid Pacific Motel (☎ 6583 2166; cnr Clarence & Short Sts; r $106; 🖳) The modern version, a high-rise that gives you great views and clean rooms.

TOP END

Four Points by Sheraton (☎ 1800 074 545; 2 Hay St; per r $149; 🖳 🖳) A new addition for those who want to pamper themselves – it will not disappoint.

Eating

Beach House (☎ 6584 5692; Horton St; mains $9-13), At the Royal Hotel, sit in beautiful surrounds with a big plate of bacon and eggs, right on the waterfront. Stay there for beer and a burger, oysters and wine or a gourmet pizza.

Café Rio (☎ 6583 3933; 74 Clarence St; mains $20) Set in the café culture that Port Macquarie nurtures, it's ideal for an espresso or a long lunch.

Signatures Bar Steak & Seafood (☎ 6584 6144; 72 Clarence St; mains $17-25; 🕑 lunch till late) Next door to Rio, this is an all-day affair that has a beachy, holiday feel about it, with good food and a busy, slick atmosphere.

Spicy Kruathai Restaurant (☎ 6583 9043; cnr Clarence & Hay Sts; mains $10-18; 🕑 dinner) Has a flamboyant way with seafood from a Thai menu that delivers, in both value and substance.

Vista Café Restaurant (☎ 6584 1422; Level 1, 74 Clarence St; mains $20) Get involved in the scene – it's a little bit hip with a lot of flavour.

Drinking & Entertainment

Like the sleeping options on offer in Port Macquarie, choices are scarce but those that are available are of good quality.

Port Macquarie Hotel (☎ 6583 1011; cnr Horton & Clarence Sts) Has live bands on weekends and a trivia night on Sunday.

Finnian's Irish Tavern (☎ 6583 4646; 97 Gordon St; mains $20) An Irish pub with delicious food that receives a lot of acclaim.

These two spots are open Wednesday to Saturday nights:

Down Under (☎ 6583 4018; cnr William & Short Sts) This is a club that's good to get down to.

Roxy's Nightclub (☎ 6583 5466; Galleria Bldg, William St; admission $5) Draws a slightly younger crowd.

Ritz Twin Cinemas (☎ 6583 8400; cnr Clarence & Horton Sts; admission $9) shows mainstream releases. Tickets are cheaper on Wednesday, Friday and Sunday.

Getting There & Around

QantasLink flies to Sydney ($152, one hour) five times a day.

McCafferty's/Greyhound (☎ 13 20 30) runs south to Sydney ($52) and north to Coffs Harbour ($36) and Byron Bay ($57). **Keans** (☎ 1800 625 587) travels across to Tamworth ($71) and up to Kempsey ($11), Nambucca Heads ($19) and Coffs Harbour ($26) three times a week. **Premier Motor Service** (☎ 13 34 10) stops daily at the Transit Centre on Hayway St on its east-coast runs.

Driving, the next major town on the Pacific Hwy is Kempsey, 50km north. The Oxley Hwy runs west through Wauchope and eventually reaches the New England tableland near Walcha. It makes for a spectacular drive.

The Settlement Point **ferry** ($3 per car, passengers free) operates 24 hours. A 10-minute trip on a flat punt gives you access to the north beach and Pilots Beach. If you are in a 4WD, you can drive to Point Plomer and on over rough roads to Crescent Head.

Renting a car, **Hertz** (☎ 6583 6599; 102 Gordon St; per day $75) is one of the big four in town. Try two wheels at **Graham Seer's Cyclery** (☎ 6583 2333; Port Marina; per day $22).

MID-NORTH COAST

Hideously exciting Coffs Harbour has an abundance of cheap, raw-adventure activities. This section of the coast is not without its natural wonders, with spectacular beaches and rainforests. The best beach can be found at South West Rocks while Dorrigo National Park is both accessible and wonderful. At its foot Bellingen is simply irresistible with street markets, a hippy feel and great food. Like it loud and heavy, or soft and chilled out, this stretch of coast delivers in spades.

KEMPSEY

☎ 02 / pop 8460

Kempsey, a large rural town serving the farms of the Macleay Valley, is a gateway of sorts to the western rainforests and the eastern coastal towns. From Kempsey comes a couple of facts that will hold you in good stead at any pub trivia competition.

The town is the home of the **Akubra hat** – if you want to know more, there's a video at the excellent **visitors centre** (☎ 6563 1555, 1800 642 480; Pacific Hwy) on the south side of town.

The late Slim Dusty was born here and, presumably, got his inspiration for songs like 'Duncan' from this unassuming town. At the time of writing, a $12 million museum focusing on the country singer had just been approved by government. The **Slim Dusty Heritage Centre** (Old Kempsey Showgrounds; ☎ 6562 6533; www.slimdustycentre.com.au) should be partly open by late 2004.

Sleeping

Ned's Bed Horse-O-Tel (☎ 6565 0085; www.nedsbed .com; 123 Kawana Lane; people/horses/dogs $88/17/11; ⚡) For those travelling with animals, this has self-contained units surrounded by long faces (horses).

Park Drive Motel (☎ 6562 1361; 161 Pacific Hwy; s/d $55/61) Well located and maintained.

Sundowner Caravan Park (☎ 6562 1361; 161 Pacific Hwy; camp sites $17) Has the best and quietest position of the five caravan parks.

Getting There & Away

McCafferty's/Greyhound (☎ 13 20 30) goes daily to Coffs Harbour ($34) and Sydney ($55).

Keans (☎ 1800 625 587) runs down to Port Macquarie ($10.50) and up to Coffs Harbour ($23) three times a week. **Premier Motor**

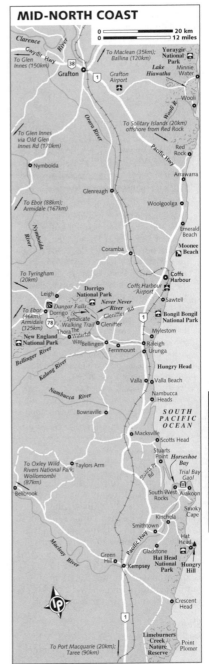

MID-NORTH COAST

Service (☎ 13 34 10) stops at the Shell service station on its daily east-coast runs.

Countrylink (☎ 13 22 32) has daily services to Sydney ($75) and north to Coffs Harbour ($17), Grafton ($32), Byron Bay ($63) and Tweed Heads ($75).

See the following Crescent Head and South West Rocks sections for local bus services.

By car, there's an interesting and largely unsealed route running west to Wollomombi (on the Dorrigo to Armidale road); head northwest to Bellbrook.

THE AUTHOR'S CHOICE Rick Starey

Australians love meat pies, and the quest for the best in the land can take you far and wide. More than likely you will end up just north of Kempsey at Frederickton, where **Fredo Pies** (☎ 02-6566 8226, 75 Macleay St, Frederickton) has a range that is as honest as the day is long. From its celebrated crocodile and kangaroo pies to the classic meat pie, it has turned pie-making into an art that makes this an essential stop on any trip up the coast. Star sighting is a possibility – Russell Crowe has introduced his Hollywood mates to an Australian institution on more than one occasion. For the historically minded, the pie has been around since the ancient Egyptians in 2000BC. During the decline of Egypt it moved to Greece, then west into Italy, France, the UK and finally Frederickton over the succeeding thousands of years.

CRESCENT HEAD
☎ 02 / pop 1190

In surfing circles, this is where the Malibu surfboard gained prominence in Australia during the '60s. Now that generation is coming back with their families to continue the surfing legacy this town cherishes. It is wonderful to watch the longboard riders surf the epic waves of **Little Nobby's Junction** when the swell's up. Crescent Head itself is an intimate town that caters mainly for family getaways and the odd backpacker who has ventured off the beaten track.

Sleeping
Mediterranean Motel (☎ 6566 0303; 35 Pacific St; s/d $70/80; 🅿 🖥) This is the best motel in town. If you are travelling in fours, it also

has fully contained shacks out the back ($90), a cheap option. The food here (Mediterranean-influenced, of course) is great (meals $20).

If it's all about location, **Crescent Head Holiday Park** (☎ 6566 0261; Pacific St; camp sites/cabins $21.50/58), at the mouth of the river, wins hands-down.

If you're here a few nights, renting a holiday apartment is both cheap and private. There are two estate agents in town.

Getting There & Away
The turn-off to Crescent Head is near the visitors centre in Kempsey. **Busways** (☎ 1300 555 611; www.busways.com.au) runs to and from Kempsey (Belgrave St) daily.

HAT HEAD NATIONAL PARK
This coastal park of 6500 hectares runs north from near Hat Head to **Smoky Cape** (south of Arakoon), protecting scrubland, swamps and some excellent beaches backed by significant dune systems. Birdlife is prolific on the wetlands. Rising up from the generally flat landscape is Hungry Hill, near Hat Head, and sloping Hat Head itself, where there's a walking track.

Surrounded by the national park, the village of **Hat Head** is much smaller and quieter than Crescent Head. **Hat Head Holiday Park** (☎ 02-6567 7501; camp sites/cabins $16/60) is close to a beautiful sheltered bay. You can camp at Hungry Head, 5km south of Hat Head. There are pit toilets and no showers, and you'll need to take your own water.

The park is accessible from the hamlet of Kinchela, on the road between Kempsey and South West Rocks. It's possible to get a lift on a school bus from Kempsey to Hat Head; phone Hat Head Holiday Park for details.

SOUTH WEST ROCKS
☎ 02 / pop 4120

This town must be Byron Bay's long-lost brother – its spectacular beach is one of the few places on the east coast where you can watch the sunset over the water. But it has learnt from Byron's rapid development and put strict expansion limitations in place – it is following an ecologically driven approach to progress.

The area is great for divers, especially **Fish Rock Cave**, south of Smoky Cape. Two outfits organise expeditions: **South West Rocks**

LOCAL LAND RIGHTS

Indigenous Australians (Aborigines) have walked, hunted and worked on Australian land for thousands of years. However, the issue of Aboriginal land rights wasn't raised in the courts until a gardener from James Cook University in Townsville by the name of Eddie Koiki Mabo turned his attention to the matter. Outraged by the fact that the Crown, rather than his family, had rights to his home on Murray Island, Eddie Mabo started court proceedings that were to span almost 10 years, and result in one of the most celebrated court decisions in Australian history. (For proof of this, watch the Australian classic film *The Castle*.) Handed down by a 6:1 majority of the High Court in 1992 – six months after Eddie Mabo died – *Mabo No 2* overrode the doctrine of *terra nullius* (which maintained that Australian land was owned by no-one) and recognised that rights to native title existed under Australian law.

In 1996, Crescent Head became the first town on mainland Australia to experience the effects of the Mabo decision, with the government recognising that the Dunghutti people had native-title rights on 12.4 hectares of land. The land in question has been turned into a residential subdivision (the Dunghutti people were reasonably compensated), so, while it may be hard to spot this historic piece of land on a drive through the town, it is strong in essence.

Dive Centre (☎ 6566 6474; 5/98 Gregory St; one dive $90) and **Fish Rock Dive Centre** (☎ 6566 6614; www .fishrock.com.au; 328-332 Gregory St; one dive $90).

Sleeping & Eating

Rock Pool Motor Inn (☎ 1800 180 133; www.rock poolmotorinn.com.au; 45 Mcintyre St; s/d $87/99; ✖ ☀) This has a fresh, new feel to it and an inviting restaurant.

Horseshoe Bay Beach Park (☎ 6566 6370; Livingstone St; camp sites/cabins $24/70) Superb position right in town and right on the sheltered Town Beach. It's usually booked out over the summer holidays.

Trial Bay Tourist Park (☎ 6566 6142; www.trial bay.com.au; 161-171 Phillip Dr; camp sites/cabins $15/75) This well-run place has a great family feel and good activities for the youngsters. The on-site **takeaway** makes 'dirty burgers' (with chips and gravy in the bun) and deep-fried Mars Bars.

South West Rocks Seafood (☎ 6566 7703; Livingstone St; basket $6) Head here for fantastic fish and chips.

Also recommended:

Geppys (☎ 6566 6169; cnr Livingstone & Memorial Sts; mains $15-28; ☾ dinner only) Specialises in local seafood and game.

Paragon Pizza (☎ 6566 7711; Paragon Ave; pizzas from $10.50) Doesn't try to hide the fact it makes a pizza with prawns, bacon, banana, avocado and pineapple.

Getting There & Away

Cavanaghs (☎ 6562 7800) has two runs daily to and from Kempsey, leaving from the town bus stop at Horse Shoe Bay (8.15am and noon).

TRIAL BAY & ARAKOON STATE RECREATION AREA

Imposing and profoundly historic, Trial Bay occupies the west headland of the town and the **Trial Bay Gaol** (admission $3) dominates the area. It was used as a gaol in the late 19th century and housed German internees during WWI. It's now a museum that exemplifies how hard the convicts lived in these idyllic surrounds.

The **Arakoon State Recreation Area** is behind the gaol and the camp sites are basic but picturesque. **Trial Bay Water Sports** (☎ 0429-041 312; Trial Bay Beach; surf-ski/sailboard/catamaran per hr $8/25/35) operates on the beach and you can try your hand at catamarans, surf-skis and ocean kayaks. Great food is on offer at the **Kiosk** (☎ 02-6566 7100; Trial Bay; mains $16) and rewards a pleasant walk up from South West Rocks along the beach: look out for the **love shack**, formerly a fisherman's abode, about halfway between South West Rocks and Trial Bay.

NAMBUCCA HEADS

☎ 02 / pop 6150

Plain and quiet, but in a good way, is Nambucca Heads (nam-*buk*-a). It is forever undergoing facelifts and re-works but, curiously, nothing seems to change. Position is the key with this town, which is neatly set overlooking the Nambucca River. The calming views prove a hit with holidaymakers.

The Nambucca Valley (which means 'many bends') was occupied solely by the Gumbainggir people until European timber cutters arrived in the 1840s. There are still strong Aboriginal communities in Nambucca Heads and up the valley in Bowraville.

Orientation & Information

The town is just off the Pacific Hwy. Riverside Drive runs alongside the estuary of the Nambucca River, then climbs a steep hill to Bowra St, the main shopping street. A right turn onto Ridge St at the top of the hill leads though the old part of town to the beaches.

The **visitors centre** (☎ 6568 6954; cnr Riverside Dr & Pacific Hwy) doubles as the main bus terminal.

Sights & Activities

The only patrolled beach in town is **Main Beach**; **Beilby's** and **Shelly beaches** are just to the

south, closer to the river mouth – where the best surf is – which can be reached by going past the Captain Cook Lookout.

For boating enthusiasts, **Beachcomber Marine** (☎ 6568 6432; Riverside Dr; 1st hr $25, every hr thereafter $11) will hire you the appropriate vessel in which to attack the river or open sea.

The **V-Wall** presents a good opportunity to soak in the atmosphere and look at some interesting art, as the hundreds of massive rocks that make up the wall have been painted by locals and visitors alike – why not leave your mark with some outrageous colours? For art of a similar genre, the **Mosaic Wall** in the town centre was created by a local artist using materials such as tiles and broken crockery.

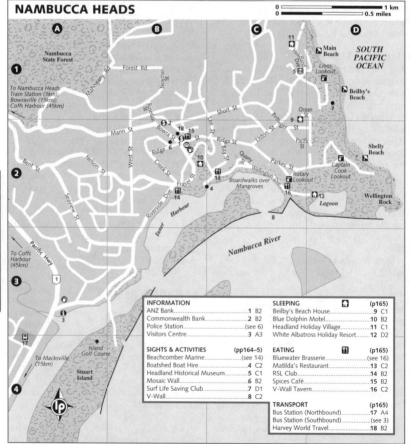

NAMBUCCA HEADS

INFORMATION		SLEEPING 🏠	(p165)
ANZ Bank.....................................**1** B2		Beilby's Beach House.....................**9** C1
Commonwealth Bank.....................**2** B2		Blue Dolphin Motel.....................**10** B2
Police Station.....................(see 6)		Headland Holiday Village.............**11** C1
Visitors Centre.....................**3** A3		White Albatross Holiday Resort.......**12** D2

SIGHTS & ACTIVITIES	(pp164–5)	EATING 🍴	(p165)
Beachcomber Marine.....................(see 14)		Bluewater Brasserie.....................(see 16)
Boatshed Boat Hire.....................**4** C2		Matilda's Restaurant.....................**13** C2
Headland Historical Museum.........**5** C1		RSL Club.....................**14** B2
Mosaic Wall.....................**6** B2		Spices Café.....................**15** B2
Surf Life Saving Club.....................**7** D1		V-Wall Tavern.....................**16** C2
V-Wall.....................**8** C2		
		TRANSPORT	(p165)
		Bus Station (Northbound).............**17** A4
		Bus Station (Southbound).............(see 3)
		Harvey World Travel.....................**18** B2

Worth a visit is the **Headland Historical Museum** (☎ 6568 6380; Main Beach; admission free; ☺ Wed, Sat & Sun 2-4pm) with local-history exhibits, including a collection of over 1000 photos and displays of early farm equipment.

Sleeping

Typical of this stretch of coast, you'll find high prices and no-vacancy signs during summer, so book ahead. There is no backpacker accommodation in town.

BUDGET

White Albatross Holiday Resort (☎ 6568 6468; www.white-albatross.com.au; Wellington Dr; camp sites/cabins $20/50) Located near the river mouth with an adjacent lagoon to swim in, this tourism award–winner has a view to die for. A deluxe waterfront villa is $105.

Headland Holiday Village (☎ 6568 6547; Liston St; camp sites/cabins $13.50/16; ☒) Close to Main Beach and equally impressive.

MID-RANGE

B&B Beilby's Beach House (☎ 6568 6466; www .beilbys.com.au; 1 Ocean St; s/d $60/75; ☒ ☐ ☒) Put simply, you can't go past this place; amazing hosts coupled with a great set-up and the beach oh so close – it's perfect. Highly recommended for travelling couples, your hosts speak German, French and English. There's also an all-you-can-eat breakfast, and children are welcome.

Blue Dolphin Motel (☎ 6568 6700; 6-10 Fraser St; s/d $50/55) Superb location with fantastic views, this motel is well above average.

Eating

Matilda's Restaurant (☎ 6568 6024; Wellington Dr; mains $20) Succulent steaks and freshly caught river and ocean seafood – and this restaurant creaks with character.

Bluewater Brasserie (☎ 6568 6394; V-Wall Tavern; Wellington Dr; mains $18) Perfect for a lazy lunch contemplating one of the most stunning views out to the river mouth, where the river's journey meets the vast sea…yes, the balcony's conducive to deep thinking.

Spices Café (☎ 6568 8877; 58 Ridge St; mains $20) Airy, cosy and slightly classy, it has a real cosmopolitan ambience.

RSL Club (☎ 6568 6288; Nelson St; lunch specials $5) Let's just say it's lucky that this boasts good views and generous serves, as it is somewhat of a concrete nightmare to dine in.

Getting There & Away

Harvey World Travel (☎ 6568 6455; Bowra St) handles bookings and a wealth of information.

Nearly all buses stop outside the visitors centre. **Keans** (☎ 1800 625 587) runs three times a week to Tamworth ($60).

Premier Motor Service (☎ 13 34 10) stops at the Country Motel coach stop daily.

The train station is about 3km out of town: follow Bowra St then Mann St. **Countrylink** (☎ 13 22 23) has trains to Coffs Harbour ($5.50), Grafton ($24), Byron Bay ($50) and south to Kempsey ($10), Broadmeadow ($63) and Sydney ($84).

URUNGA

☎ 02 / pop 2700

Urunga is a fantastic family retreat, with safe river beaches, good fishing and an innocent atmosphere. Hungry Head, just down the coast, is a very popular surf spot.

The **Bellingen Shire visitors centre** (☎ 6655 5711) is on the Pacific Hwy, just before you reach the river, and services the whole area so is well worth a stop.

The **Ocean View Hotel** (☎ 6655 6221; 15 Morgo St; s/d $36/55) is good for a **feed** (mains $12), fine views and cheap accommodation, while **Urunga Heads Holiday Park** (☎ 6655 6355; Morgo St; camp sites/cabins $18/44; ☒) is next to the Urunga Lagoon in the centre of town.

MYLESTOM

☎ 02 / pop 380

Mylestom is just north of Urunga and is another attractive, unassuming place. It has promising beaches on one side and a wide, influential river on the other.

DETOUR: THE PUB WITH NO BEER

Slim Dusty had already reached god-like status before his death, but now his legend is riding on a wave of sudden immortality. Places like the **Pub With No Beer** (☎ 02-6564 2100; Taylors Arm Rd), 25km off the Pacific Hwy from Macksville at Taylors Arm, are representative of the influence and impact this unlikely hero had on Australian culture. The Irish also embraced 'A Pub with No Beer' with unconditional love; it stayed at the top of the charts for two months. The authenticity of this pub's name lasts as long as it takes to pour a cold one, with the rusty pipes seeing new life after Slim's death.

Just south of the Raleigh Bridge is **Raleigh Winery** (☎ 02-6655 4388; www.raleighwines.com; ⊙ 10am-5pm), which happens to be the most easterly vineyard in the land. They produce a decent drop.

Sleeping & Eating

North Beach Caravan Park (☎ 6655 4250; Beach Pde; camp sites/cabins $18/60) Next to the waves is a family affair with clean facilities.

Rivers (☎ 6655 4416; 2 River St; mains $24) This gorgeous BYO restaurant on the banks of the Bellinger River has fine food and stunning views.

BELLINGEN

☎ 02 / pop 2730

Bellingen's just downright lovely. It feels as though everything necessary for fulfilment is here – great food and coffee, river swimming, rainforest walks and comfy beds. Alternative living is everyday life in this town at the foot of the magnificent New England tableland.

History

The valley was part of the extensive territory of the Gumbainggir people until European timber cutters arrived in the 1840s. The first settlement here was at Fernmount, about 5km east of Bellingen, but later the administrative centre of the region was moved to Bellingen. River craft were able to come up here until the 1940s, when dredging was discontinued. Until tourism boomed at Coffs Harbour in the 1960s, Bellingen was the most important town in this area.

Orientation & Information

The main road from the Pacific Hwy to Dorrigo and beyond becomes Hyde St through town. Next to the post office, Bridge St leads across the river to North Bellingen and Gleniffer. There is no visitors centre in town, but this place is best discovered by following your intuition and looking behind any closed doors – you're sure to find a few undiscovered gems.

Sights & Activities

To get a feel for the place, head to the magnificent **Hammond & Wheatley Emporium** (Hyde St), formerly an old department store. It's been very well restored and now houses a shop, art gallery and café.

The historic **Old Butter Factory** (☎ 6655 2150; 1 Doepel Lane) houses craft shops, a gallery, opal dealers, a masseur and a great **café**.

For a nature fix, from December to March there's a huge colony of flying foxes on **Bellingen Island**. It's an impressive sight when thousands head off at dusk to feed (best seen from the bridge). There's also an interesting walk to **rope swings** into the river, near the YHA hostel.

For a moonlight outing, **Bellingen Canoe Adventures** (☎ 6655 9955; 4 Tyson St, Fernmount; half-/full-day guided tours $44/88) are more than willing to show you Bellingen's dark side.

Heartland Didgeridoos (☎ 6655 9881; 2/25 Hyde St) sent the first 'didg' into space last year. The indigenous owners also know a thing or two about quality, with a growing international reputation. You can make your own didg here.

On the third Saturday of the month the community **market** takes to the streets and it is quite an event, with over 250 stalls. On the second and fourth Saturday of the month the **organic market** takes over the streets.

Festivals & Events

In January, Bellingen becomes a **Stamping Ground** (☎ 6655 2472; www.userland.com.au/stamping), a festival of international dance performances. The **Bellingen Jazz Festival** (www.bellingenjazzfestival.com.au) features a strong line-up of jazz names in late August. You'll find a multicultural mix of music and performances at **Global Carnival** (www.globalcarnival.com) held annually in early October.

Sleeping

Bellingen YHA Backpackers (☎ 6655 1116; 2 Short St; dm/d $23/36) Backpackers flock here in droves and it's not hard to figure out why. A tranquil, engaging atmosphere pervades a beautifully renovated weatherboard house.

Koompartoo Retreat (☎ 6655 2326; cnr Lawon & Dudley Sts; chalet $135; ✕) A delightful experience: stylish, cosy timber chalets with private balconies.

Mountside B&B (☎ 6655 2206; 309 Roses Rd; d $99; ✕ ☎) Just out of town, this offers a great little escape and country hospitality.

Casabelle Country Guest House (☎ 6655 0155; 90 Gleniffer Rd; r $195; ✕) Hard to fault in the quality stakes, the Tuscan/Mediterranean influences prove it was built with nothing but love.

Bellingen Valley Motor Inn (☎ 6655 1599; 1381 Waterfall Way, r from $95; 🆇) The only motel on the road to Dorrigo is rather plush with a price that reflects its monopoly of the market.

Federal Hotel (☎ 6655 1003; Hyde St; s/d $25/40) Reasonable rooms in the heart of town.

Bellingen Caravan Park (☎ 6655 1338; Dowle St; camp sites $18) Perched next to Bellingen Island and the bats, it's relaxing and green.

Eating

There are plenty of excellent options to choose from in this hedonistic town.

Carriageway Café (☎ 6655 1672; Hyde St; mains $15) Start with the ambient Hammond & Wheatley Emporium – good art, great cake and flavoursome food.

Swiss Patisserie (☎ 6655 0050; 7B Church St; pastries from $2.50) Satisfy your bakery-type cravings with their formidable selection of pastries.

Lodge 241 Gallery Café (☎ 6655 2470; 117-121 Hyde St; mains $16) In the old Masonic Lodge at the top of the street, this is a quality option for vegetarians.

Dreamtime Gallery Café (☎ 6655 0850; 23 Hyde St; snacks $6) For a bit of dreamtime, try the Aboriginal and modern cuisine here, surrounded by local indigenous art.

Federal Hotel (☎ 6655 1003; 77 Hyde St; mains $15) You can't go past this for pub grub at a good rate.

No 2 Oak St (☎ 6655 9000; 2 Oak St; mains $28) For a splurge, No 2 is renowned in the region for the best modern Australian cuisine with a French twist. As a bonus, it's housed in a 1910 heritage cottage. Your tastebuds will thank you for a divine experience.

Getting There & Away

Keans (☎ 1800 625 587) has buses to Coffs Harbour ($13), Tamworth, Port Macquarie, Urunga and Dorrigo three times a week.

Bellingen is about 12km west of the Pacific Hwy; turn off just south of the Raleigh Bridge. From Bellingen the Waterfall Way climbs steeply to Dorrigo – it's a spectacular drive. From Dorrigo you can continue west to the Armidale–Grafton road. A network of unsealed roads leads south to Bowraville and some tiny mountain settlements.

AROUND BELLINGEN

If you have transport, there are some beautiful spots waiting to be discovered in the surrounding valleys. The most accessible is the tiny hamlet of **Gleniffer**, 10km to the north and clearly signposted from North Bellingen. There's a good swimming hole in the **Never Never River** behind the small Gleniffer School of Arts at the crossroads. Then you can drive around Loop Rd, which takes you to the foot of the New England tableland – a great drive that words don't do justice to.

If you want to sweat, tackle the **Syndicate Ridge Walking Trail**, a strenuous 15km walk from Gleniffer to the Dorrigo Plateau, following the route of a tramline once used by timber cutters. There's a very steep 1km climb on the way up. To get to the start, take the Gordonville Rd, turning into Adams Lane soon after crossing the Never Never River. The walking track commences at the first gate.

The **Kalang Valley**, southwest of town, and the **Thora Valley**, about 10km west of town, are also worth exploring. People who pursue alternative lifestyles represent the majority around here.

DORRIGO

☎ 02 / pop 970

Beautiful wide streets, lush green forests and a sleepy feel – that's Dorrigo in a nutshell. This is densely forested mountain country, bordering the Great Dividing Range's eastern escarpment and, not surprisingly, one of the last places to be settled by Europeans in the eastwards push across the New England tableland.

The **visitors centre** (☎ 6657 2486; 36 Hickory St) is run by volunteers who share a passion for the area. The town's main attraction is **Dangar Falls**, where you can swim underneath the waterfall if you so desire.

The proposed **Steam Railway Museum** is not open, but it's well worth visiting the site – there's a long line of steam engines and lots of old railway paraphernalia scattered about.

Sleeping & Eating

Rose Cottage B&B (☎ 6657 2417; 1 Tyringham St; s/d $35/65) In a historic cottage in town, Rose Cottage offers genuine country hospitality.

Dorrigo Hotel/Motel (☎ 6657 2017; cnr Cudgery & Hickory Sts; hotel/motel $46/58) This hotel/motel has a great roomy feel about it – the mountain air is great.

Commercial Hotel (☎ 6657 2003; 15 Cudgery St; s/d $35/45) This pub is cheaper and it's reflected in the rooms.

Bridgewater Country Homestead (☎ 6657 2477; Everinghams Rd; per person $50) The cosy rooms look out to glorious country views.

Lookout Motor Inn (☎ 6657 2511; Maynard Plains Rd; s/d $66/88; 🖳) Lookout has standard motel accommodation, but for brilliant views it is unquestionably good.

Dorrigo Mountain Resort (☎ 6657 2564; www .dorrigomountainresort.com.au; Waterfall Way; camp sites/ cabins $16/55) Just north of the Dome road turn-off, this resort has basic, self-contained wooden cabins and birds-eye views.

Misty's (☎ 6657 2855; 33 Hickory St; mains $17) This is a charming little restaurant, with good service, in a renovated weatherboard house.

Dorrigo Bakery (☎ 6657 2159; 39 Hickory St) Come here for a snack or lunch.

A couple more options for cheap meals that satisfy:

Dorrigo Hotel (cnr Cudgery & Hickory Sts) Good bistro with a tantalising menu.

Commercial Hotel (15 Cudgery St) Value for money.

Getting There & Away

Three times a week **Keans** (☎ 1800 625 587) heads to Port Macquarie via Coffs Harbour, and also to Tamworth stopping at many places.

Coffs Harbour is about 60km away via Bellingen, or there's an interesting, partly unsealed route via Leigh and Coramba. You can continue west to Armidale via Ebor.

DORRIGO NATIONAL PARK

This is the most accessible of Australia's World Heritage rainforests and warrants a visit. The turn-off to the park is just south of Dorrigo. The **Rainforest Centre** (☎ 02-6657 2309; Dome Rd; 🕑 9am-5pm), at the park entrance, has information about the park's many walks. There's also an **elevated walkway** (Skywalk) over the rainforest canopy. You can see right down to the ocean on a fine day. A walking track leads to the Glade rest area, from where there's a 5.5km walk through the forest. It's well worth making the drive down to the **Never Never rest area** in the heart of the national park, from where you can walk to waterfalls or begin longer walks. Bush camping is permitted in some areas – call the Rainforest Centre for more details.

COFFS HARBOUR
☎ 02 / pop 26,080

Prepare to be bemused by a big banana, a rather large windmill and a ridiculously popular holiday destination. Coffs Harbour's popularity lies in two areas: choose from breathtakingly bad, big objects that excite kids, and wild action sports that attract adults who just want to be kids again. It is the biggest town between Newcastle and the Gold Coast, hence an important regional centre.

History

Originally called Korff's Harbour, the town was settled in the 1860s. The jetty was built in 1892 to load cedar and other logs – it fell into disrepair some years ago but is now restored to its former glory. Bananas were first grown in the area in the 1880s, but no-one made much money from them until the railway came to town in 1918.

Banana growing is still big business, but these days tourism is the mainstay of the local economy.

Orientation

The town is split into three areas: the jetty, town centre and beaches. The Pacific Hwy turns into Grafton St and then Woolgoolga Rd on its run north through town. The city centre is around the Grafton St and Harbour Dr junction. The mall runs east along Harbour Dr.

The Pacific Hwy is the best way to access the beaches and resorts to the north. South of Coffs is Sawtell, a sprawl of housing developments, fronting some fabulous surf beaches, which merge into Coffs Harbour.

Information

The **visitors centre** (☎ 6652 1522; cnr Pacific Hwy & McLean St) has a complete rundown on accommodation, activities and tours.

The main **post office** (Ground fl, Palms Centre Shopping Complex) is in the mall, with another outlet at the jetty, opposite the Pier Hotel, and a third at Park Beach Plaza.

Net access is at **Jetty Dive Centre** (☎ 6651 1611; www.jettydive.com.au; 398 Harbour Dr).

Sights

Sweeping **Park Beach** attracts plenty of swell, punters and lifeguards from October to April. **Jetty Beach** is just south and a safer option. If you have the luxury of wheels, **Diggers Beach** – to the north and partially nudist – is sensational. To get there, turn off at the Big Banana. **Moonee Beach** lies 14km further north and **Emerald Beach** is a further 6km.

The **Big Banana** (☎ 6652 4355; www.bigbanana .com; Pacific Hwy; ⏱ 9am-4.30pm) is hailed by some

as a national icon, ridiculed by others as preposterous. The park offers ice skating ($12), a snow slope ($15/10) and many other attractions. It's great for kids, not so great for the cynical visitor: either embrace the concept or loathe from a safe distance.

Clog Barn (☎ 6652 4633; www.clogbiz.com; 215 Pacific Hwy; adult/child $4.50/3.50; ⏱ 7.30am-5pm) is a

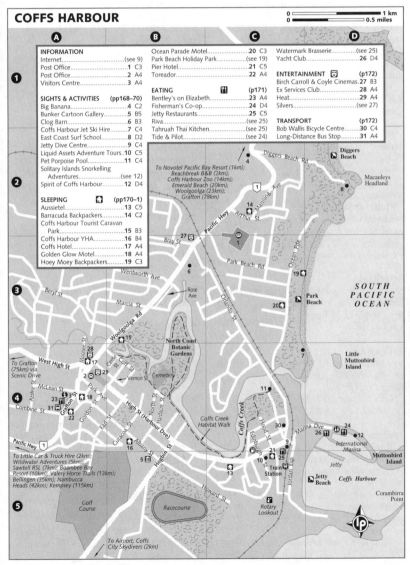

COFFS HARBOUR

INFORMATION	
Internet......................................(see 9)	
Post Office...**1** C3	
Post Office...**2** A4	
Visitors Centre..................................**3** A4	

SIGHTS & ACTIVITIES	(pp168–70)
Big Banana...**4** C2	
Bunker Cartoon Gallery...................**5** B5	
Clog Barn...**6** B3	
Coffs Harbour Jet Ski Hire...............**7** C4	
East Coast Surf School.....................**8** D2	
Jetty Dive Centre..............................**9** C4	
Liquid Assets Adventure Tours.....**10** C5	
Pet Porpoise Pool...........................**11** C4	
Solitary Islands Snorkelling	
Adventures..................................(see 12)	
Spirit of Coffs Harbour..................**12** D4	

SLEEPING	(pp170–1)
Aussitel...**13** C5	
Barracuda Backpackers....................**14** C2	
Coffs Harbour Tourist Caravan	
Park...**15** B3	
Coffs Harbour YHA.........................**16** B4	
Coffs Hotel.......................................**17** A4	
Golden Glow Motel.........................**18** A4	
Hoey Moey Backpackers.................**19** C3	

Ocean Parade Motel........................**20** C3	
Park Beach Holiday Park..............(see 19)	
Pier Hotel...**21** C5	
Toreador...**22** A4	

EATING	(p171)
Bentley's on Elizabeth....................**23** A4	
Fisherman's Co-op...........................**24** D4	
Jetty Restaurants.............................**25** C5	
Riva...(see 25)	
Tahruah Thai Kitchen...................(see 25)	
Tide & Pilot..................................(see 24)	

Watermark Brasserie.....................(see 25)	
Yacht Club..**26** D4	

ENTERTAINMENT	(p172)
Birch Carroll & Coyle Cinemas.....**27** B3	
Ex Services Club..............................**28** A4	
Heat..**29** A4	
Silvers...(see 27)	

TRANSPORT	(p172)
Bob Wallis Bicycle Centre..............**30** C4	
Long-Distance Bus Stop................**31** A4	

bizarre miniature Dutch village with windmills, a clog barn with a ridiculously large range of collectable spoons – an intriguing visit for kids.

At the **Pet Porpoise Pool** (☎ 6652 2164; Orlando St, beside Coffs Creek; shows 10.30am & 2.15pm; admission $12), dolphins, penguins and sea lions all interact with the public during the show. It's a hit with all ages. New pools were being constructed at the time of writing.

Coffs Harbour Zoo (☎ 6656 1330; Pacific Hwy; adult/child $16/8; ☽ 8.30am-4pm) has koalas, pythons and echidnas on display. As far as zoos go, this one's pretty good – well laid out and with plenty to see.

Finally, a gallery with original cartoons. **Bunker Cartoon Gallery** (☎ 6651 7343; City Hall Dr; admission $2; ☽ 10am-4pm) inspires Walt Disney creativity in all of us.

Strolling through **North Coast Botanic Gardens** (☎ 6648 4188; Hardacre St; entry by donation; ☽ 9am-5pm) emphasises the local change into subtropical surrounds. Lush rainforest and numerous endangered species make for a relaxing experience.

Muttonbird Island, at the end of the northern breakwater, is occupied by some 12,000 pairs of muttonbirds from late August to early April, with cute offspring visible in summer (December and January).

Activities

No two rides are the same at **Valery Horse Trails** (☎ 6653 4301; Gleniffer Rd; 2-hr ride $40), with their stable of 60 horses and plenty of acreage to explore.

National park kayaking can be arranged at **Liquid Assets Adventure Tours** (☎ 6658 0850; www.surfrafting.com; 328 Harbour Dr; half-day surf rafting $40), who offer good, honest fun out in nature's elements.

Coffs Harbour Jet Ski Hire (☎ 0418- 665 656; 263 Shepards Lane, Park Beach; 15 min $45) have jetskis – easy to use and high in short-term excitement.

If you ever get that urge to throw yourself out of a plane, call **Coffs City Skydivers** (☎ 6651 1167; www.coffscentral.dnet.tv/CoffsCitySkyDivers; tandem jump $310).

For the surfer in all of us, **East Coast Surf School** (☎ 6651 5515; Diggers Beach; lesson $40) will get you catching the wave of your life in no time.

You won't find many cheaper PADI courses on the coast than at **Jetty Dive Centre**

(☎ 6651 1611; www.jettydive.com.au; 398 Harbour Dr; PADI course $200), and the diving is pretty spectacular as you explore the Solitary Islands Marine Park.

Tours

Whales can now be sighted from June until late November, so the window of opportunity is widening. And dolphins can be spotted all year round.

Pacific Explorer (☎ 6652 7225; Pier 1 Marina; trike joyride $12) Seriously enthusiastic guides arrange national park tours, snorkelling and dolphin adventures.

Solitary Islands Snorkelling Adventures (☎ 6651 2401; Marina Dr; half-day snorkelling adult/child $55/45, diving $80) An effervescent marine park with a wide array of species.

Spirit of Coffs Harbour International Marina (☎ 6651 4612; International Marina; whale-watching $28) It can take you out on the water.

Wildwater Adventures (☎ 6653 3500; www.wild wateradventures.com.au; 754 Pacific Hwy; one-day trip $153) The sporadic rapids of the Nymboida River await eager participants in a well-organised outing; also runs multiday trips.

Festivals & Events

The **Pittwater to Coffs Yacht Race** starts in Sydney and finishes here, coinciding with New Year celebrations. The **Gold Cup** (☎ 6652 1488; Howard St), Coffs Harbour's premier horse race, is run in early August. On the last weekend of each year, there's the **Coffs Harbour Food & Wine Festival**.

Sleeping

Apart from the hostels and hotels, expect prices to rise by about 50% in school holidays and by as much as 100% at Christmas/ New Year.

BUDGET

If you're visiting during peak times, it's good to note that most hotel prices remain consistent all year. You are spoilt for options here with four good hostels.

Aussitel Backpackers Hostel (☎ 6651 1871; 312 High St; dm/d $18/45) Right next to the jetty, you can take the canoes for a paddle on the river or jump off the jetty as part of the experience. Diving is pretty close to the heart of what this hostel lives for.

Coffs Harbour YHA (☎ 6652 6462; 110 Albany St; dm/d $22/50) Quality is written all over this – from beds to bikes to surfboards.

Hoey-Moey Backpackers (☎ 6651 7966; Ocean Pde; dm/d $20/48) For a spot right on the beach, Hoey-Moey has many activities, with a pool comp on Monday night and karaoke on Thursday.

Barracuda Backpackers (☎ 6651 3514; 19 Arthur St; dm/d $22/55; 🛋) The quartet is complete with a reputable party atmosphere, a pool and spa.

Park Beach Holiday Park (☎ 6648 4888; Ocean Pde; camp sites/cabins $18/57) Massive and beautifully located on the beach.

MID-RANGE

Characteristic of such a town, motels command your immediate attention as you enter from the north or south. Slightly pricier but noticeably quieter, the array of motels around Park Beach is a mixed bag. Persistence does pay, or save, and hunting around normally results in a good find.

Caribbean Motel (☎ 6652 1500; www.stayincoffs .com.au; 353 High St; d $70-185, f $115-205; 🛋) Close to the creek, this is clean, bright and pretty cute. It has a pool and a little restaurant; some rooms have balconies with ocean views, others have spas.

Beachbreak B&B (☎ 6651 6468; www.beachbreak .com.au; 25A Charlesworth Bay Rd; d from $165) This modern, spacious B&B north of town is near Diggers Beach and has a pool. A couple of resorts nearby have restaurants.

Clissold Cottage (☎ 6651 2715; 4 Azalea Ave; d from $85) A little cottage in the grounds of a Federation-era house, Clissold is very private. Furnished in flowery country style, the cottage also has a big, deep claw-foot bath.

Toreador (☎ 6652 3887; 31 Grafton St; d $65; 🛋) On the southern entry into Coffs.

Golden Glow Motel (☎ 6652 2644; 19 Grafton St; s/d $60/70; 🛋) Cheap and somewhat noisy rooms near the town entrance.

Ocean Parade Motel (☎ 6652 6733; 41 Ocean Pde; s/d $60/70; 🛋) A solid option.

There is a huge range of holiday apartments and houses. The cheapest of the two-bedroom apartments go for around $70 a night in the low season (less by the week) and $140 a night in the high season. Many are vastly more expensive and a lot of places are available only by the week in the high season. The **visitors centre** (☎ 1300 369 070) has a free booking service and there are plenty of real estate agents, such as **Park Beach Realty** (☎ 6652 5374), with listings.

Novotel Pacific Bay Resort (☎ 6659 7000; cnr Pacific Hwy & Bay Dr; r $165; 🛋🛋) All the predictable features of a large resort: tennis courts, cocktail bars, volleyball courts, walking trails and fitness centre. Pleasant and reassuring.

Boambee Bay Resort (☎ 6653 2700; 8 Barber Cl; s/d $120/145; 🛋🛋) Set in tropical gardens, you are presented with plenty of activities and light, spacious villas.

Eating
CITY CENTRE

The downtown area is great for lunch and a coffee, servicing the town's office population with quick kebabs and gourmet sandwiches. Just wander through and take your pick.

Bentley's on Elizabeth (☎ 6651 7066; 18 Elizabeth St; mains $24) An international menu that caters to most taste buds.

Ex Services Club (☎ 6652 3888; cnr Grafton & Vernon Sts; mains $18) Variety of hearty mains from local seafood to steaks prepared by the in-house butcher.

HARBOUR

Tide & Pilot (☎ 6651 6888; www.tideandpilot.com; Marina Dr; mains $20) These chefs are experts in producing mouth-watering food. A glorious range of seafood is on offer.

Yacht Club (☎ 6652 5725; 30 Marina Dr; mains $18) Choose this for harbour views (of course) and a lazy lunch in front of the ocean.

Fishermans Co-op (☎ 6652 2811; 69 Marina Dr; takeaway $6.50) Excessively popular with locals for their fresh seafood, you can also let them sweat away at the stove for some outstanding fish and chips.

JETTY RESTAURANTS

Spoilt for options and blessed with quality, foodies will love this stretch.

Riva (☎ 6650 0195; 384A Harbour Dr; mains $15) This chic place has a great feel to it and the pizzas are perfect for the cosy seating arrangements.

Watermark Brasserie (☎ 6651 8221; Shop 2/394A Harbour Dr; mains $24) Renowned for its prime beef fillet that justifies the price; don't dismiss.

Tahruah Thai Kitchen (☎ 6651 5992; Harbour Dr; mains $15) Normally packed with locals (and that's always a good sign), it has exceptional stir-fries and a host of tasty vegetarian dishes.

Entertainment

Ex Services Club (☎ 6652 3888; cnr Grafton & Vernon Sts) People descend upon this place for plenty of amber liquid and the odd flutter on the pokies. Renowned for cheap drinks.

Coffs Hotel (☎ 6652 3817; cnr Pacific Hwy & West High St) Friday night sees this place take off, with the locals unwinding late into the night.

Heat (☎ 6652 6426; 15 City Centre Mall) It can get a little feisty on the Coffs club circuit, and Heat is no exception. Some come to dance, others to score. Things get really hot in the evenings.

Silvers (☎ 6652 7490; Bray St Complex) Hard joint that gets cranking late, with a party-hard dance session on offer if you're keen.

Birch Carroll & Coyle Cinemas (☎ 6651 6444; Bray St Complex) If you'd rather catch up with all your Hollywood mates, head here.

Getting There & Away

AIR

Virgin Blue (☎ 13 67 89) has flights to Sydney ($99), Melbourne ($180), Adelaide ($215), Brisbane ($115) and Perth ($300). **QantasLink** (☎ 13 13 13) flies to Sydney (one way/return $128/251). **Sunshine Express** (☎ 13 13 13) goes to Brisbane ($163) once a day.

BUS

Buses leave from adjacent to the information centre.

McCafferty's/Greyhound (☎ 13 20 30) heads daily to Grafton ($28), Byron Bay ($44), Port Macquarie ($36), Newcastle ($50) or Sydney ($57). **Keans** (☎ 1800 625 587) has services to Tamworth ($56.50), Armidale ($29.50), Ebor ($19), Kempsey ($23) and Bellingen ($13) three times a week. **Premier Motor Service** (☎ 13 34 10) stops at Urara Park on Elizabeth St daily. **Busways** (☎ 6652 2744) has local runs to Bellingen ($6.10) three times a day. Other runs include Uranga ($6.10) and Nambucca Heads ($7.70) five times a day. **Ryans Buses** (☎ 6652 3201) runs to Grafton ($17.70) twice a day and also goes to the beaches ($8.70) north of Coffs six times a day.

TRAIN

Countrylink (☎ 13 22 32) goes south to Kempsey ($16.50), Broadmeadow ($69.30) and Sydney ($83.60); and on the northern run you can get off at Grafton ($14.30), Ballina ($39.60) and Byron Bay ($44), among others.

Getting Around

All the major car-rental companies are in town. If you hire from a cheap local outfit make sure you digest the fine print.

For a cab, **Coffs District Taxi Network** (☎ 13 10 08, 6658 5922) operates a 24-hour service.

COFFS HARBOUR TO GRAFTON

Woolgoolga

☎ 02 / pop 3800

A less-developed coastal town just north of Coffs that is renowned for its surf and sizable Sikh community. As you drive in, there's the impressive Sikh **Guru Nanak Temple**, the *gurdwara* (place of worship). Don't confuse it with the **Raj Mahal**, an Indian-influenced decrepit concrete extravagance with two giant elephant statues out the front. Its origins are a mystery, but it's possible it was once a temple. If you drive straight through town up to the point, you'll get a magnificent view of the Solitary Marine Reserve.

The **Woolgoolga Beach Caravan Park** (☎ 6654 1373; Beach St; camp sites/cabins $20/50) right on the beach can't be beaten on position. For a motel, there are many good deals to be snapped up along the highway.

Opposite the temple, **Maharaja Tandoori Indian Restaurant** (☎ 6654 1122; 10-12 River St; mains $26) produces a memorable curry. On the beachfront, **Bluebottles Brasserie** (☎ 6654 1962; cnr Wharf & Beach Sts; mains $23) has jazz throughout the summer months and a versatile menu that many adore.

Red Rock

☎ 02 / pop 290

Red Rock, a site that's sacred to the Gunawarri tribe, is a sleepy village with a beautiful inlet and gorgeous surrounds. Soak up the sun or catch a fish while camping at **Red Rock Caravan Park** (☎ 6649 2730; 1 Lawson St; camp sites/cabins $11/45).

Yuraygir National Park

Yuraygir (20,000 hectares) is the southernmost in a chain of coastal national parks and nature reserves that runs almost all the way north to Ballina. The beaches are outstanding and there are some bushwalking paths where you can view endangered coastal emus. The park is in three sections, from **Red Rock** to the Wooli River (turn off the Hwy just north of Red Rock); from the township of **Wooli** to the Sandon River (turn off the Hwy 12km south of Grafton); and from near **Brooms Head** to **Angourie Point** (accessible from those towns). There is no vehicle access between the sections; on foot you'd have to cross the challenging Wooli and Sandon Rivers.

Walkers can bush camp and there are basic camping areas at Station Creek in the southern section; at the Boorkoom and Illaroo rest areas in the central section; and on the north bank of the Sandon River, and at Red Cliff at the Brooms Head end of the northern section. These are accessible by car; there are also walk-in camp sites in the northern section: Plumbago Headland, Shelly Head and Shelly Beach.

Wooli

☎ 02 / pop 560
The beauty of this town is that it is surrounded by the Yuraygir National Park on land and the Solitary Islands Marine Park by sea. This means you are encircled by wildlife and crisp waters.

On the June long weekend the locals hold their big event, the Goanna Pulling Championships. It's not all it claims to be, as contestants wrap a leather strap around their head for a good old-fashioned tug-of-war.

The **Wooli Hotel/Motel** (☎ 6649 7532; Wooli Rd; s/d $55/66) does stock-standard pub accommodation. There are two camping grounds, with the **Wooli Camping & Caravan Park** (☎ 6649 7519; North St; camp sites/cabins $16/50) your most idyllic option.

Solitary Islands Marine Park

This group of five islands is the meeting point of warm tropical currents and cooler southern currents, making for a wonderful combination of corals, reef fish and seaweeds. Dubbed the 'rivers of life', this is the best area in which to dive or snorkel (look out for extremely rough conditions).

FAR NORTH COAST

This is where the coast heats up in activity, hype and temperature. Byron Bay radiates its unbeatable glow of appeal, Yamba looks positively stunning at the mouth of the Clarence River while towers of grotesque concrete heat up Tweed Heads. You, my friend, have now entered a stretch of coast that ticks to the tourist dollar. Coupled with the beaches

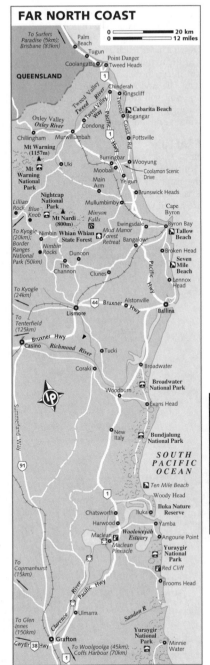

FAR NORTH COAST

and divine subtropical climate are rivers rich in depth and colour. The Clarence River can lay claim to being the most beautiful river Down Under, such as its striking blueness. The Richmond and Tweed Rivers also sprawl out into rich deltas and provide classic visuals. The land is used to produce sugar cane and you will smell it burning as you drive through. The weather is sublime – warm winters and long, lengthy summers.

GRAFTON
☎ 02 / pop 17,400

Grafton is a graceful old beast nestled on the banks of the wide, imposing Clarence River. The town has 24 parks and the streets are awash with an amazing variety of trees.

Interestingly enough, the most famous is the Brazilian jacaranda, which carpets the streets with mauve flowers in late October. The town's mainstay is in its agricultural roots – beef cattle inland and sugar cane in the Clarence River delta.

Orientation & Information

Emphasising its untouched tourist status, the Pacific Hwy bypasses the town and you enter over a lovely old double-decker (road and rail) bridge.

Clarence River visitors centre (☎ 6642 4677; cnr Spring & Charles Sts) is on the highway south of the town near the turn-off to the bridge. There is an **NPWS office** (☎ 6642 0613; 50 Victoria St) in town.

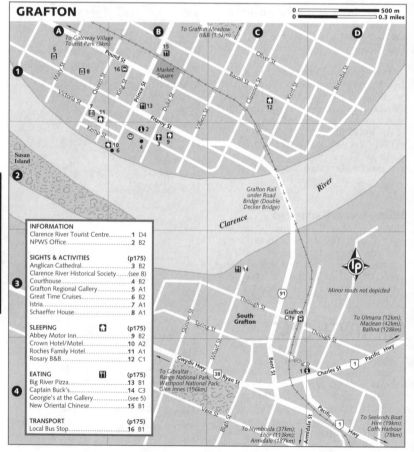

GRAFTON

INFORMATION	
Clarence River Tourist Centre	**1** D4
NPWS Office	**2** B2

SIGHTS & ACTIVITIES	(p175)
Anglican Cathedral	**3** B2
Clarence River Historical Society	(see 8)
Courthouse	**4** B2
Grafton Regional Gallery	**5** A1
Great Time Cruises	**6** B2
Istria	**7** A1
Schaeffer House	**8** A1

SLEEPING	🛏	(p175)
Abbey Motor Inn		**9** B2
Crown Hotel/Motel		**10** A2
Roches Family Hotel		**11** A1
Rosary B&B		**12** C1

EATING	🍴	(p175)
Big River Pizza		**13** B1
Captain Buck's		**14** C3
Georgie's at the Gallery		(see 5)
New Oriental Chinese		**15** B1

TRANSPORT	(p175)
Local Bus Stop	**16** B1

Sights & Activities

Victoria St is the focal point of days gone by with the **courthouse** (1862), **Roches Family Hotel** (1870), **Anglican Cathedral** (1884) and the private residence **Istria** (1899) providing glimpses of 19th-century architecture.

Fitzroy St runs parallel to Victoria St and has a couple of interesting sights. The **Grafton Regional Gallery** (☎ 6642 6996; 58 Fitzroy St; admission free; ☺ 10am-4pm Tue-Sun) is a small provincial art gallery. Further up, **Schaeffer House** (1903) is where you'll find the **Clarence River Historical Society** (190 Fitzroy St; admission free; ☺ 1-4pm Tue, Wed, Thu & Sun).

Susan Island, in the middle of the river, is home to the largest fruit-bat colony in the southern hemisphere. Their evening departure is a spectacular summer sight. Access to the river is by boat or canoe; you can hire a tinny from **Seelands Boat Hire** (☎ 6644 9381; Old Punt Rd; per day $60) or just sit on the banks and marvel.

Several outfits can help get you cruising on the lower Clarence River, such as **Great Time Cruises** (☎ 6642 3456; Prince St Wharf; 2-hr cruise inc lunch $15), which takes you around Susan Island.

Festivals & Events

Horse Racing Carnival Every July, this is the richest in country Australia.

Jacaranda Festival In the week joining October and November, Australia's longest-running floral festival sees Grafton come alive in an ocean of mauve.

Sleeping

Crown Hotel/Motel (☎ 6642 4000; 1 Prince St; hotel s/d $30/40, motel s/d $40/50) Attractively located on the Clarence River, with old beds and clean rooms, some over-looking the river and all opening onto an inviting veranda.

Roches Family Hotel (☎ 6644 2866; 85 Victoria St; s/d $30/40) Historic hotel with decent pub accommodation, pleasant common TV area, 14 rooms and licensed restaurant.

Rosary B&B (☎ 6642 2293; 41 Bacon St; d $85) A 100-year-old Federation-style home only two blocks from the main shopping area. The hosts have an intimate knowledge of the area.

Grafton Meadow B&B (☎ 6643 2331; 95 Crown St; s/d $70/85) Has classic jacarandas out the front and is set in semirural settings.

Motel-wise, there are a number of other motels along Fitzroy St that vary in quality

and price. The **Abbey Motor Inn** (☎ 6642 6122; 59 Fitzroy St; s/d $65/75; ☒) has spacious, well-maintained rooms.

A central scenic tourist park is the **Gateway Village Tourist Park** (☎ 6642 4225; 598 Sumerland Way; s/d $85/105; ☒) which has a pool and barbecue facilities.

Eating

This isn't a particularly strong point of the town but there are some respectable finds.
Crown Hotel/Motel (☎ 6642 4000, 1 Prince St; $10-20 mains) Strong Mod Oz bistro, with a stunning view on offer.
Georgie's at the Gallery (☎ 6642 6996; 158 Fitzroy St; mains $20) Great for pastas and pizzas.
Captain Buck's (Wharf St) This is good value; located at the RSL.
New Oriental Chinese (☎ 6642 3697; 117 Prince St; mains $13) Handles vegetarian-meal requests easily.
Big River Pizza (☎ 6643 1555; 100 Fitzroy St; pizzas $11) Predominantly take-away but you can snag a table.

Getting There & Away

Busways (☎ 6642 2954) runs to Yamba ($10, six times daily). **Ryans Buses** (☎ 6652 3201) goes to Coffs Harbour ($18, twice daily). **McCafferty's/Greyhound** (☎ 13 20 30) travels to Byron Bay ($41) and Coffs Harbour ($28).

Premier Motor Service (☎ 13 34 10) stops at the train station on the daily east-coast run. **Countrylink** (☎ 13 22 32) buses go south to Coffs Harbour ($15), Broadmeadow ($78.50) and Sydney ($90.50); and north to Ballina ($26.50), Byron Bay ($32) and Casino ($16.50).

The Pacific Hwy runs north to Maclean and south to Coffs Harbour. Near Grafton there are several scenic routes that parallel the highway and involve ferry crossings, such as Grafton to Maclean via the north bank and the Lawrence ferry. There's also a ferry crossing between the highway and the north bank road at Ulmarra.

There's an interesting route from Grafton to Armidale via Nymboida and Ebor, passing turn-offs to Dorrigo and the New England and Cathedral Rock National Parks. Heading west to Glen Innes, the Gwydir Hwy passes through the superb Washpool and Gibraltar Range National Parks.

Getting Around

Grafton Radio Taxis (☎ 6642 3622) operates a 24- hour service.

CLARENCE RIVER VALLEY

The Clarence River rises in Queensland's McPherson Ranges and runs south through the mountains before thundering down a gorge in the Gibraltar Range west of Grafton. It then meanders serenely northeast to the sea at Yamba, watering a beautiful and fertile valley along the way.

The delta between Grafton and the coast is a patchwork of farmland in which the now immense and branching Clarence River forms about 100 islands, some very large. If you're driving, the profusion of small bridges and waterways makes it hard to keep track of whether you're on an island or the mainland.

This is the start of sugar-cane country and also the beginning of Queensland-style domestic architecture: wooden houses with high-pitched roofs perched on stilts to allow air circulation in the hot summers. The burning of the cane fields (May to December) adds a smoky tang to the air.

Clarence Riverboats (☎ 02-6647 6232; Brushgrove; per week $1200) has reliable equipment for a break with a difference.

INLAND FROM GRAFTON

The Clarence River can be navigated as far upstream as the village of **Copmanhurst**, about 35km northwest of Grafton. Here, there's the **Rest Point Hotel** (☎ 02-6647 3125; s/d $20/30). Further up, the Clarence River descends rapidly from the Gibraltar Range through the rugged **Clarence River Gorge**, a popular but potentially dangerous site for white-water canoeing.

Private property flanks the gorge. Land on the south side is owned by the Winters family, who allow day visitors and have cabin accommodation at **Winters' Shack** (☎ 02-6647 2173). Access is via Copmanhurst. It's best to ring first to get permission and to arrange for the gates to be unlocked. On the north side, **Wave Hill Station** (☎ 02-6647 2145) has homestead or inexpensive cottage accommodation, and regular 4WD or horse-riding trips to the gorge. These trips cost $200 for the day, so a group of four would pay $50 each.

MACLEAN

☎ 02 / pop 3250

Some might say, given the tartan power poles, Maclean takes its Scottish heritage a little too seriously. That said, the town is set in charming surrounds with the imposing

Clarence River beginning its lazy sprawl over the delta. Prawn fishing is a popular activity. The **Lower Clarence visitors centre** (☎ 6645 4121; Pacific Hwy) is on the southern entry to town.

To take in the beautiful surrounds, head up the hill to **Maclean Lookout** and grab a great snap. The **Maclean Historical Society** (☎ 6645 3416; www.macleanhistory.org.au; cnr Wharf & Grafton Sts; adult/child $3/1; ⊙ Wed, Fri, Sat) gives a good insight into the town's Scottish roots.

The 1867 **Gables B&B** (☎ 6645 2452; 2b Howard St; d $95) is a great place to enjoy the epic sunsets over the Clarence.

YAMBA

☎ 02 / pop 5660

Beaches on three fronts, a relaxed pace and the stunning views make Yamba a great place to loosen up and is, quite possibly, the next BIG thing.

For a kayak tour, **Yamba Kayak** (☎ 6646 1137; pick up at Gorman's Restaurant at Yamba Bay; half-day $65) operates on demand. To use the motorised version, **Yamba Boat Hire** (☎ 6645 8525; Boat Harbour Marina, near Blue Dolphin Caravan Park; full day/8 people $120) has simple, square boats. If dry land appeals, roll through nine holes at **Yamba Golf and Country Club** (☎ 6646 1656; River St; 9/18 holes $15/25). There's a **community market** at the Yamba Oval on the fourth weekend of each month.

Sleeping

Pacific Hotel (☎ 6646 2466; 1 Pilot St; dm $18-20) Gorgeously situated overlooking the ocean, this has standard rooms but views to drink to.

Moby Dick (☎ 6646 2196; 27-29 Yamba Rd; $110 per room; ❄ ☕) Of the town's nine motels, this one, on the banks of the Clarence River, is a touch indulgent. All rooms have a private balcony, and some have spa baths and first-class amenities.

Historic Gables B&B (☎ 6645 2452; www.gables .net.au; s/d $80/100) To get an elegant view of the river, look no further than this place. This charming Federation house has six bedrooms, an extensive upstairs lounge area, open fireplace and wide veranda.

For those pitching a tent, **East's Calypso Holiday Park** (☎ 6646 2468; Harbour St; camp sites/cabins $18/70) is the best located.

Eating

Two Fat Men (☎ 6646 2619; Shop 4, 8 Yamba St; mains $6-8) For a quick hit – fill that hole in your stomach with a hearty burger.

Restaurant Castalia (☎ 6646 1155; 15 Clarence St; mains $20-30) Relaxed yet stylish. Fresh local seafood and locally grown produce are the focus of the innovative menu. The award-winning chef is not afraid to experiment and often produces great cuisine. Its trademark is the crispy skin duck. Delicious.

Tom's Chinese Restaurant (☎ 6646 2918; 3/15 Clarence St; mains $10-15) Next door to Castalia, excellent seafood dishes.

Getting There & Away

Yamba is 15km east of the Pacific Hwy; turn off at the Harbord Island bridge intersection north of Maclean. A ferry (adult/child $3.50/1.75, four times daily) runs to Iluka, on the north bank of the Clarence River.

Busways (☎ 6642 2954) runs across to Grafton ($10, six times daily).

Countrylink (☎ 13 22 32) buses go to Grafton ($12.50), Lennox Head ($16.50) and Byron Bay ($17.60).

ANGOURIE

☎ 02 / pop 210

A surf haven where epic breaks beckon, Angourie lies 5km south of Yamba. For less experienced surfers, a cool-off in the **Blue Pool**, a quarry next to the beach filled with fresh water from a spring, is a more than suitable alternative.

Angourie Rainforest Resort (☎ 6646 8600; 166 Angourie Rd; 1-/2-bedroom villas $130/155) has deluxe cabins engulfed by verdant rainforests. **Angourie Point B&B** (☎ 6646 1432; 23 Pacific St; d $130) is fashionably classic and good fun.

ILUKA

☎ 02 / pop 1860

Iluka is a carbon copy of Yamba but less developed due to its distance from the Pacific Hwy (1). Fishermen love this area as well as nature enthusiasts, the town acts as a gateway to the World Heritage–listed **Iluka Nature Reserve**.

To reach this quaint village, a ferry runs from Yamba or it's a long drive around (40km).

BUNDJALUNG NATIONAL PARK

Created in 1980, this is 4000 hectares of coastal land, with 30km of unspoilt beaches for surfing and swimming. The entrance is 60km north of Grafton or 55km south of Ballina and there are four main areas.

The **Gumma Garra** picnic area has creeks, islands, rainforests and a midden that can be seen by the river. You can get there via Evans Head on the Bundjalung road. The second is **Black Rocks & Booroora** picnic area and camping, which is tucked in behind the sand dunes of the ten-mile beach. You can sit in the shade of the Tuckeroo tree. The third area is the **Woody Head** picnic and camping area, which has rock pools and is 6km north of Iluka. The fourth is **Shark Bay**, where you can bushwalk and swim.

EVANS HEAD

☎ 02 / pop 2610

Evans Head is a great way to escape the hectic tourist lifestyle present in its northern counterparts. Locals endearingly call it 'the jewel in the crown'. It has an intense prawn and fishing industry and has been kept remarkably low-key. The **Silver Sands Caravan Park & Camping Reserve** (☎ 6682 4212; Park St; camp sites/cabins $17/53) is green, spacious and well-kept. For a pub room, try the **Hotel Illawong** (☎ 6682 4222; Evans Head; s/d $25/40). **Pacific Motor Inn** (☎ 6682 4318; 38 Woodburn St; s/d $55/60) has inviting rooms and a family feel.

NORTH COAST

NEW ITALY MUSEUM

This is an intriguing highway stop. The **New Italy Museum** (02-6682 2622) exhibition follows the Marquis de Ray's ambitious plan to colonise the New Guinea island of New Ireland. Prepare to be enthralled, yet appalled, at the tale of one man's efforts to exploit over 300 Italians by getting them to purchase land and homes in a nonexistent paradise. (The Marquis de Ray's dream were thwarted finally when he was consigned to a lunatic asylum in France.) This museum is appropriately positioned, as the survivors of de Ray's plan, who were salvaged by Australian sailors, settled around this area, making it 'New Italy'. An Italian pavilion is also on the premises with insightful information on all the Italian provinces. Adjoining is a coffee shop, licensed Italian restaurant and the Gurrigai Aboriginal arts and crafts shop, which is located towards the back of the centre and sells a variety of pieces from the outback. Admission is free.

Evans Head is 10km east of the highway; turn off at Woodburn.

BROADWATER NATIONAL PARK

Extending from north of Evans Head to Broadwater, this small coastal park (3750 hectares) protects a 7km stretch of beach backed by coastal heath. You can drive through the park on the roads between Evans Head and Broadwater. Camping is not allowed in the park.

BALLINA

☎ 02 / pop 17,000

The crossing of the Richmond River marks the end of the fishing villages and the beginning of the tourist-driven economy. Ballina is a sign of the times, basing its appeal around family holidays and nature activities. If the crossing of the river doesn't announce this, the **Big Prawn** just south certainly will.

Orientation & Information

The Pacific Hwy approaches from the south and turns into River St, the main drag.

The **visitors centre** (☎ 6686 3484; cnr Lasbalsas Plaza & River St) has detailed information on surrounding attractions. A market is held on the third Sunday of each month at the circus ground.

Sights

Behind the information centre is the **Naval & Maritime Museum** (☎ 6681 1002; Regatta Ave; admission by donation; ☺ 9am-4pm) and you will find the amazing remains of a balsawood raft that drifted across the Pacific from Ecuador as part of the Las Balsas expedition in 1973.

White and sandy, **Shelley Beach** is patrolled. For a watertight option, **Shaws Bay Lagoon** is popular with families.

Cruises up the Richmond River are a good way to get away from it all; **Richmond River Cruises** (☎ 6687 5688; Regatta Ave; 2 hrs $16) is the most established.

Just north of Ballina, the **Thursday Plantation** (☎ 1800 029 000; Pacific Hwy; admission free; ☺ 9am-5pm) has a tea-tree maze and specialises in high quality therapeutic products. It is well worth a visit.

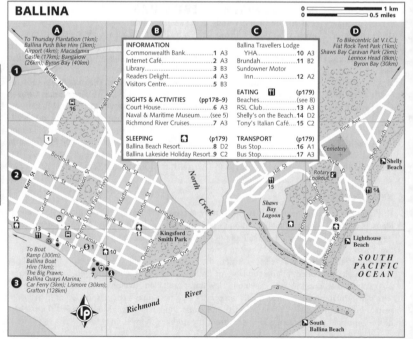

BALLINA

0 — 1 km
0 — 0.5 miles

To Thursday Plantation (1km);
Ballina Push Bike Hire (3km);
Airport (4km); Macadamia
Castle (17km); Bangalow
(26km); Byron Bay (40km)

INFORMATION
Commonwealth Bank................1 A3
Internet Café........................2 A3
Library.............................3 B3
Readers Delight.....................4 A3
Visitors Centre.....................5 B3

SIGHTS & ACTIVITIES (pp178–9)
Court House.........................6 A3
Naval & Maritime Museum......(see 5)
Richmond River Cruises..............7 A3

SLEEPING (p179)
Ballina Beach Resort................8 D2
Ballina Lakeside Holiday Resort...9 C2

Ballina Travellers Lodge
YHA...............................10 A3
Brundah............................11 B2
Sundowner Motor
Inn..............................12 A2

EATING (p179)
Beaches.........................(see 8)
RSL Club...........................13 A3
Shelly's on the Beach..............14 D2
Tony's Italian Café................15 C2

TRANSPORT (p179)
Bus Stop...........................16 A1
Bus Stop...........................17 A3

To Bikecentric (at V.I.C.);
Flat Rock Tent Park (1km);
Shaws Bay Caravan Park (2km);
Lennox Head (8km);
Byron Bay (30km)

To Boat
Ramp (300m);
Ballina Boat
Hire (1km);
The Big Prawn;
Ballina Quays Marina;
Car Ferry (3km); Lismore (30km);
Grafton (128km)

SOUTH PACIFIC OCEAN

Shelly Beach
Lighthouse Beach
South Ballina Beach

Activities

Ballina is renowned for its great walking and bike tracks, so hiring a bike can be rewarding. **Sunrise Cycles** (☎ 6686 6322; Hogan St; half-day/week $15/25) and **Ballina Push Bike Hire** (☎ 6686 8690, 0402-187 220; 27 Southern Cross Dr; half-day $23) are the people to talk to. Or for an outrageous experience, the seven-seater bike from the fittingly-named **Bikecentric** (☎ 6686 0514; Angels Beach Dr; per person $17).

Ballina Boat Hire (☎ 0403-810 277; cnr Brunswick St & Winton Lane; half hour/half day $30/50) has tinnies for fishing and catamarans for the more adventurous.

Sleeping

Ballina is an Australian holiday-maker's destination, and prices take a turn for the worse at peak times.

BUDGET

Ballina Travellers Lodge YHA (☎ 6686 6737; 36-38 Tamar St; dm/s/d $20/62/72; 🖳 🖘) Part hostel, part motel, this has friendly owners, modern dorms, and bikes and body boards available for hire if you want to leave the pool.

Shaws Bay Caravan Park (☎ 6681 1413; 1 Brighton St, camp sites/cabins $17/52) Right on the lagoon.

Ballina Lakeside Holiday Resort (☎ 6686 8755; Fenwick Dr; camp sites/cabins $17/43) Closer to Shelley's Beach, with access to fresh and saltwater swimming holes.

MID-RANGE

Brundah (☎ 6686 8166; 37 Norton St; s/d $100/130) Indulge your senses in this restored Federation home surrounded by lovely gardens. A great retreat.

Ballina Beach Resort (☎ 6686 8888; Compton Dr; s/d $110/121; 🖳 🖘) Quiet, clean and within striking distance of both Shaws Bay Lagoon and Lighthouse Beach.

The southern approach to Ballina has motels aplenty of varying class, the **Sundowner Motor Inn** (☎ 6686 2388; cnr River & Kerr Sts; s/d $53/65; 🖘) is a safe bet.

Eating

Shelly's on the Beach (☎ 6686 9844; Shelley Beach Rd; mains $15; 🕥 breakfast & lunch) Sensational food and superb views. Great for a bacon-and-eggs session before hitting the beach.

RSL Club (☎ 6686 2544; cnr Grant & River St; mains $17). For good, consistent meals head to this architectural wonder.

Tony's Italian Café (☎ 6686 6602; 3 Crompton Dr; mains $20) Great pasta and also blessed with good views.

Beaches (Compton Dr; mains $22; 🕥 daily) Attached to the Ballina Beach Resort, this restaurant focuses on local ingredients and has an enjoyable atmosphere.

Along River St there are number of cafés and the odd restaurant.

Getting There & Away

Regional Express (☎ 13 17 13) flies to Sydney ($143).

McCafferty's/Greyhound (☎ 13 20 30) runs daily to Brisbane ($32), Coffs Harbour ($41) and Sydney ($81). All stop at the Big Prawn.

Premier Motor Service (☎ 13 34 10) does pickups from the Ampol Pied Pier on its runs (three daily) up and down the coast.

Blanch's Bus Service (☎ 6686 2144) operates a service to Lennox Head, Mullumbimby, Byron Bay and Bangalow. All stop at Kmart and Tamar St.

Countrylink (☎ 13 22 32) Buses to Yamba ($14.30), Evans Head ($5.50), Lennox Head ($5.50) and Lismore ($5.50). Bus to either Byron Bay ($5.50) or Grafton ($26.40) to connect with north-or-south running trains, respectively.

If you're heading to Byron Bay, take the coast road through Lennox Head. It's much prettier than the highway and much shorter as well. Macadamia-nut fans might want to stick to the highway though, as there's the **Macadamia Castle** (☎ 6687 8432; Pacific Hwy; admission free; 🕥 8.30am-5pm) north of Ballina.

AROUND BALLINA

Inland from Ballina, the closely settled country of the north-coast hinterland begins, with winding, hilly roads running past tropical fruit farms, tiny villages and the occasional towering rainforest tree that has somehow escaped the wholesale clearing of the forest.

Lennox Head

☎ 02 / pop 5840
In surfing circles Lennox Head is a muststop destination on any east-coast adventure, with a peeling right hander off the point that has provided many fond memories. The town has the laid-back, smooth atmosphere that is associated with every surfer's quest. **Lake Ainsworth** is a freshwater

lake that is conducive to pleasant swimming and windsurfing. Swimming there can be somewhat beneficial to the skin as the dark colour is a result of tea-tree oil. If the wind's up, wind-or kite-surfing is the ticket and **Wind & Water Action Sports** (☎ 0419-686 188; www.windnwater.net; sailboard longboard per day $60; 2-hr lesson $80; kite surfing lesson $165) has a good line of equipment.

The YHA-affiliated **Lennox Head Beach House** (☎ 6687 7636; 3 Ross St; dm/d $25/55, additional $2 for non members) has immaculate rooms and a great vibe. For $5 you can use the boards, sailboards and bikes.

If you plan to stay awhile, it is worth getting in contact with the **Professionals** (☎ 6687 7209; 66 Ballina St) who hire out apartments at a good rate outside of peak time.

For a clean set-up at an affordable price, **Lake Ainsworth Caravan Park** (☎ 6687 7249; Pacific Pde; camp sites/cabins $17/40) has a nice sea breeze flowing through it.

Foodwise, **Café de Mer** (☎ 6687 7132; Ballina St; mains $7-12) is funky and stylish, and this is reflected in the popular Eggplant Stack. The **Red Rock Café** (☎ 6687 4744; 3/60 Ballina St; mains $10) is just as hip and excels with an affordable Modern Australian menu. On the beach strip, **7 Mile Café** (☎ 6687 6210; 41 Pacific Pde; mains $24) is well laid out and has some scrumptious bites.

Ruby's by the Sea (☎ 6687 5769; 17-19 Pacific Pde; pub $9-16, bistro $12-24) is part of the Lennox Point Hotel, and fills you up with all the likely options in the bar and all the delicate touches in the bistro.

Premier Motor Service (☎ 13 34 10) stops three times a day on request heading north and south; pick up is from the Countrylink Coach Stop, while **Blanch's Bus Service** (☎ 6686 2144) has services to Ballina, Byron Bay and Mullumbimby on a freedom pass ($11/33 per day/week).

BYRON BAY
☎ 02 / pop 7030

Byron Bay attracts everyone from alternative-minded Sydney millionaires to backpackers to the occasional hippy. High or low, intense or mellow, everyone embraces Byron. It's an attitude that has transformed the town into a modern-day mecca for every east-coast traveller. A cultural institution, a surfers' paradise, a place where diversity has never before been so welcome

in mainstream society, Byron Bay is a contradiction in terms of its prosperity versus its alternative ethos. The Byron Shire has implemented 'caps' on development to halt economic ambitions. In doing so, the Byron Shire has been involved in more litigation than any other Shire in the country. The weather is divine, hot in summer and mild in winter – further justification for its international acclaim.

History
Byron began as a quiet, unassuming little village until 1963. That year surfers discovered **The Pass** and over the following years it became a cauldron of artistically minded people. Surfers adore the seven different beachfronts that make up the point (almost guaranteeing a wave in the near vicinity). The council is currently flirting with infrastructural suicide by not having devised a tourism plan since 1988. This is astonishing for a town that draws 1.5 million visitors a year. What the future holds is in the lap of the gods.

Orientation
Tucked away on a magnificent piece of headland, the Pacific Hwy gets within 6km of Byron Bay. As you enter town, Bangalow Rd is the principal shopping street, with the corner of Jonson and Lawson Sts the centre of town. Cape Byron is out to your east. In fact, it's the most easterly point of the continent.

Information
Accommodation booking office (☎ 6680 8666; www.byronbayaccom.net; Old Station Masters Cottage, Jonson St) Just the ticket for the organised traveller.

Backpackers World (☎ 6685 8858; www.backpackers world.com.au; Shop 6, Byron St) A good port of call to work out the finer points of your trip.

Byron Bay Airbus (☎ 6684 3232; www.byronbaybus link.com) Very helpful Internet site with accommodation, transport and holiday ideas.

Byron Bus & Backpacker Centre (☎ 6685 5517; 84 Jonson St) Great for the first-timer: has the lowdown on buses, trains and many activities in town.

Byron Foreign Exchange (☎ 6685 7787; Central Arcade, Byron St) Cash in your travellers cheques here or swap a few euros.

Visitors centre (☎ 6680 9271; 80 Jonson St) A hive of activity and a wealth of information from enthusiastic volunteers.

Sights
BEACHES & SURF SPOTS

Main Beach has the beautiful people and is great for swimming. At its eastern end is **Clarks Beach**, good for small peeling waves when the swell's right. For the famous breaks, keep walking to **The Pass**, which leads onto **Watego's** and **Little Watego's**. Dolphin sightings are common at these spots.

South of **Cape Byron** are the hallowed sands of **Tallow Beach**, which stretch 7km down to a rockier section around **Broken Head** (named appropriately). Your next decent line of sand is **Seven Mile Beach**, running down to Lennox Head.

CAPE BYRON

George Gordon (Lord) Byron may have incessantly raved about walking in beauty like the night, but his grandfather did a little travel of his own, sailing around the world in the 1760s – Captain Cook named this headland after him. The ocean jumps to the tune of dolphins and humpback whales pass through during migration (June and July). Towering over the dolphins is the 1901 lighthouse, and you can drive right up to it. Walking is a fine way of immersing yourself in the area; try the 4km track commencing at **Captain Cook Lookout**.

Activities

Kidz Klub (☎ 6680 8585, 0429-770 147; 67 Shirley St; 5–12-year-olds per day incl food $90) keeps kids thoroughly entertained with a 'no parents' rule strictly enforced. The little devils will return with the wind well and truly out of their sails.

Just to see what lies around you, **Byron Images** (☎ 6685 8909; www.johnderrey.com; cnr Jonson & Lawson Sts) shows exquisite, powerful images from a perfectionist photographer.

If you fancy clowning around – or more to the point, getting thrown around – **Flying Trapeze** (☎ 0417-073 668; Byron Bay Beach Club; 2 hrs $40) will cure any future circus aspirations.

ALTERNATIVE THERAPIES

The *Body & Soul* guide, available from the visitors centre, is a handy guide to Byron's alternative therapies.

Ambaji (☎ 6685 6620; www.ambaji.com.au; 6 Marvell St) Unashamedly New Age, craniosacral balancing and life coaching. Sceptics will love the hour-long massage ($60) with Byron gossip thrown in.

Pure Byron Day Spa (☎ 6685 5988; 5 Jonson St; ⏲ 9.30am-5.30pm) Swedish massages, reiki, facials and a vibrating sauna ($30).

Relax Haven (☎ 6685 8304; Belongil Beachouse, Childe St; float & massage $50; ⏲ 10am-8pm) A flotation tank experience to soothe mind, body and soul.

Traditional Thai Massage (☎ 6680 9290) Get a memorable rub from the experts – they come to you.

Yoga With Flo (☎ 6685 9910; Epi Center Yoga Rooms, Border St; group lesson/private per hr $12/50) Turn yourself inside-out; pre-natal, astangar and iyengar classes.

DIVING

About 3km off shore, **Julian Rocks Marine Reserve** is where divers can sneak a peek at leopard sharks and grey nurse sharks.

Some dive outfits:

Dive Byron Bay (☎ 1800 243 483; 9 Marvell St; per dive $75) Hires out a good range of equipment and has the inside word on colourful corals.

Sundive (☎ 1800 008 755; www.sundive.com.au; Middleton St; PADI from $300; snorkel $45) Well-run and respected within the industry for its diving courses.

FLYING

Sky Limit (☎ 6684 3711, 0415-717 141; www.skylimit byronbay.com; Tyagarah Airfield; 30-min flight $145) will teach you the basics of hang-gliding.

There's also:

Byron Airwaves (☎ 6629 0354; www.byronair.cjb.net) Tandem hang-gliding ($110) and courses (from $1050)

Byron Bay Skydivers (☎ 6684 1323; www.skydive byronbay.com; Tyagarah Airport) Tandem dives ($275) and who wouldn't want to do Australia's longest freefall ($370)

Byron Gliding Club (☎ 6684 7627; www.byrongliding .com; Tyagarah Airport) Glider joy rides ($80).

KAYAKING

Byron Bay Sea Kayaks (☎ 6685 5830; tour $45) is long-established and respected by both punters and dolphins alike. Expect enthusiastic guides and a barrel of laughs.

SURFING

Blackdog Surfing (☎ 6680 9828; The Plaza, Jonson St; 3-hr lesson $45; 3 days $110) Intimate group lessons and a special course for women.

Mojosurf Adventures (☎ 1800 113 044; www.mojosurf .com.au; Byron Bay-Rainbow Beach 4 days $470, Sydney-Byron Bay $590) All about catching waves. Stop-off points are in surf shacks with all the necessities and a few luxuries.

Surfaris (☎ 1800 634 951; www.surfaris.com; Sydney-Byron Bay return $500) will have you camping under the stars listening to the waves, surfing at daybreak, then

BYRON BAY

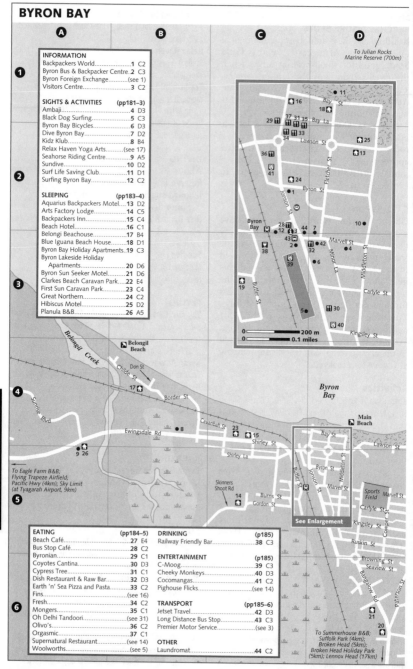

INFORMATION
Backpackers World.....................**1** C2
Byron Bus & Backpacker Centre..**2** C3
Byron Foreign Exchange...........(see 1)
Visitors Centre..........................**3** C2

SIGHTS & ACTIVITIES   (pp181–3)
Ambaji......................................**4** D3
Black Dog Surfing.....................**5** C3
Byron Bay Bicycles...................**6** D3
Dive Byron Bay........................**7** D2
Kidz Klub.................................**8** B4
Relax Haven Yoga Arts............(see 17)
Seahorse Riding Centre.............**9** A5
Sundive...................................**10** D2
Surf Life Saving Club................**11** D1
Surfing Byron Bay....................**12** C2

SLEEPING   (pp183–4)
Aquarius Backpackers Motel....**13** D2
Arts Factory Lodge..................**14** C5
Backpackers Inn......................**15** C4
Beach Hotel.............................**16** C1
Belongi Beachouse...................**17** B4
Blue Iguana Beach House.........**18** D1
Byron Bay Holiday Apartments..**19** C3
Byron Lakeside Holiday
  Apartments............................**20** D6
Byron Sun Seeker Motel...........**21** D6
Clarkes Beach Caravan Park.....**22** E4
First Sun Caravan Park.............**23** C4
Great Northern........................**24** C2
Hibiscus Motel.........................**25** D2
Planula B&B............................**26** A5

EATING   (pp184–5)
Beach Café...............................**27** E4
Bus Stop Café..........................**28** C2
Byronian..................................**29** C1
Coyotes Cantina.......................**30** D3
Cypress Tree............................**31** C1
Dish Restaurant & Raw Bar......**32** D3
Earth 'n' Sea Pizza and Pasta...**33** C2
Fins.......................................(see 16)
Fresh......................................**34** C2
Mongers..................................**35** C1
Oh Delhi Tandoori..................(see 31)
Olivo's....................................**36** C2
Orgasmic.................................**37** C1
Supernatural Restaurant..........(see 14)
Woolworths.............................(see 5)

DRINKING   (p185)
Railway Friendly Bar................**38** C3

ENTERTAINMENT   (p185)
C-Moog...................................**39** C3
Cheeky Monkeys......................**40** D3
Cocomangas............................**41** C2
Pighouse Flicks.......................(see 14)

TRANSPORT   (pp185–6)
Jetset Travel............................**42** D3
Long Distance Bus Stop............**43** C3
Premier Motor Service.............(see 3)

OTHER
Laundromat.............................**44** C2

To Julian Rocks
Marine Reserve (700m)

Belongil Creek

Belongil
Beach

Don St

Childe St

Border St

Byron
Bay

Main
Beach

Sunrise Blvd

Ewingsdale Rd

Cavanbah St

Shirley St

Shirley La

To Eagle Farm B&B;
Flying Trapeze Airfield;
Pacific Hwy (4km); Sky Limit
(at Tyagarah Airport, 9km)

Skinners
Shoot Rd

Burns St

Gordon St

See Enlargement

Bay St

Lawson St

Byron St

Marvell St

Carlyle St

Kingsley St

Sports
Field

Ruskin St

Browning St

Seaview St

Bangalow Rd

Paterson St

To Summerhouse B&B;
Suffolk Park (4km);
Broken Head (5km);
Broken Head Holiday Park
(5km); Lennox Head (17km)

0   200 m
0   0.1 miles

sinking a few of the best at night. A great back-to-nature experience.

Surfing Byron Bay (☎ 0500-853 929; Shop 5, 84 Jonson St; 3-hr lesson $45) An emphasis on having fun and, not surprisingly, getting wet.

HORSE RIDING

Seahorse Riding Centre (☎ 6680 8155; Lot 1A Ewingsdale Rd; half-day beach ride $60) has divine rides along Seven Mile Beach.

Tours

B&B Adventure Company (☎ 6685 4161) Kayaking, dolphins and many other exciting times await.

Byron on Tour (☎ 6680 7006; 3/95 Jonson St) Day trips to Nimbin, sunrise hikes up Mt Warning and all sorts of water sports.

Jim's Alternative Tours (☎ 6685 7720; www.jims alternativetours.com; tours $35) Runs an entertaining tour that will get you looking at the hinterland in a new light.

Peterpan Adventures (☎ 6680 8926, 1800 252 459; www.peterpans.com; 1/87 Jonson St) Internet access; can organise anything, anywhere.

Festivals & Events

The **East Coast International Blues & Roots Music Festival** (www.bluesfest.com.au) at Easter is gathering momentum as a national heavyweight; numerous acts from home and abroad come out into the open. Book early as accommodation and tickets sell like hot cakes. The **Byron Bay Writers Festival** (☎ 6685 5115; www.byronbaywritersfestival.com.au) is in July. The **Byron Bay Community Market** is held in the Butler St Reserve on the first Sunday of every month.

Some other festivals and events:
New Years Celebration (January)
Easter Art Classic Opening (April)
Nimbin Mardi Grass and Byron Bay Triathlon (May)
Whale-watch weekend (July) Opening of the season.
Taste of Byron & Northern Rivers Folk Festival (October)

Sleeping
BUDGET

All hostels demand your attention from the moment you step off the bus, offering special deals and promising the world, so don't feel too special too soon. Look beyond the attractive reps – there is no shortage of choice.

Arts Factory Lodge (☎ 6685 7709; www.artsfactory .com.au; Skinners Shoot Rd; dm/d $27/75; 🖳) For a taste of the *real* Byron, try this cultural haven.

The Cowboy and Indian sleeping arrangements and the Baron's insightful tour make this place one out of the box. Formerly a pig slaughterhouse, it's stunningly renovated. You'd be pink to miss it.

Aquarius Backpackers Motel (☎ 6685 7663; 16 Lawson St; dm/d $30/75; 🖳 🏊) Best described as a village, Aquarius has a bar, pool, travel agent and all home comforts. There are good double rooms, the dorms are clean, the place is great for socialising and it's close to the beach – good reasons not to leave.

Backpackers Inn (☎ 6685 8231; 29 Shirley St; dm/d $20/45; 🖳) Near the beach, this place has friendly staff and good dorms. It's ideal for party enthusiasts, with a layout and vibe conducive to big nights.

Belongil Beachouse (☎ 6685 7868; Childe St; dm/d $25/65; 🖳) Right on the beach and the facilities are reasonable with a nice walk along the sand to the centre of town. There's lots of greenery, free use of body boards and great spots hung with hammocks, perfect for a lie-down and a read.

First Sun Caravan Park (☎ 6685 6544; Main Beach; camp sites/cabins $26/80) Conveniently located close to town, but the grounds are bare in parts.

Clarkes Beach Caravan Park (☎ 6685 6496; off Lighthouse Rd; camp sites/cabins $22/85) A little further out, but this caravan park offers shade and tranquillity.

MID-RANGE

Bamboo Cottage (☎ 6685 5509; www.byron-bay.com /bamboocottage; 76 Butler St; d from $80) Great value, the bedrooms in this pretty 1930s house are sumptuous and brightly – perhaps *too* brightly – coloured. French, English, sign language and some Japanese are spoken.

Amigos (☎ 6680 8622; www.amigosbb.com; 32 Kingsley St; s $45-65, d $70-120) A cute blue and green house with hammocks in the garden and spotless rooms decorated with Mexican rugs. The cottage in the backyard is great.

Planula B&B (☎ 6680 9134; Melaleuca Dr; d $80) Tropical gardens and a nice escape just out of the town centre.

Eagle Farm B&B (☎ 6684 7563; Greys Lane; d $145) Ten minutes north of town, this has its own cute nine-hole golf course.

Great Northern (☎ 6685 6454; Jonson St; s/d $55/ 65) At the best position in town, you can sleep (or try to) listening to sensational tunes and bands playing downstairs.

Byron Sun Seeker Motel (☎ 6685 7369; www .byronsun.com.au; 100 Bangalow Rd; r $100; 🖳) Close to Tallow Beach, always good for a surf.

Recommendations for renting:

Byron Bay Holiday Apartments (☎ 6685 7391; Summerset St)

Byron Lakeside Holiday Apartments (☎ 6680 8666; www.byronbayaccom.net; 5 Old Bangalow Rd)

TOP END

Beach Hotel (☎ 6685 6402; Bay St; r from $220) This is the best outside of Watego's. It has deluxe rooms and a fantastic position.

Summerhouse B&B (☎ 6685 3090; www.thesum merhouse.com.au; 9 Cooper Shoot Rd; r $330-400; 🏊) With panoramic views and a wonderful pool. For pure comfort and enjoyment, this calls to you.

Eating

A number of smart, indulgent cafés lie behind the Beach Hotel. The main concentration of eateries can be found in the upper end of town, with some treasures dotted around the outskirts.

The kebab shops dotted along the main drag are a great late night option; many readers rate the kebabs as sublime.

CAFÉS

Supernatural Restaurant (☎ 6685 5833; Arts Factory Complex, Shinners Shoot Rd; mains $15) Romantic, quirky and stylish, this also accommodates vegans.

Orgasmic (☎ 6680 7778; 11 Bay Lane; mains $8) Some lovely falafels here threaten to do just that to your tastebuds.

Byronian (☎ 6685 6754; 58A Jonson St; mains $7-14) A relaxing café that typifies the Byron style, this will not disappoint with generous serves.

Cypress Tree (☎ 6680 8202; 4 Bay Lane; mains $14) Modern Mediterranean that caters well for vegetarians.

Bus Stop Café (☎ 6680 9200; 4/84 Jonson St; mains $9-17) A Thai and Vietnamese restaurant that offers good value and fantastic food.

QUICK EATS

Mongers (☎ 6680 8080; 1 Bay Lane; combos $9-13) A gourmet fish-and-chip experience – this place hand-cuts its chips.

Cheeky Monkey's (☎ 6685 5886; 115 Jonson St; mains $5-15) A little less particular but noticeably cheaper, this joint has unbeatable backpacker deals.

Earth 'n' Sea Pizza & Pasta (☎ 6685 6029; 11 Lawson St; mains $25) A healthy Italian fix – many succumb to its magical ways.

RESTAURANTS

Coyotes Cantina (☎ 6680 9050; Shop 3, 109 Jonson St; mains $15-20) A funky atmosphere and a genuine Mexican feel in a place where the tequilas get slammed down almost as quickly as the food.

Oh Delhi Tandoori (☎ 6680 8800; 4 Bay Lane; mains $14-20) A quality option for spice lovers.

Fresh (☎ 6685 7810; 7 Jonson St; mains $23) Attracts plenty of attention from locals and tourists alike, always a good sign.

Fins (☎ 6685 5029; The Beach Hotel; mains $35) For arguably the best seafood on the coast, the food here is absolutely delightful as the fish are line-caught and the ingredients come straight out of the chef's backyard.

Olivo's (☎ 6685 7950; 34 Jonson St; mains $24) Europe-influenced menu with gourmet dishes that excite the tastebuds.

Dish Restaurant & Raw Bar (☎ 6685 7320; cnr Jonson & Marvell Sts; mains $28) Tasty food in invigorating surrounds. Later in the night there's loud music and a nightclub atmosphere.

Drinking & Entertainment

Nightlife sees Byron at its flamboyant best.

Beach Hotel (☎ 6685 6402; cnr Bay & Jonson St) One of the best pubs in the land – spacious layout, beautiful people and plenty of entertainment results in a time one should savour.

Great Northern (☎ 6685 6454; Byron St) The town's mainstay for headline bands – a great live venue.

Railway Friendly Bar (☎ 6685 7662; 80 Jonson St) So Byron and so relaxed, a place that sums up this town's thirst for diversity; watch poets and stockbrokers mingle in unique surrounds.

Cheeky Monkeys (☎ 6685 5886; 115 Jonson St) With cheesy tunes, loose backpackers, cheap drinks and tables to dance on, this place rocks late into the night every night.

Cocomangas (☎ 6685 8493; 32 Jonson St) Local crowd in a pumping club with a touch of Europe.

C-Moog (☎ 6680 7022; The Plaza, Jonson St) Craving some harder tunes that go a little deeper into the night? It's cramped, loud and sweaty.

Pighouse Flicks (☎ 6685 5828; Arts Factory; ☿ from 6pm Tue-Sun) A bizarre cinema and an interesting night out. On Friday night an Aboriginal production takes place.

Getting There & Away

Byron Bay Airbus (☎ 6684 3232; www.byronbay buslink.com) operates three times a day from Coolangatta ($35) and Ballina ($30) airports to Byron. A useful Internet site for travel-related information.

McCafferty's/Greyhound (☎ 13 20 30) runs north to Brisbane ($31) and down the coast to Coffs Harbour ($44), Newcastle ($63) and Sydney ($81), or heads west to Tenterfield ($35).

Premier Motor Service (☎ 13 34 10) has three buses a day heading north and south down the east coast; leaves from the tourist information centre and goes to all the regular haunts on the east coast.

UNIVERSAL APPEAL...

When Tom Misner rolled into Byron and laid 40 million smackers on the table to build a university-style institution, the **SAE College** (☎ 6639 6000; www.sae.edu), many thought he was totally lacking in logic. Some may still think the German businessman is, but now there's the most extravagant, New Age, digital recording studio uncovering and educating new artists in the glamorous world of rock and roll. And what better place to do so than in a town like Byron Bay. It's a complex undertaking, which looks set to prosper. Tom Misner loves Byron and now, surely, Byron has unconditional love for him for adding an extra element of universal appeal, a university. But apparently not, with the small-town community wary, and some sectors still believing it is a cover-up for a resort, holding strong reservations about the lined palm trees, an act not in line with council guidelines. That said, it is an unquestionable asset to Byron Bay and the social impact upon the town could be unique and wonderful. If you have a few hours spare – or perhaps a couple of years for a degree – wander out and look at a university that's uniquely 'Byron'. Australian students pay approximately $12,000 annually to attend, not including accommodation costs.

Blanch's Bus Service (☎ 6686 2144) runs daily to Bangalow, Ballina, Lennox Head and Mullumbimby.

Kirklands Coaches (☎ 6622 1499) goes to Brunswick Heads, Brisbane and Lismore.

Countrylink (☎ 13 22 32) rails to Mullumbimby ($5.50) and Murwillumbah ($7.70); and south to Lismore ($7.70) Coffs Harbour ($44), Broadmeadow ($94.60) and Sydney ($102.30). Buses go to Brunswick Heads ($5.50), Evans Head ($13.20) and Yamba ($17.60).

Getting Around

Scooters can be a great way to negotiate hilly terrain. For the exercise friendly, a bicycle ride up to Cape Byron can be rewarding.

Ride On Motorcycles (☎ 6685 6304) will bring the scooter ($59 per day) to you. **Byron Bay Bicycles** (☎ 6685 6067; Woolworths Plaza, Jonson St) hires bikes ($22 per day).

Earth Car Rentals (☎ 6685 7472; small car $39) are cheap but be sure to read the fine print.

Byron Bay Taxis (☎ 6685 5008) are on call 24 hours.

BRUNSWICK HEADS

☎ 02 / pop 1860

Fresh oysters and mud crabs call the Brunswick River home, as do retirees and families who love this place as a quiet getaway with good beaches and great fishing. It is somewhat of a minnow on this coastline, wedged between the Gold Coast and Byron.

The **Terrace Reserve Caravan Park**, close to both river and sea, is extremely popular in summer with a subtle, lazy feel out of season.

Of the motels, the **Heidelberg Holiday Inn** (☎ 6685 1808; 2 The Terrace; s/d $68/78; ☒) is run by friendly staff and gives you a balcony.

Recently refurnished and very inviting, **Hotel Brunswick** (☎ 6685 1233; Mullumbimby St; r without bathroom $70) has good rooms at an affordable rate. **Bruns** (mains $14) downstairs serves tasty food in the shade of poinciana trees.

Surfside (☎ 5536 7666) has local buses up the coast and inland to Murwillumbah. They leave from Tweed Mall on Wharf St.

Countrylink (☎ 13 22 32) has buses to Byron Bay ($5.50), Tweed Heads ($9.90) and Mullumbimby ($5.50) for train connection.

THE TWEED COAST

A sense of inevitability surrounds this line of coast, which markets itself as an extension of the Gold Coast and looks like a poor man's version of it. Sadly enough, the stretch of waterfront is only getting uglier.

The new Pacific Hwy now bypasses the coastline and there is a lot to be said for sticking to this magnificent piece of road, which takes you straight to the jackpot in **Surfers Paradise**. If, however, the urge to use the coastal route overwhelms you, you will encounter the cream brick ghettos of development gone wrong and a great line of sand running all the way up to the Gold Coast.

TWEED HEADS

☎ 07 / pop 73, 800

Tweed Heads represents the beginning of the Gold Coast strip. The border between NSW and Queensland can pass by unnoticed, as there is no river or landmark, but rather an imaginary line.

Orientation & Information

The original part of Tweed Heads lies just north of Tweed River. Coming from the south, after the bypass road branches off, the old Pacific Hwy crosses the river at Boyds Bay Bridge and becomes Wharf St, the long main street. You then meet Boundary St, which will veer to the right to take you up to **Point Danger** for great views and ghastly monuments.

The **Tweed & Coolangatta tourist centre** (☎ 5536 4244; Tweed Mall, ☒ 9am-5pm), in the heart of the mall, is a good first port of call. The **visitors centre** (☎ 5536 7765; Warner St), sponsored by the Gold Coast, is in Coolangatta.

Sights & Activities

There are sweeping views back down the Tweed Coast and up to the glittering highrises of the Gold Coast from the **Mt Toonbarabah Lookout** (Mt Razorback). But beaches are what you come up here for – **Kirra Point** is a big favourite with surfers. Further round, **Kirra Beach** is patrolled year round.

The **Minjungbal Aboriginal Cultural Centre** (☎ 5524 2109; cnr Kirkwood & Duffy Sts; adult/child $15/7.50; ☒ 9am-4pm Mon-Fri, 10am-2pm Sat) gives you an insight into times prior to Europeans, when the Minjungbal people owned the land.

The **Tweed Heritage Maritime Museum** (☎ 5536 8625; Kennedy Dr; adult/child $4/50c; ☒ 11am-4pm Tue/Thu/Fri, 1-4pm Sun) has an interesting array of things, with Boyd's fishing shed well worth a look.

To catch a crab or just cruise, try **Tweed River Catch-a-Crab** (☎ 5599 9972; Dry Dock Rd; tours incl lunch & fishing $55).

Sleeping

Quality Resort Twin Resorts (☎ 5536 2121; cnr Wharf & Griffith Sts; from $169) is a towering building that provides some great views from the higher rooms.

Calico Court Motel (☎ 5524 3333; 29-33 Minjungbal Dr; s/d $59/69; ☒ ☒) One of the motels on the southern entrance to Tweed Heads. Modern, clean rooms.

Also recommended:

Boyds Bay Holiday Park (☎ 5524 3306; Dry Dock Rd; camp sites/cabins $14/67) Riverside camp sites to the tune of the old Pacific Hwy.

Tweed Fairways Motel (☎ 5524 2111; cnr Pacific Hwy & Soorley St; s/d $50/65) Has cheap rooms and is centrally located.

Eating

Scales (☎ 5536 6937; 47 Kennedy Dr; baskets $4) This is simply a top fish-and-chip shop, where you can relax and enjoy your catch by the river.

Jimbo's on the Wharf (☎ 5536 1160; River Tce; mains $22) Try this for a wide range of seafood.

Manti's Seafoods (☎ 5599 2343; 2 River Tce; basket from $5.50) Another tempting seafood option.

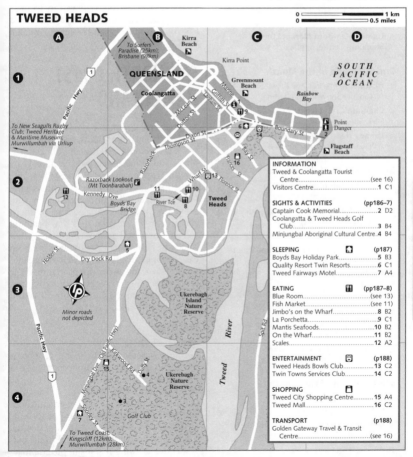

Also recommended:

Tweed Heads Bowls Club (☎ 5536 3800; cnr Wharf & Florence Sts; mains $12) Great for a cheap feed; its Blue Room's not bad for a step up in style.

La Porchetta (☎ 5536 3545; Shop 12, 87 Griffith St; mains $8) For cheap, no-fuss Italian, and it knows a thing or two about pizzas.

MARKETS OF THE HINTERLAND

Weekly Markets

- **Lismore Farmers Market** Lismore Showground, Saturday 8am-noon
- **Rainbow Region Organic Markets** Lismore Showground, Tuesday 8-11am

1st Weekend of the Month

- **Brunswick Heads** Memorial Park, Saturday
- **Lismore Car Boot Market** Lismore Shopping Centre, Sunday

2nd Weekend of the Month

- **Alstonville Market** Apex Pavilion, Alstonville Showground, Sunday
- **Channon Craft Market** Coronation Park, Sunday
- **Lennox Head Lakeside Market** Lake Ainsworth Foreshore, Sunday

3rd Weekend of the Month

- **Aquarius Fair Markets** Nimbin Community Centre, Sunday
- **Ballina Markets** Circus Ground, Sunday
- **Lismore Car Boot Market** Lismore Shopping Centre, Sunday
- **Mullumbimby Museum Market** Stuart St, Saturday
- **Uki Buttery Bazaar** Uki Village Buttery, Sunday

4th Weekend of the Month

- **Bangalow Village Market** Bangalow Showground, Sunday
- **Evans Head Riverside Market** Recreation Reserve, Saturday

5th Weekend of the Month

- **Aquarius Fair Markets** Nimbin Community Centre, Sunday
- **Lennox Head Lakeside Market** Lake Ainsworth Showground, Sunday

---

Entertainment

First-class Australian and international acts appear at the following clubs:

Twin Towns Services Club (☎ 5536 2277; www.twin towns.com.au; Wharf St)

New Seagulls Rugby Club (☎ 5536 3433; www.seagulls club.com.au; Gollan Drv, Tweed Heads West).

Getting There & Around

All long-distance buses stop at the Golden Gateway Travel & Transit Centre on Bay St.

All **Countrylink** (☎ 13 22 32) buses head south to Murwillumbah and you switch to rails down the coast.

Surfside (☎ 5536 7666) runs the local yellow buses up to the Gold Coast and south to Brunswick Heads with relentless monotony.

Several car-hire places have cars from as little as $20 a day, such as **Tweed Auto Rentals** (☎ 5536 8000) at the visitors centre. Or call a **taxi** (☎ 5536 1144).

FAR NORTH COAST HINTERLAND

Kombi vans, hippies, organic cafés, great markets, tremendous B&Bs, exquisite country and incredible waterfalls all call the hinterland home. Twenty-two million years ago an eruption of lava from Mt Warning created the northern half of the hinterland, flattening the valley and enclosing it with dramatic mountain ranges. The southern end is a maze of steep hills and beautiful valleys, some still harbouring magnificent stands of rainforest while others have been cleared for cattle grazing as well as macadamia nut, avocado and coffee plantations. The area's three national parks – Border Ranges, Mt Warning and Nightcap – are all World Heritage rainforests.

LISMORE

☎ 02 / pop 27,360

Formerly ridiculed as 'Dis-more', Lismore is starting to show promise and prominence in the region. The town leads Australia in the reprocessing of organic goods, so much so that it is the only town to have organic bins. The **Southern Cross University** campus students are filling up the cosmopolitan cafés that sell locally produced coffee from one of the biggest coffee-growing regions in the country.

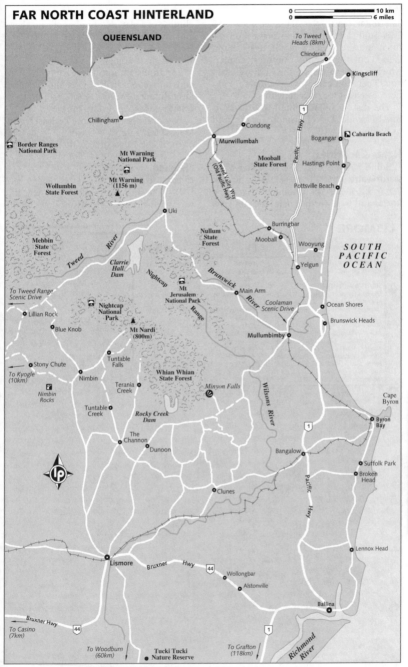

FAR NORTH COAST HINTERLAND

0 — 10 km
0 — 6 miles

QUEENSLAND

To Tweed
Heads (8km)

Chinderah

Kingscliff

Chillingham

Condong

Border Ranges
National Park

Bogangar · Cabarita Beach

Murwillumbah

Mt Warning
National Park

Mooball
State Forest

Hastings Point

Wollumbin
State Forest

Mt Warning
(1156 m)

Pottsville Beach

Uki

Burringbar

Nullum
State Forest

Mooball

Wooyung

Mebbin
State
Forest

Tweed River

Brunswick River

SOUTH
PACIFIC
OCEAN

Clarrie
Hall
Dam

Nightcap

Yelgun

Main Arm

To Tweed Range
Scenic Drive

Mt
Jerusalem
National Park

Coolaman
Scenic Drive

Ocean Shores

Lillian Rock

Nightcap
National
Park

Brunswick Heads

Blue Knob

Mt Nardi
(800m)

Range

Mullumbimby

To Kyogle
(10km)

Stony Chute

Tuntable
Falls

Cape
Byron

Nimbin

Whian Whian
State Forest

Wilsons River

Nimbin
Rocks

Terania
Creek

Minyon Falls

Byron
Bay

Tuntable
Creek

Rocky Creek
Dam

The
Channon

Bangalow

Suffolk Park

Dunoon

Broken
Head

Clunes

Pacific Hwy

Lismore

Bruxner Hwy 44

Lennox Head

Wollongbar

Alstonville

Ballina

Bruxner Hwy 44

To Casino
(7km)

To Woodburn
(60km)

Tucki Tucki
Nature Reserve

To Grafton
(118km)

Richmond River

NORTH COAST

Information

The **visitors centre** (☎ 6622 0122; cnr Molesworth & Ballina Sts) has extensive information on the town and the rainbow region to its north. Check out the famous rainforest display, which is sure to inspire the bushwalker in you. Then you can buy topographic maps here, essential for such activities.

The district's **NPWS office** (☎ 6627 0200) is in Alstonville, east of Lismore on the road to Ballina.

Sights & Activities

Wildlife is abundant. The **Koala Care & Research Centre** (☎ 6622 1233; Rifle Range Rd; admission free; ⏳ 9.30-10.30am Sat) is home to recovering koalas and well worth a visit (you can view animals from outside anytime). To get a glimpse of a platypus, head up the northern end of Kadina St and walk up to **Tucki Tucki Creek**; your best bet is at dawn or dusk to witness these animals in the wild.

For an insight into European settlement and indigenous tribes visit the **Richmond River Historical Society** (☎ 6621 9993; 165 Molesworth St; admission $2; ⏳ 10am-4pm Mon-Fri).

For local art, the Lismore **Regional Art Gallery** (☎ 6622 2209; 131 Molesworth St; ⏳ 10am-4pm Tue- Fri, 10.30am-2.30pm Sat & Sun) is child-friendly.

Sleeping

Lismore Backpackers (☎ 6621 6118; 14 Ewing St; dm/d $22/47) The only backpackers in town, this was originally a maternity hospital and the

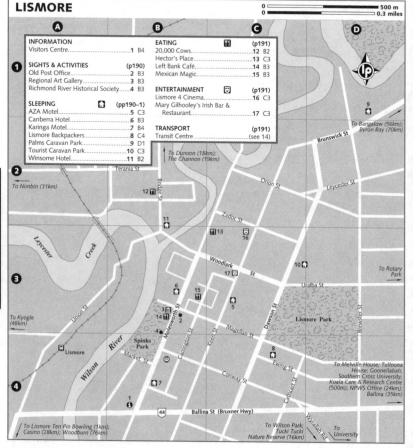

LISMORE

INFORMATION	
Visitors Centre	1 B4

SIGHTS & ACTIVITIES	(p190)
Old Post Office	2 B3
Regional Art Gallery	3 B3
Richmond River Historical Society	4 B3

SLEEPING	(pp190–1)
AZA Motel	5 C3
Canberra Hotel	6 B3
Karinga Motel	7 B4
Lismore Backpackers	8 C4
Palms Caravan Park	9 D1
Tourist Caravan Park	10 C3
Winsome Hotel	11 B2

EATING	(p191)
20,000 Cows	12 B2
Hector's Place	13 C3
Left Bank Café	14 B3
Mexican Magic	15 B3

ENTERTAINMENT	(p191)
Lismore 4 Cinema	16 C3
Mary Gilhooley's Irish Bar & Restaurant	17 C3

TRANSPORT	(p191)
Transit Centre	(see 14)

old weatherboard building is named Currendina Lodge, meaning 'place of healing' in the language of the local Bundjalung Aborigines. It's close to spotless and friendly.

Winsome Hotel (☎ 6621 2283; 75 Bridge St; s/d $35/50) This is clean and vibrant.

Canberra Hotel (☎ 6622 4736; 77 Molesworth St; r $65) For something a little different, this has themed rooms and a good level of privacy.

Karinga Motel (☎ 6621 2787; 258 Molesworth St; s/d $70/80; ⚥) Clean, affordable and central, Karinga is the best of a select few.

Also recommended:

AZA Motel (☎ 6621 9499; 114 Keen St; s/d $65/70; ⚥ ⚥) A little cheaper and barer in the rooms.

Tourist Caravan Park (☎ 6621 6581; 60 Dawson St; camp sites/cabins $17/40) Centrally located.

Palms Caravan Park (☎ 6621 7067; 42-58 Brunswick St; camp sites/cabins $15/50) Also central, welcomes dogs.

Eating

Mexican Magic (☎ 6621 8206; 6 Carrington St; mains $16) All your South American favourites at a reasonable price.

Hector's Place (☎ 6621 6566; 34 Molesworth St; mains $22) Hector the crocodile called the Wilson River home until he disappeared in the 1974 floods. Most nights here you can snap one of his relatives up for dinner.

Left Bank Café (☎ 6622 2338; 133 Molesworth St; mains $18) This has some pizzaz and innovation with its layout and menu.

20,000 Cows (☎ 6622 2517; 58 Bridge St; mains $15; ☽ dinner Wed-Sat) For vegetarians, you'll find a good array of international cuisine, from Indian to Middle Eastern.

Entertainment

Mary Gilhooley's Irish Bar & Restaurant (☎ 6622 2924; cnr Woodlark & Keen Sts) With live bands, this is a popular outing.

Canberra Hotel (☎ 6622 4736; Molesworth St) A pumping establishment, the Canberra has a nightclub and plenty of pool tables.

Lismore 4 Cinema (☎ 6621 2361; cnr Keen & Zadoc Sts; movie $10) To catch a flick, here are all Hollywood's latest.

Lismore Ten Pin Bowling (☎ 6621 2479; Krauss Ave; game $18) A family favourite that is sure to tire the little ones.

Getting There & Around

Regional Express (☎ 13 17 13) has three Sydney flights a day ($134); the airport is 3km southwest of town towards Casino.

Premier Motor Service (☎ 13 34 10) has one bus a day going north and south, departing from the Transit Centre on Molesworth St.

Kirklands Coaches (☎ 6622 1499) runs to Byron Bay, Evans Head, Brunswick Heads, Ballina and Brisbane, and also across to Casino and Tenterfield.

Wallers Bus Company (☎ 6687 8550) goes to Murwillumbah, stopping in Nimbin daily.

Countrylink (☎ 13 22 32) rails to Byron Bay ($7.70), Murwillumbah ($16.50), Grafton ($23.10), Coffs Harbour ($39.60) and Sydney ($102.30); and buses to Ballina ($5.50) and Brunswick Heads ($12.10).

Kirklands has urban-area buses, and there are 24-hour **taxis** (☎ 6621 2618).

THE CHANNON

The Channon is an intimate village between Nimbin and Lismore. If you can, time your visit for the second Sunday of the month for the 'mother of all markets', according to local pundits. It shouldn't be overlooked by the wandering traveller.

Havan's (☎ 02-6688 6108; www.rainbowregion.com /havan; Lot1, Lawler Rd; s/d $75/115) is an eco-tourist retreat set in the heart of a rainforest. It's all about connecting with nature and seeking inspiration for life.

NIGHTCAP NATIONAL PARK

South of Murwillumbah, north of Lismore and bordering Nimbin and The Channon is the Nightcap National Park, encompassing just over 8000 hectares. It was World Heritage–listed in 1989. The park's home to diverse subtropical rainforests and many species of wildlife, notably the bent-winged bat, the wompoo fruit-dove, the masked owl and the red-legged pademelon (a relative of the wallaby). With the highest annual rainfall in NSW, the park has spectacular waterfalls, gorgeous green gullies and sheer cliff walls. The exposed rock pinnacles of the **Sphinx** can be seen from Lismore.

You can choose from walks, lookouts and picnic spots to enjoy; and **Mt Nardi** (800m) offers a challenging climb. The NPWS can supply detailed maps and advice on many walks, including the Terania Creek area.

NIMBIN

☎ 02 / pop 400

'I'm livin' in the seventies' is not far from the truth with the time warp that is Nimbin.

The year was 1973 and the Aquarius Festival injected a way of life not seen before on Australian soil – it was the back-end of the hippy movement and the alternative culture transformed this dairy town into a haze of marijuana. Nowadays, Nimbin is approaching a fork in the road, for as Lismore becomes the regional centre of prominence and north-coast property prices soar, hippies are suddenly occupying valuable real estate. The local council is showing interest in the area and development could lead to the radical greens being pushed further afield.

Orientation & Information

Cullen St runs through the town and, to dispel myths, the town is in reality a small village.

The **Nimbin Connexion** (☎ 6689 1764; www.nimbinconnexion.com) is at the northern end of town and has accommodation options, bus tickets and a wealth of knowledge. Local literature should give you a gauge of the town's issues; *Nimbin & Environs* and *Nimbin News* (both $3.30) are absorbing reads.

Sights & Activities

An experience that justifies the drive up the mountain (unless you're after the effect) is the wacky and wonderful **Nimbin Museum** (☎ 6689 1123; 62 Cullen St; admission free; 9am-5pm). A kombi crashed through the front window and words of wisdom like 'love the child within yourself unconditionally' are etched on the walls.

The **Hemp Embassy** (Cullen St) is happy to discuss visas, legalisation and the fact that grass is always greener on the other side.

Many make the journey to see the **Djanbung Gardens** (☎ 6689 1430; 74 Cecil St; admission free; 10am-4pm Tue-Sat), a permaculture education centre established by Robyn Francis, a disciple of permaculture guru Bill Mollison.

Successful and world-renowned, the **Rainbow Power Company** (☎ 6689 1430; No 1 Alternative Way; admission free; 9am-5pm Mon-Fri, 9am-noon Sat) designs and produces 'appropriate home-energy systems' that use nature's forces – the sun, wind and water – to generate electricity, and they are exported to all corners of the globe. You can visit the complex and soak up the sun – but not too much, unless you can transform it into electricity.

On the third Sunday of the month a **band** comes to town and plays at the Community Centre, the curtain-raiser for a popular **market**.

Tours & Special Events

The **Nimbin Shuttle Bus** ($5; tours 2pm) is a good daily one-hour tour of the Rainbow Factory and Djanbung Gardens. The **Mardi Grass Festival**, at the end of April, ends in a big puff of smoke with the Marijuana Harvest Ball.

Sleeping

YHA Nimbin Rox Hostel (☎ 6689 0022; 74 Thornburn St; dm/d $20/48) Laid-back and chilled the Nimbin way, it's situated west of the town and has a clean layout.

Nimbin Backpackers at Granny's Farm (☎ 6689 1333; Cullen St; dm/d $20/48) A touch more upbeat, and the Oz Experience bus stops here four times a week.

Nimbin Hotel (☎ 6689 0199, Cullen St; r $20) This place has probably the loudest psychedelic-coloured rooms you will ever see. If you mix up the right cocktail, the Wiggles could well appear from out of the walls.

Eating

Rainbow Café (☎ 6689 1997; 70 Cullen St; mains $7) If you've got the munchies, the Rainbow has seen it all before, and you have never seen such delicious cakes.

Hub (☎ 6689 0084; Sibley St; mains $8) At the community centre, the Hub has some good alternative snacks and is vegetarian-friendly.

Nimbin Pizza and Trattoria, (☎ 6689 1427; 64a Cullen St; specials $5) Just up from the museum, this has good deals and the pasta is something to savour.

Pins Bistro (☎ 6689 0199; 80 Cullen St) Good grub at the Nimbin Hotel.

Entertainment

Nimbin is about spontaneous entertainment and a walk down the main street should present many free shows, be it strange people or wonderful acts.

Nimbin Hotel (☎ 6689 0199; 80 Cullen St) Constantly buzzing with activity, and gets rolling on weekends with live music, disco tunes and many wonderful characters.

At the old butter factory, the **Bush Theatre** shows films on Friday and Saturday.

Getting There & Away

The **Nimbin Shuttle** (☎ 6680 9189) operates between Byron Bay and Nimbin.

GET CONFIDENT

A lot of people get intimidated when visiting Nimbin, stemming from its open drug aspect. Once you get past its green side, it is quite a harmonious and humorous little village. As a general rule of thumb, watch out for the hippies, steer clear of the junkies and you will discover a tight-knit community with an easy philosophy on life.

Wallers Bus Company (☎ 6687 8550) stops here on its daily Lismore–Murwillumbah run.

The simplest driving routes are from Lismore from the south and from Uki in the north. If driving why not keep driving in one direction, a good way of soaking up the hinterland.

AROUND NIMBIN
Nimbin Rocks, an Aboriginal sacred site, lies about 6km south of town, well signposted off Stony Chute (Kyogle) Rd. **Hanging Rock Creek** has falls and a good swimming hole; take the road through Stony Chute for 14km, turn right at the Barkers Vale sign, then left onto Williams Rd; the falls are nearby on the right.

See Nightcap National Park (p191) for information on Mt Nardi.

BANGALOW
☎ 02 / pop 1230
Bangalow's appeal lies in the character of its main street, Byron St, where a collection of old buildings is occupied by good eateries, art and craft shops and relaxed locals. There's a great market here on the fourth Sunday of every month. Just 14km out of Byron Bay, it's well worth a trip for a relaxing lunch.

Sleeping
Riverview (☎ 6687 1317; 99 Byron St; s/d $90/95) This comes complete with a hydrotherapy spa – you are sure to relax.

Possum Creek Lodge (☎ 6687 1188; 2km out of town off Possum Creek Rd; 2 nights per person $120). A nice sleeping-hole just out of town that has a touch of class.

Eating
Cafés and the like are aplenty along the main street and you're spoilt for choice.

Urban Café (☎ 6687 2678; 39 Byron St; mains $6-14) Unbeatable for a relaxed breakfast or delicious lunch in an inviting environment.

Country Fresh (☎ 6687 1711; Byron St; mains $22) At the Bangalow Hotel, this has mouthwatering meals in luscious surrounds.

Wild about Food (☎ 6687 2555; Byron St; mains $25) This has changing art exhibitions and specialises in seafood.

I Scream for Sweets (Byron St) Here you should satisfy the kids and the kid in you.

MULLUMBIMBY
☎ 02 / pop 3000
Referred to as Mullum by most, the town is a community centre for the valley. It succeeds at this level, but fails to inspire at much else. For much of its time it was renowned for its marijuana, Mullumbimby Madness. But now the town's focus is on supplying the farming community with the more traditional fertiliser.

Orientation & Information
Burringbar St is the main shopping street and runs off Dalley St, the main road through town. There is no visitors centre in town but the locals are as friendly as they come, so don't hesitate to strike up a yarn.

Sights & Activities
Crystal Castle (☎ 6684 3111; Monet Dr; admission free; ☼ 10am-5pm) has labyrinthine gardens and an impressive collection of crystals – the energy from these beauties is all the rage.

The **Brunswick Valley Historical Society Museum** (☎ 6684 1149; Stuart St), open the third Saturday of each month, offers a comprehensive insight into days gone by, and you're likely to see some grand old buildings around town.

Sleeping
Maca's Camping Ground (☎ 6684 5211; Main Arm Rd; camp sites $17) Camping under a macadamianut plantation is what Maca's offers and delivers. The facilities aren't fantastic but the surrounds are, just 12km north of Mullum.

Commercial Hotel (☎ 6684 3229; cnr Burringbar & Stuart Sts; s/d $25/40) Standing since 1907, this is great value and the bar downstairs has an inviting atmosphere.

Mullumbimby Motel (☎ 6684 2387; 121 Dalley St; s/d $52/60; ☼) A good budget motel option on the main road.

Eating

Café Al Dente (☎ 6684 3676; Shop 1, 53 Stuart St; mains $9-18; ☺ closed Sun) A Mediterranean menu, great coffee and cosmopolitan feel.

Lulu's Café (☎ 6684 2415; Dalley St Plaza; mains $8) Lulu's is ideal for organic food lovers, excelling with a gourmet vegetarian menu.

Commercial Hotel (☎ 6684 3229; cnr Burringbar & Stuart Sts; mains $14) Reasonable counter meals with steaks to satisfy the biggest appetite.

Threeways (☎ 6684 0255; Wilson Creek Rd; mains $5-13) If you're driving, go south and turn right into Wilson Creek Rd at the golf course: a pleasant drive up the valley will bring you to this dreamy café nestled in the depths of the hinterland.

Getting There & Away

Blanch's Bus Service (☎ 6686 2144) runs daily to Byron Bay, Lennox Head and Ballina.

Mullumbimby is best reached by train as buses are a rarity. **Countrylink** (☎ 13 22 32) rails north to Murwillumbah ($5.50) and buses onto Tweed Heads ($12.10). South trains run past Byron Bay ($5.50), Lismore ($9.90), Coffs Harbour ($47.30) and Sydney ($102.30).

WHIAN WHIAN STATE FOREST

Timber is produced in this forest and is regarded as a prime example of how forestry resources can be best utilised and managed. The forest adjoins the southeast side of Nightcap National Park and is home to the Albert's lyrebird.

The spectacular **Minyon Falls** are found here, plunging 100m into a rainforest gorge and surrounded by a flora reserve with several walking tracks. Take a dip under the falls for an unforgettable experience.

The historic Nightcap Track (16km long) passes through both the state forest and Nightcap National Park and was the original track used by postal workers and others in the late 19th and early 20th century. **Rummery Park** is not far off the road down from the falls and is a well-provided picnic spot with barbecues and cold showers. Peate's Mountain Lookout, just on from Rummery Park, gives you a great panoramic view from Jerusalem Mountain in the north, to Byron Bay in the east.

The **Mud Manor Forest Retreat** (☎ 02-6688 2205; www.mudmanor.com; per couple incl buffet breakfast $80; 💻) is a perfect haven for those who just want to get away from the crowds and into the mystical magic of the hills; this hand-crafted house has beds made with love and spa baths that ooze romance.

UKI

☎ 02 / pop 210

Uki (*uke*-i) is a cute town that is overshadowed by the dominating peak of **Mt Warning**. The alternative feel of the town is indicative of the hinterland's rainbow population.

Uki Dreaming Café (☎ 6679 5351; Main St; mains $6-12) has a vegetarian menu, passionate staff and an organic feel. It has live entertainments most weekends. The town also has a unique **bead shop** and **leathergoods store**. The **Uki Dreaming Guesthouse** (☎ 6679 5777; Mitchell St; s/d $40/80) is in an old weatherboard house overlooking the town. There are a number of other places to stay in the area, including the **Midginbil Hill Country Resort** (☎ 6679 7158; Town Green; s/d with dinner $100/160) which offers you horse riding, as well as canoeing on the Clarrie Hall dam.

MT WARNING NATIONAL PARK

Relatively small in size (2380 hectares), this is the most dramatic feature of the hinterland, with Mt Warning (1156m) towering over the valley. The peak is the first part of mainland Australia to be touched by sunlight each day. This has resulted in 60,000 people each year making the 2½-hour morning trek up the mountain (don't forget a torch). Captain Cook named this mountain in 1770, to warn seamen of the offshore reefs. The Aboriginal people called it Wollumbin, meaning: 'cloud catcher', 'fighting chief of the mountain' and 'weather maker'. Speaking of weather, don't climb it in a storm as the lookout, the highest in the region, is made of steel.

You can't camp at Mt Warning, but the **Mt Warning Caravan Park & Tourist Retreat** (☎ 02-6679 5120; Mt Warning Rd; camp sites/cabins $16/46) on the Mt Warning approach road, is a viable option, with good kitchen facilities and a well-stocked kiosk.

Wallers Bus Company (☎ 6687 8550) runs from Lismore ($19) to the turn-off for Mt Warning every morning and runs past in the afternoon. Call for changing times.

Alternatively, if you stay at YHA Murwillumbah for two nights or more there is a free drop-off/pick-up service.

MURWILLUMBAH

☎ 02 / pop 7600

This town is on the plateau of the Tweed Valley, surrounded by banana and sugar-cane plantations. It is a focal point of commercial interaction in the hinterland. It's also a gateway to the NSW–Queensland Border Ranges and home to stunning views of Mt Warning (including spectacular sunsets).

Information

The **visitors centre** (☎ 6672 1340; www.tweed -coolangatta.com; cnr Alma St & Tweed Valley Way) has national park passes, information on accommodation, and a great rainforest display.

Sights

The **Tweed River Art Gallery** (☎ 6670 2790; www .tweed.nsw.gov.au/artgallery; cnr Mistral Rd & Tweed Valley Way; admission free) is newly opened and has some great Australian art. The gallery administers Australia's richest prize for traditional art, the $100,000 Doug Moran Prize. Works of past winners are on display.

The **Murwillumbah Museum** (☎ 6672 1865; 2 Queensland Rd; adult/child $2/1.50; � 11am-4pm Wed-Fri)

has a solid account of local history and an interesting radio room.

Just north of the town is a kids' paradise, **Tropical Fruit World** (☎ 6677 7222; www.tropical fruitworld.com.au; Duranbah Rd; ☉ 10am-5pm), which has the Big Avocado, a massive selection of tropical fruits and a couple of fun rides.

Tours

Northern Breeze (☎ 07-5524 2264; northernbreeze@ omcs.com.au; per person $25-40) runs tours that pick you up at your door and take you through national parks, Nimbin and attractions of the Tweed Valley.

Sleeping

Riverside YHA (☎ 6672 3763; 1 Tumbulgum Rd; dm/d $24/52) Beautifully located on the edge of the Tweed River, with views of Mt Warning; there's also free ice cream every night at 9pm, so don't be late back from the pub. Canoes and bikes are available to hire, and there's free transport to the base of the Mt Warning climb if you stay more than two nights.

Imperial Hotel (☎ 6672 2777; 115 Main St; s/d $25/40) Big and pink, it has standard pub

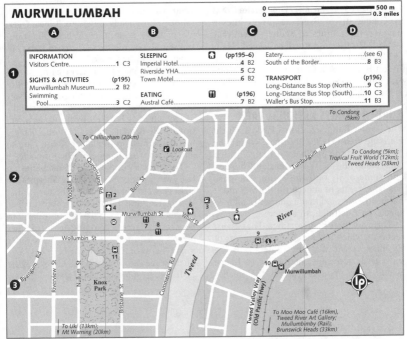

accommodation in a pub that has plenty of charm.

Town Motel (☎ 6672 8600; 3 Wharf St; s/d $55/60; ⊠) The pick of the motels, with position, facilities and local knowledge.

Eating

Austral Café (☎ 6672 2624; 88 Main St; mains $6) Good cake and coffee incorporated with 1950s elegance.

Eatery (☎ 6672 2667; 3 Wharf St; mains $20) This is a favourite among locals with its simple no-fuss menu, plus you can BYO.

South of the Border (☎ 6672 2694; 5 Wollumbi St; mains $15) There are many rich Mexican dishes here that are sure to add a bit of kick to your belly.

Moo Moo Café (☎ 6677 1230; Tweed Valley Way, Mooball; mains $8) Halfway between Murwillumbah and Brunswick Heads is an intriguing black-and-white themed café; a rather entertaining roadside stop if you enjoy cows.

Getting There & Away

McCafferty's/Greyhound (☎ 13 20 30; www.mccaffertys .com.au) Daily to the Gold Coast ($15) and Byron Bay ($13). **Premier Motor Service** (☎ 13 34 10) goes up to Brisbane three times a day and three times to Sydney. **Countrylink** (☎ 13 22 32) buses run north to Tweed Heads ($5.50) and Brisbane ($19.80). Rails to Byron Bay ($7.70), Grafton ($39.60), Coffs Harbour ($53.90) and Sydney ($110). This is the end of the northern rail.

BORDER RANGES NATIONAL PARK

The Border Ranges National Park, a World Heritage area (31,500 hectares), covers the NSW side of the McPherson Range, which runs along the NSW–Queensland border, and some of its outlying spurs. The park has large tracts of superb rainforest, and it has been estimated that a quarter of all bird species in Australia can be here.

There are three main sections. The eastern section – which includes the escarpments of the massive Mt Warning caldera – is the most easily accessible, via the Tweed Range Scenic Drive. You can access the smaller central section from the Lions Rd, which turns off the Kyogle–Woodenbong road 22km north of Kyogle. The large and rugged western section is almost inaccessible except to well-equipped bushwalkers, but there are good views of its peaks from the Kyogle–Woodenbong road.

The **Tweed Range Scenic Drive** – gravel but usable in all weather – loops through the park from Lillian Rock (midway between Uki and Kyogle) to Wiangaree (north of Kyogle on the Woodenbong road). The signposting on access roads isn't good (when in doubt take roads signposted to the national park), but it's well worth the effort of finding it. The road is unsuitable for caravans and large vehicles.

The road runs through mountain forest most of the way, with steep hills and breathtaking lookouts over the Tweed Valley to Mt Warning and the coast. The adrenaline-charging walk out to the crag called the **Pinnacle** – about half an hour's walk from the road and back – is not for vertigo sufferers! At **Antarctic Beech** there is, not surprisingly, a forest of Antarctic beeches. Some of these trees are more than 2000 years old. From here, a walking track (about 5km) leads down to **Brindle Creek**, where there is stunningly beautiful rainforest and a picnic area. The road also runs down to Brindle Creek.

From the **Sheepstation Creek** camp sites a walking track connects with the Caldera Rim Walk (three or four days) in Lamington National Park, over the border in Queensland.

Mebbin State Forest is by the eastern section of the Border Ranges National Park – this is the bush you will see if you dare to look down when you're on the Pinnacle.

There are a couple of **NPWS camp sites** on the Tweed Range Scenic Drive. **Sheepstation Creek** is about 15km north of the turn-off at Wiangaree, and **Forest Tops** is 6km further on, high on the range. There are toilets but no showers and a camping fee of $3 per person is required at both sites. Tank water might be available, but it's best to BYO. There's free camping at Byrill Creek, on the eastern side of **Mebbin State Forest**.

New England

CONTENTS

New England sits atop the Great Dividing Range, stretching north from around Newcastle to the Queensland border. The region is a vast tableland of sheep and cattle-grazing country dotted with rainforest, which tumbles over the eastern escarpment onto coastal plains below.

You can explore numerous national parks and historic towns, and enjoy country hospitality in a region that is charmingly naive about tourism. It provides a contrast to the coastal crowds and offers an opportunity to explore prime working country, with, literally, some hidden gems to uncover. If you're travelling along the eastern seaboard, it's well worth diverting inland to visit some of the area's little towns and get a glimpse of the Australian lifestyle away from the coast. The people here are passionately Australian, their attitudes refreshingly honest, and there's plenty to see along the way – from the country music scene in Tamworth, to the scenic surrounds of university town Armidale and sapphire-hunting along the Fossickers Way. Sure, the drive along the spectacular World Heritage–listed national parks that line the Waterfall Way takes a day, but with so much natural beauty on offer, why not take a few?

The New England Hwy, which runs from Hexham (northwest of Newcastle) to Brisbane, has far less traffic than the coastal roads and is an inland alternative to the Pacific Hwy.

NEW ENGLAND

HIGHLIGHTS

- Boot-scooting at the Tamworth **Country Music Festival** (p200)
- Experiencing the young blood and high altitude of **Armidale** (p204)
- Braving the fast-developing adventure-sports scene at **Manilla** (p211)
- Visiting accessible and impressive **Dangar Falls** (p207)
- Climbing **Bald Rock** (p210), the largest granite rock in the southern hemisphere
- Discovering the old-town charm of **Nundle** (p210)
- Horse riding around the countryside of **Bingara** (p212)
- Taking a helicopter trip around the **New England National Park** (p207)

NEW ENGLAND

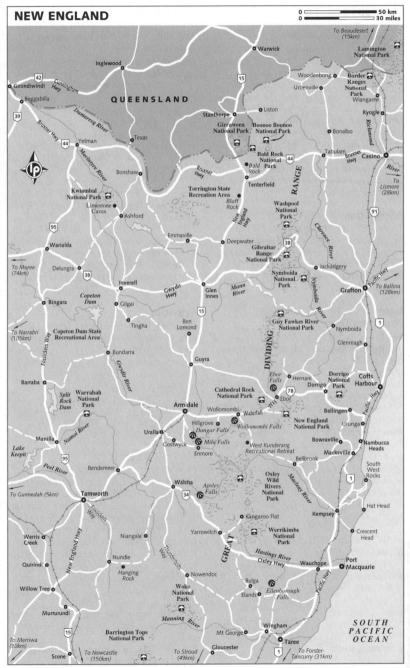

0   50 km
0   30 miles

To Beaudesert
(15km)

Warwick

Lamington
National Park

Inglewood

Woodenbong

Urbenville

Border
Ranges
National
Park

Wiangaree

Goodiwindi

Cunningham Hwy

42

Boggabilla

Dumaresq River

QUEENSLAND

Liston

Kyogle

39

Bruxner Hwy

Texas

Stanthorpe

Girraween
National Park

Boonoo Boonoo
National Park

Bonalbo

Richmond River

44

Yetman

Macintyre River

Bald Rock
National Park

Tabulam

Bruxner Hwy

Casino

Bonshaw

Bruxner
Hwy

Bald
Rock

RANGE

River

To
Lismore
(28km)

Kwiambal
National Park

Torrington State
Recreation Area

Bluff
Rock

Tenterfield

91

Limestone
Caves

Ashford

New England Hwy

Washpool
National
Park

95

Emmaville

Deepwater

Clarence River

Warialda

Gibraltar
Range
National Park

38

To Moree
(74km)

38

Inverell

Gwydir
Hwy

Glen
Innes

Mann
River

Jackadgery

Nymboida
National
Park

Grafton

Pacific Hwy

To Ballina
(128km)

Bingara

Copeton
Dam

Gilgai

15

Nymboida River

Delungra

Nymboida

To Narrabri
(105km)

Copeton Dam State
Recreational Area

Tingha

Ben
Lomond

Guy Fawkes River
National Park

Glenreagh

1

Fossickers Way

Bundarra

Gwydir River

Guyra

DIVIDING

Ebor
Falls

Hernani

Dorrigo
National
Park

Coffs
Harbour

Barraba

Warrabah
National
Park

Split
Rock
Dam

Cathedral Rock
National Park

Ebor

78

Dorrigo

Waterfall Way

Bellingen

Pacific Hwy

Manilla

Armidale

Wollomombi

Waterfall

New England
National Park

Urunga

Namoi River

Hillgrove

Wollomombi Falls

Nambucca
Heads

Lake
Keepit

Uralla

Dangar Falls

Bowraville

Peel River

Gostwyck

Mihi Falls

West Kunderang
Recreational Retreat

Macksville

95

Bendemeer

Enmore

Bellbrook

South
West
Rocks

To Gunnedah (5km)

Walcha

34

Apsley
Falls

Oxley
Wild
Rivers
National
Park

Mackay River

Hat Head

Tamworth

Fossickers Way

Kempsey

Kangaroo Flat

Werris
Creek

Niangala

New England Hwy

Yarrowitch

Werrikimbe
National
Park

GREAT

Crescent
Head

Quirindi

Nundle

Thunderbolts Way

Hastings River

1

Oxley Hwy

Wauchope

Port
Macquarie

Willow Tree

Hanging
Rock

Nowendoc

Bulga

Pacific Hwy

Murrurundi

Woko
National
Park

Elands

Ellenborough
Falls

**SOUTH
PACIFIC
OCEAN**

To Merriwa
(10km)

15

Manning River

Mt George

Wingham

To Forster-
Tuncurry (31km)

Scone

Barrington Tops
National Park

To Newcastle
(150km)

To Stroud
(49km)

Gloucester

Taree

1

TAMWORTH

☎ 02 / pop 32,550

Tamworth is not so much a town as an institution, not so much a regional centre as a holy land. The religion is country music, the god Slim Dusty and the holy grail the biggest golden guitar in the world. This is cattle country, and the locals can not only lay claim to being darn good farmers, but also the pioneers of the Australian Country Music Festival. The town is the black sheep (or should we say the white cow) of the region, and the area's heritage doesn't revolve around Scottish ancestors and misty moors, but around steel guitars and riding boots.

Information

To get into the string of things, drop into to the guitar-shaped **visitors centre** (☎ 6755 4300; www.visittamworth.com.au; cnr Peel & Murray Sts). All major **banks** are located on Peel St and there is **Internet access** at the YHA Tamworth Hostel (see p202).

Sights

COUNTRY MUSIC

For those with a thirst for country music history, the **Australian Country Music Foundation** (☎ 6766 9696; www.acmf.org.au; 93 Brisbane St; adult/child $5.50/3.30; ☾ 10am-2pm Mon-Sat) houses the backdrop to the film clip to the world-famous song 'A Pub With No Beer'.

The **Big Golden Guitar Tourist Centre** (☎ 6765 2688; New England Hwy; ☾ 8am-4pm) has a **wax museum** (adult/child $8/4) displaying effigies of 24 famous Australian country music stars (including, of course, Slim Dusty). The photo opportunity out the front is a must, but the museum a luxury even for those heavy in the pocket. To get to the centre head out of town along Goonoo Goonoo Rd which becomes New England Hwy.

Country musicians are of Hollywood status, and the **hands of fame** (cnr Kable Ave & Brisbane St) is testimony to this.

At the visitors centre is the **'walk a country mile' museum** (☎ 6755 4300; cnr Peel & Murray Sts; adult/child $4/3; ☾ 9am-5pm) which will give you an insight into Tamworth's most flaunted asset, country music.

To see where the likes of Kasey Chambers recorded hits, make an appointment to view a **recording studio**. The information centre can organise inspections.

OTHER ATTRACTIONS

There are friendly kangaroos and other native animals at the **Oxley Marsupial Park** on Endeavour Drive, the northern continuation of Brisbane St. Nearby (but accessible from the top of White St) is the **Oxley Scenic Lookout**.

The **Powerstation Museum** (☎ 6766 8324; 216 Peel St; admission $2.50; ☾ 9am-1pm Wed-Fri) pays homage to the fact that Tamworth was the first town in Australia to be switched on by electricity in 1888, and showcases a variety of unusual and interesting electrical objects.

The 1875 **Calala Cottage** (☎ 6765 7492; 142 Denison St; adult/child $4/1; ☾ 2-4pm Tue-Fri, 10am-4pm Sat & Sun) is a shepherd slab hut and part of a cluster of reconstructed historic buildings.

Tamworth City Art Gallery (☎ 6755 4459; www .tamworth.nsw.gov.au; 203 Marius St; admission free; ☾ 10am-5pm Mon-Fri, to 1pm Sat, 1-4pm Sun) has an impressive textile gallery which exhibits fibre samples from the surrounding region.

Weswal Gallery (☎ 6766 5847; 192 Brisbane St; ☾ 10am-5pm) is a commercial enterprise that has a solid collection of local art.

Activities

Leconfield Jackaroo & Jillaroo School (☎ 6768 4328; www.leconfield.com; Leconfield at Kootingal; 5 days $440) will transform you into a budding horseman/woman in no time. Experience mustering and shearing sheep or have a go at cracking the odd whip.

Of the two golf courses in Tamworth, it's worth taking a swing on the Greg Norman–designed golf course, **Longyard** (☎ 6765 2988; Sydney Rd; 9/18 holes Mon-Fri $9/18, Sat & Sun $15/22).

Festivals & Events

Held at the end of January, New England's biggest annual party, the **Country Music Festival** lasts 10 days. There are over 800 acts, of which 75% are free. People flock from afar to join in the festivities and the days are hot while the nights are even hotter. Those hesitant about 'country' music need not worry; the category is that wide and the atmosphere that jovial, you're sure to be swept up in the theatre of it all, and it's a good chance to watch gutsy guys and gals take on the bulls at a rodeo. Some other events:

Hats off to Country Music During the June long weekend, this festival usually hosts a few big names in the country music industry.

Tamworth Gold Cup & Quarter Horse Championship For horse-related events, May sees this take place.

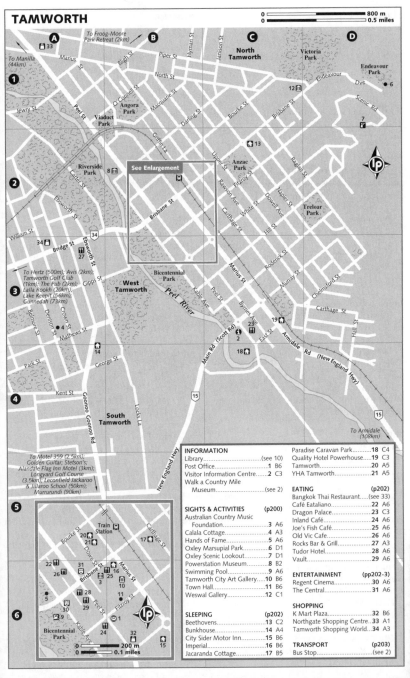

TAMWORTH

0 ————————— 800 m
0 ————————— 0.5 miles

Sleeping

Most of the accommodation in town is booked out months in advance for the Country Music Festival in January. If you miss out, the visitors centre can send you a visitors kit for the festival – it outlines temporary accommodation options when everything else is full. Tamworth is a key destination for conventions and exhibitions and you will find business-minded people fill up the motels during the week.

BUDGET

Paradise Caravan Park (☎ 6766 3120; Peel St; powered sites/cabins $19/40) Beautifully located by the river, this is the most central of all caravan parks in and around Tamworth.

YHA Tamworth (☎ 6761 2600; 169 Marius St; dm/d $20/46; **P** 🖳) Occupies a 100-year-old boarding house and has large, clean rooms.

Bunkhouse (☎ 6762 6300; bunkhouse@tpg.com.au; 118 New England Hwy; per person $20) Ideal for families, this place has a modern, stylish layout. It is located on the south side of town. Linen is provided.

Imperial (☎ 6766 2613; cnr Brisbane & Marius Sts; s/d $20/35) The rooms are freshly renovated and come at a modest rate.

Tamworth (☎ 6766 2923; Marius St; s/d $35/45) Overpriced and overstated in the room stakes, but the downstairs pub dining is great value and you take your chances at cooking your own steak. It is handily located opposite the train station.

MID-RANGE

Beethovens (☎ 6766 2735; 66 Napier St; s/d $90/110; **P**) A lovingly restored place with four en-suite rooms and a magnificent open fire in the guest lounge.

Jacaranda Cottage (☎ 6766 4281; 105 Carthage St; r $80, loft with bathroom $100; **P**) is a delightful Federation-era home, close to the centre of town, which provides a delicious home-cooked breakfast.

There are an alarming number of motels along the New England Hwy in South Tamworth en route to Armidale. Off-peak, there are bargains here aplenty.

Motel 359 (☎ 6762 4100; 359 Goonoo Goonoo Rd; 4-person r $50; **P** 🖳) No frills attached but value for money.

City Sider Motor Inn (☎ 6766 4777; 237 Marius St; d $89; **P** 🔀) Centrally located with spacious, light-filled rooms.

TOP END

Froog-Moore Park Retreat (☎ 6766 3353; 78 Bligh St; r incl 3-course breakfast $165; **P**) Definitely the pick of the bunch. Nestled away in a romantic setting, this retreats sweeping gardens, captivating design and hot-tub spa guarantee you'll walk away relaxed and rejuvenated.

Quality Hotel Powerhouse (☎ 6766 4000; www .qualityhotelpowerhouse.com.au; Marius St; r $120-180; **P** 🔀 🖳) Tamworth's five-star option at a price to match.

Eating

Joe's Fish Café (☎ 6766 2726; 181-195 Marius St; mains $16) Set in an unassuming atmosphere and serving an excellent array of fresh seafood; highly recommended.

Stetson's (☎ 6766 1771; cnr Craigends Lane & New England Hwy; mains $22) For those with a cowboy/cowgirl fantasy and an appetite for a hearty steak, you'll find this place located behind McDonald's.

Inland Café (☎ 6761 2882; 407 Peel St; mains $9) Very popular and provides generous servings, perfect for breakfast or lunch.

Old Vic Café (☎ 6766 3435; 261 Peel St; mains $10) Another downtown café with a dark interior that adds to a cosy environment.

Vault (☎ 6766 6975; 429 Peel St; mains $10) Residing in an old heritage bank, this is a great setting for a light snack or coffee.

Dragon Place (☎ 6766 6999; 528 Peel St; mains $15) A local favourite that produces a solid variety of Chinese delicacies.

Café Eataliano (☎ 6761 3221; 251 Peel St; mains $15) Covers the pasta and pizza market in style.

Bangkok Thai Restaurant (☎ 6761 3098; Northgate Shopping Centre, 18 Peel St; mains $10) Presents good value and a versatile menu.

Tudor Hotel (☎ 6766 2930; 327 Peel St; mains $14) Classically refurnished, this place also has a great steak dinner deal ($7) that attracts the locals in their droves.

Rocks Bar & Grill (☎ 6762 0033; 83-8 Ebsworth St; mains $23) An upmarket option at Ashby House (note: barramundi is its forte).

Entertainment

Note that there's a curfew in effect in Tamworth, with patrons unable to enter a bar after 1.30am.

Pub (☎ 6765 5655; cnr Gunnedah Rd & Dampier Sts) If you're looking for an injection of live country music, drop in here on a Friday night.

Imperial (☎ 6766 2613; cnr Brisbane & Marius Sts) Should impress with live bands five nights a week (Tuesday and Thursday to Sunday) and a 3am license.

Central (cnr Brisbane & Peel Sts) A good place to start the evening.

Getting There & Away

AIR

QantasLink (☎ 13 13 13; www.qantas.com.au) has four flights a day to Sydney ($158/318 one way/return).

Sunshine Express (☎ 13 13 13; www.sunshineexpress.com.au) runs one flight a day to Brisbane ($186/375 one way/return).

BUS

McCafferty's/Greyhound (☎ 13 20 30; www.mccaffertys.com.au) has daily services to Armidale ($28), Sydney ($66) and Brisbane ($68).

Keans (☎ 1800 043 339) runs to Uralla ($22.50), Coffs Harbour ($56.50) and Port Macquarie ($71) three times a week.

TRAIN

Countrylink (☎ 13 22 32; www.countrylink.info) trains go to Armidale ($17.60), Scone ($23.10) and Sydney ($74.80) daily. Buses travel to Manilla ($5.50), Barraba ($14.30) and Bingara ($23.10) daily.

Getting Around

Tamworth Coaches (☎ 6762 3999; www.tamworthbuslines.com.au) operates extensively throughout town; stops are visible and obvious. **Tamworth Taxis** (☎ 6766 1111) can be waved down around town. You can also visit one of the car-hire companies in town:

Avis (☎ 6760 7404)
Budget (☎ 6766 7255)
Hertz (☎ 6761 5545)
Tamworth Hire Cars (☎ 6766 1909) A local joint.
Thrifty (☎ 6765 3699)

OXLEY WILD RIVERS NATIONAL PARK

Now a World Heritage–listed national park, Oxley includes the largest area of dry rainforest in Australia (120,394 hectares). This vast region southeast of Armidale contains some dramatic waterfalls and gorges. **Wollomombi Falls**, 40km east of Armidale, is the highest in Australia with a drop of 220m. The spectacular **Apsley Falls** are 18km east of Walcha at the southern end of the park. In 1818 the explorer John Oxley

declared himself 'lost in astonishment at the sight of this wonderful sublimity' on viewing the falls. Down at the bottom of the gorges is a wilderness area accessible from Raspberry Rd, which runs off the Wollomombi to Kempsey road. The Armidale **National Parks & Wildlife Service** (NPWS; ☎ 02-6773 7211) office has information.

The secluded **West Kunderang Recreational Retreat** (☎ 02-6778 1264; Biston Pk; camping adult/child $7.50/2.50, 6-person cabin $90) is on a locked property in the heart of the national park. You can go horse riding (per half-day $45), canoeing (per hour $10), Bass fishing (guided three-hour tour $60) or bush hiking to view the endangered Bushtail Rock Wallaby that is exclusive to these parts.

WERRIKIMBE NATIONAL PARK

This rugged and spectacular World Heritage–listed park (35,180 hectares) has remote gorge walking as well as more gentle walks around the visitor areas; it's also great for fishing. Access is via the Kangaroo Flat road, about 50km east (45 minutes) of Walcha off the road to Wauchope or about 125km (two hours) west of Port Macquarie. The Armidale NPWS office (p204) has information.

URALLA

☎ 02 / pop 2310

Uralla's attraction lies in its country charm and its association with the NSW answer to Ned Kelly, bushranger Captain Thunderbolt. The **visitors centre** (☎ 6778 4496; New England Hwy) will happily advise you on the town's activities and also has a vibrant coffee shop.

Captain Thunderbolt roamed around New England during the 1860s and became a much-loved villain, never having shot anybody and performing as many acts of kindness as robbery. He was finally shot down near Uralla by Constable Walker in 1870, but rumours still surface that he emerged in Canada a year later. There is a **statue** of him in the main street (New England Hwy), just next to the visitors centre.

The **McCrossin's Mill Museum** (☎ 6778 3022; cnr Bridge & Salibury Sts; adult/child $4/1.50; ✆ noon-5pm Mon-Fri, 10am-5pm Sat & Sun) has nine magnificent paintings depicting the dramatic death of Thunderbolt and also houses a rare gun thought to be used by him (as well as the regular paraphernalia that goes with such icons).

NEW ENGLAND

There is minimal transport to Uralla, making it really only an option for those with their own transport.

Sleeping & Eating

Coachwood and Cedar Hotel/Motel (☎ 6778 4110; New England Hwy; s/d motel $35/55, s/d hotel $55/40) This place caters for families in an attractive environment.

Bushranger Motor Inn (☎ 6778 3777; 37-41 Bridge St; s/d $75/85; ⚙) One of a string of motels on the highway, this peppers you with quality.

Uralla Caravan Park (☎ 6778 4763; 17 Queen St; tent site/cabin $16/35; P) Well positioned with good facilities.

Chesterfield's (☎ 6778 3113; Bridge St; s/d $55/70) Ideal for backpackers with good, clean rooms at value.

Stokers Licensed Restaurant (37-41 Bridge St) Part of the Bushranger Motor Inn, this is an excellent eatery.

White Rose Café (☎ 6778 4052; New England Hwy; pies $4) Why not complete your Thunderbolt initiation with a thunderbolt pie from this place. The secret recipe has origins in China.

AROUND URALLA

A unique woolshed, a vine-covered chapel and 199 elm trees turn this unique destination, **Gostyck**, into a little piece of England. Sir Henry Dangar, of Dangar Falls/cottage/lagoon fame, built the chapel as a memorial to the men who failed to return from WWI in 1921. Gostyck is just 10 minutes' drive east of Uralla; admission is free, and as it's on public land you can visit it at any time.

Further up the road at the Dangar Falls turn-off you will witness a more colourful, slightly less tasteful **memorial** for those who 'went west' during WWI. Entry is through the gate labelled 'Nirvana', and it just so happens that a corporal with the same surname as the landowner is on top of the honour role (drastically out of alphabetical order).

ARMIDALE

☎ 02 / pop 20,270

Armidale provides a good base to attack the surrounding national parks and is a useful gateway to the gorges. More than that, though, Armidale allows you the chance to embrace a growing cosmopolitan atmosphere. Autumn is when the town flourishes, with rustic colours and fallen leaves paving the streets. It's the highest city in Australia at 980m, sitting on top of the Great Dividing Range plateau, and is home to the oldest regional university. It has a fresh, crisp feel that only young blood and a high altitude could create.

Information

The **visitors centre** (☎ 6772 4655, 1800 627 736; www.new-england.org/armidale; 83 Marsh St) is a good place to inquire about the Armidale Heritage Tour, which is a free bus tour that introduces you to the historic aspects of the town.

Just nearby is the **NPWS** (☎ 6773 7211; 85-87 Faulkner St) which will be able to sort out all your park inquiries. **Harvey World Travel** (☎ 6774 8888) is at 109 Dangar St.

Sights

HISTORIC BUILDINGS

Pick up some brochures detailing the 'heritage walking tour' and 'heritage drive' from the enthusiastic staff at the visitors centre; just strolling down the mall is enough to whet your appetite for historic buildings. The cathedrals are well worth a look as they lend a certain historical elegance to the town, particularly the imposing bluestone Anglican Church.

UNIVERSITY OF NEW ENGLAND

The university's impact upon Armidale is unquestionable. **Booloominbah** (☎ 6773 3909; University Campus, Queen Elizabeth Dr; tours $3.50; ☺ noon Mon), 5km north of the city centre, is the administration building and has a classic Victoriana aura about it. A large stained-glass window depicts events in the life (and death, in 1885) of General Charles Gordon, one-time British governor-general of Khartoum, in the Sudan, Africa. There are two museums of interest at the university: the **Zoology Museum** (cnr Trevenna & Library Rds; admission free; ☺ 9am-5pm Mon-Fri) that combines well with the **Museum of Antiquities** (admission free; ☺ 9am-5pm Mon-Fri), located next to the Art Theatre.

MUSEUMS

'Erotic and exotic' sums up the great art work on display at the **New England Regional Art Museum** (☎ 6772 5255; Kentucky St; admission free; ☺ 10.30am-5pm Tue-Sun). This, coupled with staff that are upbeat and knowledgeable,

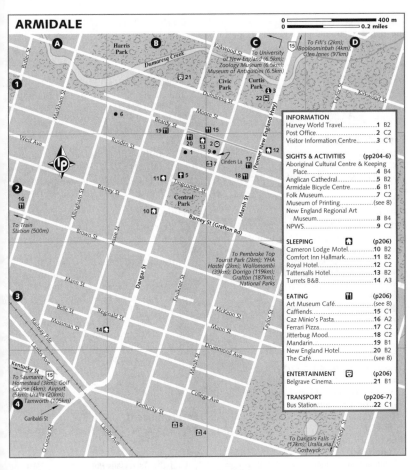

ARMIDALE

0 ————— 400 m
0 ————— 0.2 miles

make the gallery the crème de la crème of the region. The **Museum of Printing** (cnr Kentucky St & Marsh St), a little less erotic, is next door.

The **Folk Museum** (☎ 6770 3536; cnr Faulkner & Rusden Sts; admission free; ☼ 1-5pm) has a healthy selection of memorabilia collected since 1849.

At the **Aboriginal Cultural Centre & Keeping Place** (☎ 6771 1249; 128 Kentucky St; admission free; ☼ 9am-5pm Mon-Fri, 2-5pm Sat & Sun) you are invited to engulf yourself in the mystic qualities of Aboriginal art and culture.

MARKET

On the last Sunday of each month there is a **market** (Beardy St); stalls and bands are set up by both local and international students promoting multiculturalism.

Activities

The surrounding rivers are home to some of the best trout fishing in Australia; pick up a guide from the visitors centre for hot spots. If golfing is more your style, roll through 18 holes at the **Armidale Golf Club** (☎ 6772 5837; Golf Links Rd; 9/18 holes $14/19), 4km southeast of the city.

Rent a bike from **Armidale Bicycle Centre** (☎ 6772 3718; 248 Beardy St; per hr/day $5/20) to view the city from a different perspective.

If time is not on your side and heavy bushwalking not your scene, but you still want a slice of adventure, **Fleet Helicopters** (☎ 6772 2348; www.fleethelicopters.com.au; Armidale Airport) is your answer. You will be flown out to catch a close view of the gorgeous

NEW ENGLAND

gorges and given an amazing ride through the magnificent national parks. Trips for three people start at $275.

Tours

Waterfall Way Tours (☎ 6772 2018; half-/full-day tours $40/80) provides personalised natural history tours of three World Heritage–listed national parks.

Festivals & Events

Armidale is at its picturesque best in March for the **Autumn Festival**, which includes a street parade and plenty of live music.

Sleeping

BUDGET

Tattersalls Hotel (☎ 6772 2247; Beardy Street Mall; s/d $25/45) Possesses good, clean rooms in the heart of the town but can get noisy when university parties kick on.

Royal Hotel (☎ 6772 2259; Marsh St; s/d $35/45) Another good option that shouldn't be overlooked.

Pembroke Top Tourist Park (☎ 6772 6470; 39 Waterfall Way; tent site/caravan/dm $15/30/20; **P**) Friendly, leafy and with good facilities.

MID-RANGE

Cameron Lodge Motel (☎ 6772 2351; cnr Dangar & Barney Sts; s/d $60/70; **P** 🗶) A standout of the 22 motels for central location and spacious, warm rooms at value.

Comfort Inn Hallmark (☎ 6772 9800; 208 Dangar St; r from $105; **P** 🗶 🕿) A touch pricey and a little luxurious.

Turrets B&B (☎ 6772 8355; www.theturrets.com.au; 145 Mossman St; d incl breakfast $220; **P**) A heritage-acclaimed house and garden that is likely to delight.

Eating

New England Hotel (☎ 6772 7622; cnr Dangar & Beardy Sts; mains $10-15) Has the best pub grub in town.

Jitterbug Mood (☎ 6772 3022; 115 Rusden St; mains $15-20) Serves contemporary cuisine and is a popular haunt for locals.

Fifi's (☎ 6771 5733; Girraween Shopping Centre, Queen Elizabeth Dr; mains $17) If you're after a Middle Eastern dish, this Lebanese restaurant, 2km north of city centre, puts together a filling feed for a good price.

Ferrari Pizza (☎ 6772 2300; 2/110 Marsh St; mains $9) Does an impressive number of vegetarian pizzas.

Caz Minio's Pasta (☎ 6771 4555; 201A Brown St; mains $8) Produces all its pasta on-site.

If Chinese floats your boat you won't go hungry in Armidale as the town has an abundance of restaurants.

Mandarin (☎ 6772 6535; 215 Beardy St; mains $11) A universally admired Chinese restaurant.

Caffiends (☎ 6772 0277; Beardy St Mall; breakfast $8.50) Ease into the cosmopolitan lifestyle the town offers with bacon and eggs at this café.

It's worth visiting the Art Museum just for the **café** (☎ 6772 5255; Kentucky St; mains $8; 🕑 10.30am-4.30pm Tue-Sun), a light-filled, modern spot popular for lunch, coffee and cakes.

Drinking

The University of New England is Armidale's entertainment hub, with films, theatre and music.

Tattersalls Hotel (☎ 6772 2247; Beardy St) Fuelling the university's drinking culture with many sponsored events and if there's a uni occasion on, it will be at Tatts.

New England Hotel (☎ 6772 7622; cnr Dangar & Beardy Street Mall) Another favourite uni haunt is this hotel (known simply as the 'Newie'). Live bands on a Saturday night see the locals waltz through the door.

A curfew is strictly enforced in Armidale, so pick your establishment prior to 12.30am and settle in.

Entertainment

Belgrave Cinema (☎ 6772 2856, programme info 6773 3833; 137 Dumaresq St) Shows mainstream and art-house films.

Call the **Tattersalls Hotel** (☎ 6772 2247) for 'what's on' details.

Getting There & Away

AIR

The airport is 5km southeast of town. **Qantas Link** (☎ 13 13 13; www.qantas.com.au) has four flights a day to Sydney ($163/328 one way/return).

Sunshine Express (☎ 13 13 13; www.sunshine express.com.au) has one flight a day to Brisbane ($248/498 one way/return).

BUS

McCafferty's/Greyhound (☎ 13 20 30; www.mccaff ertys.com.au) runs daily to Tamworth ($28), Sydney ($74) and Brisbane ($68). **Kean's Travel** (☎ 1800 625 587) runs across to Coffs Harbour ($29.50) three times a week.

TRAIN

Countrylink (☎ 13 22 32; www.countrylink.info) goes daily to Tamworth ($17.60), Broadmeadow–Newcastle ($66) and Sydney ($83.60). There are also buses to Glen Innes ($14.30).

Getting Around

For taxi services, there's **Armidale Radio Taxis** (☎ 6771 1455).

AROUND ARMIDALE
Saumarez Homestead

Saumarez Homestead (☎ 02-6772 3616; Saumarez Rd; tour $8; ☺ grounds 10am-4pm daily, guided house tour 10.30am & 2pm Mon-Fri) is a magnificent National Trust–owned house three kilometres from Armidale Airport, that represents two eras in Australian history. The bottom floor was constructed in 1888 and the second added in 1906. It contains the effects of the wealthy pastoralists who built it and bustles with charm and historic importance.

Views & Waterfalls

The Armidale area is noted for its magnificent gorges and impressive waterfalls. These include the **Wollomombi Falls** (see Oxley Wild Rivers National Park, p203) and the **Ebor Falls**, near the hamlet of Ebor. Closer to Armidale, off the road heading south to Gostwyck, are **Dangar Falls**, the most accessible and visually impressive.

NEW ENGLAND NATIONAL PARK

Right on the escarpment, New England National Park is a spectacular 71,299 hectares,

---

THE LITTLE ITALIAN

Italians are renowned for being flamboyant, stylish and a little passionate. Signor Vertelli was no different when in 1866 he put on a one-man show that is still talked about in New England folklore. Not content with just swimming under Dangar Falls, he constructed a tightrope 600ft above the floor of the gorge. In front of an excited audience of 200 locals he walked the walk with a balancing stick, then went back the other way with a wheelbarrow, and for his encore performed somersaults across the wire. It was a raging success raising £11 for the young Signor who lived to tell the tale.

---

most of which is World Heritage–listed, with a wide range of ecosystems. Admission is free and it's good for bushwalking, with 20km of walking tracks. The park is 85km (1½ hours) east of Armidale on the Waterfall Way on unpaved roads. Access is from near Ebor, and there are camp sites with cabins near the entrance; book through the Dorrigo **NPWS** (☎ 02-6657 2309; www.nationalparks.nsw.gov.au) office.

Within the national park lies **Yaraandoo** (☎ 02-6775 9219; s/d $50/95, mains $18), a fantastic place to enjoy wonderful park views and to stop for a bite to eat. For a more romantic option, **Moffat Falls Lodge** (☎ 02-6775 9219; r $130) overlooks the falls (funnily enough).

CATHEDRAL ROCK NATIONAL PARK

Cathedral Rock National Park is also near Ebor, off the Ebor to Guyra road. It's a relatively small park (8839 hectares) with photogenic granite formations and wedge-tailed eagles. The park is 60km west of Dorrigo off the Waterfall Way (unpaved roads). There is a range of walks and camping available. Contact the Dorrigo **NPWS** (☎ 02-6657 2309; www.nationalparks.nsw.gov.au) office for more details.

GUY FAWKES RIVER NATIONAL PARK

Protecting the rugged gorges of the Guy Fawkes River, this park of 72,946 hectares offers canoeing as well as walking, with camping on the pleasant river flats. Access (not always easy) is from Hernani, 15km northeast of Ebor, and it's 30km to the Chaelundi Rest Area, with camp sites and water. The Dorrigo **NPWS** (☎ 02-6657 2309) office has all necessary information.

GLEN INNES

☎ 02 / pop 5720

Glen Innes is somewhat self-deluded in its self-portrait as a 'Scotland away from Scotland'. The town does boast strong Celtic roots and some Gaelic road signs, but is far from the real McCoy.

Orientation & Information

The town is at the intersection of the New England Hwy and Gwydir Hwy with the historic Grey St running parallel to the New England Hwy.

The **visitors centre** (☎ 6732 2397; www.gleninnes tourism.com; Church St) is on the continuation of the New England Hwy. One kilometre south is the **NPWS** (☎ 6732 5133; Church St) office.

Sights & Activities

Overlooking the town from the Centennial Parklands is the **Standing Stones**, a national monument to the Celtic people who helped pioneer Australia. It was erected in 1990 and is based on the Ring of Brodgar in Scotland's Orkney Islands comprising 33 stones that weigh up to 30 tonnes each. The Southern Cross formation brings an Australian touch to an otherwise ancient Scottish concept.

The **Land of the Beardies History House** (☎ 6732 1035; cnr Fergerson St & Western Ave; adult/child $4/1; ◷ 10am-noon Mon-Fri & 2-5pm daily), in the old hospital (1875), is a big folk museum that dedicates a room to the local Celtic influence.

Grey St has 30 heritage-listed buildings; the distinctive **town hall** (1888), **colonial courthouse** (1873) and **Club Hotel** (1906) all credit a look.

If tasting the subtle, or not so subtle, delights of kangaroo, goanna and emu ignite your tastebuds, visit the excellent **Cooramah Aboriginal Cultural Centre** (☎ 6732 5960; New England Hwy; admission free; ◷ 8am-4pm Mon-Fri, 10am-3pm Sat & Sun), which also has some inspiring local indigenous artwork.

If fossicking is more your thing then head out to **Dwyers Fossicking Reserve** (43km southeast; honest box $5) to find that elusive sapphire. The visitors centre has information and maps for the area and also has pans and other such fossicking equipment.

Festivals & Events

In early March the gem and mineral festival, **Minerama**, takes centre stage. The **Celtic Festival in Glen Innes**, naturally, transforms the town into a swirl of kilts in May.

Sleeping

Imperial Hotel (☎ 6732 3107; cnr Grey & Mead Sts; s/d $25/45) Good value, in a spacious old pub. Other pubs in town offer a similar deal.

Central Motel (☎ 6732 2200; Meade St, s/d $65/75; ▨) Tucked away from the highway, this motel offers clean modern rooms a stone's throw from Grey St. There is a string of motels along the highway that vary in standard.

Kings Plains Castle (☎ 6733 6807; www.kingsplainscastle.gleninnes.biz; Kings Plain Rd; r $150) Visit this exclusive and unique B&B and it could turn you Scottish with delight. Sip your complimentary port in the engaging atmosphere.

Red Lion Tavern (☎ 6733 3271; Glencoe; s/d $58/69) Situated 22km south of Glen Innes, it has a strong Celtic flavour and good country charm constructed with second-hand goods. Check out the portholes inside.

Craigieburn Tourist Park (☎ 6732 2215; New England Hwy; tent sites/cabins $8/40) Has the best location and greenest grounds of the five caravan parks.

Eating

Super Strawberry (☎ 6732 1210; 9922 New England Hwy; ◷ 9am-5.30pm) Super does everything imaginable to strawberries and is a great spot for a snack.

Café Heritage (☎ 6732 6123; 215 Grey St; mains $10) Renowned for variety with feisty burgers and focaccias, these are solid options in wood-laden surrounds.

Gum Wah (☎ 6732 3211; 292 Grey St; mains $8-14) Stock-standard Chinese feed that yields no surprises.

Hereford Steakhouse (☎ 6732 2255; Comfort Inn, 72 Church St, New England Hwy; mains $15-25) This place pulls plenty of punches and locals love its knockout rump steak.

Getting There & Away

McCafferty's/Greyhound (☎ 13 20 30; www.mccaffertys.com.au) runs to Armidale ($35), Tamworth ($44), Sydney ($74) and Brisbane ($68) daily and stops near the visitors centre.

Black & White (☎ 6732 3687; www.blackandwhitebus.com) runs to Inverell twice a day.

Countrylink (☎ 13 22 32; www.countrylink.info) has buses to Armidale ($14.30) and Grafton ($26.40).

The Gwydir Hwy to Grafton is a scenic road and a good way to get off the beaten track; take the Old Grafton Rd to where it turns off the Gwydir Hwy, about 40km east of Glen Innes. The road, mostly unsealed but in fair condition, passes through a convict-built tunnel, and there are good camping and fishing spots along the river.

AROUND GLEN INNES

Spend days crossing rivers and galloping up the plains, and nights in true country hospitality in a fine old pub (with plenty of amber liquid and luscious food) with **Pub Crawls on Horseback** (☎ 02-6732 1599; www.pubcrawlsonhorseback.com.au; 1192 Bullock Mountain Rd, Glen Innes; weekend/7 days $325/1350). Also on the property is **Bullock Mountain Homestead**

Backpackers (www.bullockmountainbackpackers.com; r incl meals & ride $80).

Emmaville Mining Museum (☎ 02-6734 7025; Moore St, Emmaville; admission gold coin donation; ⏲ 10am-4pm Fri-Tue), on the edge of the granite belt, 38km northwest of Glen Innes, features internationally recognised mineral collections and other enticing displays.

GIBRALTAR RANGE & WASHPOOL NATIONAL PARKS

These two national parks – dramatic, forested and wild – lie between Glen Innes and Grafton off the Gwydir Hwy. Together they form a World Heritage–listed area. Main features are the enormous granite tors, needles, old man's hat and anvil rock in the Gibraltar Range (25,346 hectares), and the river gorges in the Washpool National Park (60,068 hectares) which are also home to the world's largest coachwood rainforest and rare bird species like the wompoo fruit-dove and the paradise rifle bird. Countrylink buses between Glen Innes and Grafton stop at the Gibraltar Range visitors centre and at the entrance to Washpool. The **NPWS** (Grafton ☎ 02-6640 3910; Glen Innes ☎ 02-6732 5133) offices have more information on camping, walks etc.

NYMBOIDA NATIONAL PARK

The Nymboida River and its tributary, the Mann River, flow through this wilderness and offer excellent canoeing and whitewater rafting (best organised in Coffs Harbour). Much of the park (31,566 hectares) is rugged wilderness, and the only camping facilities are at the Nymboida River Camping Area. To get there, head east from Glen Innes on the Gwydir Hwy for 45km, turn off onto the Narlala road and travel for another 35km. You can reach the eastern end of the park from Jackadgery, further east on the highway. The **NPWS** (Grafton ☎ 02-6640 3910; Glen Innes ☎ 02-6732 5133) offices have more details on camping and walks in the park.

TENTERFIELD

☎ 02 / pop 3190
Tenterfield, just 15km from the Queensland border is a town bustling with character and high on history. It was here in 1889 that Sir Henry Parkes proclaimed his vision of 'one people, one destiny', thus beginning Australia's road to federation; Peter Allen rose from these parts to take Broadway by storm and put his childhood town on the international map with the song 'Tenterfield Saddler'. Nowadays, the town has an intimate feel and gives travellers an opportunity to see the 'real' Australia.

Information

Tenterfield **Gateway Information Centre** (☎ 6736 1082; 157 Rouse St) is just south of the town centre on the New England Hwy. Note that the New England Hwy turns into Rouse St throughout the town.

Sights & Activities

Henry Parkes speech that shaped the nation took place at the **School of Arts** (☎ 6736 3592; cnr Manners & Rouse Sts; admission $5; ⏲ 10am-4pm) now a library that houses a small museum with exhibits relating to the politician's career.

Centenary Cottage Complex (☎ 6736 2844; cnr High & Logan Sts; adult/child $3/1; ⏲ 10am-4pm Wed-Sun) houses local history accompanied by the works of one of Australia's first internationally renowned women artists, Lillian Chauvel. Just round the corner on High St stands the old stone saddler's shop that was put on the map through Allen's lyrics; it used to belong to his grandfather and now sells quality Australian leather products. Back on the main drag the **post office** (1881) is well worth a look.

The notorious bushranger Captain Thunderbolt found safety in the granite rocks 11km northeast of the town at **Thunderbolt's Hideout**. Further north is the **Girraween National Park** (11,700 hectares) and wineries of the granite belt.

Tours

Tenterfield Tours (☎ 6736 1864, 0413-752 469) provides trips around surrounding national parks and local wineries, which offer a unique insight into local history (note that tailored tours are available on request).

Festivals & Events

The **Tenterfield Show** takes to the streets in February, and always draws a celebrity. In March the **German Beer Festival** celebrates the recognition of the 2002 friendship and sister-town agreement with its German counterpart Ottobeuren. **Oracles of the Bush** is an April celebration.

NEW ENGLAND

Sleeping

Royal (☎ 6736 3008; theroyal@halenet.com.au; 130 High St; r hotel $35, s motel $45-50, d motel $60) Definitely the pick of the pubs, it serves up massive meals, has a great open fireplace in the Shed Bar and is perfect for backpackers or families.

Peter Allen Motor Inn (☎ 6736 2499; New England Hwy; s/d $65/75; 🔀) Outrageously pink yet offering all the creature comforts of a three-star motel.

Tenterfield Lodge and Caravan Park (☎ 6736 1477; 2 Manners St; tent sites/dm/d $13/21/42; 🖳) Situated on the west side of town, this place emits a peaceful feel. The manager can arrange work on nearby farms in the area for cash-shortage-stricken backpackers.

Getting There & Away

McCafferty's/Greyhound (☎ 13 20 30; www.mccaffertys.com.au) buses daily to Lismore ($26), Brisbane ($55) and Sydney ($74).

Kirklands Coaches (☎ 6622 1499; www.kirklands.com.au) runs from Tenterfield across to Casino ($23.40, Monday to Friday).

Countrylink (☎ 13 22 32; www.countrylink.info) has bus services to Glen Innes ($14.30) and to Armidale ($31.90).

If you've driven or ridden across from the coast or up the relatively busy New England Hwy, a journey west from Tenterfield is a delight – the Bruxner Hwy is a wide, almost deserted road. It runs west to Boggabilla, on the Newell Hwy, or heading east it twists and turns over the ranges to Casino, then on to Lismore.

BALD ROCK NATIONAL PARK

Bloody big and bloody impressive, **Bald Rock** is the largest granite rock in the southern hemisphere (750m long, 500m wide and 200m high). It the centrepiece of **Bald Rock**

THE LEGEND OF BLUFF ROCK

Bluff Rock is situated 10km south of Tenterfield on the New England Hwy. In 1844 landowner Edward Irby took revenge on the Aboriginal tribe he accused of killing one of his shepherds by chasing them to Bluff Rock where the tribe was allegedly thrown off the edge, killing most. Mr Irby is quoted as writing, 'we punished them severely and proved our superiority to them'. Impressive by sight and terrifying by legend.

National Park (admission $6), lying 30km north of Tenterfield on an unsealed road that continues into Queensland. It takes two hours (3km) of casual walking to reach the top and you're sure to pass many kangaroos. There's a basic camping area near the base with pit toilets and barbecues.

Access is from Tenterfield, off the partly sealed Mt Lindsay Rd to Warwick.

BOONOO BOONOO NATIONAL PARK

Near Bald Rock, the 4377-hectare **Boonoo Boonoo** (bun-na-b'*noo*) costs $6 per vehicle. It comprises a pretty forest and a towering 210m waterfall, and is particularly noted for Australian native flowering plants like grevilleas and banksias. The endangered glossy black cockatoo also calls these parts home.

CASINO

Casino, oh, if only it did have one. Little to inspire the visitor but is renowned as Australia's beef capital so you're sure to see many cows. The **visitors centre** (☎ 02-6662 1572; Glen-Villa Resort, Bruxner Hwy) is just over the Richmond River.

THE FOSSICKERS WAY

The Fossickers Way conjures up history, revels in adventure and emits a powerful country atmosphere, making it an enjoyable, picturesque drive through New England. The Fossickers Way is so named because of the many sites where you might unearth anything from fossilised wood to diamonds. It also boasts other rousing activities like quality fishing, adventure sports and great historical angles. The 'Way' begins in the hills of Nundle and passes through Tamworth and then skirts the western edges of the ranges up to Warialda.

NUNDLE

☎ 02 / pop 260

Nundle is a quaint little village on the Peel River and combines renowned trout fishing, optimistic fossicking and a rich history of gold mining to mark the beginning of the Fossickers Way. The **visitors centre** (☎ 6769 3158; 96 Jenkins St) is part of the Nundle Country Café, and while you're there, if you can, get your mouth around a Nundle Pounder. It should satisfy any appetite.

Hanging Rock is 10km to the east and yet a staggering 2000ft higher, offering superb views and picnic opportunities; you can camp here by the **Sheba Dams**, which were built during the gold rushes; there is no camping fee.

Sleeping & Eating

Peel Inn (☎ 6769 3377; www.peelinn.com.au; s/d $35/65, mains $10-20) Dating back to 1860, this place has a genuine old feel and presents good accommodation and great food; try the sheep shanks ($17) marinated in Guinness.

Jenkins St Guest House (☎ 6769 3239; 85 Jenkins St; r $120-150, mains $15-25) Self proclaimed as the 'sexiest place in NSW', it's not far off the mark, oozing romance with an ambient atmosphere and luscious gardens. Its restaurant downstairs is cutting-edge and presents a wonderful dining experience. At the very least, drop by for a coffee and soak in the glorious surrounds.

Nundle Caravan Park (☎ 6769 3355; Jenkins St; tent sites/cabins $12/40) Opposite the visitors centre, this caravan park has a wealth of activities on offer, ranging from fossicking to swimming to bird-watching.

Getting There & Away

There's a sealed road from Nundle to Tamworth. A largely unsealed and hilly road runs to Walcha, passing through some lovely forest. Other minor roads head southeast to Nowendoc, then on to Taree and Gloucester, offering spectacular drives that skirt the Barrington Tops National Park. You can also head south to Scone from Nundle.

MANILLA

☎ 02 / pop 2040

Manilla is fast developing into an adventure-sports haven. Located at the junction of the Namoi and Manilla Rivers, its name derives from the local Aborigines, the Manellae people.

Paragliding is big business out this way, and if you feel the urge to get an aerial view of these glorious surroundings get in touch with **Sky Manilla** (☎ 6785 6545; www.flymanilla.com) who offer a tandem flight for half an hour at a very reasonable $125. If your thirst for adventure has not been quenched, drop into the **River Gums Caravan Park** (see Sleeping, below), which will sort you out

with a canoe trip down the river, a spot of volleyball or a mountain bike ride through the ranges. Prices vary depending on the time of year.

The national paragliding championships are held every February/March and attract a lot of international interest.

Warrabah National Park (3471 hectares), 35km northeast of Manilla, is centred on a gorge in the Namoi River and has bushwalking, climbing, great fishing, canoeing and basic camp sites. There's a challenging three-day canoe trip from the village of Retreat, east of the park, to Lowry Creek within the park – a 250m drop over 15km, with plenty of rapids. It's for experienced or stupid canoeists only.

For the historically minded, the **Manilla Heritage Museum** (☎ 6785 1207; 197 Manilla St; adult/child $4/2; ☼ 9am-noon Sat & Sun) offers a step back in time with many interesting exhibits, including a digital watch that dates back to 1822! **Dutton's Meadery** (☎ 6785 1148; admission free) is located just over the river and is home to meads and melomels (meads fermented with fruit juices) as well as many other peculiar collectables. Phone ahead for visiting hours and details.

Sleeping

Manilla's three pubs all offer accommodation, the **Manilla Motel** (☎ 6785 1306; cnr Namoi & Court Sts; s/d 65/80; ✗) is a viable option. **River Gums Caravan Park** (☎ 6785 1166; www.users.bigpond.com/therivergums; 86 Strafford St; tent site/cabin $12/15) is well presented and good value.

VIEW FROM ABOVE

Receiving sporting medals from the Prime Minister alongside Steve Waugh and Kieran Perkins was a less-celebrated man who has certainly gone the distance. Meet Godfrey Wenness, the man who bought his own mountain and proceeded to fly the very first hill-launched Open Distance Hang Gliding World Record from it. Not content with the solo record, his girlfriend Suzi joined him up in the clouds for a tandem flight of 223km that netted the world record and saw them land near the Queensland border.

Manilla has become world-famous in the flying community for long-distance flights and Godfrey's mountain is known in flying circles as God's takeoff point.

BARRABA

☎ 02 / pop 1200

Barraba lies on the upper reaches of the Manilla river and claims to be 'the most generous town in the land'. It has a gentle, small-town air with fossicking, bushwalking and relaxation the main activities on offer.

The **visitors centre** (☎ 6782 1255; 116 Queen St) can organise the museum of local history to be opened for you and **Andy's Backpackers Lodge** (☎ 6782 1916; 98 Queen St; dm $20, meals by donation) is an experience in itself, an epic front room where music takes centre stage and enjoying country life is unavoidable.

Mt Kaputar National Park (permit available at Barraba visitors centre, see above) is accessible by 4WD and is renowned for stunning scenery and secluded camp sites.

BINGARA

☎ 02 / pop 1230

Bingara is the self proclaimed 'centre of the Fossickers Way' and lies on the edge of the Gwydir River. The **visitors centre** (☎ 6724 0066; www.bingara.nsw.gov.au; 74 Maitland St) is situated in the Roxy Theatre Building which is a Greek influenced, refurnished Art Deco cinema.

The town's **museum** (1860; Maitland St; ☯ 10am-2pm Fri & Sat) was originally known as the Post Office Hotel and features a puddled iron roof, corrugated iron's grandfather. See the visitors centre for information; it can be opened by appointment.

Finch Street is lined with orange trees as a special **war memorial** and each July the trees are picked by the school children, a long-standing tradition.

Horse riding attracts backpackers in their droves with **Gwydir River Trail Rides** (☎ 6724 1562; 17 Keera St; trail ride $40) offering a seven-day package that includes five rides, meals and accommodation for $351. It comes highly recommended and many other activities are on offer. The nearby **Copeton Dam State Recreation Area** excels in water sports and is a great way to spend a couple of days.

Sleeping

Riverside Caravan Park (☎ 6724 1209; Keera Rd; tent sites/cabins $12/34) This pleasant park is well located and decent value.

Imperial Hotel (☎ 6724 1629; Maitland St; s/d $20/35) This 1879 hotel runs in conjunction with the trail rides and is a good accommodation option.

Fossickers Way Motel (☎ 6724 1373; 2 Finch St; s/d $60/65; ☒) Has a tidy appearance and a very quiet setting on the edge of parkland, just across the road from the Gwydir River. There are 12 modern units with air-con.

INVERELL

☎ 02 / pop 9540

Located on the picturesque Macintyre River, Inverell ('inv' means meeting place, 'ell' means swans) was founded by the Scottish. It is a sapphire-mining area and other stones, such as diamonds, are also found.

Until they are cut, sapphires aren't especially impressive. There's a story, probably questionable, that some years ago the council was resurfacing a stretch of road and one truckload of gravel had a bluish look to it. 'Couldn't be, there's too many of the bastards', was the road crew's verdict, but who knows?

Information

The converted water tower is home to the **visitors centre** (☎ 6728 8161; www.inverell-online.com.au; Campbell St) where you can pick up a map of the area's fossicking sites.

Sights & Activities

The **Inverell Pioneer Village** (☎ 6722 1717; Tingha Rd; adult/child $6.60/3.50; ☯ 10am-5pm Tue-Sun) provides an historic venue to fossick, stroll and soak up the region's history. The **Draught Horse Centre & Museum** (☎ 6722 1461; Glen Innes Rd; adult/child $6/3; ☯ 10am-4pm Thu-Mon), near Fishers Rd, breeds the endangered Suffock horses, the only ones in Australia, as well as four other imposing breeds. The museum is worth a visit for the horse-minded.

Around town you will find some interesting old buildings, such as the superb 1886 **court house** (Otho St) and the equally elegant **town hall**. The **Inverell Art Centre** (☎ 6722 4983; 5 Evans St; admission gold-coin donation; ☯ 10am-5pm Mon-Fri, to 4pm Sat) has a good selection of local art with paintings, pottery and copperware all prominent.

Festivals & Events

The **Grafton to Inverell International Cycling Classic** in September ignites sporting fans. The **Inverell Sapphire City Floral Festival** brings the city to life in October, and in December the **Great Inland Fishing Festival** is held in and around this sapphire region.

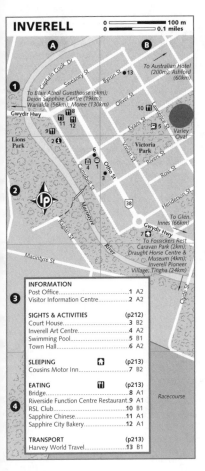

Sleeping

Australian Hotel (☎ 6722 1611; Byron St; s/d $25/35) Absolute gem of a place and high on value.

Cousins Motor Inn (☎ 6722 3566; Glen Innes Rd; s/d $85/95; ✴) For a bigger carat and a few modern motel luxuries.

Blair Athol Guesthouse (☎ 6722 4288; Warialda Rd; r $80-180) In magnificent gardens, this great old mansion (1904) is just west of the town.

Fossickers Rest Caravan Park (☎ 6722 2261; Lake Inverell Dr; tent sites/cabins $16/43) Friendly and well positioned, with on-site fossicking.

Eating

Bridge (☎ 6722 4925; 1 Otho St; meals $7-10) For a hearty breakfast or solid lunch, this place is more than competent.

Sapphire City Bakery (☎ 6722 3300; 58 Otho St; pies $3) Simply put, the best pies in town at sparkling value.

Sapphire Chinese (☎ 6722 2266; 23 Byron St; mains $10-15) A great spot to try classic Chinese cuisine.

RSL Club (☎ 6722 3066; Evans St; mains $7-15) Excels at providing a fulfilling feed for little to nothing.

Riverside Function Centre Restaurant (☎ 6721 1244; Campbell St; mains $15-30) A modern Australian menu and a great view, one of the best in town.

Getting There & Away

Black & White (☎ 6732 3687; www.blackandwhitebus .com) has trips to Glen Innes twice a day.

Countrylink (☎ 13 22 32, www.countrylink.info) buses go to Glen Innes ($12.10), Bingara ($16.50), Manilla ($31.90) and Tamworth ($41.80). You can also catch a bus then train to Sydney ($94.60).

Harvey World Travel (☎ 6722 3011; 45 Byron St) has extensive knowledge on all things travel. At the time of writing Big Sky Express was planning to fly into Inverell; inquire here.

AROUND INVERELL

The **Dejon Sapphire Centre** (☎ 02-6723 2222; Gwydir Hwy; admission free; ☾ 9am-5pm) has a wonderful display of gems. The centre is 19km east of Inverell on the Gwydir Hwy and is well signposted.

Thomas New England Estate Wines (☎ 02-6724 8508; Delungra), northwest of Inverell, is growing in reputation and is a good drinks break on any trip.

Green Valley Farm (☎ 02-6723 3370; Tingha; adult/child $5/3; ☾ Sat, Sun & public hols) offers mini golf ($2), water slides ($6), a museum, a zoo and topiary grotesqueries, such as an 'eight-legged kitten' and 'Siamese pigs'.

KWIAMBAL NATIONAL PARK

On the way to the Queensland border is the Kwiambal (Ki-am-bal) National Park (1301 hectares) with impressive waterfalls and waterholes. It is renowned for its Limestone Caves – the main cave is over 500m long and leads on to the great cave, nearly as large. They were mined for bat droppings called guano, a low-grade fertiliser, in the 1960s. Close by on the Macintyre River are the Macintyre Falls, holding some rugged gorges, swimming holes and basic camp sites.

Central West

CONTENTS

Stretching 400km inland from the Blue Mountains, the NSW central west gradually shifts from fields to vast plains and finally the harsh outback. The area appears utterly typical but is unique in the state for its relatively close settlement and liberal sprinkling of fair-sized towns. These are steeped in bushranger and gold rush history; the streets are lined with stately buildings, the parks with manicured English gardens. Local history is strong; folk museums are filled to bursting with memorabilia; roads are named after admired drovers. The central west is solid, respectable and, above all, rural. With some notable exceptions, such as the Western Plains Zoo in Dubbo, there isn't a lot in the way of tourist-oriented attractions – but this in itself is an attraction.

It was gold that began it, and it is the history of gold that you feel every time you enter one of the region's fascinating towns. It started with Edward Hargraves, a clever man with an intense dislike for work. Returning empty-handed from the Californian goldfields, he was inspired by a government reward for discovering payable gold, so he headed west in 1851 and found gold in Lewis Ponds Creek. He named the field Ophir after the biblical city of gold. Within a week gold fever gripped the region; for the rest of the century tens of thousands of fossickers came to the central west in the hope the streams and hillsides would yield enough of the promised metal to change their lives forever.

HIGHLIGHTS

- Coming face to face with the rare black rhinos at Dubbo's **Western Plains Zoo** (p226)

- Feeling satisfied after a good meal of local produce at **Eda-Bull** (p229) in Forbes, one of the region's many fine restaurants

- Strolling in the serene Japanese Gardens in **Cowra** (p230)

- Watching Stephen Doyle hand-prune his vines (and enjoying one of Rhonda's quiches) at **Bloodwood Winery** (p223) near Orange

- Dreaming of being a moon-walker at **Parkes Radio Telescope** (p228)

- Exploring the subterranean wonderland of the magnificent **Abercrombie Caves** (p219)

- Picking your own succulent red cherries at an orchard in **Young** (p231)

- Travelling through time at the **Gulgong Pioneer Museum** (p222)

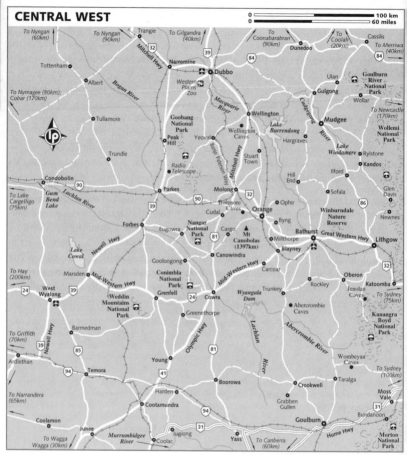

CENTRAL WEST

BATHURST

☎ 02 / pop 30,100

Laid out on a grand scale, Bathurst is Australia's oldest inland settlement. It boasts European trees and a cool climate. As well as its architectural and historical interest, Bathurst is a bastion of Australian motor sport, hosting numerous events.

Orientation & Information

The city is laid out on a large grid of wide streets. William St between Durham and Keppel Sts is the main shopping area.

The **visitors centre** (☎ 6332 1444; Kendall Ave; www.bathurst.nsw.gov.au; 9am-5pm) is particularly helpful. Internet is free at the **Bathurst Library** (☎ 6332 2130; Keppel St).

Sights & Activities

Although not open at the time of writing, the **Australian Fossil & Mineral Museum** (☎ 6332 1444; 244 Howick St; adult/child $8/5; 10am-5pm) will display the internationally renowned Somerville Collection, the personal collection of geologist Warren Somerville. Over 6000 fossils will be exhibited from every period of the earth's history, some specimens being the only examples in the world. The museum will also house Australia's only complete Tyrannosaurus Rex skeleton, the country's finest collection of fossils in amber, and opalised dinosaur teeth. This is a significant collection and a visit is definitely warranted.

The **Bathurst Regional Art Gallery** (☎ 6331 6066; 70-78 Keppel St; admission free; 10am-5pm Tue-Sat,

Divers and a blue groper, Coffs Harbour (p168)

Main street, Nimbin (p191)

OLIVER

ROSS BARNETT

Bald Rock National Park (p210)

CHRIS MELLOR

Hot-air balloon, Hunter Valley (p143)

Purple swamphen, Macquarie Marshes (p240)

MITCH RE

11am-2pm Sun) has a dynamic collection of work, featuring local artists as well as exciting touring exhibitions. The work of Grace Cossington Smith, whose paintings of the Sydney Harbour Bridge under construction defined the event for many Australians, is well represented but restricted; you must ask at the front desk.

The **courthouse** (1880), on Russell St, is the most impressive of Bathurst's many interesting old buildings. Local myth has it that there was a mix-up of the plans with those intended for India's magnificent Court of Appeals! The court, the central section of the building, can be visited from 9.30am to 1pm and from 2pm to 4pm weekdays. In the east wing is the small **Historical Museum** (☎ 6332

4755; adult/child $2/1; ☺ Tue-Sun). **Machattie Park**, behind the courthouse, was once the site of the jail and is now a pleasant formal park, known for its begonias, which flower from late summer to early autumn.

Ben Chifley, prime minister from 1945 to 1949, lived in Bathurst and the modest **Chifley Home** (☎ 6332 1444; 10 Busby St; adult/child $5/3; ☺ 2-4pm Sat-Mon) is on display. The Chifley government's initiatives in welcoming European refugees as immigrants were important to Australia's cultural and economic development. Before entering politics Chifley had been a train driver and he maintained a simple lifestyle even when in office.

Near the city centre is the 6.2km **Mt Panorama Motor Racing Circuit**, the venue for some

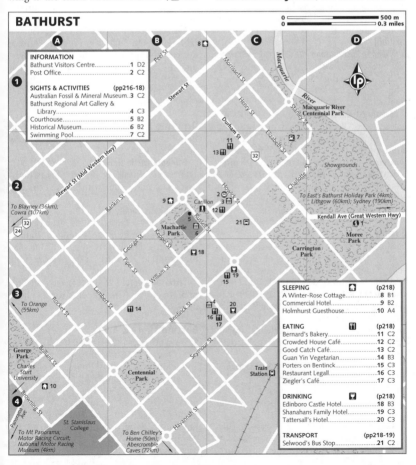

BATHURST

0 — 500 m
0 — 0.3 miles

INFORMATION	
Bathurst Visitors Centre	1 D2
Post Office	2 C2

SIGHTS & ACTIVITIES	(pp216-18)
Australian Fossil & Mineral Museum	3 C2
Bathurst Regional Art Gallery & Library	4 C3
Courthouse	5 B2
Historical Museum	6 B2
Swimming Pool	7 C2

To Blayney (36km); Cowra (107km)

To Orange (55km)

Stewart St (Mid Western Hwy)

Macquarie River Centennial Park

Showgrounds

To East's Bathurst Holiday Park (4km); Lithgow (60km); Sydney (190km)

Kendall Ave (Great Western Hwy)

Carrington Park

Moree Park

Machattie Park

Centennial Park

Train Station

George Park

Charles Sturt University

St. Stanislaus College

To Mt Panorama; Motor Racing Circuit; National Motor Racing Museum (4km)

To Ben Chifley's Home (50km); Abercrombie Caves (72km)

SLEEPING		(p218)
A Winter-Rose Cottage	8	B1
Commercial Hotel	9	B2
Holmhurst Guesthouse	10	A4

EATING		(p218)
Bernard's Bakery	11	C2
Crowded House Café	12	C2
Good Catch Café	13	C2
Guan Yin Vegetarian	14	B3
Porters on Bentinck	15	C3
Restaurant Legall	16	C3
Ziegler's Café	17	C3

DRINKING		(p218)
Edinboro Castle Hotel	18	B3
Shanahans Family Hotel	19	C3
Tattersall's Hotel	20	C3

TRANSPORT	(pp218-19)
Selwood's Bus Stop	21 C2

of Australia's most popular car races: the Bathurst Motorsport Spectacular in October; the FAI 1000 for 5L production cars, held in November; and motorcycle racing over Easter. You can drive around the circuit, which is a two-way public road with a 60km limit (boring!). Rev-heads will enjoy the **National Motor Racing Museum** (☎ 6332 1872; Pit Straight; adult $7; ⊕ 9am-4.30pm).

Sleeping

During the motor racing, the visitors centre runs a home-share scheme.

Commercial Hotel (☎ 6331 2712; 135 George St; www.geocities.com/commercialhotelbathurst; s/d $25/44) This pub has a cosy bar downstairs and small but inviting rooms upstairs. The Commercial is encouraging a backpacker market so the shared kitchen is well stocked, the pub grub is first-rate and there are good weekly deals available.

A Winter-Rose Cottage (☎ 6332 2661; www.winter -rose.com.au; 79 Morrissett St; d $90-110) A snug B&B with a well-loved garden. If you're staying a while, opt for the self-contained cottage out the back.

Holmhurst Guest House (☎ 6332 4141; 306 William St; s/d $85/110; ℗) Located in a beautiful old orphanage, this comfortable B&B has some of the best views in Bathurst and a wraparound veranda to enjoy them from.

East's Bathurst Holiday Park (☎ 6331 8286; Great Western Hwy; camp sites $18, cabins from $55; ⊠) This is the main caravan park, but at race periods other camping areas are opened.

Eating

Good Catch Café (☎ 6331 1333; 85 George St; mains $8-16; ⊕ 11am-9pm Wed-Sun) This cheerful café sells a range of wonderfully fresh seafood and salads from its slickly tiled shop front.

Bernard's Bakery (☎ 6331 2042; 81 George St; sandwiches around $6; ⊕ breakfast & lunch) Bernard's packs the local workers in with crusty rolls and its home-made version of the Australian school-yard classic the 'snot block', delicious vanilla slices!

Porters on Bentinck (☎ 6331 8108; 92 Bentinck St; mains $8-15; ⊕ 10am-5pm Sun-Thu, to 10pm Fri, to 2pm Sat) An upmarket deli-cum-wine bar with a soothing atmosphere and a focus on local produce.

Ziegler's Café (☎ 6332 1565; 52 Keppel St; mains $10-20; ⊕ 9.30am-10pm Mon-Fri, 9am-10pm Sat & Sun) You could sit for hours in the leafy courtyard at Ziegler's; it's the perfect place for coffee and a book, though it also has tasty main dishes.

Guan Yin Vegetarian (☎ 6332 5388; 166A William St; mains $8-14; ⊕ lunch Mon-Fri, dinner Wed-Sat) It seems an unlikely find in a country town, but Guan Yin serves up popular 'I can't believe it's not meat' smorgasbords where vegetarian Mongolian lamb is the order of the day.

Crowded House (☎ 6334 2300; 1 Ribbon Gang Lane off William St; mains $12-25; ⊕ 10am-3.30pm Mon-Sat, dinner Tue-Sat) From a restored 1850 church with soaring ceilings, the restaurant spills out onto a courtyard dotted with olive trees and lavender bushes. While lunch is above average café fare, at night the food is more sophisticated – ocean trout on wilted greens, kipfler potatoes, feta and lemon myrtle olive oil ($25) might be on offer.

Restaurant Legall (☎ 6331 5800; 56 Keppel St; mains $25-7; ⊕ dinner Tue-Sat) In a sweet yellow terrace it is easy to mistake the solicitors' office next door for this restaurant. However, while it may provide the same country warmth, one doubts the lawyers could make such good provincial French fare.

Drinking

Bathurst is a student town and they know how to party.

Edinboro Castle Hotel (The Eddy; ☎ 6331 5020; 134 William St; ⊕ until 5am Thu-Sat) This is Bathurst's late-night spot with big screens and big noise.

Shanahans Family Hotel (The Family; ☎ 6331 1353; cnr Russell & Bentinck Sts) is exactly that, with a pleasant beer garden and an Italian-style bistro. There is free jazz on Thursday nights and local bands get the place rocking on Friday and Saturday.

Tattersall's Hotel (☎ 6331 5544; Keppel St) This pub is popular with students for its cheap drinks.

Getting There & Away

Selwood's Coaches (☎ 6362 7963) links Bathurst with Orange ($7.80, 45 minutes, once daily) and Sydney ($28, three hours, once daily).

The quickest **CountryLink** (☎ 13 22 32) trains from Sydney ($37.50, three hours) operate during rush hours; CountryLink coaches go to Orange ($10) and Dubbo ($33, two hours, once daily). CountryLink coach/train combinations also run to Melbourne ($98, nine hours).

Getting Around

Taxis (☎ 6331 1511) run 24 hours a day. Bathurst Coaches runs a local bus service, which stops outside East's Bathurst Holiday Park every day except Sunday. Grab a timetable from the tourist office.

AROUND BATHURST

About 70km south of Bathurst along awesomely winding roads are the famous **Abercrombie Caves** (☎ 6368 8603; www.jenolancaves .org.au; self-guided, admission $12; ☉ 10am-4pm). The Grand Arch is one of the world's largest natural tunnels and even the side passages are huge. In the Hall of Terpsichore you can still see the dance floor installed by miners last century. Beneath all the limestone is a river with a few particularly beautiful pools. There's swimming and **camping** (☎ 6368 8603; per person $6.50) near the cave.

Sofala, Australia's oldest surviving gold town, is a good-looking little place with some unusually well-preserved timber buildings. Peter Weir shot his 1974 film *The Cars that Ate Paris* here.

Thirty-five kilometres northwest of Sofala, down an unsealed road, the ghost town of **Hill End** was the scene of an 1870s gold rush. The **National Parks & Wildlife Service (NPWS) visitors centre** (☎ 6337 8206; Hospital Lane; admission $2.20; ☉ 9.30am-12.30pm & 1.30-4.30pm), inside the old hospital, includes a fascinating **museum** (admission $2.50). Book here for the three **NPWS camping grounds** (adult/child $5/3). There are a few residents hanging on in this enviably pretty locale, and many of them can be found at the dusty **Royal Hotel** (☎ 6337 8261; Beyers Ave; s/d/f $33/55/90), the only pub remaining of an original 28.

Further northeast towards Mudgee, the village of **Rylstone** has pretty sandstone buildings and access to **Wollemi National Park**.

MUDGEE

☎ 02 / pop 8600

Mudgee, an Aboriginal word for 'nest in the hills', doesn't stand out as a country town, but it does as a centre for the new regional gourmet food and wine industries. This makes it a popular weekend getaway for those interested in combining attractive natural surroundings with gastronomic exploration. Local farms are now specialising in sheep and goat cheeses and, of course, the renowned Mudgee honey.

Orientation & Information

Mudgee is about 120km north of Bathurst and Lithgow, on the banks of the Cudgegong River. Most wineries are north of the river. The main shopping street is Church St.

The **visitors centre** (☎ 1800 816 304, 6372 1020; www.mudgee-gulgong.org; 84 Market St; ☉ 9am-5pm Mon-Fri, to 3.30pm Sat, 9.30am-2pm Sun) is near the post office. If you're going wine tasting, grab a copy of the Mudgee-Gulgong visitors guide.

Sights & Activities
WINERIES

The vineyards are clustered together, making the region ideal for cycling. The vintage is later than in the Hunter Valley because of Mudgee's higher altitude.

Formerly Craigmoor, **Poet's Corner** (☎ 6372 2208; Craigmoor Rd, 2.5km off Henry Lawson Rd; ☉ 10am-4.30pm Mon-Sat, to 4pm Sun) has produced a vintage annually since 1858, making it one of Australia's oldest. (These days it's owned by the Pernod company.)

Get some old-fashioned winery atmosphere at **Pieter Ven Gent** (☎ 6373 3807; Black Springs Rd; ☉ 9am-5pm Mon-Sat, 10am-4pm Sun), where tastings can be taken in old choir stalls.

Try the excellent shiraz at **Platts Wines** (☎ 6372 7041; platt@hwy.com.au; cnr Henry Lawson Dr & Cassilis Rd; ☉ 9am-5pm), and don't leave without a bottle of this winery's celebrated verjuice.

See also p219 for more winery-related events.

OTHER ATTRACTIONS

If you really want to embrace the foodie experience, **Heart of Mudgee** (☎ 6372 3224; www .mudgeehampers.com.au; cnr Court & Short Sts; ☉ 9am-5pm) is a good place to start. Selling only products produced by people living in Mudgee, a tasting table runs down the middle of the store, showcasing the best this region has to offer; remember, no double-dipping!

If that wasn't enough, **Honey Haven** (☎ 6372 4478; cnr Gulgong & Hargraves Rds; ☉ 10am-4pm Tue-Sun) has endless varieties to trial (the wonderfully named *Beeagra* included!); kids can watch the bees hard at work in their hive.

Festivals & Events

In September, there's a fabulous **wine festival** (www.mudgeewines.com.au) to celebrate the region's new-release wines, complete with wine show, tastings, food and concerts.

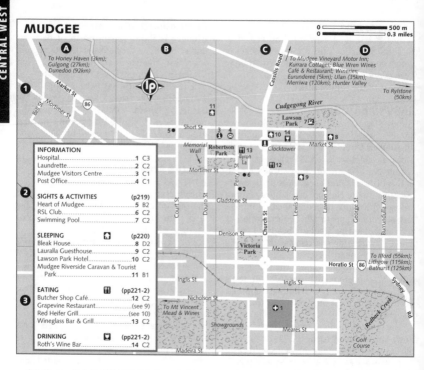

MUDGEE

0 ————— 500 m
0 ————— 0.3 miles

To Honey Haven (3km);
Gulgong (27km);
Dunedoo (92km)

To Mudgee Vineyard Motor Inn;
Kurrara Cottages; Blue Wren Wines
Café & Restaurant; Wineries;
Eurunderee (5km); Ulan (35km);
Merriwa (120km); Hunter Valley

To Rylstone
(50km)

Cudgegong River

Lawson Park

Clocktower

Market St

INFORMATION	
Hospital	1 C3
Laundrette	2 C2
Mudgee Visitors Centre	3 C1
Post Office	4 C1

SIGHTS & ACTIVITIES	(p219)
Heart of Mudgee	5 B2
RSL Club	6 C2
Swimming Pool	7 C2

SLEEPING	(p220)
Bleak House	8 D2
Lauralla Guesthouse	9 C2
Lawson Park Hotel	10 C2
Mudgee Riverside Caravan & Tourist Park	11 B1

EATING	(pp221-2)
Butcher Shop Café	12 C2
Grapevine Restaurant	(see 9)
Red Heifer Grill	(see 10)
Wineglass Bar & Grill	13 C2

DRINKING	(pp221-2)
Roth's Wine Bar	14 C2

Memorial Wall
Robertson Park
Byron La
Mortimer St

Victoria Park

To Ilford (55km);
Lithgow (115km);
Bathurst (125km)

To Mt Vincent
Mead & Wines

Showgrounds

Golf Course

Redbank Creek

Sydney Rd

Huntington Estate (☎ 6373 3825; huntwine@hwy .com.au; Cassilis Rd; 9am-5pm Mon-Fri, 10am-5pm Sat, to 4pm Sun) hosts the immensely popular **Huntington Music Festival** in early December, featuring the Australian Chamber Orchestra.

Sleeping

If you come to Mudgee on a weekend or during the wine festival you should book. There is a staggering number of B&Bs in the Mudgee Valley – over 80 at last count; a full list is available at the visitors centre.

Lawson Park Hotel (☎ 6372 2183; cnr Church & Short Sts; s/d $40/55) This beautiful, historic hotel has a cosy living area and comfortable rooms, most with direct access to the veranda.

Mudgee Vineyard Motor Inn (☎ 6372 1022; 252 Henry Lawson Dr; s/d $60/70 Mon-Thu, $65/75 Fri-Sun;) Put this motel on a busy highway strip and it wouldn't look out of place. But it isn't, instead it's smack bang in the heart of the vineyards.

Bleak House (☎ 6372 4888; www.geocities.com /bleakhousemudgee; 7 Lawson St; $160 Mon-Thu, $185 Fri-Sun;) Built in 1860, this superior B&B with its gracious verandas, soaring ceilings

and pretty gardens is anything but bleak. The rooms are tastefully decorated and the scrumptious breakfasts will have you powering through the vineyards.

Kurrara Cottages (☎ 6373 3734; www.kurrara.com .au; Henry Lawson Dr; 1-/2-bedroom with breakfast $150/ 260;) For romance, sunken spa pools and fluffy bathrobes, this is the place to come.

Mudgee Riverside Caravan & Tourist Park (☎ 6372 2531; 22 Short St; camp sites from $16, cabins $50-70) In a leafy setting, this relaxed caravan park is a real beauty. They also have mountain-bike rental ($15 half-day).

Eating & Drinking

Butcher Shop Café (☎ 6372 7373; 49 Church St; mains $9-20; breakfast & lunch daily, dinner Fri & Sat) A hip eatery in an old butchery. Menus are scribbled on butcher's paper attached to gleaming tiled walls – but you won't get half-a-dozen pork chops here. Scrambled eggs and salmon roe with freshly roasted coffee for breakfast, with dinners moving into smart modern-Australian territory.

Red Heifer Grill (Lawson Park Hotel; mains $11-18; dinner) Locals swear on this place; a communal BBQ every night of the week with a choice of big, spiced-up steaks you can slap on the central grill, or try a trout wrapped in foil. Match it with a local wine from the bar.

Blue Wren Wines Café & Restaurant (☎ 6372 6205; Cassilis Rd; mains $18-26; ⓦ lunch, dinner Wed-Sat) An exceptional restaurant in an interesting space, Blue Wren is the place to indulge in handmade prawn ravioli and barramundi chowder. There is also a very generous BYO policy – considering it *is* a winery.

Other spots to try superb local food are the **Wineglass Bar & Grill** (☎ 6372 3417; Cobb & Co Ct, cnr Market & Perry Sts), and the **Grapevine Restaurant** (☎ 6372 4480; www.lauralla.com.au; cnr Lewis & Mortimer Sts) at the Lauralla Guesthouse, which serves seven-stage degustation dinners ($70).

Roth's Wine Bar (☎ 6372 1222; 30 Market St; ⓦ noon-6.30pm Mon-Fri, 10am-noon Sat) After a day in the vineyards a late-afternoon tipple is probably the last thing on your mind, but Roth's is the oldest wine bar in NSW and the atmosphere is still there.

Getting There & Away

CountryLink (☎ 13 22 32) buses to Lithgow are timed to meet Sydney trains ($45.50, five hours 20 minutes).

GULGONG
☎ 02 / pop 2020

Gulgong was known as 'the hub of the world' during the roaring days of gold fever; the settlement was created almost overnight in the rush that began in 1870. After 1880 the rush tapered off, but it left behind a well-established town that is today classified by the National Trust. Gulgong later called itself 'the town on the $10 note', but since the introduction of the plastic $10 note, it isn't.

Orientation & Information

Gulgong's main street is Herbert St, which leads south to Mudgee. Originally, it was Mayne St, a delightful old thoroughfare that winds across town from the Wellington road. The **visitors centre** (☎ 6374 1202; 109 Herbert St; ⓦ 8am-12.30pm, 1.30-4.30pm Mon-Fri) has guides to some terrific walks around the area.

PRIDE & PRODUCE

Orange, Dubbo, Young, Mudgee, Cowra, Bathurst...the names trip off the tongue. The NSW Central West preserves the best of the old while embracing the new. The products may have changed, but the spirit that cleared the early acres and saw off the droughts and the floods remains. Driving through the countryside in spring to visit the Orange Field Days, your senses are overwhelmed by the blue-purple haze of the Patterson's Curse, the buzz of the native bees and the smell of newly cut forage. You know this area had a winter, that it was frosty and that it is over. New season, new hope. Cherry blossom in Young, young vines in Mudgee and lambs almost everywhere.

The central west is Victorian towns and 21st-century agribusiness. It is the university city of Bathurst, the public service enclave of Orange and the thrusting new small businesses of Mudgee. These 'regions' are flexing their political muscles to ensure they have the same access to modern infrastructure as their city cousins. Now every small holder is on the Net and trading electronically. The centres are being sympathetically renovated. New uses are being found for old building stock and if many of them are service- or tourist-oriented, that's because these industries lead the way in providing opportunity and employment.

In early summer the stone fruit begins to ripen, the lambs fatten and the vines bud. Each year new products reach the markets, encouraged by both local and city chefs and gastronomes. Once asparagus was green and came in tins. Now it is white and purple and delivered daily to Sydney's Flemington. Once there was leg of mutton, now there is lamb and baby goat. Once Mudgee and Orange wineries were an aberration, now they are appellation-controlled. And there is cheese of every variety, virgin olive oil and verjuice.

The towns compete to provide the best services to visitors and take pride in their locality. The staff in the visitors centres are well informed and informative. On a slow day you could be given a tour of the local wineries and honey producers, on a busy day a map. Local history thrives and the museums are relevant and interesting. The central west is not in the heart of Australia, but it gives out an aura of being its heart. Spend a few days absorbing the atmosphere and you will see what that means.

Sights & Activities

The **Gulgong Pioneer Museum** (☎ 6374 1513; 73 Herbert St; admission $5; ☉ 9am-5pm) is one of the most eclectic country-town museums in the state. The huge collection of the important and the trivial borders on chaos, but it's all fascinating. Photographs of early Gulgong from the Holterman Collection are displayed, and there are also pin-up photos of the stars who drove the diggers wild at the local opera. Music aficionados can get their fix a few doors down in the sight and sound section and might even get to play a record on the gramophone run by car batteries.

Author Henry Lawson spent part of his childhood in the area after his parents followed the rush to the goldfields. The **Henry Lawson Centre** (☎ 6374 2049; 147 Mayne St; adult/child $4/2.50; ☉ 10am-3.30pm Wed-Sat, to 1pm Sun-Tue) looks at Lawson's early memories of Gulgong; it was here he learned to dislike the squalor, meanness and brutalising hard work and poverty of the goldfields – a bitterness that never quite faded. There is a good selection of his works for sale.

Originally built from bark, the **opera house** (☎ 6374 1162; 99-101 Mayne St) is one of the oldest surviving theatres in Australia. It was immortalised in Henry Lawson's poem, 'The Last View', and played host to such stars as Dame Nellie Melba.

Festivals & Events

The second weekend in June is the time for the big **Henry Lawson Festival**. There is music, dramatisation of Lawson stories at the Opera House, and literary awards, some of them sponsored by Norwegian organisations – given that Lawson's father was a Norwegian immigrant.

Gulgong also hosts a popular folk-music festival over the New Year period.

Sleeping & Eating

Stables Guesthouse (☎ 6374 1668; 149 Mayne St; s/d Mon-Thu $80-95/120-150, Fri-Sun $100-110/140-170; ✄ ✎) An attractive B&B which has been authentically renovated, designed to provide privacy while being right in the centre of town.

Ten Dollar Town Motel (☎ 6374 1204; www .tendollartownmotel.com.au; cnr Mayne & Medley Sts; s/d $85/95; ✄) The charming heritage façade hides a standard motel complex. However,

the service is friendly and it's close to all the action.

Henry Lawson Van Park (☎ 6374 1294; Mayne St; camp sites $12-16, cabins $38-55) Although a little way out of town on the road to Wellington, this park has a sweet animal farm with some friendly llamas.

Bank Onya Pizza (☎ 6374 1908; 117 Mayne St; pizzas $9-16; ☉ lunch & dinner) Besides pizzas this restaurant does some hearty baked potato and pasta dishes.

Larsen's Brasserie (☎ 6374 2822; 137 Mayne St; mains $14-25; ☉ 10am-10pm Fri-Sun) Relax in the nice courtyard at the weekend while enjoying some home-made fare and a fine selection of local wines.

Getting There & Away

CountryLink (☎ 13 22 32) runs two buses to Mudgee ($5.50, 25 minutes, twice daily) from Gulgong.

ORANGE
☎ 02 / pop 32,000

The city of Orange is in a fertile agricultural area, but it does not grow oranges! Rather, it was named in 1846 after Prince William of Orange. With four distinct seasons (due to an altitude of 950m), the city's parks and gardens are a kaleidoscope of colours throughout the year; cold winters bring occasional snowfalls.

Orientation & Information

Suburban Orange sprawls over quite a large area, but the city centre, with its grid-pattern streets, is compact and easy to get around. Summer St is the main street and the town centre begins just west of the train line.

The **visitors centre** (☎ 6393 8226; Byng St; ☉ 9am-5pm) has a range of handy brochures, including a walking tour of the city and winery tours around the district.

Internet access is available at **Octec** (247 Anson St; per hr $5; ☉ 9am-5pm Mon-Fri).

The autumn apple-picking season lasts for about six weeks. Octec's **employment service** (☎ 6362 8169; http://cww.octec.org.au) can help you find work. Some orchards have accommodation.

Sights & Activities

The excellent **Orange Regional Gallery** (☎ 6393 8136; Civic Sq; admission free; ☉ 10am-5pm Tue-Sat, 1-4pm Sun) has an ambitious, varied programme of exhibitions as well as works by modern Australian masters.

The **Botanic Gardens** (☎ 6361 5186; Kearneys Dr; admission free; ☼ 7.30am-dusk) are on Clover Hill (with good views of the city), 2km north of the city. The gardens were established in 1981 to preserve the native woodlands of the area and to grow other plants suited to this cool climate. This is an interesting project, as most botanic gardens in the state were established long ago and are rigidly formal, echoing the gardens 'back home' in Britain.

Poet Banjo Paterson (who wrote the lyrics to 'Waltzing Matilda') was born on Narrambla Station near Orange in 1864. The site of the station is now **Banjo Paterson Memorial Park**, about 3km northeast of Orange on the Ophir road, with picnic facilities under the giant oak trees.

Orange is developing a reputation for distinctive cool-climate wines, and many award-winning vineyards lie southwest of town. The *Orange Region Wines* brochure is available from the visitors centre. But if you're fighting over who will do the driving,

Reds & Whites of Orange Winery Tours (☎ 6362 2344; adult $49.90) runs trips on the weekends that take in four wineries as well as a light lunch. Two not to miss are **Pinnacle** (☎ 6365 3316) and **Bloodwood** (☎ 6362 5631) – phone for bookings.

Australia's first real gold rush took place at **Ophir**, 27km north of Orange along mostly unsealed roads. After the diggers left, deep mining was begun and continues today at Doctors Hill. A few fossickers still come here, and small finds by visitors aren't uncommon. You can buy a licence and a pan at the site (☎ 6366 0445).

Festivals & Events

Orange Food Week (www.orangefoodweek.com.au) is the city's annual celebration of all things epicurean and gustatory. Held during the middle of April, events range from cooking classes to **Opera in the Vineyard**.

Orange National Field Days, the largest in the state, are held in the middle of October. Here you can check out the latest farm machinery and watch events such as sheepdog trials.

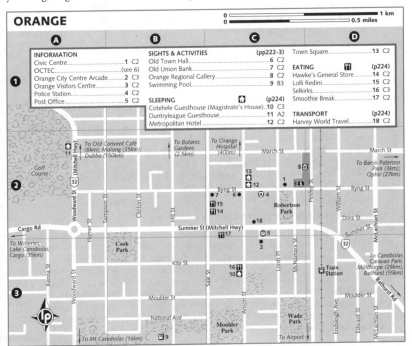

ORANGE

0 ———— 1 km
0 ———— 0.5 miles

INFORMATION	
Civic Centre	1 C2
OCTEC	(see 6)
Orange City Centre Arcade	2 C3
Orange Visitors Centre	3 C2
Police Station	4 C2
Post Office	5 C2

SIGHTS & ACTIVITIES	(pp222-3)
Old Town Hall	6 C2
Old Union Bank	7 C2
Orange Regional Gallery	8 C2
Swimming Pool	9 B3

SLEEPING	(p224)
Cotehele Guesthouse (Magistrate's House)	10 C3
Duntryleague Guesthouse	11 A2
Metropolitan Hotel	12 C2

Town Square	13 C2

EATING	(p224)
Hawke's General Store	14 C2
Lolli Redini	15 C3
Selkirks	16 C3
Smoothie Break	17 C2

TRANSPORT	(p224)
Harvey World Travel	18 C2

To Old Convent Café (8km); Molong (35km); Dubbo (150km)

To Botanic Gardens (2.5km)

To Orange Hospital (400m)

March St

To Banjo Paterson Park (3km); Ophir (27km)

Golf Course

Woodward St (Mitchell Hwy)

Byng St

Robertson Park

Dora St

Cargo Rd

Summer St (Mitchell Hwy)

To Wineries; Lake Canobolas; Cargo (35km)

Cook Park

Summer St

To Canobolas Caravan Park; Millthorpe (29km); Bathurst (55km)

Kite St

Train Station

Bathurst Rd

Moulder St

Moulder St

National Ave

Wade Park

To Mt Canobolas (16km)

Moulder Park

To Airport

Sleeping

Town Square (☎ 6369 1444; tsm@netwit.net.au; 246 Anson St; s/d $95/110; ⊠) In a convenient central location behind the Metropolitan Hotel, the Town Square is one of the newer motels.

Cotehele Guest House (The Magistrate's House; ☎ 6361 2520; 177 Anson St; www.cotehele.com.au; s/d $120/185; ⊠) A beautifully restored Victorian home with a lush garden full of rambling roses and deciduous trees. Full of character, it still retains the history of its previous owner, local magistrate and gold commissioner John Tom Lane (1878).

Duntryleague Guest House (☎ 6362 3822; www .duntryleague.com.au; Woodward St; s/d $100/120 incl breakfast; ⊠) An elegant mansion built in 1876, with the Orange golf course constructed in its grounds in 1920.

Canobolas Caravan Park (☎ 6362 7279; www .canobolasmarine.com.au; 166 Bathurst Rd; camp sites $10-15, cabins with bathroom $50-60) Southeast of the city centre, there is a large grass camping area here.

Eating

Two restaurants in Orange have been heavily acclaimed, and a visit to at least one is certainly recommended; booking is advised.

Lolli Redini (☎ 6361 7748; 48 Sale St; mains $25-30; ⊠ lunch & dinner Wed-Sat, plus 10am-2pm Sat) A sassy family-owned bistro where an Italian flavour presides. The menu changes daily but you might find a *crepinette* of local venison wild-mushroom ragout, *boulangère* potato and sweet onions or a bright green pea risotto with artichoke on offer. Beware – the desserts are as equally tempting.

Selkirks (☎ 6361 1179; 179 Anson St; mains $25-30; ⊠ dinner Tue-Sat) In a lovely old sand-stone house is one of NSW's premier restaurants,

Selkirks, passionate advocate for the region's food and wine. The menu follows the seasons, and there's a local wine chosen for every dish – such as the Bloodwood Shiraz for a charcuterie plate of paté, terrine and sausage. Don't miss the dessert platter – trifle, tarts and gelato are absolute bliss.

For a quick bite there are several places along Summer St.

Smoothie Break (☎ 6360 4860; 142 Summer St; dishes $3-8; ⊠ 8am-8.30pm) Delicious sorbets are served up here, as well as fresh juices and sandwiches.

Hawkes General Store (☎ 6362 5851; 46 Sale St; mains $6-14; ⊠ 9.30am-5.30pm Mon-Fri, 10am-1.30pm Sat) Around the corner from Smoothie Break, this is a popular meeting place for Orange's ladies who lunch. It has an excellent selection of coffee and a pretty outdoor area.

Old Convent Café (☎ 6365 2420; Convent Rd, Borenore; mains $18; ⊠ breakfast & lunch Sat & Sun) It's only a pretty 10-minute drive through the countryside to this popular weekend brunch spot. The food is unpretentious and delicious and the service friendly.

Getting There & Away

Regional Express Airlines (Rex; ☎ 6361 5888) flies to Sydney ($120) daily. The airport is 13km southeast of Orange. Shuttle buses leave from Harvey World Travel on 249 Summer St.

McCafferty's/Greyhound (☎ 13 14 99) has daily services to Dubbo ($27.50, one hour 45 minutes). **Selwood's** (☎ 6362 7963; www.selwoods .com.au) departs for Sydney ($33, four hours 15 minutes, once daily) and Bathurst ($7.80, 45 minutes, once daily) from the train station. **CountryLink** (☎ 13 22 32) trains go to Sydney ($45, five hours, once daily) and Dubbo ($22, one hour 45 minutes, once daily).

DETOUR: MILLTHORPE TO MT CANOBOLAS

From Bathurst take the Mid Western Hwy (24) to Blayney before veering right onto the Millthorpe road. Millthorpe is a sweet village that appears to be waking from a long slumber. The gently sloping streets are abuzz on weekends and well worth a stop. Try **Tonic** (☎ 6366 3811; ⊠ lunch & dinner Thu-Sun, brunch Sat & Sun) for a taste of local produce. Browsers will delight in the several antique stores. From Millthorpe it is a pretty 10km drive west through the picturesque hills to the **Forest Reefs Tavern,** a classic miners pub. Follow the signs to **Mt Canobolas** (1395m), a steep, extinct volcano. Drive or walk to the top and enjoy views that stretch a long way across the western plains; in winter there's often snow on the peak. At the bottom of the mountain is **Lake Canobolas**, where you can see deer and lots of birds.

WELLINGTON

☎ 02 / pop 4670

Wellington was the first settlement to be established west of Bathurst and while it may seem like another typical rural town, it is a very appealing place. With its steep green hills overlooking the town, and the wide Bell River running through, it makes as pleasant a stop as its more touristy neighbours.

Orientation & Information

The town meanders along the east bank of the Bell River, which joins the Macquarie River just north of the town centre. Nanima Crescent curves past Bell River; Cameron Park runs down to the river from Nanima Crescent, and across the river is the pleasant Pioneer Park.

Next to the library in Cameron Park, **Wellington Travel** (☎ 1800 621 614; ☺ 9am-5pm) is also a helpful information centre.

Sights & Activities

The **Wellington Caves & Phosphate Mine** (☎ 6845 1733; adult/child 1 cave $12/8, 2 caves or cave & mine $21/14) are the area's big attraction. Thought to have been discovered in 1830 by a colonist, George Ranken, who accidentally fell into the entrance of one of the caves, these exquisite and unusual formations can be visited on guided tours, which run several times daily. The Cathedral Cave is famous for its majestic stalagmite known as the Altar Rock (or the Madonna) which is 32m wide and 15m high! The mine is wheelchair friendly.

Across the road from the caves is a **Japanese Garden** (admission free; ☺ 9am-4pm), a gift from Wellington's Japanese sister city Osawanao.

Whether or not you are a plant lover, you can't help but be entranced by the **Burrendong Arboretum** (☎ 6846 7454; per car $4; ☺ 7.30am-5pm). The area overlooking Lake Burrendong has been transformed into a wonderland of native vegetation – 50,000 plants at last count! The colour and variety is spectacular, especially in the dry bush gully that has been turned into a lush rainforest.

Festivals & Events

The horse-racing carnival in March culminates in the running of the town's answer to the Golden Slipper (Australia's premier event for two-year-olds), the **Wellington Boot**. At the same time there is the annual **Wellington Vintage Fair**, the largest swap meet in NSW – certainly the place to come if you are into antique motors.

Sleeping & Eating

Carinya B&B (☎ 6845 4320; 111 Arthur St; s/d $70/80) This pretty Edwardian house offers comfortable rooms and a hearty breakfast – walk it off with a game of boules on the main lawn.

Wellington Caves Holiday Complex (☎ 6845 2970; Caves Rd; camp sites $14-17, cabins/units from $50; ☒) You can camp out near the caves at this camping ground.

Cactus Café & Gallery (☎ 6845 4647; 33-35 Warne St; ☺ Wed-Sun). If you're after a coffee or a bite to eat you can't go past this unique café situated in the former Sacred Hearts Infants' School, built in 1929–30 in the Spanish mission style. The gallery features local artists and there are Mexican handicrafts for sale.

The Wellington **Rugby Club** (☎ 6845 1595; 36 Swift St) has a popular Thai restaurant downstairs.

Getting There & Away

All long-distance buses leave from the post office. **Rendell Coaches** (☎ 1800 023 328) has a daily service to Sydney ($50). The Dubbo XPT stops daily at Wellington ($63).

DUBBO

☎ 02 / pop 31,000

One of the larger towns in the state, Dubbo is a rural centre and a transport crossroads on the northern fringe of the Central West region. Go north or west from Dubbo and you'll find that the population density drops dramatically and the outback begins.

Orientation & Information

Dubbo's grid-pattern city centre lies just east of the Macquarie River, with parkland bordering both banks of the river.

The Mitchell and Newell Hwys cross at a roundabout just west of the river. The Newell Hwy becomes Whylandra St then Erskine St as it bends east around the top end of the city centre; the Mitchell Hwy becomes Cobra St and skirts the city centre to the south. The main shopping street is Macquarie St, which runs between the two.

The **visitors centre** (☎ 1800 674 443, 6884 1422; www.dubbo.com.au; ☺ 9am-5pm) is at the northern end of town on the corner of Macquarie and Erskine Sts.

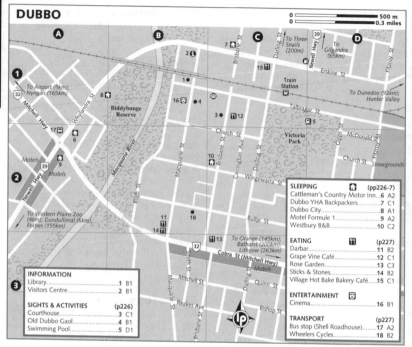

DUBBO

0 —— 500 m
0 —— 0.3 miles

To Three Snails (200m)

To Gilgandra (65km)

To Airport (5km); Nyngan (165km)

Biddybunge Reserve

Train Station

To Dunedoo (92km); Hunter Valley

Talbragar St

Victoria Park

McDonald St

Church St

Showgrounds

Motels

To Western Plains Zoo (4km); Dundullimal (6km); Forbes (155km)

Wingewarra St

Bultje St

To Orange (145km); Bathurst (200km); Lithgow (263km)

Cobra St (Mitchell Hwy)

Motels

Mitchell St

Quinn St

Reakes Ave

Bishop St

SLEEPING	⬛	(pp226–7)
Cattleman's Country Motor Inn...6		A2
Dubbo YHA Backpackers..........7		C1
Dubbo City.............................8		A1
Motel Formule 1......................9		A2
Westbury B&B........................10		C2

EATING	🍴	(p227)
Darbar....................................11		B2
Grape Vine Café.....................12		C1
Rose Garden...........................13		C3
Sticks & Stones......................14		B2
Village Hot Bake Bakery Café...15		C1

ENTERTAINMENT	🎟	
Cinema...................................16		B1

TRANSPORT		(p227)
Bus stop (Shell Roadhouse)......17		A2
Wheelers Cycles.....................18		B2

INFORMATION		
Library....................................1		B1
Visitors Centre........................2		B1

SIGHTS & ACTIVITIES		(p226)
Courthouse.............................3		C1
Old Dubbo Gaol......................4		B1
Swimming Pool.......................5		D1

The library on Talbragar St provides free Internet access. There is a laundrette on Brisbane St near the corner of Bultje St.

Sights & Activities

With more than 1500 animals, the **Western Plains Zoo** (☎ 6882 5888; www.zootopia.com.au; Obley Rd; 2-day pass adult/child/family $25/13.50/65; ☼ 9am-5pm, last entry 4pm) is Dubbo's star attraction. Rare black rhinos were flown in from Zimbabwe as part of an international project to save these magnificent beasts from extinction. There is also an exciting Asian Wetlands exhibit which brings you up close to crazy acrobatic otters and other wildlife found in a Nepalese village. The Bengal tigers alone are worth the admission price. You can walk the 6km, hire a bike ($13) or join the crawling line of cars. Guided morning zoo walks start at 6.45am ($3) every Saturday and Sunday.

The large **Old Dubbo Gaol** (☎ 6882 8122; Macquarie St; adult/child $8/4; ☼ 9am-4.30pm) is open as a museum. 'Animatronic' characters tell their stories, including that of a condemned man due for a meeting with the gallows. Rather creepy night tours are also available.

Dubbo has some lovely old country-town buildings such as the **courthouse** on Brisbane St, an impressive neoclassical edifice. The visitors centre has maps for both a heritage walk and a heritage drive.

Dundullimal (☎ 6884 9984; Obley Rd; adult/child $6/3; ☼ 10am-5pm), about 2km beyond the Western Plains Zoo, is a timber slab homestead built in the 1840s. Slab houses, made from rough-cut tree trunks laid vertically around the frame, were the earliest form of permanent European housing in the newly settled areas of NSW.

Sleeping

Westbury B&B (☎ 6884 9445; westburydubbo@bigpond .com; cnr Brisbane & Wingewarra Sts; s/d $80/110; 🅿) The good-value Westbury, more a boutique hotel than a B&B, is decorated in an old-fashioned style to match the heritage building, but all the trappings are very modern.

Dubbo is not short of motels and they build more every day. Most are to be found along Cobra and Whylandra Sts. Average prices are $75/95 for a single/double with a pool.

Cattleman's Country Motor Inn (☎ 6884 5222; 8 Whylandra St; s/d $85/95; P X 🔁) This is currently the swankiest place in town.

Motel Formule 1 (☎ 6882 9311; Whylandra St; 3 people $45; P 🔁) Cheap and cheerful, a good option if passing through town.

Here are a couple of picks from Dubbo's six caravan parks :

Dubbo City (☎ 6882 4820; Whylandra St; camp sites/cabins from $14/45; 🔁) On the riverbank, this park is an easy 20-minute walk from town, but highway noise can be an issue – a problem also facing the caravan parks closer to the zoo.

Dubbo YHA Backpackers (☎ 6882 0922; yhadubbo@ hwy.net.au; 87 Brisbane St; camp sites from $8, dm/d $17/ 45; 💻) A homey little place that fills up quickly, despite the managers letting guests camp in their living room. Discount zoo tickets and bike hire ($8) are also available here.

Eating

Village Hot Bake Bakery Café (☎ 6884 5454; 113 Darling St; pies $3.95, pie & salad $5) The awards on the wall here prove that it has Australia's best pies.

Grape Vine Café (☎ 6884 7354; 144 Brisbane St; mains $5-10; 💻) Enjoy snacks, cakes and light meals in a coffee-house atmosphere. Take your cup out the back and get some sun in the lovely courtyard.

Sticks & Stones (☎ 6885 4852; 215 Macquarie St; mains $17; ⏰ dinner) The meals may be slightly overpriced, but the wood-fired pizza and pasta are pretty good, and the servings country style (aka huge!).

Rose Garden (☎ 6882 8322, 208 Brisbane St; mains $14-17; ⏰ lunch & dinner) A local institution in Dubbo, probably due to above-average Thai cuisine, rich décor and friendly staff.

Darbar (☎ 6884 4338; 215 Macquarie St; mains $14-16; ⏰ dinner) This licensed Indian joint serves excellent curries and tandoori grills in a leafy courtyard below street level.

Three Snails (☎ 6884 9994; 36 Darling St; mains $25; ⏰ lunch Wed-Fri, dinner Tue-Sat) Dubbo's most exciting restaurant has outlasted the early raves to produce a seasonal menu with delights such as slow-cooked beef cheek with celeriac mash.

Getting There & Away

One-way flights from Sydney with **Qantas** (☎ 13 13 13) start at $160 (one hour). **Rex** (☎ 13 17 13) does the same trip for $130.

Major coach companies all pass through Dubbo – expect to pay about $84 to Sydney

(12 hours), $83 to Melbourne (11 hours), $56 to Adelaide (11 hours) and $79 to Brisbane (15 hours). **Rendell Coaches** (☎ 1800 023 328; Dubbo Bus Station) depart from the Shell Roadhouse at the corner of Whylandra and Victoria Sts for Sydney ($50, 6½ hours), stopping at Orange ($33) and Bathurst ($38). In school holidays Rendell also goes to Canberra ($50, 6¼ hours) via Orange and Cowra.

CountryLink (☎ 13 22 32) trains to Sydney cost $66 (6½ hours).

Getting Around

Darren Wheelers (☎ 6882 9899; 25 Bultje St; ⏰ closed Sun) rents mountain bikes for $15 per day.

PARKES

☎ 02 / pop 9800

A visit to the Parkes gold diggings by NSW premier Sir Henry Parkes in 1871 prompted the locals to change the name of their village from Currajong and name the main street after Parkes' wife, Clarinda. It's said that Parkes influenced the decision to route the railway through the town, so this sycophancy paid off.

Today, Parkes is happy to be known as the home of the radio telescope, made famous by the independent Australian film *The Dish*.

Orientation & Information

From the south, the Newell Hwy takes a twisting route through the centre of Parkes, becoming Grenfell St, Welcome St and finally joining Clarinda St, the main shopping street, to begin its run north to Dubbo. This is a three-way intersection, with Dalton St, the road running west to Condobolin, also joining Clarinda St here. South of this intersection, Clarinda St curves eastwards and becomes the main route to Orange.

The **visitors centre** (☎ 6861 2365; cnr Newell Hwy & Thomas St; ⏰ 9am-5pm Mon-Fri, 10am-4pm Sat & Sun) is in Kelly Reserve. Parkes Shire **library** (☎ 6861 2309; Bogan St; ⏰ 10am-7pm Mon-Fri, to noon Sat) has Internet access.

Sights & Activities
MUSEUMS

Along the Newell Hwy on the Dubbo side of town the **Sir Henry Parkes Museum** (☎ 6862 3509; adult $5; ⏰ 10am-3.30pm Mon-Sat) is more like someone's house than a traditional exhibition space, but it has some Parkes memorabilia and you can walk through the antique machinery collection which has over 5000 items. A reconstruction of Moat House Cottage in Coventry where Parkes was born in 1815 is currently being constructed on the site and it is expected to contain a gallery as well as an audiovisual story of Federation.

PARKES RADIO TELESCOPE

The Parkes Radio Telescope, built by the Commonwealth Scientific and Industrial Research Organisation (CSIRO) in 1961, is 6km east of the Newell Hwy, about 20km north of Parkes. As one of the world's most powerful telescopes it has helped Australian radio astronomers become leaders in their science, and brought pictures of the *Apollo 11* moon landing to an audience of 600 million people. The telescope has also played a vital role in detecting thousands of new galaxies at the edge of the known universe. Over half the known pulsars (rapidly spinning 'cores' of dead stars) have been discovered at Parkes.

Although the telescope is off limits, you can get close enough for a good look. Anyone with even a slight interest in astronomy will enjoy the renovated **visitors centre** (☎ 6861 1777; admission free; ☽ 8.30am-4.15pm), with hands-on displays and screens that show you what the astronomers see. Three-D films such as *Journey to Mars* screen regularly during the day (adult/child $6.50/5.00). The **Dish Café** (☽ 8.30am-4.15pm), in the shade of the telescope, makes good coffee, and does a delicious breakfast on weekends.

Festivals & Events

There's a Country Music Jamboree on the Labour Day long weekend in early October, when there's also an antique motorcycle rally. But perhaps the most unusual event is the annual **Parkes Elvis Revival Festival** (www.visitparkes.com.au/elvis.htm; held in conjunction with Elvis's birthday in early Jan), which has Elvis lookalike, soundalike, and even movealike competitions.

Sleeping & Eating

Parkes is well supplied with motels.

All Settlers Motor Inn (☎ 6862 2022; 20 Welcome St; s/d $75/90; ☒ ☒) This motel, across from Cooke Park, is quite plush.

Bushmans Motor Inn (☎ 6862 2199; Currajong Rd; r $95; ☒ ☒) This one gets a mention because

it actually supplies the weary traveller with somewhere to stable their horse – a lush paddock at the rear of the hotel.

Parkes Overnighter Caravans (☎ 6862 1707; 48 Bushman St; camp sites from $15, cabins from $40; ☒ ☒) West of the town centre, this camping ground is hidden behind a house on a quiet street.

The locals rave about the scones, but the cook refuses to give away her recipe; try them at **Cedar Café & Art Gallery** (☎ 6862 6212; Greenparkes Centre, cnr Forbes Rd & Medlyn St; mains $4-10; ☽ 9am-5pm).

Getting There & Away

Rex (☎ 13 17 13) has daily flights to Sydney (excluding Sunday) which cost about $120 standard one way.

Countrylink (☎ 13 22 32) buses connect to trains daily departing Orange and Lithgow for Sydney (combined ticket $66, 6½ hours). The *Indian Pacific* train stops here on the run between Sydney and Perth. The Broken Hill Outback Explorer train also stops en route.

FORBES

☎ 02 / pop 7100

Perched on the banks of the Lachlan River, Forbes is one of NSW's prettiest towns, retaining much of its 19th-century flavour thanks to its beautifully restored buildings. It is also famous for its connections with Ben Hall, a landowner who became Australia's first official bushranger, and who was betrayed and shot near Forbes. He's buried in the town's cemetery: people still miss him, if the notes on his grave are anything to go by.

The first Europeans to set foot on the future town site were members of explorer John Oxley's party in 1817. Oxley is said to have been so unimpressed with the clay soil, poor timber and swamps that he concluded, 'It is impossible to imagine a worse country'. How wrong that would have seemed to the men who profited from the gold rush in the early 1860s. Apparently over 8000kg of gold were found!

Orientation & Information

Forbes has two main roads: Dowling St (Newell Hwy) and, parallel, Rankin St. The cheerful **visitors centre** (☎ 6852 4155) in the old train station at the northern end of town also exhibits works by local artists.

Internet access is available at **Western Internet Services** (☎ 6851 1624; Lachlan St; per hr $5; ☺ Mon-Sat).

One of Australia's yarn-spinning champions, John Rennick, runs **Ben Hall Country Tours** (☎ 6852 2452; adult/child $25/12; ☺ 1-4pm Mon-Fri, 2-5pm during daylight saving) from the visitors centre.

Sights & Activities

Forbes' wide streets are lined with grand 19th-century gold rush–funded buildings including the **Town Hall** (1891) and **courthouse** (1880). At the tower atop the **Albion Hotel** on Lachlan St a watch was kept for Cobb & Co coaches.

The Albion also contains the interesting **Bushrangers Hall of Fame** (☎ 6851 1881; 135 Lachlan St; adult/child $5/3; ☺ 10am-6pm), which has guided tours of old underground tunnels used to transfer gold from banks into waiting coaches. On the corner of Court and Lachlan St is the **post office** (1879–81) that has an unusual three-storey clock tower.

Osborne Hall on Cross St was the dance hall of the Osborne Hotel and now houses the **Forbes Museum** (☎ 6852 1694; $2/1; ☺ 3-5pm Oct-May, 2-4pm Jun-Sep) of local history, with Ben Hall relics. One kilometre south of Forbes on the Newell Hwy is the **Lachlan Vintage Village** (☎ 6852 2655; ☺ 8am-5.30pm) on the site of the old goldfields. Henry Lawson's home has been moved to the village and you can pan for gold.

Just off the Newell Hwy about 4km south of Forbes, **Gum Swamp** is an enchanting wetland area that is home to many species of birds. There's a hide to watch them from. While sunset and sunrise are the best viewing times, it is an idyllic spot at any hour.

Sleeping & Eating

Albion Hotel (☎ 6851 1881, 135 Lachlan St; s/d $35/60) This impressive building has comfortable but basic rooms.

Ben Hall Motor Inn (☎ 6851 2345; 5-7 Cross St; r $70; ☒) Despite being a budget motel, this place retains a bit of charm.

Forbes River Meadows Caravan Park (☎ 6852 2694; camp sites $14-19, cabins $50-100 ☒ ☒) By the Lachlan River on the Newell Hwy southwest of town.

Eda-Bull (☎ 6852 1000; 137 Rankin St; mains $16-20; ☺ lunch Wed-Sun, dinner Wed-Sat) Forbes' finest restaurant makes a relaxed place to enjoy a

great selection of regional wine and produce, such as the district's lamb and beef – the source of much local pride.

Cobb & Co Restaurant (mains $14-22; ☺ lunch & dinner Mon-Sat) At the Albion Hotel, Cobb serves good food and has a nice balcony outlook onto Lachlan St.

Getting There & Away

CountryLink (☎ 13 22 32) buses connect to trains to Sydney. **McCafferty's/Greyhound** (☎ 13 14 99) runs buses to Brisbane ($125) and Melbourne ($110).

THE LACHLAN VALLEY

Surrounded by five major highways, the Lachlan Valley and its environs make a pleasing alternative route if you want to free yourself from the traffic and the road trains on the main roads. The scenic Lachlan Valley Way runs by the Lachlan River from Forbes to **Condobolin**, the main service centre, and there are several camping sites and fishing spots along the winding road.

The 40-hectare **Gum Bend Lake**, 3km west of Condobolin, is the area's water playground; however, it is sometimes closed in summer due to low water levels. About 8km north of 'Condo' is **Mt Tilga**, officially the geographical centre of NSW.

North of Condobolin, the farmland begins to blur into the outback. If you're heading north to the Barrier Hwy (and have a decent map) there are several routes (with stretches of well-maintained gravel road) from Condobolin that don't involve backtracking to the Newell Hwy.

COWRA

☎ 02 / pop 8700

Ever since August 1944, when 1000 Japanese prisoners broke out of a POW camp here (231 of them died, along with four Australians), Cowra has aligned itself with Japan and with the cause of furthering world peace. The break-out is immortalised in the film *Die Like the Carp!*

Orientation & Information

Cowra straggles up the side of a steep hill above Lachlan River. The main landmark's a set of traffic lights, on the corner of Kendal (Mid Western Hwy) and Brisbane Sts.

The **visitors centre** (☎ 6342 4333; www.cowra tourism.com.au; Olympic Park, Mid Western Hwy; ☺ 9am-

5pm) has a great introduction to the break-out, with a strange but fascinating hologram film on the subject. The **Japanese War Cemetery** is five kilometres north of town on Binni Creek Rd (Brisbane St). A nearby **memorial** marks the site of the break-out, and you can still see the camp foundations.

Sights & Activities

Built as a token of Cowra's connection with Japanese POWs (but with no overt mention of the war or the break-out), the **Japanese Garden** (☎ 6341 2233; Binni Creek Rd; adult/child $8.50/$5; ☒ 8.30am-5pm) and the attached cultural centre on Bellevue Hill are well worth visiting. The large garden, serene and beautifully maintained, was a gift from the Japanese government. The cultural centre is a peaceful place, with displays of modern Japanese art, some modern Japanese kitsch and some antiques. There's a collection of *ukiyo-e* paintings, depicting everyday events in the lives of ordinary people in pre-industrial Japan. A **sakura** (cherry-blossom festival) is held around the second weekend in October.

Nearby is the **Bellevue Hill Flora & Fauna Reserve**, a complete contrast to the formality of its neighbour.

The darkest place for star gazing in all of Australia is **Darby Falls Observatory** (☎ 6345 1900; Mt McDonald Rd; adult/child $8/4; ☒ 7-10pm, 8.30-11pm during daylight saving). From town, take Wyangala Dam Rd for 22km and turn onto Mt McDonald Rd, then follow the signs. Turn off your headlights as soon as you see the red fairy lights leading up to the observatory.

Kids will enjoy the **War, Rail & Rural Museum** (☎ Mid Western Hwy; adult/child $7.50/5; ☒ 9am-5pm) with its hands-on displays about the railway, local farming industry and the POW camp.

WINERIES

There are some excellent wineries in the area; the visitors centre has a guide to cellar doors around Cowra and Canowindra. **Ideal Tours** (☎ 6341 3350; www.australianacorner.com; 1 Kendal St) runs bus tours of the area. Right in town is the **Mill** (☎ 6341 4141; 6 Vaux St; ☒ 10am-6pm), Cowra's oldest building, and a well-regarded winery. Taste some of the region's famous chardonnay with a platter of local produce ($22 for two people).

Sleeping & Eating

Imperial Hotel (☎ 6341 2588; 16 Kendal St; s/d with breakfast $30-50/50-65) This is the best of Cowra's pubs. Rooms are comfortable, modern and motel-like.

There are several motels in Cowra; almost all increase their tariff on the weekends.

Vineyard Motel (☎ 6342 3641; Fagan@ix.net.au; Chardonnay Rd; s/d $90/100; ☒ ☒) Surrounded by fields of grapevines and overlooking the lush Lachlan Valley, the Vineyard is secluded and peaceful, a welcome change from the run-of-the-mill motel strip.

Country Gardens (☎ 6341 1100; 75 Grenfell Rd; s/d $90/140; ☒ ☒) The most upmarket motor inn in town, with bright, comfortable rooms and helpful staff.

Smokehouse Deli & Cafe (☎ 6341 1489; Mid Western Hwy; mains $9-15; ☒ 9.30am-6pm Wed-Mon) It may be in a massive container shed on the highway, but the Smokehouse has the monopoly on the best of local produce. Smoked

---

DETOUR: EUGOWRA & CANOWINDRA

To the west of Cowra the Lachlan River flows through picturesque, fertile farmland. The road to Forbes (turn off the Mid Western Hwy about 5km south of Cowra) runs along the Lachlan River and is a lovely drive. At Paynters Bridge, about 45km on from the turn-off, cross the Lachlan to visit **Eugowra**, a rambling village in the shadow of bush-clad hills. Eugowra was held up by Ben Hall in 1863, and there is a re-enactment every October. Follow the signs to **Canowindra**, via a road along the Lachlan River's northern side. Canowindra's main thoroughfare, Gaskill St, follows the crooked route of the old bullock track and every building is heritage listed. The **Age of Fishes Museum** (☎ 6344 1008; cnr Gaskill & Ferguson Sts; admission $7.70; ☒ 10am-4pm) is very proud of its display of unique fossil fishes found nearby. With the gentle winds and attractive countryside **ballooning** is popular; several outfits offer flights including **Balloon Aloft** (☎ 6344 1797; www.balloonaloft.com). Drive through fields of yellow canola and budding vineyards on your way back to Orange (60km).

trout salad ($13) is so fresh you know the fish was swimming around the huge water troughs next door not so long ago.

Neila (☎ 6341 2188; 5 Kendal St; mains $26; ✆ dinner Thu-Sat) A brief but innovative Mediterranean menu fused with bold Asian flavours is supported by proudly local produce at this small gem on Cowra's main drag. The food is outstanding and the atmosphere decidedly laid-back.

Getting There & Away

CountryLink (☎ 13 22 32) runs a coach/train combination to Brisbane ($129, 24 hours), Melbourne ($86, 7½ hours) and Sydney ($52, 5½ hours) and coaches to Canberra ($27, six hours) and Bathurst ($16.50, one hour 50 minutes).

AROUND COWRA

About 40km west of Cowra, Grenfell is a quiet country town with a curvy Main St, and some beautiful old buildings.

The town's main claim to fame is that Henry Lawson was born here in 1867; a memorial marking his birthplace is off the highway at the eastern edge of town. The annual Henry Lawson Arts Festival is held around the writer's birthday on 17 June. For something completely different, Grenfell hosts the National Guinea Pig Races during Easter and in June.

Nineteen kilometres southwest of Grenfell, **Weddin National Park** isn't large (8361 hectares), but it's a rugged place with lots of wildlife, Aboriginal sites and some good walking trails. **Holy Camp** in the northwest and **Seatons Camp** in the northeast are camping areas; both have road access and you can walk between them. The **NPWS office** (☎ 6851 4429; 83 Lachlan St; ✆ 8.30am-4.30pm Mon-Fri) in Forbes has more information.

YOUNG

☎ 02 / pop 6800

Young, Australia's 'cherry capital', is on the edge of the western slopes of the Great Dividing Range. East of here is rolling country; to the west the plains of the Riverina begin.

Nicole Jasprizza, who arrived during the gold rush, first planted cherries here in 1860. His orchard was an immediate success and expanded rapidly.

Today there are about 130 orchards producing a large proportion of Australia's crop. Prunes are also an important local industry, but 'prune capital' doesn't have quite the same ring.

The notorious White Australia policy of Australia's early years had its origins near Young – goldfield riots at Lambing Flat in 1861 led to the government restriction on Chinese immigration.

Information

The **visitors centre** (☎ 6382 3394; 2 Short St; ✆ 9am-5pm Mon-Fri, 9.30am-4pm Sat & Sun) is near the creek as you enter town from the south.

The cherry harvest is in November and December. In January other stone fruits are harvested and in February the prune harvest begins. The **Employment National office** (☎ 13 3400; 187 Boorowa St) can help you find fruit-picking work.

Sights & Activities

WINERIES

This area produced wine grapes from the 1880s until the 1930s, when the more profitable cherry orchards took over. In the 1970s the Barwang vineyard was established, and there are now about 15 small vineyards in the area, with a couple you can visit for wine tastings and sales. **Lindsay's Woodonga Hill** (☎ 6389 2972; ✆ daily) is northeast of Young on the Cowra road; **Demondrille Vineyards** (☎ 6384 4272; ✆ Fri-Sun) is south on the Prunevale road near Kingsvale.

OTHER ATTRACTIONS

The **Lambing Flat Folk Museum** (☎ 6382 2248; Campbell St; adult/child $4/1; ✆ 10am-4pm) displays artefacts from the goldfields including the remarkable 'Roll Up' banner carried by European miners prior to assaults on the local Chinese community in 1861. It still bears the large inscription, 'No Chinese'. Several years ago the Sydney Chinese community raised money for a monument recognising the contribution their brethren made at the time and the **Chinese Tribute Garden** (Pitstone Rd; admission free; ✆ daily) is a tranquil spot featuring a pagoda and dam. The dam remembers the Chinese miners who obtained water for their diggings using clever trough-like structures to transport the water up to 3km away.

The visitors centre staff can tell you about orchards open for inspection and where you can pick your own fruit; in fact they will even supply you with a bag! **JD's Jam Factory** (☎ 6382 4060; Grenfell Rd; admission free; ⌚ 8am-6pm) is worth a stop to have a look at how a small jam factory, which started life as a road-side stall and now supplies companies like SPC and Yoplait, operates. You can also sample or buy some of the produce; don't leave Young without having at least a mouthful of their glorious cherry pie.

There are some spectacular gardens in the area that you can wander through for a small fee; the **Price of Peace** (☎ 6382 2465; Willawong St) and **Jacaranda Hill** (☎ 6382 4657; Noonan Rd) are two.

Festivals & Events
The **Cherry Festival** is held on the last weekend in November and the first weekend in December – but if you want to see the trees in blossom, come in early October.

Sleeping & Eating
Australian Hotel (☎ 6382 5544; 222 Boorowa St; s/d $30/50 incl breakfast) The hotel has renovated its pub accommodation, making it an especially clean, convenient and comfortable place to stay.

Young Federation Motor Inn (☎ 6382 5644; www .youngfederation.com.au; 109 Main St; s/d $120; 🖳 🖳) The newest motel in Young attracts honeymooners and Club Keno–playing oldies alike. The suites are pretty luxurious and you can work off all that cherry pie with a few laps in the huge corner spa baths.

Young Tourist Park (☎ 6382 2190; Zouch St; camp sites $15-17, cabins $40-60; 🖳) A new camp kitchen and drive-through van bathrooms make this a comfortable option.

Cherrywood (☎ 6382 7255; 143 Boorowa St; mains $8-14; ⌚ lunch & dinner) This is the place for some decent Italian fare. The joint is really jumping on Friday nights when it turns into a pizzeria.

Café Dujour (☎ 6382 1413; cnr Lovell & Zouch Sts; mains $12-20; ⌚ lunch & dinner Tue-Sat) An eatery that is very popular with the local food critics.

Zouch (☎ 6382 2775; 26 Zouch St; mains $16-26; ⌚ lunch Wed-Mon, dinner Thu-Sat) The old Masonic hall has been put to good use in housing this charming restaurant serving up lashings of exotic country cooking. The plum, pear and apricot crumble topped with shortbread and macadamia nuts is a must-have.

Getting There & Away
Buses stop at the old train station on Lovell St. **Countrylink** (☎ 13 22 32) buses run to Cootamundra and Bathurst.

Northwest

CONTENTS

NORTHWEST

Most people pass through this wedge of NSW on the Newell Hwy, barely pausing on their way to or from Queensland. The country is flat and dry but largely fertile, especially in the broad valley of the Namoi River. Cattle and cotton are the main industries.

Many of the towns in the area are small, relaxed places, still conscious of the hard work that went into their establishment, and aware that their status as outposts of settlement gives them an importance greater than their size. It's only since WWII that good roads have linked many towns, and even today they can be isolated by floods.

The large slice of country between the Castlereagh and Mitchell Hwys is a flat artesian basin. In spring this is a beautiful area, with the vast, steamy plains bursting into life. Much of the area is black-soil country, with the dry outback beginning as you approach the Mitchell Hwy.

The Northwest doesn't see many tourists, excepting those visiting Warrumbungle National Park and Lightning Ridge. The latter is getting an increasing stream of visitors who are drawn to its opal mining culture, and is possibly the best reason to venture deep into the region. Otherwise you can drive for quite a way without seeing another car, on roads that follow incongruously sinuous routes across the flat landscape.

HIGHLIGHTS

- Bushwalking in the **Warrumbungle Range** (p237) in spring
- Taking in the view from the summit of **Mt Kaputa**r (p239)
- Soaking in the hot spa baths at **Moree** (p239) after a long day's drive
- Meeting some of the characters who mine for opals at **Lightning Ridge** (p240)
- Bird-watching in the **Macquarie Marshes** (p240)
- Looking for Pluto at the **Skywatch Observatory** (p236) near Coonabarabran
- Enjoying the wide-open spaces on the long country drives
- Pondering the depths of the cosmos at **Australia Telescope** (p238)

GILGANDRA

☎ 02 / pop 2720

Gilgandra is a sizable town on the Castlereagh River, at the junction of the Newell, Castlereagh and Oxley Hwys. During WWI, Gilgandra was the starting point for the Coo-ee March, when 26 volunteers set off for Sydney to enlist. Along the way their numbers grew to 351, of whom 263 were duly shipped to the trenches.

Information

The **visitors centre** (☎ 6847 2045; www.gilgandra.nsw .gov.au; Newell Hwy; 🕑 9am-5pm) is in the Coo-ee March Memorial Park, south of the town centre.

Sights

Attached to the visitors centre is a small **museum** (admission $3) recalling the Coo-ee March. Just 200m south is the new **Rural Museum** (adult/child $5/3; 🕑 10am-4pm Sat & Sun), marked by a large windmill and featuring notable hoes and ploughs. The privately run **Gilgandra Observatory** (☎ 6847 2646; www.gilobs.com.au; Willie St; adult/child $9/6; 🕑 7-10pm Mon-Sat) has a 31cm telescope. You can look for the rings of Saturn and comets or, possibly, spot a Martian on their way to see the notable hoes.

Sleeping

Gilgandra has numerous motels north and south of the centre.

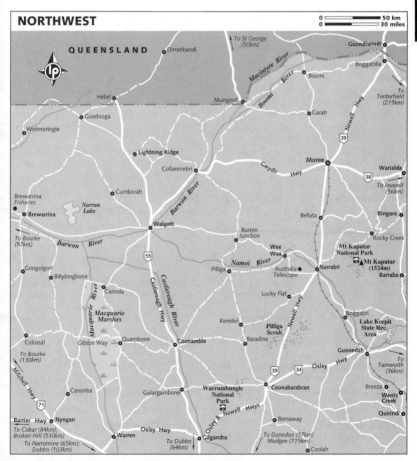

Cooee Motel (☎ 6847 2981, 800 266 333; cooeegil@ tpg.com.au; Hargraves Lane, off Newell Hwy; s/d $65/69; ⊠) A simple 12-unit motel with lovely grounds. Dinners are served in the rooms.

Gilgandra Rotary Caravan Park (☎ 6847 2423; Newell Hwy; tent/riverfront site $4/16-20; ⊠) By the river, 300m north of the bridge, this pleasant park is close to town and has a playground to go with the pool.

Getting There & Away

Countrylink (13 22 32) buses run north to Lightning Ridge ($44, once daily, four hours) and south to Dubbo ($10, once daily, one hour).

COONABARABRAN

☎ 02 / pop 2750

Coonabarabran (*coo*-na-*bar*-ra-*brn*) is a country town that has retained its shady main street (John St), despite the street being both the Newell and Oxley Hwys.

As well as serving as a base for visits to the Warrumbungle National Park, Coonabarabran is a handy stop roughly halfway between Brisbane and Melbourne. It's about 450km from Sydney, an easy day's drive.

The town's name comes from Cooleburbarun, a squatting lease that was taken up in 1839, 20 years after John Oxley's party made the first European foray into the homelands of the Kamilario people.

Information

The **visitors centre** (☎ 6842 1441; www.coonabarabran .com; Newell Hwy/John St; ☽ 9am-5pm), south of the town centre, has details on the area and the Warrumbungle National Park. Its best feature (beyond the clean toilets) is the exhibition of a nearly complete skeleton of a diprotodon, the largest known marsupial. About the size of a small elephant, the creature lived at least 20,000 years ago and stood 2m tall. Look for the mysterious hole in one of its bones.

The **National Parks & Wildlife Service office** (NPWS; ☎ 6842 1311; 30 Timor St; ☽ 9am-4pm Mon-Fri) has area park information, including details on Warrumbungle National Park.

For outdoor supplies and licences, try **Top Shop** (☎ 6842 2066; Camp St; ☽ 9am-5pm).

There's Internet access at **CTC** (☎ 6842 2920; 71 John St; per hr $2; ☽ 9am-5pm Mon-Fri).

Sights & Activities

The area's main attraction is the nearby national park. These are some tour options:

Dave's Outback Wildlife Adventures (☎ 6842 4940; 96 Cassilis St; tours for up to 6 people $120-180) Everything from koalas to birds.

Warrumbungle Light (☎ 6843 4446) Variety of tours focusing on local Aboriginal culture and history.

The **Skywatch Observatory** (☎ 6842 3303; Timor Rd; adult/child $14/9; ☽ exhibits 2-5pm), 2km west of the town centre, has a planetarium and astronomy exhibition but the main event is the night-time telescope viewing. Viewing times vary by season. Nongalactic-minded day visitors can try the mini-golf at the observatory.

Sleeping

There are more than a dozen motels in town.

Coachman's Rest Motor Lodge (☎ 6842 2111; www.bestwestern.com.au/coachmansrest; Newell Hwy; s/d $90/115; ⊠) Small and quiet, the Coachman's has a good pool area as well as a restaurant. Rooms are well-equipped.

Imperial Hotel (☎ 6842 1023; imphotel@tpg.com.au; John St; r $22-45) Located across from the clock tower, this is a well-maintained, family-run pub. The food's basic but good and it's the best place in town for a drink after a long day.

John Oxley Caravan Park (☎ 6842 1635; Newell Hwy; camp sites $12-16, cabins from $45) This pleasant spot is 1km north of the centre.

Eating

Golden Sea Dragon (☎ 6842 2388; 8 John St; mains $9-13; ☽ lunch & dinner; ⊠) The lavish interior at this Chinese restaurant is a sure sign it is a cut above the usual. Among the noteworthy dishes are sizzling steak and duck in plum sauce.

Woop Woop Café (☎ 6842 4755; 38A John St; mains $6-12; ☽ breakfast & lunch Tue-Sun, dinner Fri & Sat) Organic salads are among the creative highlights at this café, which boasts good coffee and an art gallery.

Jolly Cauli Coffee Shop (☎ 6842 2021; 30 John St; mains $4-8; ☽ breakfast & lunch Mon-Fri, breakfast Sat; ⊠ ▯) This bustling place has tables inside, outside on the footpath and in an adjoining patio. The juices and sandwiches are fresh and good.

Getting There & Away

The major bus lines stop here on their Newell Hwy services. **Countrylink** (☎ 13 22

32) buses meet some trains at Lithgow and run to Coonabarabran ($60, five hours, one daily) via Mudgee.

WARRUMBUNGLE NATIONAL PARK

The Warrumbungle Range makes an abrupt appearance in the midst of the region's gentle slopes. It was formed by volcanic activity an estimated 13 million years ago, and has been eroded into a strikingly rugged mountain range. In 1818 explorer John Oxley described the Warrumbungle Range as '...lofty hills arising from the midst of lesser elevations, their summits crowned with perpendicular rocks, in every variety of shape and form that the wildest imagination could paint...'.

The national park (23,198 hectares), a highlight of the area, is popular with sightseers, bushwalkers and rock climbers. There are many walking trails, both short and long. Bizarre geological formations, including the Breadknife, can be seen from the series of peaks known as the **Grand High Tops**.

There's a great range of flora and fauna, with spectacular displays of wild flowers in the spring. (Wild flowers aren't the only plants to thrive in the area – the national park grew by 620 hectares in 1993, when land confiscated from a marijuana grower was added to it.)

Summers can be hot but it usually cools down at night, and while winter days are often sunny, there can be heavy night frosts. The best time to visit is spring or autumn.

Information

The daily user fee is $6 per car.

Thirty-seven kilometres west of Coonabarabran, the **Warrumbungle National Park visitors centre** (☎ 6825 4364; ☺ 9am-4pm) has lots of highly useful activity information, as well as details of the park's flora, fauna and facilities. A shop sells ice and camping supplies. You can also get park information from Coonabarabran's **NPWS office** (☎ 6842 1311).

For more information on the park, *Warrumbungle National Park* by Peter Fox is an excellent guide published by the NPWS. It has detailed walking information. Lonely Planet's *Walking in Australia* details the Grand High Tops walk.

Sleeping

There are some interesting sleeping options outside of the park.

Tibuc Cabins (☎ 6842 1740; yurruunda@tpg.com.au) Tiboc is an organic farm on the boundary of the park, with accommodation in two mud-brick buildings and an old cabin. The facilities range from no electricity to solar or mains power. Each building costs $72 per night (less for each additional night) and sleeps up to six people. Catering facilities are provided, but you need to bring your own linen and bedding, or rent onsite. The turn-off to the farm is 17km from Coonabarabran on the road to the park.

Gumin-Gumin (☎ 6825 4368; gumin@tpg.com.au; d/f $77/88) This beautiful old 1870s homestead rambles across a lovely setting 9km from the west entrance to the park.

The park has three camping grounds; book through the visitors centre.

Camp Blackman (powered/unpowered sites $7.50/5) 102 sites.

Camp Wambelong (camp sites $5) 30 sites.

Walaay (camp sites $5) Five sites.

Camping in the back country is possible in many areas and is free.

Getting There & Away

The park entrance is 33km west of Coonabarabran, and most people come via that town, but you can also get here on smaller roads from Gulargambone or Coonamble, both on the Castlereagh Hwy to the west of the park.

There are also tour options from Coonabarabran (opposite).

THE PILLIGA SCRUB

This 400,000-hectare forest and its large koala population is between Coonabarabran and Narrabri – it has an interesting history that you can read about in Eric Rolls' outstanding book *A Million Wild Acres* (1981). Rolls says that when the early settlers cleared the land, they wiped out the small marsupials that would have eaten many of the tree seedlings. As a result, the new forest exploded into life after the farms failed because of unsuitable soils. A good amount, but not all, of the scrub is designated the Pilliga Nature Reserve.

Baradine, northwest of Coonabarabran, is the main town in these parts, and roads into the Pilliga Scrub run east from here and from **Kenebri**, 20km farther north. Baradine's **Forestry Office** (☎ 6843 1607; ☺ 9am-4pm) has maps of drives through the Scrub.

GUNNEDAH
☎ 02 / pop 7870

Gunnedah is a large country town on the Oxley Hwy at the edge of the Namoi Valley's plains. Its claim to fame – and good luck to you if you can ignore it – is that it's the self-proclaimed Koala Capital of the World.

Information
The **visitors centre** (☎ 6740 2230; www.infogunnedah .com.au; Anzac Park off South St; ☻ 9am-5pm Mon-Fri, 10am-3pm Sat & Sun) is just south of the railway lines from the town centre.

Sights
The town's trademark koalas can be seen in the trees across from the visitors centre. Another good option is along the **Bindeah Walking Track**, which leads from the visitors centre to **Porcupine Lookout**.

Just uphill from the visitors centre is the **Water Tower Museum** (adult/child $3/1; ☻ 2-5pm Mon & Sat), with the usual array of old local items. Opposite is the **Dorothea Mackellar memorial**. The poet's work 'My Country' contains arguably the most famous stanza in Australian poetry:

I love a sunburnt country,
A land of sweeping plains,
Of ragged mountain ranges,
Of droughts and flooding rains.

The **Rural Museum** (☎ 6742 4690; Oxley Hwy; adult/child $5/2; ☻ 9am-3pm), 1km west of the visitors centre, is the place for superlatives, with 'the largest gun display in northern NSW' as well as 'the biggest vintage tractor collection in Australia'.

Across from the police station, is the **grave-site of Cumbo Gunnerah** (cnr Abbott & Little Conadilly Sts), an 18th-century Aboriginal leader known as Red Kangaroo. His burial place is marked by a bronze cast of the carved tree that once stood over the site. It's rare to have any physical reminder of individual Aborigines who lived before European contact. The events of Cumbo Gunnerah's life are related in *The Red Chief* by Ion Idriess, available at the visitors centre.

Sleeping & Eating
There are numerous motels to choose from.
Alyn Motel (☎ 6742 5028; alynmotel@telstra.easymail .com; 351 Conadilly St; s/d $68/78; ☒ ☐) This tidy

and modern place has 13 rooms, all of which have access to the on-site spa. The pool is a good place to relax at the end of a long day's koala-watching.

Regal Hotel (☎ 6742 2355; 298 Conadilly St; s/d $40/45; ☒) A nicely renovated pub with decent rooms; be sure to get one with aircon. There's a beer garden, and a bistro and restaurant (mains $5-15; ☻ lunch & dinner Mon-Sat). The pub has live entertainment on weekends.

Getting There & Away
Trains stop in Gunnedah on the way from Sydney to Moree.

NARRABRI
☎ 02 / pop 6250

As in so many other areas of the northwest, surveyor-general Major Thomas Mitchell made the first European foray and was quickly followed by others who took up land as squatters. Mitchell's visit was perhaps inevitable, but it was sparked by the capture of George Clark, a runaway convict who had lived with Aborigines for six years. The unfortunate Clark was sent to Norfolk Island, but before leaving he told of rich lands and a big river flowing to an inland sea.

Split by the Namoi River and the Narrabri Creek, this old town is today a bustling stop on the busy Newell Hwy.

Information
NPWS Office (☎ 6799 1740; 1/100 Maitland St; ☻ 8.30am-4.30pm) Good source of information on Mt Kaputar National Park.
Visitors centre (☎ 6799 6760; www.visitnarrabri.com.au; Newell Hwy; ☻ 9am-5pm Mon-Fri, to 1pm Sat & Sun) Adjoins the Australian Cotton Centre, and has lists of local farmstays.

Sights & Activities
In the centre of town. the **Australian Cotton Centre** (☎ 6792 6443; Newell Hwy; adult/child $7/5.50; ☻ 9am-5pm) is a large, new exhibition dedicated to the region's big cash crop. Nine interactive exhibits take you from cotton seed to finished T-shirt, and impart such compelling facts as that one standard 225kg bale of cotton can be made into 3085 nappies.

Australia Telescope, 20km west of Narrabri, comprises an array of radio telescopes, including five that move on 3km of rail tracks. It began operating in 1990 and helps keep Australia at the forefront of radio astronomy, which is used to map the universe far beyond the capabilities of optical telescopes. The **visitors centre** (☎ 6790 4070; admission free; ☺ 8am-4pm), near the car park, has displays and a shop.

There's good fossicking, especially for agates and petrified wood, near the township of **Bellata**, 40km north of Narrabri on the Newell Hwy.

Sleeping & Eating

Motels line Newell Hwy. There are bakeries and pubs in the centre on Maitland St.

Adelong Motel (☎ 6792 1488, 800 421 488; adelong motel@northnet.com.au; 174 Maitland St; s/d $85/92; ☒ ☒) This tidy place has lovely grounds and is close to everything. There's a licensed restaurant and room service. An extra $10 gets you a deluxe room with amenities like a fridge.

There are several caravan parks in town. **Narrabri Council Caravan Park** (☎ 6792 1294; Tibbereena St; sites $12-17, cabins $35-46) is a block back from the highway and has a camping area by the river.

Getting There & Away

QantasLink (☎ 13 13 13) flies to/from Sydney daily.

The major bus lines stop here on their Newell Hwy services. **Countrylink** (☎ 13 22 32) runs to Wee Waa and other small towns.

The train running between Sydney and Moree ($84, 7½ hours, daily) stops here.

MT KAPUTAR NATIONAL PARK

A rugged park on the westernmost spur of the Nandewar Range, Mt Kaputar National Park (36,817 hectares) is popular for **bushwalking**, **rock climbing** and, between August and October, **wild flowers**. Mt Kaputar rises to 1524m and snow has been known to fall on its peak. A road (unsuitable for caravans) runs close to the summit. From the **Doug-Sky Lookout** near the summit you can see 10 per cent of NSW. There are numerous striking geological features formed by volcanic activity millions of years ago.

There are two established **camp sites** (camp sites per adult/child $3/2) with good facilities: Dawsons Springs and Bark Hut, both accessible from the road up the mountain. Facilities include flush toilets, showers and picnic tables. There are also two cabins ($55) at Dawsons Springs – you have to book through the **NPWS office** (☎ 6799 1740) in Narrabri, and there's a minimum stay of two nights. The road to Mt Kaputar runs northeast from Narrabri.

Sawn Rocks, at the northern end of the park, is a spectacular 40m cliff formed of octagonal columns of basalt. The site is signposted off the Bingara road about 40km northeast of Narrabri. There's a 900m walking trail that starts at the car park (suitable for wheelchairs).

MOREE

☎ 02 / pop 9270

Moree was first settled in the 1840s and is the largest town on the northwest plains. It's known for its mineral springs. The extensive, landscaped gardens of Moree's residential districts are examples of the wealth derived from the surrounding lush farmlands. In addition to cotton, the region is known for growing pecans, olives and other food crops.

Information

The **Moree visitors centre** (☎ 6757 3350; Newell & Gwydir Hwys; ☺ 9am-5.30pm Mon-Fri, to 1pm Sat & Sun) has information on historic buildings and tours of local farms.

Sights

Moree's **Spa Baths** (☎ 6757 3450; Anne St; adult/child $5/3; ☺ 7am-8.30pm Mon-Fri, to 7pm Sat & Sun) are a good way to get the cricks out of your back after a long day in a bus or car. The baths are filled with hot (41°C) artesian water, which pours out of a bore at the rate of 13 million litres a day. Facilities include two artesian pools and a 27°C Olympic-sized pool.

The **Moree Plains Gallery** (☎ 6757 3320; Heber St; admission by donation; ☺ 10am-5pm Mon-Fri, to 2pm Sat) is in an impressive old building, formerly a bank (1910), and specialises in Aboriginal art.

There are several other interesting buildings near the art gallery. These include the **Lands Department office** (Frome St) and the nearby **courthouse**.

Sleeping & Eating

Scores of motels line Newell Hwy south of the centre. However the street is busy and less than scenic.

NORTHWEST

Sundowner Moree Motel (☎ 6752 2466, 800 654 576; moree@sundownermotorinns.com.au; 2 Webb Ave; r $65-150; 🅿 🖳) Set on lush grounds on Broadway Creek, this is the best place to stay in town. An outdoor pool is next to a large indoor spa pool. Rooms range from fairly basic to quite nice, with fridges as well as patios on the creek. There's a good restaurant as well.

Dover Motel (☎ 6752 2880; 20 Dover St; r $58-70; 🖳) A small and clean place, the Dover is on a quiet street one block off of the Newell Hwy strip. The spa baths are 100m east.

Mehi River Van Park (☎ 6752 7188; site $15-19; 🖳) On the river at the eastern end of Alice St, this good facility has a range of amenities.

Vision Café (☎ 6752 2020; 63 Balo St; mains $4-8; 🕒 breakfast, lunch & dinner; 🖳) Just north of the centre off the Newell Hwy, this stylish café has excellent baked goods, sandwiches, fresh juices and more.

Getting There & Away

QantasLink (☎ 13 13 13) flies to/from Sydney daily.

The major bus lines stop here on their Newell Hwy services. Most buses leave from the Shell roadhouse on the corner of Gwydir & Balo Sts.

Moree is the terminus of the passenger rail line from Sydney; trains run once daily ($90, nine hours).

WALGETT & AROUND

The small town of Walgett is near the junction of the Namoi and Barwon (a tributary of the Darling) Rivers. Walgett and the Barwon River feature in Banjo Paterson's poem 'Been There Before'. Other than this, there isn't a lot of interest in this quiet little town.

As well as the opal fields around Lightning Ridge, there are the smaller **Grawin**, **Glengarry** and **Sheepyard** opal fields west of Cumborah, a hamlet 47km northwest of Walgett on the secondary Walgett–Goodooga road.

Collarenebri is 75km northeast of Walgett on the Moree road. Its name is an Aboriginal word meaning 'place of many flowers', and in spring that is very appropriate. The weir near town is supposed to be one of the best fishing holes in the state.

Some 134km west of Walgett on the partially paved Kamilardi Hwy, **Brewarrina** (known locally as Bree) is a pleasant little town that's bright with coral-tree blossom from July to September.

One of the most important Aboriginal sites in the country is the **Brewarrina Fisheries** *(Ngunnhu)*, a series of low-walled rock traps on the Darling River where, perhaps for thousands of years, the Ngemba people caught fish to feed the huge intertribal gatherings that they hosted. Adjacent to the fisheries is the excellent **Brewarrina Aboriginal Cultural Museum** (☎ 6839 2421; adult/child $6/3; 🕒 8.30am-4.30pm Mon-Fri).

LIGHTNING RIDGE

☎ 02 / pop 1830

Lightning Ridge is a scruffy little town that was once entirely dependent on opal mining. Now tourism has followed and the town is showing signs of prosperity while enjoying its role as a place worth a special trip in the Northwest.

DETOUR: MACQUARIE MARSHES

Covering some 200,000 hectares, 90% of the **Macquarie Marshes** are privately owned. Birdlife on the marshes is varied and prolific, with native and migratory species breeding here. In the 1930s one casual observer reckoned that 3000 birds flew overhead in an hour. The wetlands have suffered from the damming of rivers and are receding, but while the skies are no longer dark with birds there are still plenty to be seen. The best time to visit is during the breeding season, generally in spring but varying according to the water level. Key parts of the area are preserved in the **Macquarie Marshes Nature Reserve** (☎ 6842 1311).

The main area of the nature reserve is on the west side, about 100km north of Warren (a small town notable mostly as a gateway to the Marshes), and off the sealed road from Warren to Carinda. From here the unsealed Gibson Way runs east to Quambone and it's along here that you're most likely to see birds. A sealed road runs from Quambone back to Warren, so you can make a round trip. **Tiger Bay Wildlife Park**, off the Oxley Hwy 1km northeast of Warren, has been created to provide birds and other wildlife with a refuge. The Gibson Way floods in a good season, but usually doesn't close just because of rain. Other unsealed roads in this area should be treated with caution as this is black-soil country and you can easily get bogged.

Although the entire town is geared towards relieving you of some cash, Lightning Ridge is no slick tourist trap. It has a decidedly eccentric feel to it and there are some interesting characters to meet.

Opal mining is still the domain of the battler, the bloke or sheila whose hard work and tenacity pays off – sometimes. For those who don't make it, scraping a living among rusting car bodies and extremely basic huts is not considered socially demeaning. Towns like Lightning Ridge (and there aren't many) are the last refuge of the 'bushie', usually down on their luck but infinitely resourceful and wary of authority. These true-blue types sell their finds to visiting opal buyers who set up shop in motel rooms, and the meeting of these two very different worlds is an odd contrast. Some buyers come all the way from Hong Kong to buy black opals, the speciality of the area.

Most claims are good for one year and are 50 sq metres. No one can hold more than two claims, although given the tough, troglodyte existence, it's hard to imagine anyone being able to.

Orientation & Information

Bill O'Brien's Way, the road in from the highway, becomes Morilla St, which is the main street. The corner of Morilla and Opal Sts is pretty much the centre of town.

Lightning Ridge visitors centre (☎ 6829 1670; www.lightningridge.net.au; Morilla St; ☼ 9am-5pm) sells local art.

Sights & Activities

On the north and west sides, the town is surrounded by intensively mined opal fields. Be careful walking around the diggings, as they're riddled with deep, unmarked holes; young children are especially at risk. Dropping anything down a hole won't make you popular if someone is working at the bottom.

Some of the local community have shown their wit by organising four **car-door tours** which explore different areas of interest around town. Each of the tours is marked by coloured car doors (green, blue, yellow and red), easily followed using the excellent map from the visitors centre.

The **Walk-In Mine** (☎ 6829 0473; adult/child $7/3; ☼ 9am-5pm), on the blue tour northeast

of town off Gem St, lets you explore an old opal site. It's amazing to think of the toil and sweat that went into creating the tunnels. Nearby, **Bevan's Black Opal & Cactus Nursery** (☎ 6829 0429; adult/child $4/2; ☼ daylight hr) has many species of cactus including some very old plants.

The **Big Opal** (☎ 6829 0247; adult/child $12/4; ☼ tour 10am), on the yellow tour southwest of town off Bill O'Brien's Way, is the deepest mine open for tours, with visitors navigating a 113-step spiral staircase. At busy times there is also a 2pm tour.

The **Bottle House** (☎ 6829 0618; Opal St; adult/child $5/1; ☼ 9am-5pm) is built from bottles and contains mining memorabilia as well as souvenirs and opals.

If you need to relax (but not cool off!), try the 52°C **hot artesian baths** (Pandora St; admission free; ☼ 24hr) at the northern edge of town.

As well as miners and jewellers, Lightning Ridge is home to many artists and craftspeople. John Murray's engaging paintings and limited-edition prints of outback life, along with B&W photos, are displayed at his **gallery** (☎ 6829 1130; Opal St; ☼ 9am-5pm Mon-Fri, to 1pm Sat & Sun).

The **Opal Cave** (☎ 6829 0333; Morilla St; ☼ 9am-6pm) is where you can view opals and learn about their value. The mural outside is a good representation of the hard-scrabble lives of the miners.

Tours

Black Opal Tours (☎ 6829 0368; adult/child tour $35/15; ☼ tours 9.30am, at busy times 1.30pm) runs 2½-hour tours of the town and surrounding opal fields and mines.

Festivals & Events

The **Great Goat Race** is held on Easter Saturday along with horse races. The **Opal & Gem Festival** is held at the end of July. See www.lightningridge.net.au for details.

Sleeping & Eating

Lightning Ridge Hotel Motel (☎ 6829 0304, ridgehotel@hotmail.com; Onyx St; s/d $65/85; 🔀 🔊) Set on nicely landscaped grounds, this sprawling motel has camp sites, as well as a fun pub with a large shaded patio. Locals consider the motel's **Ridge Rock Café** (mains $8-16; ☼ breakfast, lunch & dinner; 🔀) to have the best food in town. The steaks and fish are popular.

Bluey Motel (☎ 6829 0380; 32 Morilla St; s/d $39/49; 🕸 🖳) This simple place is one of several in the centre of town. Rooms have TVs and bathrooms, and the motel has a barbecue area. The owner also operates a small bookstore on-site; there's a good selection of books on opals and the folks who mine them.

Wong's Chinese (☎ 6829 2330; 12 Opal St; mains $7-12; 🕒 lunch Mon-Fri, dinner daily; 🕸) Decent food.

Two supermarkets on Opal St sell the best selection of foods in the Northwest. This is the place to stock up before heading further afield.

Getting There & Away
Countrylink (☎ 13 22 32) runs daily on the Castlereagh Hwy north to St George in Queensland and south to Dubbo ($60).

Far West

A startlingly empty land of vast sunburnt plains, crimson sunsets and empty horizons, far west NSW is rough and rugged. But this expanse of dry country is one of the most interesting areas in the state, and much more diverse than it first appears. It produces much of NSW's wealth, particularly from the mines of Broken Hill. The far west is home to some of the state's most interesting national parks; a wondrous combination of stunning natural environments and vastly significant Aboriginal heritage.

The outback is sparsely populated but the people you meet are often much larger than life – they have room to grow, sometimes in pretty quirky ways.

From November to February the heat is intense. By 10am the Celsius landmark, 40°C, is passed. That leaves another 10 hours of daylight for the current record, 51.7°C, to be broken.

You'll see a lot more of the outback if you venture off the sealed roads. Seek local advice first; many dirt roads are traversable for 2WDs, but they can be very corrugated, and sandy or dusty in patches. Much of the country is flat and featureless into the distance, but there are plenty of birds, mobs of emus, and kangaroos along the roadside to watch – and to watch out for!

FAR WEST

HIGHLIGHTS

- Enjoying a sunset walk around the sandstone sculpture symposium at **Broken Hill** (p256)
- Being taken on a guided bush walk in **Mutawintji National Park** (p253) by the traditional owners
- Getting into the action at the annual **Louth Races** (p248)
- Camping under the stars, then waking up to a full outback sunrise on top of **Mt Oxley** (p247)
- Staying underground at **White Cliffs** (p252)
- After a long day of driving, enjoying a cold beer and a yarn at the **Tilpa Hotel** (p248)
- Slowing down to allow an emu and his chicks to cross the **Silver City Hwy** (p249)
- Uncovering the extraordinary archaeological record at **Mungo National Park** (p259)

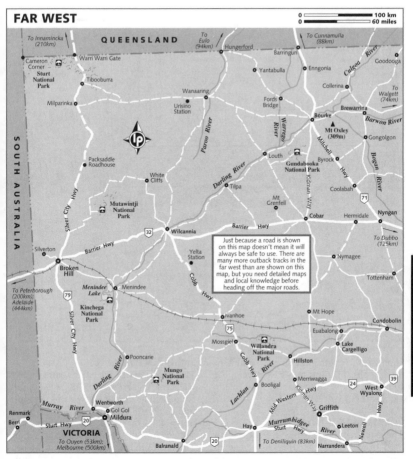

FAR WEST

Just because a road is shown on this map doesn't mean it will always be safe to use. There are many more outback tracks in the far west than are shown on this map, but you need detailed maps and local knowledge before heading off the major roads.

BOURKE

☎ 02 / pop 2560

Immortalised in the expression 'Back of Bourke' (describing anything remote), this easy-going town on the Darling River sits on the edge of the outback. Beyond Bourke, settlements of any sort are few and the country is flat and featureless. Bourke is attractive and the surrounding country can be beautiful; the space is exhilarating, and its very remoteness attracts a steady stream of visitors.

History

The Ngemba people lived in a large area centred on the Brewarrina Fisheries, a series of stone traps on the Darling River, including Bourke and Louth.

The first Europeans to see this area were in Charles Sturt's party of 1828. Sturt was unenthusiastic about the country but by 1860 there were enough grazier settlers for a paddle-wheeler to risk the difficult journey up to Bourke. By the 1880s, many of the Darling River's 200 paddle-steamers were calling at Bourke; it was possible for wool leaving here to be in London in just six weeks.

Bourke is still a major wool-producing area, but droughts and low prices have forced farmers to look to products such as cotton and rock melons. There's even a vineyard.

Bourke has hosted Australian legends. Poet and writer Henry Lawson lived at the Carriers Arms Hotel in 1892 while painting the Great Western Hotel. Fred

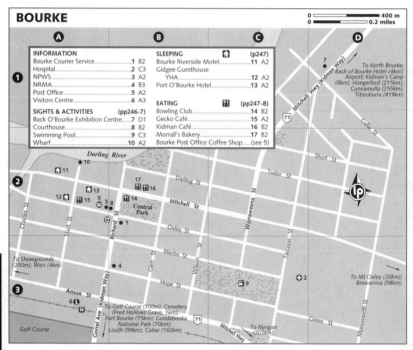

BOURKE

0 —————— 400 m
0 —————— 0.2 miles

INFORMATION	
Bourke Courier Service................**1** B2	
Hospital..**2** C3	
NPWS...**3** A2	
NRMA...**4** B3	
Post Office.....................................**5** A2	
Visitors Centre...............................**6** A3	

SIGHTS & ACTIVITIES	(pp246-7)
Back O'Bourke Exhibition Centre.....**7** D1	
Courthouse....................................**8** B2	
Swimming Pool...............................**9** C3	
Wharf...**10** A2	

SLEEPING 🏠	(p247)
Bourke Riverside Motel..................**11** A2	
Gidgee Guesthouse	
YHA...**12** A2	
Port O'Bourke Hotel......................**13** A2	

EATING 🍴	(pp247-8)
Bowling Club..................................**14** B2	
Gecko Café....................................**15** A2	
Kidman Café...................................**16** B2	
Morrall's Bakery.............................**17** B2	
Bourke Post Office Coffee Shop.....(see 5)	

Darling River

To North Bourke;
Back of Bourke Hotel (4km);
Airport; Kidman's Camp
(8km); Hungerford (215km);
Cunnamulla (255km);
Tibooburra (419km)

To Showgrounds
(200m); Weir (4km)

To Golf Course (100m); Cemetery
(Fred Hollows Grave, 1km);
Fort Bourke (15km); Gundabooka
National Park (70km);
Louth (99km); Cobar (160km)

To Nyngan
(203km)

To Mt Oxley (30km);
Brewarrina (98km)

Golf Course

Hollows, the ophthalmic surgeon and hero for his philanthropic work in developing countries, chose to be buried here in the 'land without fences'.

Orientation & Information

The Mitchell Hwy winds through town then heads out across the old bridge to North Bourke (just a pub) 6km away. The shopping centre is in Oxley St between Sturt St and Richard St (the highway).

The **visitors centre** (☎ 6872 1222/2800; tourinfo@ lisp.com.au; Anson St; ☼ 9am-5pm daily Easter-Oct, Mon-Fri at other times) has an excellent leaflet called *Bourke Mud Map Tours*, detailing a town walk and drives to places in the district.

Limited seasonal work is available in the Bourke area: picking grapes (December to January), rock melons (November or December), citrus fruits (May to October) and cotton chipping (weeding; November or December). Nearly all these activities take place in summer and it can be *hot*! For work opportunities contact **Bourke Joblink** (☎ 6870 1041) or **Orana Education Centre** (OEC; ☎ 6872 1949).

Sights & Activities

The **Back O'Bourke Exhibition Centre** (☎ 6872 1321; Kidman Way; adult/child $15/7.50) was not fully completed at the time of writing (completion could still be another two years away). But judging by stage one, it will provide a great overview of this amazing region. The centre follows the legends of the back country from both indigenous and settler perspectives by using oral histories and innovative displays. Certainly worth a visit now, the final form of the exhibition promises a unique experience.

There are many reminders of the time when the big paddle-wheelers were Bourke's lifeline. The impressive three-tiered **wharf** at the northern end of Sturt St is a faithful reconstruction of the original built in 1897 and, on the river, the **PV Jandra** (☎ 6872 1321; Kidman's Camp; adult/child $13/10) is a replica of an 1895 paddle-wheeler. A one-hour cruise on the *Jandra* departs at 9am, 11am and 3pm Monday to Saturday (2.30pm on Sunday).

Many old buildings in town are reminders of Bourke's important past. The **courthouse**

(1900), on the corner of Oxley and Richard Sts, is topped by a crowned spire, signifying that it can hear maritime cases!

Having a beer and a yarn with the locals is a highlight of staying in Bourke. **Back of Bourke Hotel** (☎ 6872 2614; 2 Darling St, North Bourke) is a good meeting place. The **Port O'Bourke Hotel** (Mitchell St) is comparatively sedate, but very friendly.

Cotton is picked in March and April. From about May to August you can see the cotton gin in action by phoning **Clyde Agriculture** (☎ 6872 2528).

Tours

Both Mateship Country Tours and Thomo's Back O'Bourke Tours are excellent ways to explore the town and surrounding areas; call to arrange tours. Trips offered by **Mateship Country Tours** (☎ 6872 1222; 3½hr; adult/child $22/11) depart daily. **Thomo's** (☎ 6872 4189; 4-hr town tour $24) town tours depart at 8.45am Monday to Saturday. There are also Mt Oxley tours twice a week.

For a challenge, Wapweelah Station and the Bourke YHA run a camel-handling as well as trek-training course. **Camel Trekking** (☎ 6874 7606; wapweelah@bigpond.au; 8 nights per person $870) includes tuition in bush skills, tracking, and camel love!

Festivals & Events

Held around September to October, the **Mateship Festival** derives its name from Henry Lawson's literary theme of male bonding in the bush, a powerful strain in Aussie culture.

Sleeping

Bourke Riverside Motel (☎ 6872 2539; bourke riverside@ozemail.com.au; 3 Mitchell St; s/d with bathroom $55-95; 🔌 🖳 🔄) Occupying the historic Telegraph Hotel, this is a friendly place in an enchanting riverside garden setting offering some unique accommodation.

Gidgee Guesthouse YHA (☎ 6870 1017; gidgee@ auzzie.net; 17 Oxley St; dm/d $20-4/52-7; 🖳) Located in the old London Bank building. Gidgee has a distinct arts focus with changing exhibitions, music gear for use and a peaceful sculpture garden.

Port O'Bourke Hotel (☎ 6872 2544; 32 Mitchell St; s/d $38/59, d with bathroom $85; 🔌) Recently renovated pub accommodation in the best of Bourke's hotels.

Kidman's Camp Tourist Park (☎ 6872 1612; Kidman Way; camp sites $14, cabins s/d $36/44; 🔌) This quiet camping ground, 8km north of town, runs down towards the river. New deluxe cabins make it a good place to stay for noncampers.

Eating

Port O'Bourke Hotel (☎ 6872 2544; Mitchell St; 🕑 bistro Tue, Fri & Sat nights, lunch Mon-Sat, dinner Mon, Wed & Thu; dinner mains $15) The best place in town for dinner, with decent pub grub and a welcoming atmosphere.

Gecko Café Oxley (☎ 6872 2701; 🕑 8.30am-5pm Mon-Fri, to 2pm Sat) A charming place serving excellent coffee.

Bowling Club (☎ 6872 2190; Richard St; 🕑 lunch & dinner Tue-Sun) A Chinese restaurant hidden away upstairs is well worth the search.

Bourke Post Office Coffee Shop (☎ 6872 1028; Oxley St; 🕑 9am-2pm Easter-Christmas) Has great opportunities for people-watching in the shade of hanging plants.

DETOUR: MT OXLEY & GUNDABOOKA NATIONAL PARK

From Bourke, take a detour to **Mt Oxley** (☎ 6872 3275; stalley@auzzie.net), 30km southeast off the Brewarrina road, for views at sunset and sunrise. There are very good **camping facilities** (per person $10) atop the mountain; there's little better than a barbecue under the stars while taking in the panorama. However, it is rocky, so take an air mattress.

There are more good views and abundant flora at **Gundabooka National Park**, about 70km to the southwest off the Kidman Way. The rock pools here often have water in them and the mountain is of great cultural significance to the Ngemba and Paakintji Aboriginal people, whose rock-art painting can still be seen. Camping is available at Dry Tank, or you can stay in shearers' quarters or the Belah Governess's Cottage. Watch carefully for the turn-offs from the Kidman Way. Before you go, pick up a key for Mt Oxley from the visitors centre, or visit **NPWS** (☎ 6872 2744; 51 Oxley St; 🕑 8.30am-4.30pm Mon-Fri) for the Gundabooka key (needed to open gates to see rock art) and to book accommodation. If plans to develop Bennets Gorge eventuate, there will be a spectacular walk to the summit of Gundabooka.

Kidman Café (Mitchell St; ⏰ 8am-10pm) A pleasant café next to the Towers Drug Co building (1890).

Morrall's Bakery (☎ 6872 2086; 37 Mitchell St) Makes award-winning meat pies and turns into a pizzeria Friday to Sunday nights.

Getting There & Away

Air Link (☎ 13 17 13) has five flights a week from Dubbo to Bourke ($220 one way). **CountryLink** (☎ 13 22 32) buses run to Dubbo ($56, four times a week) and connect with trains to Sydney ($66). **Bourke Courier Service** (☎ 6872 2092; cnr Oxley & Richard Sts) sells bus and plane tickets (opening hours depend on flight times).

DARLING RIVER

Although it passes through some of the driest country in the state, the Darling River usually has some water and its banks are lined with massive river red gums. With the Murray, the Darling forms one of the world's longest exotic rivers – one that for much of its length flows through country from which it receives no water.

The unsealed road that runs along the south bank is the main route downstream from Bourke. Apart from kangaroos and emus, you won't encounter much along the way.

Fort Bourke, signposted off the Louth road about 15km southwest of Bourke, is a replica of the crude stockade built by Major Mitchell in 1833. The area is a wildlife refuge with lots of water birds. The road in affords excellent river views.

The tiny town of **Louth** (population 34), about 100km from Bourke, hosts up to 4000 people during the annual race meeting on the second Saturday in August. During the week before the races the local Shindy's Inn comes alive each night with events such as a damper bake-off.

Old Louth Post Office (☎ 6874 7362; dr.white@ bigpond.com; s/d $45/90) has been lovingly restored and now operates as a B&B.

Twenty kilometres from Louth is **Trilby Station** (☎ 6874 7420; www.trilbystation.com.au; cottages from $80, bunkhouse per person $25; camping from $17) offering an insight into outback life, including watching cattle mustering, sheep shearing and station kids learning on School of the Air. Like other farmers in the region, the Murray family has opened their home to tourism after many years of drought. There are several accommodation options from roomy self-contained cottages, to the bunkhouse, as well as camping on secluded riverside spots.

Kallara Station (☎ 6837 3963; www.kallarastation .com.au; camping from $5, bunkhouse s/d $25/35, lodge s/d $60/85; ♨) If you are keen on fishing, this station has a punt for hire and large populations of carp, yellow belly and perch.

About 90km downstream is the classic **Tilpa Hotel** (☎ 6837 3928; Tilpa; s/d $30/40) with meals, fuel and, of course, beer. See below.

TOP FIVE OUTBACK PUBS

The owner might drink you under the table, and the paint might be falling off the walls, but these pubs will give you an insight into outback Australia that no guidebook can equal.

Back of Bourke Hotel (☎ 6872 2614; 2 Darling St, North Bourke) Known affectionately as the Northy, this hotel was built when the flood of 1890 caused most of the town's residents to camp at North Bourke until the water subsided. Right next to the historic North Bourke Bridge, the hotel continues to be the most raucous in town.

Tilpa Hotel (☎ 6837 3928; Darling St, Tilpa) Perched on the bank of the Darling River with a shady beer garden, this is a classic bush pub. Have a yarn with the shearers or donate some money to the Flying Doctor Service for your chance to scribble on the walls. See above.

Royal Mail (☎ 07-4655 4093; Archenar St; Hungerford) Writer Henry Lawson walked from Bourke to Hungerford in 1892 and he wasn't all that impressed with what he saw there. Read about it in his story, 'Hungerford'. But this beautiful old hotel is still going strong.

Family Hotel (☎ 08-8091 3314; Briscoe St, Tibooburra) Built in 1883, the Family is covered in original works of the artists Clifton Pugh, Russell Drysdale and Rick Amor who, fascinated by the desert, came to the area to paint a couple of decades ago. See p249.

Silverton Hotel (☎ 08-8088 5313; Laynard St, Silverton) Make like Mad Max and take a drink at the pub that has been used as a film location at least 140 times. See p258.

MARK PARKES

Kosciuszko National Park (p290)

Moored boats, Merimbula (p326)

ROSS BARNETT

MITCH REARDON

Penguins, Montague Island
(p321), Narooma

View down Anzac Parade to Parliament House (p337), Canberra

RICHARD NEBESKY

DENNIS JONES

Black rhino, Western Plains Zoo
(p226), Dubbo

CHRISTOPHER GR

Sculpture Symposium (p256), Broken Hill

Outback road signs, Silver City Highway, near Tibooburra (p249)

CLAVER

From Tilpa, the Darling flows down to **Wilcannia** (p251), then through a system of lakes at **Menindee** (p259), surrounded by **Kinchega National Park** (p259). These places are accessible by sealed roads from Broken Hill.

Beyond Menindee, another 125km of dirt road brings you to **Pooncarie**, a pretty hamlet and a jumping-off point for Mungo National Park (p259).

CORNER COUNTRY

There's no sealed road west of Bourke – the 713km from Bourke to Tibooburra via Wanaaring can be an adventurous drive. The far western corner of NSW is a semi-desert of red plains, heat, dust and flies; to quote Henry Lawson (1893): 'There are no "mountains" out west, only ridges on the floor of hell'. But it's worth seeing for its interesting physical features and wildlife. As well as kangaroos and emus, watch out for goannas and other lizards on the road, and wedge-tailed eagles above. Along the Queensland border is the dingo-proof fence, patrolled daily by boundary riders.

Tibooburra
☎ 08 / pop 150

Tiny Tibooburra, the hottest town in the state, boasts two fine sandstone pubs and a small outdoor cinema. Tibooburra used to be called the Granites after the 400 million–year-old granite outcrops nearby, which are good to visit on a sunset walk. Tibooburra is the closest town to Sturt National Park and there's a large **NPWS office** (☎ 8091 3308; ☺ 8.30am-4.30pm Mon-Fri) in the main street. Next to the office is the well-presented **Courthouse Museum. Keeping Place** (☎ 8091 3435) features indigenous artefacts as well as art for sale from the Wadigali, Wengkumara and Malyangapa tribes.

Internet access is available at the **Telecentre** (☎ 08 8091 3388; Sturt St; ☺ 9am-5pm Mon-Fri; per hr $6).

For a small fee you can camp in the national park north of town at **Dead Horse Gully**; despite the immediate beauty it is rather exposed and dusty. In town, **Granites Motel** (☎ 8091 3305; Brown St; camp sites/cabins/units from $10/50/60) has its reception at TJ's Roadhouse.

Both pubs, the **Family Hotel** (☎ 8091 3314; units, s/d $60/70; ☒) and **Tibooburra Hotel** (☎ 8091 3310; s/d $30/55), have accommodation. Both

bars have character; the Tibooburra has a collection of more than 60 well-worn hats on the walls. **Corner Country Store** (☎ 8091 3333) serves fantastic home-cooked meals, and breakfast all day. It also sells fuel, groceries and camping equipment.

Milparinka

This hamlet (population approximately 20) appears deceptively moribund, but what remains of a town formerly of 3000 souls is being lovingly restored by a group of determined locals who firmly believe in the motto 'never say die'. The courthouse is a fine sandstone building, which now houses a local history centre. There is a heritage walking trail.

In 1845 members of Charles Sturt's expedition were forced to camp near here for six months. About 14km northwest of the settlement at **Depot Glen** is the grave of James Poole, Sturt's second-in-command, who died of scurvy.

The only fuel between Milparinka and Broken Hill is at the Packsaddle roadhouse, about halfway along the partially sealed Silver City Hwy.

Sturt National Park

Taking in vast stony plains, the towering red sand hills of the great Strzelecki Desert and the unusual flat-topped mesas around the Olive Downs, this park covers 340,000 hectares of classic outback terrain. Thanks to the protection of the dingo-proof fence, there are large populations of western grey and red kangaroos.

Sturt has 300km of drivable tracks, camping areas and walks. The NPWS at Tibooburra has brochures for each. A favourite destination for visitors is **Cameron Corner**; a post marks the spot where Queensland, SA and NSW meet. The Corner lies 140km northwest of Tibooburra and is reached by a good, well-signposted dirt road (allow two hours). In the Queensland corner, **Cameron Corner Store** (!) has good advice on road conditions.

BARRIER HIGHWAY

The Barrier Hwy is the main sealed route heading from Nyngan 594km to Broken Hill. It's an alternative route to Adelaide and the most direct one between Sydney and Western Australia.

Nyngan

☎ 02 / pop 2070

Nyngan is a leafy country town on the banks of the Bogan River at the junction of the Barrier and Mitchell Hwys. Nyngan is also close to the centre of NSW; a cairn marks the exact spot 72km south.

The great flood of 1990, when the Bogan River overwhelmed the town and the entire population was evacuated by helicopter, still looms large in local memory. You can see photos of the flood at the **Railway Station Museum** (adult/child $2/50c; ⊙ 10am-4pm). There is good bird-watching in Nyngan. An ideal spot is the **Rotary Park** near the Peter Sinclair Bridge. Nyngan makes an excellent jumping-off point for visiting the Macquarie Marshes Nature Reserve (p240). **Nyngan Video Parlour** (☎ 6832 1155) doubes as a visitors centre.

Beancounters House (☎ 6832 1610; www.bean countershouse.com.au; 103 Pangee St; d $100-30; 🖳) is a wonderful find on top of the Westpac bank. Situated in the manager's residence, it is a very comfortable B&B.

Burnside on the Bogan B&B (☎ 6832 1827; Temples Lane; s/d with cooked breakfast $100, with continental breakfast $90) has wraparound verandas to enjoy the river from. **Canonba Hotel** (☎ 6832 1559; 129 Pangee St) has pub accommodation as well as decent counter meals.

There are several caravan parks; the nicest is the **Riverside** (☎ 6832 1729; Barrier Hwy; camp sites $14-18, cabins $45-65) west of town. But you can easily find some lovely camping spots off Temples Lane which won't set you back a cent.

The charming owners of Beancounters House also run the **Beancounters Café** (☎ 6832 2270; www.beancountershouse.com.au; 103 Pangee St; ⊙ breakfast & lunch) set in a verdant herb garden.

Countrylink (☎ 13 22 32) bu services run to Dubbo, Broken Hill, Brewarrina, Bourke, and Sydney.

Cobar

☎ 02 / pop 4120

Cobar is a bustling mining town with a productive copper mine. Rich copper ore was discovered in 1871. Both the Great Cobar and Cornish, Scottish & Australian (CSA) mines closed in the 1920s. The CSA mine reopened in the 1960s; it is 1km deep. The Endeavor mine, 47km west of Cobar, is currently exploiting a rich plug of zinc, lead and silver.

INFORMATION

The **visitors centre** (☎ 6836 2448; Barrier Hwy, Cobar; ⊙ 8.30am-5pm Mon-Fri, 9am-5pm Sat & Sun), at the eastern end of town, is in the Great Cobar Heritage Centre, which also houses the museum. There's also a **NPWS office** (☎ 6836 2692; 16 Barton St).

SIGHTS & ACTIVITIES

Don't think the **Cobar Museum** (adult/child $5.50/3.50; ⊙ 8.30am-5pm Mon-Fri, 9am-5pm Sat & Sun) is just another small-town history exhibition.

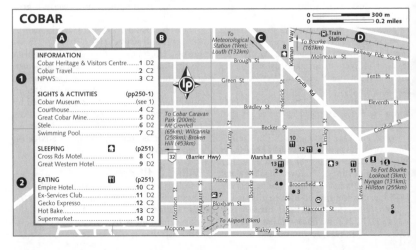

COBAR

0 —————— 300 m
0 —————— 0.2 miles

INFORMATION	
Cobar Heritage & Visitors Centre	1 D2
Cobar Travel	2 C2
NPWS	3 C2

SIGHTS & ACTIVITIES	(pp250-1)
Cobar Museum	(see 1)
Courthouse	4 C2
Great Cobar Mine	5 D2
Stele	6 D2
Swimming Pool	7 C2

SLEEPING	🏠	(p251)
Cross Rds Motel		8 C1
Great Western Hotel		9 D2

EATING	🍴	(p251)
Empire Hotel		10 C2
Ex-Services Club		11 D2
Gecko Expresso		12 C2
Hot Bake		13 C2
Supermarket		14 D2

To Meteorological Station (1km); Louth (132km)
To Bourke (161km)
Brough St
Green St
Kidman Way
Molineaux St
Railway Pde South
Tenth St
Bradley St
Louth Rd
Eleventh St
To Cobar Caravan Park (200m); Mt Grenfell (65km); Wilcannia (258km); Broken Hill (453km)
Becker St
Conduit St
Frederick St
Murray St
Linsley St
(Barrier Hwy)
Marshall St
Prince St
Broomfield St
To Fort Bourke Lookout (3km); Nyngan (131km); Hillston (255km)
Bourke St
Lewis St
Morrison St
Margaret St
Bloxham St
Barton St
Harcourt St
To Airport (8km)
Mopone St
Blakey St

It's housed in the former Mines Office (1910) and many of the displays reflect this association. The hospital train carriage is interesting and there are also sophisticated displays on the environment, local Aboriginal life and the early Europeans. Don't miss it.

Next to the museum is the **Stele Monument**, dedicated to the town and its mining past. Pick up a Cobar mud map from the visitors centre. There is a surprising number of interesting buildings including the enormous **Great Western Hotel** (1898), which has perhaps the longest pub veranda in the state. The town also has some legendary characters; stories can be found at the visitors centre.

Take a sealed road to **Fort Bourke Lookout** and view Cobar and its surroundings. There is a viewing platform, which looks down on the working gold mine.

Weather balloons are released at 9.15am (10.15am during daylight saving) from the meteorological station on the edge of town, off the Louth road.

SLEEPING & EATING
Several pubs have accommodation.

Cross Roads Motel (☎ 6836 2711; cnr Bourke & Louth Rds; s/d $65/75; 🅿 🏊) A quiet option to the bigger motels along the main highway.

Great Western Hotel (☎ 6836 2053; Marshall St; d with breakfast $50) A popular hotel that has basic motel-style units. From 5.30am it serves up a breakfast of chops and eggs.

Gecko Espresso (☎ 6836 4888; 35 Marshall St; meals $5-8) A slick new coffee bar with good cakes and wraps. See boxed text, p252.

Empire Hotel (☎ 6836 2725; 6 Barton St; meals $6-14) The best bet for dinner is the bustling Empire, for a good steak. Finding somewhere to eat in Cobar on a Sunday night is a difficult task.

Cobar Hot Bake (☎ 6836 2007; 13 Barton St; meals $2-5) Sells decent pies.

Mt Grenfell Historic Site

Taking in part of the Mt Grenfell station, the Mt Grenfell historic site protects Aboriginal rock art in several caves along a well-watered gully, an important place for the local Ngiyampaa people. Apart from the art, which features well-preserved and brilliantly coloured ochre paintings, the site is worth visiting for the chance to walk through some pretty

country on the 5km walking track. You will probably see feral goats and pigs in the area and there are also plenty of kangaroos and emus. Like many national park sites in the region, Mt Grenfell is currently in the process of being handed back to its traditional owners (see boxed text, p253). Inquire at the NPWS in Cobar about Ngiyampaa tours, a two-hour guided walk around the area.

Travel west from Cobar on the Barrier Hwy and turn off after 40km (it's signposted). The site is another 32km away on a good dirt road. There's water at the site but camping is not allowed.

Wilcannia
☎ 02 / pop 700

The small town of Wilcannia on the banks of the Darling River was a busy, prosperous port in the 1880s, despite being 1000km from the sea! Today it's a dilapidated town trying to shake off some bad press in the last few years as a rough and ragged place, but that shouldn't deter a stop. Some fine old buildings remain – the impressive sandstone police station and courthouse (1881), as well as the **Athenaeum Chambers** (☎ 8083 8900) which house the local **museum** and a **gallery** that displays local indigenous art and is an Internet centre ($6 per hour).

Wilcannia has a large indigenous community and is the traditional home of the Barkindji people.

WHITE CLIFFS
☎ 08 / pop 225

There are few stranger places in Australia than the tiny opal-mining town of White Cliffs. Surrounded by some of the harshest country the outback has to offer, many residents have gone underground to escape the heat. Although the town is still a key opal producer, tourism brings in almost as much money these days. The owners of PJ's Underground often tell guests how, in digging 10m underground to build their hotel, they found enough opal to cover the cost of their paint!

The town centre (a pub, a post office and a general store) is on flat land south of the main digging area. At the digging area, there are thousands of holes in the ground and miners' camps surrounded by car graveyards. The two bare hills, Turley's Hill (with the radiotelephone mast on top) and

HOME SWEET HOME

Michelle Hush left home when she was 15 years old. Swapping the wide streets and quiet nights of Cobar for the big city, she 'went to Sydney on a holiday, and never came back'.

She wasn't the only one. Almost all of her school classmates, and those of her siblings, also disappeared. 'In Cobar you reach 16 and suddenly there is nothing to do. It's a real problem if you aren't a sporting person – artistic things are few and far between,' she says.

Twenty years later, Michelle makes coffee for high-school girlfriends as the owner of a slick new café, Gecko Espresso, in Cobar's main street.

Returning to the town she spurned was hard, but she speaks only of its benefits: 'This was a transitional time in my life. I needed a grounding spot for that and Cobar was a natural choice.'

Travelling through the far west of NSW, strike up a conversation in any town, and you will come across people who have returned to their roots. It's an increasing trend, with those returning bringing a fresh approach.

'It's the changing of the guard,' says Ian Perkins, who has made a home in Nyngan (132km east of Cobar). 'Older people say, "We're a dying town; let's not put in any effort". So younger people are taking over businesses. Out here there's a new bakery, a nursery, they all feed off each other.'

Ian fled Mt Molloy for Sydney: 'I wanted to go somewhere I wasn't related to everybody! I wanted a house on the water, a corporate career and all the choices the city offers.'

But after too many years of working too hard and taking those choices for granted, he realised he wanted out.

'I missed that sense of community, of knowing my neighbours,' he says.

And the neighbours certainly know him now. As local solicitor, Westpac agent, as well as café and B&B owner, he's thrown himself into small-town life.

'I have absolute freedom,' Ian says. 'It's very exciting. I work just as hard as I did in the city and earn less money, but I'm doing exactly what I want to be doing – following my own route – not one a thousand other people have trodden.'

For both returnees there is a sense of achievement in helping build up their communities. 'We looked at what we could give to the town, and it was a gamble, opening a business so different and upmarket, but it's worked,' says Michelle.

Ian agrees: 'To run any facility in a small town is an effort but everyone realises that, and they are so appreciative.'

With less than 40,000 people living in the Far West, one member of parliament, and constantly decreasing services, the old adage of bush folk – 'make do and have a go' is being reinvented. Says Ian, 'People are now thinking, we used to look after ourselves and we can keep on doing it!'

Smith's Hill (south of the centre), command the plains like diminutive city-states.

You can fossick for opals around the old diggings, but watch the kids around those deep, unfenced holes. There are a number of opal showrooms and underground homes open for inspection. A visit to **Jock's Place** on Turley's Hill is a wonderful starting point. For $4 Jock and his dog Lily will give you a tour of his rambling abode and relic collection, and keep you up-to-date with the town gossip. But keep in mind, as Jock says, '35 years in this place and even the dogs go mad'.

In the town's centre is the **solar power station** where emus often graze out the front. Up until 15 years ago, businesses in White Cliffs each spent up to $60,000 a year on a diesel generator for electricity before the Australian National University updated their original solar power project in 1993 and got them on the grid. The station is open for inspection at 2pm daily.

Sleeping & Eating

White Cliffs is busy during holiday periods, so it's advisable to book ahead.

PJ's Underground (☎ 8091 6626; s/d with breakfast $100/120; 3-course dinners $44) On Turley's Hill and with only five rooms, PJ's is usually heavily booked. Its reputation as the place to stay is well founded – especially after a dip in the spa in the sunken garden. Energetic owners Peter and Joanne Pedler have performed miracles in converting their old mine workings into a cool sanctuary with whitewashed walls and stone floors. Self-caterers can pay $5 to use the barbecue in the evening.

White Cliffs Underground Motel (☎ 8091 6677; www.undergroundmotel.com.au; s/d $67/87; 3-course set-menu dinners $27; 🐾) The other option here, which is popular with tour groups. Custom-built with a tunnelling machine, the place is quite a maze (you get a map when you check in) but surprisingly comfortable. Separated by several metres of rock, when the lights are off the silence is total. Claustrophobics need not despair; there are three above-ground rooms for rent.

Getting There & Away
The emergence of White Cliffs as a tourist destination has led to an upgrading of the road south to Wilcannia. The 97km road is now completely sealed. All other roads out of White Cliffs are unsealed. Information on road conditions is posted outside the general store.

MUTAWINTJI NATIONAL PARK
Mutawintji National Park lies in the Byngnano Ranges, 131km northeast of Broken Hill. The area teems with wildlife and is a place of exceptional, rough beauty with stunning gorges, dark rock pools and mulga plains stretching to the horizon.

The reliable water supply in the range was vital to the Malyankapa and Pandjikali people who lived in the area for over 8000 years. There are important **rock engravings**, stencils and paintings as well as the scattered remains of the day-to-day life of the people. Some rock art has been badly damaged by vandals and the major site is off limits to visitors except on escorted tours by Aboriginal guides on Wednesday and Saturday morning at 11am (adult/child $20/10) between April and November. The Broken Hill NPWS office (p255) has details.

There are walks through the crumbling sandstone hills to rock pools, and rock paintings can be seen in the unrestricted areas.

There's a **camping ground** (small fee) at Homestead Creek, with toilets, showers and gas barbecues. Fuel and food are not available in the park; collect firewood from the signposted areas near the park entrance.

'...A CHANGE FROM THE INSULTS OF THE PAST...'

In 1983 Mutawintji National Park made headlines after a group of Aboriginal people from the far west of New South Wales (NSW) blockaded the park to visitors. They were concerned at the way the NPWS was interpreting the park's major historic sites. Our heading quotes part of a 1984 speech summing up Aboriginal feelings about the blockade.

The closure fractured the relationship between the Aboriginal people and local landholders. However, by 1990, Aboriginal owners and descendants had become increasingly involved with the management of the park, employed as guides, rangers and maintenance workers. The following year, the Royal Commission into Aboriginal Deaths in Custody found that control of native lands was an important step in fostering pride and cultural understanding in Aboriginal people – a direct result was the development of Indigenous Land Use Agreements with native titleholders.

Many of the group who closed the park attended the hand-back ceremony in 1998, where Mutawintji was officially returned to its traditional custodians. Subsequently, the park was leased back to the State Government and managed by a board incorporating Mutawintji Aboriginal Land Council, local landowners, Broken Hill Council and the NPWS. Most important, the Aboriginal people are now engaged in the decision-making processes of this area.

But it goes further; Kinchega and Mungo National Parks now have a comanagement agreement with councils of elders; Mungo has formed a concept of shared heritage between the three tribal groups who are descendants of the land. Mt Grenfell is in the process of being handed back.

The relevance to the traveller is that Australia now has national parks that are truly national.

Getting There & Away
Most people head out to Mutawintji from Broken Hill. The turn-off is 56km north of town along the Silver City Hwy and then 68km to the park entrance along a good unsealed road – impassable in the rain. The back road to White Cliffs is also good.

BROKEN HILL
☎ 08 / pop 19,830

The Silver City, as Broken Hill is known, is a fascinating destination for its comfortable oasis-like existence in an extremely unwelcoming environment. Some of the state's best national parks are in the area, plus interesting near-ghost towns. Elements of 'traditional' Australian culture that are disappearing in other cities can still be found in Broken Hill: physical labour, hard drinking and the sensibilities that come with access to a huge, unpopulated landscape. The less attractive aspects of this culture have been considerably mellowed by the city becoming a major arts centre, most of it local – a surprising but delightful development.

History

The Broken Hill Proprietary Company (now international giant BHP Billiton) was formed in 1885 after a boundary rider, Charles Rasp, discovered a silver lode. Other mining claims were staked, but BHP was always the 'big mine' and dominated the town. Rasp went on to amass a personal fortune and BHP, which later diversified into steel production, became Australia's largest company.

Early conditions in the mine were appalling. Hundreds of miners died and many more suffered from lead poisoning and lung disease. This gave rise to the other great force in Broken Hill, the unions. Many miners were immigrants, but all were united in their efforts to improve mining conditions.

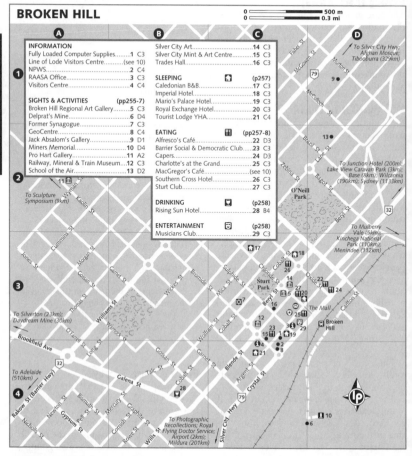

BROKEN HILL

0 —————— 500 m
0 —————— 0.3 mi

INFORMATION
Fully Loaded Computer Supplies........1 C3
Line of Lode Visitors Centre...........(see 10)
NPWS....................................2 C4
RAASA Office............................3 C3
Visitors Centre.........................4 C4

SIGHTS & ACTIVITIES   (pp255-7)
Broken Hill Regional Art Gallery........5 C3
Delprat's Mine..........................6 D4
Former Synagogue........................7 C3
GeoCentre...............................8 C4
Jack Absalom's Gallery..................9 D1
Miners Memorial........................10 D4
Pro Hart Gallery.......................11 A2
Railway, Mineral & Train Museum....12 C3
School of the Air......................13 D2

Silver City Art........................14 C3
Silver City Mint & Art Centre..........15 C3
Trades Hall............................16 C3

SLEEPING 🏠   (p257)
Caledonian B&B.........................17 C3
Imperial Hotel.........................18 C3
Mario's Palace Hotel...................19 C3
Royal Exchange Hotel...................20 C3
Tourist Lodge YHA......................21 C4

EATING 🍽   (pp257-8)
Alfresco's Café........................22 D3
Barrier Social & Democratic Club.....23 C3
Capers.................................24 D3
Charlotte's at the Grand...............25 C3
MacGregor's Café.....................(see 10)
Southern Cross Hotel...................26 C3
Sturt Club.............................27 C3

DRINKING 🍸   (p258)
Rising Sun Hotel.......................28 B4

ENTERTAINMENT 🎭   (p258)
Musicians Club.........................29 C3

To Silver City Hwy;
Afghan Mosque;
Tibooburra (329km)

To Junction Hotel (200m);
Lake View Caravan Park (3km);
Base (8km); Wilcannia
(190km); Sydney (1133km)

To Mulberry
Vale (5km);
Kinchega National
Park (110km);
Menindee (112km)

To Sculpture
Symposium (9km)

To Silverton (23km);
Daydream Mine (30km)

To Adelaide
(510km)

To Photographic
Recollections; Royal
Flying Doctor Service;
Airport (2km);
Mildura (201km)

O'Neill
Park

Sturt
Park

The Mall

Broken
Hill

The first 35 years of Broken Hill saw a militancy rarely matched in Australian industrial relations. After many unsuccessful campaigns the turning point was the Big Strike of 1919–20, which lasted for over 18 months. The miners won a great victory, achieving a 35-hour week and the end of dry drilling, responsible for the dust that afflicted so many miners.

The concept of one big union, which had helped to win the strike, was formalised in 1923 with the formation of the Barrier Industrial Council.

Today the world's richest silver, lead and zinc deposit is still worked, though not by BHP, which ceased work in 1940, but by Pasminco, the only remaining operator. The ore body is diminishing and modern technology has greatly reduced the number of jobs. But while mining has declined, art has thrived.

Orientation & Information

The city is laid out in a grid. Argent St is the main street.

The **visitors centre** (☎ 8087 6077; www.murray outback.org.au; cnr Blende & Bromide Sts; ⏰ 8.30am-5pm) has the excellent free booklet *Broken Hill, the Accessible Outback*, which is full of helpful regional information. There is also a handy guide to the art around town.

The visitors centre is also where buses arrive (book through the town's travel agents) and there's a car-rental desk on the premises.

TIME

Broken Hill operates on SA time (Central Standard), which is half an hour behind the time in the rest of NSW. Towns near Broken Hill don't follow the Silver City's lead, keeping NSW time instead.

The **NPWS office** (☎ 8080 3200; 183 Argent St; ⏰ 8.30am-4.30pm Mon-Fri) can help with local national park inquiries and bookings.

The **Royal Automobile Association of South Australia** (RAASA; ☎ 8088 4999; 261 Argent St; ⏰ 8.30am-5pm Mon-Fri, to 11.30am Sat) provides reciprocal service to other auto club members.

Internet access is available at **Fully Loaded Computer Supplies** (☎ 8088 4255; 195a Argent St; ⏰ 10am-5pm).

Sights & Activities

MINES

There's an excellent underground tour at **Delprat's Mine** (☎ 8088 1604; adult/child $38/34; ⏰ Mon-Sat) where you don miners gear and descend 130m for a tour lasting nearly two hours. Children under six are prohibited. Delprat's is up Iodide St; cross the railway tracks and then follow the signs – a five-minute drive.

Before caged lifts and big drills were the walk-in, pick and shovel mines of the last century. You can tour the historic **Daydream Mine** (☎ 8087 6077; adult/child $15/8), 33km from Broken Hill, off the Silverton road. Daydream was established in 1882 and the guide has a few tales of baby-faced miners, which should have any youngsters with you giggling nervously. Sturdy footwear is essential for the one-hour tour.

LINE OF LODE

The huge silver skimp dump, which makes up Broken Hill's stark backdrop, also features the moving **Miners Memorial** (☎ 8088 6000; Federation Hill; memorial admission $2.50; ⏰ 9am-10pm). The memorial commemorates the deaths of over 800 men who have died in the mines since 1883. The list of the dead also includes Dario Palumbo, an architecture student from the University of South Australia, who died suddenly during his work on the project, which through its severe structure truly captures the emotions. There's McGregor's, a good café/restaurant, attached (see Eating, p257).

ROYAL FLYING DOCTOR SERVICE

You can visit the **Royal Flying Doctor Service** (☎ 8080 1777; adult/child $5.50/2.20; ⏰ 9am-5pm Mon-Fri, 11am-4pm Sat & Sun) at the airport, which includes the fascinating **Mantle of Safety Museum**. The tour includes a film about the service, and you inspect the headquarters, aircraft and the radio room that handles calls from remote towns and stations. While tours run only during the week you can visit the museum, which is well presented with lots of quirky stories and things to see, at any time.

SCHOOL OF THE AIR

You can sit in on School of the Air, which broadcasts to kids in isolated homesteads at 8.30am sharp on weekdays. The one-hour session costs $3; book through the visitors centre. You can visit even when school is out, as a tape recording is played for visitors during vacations.

GALLERIES

With its dramatic scenery and empty spaces Broken Hill is an inspiring place, so it's not strange to find that the city houses a vibrant community of artists, from painters to performers. There is an abundance of galleries, including the **Pro Hart Gallery**, (☎ 8087 2441;108 Wyman St; adult $2; ☺ 10am-5pm Mon-Sat), and **Jack Absalom's Gallery** (☎ 8087 5881; 638 Chapple St; admission free).

Pro Hart, a former miner, is Broken Hill's best-known artist and a local personality. His gallery displays his own work, minor works of major artists (such as Picasso and Dali) and a superb collection of Australian art.

Broken Hill Regional Art Gallery (☎ 8088 5491; 142-cnr Chloride & Blende Sts; adult $3; ☺ 1-4pm Mon, 8.30am-5pm Tue & Fri, 10am-5pm Wed, Thu & Sat, to 4pm Sun) was established in 1904 to meet the cultural needs of a 'city in isolation', making it the oldest regional gallery in NSW and with 1500 works in its permanent collection, possibly the largest. You can see *Silver Tree*, an intricate silver sculpture that was commissioned by Charles Rasp (p254). One room of the gallery is devoted to the artists of Broken Hill.

Thankakali (☎ 8087 6111; cnr Buck & Beryl Sts; ☺ 9am-4pm Mon-Fri, 10am-3pm Sat & Sun) is the Aboriginal cultural centre, located in an old brewery. There is an extensive gallery downstairs as well as a huge range of hand-painted arts and crafts by local artists – all for sale.

While on Argent St make sure you have a look at the murals inside the residential entrance of Mario's Palace Hotel (opposite).

SCULPTURE SYMPOSIUM

In 1993, 12 international sculptors were invited to record their impressions of Broken Hill at a hilltop site 8km northwest of town. Responding to the limitless landscape, the sculptors have created a striking range of work using little more than Wilcannia sandstone and chisels. The colours of the stone change constantly with the light. To get here, follow Kaolin St out of town on to Nine Mile Rd and the sculptures are signposted to the right. From the lower car park

it's a 15-minute climb to the sculpture site. Bring water in summer. There's wheelchair access to the sculptures from the upper car park, but you need to get the keys for the gate from the Broken Hill visitors centre.

HISTORIC BUILDINGS

Broken Hill has a rich and varied architectural heritage. It is well worth buying a copy of the *Heritage Trails* booklet from the visitors centre ($2.20). The many listed sights include the old miners cottages and the slag heap. Locals say there is millions of dollars worth of silver left in the slag heap but it can't be touched because of the heritage listing!

Trades Hall (cnr Sulphide & Blende Sts; ☺ 9am-5pm Mon-Fri), built between 1898 and 1904, houses the Barrier Industrial Council. It features a pressed-iron ceiling and an elaborately detailed interior restored in 1988.

Afghan Mosque (cnr William & Buck Sts, North Broken Hill; admission $2.50; ☺ 2-4pm Sun) is a simple corrugated-iron building circa 1891. Afghan cameleers helped to open up the outback and the mosque was built on the site of a camel camp.

The **Synagogue** on Wolfram St dates from 1900 when there was a Jewish community of more than 150 people. It closed in 1962 and the religious scrolls were sent to Melbourne.

OTHER ATTRACTIONS

The wonderful **Photographic Recollections** (☎ 8087 9322; old Central Power Station, Eyre St, Broken Hill South; adult/child $4.50/1.50; ☺ 10am-4.30pm Mon-Fri, 1-4.30pm Sat & Sun) exhibition is a pictorial history of Broken Hill.

There is more local history at the **Sulphide St Station Railway & Historical Museum** (☎ 8088 4660; cnr Blende & Bromide Sts; adult/child $2.50/$2; ☺ 10am-3pm). The museum is in the Silverton Tramway Company's old station. The tramway was a private railway running between Cockburn (SA) and Broken Hill via Silverton until 1970.

GeoCentre (☎ 8087 6538; cnr Bromide & Crystal Sts; adult/child $3.50/2.50; ☺ 10am-4.45pm Mon-Fri, 1-4.45pm Sat & Sun) is an interactive geology museum. There are lots of touch-and-feel exhibits that display the story of Broken Hill's geological history from its formation to its transformation into a significant industrial centre.

Silver City Mint & Art Centre, (☎ 80886166; 66 Chloride St; ☺ 10 am-4 pm) is home to the *Big Picture*, the largest continuous canvas in Australia. There is a $4.95 admission fee to see the 12m-high diorama of the Broken Hill outback.

Tours

Free two-hour guided walks of Broken Hill commence from the tourist centre at 10am Monday, Wednesday and Friday. Plenty of companies offer tours of the town and nearby attractions, some going further out to White Cliffs, Mutawintji National Park and other outback destinations. The visitors centre has information and takes bookings.

Several outfits have longer 4WD tours of the area. **Broken Hill's Outback Tours** (☎ 8087 7800; www.outbacktours.net) has deluxe tours of the surrounding areas for up to nine days, starting either in Sydney, Adelaide or Broken Hill. You can also hitch a ride with the **Bush Mail Run** (☎ 8087 2164; adults $77), an outback mail delivery service that operates every Wednesday and Saturday. The day starts at 7am and you cover over 500km, stopping at isolated homesteads for the occasional cuppa.

Festivals & Events

Held annually on the Saturday two weeks before Easter is **St Patrick's Race Day**. Thousands of people flock to the dirt-track racecourse on the outskirts of the city. Celebrations begin in town on the preceding Wednesday, and the actual event is followed by a recovery party at the Silverton pub on the Sunday.

Sleeping

BUDGET

Tourist Lodge YHA (☎ 8088 2086; 100 Argent St; dm/s/d $18/22/28; ☺ ☐ ☎) This popular and central YHA has a laid-back atmosphere. The small pool may be empty (depending on the weather). The Lodge has no stairs so it is also popular with seniors. Bike rental costs $15 a day.

Lake View Caravan Park (☎ /fax 8088 2250; 1 Mann St; camp sites from $18, cabins $50; P ☺) Three kilometres northeast of town, this is in a quiet, prime location on the edge of the bush.

MID-RANGE

Caledonian B&B (☎ 8087 1945; 140 Chloride St; cally bnb@iinet.net.au; s/d with breakfast $44/66; P ☺) This good-value B&B is in a refurbished pub

(1898) that lost its licence to a Sydney establishment during the 2000 Olympic Games. It has charming hosts, a cosy interior, and delicious home cooked breakfasts.

Mulberry Vale (☎ 8088 1597; Menindee Rd; cabin with bathroom $77 per night, cheaper if staying longer; ☺ ☎) About 5km out of Broken Hill is this scrap of desert that congenial owner Pam Wright has turned into a small oasis. The accommodation is comfortable; however, it's the peaceful environment that is the drawcard.

Broken Hill Historic Cottages (☎ 8087 9966; from $95; ☺) This is a booking service for a range of homes available for holiday rentals, all fully equipped and sleeping up to six people.

Mario's Palace Hotel (☎ 8088 1699; cnr Argent & Sulphide Sts; s/d with bathroom $48/67; P ☺) Star of the hit Australian movie *The Adventures of Priscilla, Queen of the Desert*, it has taken Mario's almost ten years to shake the Aussywood image. It is an impressive old pub (1888) in its own right, but its coating of murals makes it extraordinary. It features the owner Mario Celetto's tribute to Botticelli's *Birth of Venus* on the ceiling, as well as walls and walls of lavishly kitsch Australiana landscapes.

TOP END

Imperial (☎ 8087 7444; imperial@pcpro.net.au; 88 Oxide St; with bathroom $180; P ☺ ☎) Five luxurious rooms that retain the feel of the grand old hotel the Imperial once was. There is a full-size billiard table in the guest lounge.

Royal Exchange Hotel (☎ 8087 2308; www.royalexchangehotel.com; 320 Argent St; with bathroom from $150; P ☺ ☐) This elegant hotel has recently been revamped, but has kept its wonderful Art Deco style. There is also an impressive lounge bar.

Eating

Broken Hill's many clubs welcome visitors.

McGregor's Café (☎ 8088 6000; Line of Lode visitors centre; meals $12-25; ☺ 10am-10pm) With its stunning views over Broken Hill, airy modern design and something-for-everyone menu of modern Australian dishes, McGregor's is certainly the best restaurant in town.

Southern Cross Hotel (☎ 8088 4122; 357 Cobalt St; meals $12-16; ☺ dinner) Has a good pub restaurant menu with standouts being the fresh fish. The dining room is pleasant and the staff genuinely friendly.

Sturt Club (☎ 8087 4541; 321 Blende St; meals $12-22; ☽ lunch & dinner) This club has interesting French cuisine and the chef is not afraid to try new things on his daily specials board (not always the case in outback NSW).

Alfresco's Cafe (☎ 8087 5599; cnr Argent & Oxide Sts; meals $8-16; ☽ breakfast, lunch & dinner) Always busy, serving plates of pancakes and pasta dishes.

Capers (☎ 8088 1727; 397 Argent St; meals $9-20; ☽ breakfast, lunch & dinner) Next door to Alfresco's, and mainly a takeaway business, Capers makes gourmet pizzas. There are a few tables outside.

Charlotte's at the Grand (☎ 8087 2230; 317 Argent St; meals $6-12; ☽ breakfast & lunch Tue-Sun) A good place for lunch, with lots of tasty vegetarian options, sandwiches and smoothies.

Barclays at the 'J' (☎ 8088 4380; Junction Hotel, 560 Argent St; meals $12-16; ☽ dinner Mon-Sat) Barclays has tasty dishes.

Barrier Social & Democratic Club (Demo; ☎ 8088 4477; 218 Argent St; meals from $8; ☽ breakfast & lunch) The Demo starts early with breakfast from 6am (7am at weekends) and closes at 8.30pm.

Drinking & Entertainment

Broken Hill stays up late; you can find pubs doing a roaring trade until almost dawn on Thursday, Friday and Saturday.

Rising Sun Hotel (☎ 8087 4856; 2 Beryl St) Has free games of pool and gets very lively on Friday night.

Southern Cross Hotel (☎ 8088 4122; 357 Cobalt St) Here you'll find a mellow atmosphere with an extensive cocktail list.

Musicians Club (267 Crystal St) A jolly place with a heaving mix of young and old. Country music bands play on the weekends and the drinks continue to flow until 1am. Two-up (gambling on the fall of two coins) is played here on Friday and Saturday night from 10pm to 2am. Broken Hill claims to have retained the atmosphere of a real two-up school, unlike the sanitised versions played in casinos. The locals are happy to give you lessons if you get in early.

Getting There & Away

Standard one-way airfares on **Regional Express Airlines (Rex)** (☎ 13 17 13) from Broken Hill include $90 to Adelaide, $470 to Melbourne via Sydney and $250 to Sydney, via Dubbo.

McCafferty's/Greyhound (☎ 13 20 30) runs buses daily to Adelaide (from $58) and Sydney (from $89).

There's a CountryLink service on Tuesday direct to Sydney ($125, around 14 hours) departing 7.30am. The **CountryLink booking office** (☎ 8087 1400; ☽ 8am-5pm Mon-Fri) is at the train station. The **Indian Pacific** (☎ 13 21 47; www.trainways.com.au) goes through Broken Hill on Tuesday and Friday (departing 6.15pm CST) bound for Sydney ($165), and on Thursday and Sunday (8.20am) heading for Perth (from $375) and Adelaide ($64).

Getting Around

The Sturt and Musicians clubs have a free bus to drive you home after a night's drinking. It leaves hourly between 6pm and midnight.

Murton's Citybus (☎ 8087 3311) operates four routes around Broken Hill. Pick up a timetable at the visitors centre.

Hertz (☎ 8087 2719) has an office at the visitors centre. There are several other car rental companies or you can call for a **taxi** (☎ 8087 2222).

SILVERTON

☎ 08 / pop 50

Silverton, 25km northwest of Broken Hill, is an old silver-mining town. Its fortunes peaked in 1885, when it had a population of 3000 and public buildings designed to last for centuries, but in 1889 the mines closed and the people (and many of the houses) moved to the new boom town at Broken Hill.

Today it is an interesting ghost town, which has received a new lease of life due to a small community of artists. Several, including Peter Browne and John Dynon, have studios here.

Silverton is used as a setting in films such as *Mad Max II* and *A Town Like Alice*. A number of buildings survive, including the old jail (now the museum) and the **Silverton Hotel** (☎ 8088 5313; ☽ 9am-9pm). The hotel displays photographs taken on the film sets; ask at the bar about the infamous 'Silverton test'. The pub and galleries have a walking-tour map. The friendly **café** (☎ 8088 6601; ☽ Tue-Thu, Sat & Sun 10am-4pm, Sat & Sun only in summer) has a traditional Aussie menu with staples such as damper and drovers stew. **Barrier Ranges Camel Safaris** (☎ 8088 5316; 15min/1-hr tours $5/25,

2-hr sunset ride $50) runs a variety of **camel tours** from Silverton.

There's accommodation at **Penrose Park** (☎ 8088 5307; camp sites from $12, bunkhouse $35-40), located in a desert camp setting. The road beyond Silverton leads directly into the vast expanse of the Mundi Mundi Plain. If you aren't heading out that way, it is still worthwhile driving an extra 4km to the **Mundi Mundi Lookout**.

MENINDEE
☎ 08 / pop 400

This small town on the Darling River, 112km southeast of Broken Hill, provides access to the Menindee Lakes and Kinchega National Park.

The **visitors centre** (Yartla St) is open from 10am to 1pm daily.

Menindee Lakes are a series of nine natural, ephemeral lakes adjacent to the Darling River, but they have been dammed to ensure year-round water. Water was transported to Broken Hill by rail until 1960. The last water train to leave Menindee was derailed by floodwaters that broke the drought! **Copi Hollow** is a lovely swimming hole and is very popular during summer. Jeff Looney runs **boat tours** from the visitors centre.

Explorers Burke and Wills stayed at the **Maidens Hotel** (☎ 8091 4208), but you'll have to make do with the **Burke & Wills Motel** (☎ 8091 4313; s/d with bathroom $55/65) across the road.

There are caravan parks and cabins out of town by the lakes. There's also camping in Kinchega National Park, with some excellent sites among the red gums along the banks of the Darling River.

Menindee is on the main railway line between Sydney and Adelaide. A bus service departs Menindee for Broken Hill from outside the post office at 9am (EST) Monday to Friday. The same bus leaves Broken Hill for the return trip at 3.15pm (CST).

KINCHEGA NATIONAL PARK
Kinchega National Park is close to Menindee and includes the Darling River and several of the lakes in the Menindee system. These glittering lakes are a haven for water birds living among the backwaters and drowned forests. The visitors centre is at the site of the old Kinchega homestead, about 16km from the park entrance. Kinchega shearing shed has been beautifully restored. Bunk accommodation is available at the shearers' quarters (book at the Broken Hill NPWS office) and there are plenty of camp sites ($5) along the river. There is a $6 per day vehicle fee that can be paid at the self-registration box near the woolshed.

MUNGO NATIONAL PARK
Mungo National Park (27,850 hectares), part of the Willandra Lakes World Heritage area, is remote, beautiful and a most important place, full of great significance for the human species. The echoes of over 400 centuries of continuous human habitation are almost tangible.

The story of both Australia and its oldest inhabitants is told in the dunes of Mungo. At least 60,000 years ago, Aborigines settled on the banks of the fertile lakes, living on the plentiful fish, mussels, birds and animals. Some of the animals were much larger than their modern relatives. After 45,000 years the climate changed, the lakes dried up and the Aborigines adapted to life in a harsh semidesert, with only periodic floods filling the lakes. The constant westerly wind drifted sand from the lakebed up onto the dunes, gradually burying old camp sites.

The people maintained their culture for another 15,000 years, but it was destroyed when Europeans arrived with their sheep in the early 19th century. Along with the remains of incredibly ancient animals and people, the dunes hold tracks of the Cobb & Co coaches, which cut across the lake last century. A 25km semicircle (lunette) of huge sand dunes has been created by the unceasing westerly wind, which continually exposes fabulously ancient remains. These shimmering white dunes are known as the **Walls of China**.

Information
There's a visitors centre (not always staffed) in the park, by the old Mungo woolshed. Pay your day-use fee of $6 per car on an honesty system here. A road leads across the dry lake bed to the Walls of China, and you can drive a complete 70km loop of the dunes when it's dry. There's a self-guided drive brochure at the visitors centre. Mungo is 110km from Mildura and 150km from Balranald on good, unsealed roads that become instantly impassable after rain. These towns are the closest places selling fuel.

Tours

Award-winning **Harry Nanya Tours** (☎ 1800 630 864, 03-5027 2076; carnma@ruralnet.net.au) has daily tours to Lake Mungo from Mildura and Wentworth, employing culturally informed Aboriginal guides. Some tours may be cancelled due to insufficient numbers, so check, especially if travelling into Wentworth.

Sleeping

Places fill up during the school holidays. Book through the **NPWS** (☎ 03-5021 8900) at Buronga.

Mungo Lodge (☎ 03-5029 7297; mungoldg@rur alnet.net.au; s/d $78/88) On the Mildura road, about 4km from the visitors centre, this is a comfortable quiet spot with a restaurant (book ahead).

The **Shearers' Quarters** (bunkhouses adult/child $17/5.50) are next to the visitors centre.

The **Main Camp** (camp sites per person $3) is 2km from the visitors centre. **Belah Camp** (camp sites per person $3) is on the eastern side of the dunes.

To pay your camp fees, put money in an envelope at the visitors centre.

The Riverina

The mighty Murray and Murrumbidgee Rivers are the lifeblood of this region, and the reason it's called the Riverina. This is green, endlessly rolling country with some of the state's best farming and grazing areas. Irrigation schemes have allowed crops, such as rice, lettuce and grapes, to flourish in several centres, while the small towns of the Riverina region are welcoming oases, especially for visitors who are serious about food and wine.

Before the Europeans arrived, the rivers of the region provided an idyllic home for the Aborigines, and the area around Deniliquin was probably the most densely populated part of the continent. But John Oxley, the first European to visit the area, wasn't impressed with the arid plains carved by the waterways as they changed course over the millennia, saying: 'There is a uniformity in the barren desolation of this country which wearies one more than I am able to express...I am the first white man to see it and I think I will undoubtedly be the last'.

A century later, graziers had established sheep stations on the plains, and the Murrumbidgee Irrigation Area (MIA) had turned those dry flatlands into fertile farmland. Away from the rivers, which are popular for fishing holidays, much of this region sees few visitors. This is part of the Riverina's attraction – you can meet locals who are as interested in you as you are in them.

HIGHLIGHTS

- Feasting on traditional Southern Italian fare in **Griffith** (p271)
- Sinking beers at the grand old pubs in **Junee** (p267)
- Embracing the sights and smells of the **livestock sales market** (p265) in Wagga Wagga
- Capturing the vast beauty of the salt plains with a drive through these open grasslands outside **Hay** (p275)
- Watching wildlife from the beautifully restored homestead at **Willandra National Park** (p275)
- Taking in the colour and diversity of the **National Glass Art Collection** (p265) in Wagga Wagga
- Getting cosy in the back of a truck at Deniliquin's annual **Ute Muster** (p278)
- Lazing the days away on a sandy river-beach near **Tocumwal** (p277)

★ Willandra National Park

★ Hay ★ Griffith

★ Junee

★ Wagga Wagga

★ Deniliquin

★ Tocumwal

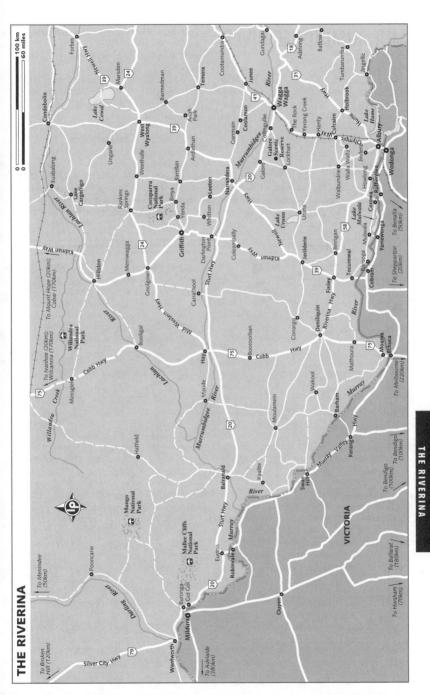

THE RIVERINA

100 km
60 miles

To Menindee
(50km)

To Broken
Hill (120km)

Darling River

Pooncarie

Silver City Hwy

Wentworth

To Adelaide
(380km)

Mildura

Buronga
Gol Gol

Mallee Cliffs
National Park

Mungo
National Park

Hatfield

Mossgiel

Willandra
Creek

Willandra
National Park

Booligal

Lachlan River

Euabalong

Lake
Cargelligo

Condobolin

Forbes

Newell Hwy

Marsden

Ungarie

West
Wyalong

Weethalle

Rankins
Springs

Hillston

Merriwagga

Goolgowi

Carrathool

Mid Western Hwy

Maude

Balranald

Kyalite

Swan Hill

Murrumbidgee River

Lachlan

Cobb Hwy

Cobb

Booroorban

Hay

Wakool

Moulamein

Barham

Kerang

To Bendigo
(100km)

Murray Valley Hwy

Echuca
Moama

To Melbourne
(220km)

Mathoura

Conargo

Deniliquin

Finley

Tocumwal

Cobram

Barooga

Mulwala

Berrigan

Jerilderie

Urana

Lake
Urana

Coleambally

Darlington
Point

Whitton

Leeton

Narrandera

Griffith

Yenda

Binya

Cocoparra
National Park

Ardlethan

Barellan

Ganmain

Coolamon

Junee

Temora

Barmedman

Auch
Park

Cootamundra

Gundagai

Adelong

Batlow

Tumbarumba

Jingellic

Holbrook

Hume Hwy

Lake
Hume

Albury

Wodonga

Rutherglen

Corowa

Howlong

Wahgunyah

Lake
Mulwala

Yarrawonga

To Shepparton
(20km)

To Benalla
(50km)

Jindera

Walla Walla

Walbundrie

Henty

Yerong Creek

Culcairn

The Rock

Olympic Way

Galore

Lockhart

Galore
Scenic
Reserve

Collingullie

Wagga
Wagga

Murrumbidgee

River

Sturt Hwy

Newell Hwy

Kidman Way

Riverina Hwy

Sturt Hwy

VICTORIA

THE RIVERINA

Murray River

Robinvale

Euston

Gol Gol

Ouyen

To Horsham
(70km)

To Ballarat
(180km)

Eugowra

Lake
Cowal

MURRUMBIDGEE RIVER

Murrumbidgee is an Aboriginal word for 'big river', and true to its name the Murrumbidgee flows 1578km from the Snowy Mountains to its confluence with the Murray River. The Murrumbidgee is the most important source of irrigation water for the lush Riverina region.

WAGGA WAGGA

☎ 02 / pop 44,450

Wagga Wagga is the state's largest inland city. Though it sprawls across a large area, it has the feel of a relaxed country town, with the nearby Charles Sturt University

and some interesting cultural attractions adding diversity. 'Wagga' is a pretty city with fine buildings, wide tree-lined streets and lovely riverside gardens.

The name means 'place of many crows' in the language of the local Wiradjuri people, but an alternate meaning is 'dancing like a drunken man'.

Orientation & Information

The long main street, Baylis St, which runs north from the train station, becomes Fitzmaurice St at the northern end. The **visitors centre** (☎ 6926 9621; www.tourismwaggawagga.com.au; Tarcutta St; ☺ 9am-5pm) is close to the river.

There's Internet access at **Civic Video** (☎ 6921 8866; 21 Forsyth St; per hr $5; ☺ 10am-10pm).

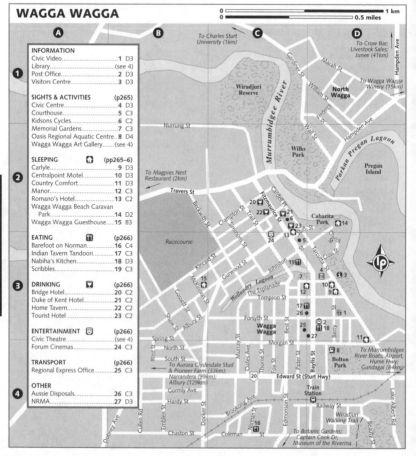

WAGGA WAGGA

INFORMATION	
Civic Video	1 D3
Library	(see 4)
Post Office	2 D3
Visitors Centre	3 D3

SIGHTS & ACTIVITIES	(p265)
Civic Centre	4 D3
Courthouse	5 C3
Kidsons Cycles	6 C2
Memorial Gardens	7 C3
Oasis Regional Aquatic Centre	8 D4
Wagga Wagga Art Gallery	(see 4)

SLEEPING	(pp265–6)
Carlyle	9 D3
Centralpoint Motel	10 D3
Country Comfort	11 D3
Manor	12 C3
Romano's Hotel	13 C2
Wagga Wagga Beach Caravan Park	14 D2
Wagga Wagga Guesthouse	15 B3

EATING	(p266)
Barefoot on Norman	16 C4
Indian Tavern Tandoori	17 C3
Nabiha's Kitchen	18 D3
Scribbles	19 C3

DRINKING	(p266)
Bridge Hotel	20 C2
Duke of Kent Hotel	21 C2
Home Tavern	22 C2
Tourist Hotel	23 C2

ENTERTAINMENT	(p266)
Civic Theatre	(see 4)
Forum Cinemas	24 C3

TRANSPORT	(p266)
Regional Express Office	25 C3

OTHER	
Aussie Disposals	26 C3
NRMA	27 D3

Sights & Activities

The Civic Centre houses the **Wagga Wagga Art Gallery** (☎ 6926 9660; admission free; ✆ 10am-5pm Tue-Sat, noon-4pm Sun), home to the wonderful **National Art Glass Collection**. The Glass Collection provides an overview of the history and development of the studio glass movement in Australia from the 1970s. Not only is the actual gallery space a superb configuration of water, light and glass, but the permanent exhibition is one of diverse colour and beauty.

To check out the town, make use of Wagga Wagga's bikeways, flat paths that completely circle the city. **Kidsons Cycles** (107 Fitzmaurice St; per day $40; ✆ 9am-5.30pm Mon-Sat, to 1pm Sat) rents bicycles. The **Oasis Regional Aquatic Centre** (☎ 6937 3737; Morgan St; adult/child $4.40/3; ✆ 6.30am-9pm Mon-Fri, 8.30am-6pm Sat & Sun) is a brand-new swimming complex that will impress kids and adults alike.

The excellent **Botanic Gardens** (Macleay St; ✆ sunrise-sunset) have a small **zoo**. Geese and peacocks roam free, and there's a free-flight aviary containing some colourful native birds. The gardens are south of the town centre; turn south off Edward St onto Edmondson St (which becomes Mitchelmore St), then follow the signs. The entrance is on the right, just before the archway telling you that you're entering Lord Baden Powell Drive, which itself leads to a good lookout and the scenic **Captain Cook Drive**.

Wagga Wagga is a major centre for **livestock sales**, and you can see the farmers (and animals) in action every week. Cattle are sold every Monday in an amphitheatre-style ring, while sheep are sold outdoors by the thousands on Thursday. While traditionalists might bridle at computerised stock information, the essence of a large-scale livestock market can never be lost; the smells and sounds are what bring this place to life. Follow the signs from the centre of town to the Boman industrial area.

The **Museum of the Riverina** (☎ 6925 2934; Baden Powell Dr; admission free; ✆ 10am-5pm Tue-Sat, noon-4pm Sun) operates from both the Civic Centre and the Botanic Gardens; the latter site has recently been refurbished and focuses on the people, places and events of Wagga Wagga. The section on the Wiradjuri people, then and now, is particularly good, but the locals are most proud of the Sporting Hall of Fame. Countless sports stars

grew up in the area, from AFL luminary Wayne Carey to test cricketer Mark Taylor.

Murrumbidgee River Boats (☎ 6925 8700; 175 Eunony Bridge Rd; adult/child $12/6; ✆ Thu-Mon) operates a one-hour cruise at 2pm. You can bring your own picnic lunch, making for a very pleasant afternoon on the river.

The **Wiradjuri Walking Track** begins at the visitors centre, where they have maps of the track, and returns there after a 30km circuit of the area, which includes some good lookouts and places of Aboriginal significance. There's a shorter 10km loop past the **Wollundry Lagoon**. From the **beach** near Cabarita Park you can swim and fish, and ponder the famous 'Five O'Clock Wave' (ask a local for an explanation).

The **Wagga Wagga Winery** (☎ 6922 1221; ✆ 11am-10pm or 11pm) is midway between Wagga Wagga and Oura on the Gundagai road. Delicious BBQ meals (from $16) are available. Charles Sturt University, north of town, has an award-winning **winery** (☎ 6933 2435; ✆ 11am-5pm Mon-Fri, to 4pm Sat & Sun), which is reached through the Agriculture Research Unit, about 3km north of Wagga Wagga, off the Olympic Way.

Festivals & Events

The **Wagga Wagga Jazz Festival** (www.waggajazz .org.au), held annually in September, hosts international and national musicians, who play in a variety of locations. The festival is well regarded, and prices for single sessions are reasonable.

Sleeping

BUDGET

Wagga Wagga Guesthouse (☎ 6931 8712; www .nomadsworld.com; 149 Gurwood St; s/d $25/45; P ⌨) The only backpackers in town offers cheap weekly rates if you have seasonal work in the area. Housed in a renovated weatherboard cottage, it has a friendly atmosphere and clean communal areas. It also has bikes for hire (per day $15).

Romano's Hotel (☎ 6921 2013; cnr Fitzmaurice & Sturt Sts; s/d $35/50, d with bathroom $75) An airy old pub – ask for a room on the quieter 2nd floor.

Of the several caravan parks in the area, the **Wagga Wagga Beach Caravan Park** (☎ 6931 0603; 2 Johnston St; camp sites $15-20, cabins $55-95; ▨) has the best location. It's on the river next to a swimming beach and is only a couple of blocks from the town centre.

THE RIVERINA

MID-RANGE

Manor (☎ 6921 5962; 38 Morrow St; s/d with breakfast $70/90; **P**) A small, well-restored guesthouse in a perfect position opposite the Memorial Gardens, the Manor has gorgeous rooms furnished with antiques, as well as a fine restaurant.

There are many motels to choose from. There are several along Tarcutta St, which fronts the Murrumbidgee River and is close to the centre of town.

Centralpoint (☎ 6921 7272; 164-166 Tarcutta St; s/d $85/105) Describes itself as 'allergy-conscious' and has self-contained rooms.

Country Comfort (☎ 6921 6444; cnr Morgan & Tarcutta Sts; d from $120; **P** **⊡**) This sprawling place is in some pretty gardens.

Carlyle (☎ 6931 0968; www.thecarlyle.com.au; 148 Tarcutta St; r $117; **P** **⊠**) An elegant terrace with modern furnishings and particularly spacious suites.

Eating

Along Fitzmaurice and Baylis Sts there is a range of good places to eat.

Nabiha's Kitchen (☎ 6921 7813; Neslo Arcade, Baylis St; mains $5-10; ⏲ lunch & dinner Mon-Sat) A small Lebanese takeaway (with tables) where everything is cooked in front of you. The mostly vegetarian menu of simple, inexpensive dishes includes some Indian items, home-grown vegetables and free-range eggs. It's well worth checking out.

Scribbles (☎ 6921 8860; 22 Fitzmaurice St; mains $8-15; ⏲ breakfast & lunch daily, dinner Thu-Sat) Shabby but fun, with paper tablecloths for doodling and a pile of favourite boardgames for you (or your children).

Barefoot on Norman (☎ 6925 2644; 67 Coleman St; mains $8-15; ⏲ lunch daily, dinner Wed) This laid-back haunt serves inexpensive home-style food, and often has acoustic music on Wednesday nights.

Indian Tavern Tandoori (☎ 6921 3121; 176 Baylis St; dishes $8-17; ⏲ dinner) Locals who love a tasty vindaloo support this multi award eatery in D'Hudson arcade, perhaps the best regional Indian restaurant in NSW.

Magpies Nest Restaurant (☎ 6933 1523; cnr Old Narrandera & Pine Gully Rds; dishes $15-27; ⏲ lunch & dinner Wed-Sun) Housed in restored stone stables, with outside seating offering sweeping views of the town. The focus is on local produce; vegetables come straight from the garden! Meals are huge and often delightful, but the setting wins out.

Drinking

This is a university town of sorts, and the pubs can get really packed.

Tourist Hotel (☎ 6921 2264; 91 Fitzmaurice St) This is a rather grungy place, but it does have regular live music and a relaxed atmosphere.

Home Tavern Hotel (☎ 6921 3117; 142 Fitzmaurice St) This place is more of a pool hall with a pub, rather than the other way around. But it's a popular spot, and there are nightly competitions.

Crow Bar (☎ 6933 2040; Charles Sturt University) Has cheap drinks and a line-up of local bands; visitors are welcome – get a student to sign you in.

Duke of Kent (☎ 6921 3231; Fitzmaurice St) The Duke is popular with local agriculture students; rowdy but fun.

Entertainment

Wagga Wagga often has a number of arts events going on at any one time; they just aren't highly publicised.

Civic Theatre (☎ 6926 9680; ⏲ 10am-5.30pm Mon-Fri, to 12.30pm Sat) The Civic has a booking office, not only for its own productions but for much of the locally created entertainment, from youth theatre to performances by the Riverina Conservatorium.

Forum Cinemas (☎ 6921 6863; 77 Trail St) Six huge screens show both the latest blockbusters and arthouse flicks.

Getting There & Away

From Wagga, **Qantas** (☎ 13 13 13) flies daily to Sydney (one way from $160) and **Regional Express** (Rex; ☎ 13 17 13) flies daily to Melbourne (one way from $130).

CountryLink (☎ 13 22 42) buses leave from the train station (☎ 13 22 32, 6939 5488), where you can make bookings. Wagga is on the railway line between Sydney (6¼ hours) and Melbourne (4¼ hours); the one-way fare to both cities is $75 and there are daily services. **McCafferty's/Greyhound** (☎ 13 14 99) and **Fearnes** (☎ 6921 2316) run daily to Sydney ($48, seven hours) and Brisbane ($140, 18 hours).

Avis (☎ 6921 9977) car rentals is near the train station at the corner of Edward and Fitzharding Sts.

AROUND WAGGA WAGGA
Aurora Clydesdale Stud & Pioneer Farm

About 35km west of Wagga Wagga, on the Sturt Hwy, **Aurora Stud** (☎ 6928 2215; adult/child

$2.50; ◯ 9am-4pm, closed Thu & Sun) is a work-ing farm where you can see magnificent Clydesdales in action.

The Rock & Around

On the Olympic Way about 25km south-west of Wagga Wagga, The Rock is a small village near a large craggy hill rising out of the flat plain. The town was called Hanging Rock until the boulder balanced on top of the hill fell off late in the 19th century.

The hill is in **The Rock Nature Reserve**; there's a 3km walking trail to the summit, from which you can see Mount Kosciuszko and the Victorian Alps on a clear day. Near the top, the going is steep and you have to be careful of falling rocks.

Galore Scenic Reserve

Henry Osborne (owner of the first station in the region) walked from Wollongong to Adelaide in 1840 and on the way he climbed this sudden hill (it rises 215m from an almost flat plain), exclaiming at the top, 'There's land, and galore'. Now a scenic reserve, Galore Hill is worth a visit for its bush, the plantings near the base of the hill, and the 360-degree views from the platform at the top. You can't camp here.

MORGAN COUNTRY

The area known as Morgan Country is a rough circle of pretty country south of Wagga Wagga, west of Holbrook and north of Al-bury, containing some interesting little towns, including Henty, Culcairn and Jindera.

This was once the stamping-ground of Dan 'Mad Dog' Morgan, allegedly the most brutal and callous bushranger in Australia's history. Unlike Ned Kelly, Morgan was a bushranger no-one respected. He began his career in Victoria in the 1850s but was cap-tured and spent six years on a prison hulk in Port Phillip Bay. On receiving parole he esca-ped and moved into NSW, where for two years he terrorised this small area. Declared an outlaw, he fled to Victoria (where he was still wanted) in 1865, resolving to 'take the flashness out of the Victorian people and police'. With a £1000 bounty on his head he didn't get very far. At Peechelba station, just south of the Murray River, he was shot dead. His head was cut off and it's said that his scrotum became a tobacco pouch.

Galore Hill is 14km south of the Sturt Hwy – turn off about 60km west of Wagga Wagga. It's also accessible from **Lockhart**, a little town 65km southwest of Wagga, known for its beautiful, late-19th-century verandas – both sides of the main street, are lined with them.

Culcairn

☎ 02 / pop 1020

Culcairn was once a major overnight stop for people travelling by train between Syd-ney and Melbourne, and the town's main feature, the **Culcairn Hotel** (1891), reflects this status. It's a majestic hotel, the largest between the two cities until the 1930s, with a beer garden that deserves a more lavish name – there's even a fountain!

Across the tracks from the Culcairn Pub, the old stationmaster's residence has been lovingly restored as a **museum** (admission free; ◯ 10am-4pm Sat). There are several other historic buildings, with half the main street classified by the National Trust.

Morgan's Lookout is a low hill with a cluster of huge boulders on top. Allegedly this was Mad Dog's lookout where he watched for approaching victims and police (see boxed text, this page). You can climb up for great views, and there are gas barbecues. The lookout is about 18km southwest of Cul-cairn on the sealed road to Walla Walla.

Henty

☎ 02 / pop 860

Henty is 'Home of the Header' because, in 1913, local farmer Headlie Taylor invented the header harvester, which revolutionised grain harvesting around the world. There's a display commemorating this claim to fame in **Henty Memorial Park**.

Each year the **Henty Machinery Field Days** are held in the third week in September. If you're interested in farm equipment (or in the people who are), this is the place to come. About 50,000 people turn up for this event, perhaps the best of its type in Australia.

JUNEE

☎ 02 / pop 3590

Junee, once known as the 'Rail Centre of the South', is a small, friendly country town with a disproportionate number of impres-sive buildings. Get tourist information from the Junee **visitors centre** (☎ 6924 4200) in the station's Railway Refreshment Room.

THE RIVERINA

Sights & Activities

MONTE CRISTO

Built in 1884, the mansion of **Monte Cristo** (☎ 6924 1637; adult/child $7.50/3.80; ☼ 10am-4pm) was the home of Christopher Crawley, a shrewd landowner who predicted or, rather, manipulated, the railway's arrival (via his land) in Junee, and the subsequent boom in land prices.

Monte Cristo homestead has been faithfully decorated in high Victorian style, and it's full of superb antiques collected by the owners during their 30-year restoration of the property. It had nearly been destroyed by weather, and vandals who weren't deterred by the house's reputation for supernatural goings-on.

Entry includes an informative guided tour. You can get to Monte Cristo from John Potts Drive.

RAILWAY ROUNDHOUSE

The only surviving, working roundhouse in Australia, the **Junee Roundhouse** (☎ 6924 2909; Harold St; adult/child $5/2.50; ☼ 10am-4pm, closed Mon & Fri) was built in 1947. Back then, its 30m turntable was the largest in the southern hemisphere. Railway enthusiasts should visit the **Roundhouse Museum** in the same complex. As well as the large display about the history of rail in Australia, and an impressively large model-train set, there's also an interesting general transport display.

OLD BUILDINGS

If you like pubs, you'll lament the closing of many of Junee's watering holes. Some magnificent old pubs with massive verandas dripping with iron lace now stand empty.

The 1915 **Commercial Hotel** (cnr Lorne & Waratah Sts) still has a busy bar crowded with after-work drinkers. The **Loftus** (☎ 6924 1511; 6 Humphreys St) was the town's grandest hotel, with a frontage running for an entire block. It was sold in late 1999 for only $32,000!

Across the tracks, the **Junee Hotel** (☎ 6924 1124; Seignior St) was built by Christopher Crawley in 1876. The pub hasn't had a lot done to it over the years, but that means the original fittings are still intact.

LICORICE FACTORY

If you have a sweet tooth you will enjoy watching **Green Grove Organics** (☎ 6924 3574; 8-18 Lord St; adults $4; ☼ 8.30am-4pm Mon-Fri, 10am-4pm Sat & Sun) make licorice and chocolate in the old Junee Flour Mill (1935). Tours run three times a day.

Sleeping

There are motels, but this is a town where you should try a pub.

Loftus B&B (☎ 6924 1511; 6 Humphreys St; s/d $35/70) You can get lost in this 100-year-old pub in the centre of town, complete with sweeping staircases and an endless balcony. The owner and her young son will accommodate most needs, and the pub food is perhaps the best in town.

Junee Caravan Park (☎ 6924 2530; Broadway St; camp sites from $20) This small but pleasant caravan park is on the outskirts of town.

Getting There & Away

McCafferty's/Greyhound (☎ 13 14 99) buses go through Junee on the run between Melbourne and Brisbane ($170). **Junee Buses** (☎ 6924 2244), on Main St near the railway level crossing, runs weekday services to Wagga Wagga (one way $7).

Junee is on the main Sydney–Melbourne rail line.

COOTAMUNDRA

☎ 02 / pop 5490

Cootamundra, founded around 1860, is a prosperous service centre for surrounding farmland and an important railway junction. Most well known for being the birthplace of cricket great Don Bradman, the town's neat grid of streets contains many fine examples of Federation-style houses and a few earlier Victorian gems. Cootamundra is in the foothills of the Great Dividing Range.

Orientation & Information

Parker St is the main shopping street, and its intersection with Wallendoon St, where you'll find the impressive post office, town hall and several banks, is the centre of town. At the train station on Hovell St there's a **visitors centre** (☎ 6942 4212; ☼ 10am-4pm).

Sights & Activities

Donald Bradman, Australia's greatest cricketer, was born here in 1908. His birthplace, an old weatherboard hospital, is now a **museum** (☎ 6942 2744; 89 Adams St; adult $2; ☼ 9am-5pm). The Bradmans moved to Bowral when

THE RIVERINA

the Don was still very young, and it's there he learned his craft (see p119).

Cootamundra's climate means that European trees flourish (the elms along Cooper St are over 100 years old) and there are several formal parks. **Albert Park** (Hovell St) is near the train station and **Jubilee Park**, on the other side of the city centre, features the **Captains' Walk**, a series of busts of Australia's cricket captains.

Cootamundra is also known for the **Cootamundra wattle** (*Acacia baileyana*); its profuse yellow flowers bloom in July and August each year. Although native to this area, Cootamundra wattle has been planted throughout the cooler areas of southern Australia. The **Wattle Time Festival** is held in August.

Sleeping & Eating

Cootamundra Hotel (☎ 6942 1290; 96 Parker St; s/d $35/45) One of two large, old pubs that offer accommodation, this place is pretty basic and it can get pretty loud on weekends.

White Ibis B&B (☎ 6942 1850; whiteibis@yol.net.au; 21 Wallendoon St; s/d $50/80) The Ibis has been restored to a boutique hotel.

Cootamundra Caravan Park (☎ 6942 1080; camp sites from $15, cabins from $50) In pretty Jubilee Park, this sits beside Muttama Creek.

There are also several motels in Cootamundra.

Platypus Cottage (☎ 6942 6780; 132 Parker St; mains $6-12) does a busy lunch-time trade in chunky melts and fresh wraps. Some of the town's pubs also have good food, notably **Matilda's on Parker** (☎ 6942 1446; 1 Parker St; mains $8-15) at the Globe Hotel.

Getting There & Away

There's a **Countrylink Travel Centre** (☎ 6940 1246) at the train station. Fast trains (XPTs) running between Sydney and Melbourne stop here twice daily.

NARRANDERA

☎ 02 / pop 4120

On the banks of Lake Talbot and the Murrumbidgee River, Narrandera is known for its beautiful green avenues and parks. With good services and accommodation, it makes a pleasant stopover for a day or two.

Orientation & Information

The Newell Hwy runs through town as Cadell St; the Sturt Hwy passes just south of the town. East St is the commercial centre. The helpful **visitors centre** (☎ 1800 672 392; Narrandera St; ☺ 9am-5pm Mon-Fri, 10am-4pm Sat & Sun) is in Cadell St. Here you'll find 'the largest playable guitar in the southern hemisphere' – although you need two people to play, and you wouldn't get much of a tune out of it.

Sights & Activities

In the best tradition of small-town museums, the **Parkside Cottage Museum** (☎ 6959 1372; Twynam St; adult/child $2/50c; ☺ 2-5pm Mon & Tue, 11am-5pm Wed & Sun) has an extremely eclectic collection, from '1000 years of monarchy' to skis from Scott's Antarctic expedition.

Lake Talbot Complex (☎ 6959 1211; Lake Drive; adult/child $2.50/1.50; ☺ 6-8am, 10am-1pm, 4-6pm Mon-Fri, 10am-7pm Sat & Sun) is a beautiful but faded water-sports reserve, partly a long artificial lake and partly a swimming centre with an exhilarating 100m water slide.

Bush (including a koala regeneration area) surrounds the lake and a number of trails make up the **Bundidgerry Walking Track**. The visitors centre has a map and brochure.

The **John Lake Centre** (☎ 6959 9021; Buckingbong Rd; adult/child $5.50/2.75; ☺ 8.30am-4pm), at the Narrandera Fisheries, breeds endangered fish species of the Murray Darling river system. There are guided tours at 10.30am (look out for a huge Murray cod named Agro).

Festivals & Events

In early January, **water-skiing championships** take place on Lake Talbot. March sees the **John O'Brian Bush Festival**, which celebrates the bush poetry of Father Hartigan ('We'll all be rooned said Hanrahan, in accent most forlorn'). In October there's the **Tree-mendous Celebration** (centred on Narrandera's trees but including a home-brewing competition).

Sleeping

Murrumbidgee (☎ 6959 2011; cnr East & Audley Sts; s/d $25/35) This nice old place has big, clean rooms and friendly service.

Old Edgerton Country B&B (☎ 6959 3644; 48 Victoria Ave; d $95-150) A handsome home with charming hosts, this B&B is the perfect place if you're exploring the area or trying to relax after a lengthy drive; a long soak in the claw-foot tub might just hit the spot.

THE RIVERINA

Historic Star Lodge (☎ 6959 1768, 64 Whitton St; www.historicstarlodge.com.au; r with/without bathroom $115/95) This impressive old hotel, complete with verandas and iron lace, is now a beautiful, if old-fashioned, B&B.

Narrandera Club Motor Inn (☎ 6959 3123; fax 6959 3169; Bolton St; s/d $85/90; 🖳) Narrandera has many motels along the Newell Hwy, but this one is in a location that's both central and quiet.

Lake Talbot Caravan Park (☎ 6959 1302; fax 6959 1949; camp sites $15-20, cabins with bathroom $45-70) In a picturesque setting on a hill overlooking Lake Talbot, with dense red-gum forest stretching to the horizon.

Eating

Classique Café Restaurant (☎ 6959 1411; 124 East St; mains $8-18; 🕑 9am-5.30pm Mon-Fri, to 4.30pm Sat, dinner Fri & Sat) A pleasant place for an alfresco coffee during the day, the Classique Café goes upmarket for weekend dinners with standard modern Australian fare.

Franks Bellissimo Pizza & Pasta (☎ 6959 3010; 131 East St; dishes $6-15; 🕑 dinner) A friendly family restaurant that the locals unashamedly recommend for the cheap but tasty Italian dishes.

Narrandera Bakery (☎ 6959 3677; cnr East & Bolton Sts; dishes $3-6; 🕑 7.30am-5.45pm Mon-Fri, to 2.30pm Sat & Sun) Serves sandwiches and fresh baked pies, and judging by the queues they taste as good as they smell.

Star Lodge Restaurant (☎ 6959 1768; 64 Whitton St; mains $15-25; 🕑 dinner Tue-Sat) One-time award-winning place features regional food and an extensive wine list, but there's been mixed reports of late.

Murrumbidgee Hotel (☎ 6959 2011; cnr East & Audley Sts; dishes $4.50-10; 🕑 lunch & dinner Tue-Sun) The best pub meals in town can be eaten in an agreeable beer garden or scoffed at the bar. Either way, it's hard to go past the two-course roast on Sundays ($8.50).

Getting There & Away

McCafferty's/Greyhound (☎ 13 14 99) goes to Sydney ($55, 10 hours) and Adelaide ($124, 12 hours), stopping at the Mobil roadhouse on the Stuart Hwy.

LEETON

☎ 02 / pop 6930

As the headquarters of the Murray Irrigation Scheme (MIA), Leeton is at the centre of one of the largest fruit- and vegetable-growing regions in Australia.

Leeton was founded as a MIA town in 1913; there was no settlement here before the water came. The first of the Walter Burley Griffin–designed towns, it remains close to the architect's original vision, and is developing into a thriving commercial centre.

Orientation & Information

Most streets are named after trees or local products; the main street is Pine Ave, named after the Murray pine, a native species.

The **visitors centre** (☎ 6953 6481; 8-10 Yanco Ave; 🕑 9am-5pm Mon-Fri, 9.30am-12.30pm Sat & Sun) formerly housed the manager of the MIA. It has several walking-tour maps.

There's Internet access at **Leeton Internet Café** (☎ 6953 6636; 32 Kurrajong Ave; per hr $6).

Sights & Activities

Rice-growing began near Leeton in 1924, and today the Riverina exports 85% of its 1.2 million-tonne crop each year – learn all about it at the **SunRice Centre** (☎ 6953 0596; Calrose St; admission free; 🕑 9am-5pm), which has presentations at 9.30am and 2.45pm, weekdays.

Lillypilly Estate (☎ 6953 4069; 🕑 tours 4pm Sat & Sun) and **Toorak Wines** (☎ 6953 2333; 🕑 tours 11.30am Sat & Sun) are two wineries near Leeton, open Monday to Saturday for tastings, and on weekdays for tours.

Leeton has several Art Deco gems, including the majestic **Roxy cinema** (1930), which still operates in all its neon glory on Friday and Saturday nights. The visitors centre has a map outlining other buildings of note.

Sleeping & Eating

Historic Hydro Motor Inn (☎ 6953 2355; Chelmsford Pl; s/d $60/80) The well-positioned Hydro is a huge old home with a National Trust listing. Despite its restoration, it's somewhat faded. There are daily tours.

Madalock Country B&B (☎ 6953 3784; 81 Kurrajong Ave; r with/without spa $89/110) A sweet guesthouse on the main street.

Oasis Holiday Park (☎ 6953 3882; fax 6953 6256; Corbie Hill Rd; camp sites $13-15, cabins $45-55; 🕑 6.30am-5.30pm Mon-Fri, 7am-1pm Sat & Sun) In a quiet bush setting.

Mick's Bakehouse (☎ 6953 2212; 56 Pine Ave; mains $3-9) Has excellent pies (including hard to get vegie varieties).

Pages on Pine (☎ 6953 7300; 119 Pine Ave; mains $10-20) The ubiquitous Mod Oz dining experience in Leeton; but $25 buys you a three-course meal on weekends, perfect before a night at the flicks across the road.

Also recommended:

Benvenuti (☎ 6953 7744; 18A Pine Ave) A very popular Italian joint.

Chan's Hong Kong (☎ 6953 4111; 81 Pine Ave; mains $6-14) Serves decent Chinese food.

Leeton Soldiers' Club (☎ 6953 3444; Acacia Ave; mains $6-15; ☼ noon-2pm & 6-9pm) Recommended by locals.

Getting There & Away

Countrylink buses (☎ 13 22 42, 13 22 32) stop daily at the visitors centre on the runs between Griffith ($8, one hour) and Cootamundra or Wagga Wagga ($14, one hour 55 minutes), and connect with the trains in those towns.

GRIFFITH
☎ 02 / pop 16,000

Griffith is small but sophisticated; its cultural mix of Europeans, Indians and South Pacific Islanders gives it a cosmopolitan

---

FORZA ITALIA!

Griffith used to make headlines for its alleged links to the Mafia, the murder of an anti-drugs crusader and police corruption. But today the emphasis is more on tasty produce, and the large Italian community is working hard to free itself of a quarter of a century of unwanted and, generally speaking, undeserved infamy.

Italians have been in Griffith since the early days of the Murrumbidgee Irrigation Scheme; having tried their luck at mining in Broken Hill (p254), three pioneering Italians, Enrico Lucca, Luigi Gulielmini and Francesco Bicego took up farming in 1913. The outbreak of war a year later started an exodus of Italian miners from the Silver City, as well as from the Burrinjuck Dam construction camps. Originally from the Veneti region around Verona, the miners lived in shacks, working from daylight till dark trying to repay the cost of their fare (and that of their wives) for the trip from Italy.

Valentino Ceccata was one of these irrigation pioneers. He slowly started a modest building business and got occasional contract work through the MIA Commission. When the Italian consulate in Sydney heard about this, it got so excited by his success that it directed all new immigrants to Valentino's home. Within a few months he had over 40 people camped on his property. Knowing the difficulties of arriving in a strange country with no language and no contacts, Valentino rotated his six staff every week to give everyone a chance at earning some pay. Eventually the stream of arrivals became too much to cope with, and Valentino had to travel to Sydney to inform the consul.

It was a difficult time for these men and their families: during the depression prices collapsed and fruit was left to rot.

An Italian farmer who lived in a tent couldn't sell his Griffith grapes, so he decided to make some wine for his friends. Eighty years later his grandson, Darren de Bortoli, is the managing director of a company that makes half a million cases of wine a year.

Others were not so lucky. Valerio Recitti, who arrived in Australia in 1916, had a serious run of bad luck. Passing through Griffith in the 1920s, he sought refuge in a local cave and decided to stay. Valerio believed he was the only Italian in the area and kept entirely to himself, creating a private utopia of massive stone galleries, cliff-side gardens and floral painted walls. After falling and injuring himself he was discovered and later interned at Hay during WWII on suspicion of being a spy.

While Australian-born farmers and inexperienced soldier settlers went broke and left for the cities, this was not an option for the Italians whose extended families and support networks were confined to the area. It was at this time that they pooled their resources and bought out farmers at bedrock prices. In 1929 Italians held 67 small lots; by 2003 they had bought up almost all the irrigated farms. Many of the people who own the farms today came to Griffith from Calabria, in southern Italy, after WWII. In the last 30 years, 'tribal' distinctions between the Veneto and Calabrese communities have become less distinct, and all Italians join together to support the Azzuri.

THE RIVERINA

atmosphere. Quite clearly the wine-and-food capital of the Riverina, Griffith's vineyards, Cafés and restaurants offer a variety and quality unmatched in the region, and recognised nationally.

Information

The **visitors centre** (☎ 6962 4145; www.griffith.nsw .gov.au; cnr Banna Ave & Jondaryan St; ☯ 9am-5pm) has a life-size WWII Fairey Firefly plane outside. The **NPWS office** (☎ 6966 8100; www .npws.nsw.gov.au; 200 Yambil St; ☯ 8.30am-4.30pm Mon-Fri) has information on Cocoparra, Willandra and Oolambeyan National Parks. The library offers Internet access ($3 for 30 minutes).

With the lowest unemployment rate in Australia, it's hard *not* to get a job in Griffith; there is seasonal work harvesting grapes, which usually begins in February and lasts six to eight weeks. A multitude of other crops such as oranges, melons and onions are harvested during the year. The **Griffith Employment National Office** (☎ 13 34 44; 108b Yambil St) can help you find harvest work.

Fewer than half the vineyards and almost none of the other properties have accommodation, or even space to camp, so you'll probably have to stay in Griffith, which means that you'll need your own transport.

Sights & Activities

High on a hill north of the town centre, **Pioneer Park Museum** (☎ 6962 4196; cnr Remembrance & Scenic Drs; adult/child $7/3; ☯ 9am-4.30pm) is a re-creation of an early Riverina village. There are about 40 displays, and many of the old buildings are original. Ask about the Italian museum under construction.

Not far from Pioneer Park is the **Rotary Lookout**, with great views of the town and the surrounding farmland. Also up here on Scenic Hill are three **walking tracks**: Trates Loop (2km), Barinji Loop (5km) and Narinari Loop (6.5km). About 1.5km east of Pioneer Park is **Sir Dudley de Chair's Lookout**. Just below is the **hermit's cave**, home of an Italian recluse for many years (see boxed text, p271).

With the high quality of produce in the area, a stop at **Riverina Grove** (☎ 6962 7988; www .riverinagrove.com.au; 4 Whybrow St; ☯ 8am-5pm Mon-Fri, 9am-noon Sat) is a real indulgence. This mecca of gourmet food allows you to sample everything from marinated fetta to rich nougat; and you won't leave empty handed.

Though small, the Art Deco **Griffith Regional Art Gallery** (☎ 6962 5991; 167-185 Banna Ave; adult/child $2/1; ☯ 10.30am-4.30pm Tue-Sat) has a lovely sense of space. Exhibitions change monthly and there's also a permanent collection of contemporary Australian jewellery.

The **Griffith Regional Theatre** (☎ 6962 7466; Neville Pl; admission free; ☯ 9am-5pm Mon-Fri), has a massive, community-produced soft-sculpture curtain depicting the region and its activities. You can see it at 11am, 2.30pm and 4pm on weekdays provided there are no productions under way. The theatre is also home to the interesting **Griffith Photographic Collection**, dating back to the foundation of the city.

WINERIES

The Griffith area has a large number of wineries that can be visited. **McWilliams** (☎ 6963 0001; Jack McWilliam Rd, Hanwood; ☯ tastings 9am-5pm Mon-Sat) is the oldest (1913), but among the best in terms of quality and range are **Westend Estate** (☎ 6964 1506; Brayne Rd; ☯ 8am-5pm Mon-Fri, 10am-4pm Sat & Sun), started in 1945, which has a range of reds of high quality, and **Riverina Estate** (☎ 6963 8300; 700 Kidman Way, ☯ tastings 9am-5pm Mon-Fri; 10am-4pm Sat). Check out www.griffith.nsw.gov.au /GriffithVisitorsCentreTheCellarDoor.htm for a map of Griffith's wineries, as well as opening times.

Festivals & Events

Held on Easter Saturday, **La Festa** is a big occasion, when the wineries come to town and food stalls cover the streets.

Sleeping

If you are doing seasonal work in Griffith, there are two options for cheap longer-term accommodation, but they fill up quickly.

Pioneer Park (☎ 6962 4196; Remembrance Dr; d $15) Dorms are in former shearers' quarters. While the rooms are small and basic (this is a historic building), there's a good communal kitchen and lounge. Unfortunately it's a steep walk from town and there's no public transport.

Griffith International Hostel (☎ 6964 4236; 112 Binya St; d $19; ▯) On a pleasant street near the town centre, this Griffith Hostel is a little rough around the edges.

Victoria Hotel (☎ 6962 1299; 384 Banna Ave; s/d includes breakfast $75/90; ▣ ▨ ▯) The Victoria

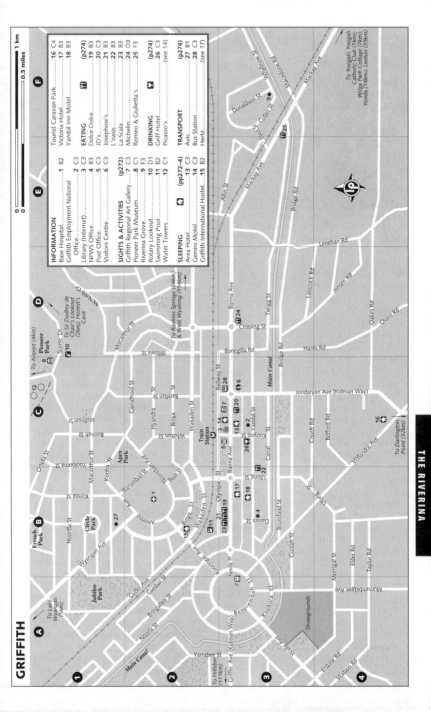

GRIFFITH

has recently renovated rooms and friendly staff, but it's also a pub and the noise can be a problem on Saturday nights.

There are many motels in Griffith.

Gemini Motel (☎ 6962 3833; 201-227 Banna Ave; s/d $80-120/$80-130; P 🔀) A comfortable place in the perfect location, right in the middle of a main street, with a popular cocktail bar.

Yambil Inn Motel (☎ 6964 1233; 155 Yambil St; s/d $85/100; 🖳 P 🔀) This place has a pretty tropical-garden feel with a good pool to relax by on hot Riverina days.

Wilga Park Cottage (☎ 6968 1661; 6 Condon Rd, Bilbul; s/d with breakfast $110/135) There are no B&Bs in the centre of Griffith, but if you want an alternative to an impersonal motel, this stylish cottage is only 10km away, in the middle of lush farmland.

There are several caravan parks. The most convenient for the town centre is the small **Tourist Caravan Park** (☎ 6962 4537; 919 Willandra Ave; camp sites $18, cabins $50-55; 🖳).

Eating

The quality of the food in Griffith, in particular the Italian cuisine, is outstanding; it's hard not to spend the whole day eating!

La Scala (☎ 6962 4322; 455b Banna Ave; dishes $10-25; 🕑 dinner Tue-Sat) Hidden down some sloping steps, this place run by the Vico family is perhaps the best of the Italian restaurants. The menu includes a good range of traditional dishes and there's an extensive wine list.

Dolce Dolce (☎ 6962 1888; 449 Banna Ave; mains $3-10; 🕑 Wed-Sun) Come here for fine Italian torte and pastries; a morning break of coffee and *millefoglie* (Italian custard sponge with liqueur) is nothing short of bliss.

Josephine's (☎ 6962 9977; 453 Banna Ave; dishes $8-20; 🕑 breakfast & lunch daily; dinner Thu-Sun) A few doors up, this place serves true southern Italian fare, with delights such as *penne arrabiata* (pasta with tomato, chilli and garlic).

JD's (☎ 6962 7777; Banna Ave; 🕑) You can't go past this joint for its homemade pasta lunch ($6).

Romeo & Giulietta's (☎ 6962 7728; 40 Mackay Ave; dishes $12-25; 🕑 dinner Thu-Sun) Try this place for traditional wood-oven pizzas.

Michelin (☎ 6964 9006; 72 Banna Ave; dishes $20-26; 🕑 lunch daily, dinner Mon-Sat, brunch Sun) If you've done your dash on the pizza/pasta front, the elegant dining room of the lauded Michelin provides regional produce with a distinct French flair. Despite being so far inland, the dishes are full of fresh seafood, and there is an additional 'Riverina' menu featuring local produce.

L'Oasis (☎ 6964 5588; 150 Yambil St; dishes $15-25; 🕑 lunch Mon-Sat, dinner Tue-Sat) Here is a modern brasserie producing light Asian flavours; a huge bowl of *tom yum* soup goes down well with a selection from the proudly local wine list.

Drinking

Yoogali Catholic Club (Leeton Rd) The biggest night out in Griffith is Dusk til Dawn, held here on a Saturday night each month.

Victoria Hotel (384 Banna Ave) If you miss out on Dusk til Dawn, console yourself at this popular watering hole.

Picasso's (201-227 Banna Ave) At the Gemini Motel (this page), Picasso's has an extensive cocktail list and a relaxed atmosphere.

Griff nightclub (☎ 6962 4325; cnr Kooyoo & Yambil Sts) At the Griff Hotel, this can be rowdy. It often has local bands and is open late.

Getting There & Away

Regional Express (☎ 13 1713) flies between Griffith and Sydney (one way $180).

All buses, except Countrylink (which stops at the train station), stop at the **Griffith Travel & Transit Centre** (121 Banna Ave; ☎ 6962 7199) in the Mobil petrol station. You can book McCafferty's/Greyhound, V/Line and Countrylink tickets here, with connections to regional coach lines. Typical prices are $70 to Sydney, $95 to Melbourne, $135 to Adelaide, $55 to Canberra, and $40 to Wagga Wagga. All services run daily.

Getting Around

Griffith has a **taxi service** (☎ 6964 1444).

Car-rental companies include:

Avis (☎ 6962 6266; 7 Wyangan Ave)

Hertz (☎ 6964 1233; Yambil St) At the Yambil Inn Motel.

Thrifty (☎ 6962 9122; 2 Griffin Ave) Also at the airport.

LAKE CARGELLIGO

☎ 02 / pop 1300

On the flat western plains north of Griffith, **Lake Cargelligo** (the town is known locally as 'the Lake') is an unexpected oasis.

The 8km lake is home to numerous species of birds, including pelicans, swans and black cockatoos, and is popular for **water sports**.

Lake View Caravan Park (☎ 6898 1077; Naradhan & Womboyn Sts; camp sites $11-15, cabins $44; ⚌) is right by the lake, and has a large BBQ area.

There are a couple of motels:

Lake Cargelligo (☎ 6898 1303; Canada St)

Lachlan Way (☎ 6898 1201; Foster St)

WILLANDRA NATIONAL PARK

Like Mungo National Park (p259), **Willandra** is part of a huge sheep station on a system of dry lakes. The lakes here, especially **Hall's Lake**, tend to become temporary wetlands more often than Mungo's ancient basins, and **birdlife** is abundant. During spring there are magnificent displays of **wild flowers**, and **emus** and **kangaroos** can be found on the open plains throughout the year.

The historical interest of Willandra centres on the wool industry and station life, although there were certainly Aboriginal civilisations in the area, probably of the same antiquity as those at Lake Mungo. In 1869 some enterprising Melbourne grocers formed the sheep station **Big Willandra** – the national park (about 19,400 hectares), formed in 1972, is less than 10% of Big Willandra.

One of the highlights of visiting the park is staying in the newly restored **Willandra Homestead** (r $60). Built in 1918 (the third to be built on the increasingly busy station) to a U-shaped plan traditional for the Riverina, it has sweeping verandas and established rose gardens. The homestead was the centre of station life.

The custom on sheep stations was that the distance of accommodation from the homestead indicated the status of the workers; furthest away is the tin-lined shearers' quarters (take time to explore the graffiti in each room) – much less comfortable in the heat, one would imagine, than the thatched ram shed, where the kings of the station (ie the rams who made all the money) lived.

There are walking tracks in the park, none of them very long, and the **Merton Motor Trail**, which takes you on a loop around the eastern half of the park.

Sleeping

There's accommodation available in the old station's **men's quarters** (r $25) which has six bedrooms containing two double bunks per room, or in a **cottage** (up to 4 adults $40, per extra person $10) which sleeps eight. Book through **Griffith NPWS** (☎ 6962 7755).

Other than staying at the Willandra Homestead, you can **camp** (adult/child $3/2) at sites near the homestead or, with permission, anywhere else in the park.

Getting There & Away

Main access to the park, around 40km west of Hillston, is via the Hillston–Mossgiel road. It takes very little rain to close roads here; phone the **park manager** (☎ 6967 8159) or the **NPWS office** (☎ 6962 7755) in Griffith to check conditions. Note that there's a $6 per day vehicle fee.

HAY

☎ 02 / pop 2700

In flat, treeless country, Hay is a substantial town, and its position at the junction of the Sturt and Cobb Hwys makes it an important transit point.

It's very much a rural service centre and on Saturday morning the main street is full of utes (utility vans). Station hands from the big merino properties in the area make good use of the half-dozen pubs on weekends.

The **Tourist & Amenities Centre** (☎ 6993 4045; www.visithay.com.au; 407 Moppett St; ⏱ 9am-5pm Mon-Fri, to noon Sat & Sun) has clean showers and a screened picnic area; both are free and open 24 hours.

There is Internet access at the **Hay Telecentre** (⏱ 8.30am-5pm Mon-Fri) at the old railway station.

Sights & Activities

Shearers enjoy legendary status in this part of Australia, and the innovative **Shear Outback** (☎ 6993 4000; cnr Sturt & Cobb Hwys; adult/child $15/8; ⏱ 9am-5pm) is devoted to these colourful characters. If you've ever felt the draw of a bushman's life, Shear Outback's interactive displays will give you all the incentive you need.

Hay housed three internment camps during WWII, and the **Hay POW & Internment Camp Interpretive Centre** (☎ 6993 2112; Murray St; adult $2; ⏱ 9am-5pm Mon-Fri) at the old railway station gives an insight into that time, telling the stories of the 'Dunera boys', and Japanese and Italian detainees.

There are several impressive old buildings in town, including **Bishop's Lodge** (☎ 6993 1727; Roset St; adult $4; ⏱ 2-4.30pm Mon-Sat Apr-Dec, 10am-12.30pm Jan-Mar), a mansion built entirely of corrugated iron as a residence for the

THE RIVERINA

DETOUR: TABBITA

If you want to see salt-plains country at its best, and you're travelling from Griffith, get off the highway, at least for a few kilometres! If you're heading to Hay follow Griffin Ave out of town on to the Tabbita Rd. **Tabbita** is a huge, productive property, and this drive takes you straight through the feed lot (where they fatten up the cows with special grain before exporting them to Japan). Not only is this a picturesque road, but the constant action in the fields gives you an idea of the seasonal rhythms of this massive pastoral area. At Goolgowi turn left on to the Mid-Western Highway that takes you to Hay.

Anglican bishop in 1888. From the highway it doesn't look especially inviting, but the building faces the other way, towards the river, and there's an acclaimed heritage rose garden at the front.

From an insane asylum to a maternity hospital, the **Old Hay Gaol** (Church St; adult/child $2/1; 🕑 9am-5pm) has had many uses. Now a museum, the old cells are filled with a fairly random collection of the district's memorabilia and detritus. It's like a good junk shop. One cell is set up as it was when the gaol was a detention centre for wayward girls, its last incarnation before it closed in 1973.

Festivals & Events
On Australia Day (26 January), Hay holds a fun **Surf Carnival** at Sandy Point beach on the Murrumbidgee River (a good place for a swim at any time).

Sleeping & Eating
Bank B&B (☎ 6993 1730; www.users.tpg.com.au/users /tssk; 86 Lachlan St; s/d $70/90; 🔀) On the main street, this is a charming place in a building with heaps of character.

Nicholas Royal (☎ 6993 1603; 152 Lachlan St; s/d $75-$100; P 🔀) There are other motels nearby, but the Nicholas has a central location, and there isn't any highway noise.

Blue Bush (☎ 6993 4099; powered camp sites $25) Of the several caravan parks, this one, situated on a small farm 11km east of Hay, off the Sturt Hwy, is the nicest. You can camp right on the Murrumbidgee and there is a sandy beach for swimming.

For snacks and meals:
Wok in Hay (☎ 6993 2031; 101 Lachlan St) Serves decent Thai food, a change from small-town Chinese.

Cumquats (☎ 6993 4399; 161 Lachlan St) Here you can have nice coffee among buckets of fresh flowers.

Riverina Hotel (☎ 6993 1137; 148 Lachlan St) The best pub meals in town.

Getting There & Away
Long-distance buses stop at the Caltex petrol station on the Sturt Hwy. **McCafferty's/ Greyhound** (☎ 13 14 99) buses come through on the run between Adelaide ($135) and Brisbane or Sydney ($100).

Countrylink's (☎ 132242) Balranald to Cootamundra buses also stop here.

THE SOUTHERN RIVERINA

Albury, the largest town on the Murray River, is covered on p303.

COROWA
☎ 02/ pop 5220
This historic river town's claim to fame is its reputation as the 'Birthplace of Federation'. The proclamation of the Colony of Victoria in 1850 and the ensuing customs hassles across the Murray River caused many people in the area to push for federation of the colonies. In 1893 a conference was held in Corowa that began the process of Federation, achieved in 1901. There had been previous conferences, but Corowa's was the first to capture the attention of the public.

Another lasting product from Corowa is the Tom Roberts painting *Shearing the Rams*, which was researched in the woolshed of Brocklesby station.

Orientation & Information
The main street, where you'll find most of the pubs and shops, is Sanger St. It leads down to the Foord Bridge across the Murray River to Wahgunyah. Federation Ave is a leafy street cutting through town to the Mulwala road. The **visitors centre** (☎ 6033 3221; 88 Sangar St; 🕑 10am-5pm Mon-Sat, 10am-1pm Sun) hires bikes ($10 per day).

Sights & Activities

The **Federation Museum** (☎ 6033 1568; Queen St; adult/child $2/50c; ☯ 2-5pm Sat & Sun), opposite the neat Ellerslie Gardens, is worth a look for the display on the history of Federation and to see some of Tommy McCrae's sketches. McCrae was a member of the Bangerang people who lived in the area at the time of first contact with Europeans. The sketches are among the few records of an indigenous people's reaction to European arrival.

The **Star Hotel** (Sanger St) has veritable catacombs in its old cellars which are filled with memorabilia from the town; ask here at the pub for access.

You can catch your own yabbies and cook them at the **Murray Bank Yabby Farm** (☎ 6033 2922; 76 Federation Ave; family $15; ☯ 11am-4pm Nov-Apr).

There are about a dozen **wineries** open for tasting in Victoria's Rutherglen region about 10km away.

Festivals & Events

The premier event on the Victorian wine-buff's calendar is the **Rutherglen Winery Walkabout** in June, and Corowa is a good place to base yourself for the festivities.

Sleeping & Eating

Easdown House (☎ 6033 4077; easedown@dragnet .com.au; 1 Sanger St; r $145, meals $15-25) A luxurious B&B in the town centre, Easdown's two rooms are stunningly decorated, and share a veranda which wraps around the heritage-listed building. It also has a fine restaurant (open whenever there are bookings), specialising in local produce including yabbies and silver perch.

There are lots of motels and the cluster on Federation Avenue is in hot competition; singles and doubles cost about $60 and $80 respectively, with prices rising in summer and around holidays.

There are several caravan parks in the area, including the riverside **Rivergum Top Tourist Park** (☎ 6033 1990; 38 Honour Ave; camp sites $16-25, cabins with bathroom $50-80; ☒).

To dine in Corowa:

Royal Hotel (☎ 6033 1295; 95 Sanger St) Newly renovated, with the best pub meals in town

D'Amico's (☎ 6033 0666; 235 Sanger St) Does decent Italian dishes.

See also the review of Easdown House's restaurant above.

Getting There & Around

Countrylink (☎ 13 22 42) buses stop here daily on the run between Albury and Echuca (Victoria), via Cobram (Victoria), Tocumwal, and Deniliquin ($5.50, 48 minutes).

Taxis (☎ 6033 1634) are available 24 hours.

TOCUMWAL

☎ 03 / pop 1530

With its mild winters, long summers and lovely river beaches Tocumwal is an attractive holiday town well worth a stop. The **visitors centre** (☎ 1800 677 271; Deniliquin St; ☯ 9am-5pm) can book accommodation for you.

A huge statue of a **Murray cod** stands in the centre of town; in the bar of Tattersalls Hotel across the road you'll see some stuffed Murray cod almost as big. There are **riverboat cruises** (☎ 5872 2132; Thompsons Beach, Cobram; adult/child with afternoon tea $20/10) on the *Matilda*, which run at 1.30pm every Wednesday and Saturday, daily during summer; book at the tourist office.

The **Railway Store** (cnr Newell Hwy & Deniliquin Rd) has an impressive miniature train display, complete with special effects.

Tocumwal is a centre for **gliding** and you can also get your ultralight pilot's licence here. The **Sportavia Soaring Centre** (☎ 5874 2063) at the aerodrome (a very large airbase during WWII) has package deals including flights, tuition and accommodation. For $88 you can try a glider flight.

Tocumwal is a haven for golfers during winter (summers are scorchers!) with its 36-hole championship **golf course** (☎ 5874 2179).

Sleeping & Eating

Tocumwal Motel (☎ 5874 3022; 11 Murray St; s/d with breakfast $65/80; ☒) Centrally located, with a very friendly owner.

There are several nice B&Bs in the area; the tourist office (in the visitors centre) can give you a list.

There are several basic camp sites, such as Mulberry and Pebbly beaches, by the river, but most are across the river from town and quite a distance away on winding tracks.

Bushlands on the Murray (☎ 5874 2752; Lot 4 Barooga Rd; camp sites per person $7-9, units $50-70; ☒ ☒) About 3km east of town, this is a good place to laze around, being only minutes from the beach. For the more active there is fishing, horse riding and a bus that turns into a boat.

THE RIVERINA

Lime Spider (☎ 5874 3166; Foreshore Reserve; ☉ 9.30am-5.30pm, to 10pm or 11pm summer) Perfect for a delicious breakfast or a post-swim ice-cream. the Spider also makes a wide range of gourmet snacks, and excellent coffee.

Tocumwal Pizza & Pasta (☎ 5874 2651; 2 Deniliquin Rd; meals $6-14; ☉ 5pm-midnight Wed-Sun) Popular with locals and closes late.

Getting There & Away

Countrylink (☎ 13 22 42) buses pass through Tocumwal three times weekly on the Echuca–Albury service.

DENILIQUIN

☎ 03 / pop 7790

Deniliquin is a busy town, big enough to offer most services but small enough to retain an easygoing rural feel.

History

Before whites arrived, the Deniliquin area was the most densely populated part of Australia. The flood plains and their networks of creeks and billabongs provided plenty of food, although stone for tools was hard to come by in this vast expanse of rich soil.

The enterprising Ben Boyd found the river in 1842 and established a station and a pub called Deniliquin, after a local Aboriginal wrestler who was respected for his size and strength. Boyd's shaky empire fell apart soon after, but the town kept growing, and by 1849 it was officially recognised. It prospered because it was at the end of major droving routes leading down from Queensland. Later, it became a wool and sheep centre.

Orientation & Information

Deniliquin is on a bend in the Edward River. Although the town covers a wide area, its centre, the blocks around Napier and Cressy Sts, is compact.

The **visitors centre** (☎ 1800 650 712; George St; ☉ 9am-4pm) is part of the Peppin Heritage Centre.

Sights & Activities

The **Island Sanctuary**, on the riverbank in town, has a pleasant walking track among the river redgums. It's home to plenty of wildlife including kangaroos, possums and birds.

The attractive **Peppin Heritage Centre** (☎ 1800 650 712, 03 5881 4150; George St; admission free; ☉ 9am-4pm) is devoted to the wool industry. Photos of the winning 'Riverina Rams of the Year' (and their owners) are as interesting as the historical displays.

The Graeco-Roman style **courthouse** (Poictiers St) is an extremely imposing building constructed in 1883.

For swimming, try **McLean Beach**, said to be the finest riverside beach in Australia. There are picnic facilities and a walking track.

Festivals & Events

Deniliquin holds an annual **Ute Muster**, when bush boys – and some girls – get together for an action-packed weekend in their utility vehicles, about 3000 of them! The event is part of the **Play on the Plains Festival**, held on the Labour Day long weekend in October. It also features country music and competitions such as 'Best Chick's Ute' and 'Most Feral Ute'.

Sleeping

There are several caravan parks and plenty of motels, but as trucks roll through town all night, choose one off the highway.

Riverview Motel (☎ 5881 2311; 1 Butler St; s/d $60/70; ▨) Certainly has the best position, overlooking the river.

Both the following have a more bustling feel than the Riverview:

Deniliquin Motel (☎ 5881 1820; 286 Wick St; s/d $60/70; ▨ ▨)

Country Club Motor Inn (☎ 5881 5279; 68-72 Crispe St; s/d $80/90; ▨)

Right on the swimming beach, **McLean Beach Caravan Park** (☎ 5881 2448; www.mcleanbeachcaravanpark.com.au; Butler St; camp sites $16-18, cabins $55-65) is shady and pleasant.

Eating

Crossing Café (☎ 5881 7827; Peppin Heritage Centre; dishes $15; ☉ 9am-5pm, dinner Thu-Sat). Make sure you arrive while it's still light so you can soak up the idyllic setting. Wood-fired pizzas and understated gourmet meals are on offer, as is a drop of fine local wine.

Bronte's Café (Napier St) Has a slick inner-city ambience, and serves light meals. Pass on the coffee.

Globe Hotel (☎ 5881 2030; 202 Cressy St) Has the most popular counter meals.

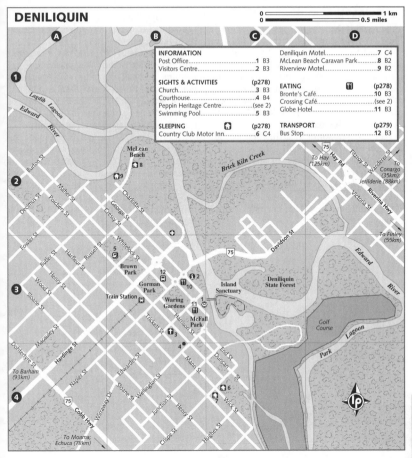

DENILIQUIN

0 ————————————————— 1 km
0 ————————————————— 0.5 miles

INFORMATION		Deniliquin Motel.......................7 C4
Post Office.......................1 B3		McLean Beach Caravan Park.........8 B2
Visitors Centre.......................2 B3		Riverview Motel.......................9 B2
SIGHTS & ACTIVITIES (p278)		EATING (p278)
Church.......................3 B3		Bronte's Café.......................10 B3
Courthouse.......................4 B4		Crossing Café.......................(see 2)
Peppin Heritage Centre.......(see 2)		Globe Hotel.......................11 B3
Swimming Pool.......................5 B3		
		TRANSPORT (p279)
SLEEPING (p278)		Bus Stop.......................12 B3
Country Club Motor Inn.......6 C4		

Getting There & Away

Long-distance buses stop at the defunct Bus Stop Café on Whitelock St. **CountryLink** (☎ 13 22 42) runs to Wagga ($45) on Wednesday, Friday and Sunday (from where trains run to Sydney and Melbourne), and to Albury ($23) on Tuesday, Thursday and Saturday. **V/Line** (☎ 13 61 96) also runs daily to Melbourne ($32). **Deniliquin Travel Centre** (Cressy St) is the ticket agent.

JERILDERIE

☎ 03 / pop 800

The Kelly Gang held up Jerilderie for three days in 1879, earning themselves an Australia-wide reputation for brazenness. The speech Ned Kelly made to his captives in the Royal Mail Hotel (still operating as a pub) and the letter he wrote complaining of his treatment at the hands of the authorities aroused the suspicion that young Ned might be a latent political activist. Holding up the town sealed Kelly's fate, for the NSW government declared him an outlaw and the colony was no longer a safe haven.

Next door to the **blacksmith's shop** (Powell St) where the Kelly gang had their horses shod and charged it to the NSW government, is the **Do Book Inn** (☎ 5886 1513; horseshoebendjerild erie@bigpond.com; 17 Powell St; r with breakfast $75), a very interesting place to stop for the night. This lovely cottage, made mostly of recycled materials, overlooks the billabong. There are wonderful sculptures in the garden.

THE RIVERINA

WENTWORTH

☎ 03 / pop 1440

This old river port lies at the confluence of the Murray and Darling Rivers, 30km northwest of Mildura. Enormous river redgums shade the banks, and there are numerous lookouts and walking tracks. The **visitors centre** (☎ 5027 3624; www.wentworth.nsw .gov.au; 28 Darling St; ⏱ 9.30am-4pm Mon-Fri, 10am-2pm Sat & Sun) is on the main road.

You can see some local history in the **Old Wentworth Gaol** (☎ 5027 3327; Beverley St; adult $6; ⏱ 10am-5pm) and across the road in the interesting **Pioneer World Folk Museum** (☎ 5027 3337; adult $2; ⏱ 10.30am-5pm Sat-Wed). The latter has a large collection of photos of the paddle-steamers that once made this a major port.

The **Perry Dunes** are impressive orange sand dunes 6km north of town, off the road to Broken Hill.

Harry Nanya Tours (☎ 1800 630 864; www.harrynan yatours.com.au; Shop 11, Sandwych St), based in town, runs full- and half-day tours, with Aboriginal guides, into Mungo National Park (p259).

Red Gum Lagoon (☎ 5027 2063; 210 Adams St; s/d $95/110; 🔀) has a number os peaceful self-contained cottages on the waterfront.

Staying on a houseboat is popular. The boats accommodate from six to eight people. Expect to pay around $600 for three nights on an eight-berth boat. The visitors' centre has a complete listing of boat operators.

Most long-distance buses run through Mildura. **Coomeallan Bus Lines** (☎ 5027 4704) runs to Mildura ($5, three times daily).

Southeast

CONTENTS

Dominated by the Kosciuszko National Park and home to Australia's highest peak, the southeast has some of New South Wales' (NSW) most spectacular scenery. East of the Great Dividing Range are soaring mountains, stately forests and the massive artificial lakes of the Snowy Mountains hydro-electric scheme. To the north is the elevated but flat expanse of the Monaro Tableland, where farmers battle the elements, struggling to make a living from the sometimes unforgiving soil. To the east lies lush agricultural land which produces food not only for the region, but for many parts of the rest of Australia as well.

Going for a drive can be one of the most rewarding pastimes in this part of the world. The Alpine Way, an all-weather road that passes through the southern ski fields, is a favourite for car drivers and motorcyclists alike as it winds its way through mountain passes, opening up magnificent vistas at nearly every turn.

Many visitors choose to focus on the Snowy Mountains and the range of summer and winter activities (you name it, you can probably do it) centred around there. If you don't want to stay on the mountain in wintertime, Khancoban, Jindabyne and, to a lesser extent, Cooma are all good bases for exploring the area. Some of the smaller towns between the Snowies and the Hume Highway are well worth a visit, too, for their laid-back charm.

HIGHLIGHTS

- Admiring the view from **Mt Kosciuszko** (p290), Australia's tallest mountain
- Dodging stalactites at **Yarrangobilly Caves** (p294) before slipping into the nearby thermal pool
- Sailing, waterskiing or just lounging about on the shores of spectacular **Lake Jindabyne** (p288)
- Dropping in for a beer or three at the famous **Ettamogah Pub** (p306)
- Getting away from it all in the delightfully named **Wee Jasper** (p301)
- Taking a trip down memory lane in **Batlow** (p296), a small town that hasn't 'reinvented' itself one inch
- Catching a cool breeze in the shade of a tree at a riverside park in **Yass** (p300)
- Following (at least some of) the footsteps of early European trailblazers on the **Hume and Hovell Track** (p301)

MONARO TABLELAND

Getting There & Away

There are regular flights with Macair through **Qantas** (☎ 13 13 13; www.qantas.com.au) from Sydney to the Snowy Mountains airport near Cooma.

Bus services are more frequent in winter, with crowds coming to the ski-fields from Canberra and Sydney. Cooma is the main transport hub; buses from Melbourne, Sydney and Canberra run there.

If driving from Canberra, the Monaro Hwy runs down to Cooma (1½ hours). The quickest route from Sydney is to take the Hume Hwy to Goulburn, then the Federal Hwy to Canberra. A longer alternative is to take the Princes Hwy then head to Cooma from the coast at Batemans Bay or Bega. From Cooma, the Monaro Hwy heads south to Bombala and the Victorian border.

The Barry Way is a largely unsealed, narrow and winding mountain road running from near Jindabyne to Buchan in Victoria. It's a spectacular route through national parks, but it can be difficult when wet. Fuel isn't available anywhere along this road.

The Alpine Way, a spectacular mountain road, runs from Khancoban past the southern end of the ski-fields, through Thredbo to Jindabyne.

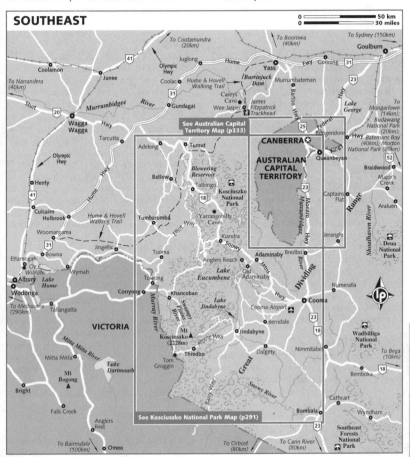

BRAIDWOOD

☎ 02 / pop 1000

Classified by the National Trust, Braidwood is a well-preserved town with a broad main street. Most historic buildings date from the 1850s, when it was the main town in the southern goldfields. Today, Braidwood is a base for visiting the national parks and a popular weekend trip for Canberrans. It also has a thriving arts and crafts community.

Information

Braidwood visitors centre (☎ 4842 1144; www .braidwood-tourism.com; 92 Wallace St; ☒ 10am-4pm) has a good range of information, including a walking-tour map of the town (free) and maps and books on scenic drives and bushwalks in the nearby national parks.

The post office is on Wallace St.

Sights

A stroll along **Wallace St**, with its restored Victorian buildings and wrought-iron lacework, is a pleasant experience.

Braidwood Museum (Wallace St; adult/child $3/50c; ☒ 10am-4pm) has displays on gold mining and local history, and the suit of armour worn by Mick Jagger in the 1970 film *Ned Kelly*, which was shot in Braidwood.

There are a few galleries and studios. Don't miss the Italianate **Studio Altenburg** (☎ 4842 2384; 104 Wallace St; ☒ 1-5pm), in the impressive old bank (1888). The gallery displays the work of local artists and craftspeople.

St Andrews Church (Elrington St) has a restored pipe organ and a fine collection of gargoyles leering from its tower.

Bedervale (☎ 4842 2421; Monkitee St), an impressive homestead, was built in 1836 to the design of John Verge, architect of Elizabeth Bay House in Sydney (see p54). It's still a working farm but opens to the public on the first Sunday of the month (homestead and gardens $8; gardens $4).

Festivals & Events

On the first Saturday in February, the **Braidwood Cup** is one of those great country race meetings. The **Braidwood Heritage Festival** is a week-long event of arts and music in early April.

Sleeping

Doncaster Inn (☎ 4842 2356; www.doncasterinn.com .au; 1 Wilson St; d $130-145 Fri & Sat, $90 Sun-Thu) A B&B with an impressive garden and restored rooms, this large building (formerly a convent, then a pub) is across the park from the courthouse. It's undergoing renovations and will reopen in November 2004.

Snow Lion (☎ 4842 2023; snowlion@ozemail.com.au; 58 Wilson St; s/d with breakfast from $75/100) A cute place with spacious, understated rooms.

Royal Mail Hotel (☎ 4842 2488; rmhotel@ispsd .net.au; 147 Wallace St; s/d $30/50) Spotless pub rooms (some with balcony overlooking the park). The shared bathrooms are possibly the least grimy in all of NSW.

Torpy's (☎ 4842 2551; www.torpys.com.au; 18 Mc-Kellar St; guesthouse with breakfast s/d $80/120, motel s/d with breakfast $60/80) Charming colonial-style guesthouse rooms with four-poster beds. There are also comfortable motel units. It's just off the north end of Wallace St.

Eating

La Luna (☎ 4842 1666; 123 Wallace St; mains $18; ☒ lunch Wed-Sat, dinner Thu-Sat) An upmarket restaurant serving vaguely imaginative Italian food. Try the king prawn and mussel pasta ($18.50). BYO wine, fully licensed.

Pit Stop Café (☎ 4842 2809; 143 Wallace St; mains $8; ☒ breakfast, lunch & dinner) Good cheap breakfasts and healthy home-style meals in casual surrounds. Dinner is served until 8pm.

Café Altenburg (☎ 4842 2077; 104 Wallace St; mains $8-13; ☒ 10am-5pm) This pleasant and relaxing café in the courtyard of Studio Altenburg (this page) has home-made soups, pies, pastries, savoury tarts, cakes, tempting pastas and salads, all at reasonable prices.

Getting There & Away

Murrays (☎ 13 22 51; www.murrays.com.au) has a bus that stops daily in each direction on its run between Canberra and Batemans Bay. The bus stop is outside the post office on Wallace St.

Braidwood is on the Kings Hwy between Canberra (89km) and Batemans Bay (59km). An alternative route to the south coast at Moruya runs through Araluen and some beautiful country on the northern edge of Deua National Park. The road is sealed as far as Araluen, but after that it's not suitable for caravans.

If you're heading to Cooma, consider taking the scenic, partly-sealed road via Numeralla. It follows the Shoalhaven River to its source, Big Badja Hill. Several sections of this road can be cut by floods, so if it has been raining be prepared to change your plans.

AROUND BRAIDWOOD

Both **Budawang National Park** and the southern end of **Morton National Park** are accessible from Braidwood. At 23,731 hectares, Budawang is much smaller than Morton but offers rugged scenery and wilderness walking. There are no roads through the park, nor any facilities in it. The easiest access is from tiny **Mongarlowe**, 14km east of Braidwood.

The **Corn Trail**, in the Buckenbowra State Forest, is a 13km walking trail down the Buckenbowra River from Clyde Mountain (774m). It starts about 25km out of Braidwood, just off the Kings Hwy as it begins its steep descent to Batemans Bay.

Major's Creek, an old gold-mining town 16km south of Braidwood, has a number of historic buildings and a good country pub with comfortable rooms – the **Elrington Hotel** (☎ 02-4846 1145; s/d $30/40).

LAKE EUCUMBENE

Lake Eucumbene is a massive dam, built as part of the Snowy Mountains hydro-electric scheme near the central section of Kosciuszko National Park. Some of the lake's forested arms and inlets are scenic, although much of the area has been cleared of trees. The lake is popular for trout fishing and boating in summer, and there are several small communities on the shores with camping and other accommodation.

Adaminaby
☎ 02 / pop 460
Adaminaby (1017m) is a tiny town on the Snowy Mountains Hwy, built to replace the old town now lying beneath Lake Eucumbene 10km away. In fact, 101 buildings were moved here in 1956, when the lake flooded the original town. It's shrunk a bit since then, but is still the biggest place between Cooma and Tumut and there's a good range of services. Fishing in Lake Eucumbene is a big attraction, which accounts for the giant rainbow trout greeting visitors in the town park.

Adaminaby is the closest town to the **Mt Selwyn ski-fields**, and the **Adaminaby Bus Service** (☎ 6454 2318) runs there (return $25) and to Cooma ($30). It also offers a charter

transport service for bushwalkers in summer. You can hire ski gear at **Adaminaby Ski Hire** (☎ 6454 2455; 2/16 Denison St).

SLEEPING & EATING
Tanderra Lodge (☎ 6454 2470; www.tanderra.com; 21 Denison St; low season s/d & tw $55/84, high season s/d & tw $89/115) Plenty of '70s fishing and skiing ambience here. Rooms are basic but comfortable, with dorm beds ($42) a cheaper option all year round. All rates include breakfast.

Snow Goose Hotel/Motel (☎ 6454 2202; cnr Denison & Baker Sts; pub r s/d $40/60, motel s/d $55/85) Decent pub and motel rooms, both including a cooked breakfast. The Snow Goose also offers bistro and counter meals, and is one of the few places open in the evening (till 9pm) year-round.

Alpine Tourist Park (☎ 6454 2438; www.alpine touristpark.com.au; cnr Snowy Mountains Hwy & Lett St; powered/unpowered $18/20, caravans $45, cabins $45-110) On the edge of town.

During winter these places might be booked out by groups on ski packages.

There are several cafés on Denison St, all serving smoked trout pâté in various snack and sandwich forms.

Farmstays
A working sheep and cattle property, **Reynella** (☎ 6454 2386, 1800 029 909; www.reynellarides.com .au; Kingston Rd, s/d $99/198) offers accommodation and horse riding. Day rides are available, as well as treks of up to five days through the north of Kosciuszko National Park. A three-day ride costs $510 per person. The Reynella turn-off from the Snowy Mountains Hwy is about 8km south of Adaminaby.

The **Cooma visitors centre** (☎ 1800 636 525) can point you towards other farmstays in the region.

COOMA
☎ 02 / pop 6950
Cooma is the largest town on the Monaro Tableland, but it retains a small country-town feel. Some unkind souls drop the second 'o' from its name. In the 1950s and '60s, during the construction of the Snowy Mountains hydro-electric scheme (for which it was the headquarters), 16,000 people crowded into the town. The streetscape has changed significantly since then; when a TV mini-series about the Snowy

Mountains scheme was being filmed in 1993, the producers chose the central Victorian town of Castlemaine to recreate Cooma's street scenes because Cooma had grown too modern.

Orientation & Information

The main shopping street in Cooma is Sharp St, which becomes the Snowy Mountains Hwy to the west of town and the Monaro Hwy to the east.

The **Cooma visitors centre** (☎ 1800 636 525; www.visitcooma.com.au; 119 Sharp St; ⊗ 9am-5pm Mon-Sat) is next to Centennial Park. It makes accommodation bookings and may know of special deals being offered. There's Internet access at the **library** (Vale St; per hr $6).

Sights & Activities

In **Centennial Park** there is a series of mosaic scenes from the history of the Monaro. There's also a relief map of the mountains cast in metal.

The visitors centre has a map of the **Lambie Town Walk** (4km), which details the town's main points of interest. Interpretive boards are scattered around town to explain its history.

Off the Monaro Hwy, just a couple of kilometres north of the town centre is the **Snowy Mountains Scheme Information Centre** (☎ 1800 623 776; www.snowyhydro.com.au; admission free; ⊗ 8am-5pm Mon-Fri, to 1pm Sat & Sun). It has models of the tunnels and power stations, a large 3D map and a video about the project.

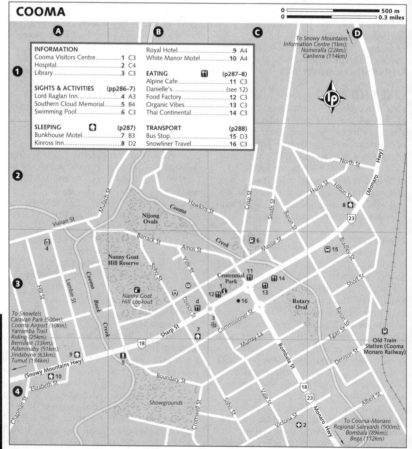

COOMA

0   500 m
0   0.3 miles

INFORMATION
Cooma Visitors Centre.............1 C3
Hospital.....................................2 C4
Library......................................3 C3

SIGHTS & ACTIVITIES (pp286–7)
Lord Raglan Inn........................4 A3
Southern Cloud Memorial........5 B4
Swimming Pool........................6 C3

SLEEPING (p287)
Bunkhouse Motel......................7 B3
Kinross Inn...............................8 D2

Royal Hotel...............................9 A4
White Manor Motel.................10 A4

EATING (p287–8)
Alpine Cafe.............................11 C3
Danielle's..........................(see 12)
Food Factory...........................12 C3
Organic Vibes.........................13 C3
Thai Continental.....................14 C3

TRANSPORT (p288)
Bus Stop.................................15 D3
Snowliner Travel....................16 C3

To Snowy Mountains Information Centre (1km); Numeralla (22km); Canberra (114km)

North St

Harris St

Hilton St

(Monaro Hwy)

Budley St

Mulach St

Hawkins St

Crisp St

Smith St

Baron St

8

23

Vulcan St

Cooma

Nijong Ovals

Barrack St

Amos St

Creek

Massie St

6

15

Short St

Nanny Goat Hill Reserve

Soho St

Vale St

Centennial Park

11

14

Hill St

Lambie St

Cooma

Buck

12

1

16

13

Nanny Goat Hill Lookout

d

Dawson St

Rotary Oval

Baron St

To Snowtels Caravan Park (500m); Cooma Airport (10km); Yarramba Trail Riding (25km); Berridale (33km); Adaminaby (51km); Jindabyne (63km); Tumut (184km)

Creek

Sharp St

3

7

Commissioner St

Murray La

Bombala St

Egan St

Old Train Station (Cooma Monaro Railway)

9

(Snowy Mountains Hwy)

10

Elizabeth St

5

Boundary St

18

Denison St

Chapman St

Showgrounds

Cromwell St

Soho St

Vale St

Victoria St

18

23

Monaro Hwy

Albert St

2

To Cooma-Monaro Regional Saleyards (500m); Bombala (89km); Bega (112km)

SOUTHEAST

THE SNOWY MOUNTAINS HYDRO-ELECTRIC SCHEME

More than 50 years after it began, the extraordinary Snowy Mountains hydro-electric scheme is still hailed as one of Australia's greatest engineering feats. In 1947 work began in untamed, mountainous country. Workers from around the world were recruited to the project – many from postwar eastern and southern Europe. Seventeen large dams were built (Lake Eucumbene alone could hold the water of eight Sydney Harbours), rivers were diverted and all sorts of tunnelling and building records were smashed.

The project was completed in 1974 and today provides electricity to Canberra, New South Wales and Victoria. Water from the diverted rivers irrigates the Murray, Murrumbidgee and Riverina areas inland. It's estimated that if the electricity produced by the scheme were produced by coal-fired turbines, five million tonnes of carbon dioxide would be released into the atmosphere each year.

Although little account was taken of the environmental impact of diverting the waters of the Eucumbene, Murrumbidgee, Murray, Snowy, Tooma and Tumut Rivers, the project did have an unexpected social benefit. Australia in the '50s was a parochial island and the postwar turmoil in Europe and Asia didn't do much to change that. With workers from 30 countries vital to a project that was a source of immense national pride, attitudes to new immigrants changed and Australia's multiculturalism began.

Today you can visit three power stations, as well as the information centre in Cooma. Murray 1, near Khancoban, has a good interactive visitors centre; Tumut 2, near Cabramurra, has underground tours; and Tumut 3, near Talbingo, has daily tours.

The **Southern Cloud Memorial**, by the Cooma Back Creek bridge, incorporates some of the wreckage of the *Southern Cloud* – an aircraft that crashed in the Snowies in 1931, but wasn't discovered until 1958.

On **Lambie St**, Cooma's oldest street, are several historic buildings classified by the National Trust. The **Lord Raglan Inn** (☎ 6452 3377; 9 Lambie St; entry by donation; ☉ 10am-4pm Wed-Sat) was built in 1854 and is now a gallery and cultural centre for Monaro Tableland artists.

The **Cooma Monaro Railway** (☎ 6452 7791; ☉ 11am, 1pm & 2 pm Sat & Sun) runs 45-minute train rides ($12) aboard restored 1923 CPH rail motors. The line, which closed in 1989, originally ran from Bombala to Queanbeyan.

Cooma is a major centre for **cattle sales** and a big sale is worth seeing. The saleyards are just southeast of town on the Monaro Hwy. For sale days see http://cooma.saleyards.info/sales/calendar.asp.

There are several **horse-riding** outfits in the area. **Yarramba Trail Riding** (☎ 6453 7204; Dry Plains Rd), midway between Adaminaby and Cooma, has rides along the upper Murrumbidgee River for $30 an hour or $100 for a full day including lunch. It offers tuition for novices.

Festivals & Events
Held in early March is the **Cooma Show**. **Coomafest** is a big event with street parades,

bands and performing arts held over 10 days in mid-October. The local **Race Day** is on the first Saturday in December.

Sleeping
Kinross Inn (☎ 6452 4133; 15 Sharp St; s/d from $75/80; ☑) A neatly manicured lawn, spas and cable TV make the Kinross a good option.

White Manor Motel (☎ 6452 1152; 252 Sharp St; s/d $63/68; ☑) This place has a modicum of style, with clean rooms and a jungle of pot plants.

Royal Hotel (☎ 6452 2132; 59 Sharp St; s/d $28/45) The oldest licensed hotel in Cooma is a beautiful old sandstone place – try to get a room leading onto the wonderful veranda.

Bunkhouse Motel (☎ /fax 6452 2983; 28 Soho St; dm/s/d from $20/35/50) Reasonable backpacker accommodation – a neat, friendly place with a slightly cramped and rustic feel.

Snowtels Caravan Park (☎ 6452 1828; www.ski.com.au/snowtels; 286 Sharp St; powered/unpowered sites $20/15, cabins from $45) On the highway, 1.5km west of town, this is a big, well-equipped place. All rates go up in winter.

Eating
Food Factory (123 Sharp St; ☉ lunch & dinner) Next to the visitors centre, this is a good place for filling fast food; it does huge hamburgers ($3.50), pizzas and sandwiches.

SOUTHEAST

Danielle's (☎ 6452 4488; mains $16-25; ☺ lunch & dinner Tue-Sat, breakfast Sat & Sun) Directly above the Food Factory, this is probably Cooma's best restaurant. It's licensed and has a wide menu of Italian-influenced dishes.

Organic Vibes (☎ 6452 6566; 82a Sharp St; mains around $9; ☺ lunch) Healthy meals and good fresh juices are the go here.

Alpine Café (cnr Sharp & Bombala Sts; meals from $9; ☺ breakfast & lunch) Huge breakfasts – a great way to start the day.

Thai Continental (☎ 6452 5782; 76 Sharp St; meals $10-15; ☺ lunch & dinner) Readers have recommended the Thai and Asian food here.

Australian Hotel (137 Sharp St; ☺ lunch & dinner) A bistro with good-value lunch-time roasts ($7) and the usual dinner-time selection.

Getting There & Away

Macair, Horizon and Aero Pelican share flights between them from Sydney ($200, daily. Book through **Qantas** (☎ 13 13 13). The airport is about 10km southwest of Cooma on the Snowy Mountains Hwy.

Snowliner Travel (☎ 6452 1584; Sharp St), opposite the visitors centre, handles bus bookings. **Summit Coaches** (☎ 6297 2588) goes to Canberra ($35) where you can connect with a Greyhound to Sydney.

Thrice a week **Countrylink** (☎ 13 22 32) buses run via Cooma on the Canberra–Eden run.

Victoria's **V/Line** (☎ 136 196; www.vlinepassenger.com.au) has an interesting twice-weekly run between Melbourne and Canberra via Cooma. The nine-hour trip from Melbourne takes you by train to Sale, then by bus.

Heading to Batemans Bay, you can travel via Numeralla to Braidwood on a partly sealed road skirting Deua National Park.

NIMMITABEL

☎ 02 / pop 240

Pretty Nimmitabel, on the Monaro Hwy 35km south of Cooma, is a good place for a break, although its only real 'attraction' is the impressive old **windmill**.

A German immigrant spent seven years building the mill in the 19th century, but when it was finished he was told he couldn't use it because the spinning sails would frighten horses.

Another thing that might frighten the horses is the more recent addition of a life-size eight-tonne elephant on the main street (the Monaro Hwy) next to the bakery. The

owner of the bakery took a shine to the statue and had it shipped over from Bali. There are several antique shops along the main street and the **Milkwood Gallery**, which shows mostly local arts and crafts.

The **Royal Arms** (☎ 6454 6422; www.royalarms.com.au; s/d from $68/98) is a handsome restored hotel on the main road through town. The rooms have period furnishings, and include a cooked breakfast.

The **Baker's Shop** (☺ 6am-7pm; bread & pastries $3, mains $9) has good gourmet sandwiches, pies and snazzy pastas in a clean, leafy sitting area. Check out the attached sculpture garden.

The **Countrylink** (☎ 13 22 32) bus between Canberra and Eden passes through three times a week. It stops outside the elephant.

SOUTHEAST FORESTS NATIONAL PARK

This national park (90,000 hectares) combines state forests and former smaller national parks, extending south from Nimmitabel to the Victorian border and east towards the coast near Eden. The park was created in 1997 after a protracted battle between loggers and environmentalists.

There are many **picnic areas** within the park. Six Mile Creek, between Cathcart and Candelo on the Tantawangalo Mountain Rd, has camping facilities and access to walking tracks. Contact the **National Parks & Wildlife Service** (NPWS; ☎ 6458 4080) office in Bombala for more information.

JINDABYNE

☎ 02 / pop 4420

Jindabyne is the closest town to the major ski resorts in Kosciuszko National Park. It's a sizable place, with two modern shopping centres and a lot of new development. It's relatively peaceful in summer, but in winter the town sleeps more than 20,000 visitors!

Orientation & Information

As with many other towns on the Monaro Tableland, today's Jindabyne is a modern incarnation of an original settlement that is now submerged in Lake Jindabyne.

The impressive **Snowy Region visitors centre** (☎ 6450 5600; fax 6456 1249; www.snowymountains.com.au; Kosciuszko Rd; ☺ 8am-5pm) is on the main road in from Cooma or Thredbo. It's operated by the NPWS and has information on the whole region. There are display areas, a cinema and a good café.

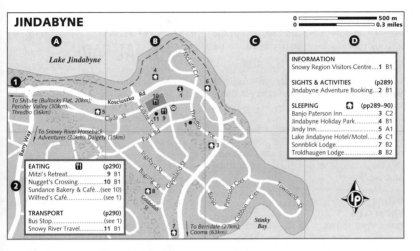

JINDABYNE

0   500 m
0   0.3 miles

Lake Jindabyne

To Skitube (Bullocks Flat, 20km);
Perisher Valley (30km);
Thredbo (36km)

To Snowy River Horseback
Adventures (30km), Dalgety (35km)

Kosciuszko Rd

Clyde St

Barry Way

Park Rd

Ingebyra St

Bogong St

Cobbodah St

Gippsland St

Thredbo Tce

Patterson Cres

Cobbon Cres

Townsend St

Banjo

Stinky
Bay

To Berridale (27km);
Cooma (63km)

INFORMATION	
Snowy Region Visitors Centre....1	B1

SIGHTS & ACTIVITIES	(p289)
Jindabyne Adventure Booking...2	B1

SLEEPING	(pp289–90)
Banjo Paterson Inn....................3	C2
Jindabyne Holiday Park............4	B1
Jindy Inn.................................5	A1
Lake Jindabyne Hotel/Motel......6	C1
Sonnblick Lodge.......................7	B2
Troldhaugen Lodge...................8	B2

EATING	(p290)
Mitzi's Retreat.......................9	B1
Nugget's Crossing................10	B1
Sundance Bakery & Café...(see 10)	
Wilfred's Café...................(see 1)	

TRANSPORT	(p290)
Bus Stop..........................(see 1)	
Snowy River Travel.............11	B1

There's a bank and a post office in **Nugget's Crossing** (Kosciuszko Rd), a shopping centre.

Summer Activities

Outside of the ski season, there's still plenty to do.

Jindabyne Adventure Booking (☎ 1800 815588; 2 Thredbo Tce) is a good one-stop shop for activities in the area. They offer various tours and packages including wake boarding, mountain biking, kite boarding, whitewater rafting, guided walks and abseiling, amongst others.

This is a prime area for horse riding. **Snowy River Horseback Adventure** (☎ 6453 7260), on the Barry Way about 30km southwest of Jindabyne, suits more experienced riders, and has half-day rides ($70), as well as longer ones with overnight stops (two/five days $460/1575).

Upper Murray Rafting (☎ 1800 677 179; 7 North St, Cooma) operates white-water rafting trips out of Jindabyne and Khancoban, starting near Tom Groggin. Day trips cost $140, while the two-day camping trip is $280. It's also possible to get on a half-day trip ($75) at short notice.

Paddy Pallin (☎ 6456 2922; www.paddypallin.com.au; cnr Kosciuszko & Thredbo Rds), next to the Snowline Caravan Park, rents out tents and other walking equipment, and offers an impressive range of summer activities, including guided alpine hikes, from leisurely day walks ($23) to seven-day walks in Kosciuszko National Park ($850).

Sleeping

The influx of snow bunnies in winter sends prices through the roof, but it's still generally cheaper in Jindabyne than at the resorts and you'll at least have a chance of finding overnight accommodation. Still, many places book out months in advance, so if you're coming to ski, plan well ahead and check out the various packages offered by the resorts and lodges.

Jindy Inn (☎ 6456 1957; 18 Clyde St; s/d from $35/55) The best value for money in summertime, well-equipped rooms with private bathrooms.

Lake Jindabyne Hotel/Motel (☎ 1800 646 818; Kosciuszko Rd; s/d with breakfast $70/80; ☒) A big place by the lake in the centre of town, with a heated pool, spa and sauna. Rates nearly double in winter.

Banjo Paterson Inn (☎ 1800 046 275; www.banjo patersoninn.com.au; 1 Kosciuszko Rd; d $70-250) A flash, refurbished place with two bars, a restaurant and some very nice lake-view rooms.

Also recommended:

Sonnblick Lodge (☎ 6456 2472; 49 Gippsland St; s/d with breakfast $45/70)

Troldhaugen Lodge (☎ /fax 6456 2718; 13 Cobbodah St; s/d with breakfast from $30/60)

There are many places offering accommodation in flats, apartments and lodges, but they can fill up quickly. Although getting a single night in winter is almost impossible, booking a weekend or longer shouldn't be a problem. There are five pricing seasons.

SOUTHEAST

Cheaper, fully equipped apartments that sleep six cost from around $540/750 in the low/high season. You can pay a hell of a lot more. Agents in Jindabyne:

Alpine Resorts & Travel Centre (☎ 1800 802 315)
Kosciuszko Accommodation Centre (☎ 1800 026 354)
Snowy Mountains Reservations Centre (☎ 1800 020 622)

In town and positioned by the lake, **Jindabyne Holiday Park** (☎ 6456 2249; www.jindabyne holidaypark.com.au; Kosciuszko Rd; powered/unpowered sites $20/18, cabins from $60) offers canoe, bike and ski hire.

Eating

Wilfred's Cafe (☎ 6457 2111; mains $12; ☼ breakfast, lunch & dinner) Situated in the visitors centre complex, with a great patio, good food and a wide range of dishes.

Sundance Bakery & Café (Nugget's Crossing; pies $5, pastries $2.50; ☼ breakfast & lunch) A good place for coffee, cakes, sandwiches and snacks.

Mitzi's Retreat (☎ 6457 2888; upstairs, Central Park shops, 1 Snowy River Ave; mains $20-26; ☼ dinner) Euro ski-field food like veal Zurich ($21) and Bauer Schmaus (a pork extravaganza; $26) in ambient surrounds.

Lake Jindabyne Hotel (☎ 1800 646 818; Kosciuszko Rd) Has an excellent bistro open all year.

Nugget's Crossing on Kosciuszko Rd is a well-stocked shopping centre with a supermarket and numerous places to eat.

Getting There & Away

For transport bookings contact **Snowy River Travel** (☎ 6456 2184) behind Nugget's Crossing.

Summit Coaches (☎ 6297 2588) has a bus from Canberra to Jindabyne ($49, three hours), which continues on to Thredbo ($53). This bus connects with the Sydney–Canberra bus. The bus stop is outside the visitors centre.

The Skitube terminal at Bullocks Flat is less than half an hour from Jindabyne by car.

McCafferty's/Greyhound (☎ 13 20 30) runs daily shuttles to Bullocks Flat ($11), Thredbo ($17), Sawpit Creek, Smiggin Holes ($17) and Perisher Valley ($15) in winter. The trip to Perisher Valley takes 45 minutes; to Thredbo it's about an hour.

Jindabyne Coaches (☎ 6457 2117) runs buses to Bullocks Flat in winter, and may go as far as Thredbo depending on demand.

KOSCIUSZKO NATIONAL PARK

NSW's largest and most spectacular national park (690,000 hectares) includes caves, glacial lakes, forest and all of the state's ski resorts, as well as Australia's highest mountain (2228m). **Mt Kosciuszko** (koz-zy-*os*-ko) was named by the Polish explorer Paul Edmund Strzelecki after a Polish hero of the American War of Independence.

Famous for its snow, the national park is becoming popular in summer when there are excellent bushwalks and marvellous alpine wild flowers. Outside the snow season you can drive to within 8km of the top of Mt Kosciuszko from Jindabyne to Charlotte Pass. Thredbo is the best summer base, but if you have your own transport there are many free camping areas scattered around the park.

Orientation & Information

Mt Kosciuszko and the main ski resorts are in the south-central area of the park. From Jindabyne, Kosciuszko Rd leads to the resorts of Smiggin Holes (30km), Perisher Valley (33km) and Charlotte Pass (40km), with a turn-off before Perisher Valley to Guthega and Mt Blue Cow.

The main visitors centre for the park, run by the NPWS, is at Jindabyne (p288).

There's an **education centre** (☎ 02-6450 5666) at Sawpit Creek, which runs programs during school holidays (but is otherwise closed to the public), and another visitors centre at Yarrangobilly Caves (p294) in the north of the park. For more information, there are also the **park-ranger stations** (Perisher Valley ☎ 02-6457 5214; Thredbo ☎ 02-6457 6255).

Entry to the national park costs $15 per car, per day. If you intend to spend a few days here, consider buying the $80 annual parks permit, which gives you unlimited access to almost every national park in NSW, although no other park costs as much to enter as Kosciuszko.

Bushwalking

Contact the NPWS visitors centres in Jindabyne (p288) or Khancoban (p298) for information on the many walks in the park.

From Charlotte Pass you can walk to the summit of Mt Kosciuszko (16km return),

KOSCIUSZKO NATIONAL PARK

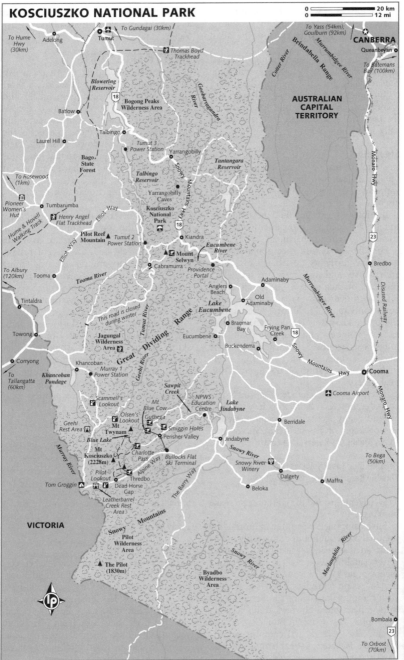

0 ———— 20 km
0 ———— 12 mi

To Hume Hwy (30km)

Adelong

To Gundagai (30km)

Tumut

Thomas Boyd Trackhead

To Yass (54km); Goulburn (92km)

CANBERRA

Queanbeyan

To Batemans Bay (100km)

Cotter River

Brindabella Range

Murrumbidgee River

Blowering Reservoir

18

Bogong Peaks Wilderness Area

Batlow

Goobragandra River

AUSTRALIAN CAPITAL TERRITORY

Talbingo

Tumut 3 Power Station

Yarrangobilly

Laurel Hill

Bago State Forest

Talbingo Reservoir

Snowy Mountains Hwy

Tantangara Reservoir

To Rosewood (1km)

Yarrangobilly Caves

Tumbarumba

Pioneer Women's Hut

Henry Angel Flat Trackhead

Elliot Way

Kosciuszko National Park

18

Hume & Hovell Walking Track

Pilot Reef Mountain

Tumut 2 Power Station

Kiandra

Eucumbene River

Monaro Hwy

23

To Albury (120km)

Tooma

Elliot Way

Mount Selwyn

Cabramurra

Providence Portal

Adaminaby

Murrumbidgee River

Bredbo

Tintaldra

Tooma River

This road is closed during winter

Tumut River

Anglers Beach

Old Adaminaby

Lake Eucumbene

Disused Railway

Towong

Great Dividing Range

Eucumbene

Braemar Bay

Frying Pan Creek

18

Snowy Mountains Hwy

Buckenderra

Corryong

Khancoban

Geehi River

Jagungal Wilderness Area

Murray 1 Power Station

Cooma

To Tallangatta (60km)

Khancoban Pondage

Scammell's Lookout

Sawpit Creek

NPWS Education Centre

Lake Jindabyne

Cooma Airport

Mt Blue Cow

Olsen's Lookout

Guthega

Berridale

Monaro Hwy

Geehi Rest Area

Mt Twynam

Smiggin Holes

Perisher Valley

Jindabyne

Snowy River

Blue Lake

Charlotte Pass

Bullocks Flat Ski Terminal

Snowy River Winery

To Bega (50km)

Mt Kosciuszko (2228m)

Alpine Way

Pilot Lookout

Thredbo

The Barry Way

Dalgety

Maffra

Tom Groggin

Dead Horse Gap

Beloka

Murray River

Leatherbarrel Creek Rest Area

VICTORIA

Snowy Mountains

Macalister River

Snowy Pilot Wilderness Area

Snowy River

The Pilot (1830m)

Byadbo Wilderness Area

Bombala

23

To Orbost (70km)

LP

or take the easier walk to the summit from Thredbo (12km return). Other walking trails from Charlotte Pass include the 20km glacial lakes walk.

There are longer walks through the vast Jagungal Wilderness area, with several alpine huts available for camping, but these treks require planning (including good maps and a compass), experience, and knowledge of the conditions, which can change dramatically at any time of year.

Sleeping

In summer most of the resort lodges close, but good deals can be found at Thredbo (opposite), and guesthouses and retreats elsewhere in the park.

In winter, the cheapest (and most fun) way to take to the slopes is to gather a bunch of friends and rent an apartment.

For the ski season, begin making inquiries as early as possible. Costs vary enormously and new rates are set before the start of each season. As rough examples, a two-bedroom apartment in Thredbo costs from about $3000 for a week during the peak ski season (roughly mid-July to early September) and a double room in a lodge costs around $1000, including some meals. It's unlikely that you'll find overnight accommodation on the mountain in peak season.

There's a good chance that you'll pay considerably less than this if you shop around. Many agents book accommodation and packages on the ski-fields. Specialists:
Snowy Mountains Reservation Centre (☎ 1800 020 622)
Perisher Blue Snow Holidays (☎ 1300 655 811)
Thredbo Resort Centre (☎ 1800 020 589)

Travel agents around the country also make bookings.

Bush camping is permitted in most of the national park, but not in ecologically fragile areas (such as near the glacial lakes or other water catchment areas). Some riverside picnic areas, where you can camp, have fireplaces and pit toilets. There's a string of such camping areas along the Barry Way at the southern end of the park, and five along the Alpine Way between Bullocks Flat and Geehi. The only formal camping area is **Kosciuszko Mountain Retreat** (☎ 02-6456 2224; www.kositreat.com.au; powered/unpowered sites $21/16,

cabins from $66), a tranquil place in bushland at Sawpit Creek along the road to Perisher Valley.

SKIING & SKI RESORTS

Skiing or snowboarding in Australia can be a marginal activity. The season is short (July, August and early September) and good snow isn't always guaranteed, although the increased use of snow-making machines is making it more so. Nor are the mountains ideal for downhill skiing; their gently rounded shapes mean that long runs are relatively easy and the harder runs short and sharp. Worse, the short seasons mean operators have to get their returns quickly, so costs are high.

The good news is that when the snow is there and the sun is shining, the skiing can be superb and the resorts are great fun. You'll find lively nightlife, decent restaurants, fine scenery and enough frightening slopes to keep you interested. The resorts tend to be particularly crowded on weekends because they're so convenient to reach, particularly from Canberra.

The open slopes are a ski-tourer's paradise – Nordic (cross-country or *langlauf*) skiing is popular and most resorts offer lessons and hire out equipment. The national park includes some of the country's best trails, and often old cattle-herders' huts are the only form of accommodation apart from your tent.

Information

For snow and road reports ring the various visitors centres. **Thredbo** (☎ 1900 934 320) and **Perisher Blue** (☎ 1900 926 664) have their own numbers. On the Internet try www .ski.com.au for information on all resorts. Snow chains must be carried during winter even if there's no snow – heavy penalties apply if you don't.

Costs

Group lessons, including a lift ticket, cost about $110/60 a day for an adult/child. Boots, skis and stocks can be hired for around $40 a day. It will cost less for longer periods; less, too, if you hire them away from the mountain, but if you have a problem with the fit you may be stuck. There are hire places in towns close to the resorts and many garages hire out ski equipment and chains.

Thredbo

☎ 02 / pop 2930

At 1370m, with the longest runs (the longest is more than 3km through 670m of vertical drop), **Thredbo** (www.thredbo.com.au) has some of the best skiing in Australia. An adult lift-only ticket costs $80 a day, a five-day pass $360 and a five-day lift-and-lesson package costs $455. Beginner/experienced-skier lift and lesson packages cost from $222/166 for two days and from $455/360 for five days. Friday Flat is a purpose built beginners' area with its own slow-speed quad chairlift ($43).

Unlike the other resorts, Thredbo is also a great place to visit in summer. It's a popular bushwalking centre with excellent, scenic tracks, a good starting point for mountain-biking tours and even a bobsled ride. Although Thredbo Village covers only a small area, streets wind around the steep valley side and it's tightly packed with lodges. Pick up a map of the village in Jindabyne or Khancoban before you arrive. There's an information centre in the **Valley Terminal** (☎ 6459 4100) at Thredbo Village across the wooden footbridge from the shopping centre.

The chairlift to the top of Mt Crackenback runs right through the summer (adult/child return $22/11). It's a very steep walk if you don't take the lift. From the top it's an easy 2km walk or cross-country ski to a good lookout to Mt Kosciuszko (which, from here, looks more like a small hill), or 6km to the top of the mountain itself. Other walks leave from the top of the lift; maps are available at the information centre. Remember to carry adequate clothing and be prepared for all conditions, even in summer.

The **Thredbo Leisure Centre** (☎ 6459 4100/4151) organises all sorts of activities including hiking, mountain-biking, canoeing, whitewater rafting, abseiling and horse riding.

Raw NRG (☎ 6457 6990), located in the Valley Terminal, specialises in mountain-bike rides. A half-day ride from Dead Horse Gap down to Tom Groggin (a drop of over 1000m) costs $99, including lunch and equipment.

FESTIVALS & EVENTS

The hills come alive in summer. There's the **Blues Festival** in mid-January; the **Thredbo** **World Music Festival** in mid-March and the **Jazz Festival** in late April/early May.

SLEEPING

Kasee's (☎ 6457 6370; www.kasees.com.au; d summer from $100, winter from $160) A very cosy place – rooms have kitchen and balconies (with a great view) and guests can use the Finnish sauna or mellow out around the open fire.

Candlelight Lodge (☎ 1800 020 900; www.candlelightlodge.com.au; s/d summer $75/220, winter $130/190) B&B with a licensed restaurant on the premises.

Thredbo YHA Lodge (☎ 6457 6376; thredbo@yha nsw.org.au; 8 Jack Adams Path; dm/d summer $18/40, winter $62/77) Well appointed, with great common areas, a good kitchen and balcony. There's a two-night minimum stay in winter. Not surprisingly, there's stiff competition for beds in winter. A ballot is held for winter places and you have to enter by April, but it's always worth checking to see if there are cancellations. There's plenty of room in the off-season. Contact the **YHA Travel Centre** (☎ 9261 1111) in Sydney for ballot forms or register online at www.yha.com.au.

Perisher Blue

☎ 02 / elevation 1680m

In 1995 the resorts of Perisher Valley, Smiggin Holes, Mt Blue Cow and Guthega combined to become **Perisher Blue** (☎ 6459 4495; 1300 655 811; www.perisherblue.com.au), providing skiing on seven peaks across 1245 hectares, with 53 lifts, including the Skitube, and one ticketing system.

Perisher Valley (1720m) has a good selection of intermediate runs. Smiggin Holes (1680m) is just down the road. Guthega (1640m) is mainly a day resort best suited to intermediate and beginner skiers, as it's smaller and less crowded than other places; from here, cross-country skiers head to the Main Range or Rolling Ground. Mt Blue Cow (1640m), between Perisher Valley and Guthega in the Perisher Range, has beginner to intermediate skiing. Mt Blue Cow is a day resort (no accommodation) accessible via the **Skitube** (☎ 6456 2010; adult/child same-day return $27/16).

An adult one-/five-day lift ticket costs $80/340; other passes are also available. A combined lesson and lift pass costs $80/300 (for beginners) and $110/440 (for experienced skiers).

SOUTHEAST

SLEEPING

Most accommodation is in Perisher Valley and Smiggin Holes.

Sundeck Hotel (☎ 6457 5222; www.ski.com.au /sundeck/info.html; d/tw per person winter low $150/170, winter peak $230/270) One of the oldest lodges in Perisher, with a comfy bar and great views from the guest lounge. There are also triple/quad rooms (winter low/peak $140/215), and all rates include breakfast and lunch.

Chalet Sonnenhof (☎ 6457 5256; www.sonnenhof .com.au; s/d summer $100/200, tw winter per person with breakfast & dinner from $140) This is one of the few Perisher lodges open in summer.

Lodge (☎ 6457 5012; www.ski.com.au/thelodge; 3-night packages $660) This is close to the ski runs, but only open June to October. The three-night package includes ski hire, dinner and a light breakfast.

Charlotte Pass

☎ 02 / elevation 1780m

At the base of Mt Kosciuszko, this is one of the highest (1780m), oldest and most isolated resorts in Australia. In winter you have to snowcat the last 8km from Perisher Valley ($30 each way, book ahead). Five lifts service rather short, but uncrowded, runs and this is good ski-touring country. In summer, this is the start for a number of walks including to the summit of Mt Kosciuszko (18km return), the Main Range (25km) and the Blue Lake Lookout (10km).

Kosciuszko Chalet (☎ 1800 026 369; www.charlotte pass.com.au; weekend package $688) is a grand old place dating from the 1930s. The weekend package (Friday and Saturday) includes dinner, breakfast, transport and lift passes. The **Southern Alps Ski Club** (☎ 6457 5223; s/d summer $34/42) is open in summer. Kitchen facilities are available and you need to bring your own linen (or hire it from them). **Stillwell Lodge** (☎ 6457 5073; www.stillwell-lodge.com.au; d summer $99, d winter from $130) also opens year-round.

Bullocks Flat

☎ 02

Bullocks Flat, on the Alpine Way between Jindabyne and Thredbo, is the site of the Skitube terminal. The **Skitube train** (☎ 6456 2010; adult/child same-day return $27/16) runs from here mostly underground to Perisher Valley and Mt Blue Cow. In summer the Skitube runs to a reduced timetable but operates daily during school holidays.

The **Novotel Lake Crackenback Resort** (☎ 1800 020 524; www.novotellakecrackenback.com.au; d summer from $230, d winter from $310) is an excellent complex within walking distance of the Skitube terminal. There are lower rates available for longer stays or for up to four people sharing a room. There are also winter packages, which include accommodation, some meals and lift tickets. The complex has everything you can shake a ski-pole at, and some of the summer activities include canoeing and horse riding.

Crackenback Cottage (☎ 6456 2198; www.cracken back.com.au; s/d with breakfast $75/90; 🐾), on the road towards Jindabyne, has a cosy little restaurant and luscious day-spa treatments.

Thredbo Diggings is a pretty-but-basic free camp site near the Skitube.

Cabramurra

☎ 02

Australia's highest town (1488m), Cabramurra has some nice views (when not enveloped in cloud) and a photo gallery in the general store, but the main reason to come up here is to visit the nearby **Tumut 2 Power Station** (☎ 1800 623 776; adult/child $12/8; ☾ tours 11am & 2pm).

Yarrangobilly Caves

Although not as well known as some other caves in NSW, the **Yarrangobilly Caves** (☎ 6454 9597; car entry $3, cave admission $11-13; ☾ 9.30am-4pm) are among the most interesting. You can visit the Glory Hole by yourself, or there are guided tours at 11am, 1pm and 3pm, as well there are guided tours of other caves.

There's a good **NPWS visitors centre** (☎ 6454 9597), some short walks and a thermal pool where you can swim in 27°C water.

You don't have to pay the park fee if you're only visiting the caves – provided you pay the cave admission fee.

Getting There & Around

Summit Coaches (☎ 6297 2588) is the main carrier in this area. There are services from Sydney and Canberra to Cooma and Jindabyne, from where shuttles run to the resorts in winter. In summer, buses run to Thredbo from Canberra ($54).

In winter you can normally drive as far as Perisher Valley, but snow chains must be carried and fitted where directed. The simplest, safest way to get to Perisher Valley and Smiggin Holes in winter is to take the Skitube, a tunnel railway starting below the snowline at Bullocks Flat. Luggage lockers and overnight parking are available.

See below for western routes into the national park.

THE ALPINE WAY

From Khancoban, this spectacular route runs through dense forest, around the southern end of Kosciuszko National Park to Thredbo and on to Jindabyne. The road has been upgraded in recent years and the final sections of gravel were sealed in mid-2000. Caravans and trailers can be towed on the Alpine Way but there are some very steep sections, particularly between Thredbo and Tom Groggin. In winter, check conditions at Khancoban or Jindabyne. There's no fuel available between Khancoban and Thredbo (71km). If you're driving between Khancoban and Jindabyne, you can get a free transit pass, but if you stop en route you must have a day pass ($14 for 24 hours).

Murray 1 Power Station (☎ 6076 5115; admission free; ⊙ tours 10am & 2pm), off the Alpine Way south of Khancoban, has a hi-tech, interactive visitors centre explaining the construction and role of the Snowy Mountains hydro-electric scheme. Brief (10 minute) guided tours run daily, but it's best to book ahead.

Farther south is **Scammels Lookout**, offering superb views. Farther on you can camp at **Geehi**, a grassy picnic area with good facilities, on the Swampy Plains River.

At **Tom Groggin**, home of the original Man from Snowy River, the road skirts the upper Murray River, a clear, cool stretch that's good for a swim on a hot day. There's a good camping and picnic site here and a smaller site at **Leatherbarrel Creek**, about 7km farther on. After Tom Groggin the road climbs 800m to the **Pilot Lookout** (1300m), with views across a wilderness area to The Pilot (1830m), the source of the Murray River. There's another climb to **Dead Horse Gap** (1580m), named after some brumbies that froze here, then a descent to Thredbo Village (1400m), the Skitube terminal at Bullocks Flat, and Jindabyne. **Thredbo Diggings** and **Ngarigo** are two more picnic and camping areas on the banks of the Thredbo River near Bullock's Flat.

WEST OF THE SNOWIES

The western slopes of the Snowy Mountains are steeper than on the east, and the area is more intensively farmed, although there's still plenty of bush. The farms and small towns in the area blaze with colour in the autumn when poplars and fruit trees prepare to shed their leaves. This is a rural area with a thriving fruit-growing industry.

Getting There & Around

Countrylink (☎ 13 22 32) runs a bus from Cootamundra to Gundagai, Tumut, Adelong, Batlow and Tumbarumba daily except Saturday. At Cootamundra it connects with the Sydney to Melbourne XPT (express) train.

If driving or riding a motorcycle, there are several approaches to the Snowies from the west, all accessible from the Hume Hwy. The main route, the Snowy Mountains Hwy (18), leaves the Hume about 30km south of Gundagai and takes you to Tumut, Kiandra, Adaminaby and Cooma.

From Albury you can travel on Victoria's Murray Valley Hwy to Corryong, then head across the river to Khancoban for the Alpine Way. Another road in Victoria parallels the Murray Valley Hwy, but follows closely the south bank of the Murray. This route is longer, but perhaps more scenic, than the Murray Valley Hwy.

From Holbrook on the Hume Hwy, a sealed road runs through to Jingellic, while another sealed road runs from the Hume to Tumbarumba. From Tumbarumba you can cross the mountains on the winding Elliott Way to get to Mt Selwyn and the Snowy Mountains Hwy at Kiandra.

TUMUT

☎ 02 / pop 6240

Tumut is the closest centre to the northern end of Kosciuszko National Park. In the area are many pine plantations (timber is Tumut's biggest industry) and orchards.

Tumut was once a meeting place for three Aboriginal tribes, the Ngunawal, Walgalu and Wiradjuri. The explorers Hume and Hovell first came through in 1824, but development of the town was slow. One of the area's most famous early residents was author Miles Franklin (*My Brilliant Career*), who was born at Talbingo.

Information

The **Tumut visitors centre** (☎ 6947 7025; www
.tumut.nsw.gov.au/trvc/trvc.html; 5 Adelong Rd; ☺ 9am-
5pm) is in the refurbished Old Butter Factory
north of the town centre. This is also the
NPWS office for the region.

The **library** (☎ 6947 1969; 169 Wynyard St; ☺ 10am-
6pm Mon-Fri, 9am-noon Sat) has Internet access
($5 per hour).

Sights & Activities

There's a paved **river walk** along the shady
bank of the Tumut River (probably better
than swimming in the freezing water).

Opposite the visitors centre is the **Tumut
Broom Factory** (☎ 6947 2804; admission free; ☺ 9am-
12.30pm, 1.30-4pm Mon-Fri) where brooms are still
made from millet. The small **Tumut & District
Historical Museum** (cnr Capper & Merivale Sts; admission
$2; ☺ 2-4pm Wed & Sat) has a room devoted to
Miles Franklin.

Tumut is a popular spot for powered
hang-gliding. A half-hour microlight 'trike'
flight out over the Tumut Valley costs $77.
Contact **Air Escape** (☎ 6947 1159) to organise a
hang-gliding session.

Selwyn Snow & Water (☎ 6947 6225), near the
swimming pool on Fitzroy St, hires bikes as
well as ski and water-sports gear.

Sleeping

Oriental Hotel (☎ 6947 1174; cnr Fitzroy & Wynyard
Sts; r per person $25) A nice old pub with rooms
leading onto the big balcony.

Royal Hotel (☎ 6947 1129; 88 Wynyard St; s/d from
$42/55) Large, with motel-style units and
hotel rooms.

Tumut Log Cabins (☎ 6947 4042; 30 Fitzroy St; d
$60) Good-value self-contained cedar units
by the river, and comfortable.

Riverglade Caravan Park (☎ 6947 2528; glade@
dragnet.com.au; powered/unpowered sites $16/12, cabins
from $35) This immaculate place is on the
Snowy Mountains Hwy a few blocks from
the town centre, on the Tumut River.

Eating

Coach House Gourmet Eatery (Russell St; mains $8-10;
☺ breakfast & lunch) Excellent coffee, gourmet
sandwiches and a couple of tasty hot dishes
that change daily.

Brandy's (☎ 124 Wynyard St; mains $20-25; ☺ din-
ner) Tumut's best restaurant, serving mostly
steaks and seafood. If you can't decide, try
both with Brandy's beef Neptune ($25).

Rusty's (☺ 43 Wynyard St; mains $10-20; ☺ lunch
& dinner; ☒) A comfortable BYO restaurant
serving steak, chicken and local fish. The
camembert steak with cranberry sauce ($21)
is close to – but not quite – too much.

Heritage Coffee Lounge (44 Wynyard St; ☺ breakfast & lunch) Opens early (7am) for breakfast.

Getting There & Away

Countrylink (☎ 13 22 32) buses, which run to
Cootamundra, Adelong, Gundagai, Batlow
and Tumbarumba, stop daily (except Saturday) outside the National Bank on the
corner of Russell and Wynyard Sts. **Harvey
World Travel** (☎ 6947 3055), in the Hub centre
on Wynyard St, sells tickets.

There's a handy little road from Tumut
north to Wee Jasper (69km), from where you
can get to Yass, and another running east
through the Brindabella Range to Canberra
(125km). These roads are mostly unsealed
but are in reasonable condition – the visitors
centre has information and maps.

AROUND TUMUT

The Thomas Boyd Trackhead of the **Hume
and Hovell Walking Track** is 23km southeast of
Tumut and it has camping facilities.

Blowering Reservoir, nearly 20km long, is
part of the Snowy Mountains hydro-electric
scheme. There are walks along the forested
shores and numerous picnic and camping
areas, and the lake is popular for water
sports. You can drive or walk up to the
top of the 112m-high Blowering Dam for
a good view; the gates close at 4pm. At the
southern end of the reservoir is the small
town of **Talbingo**, and 2km farther south
is the **Tumut 3 Power Station** (☎ 1800 623 776;
Murray Jackson Drive; adult/child $10/7; ☺ tours 10am,
11am, noon, 1.30pm & 2.30pm). It's the largest of the
Snowy power stations and has informative,
one-hour guided tours.

Batlow

☎ 02 / pop 970
Batlow, on one side of a bowl-shaped valley,
is an apple-orchard town. Tourist information for the area (and fresh fruit) can be
found at **Springfield Orchard** (☎ 6949 1021), just
north of town.

The trees blossom in October and the
apple harvest starts around mid-March
(when there's a local festival), but there are
also stone fruits and cherries, so picking

work is usually available from December to May. The best way to find work is to approach the orchards directly – the **Tumut visitors centre** (☎ 6947 7025) has a list.

Apple-picking aside, Batlow is a sleepy little place. If you've never seen the inside of an apple-packing factory, **Fruits of Batlow** (☎ 6949 1835; 1 Cottams Rd), 6km south of town, is the place for a short guided tour ($3) from Monday to Friday.

Digger's Rest Motel (☎ 6949 1342; Tumbarumba Rd; s/d $60/70) fits in nicely with the authentic feel of Batlow. The colour scheme is overwhelmingly brown and some furnishings are so retro that they've actually become fashionable again. **Batlow Hotel** (☎ 6949 1001; 12 Pioneer St; s/d $25/35) has good honest pub rooms. **Batlow Caravan Park** (☎ 6949 1444; off Kurrajong Ave; s/d camp sites $9/11, on-site vans $20-30) is down by the creek.

BAGO STATE FOREST

The Adelong road from Batlow to Tumbarumba slices down the western edge of the Bago State Forest, a large area of pine plantations and native hardwood stretching across to the Blowering and Talbingo Reservoirs. You can enter the forest from Laurel Hill, about 15km south of Batlow, and explore a number of walks and drives. The short stroll through a stand of **sugar pines** on Kopsens Rd is worthwhile, and farther in is the **Pilot Hill Forest Park** with a tidy little picnic and camping area. Heading up towards Blowering Reservoir is the **Hume and Hovell Lookout**. These roads are unsealed but in good condition.

TUMBARUMBA

☎ 02 / pop 1500

Tumbarumba (usually called just Tumba) is a small town, though it may seem large for this part of the world. The area was first settled by graziers, who wintered their cattle here when the snows came to the high plains, and a small gold rush in the 1860s boosted the population. Today, forestry is the major industry, along with orchards growing cool-climate fruits.

Orientation & Information

The main street through town, Tumbarumba Parade, is known simply as the Parade.

The best place for tourist information is the **Wool & Craft Centre** (☎ 6948 2805; Bridge St;

⏰ 9am-5pm) at the southern end of The Parade. The **Forestry Commission office** (☎ 6948 2400; Winton St) has details of the area's state forests, including camp sites and walking tracks. There's Internet access at the **library** (☎ 6948 2725; ⏰ 9am-5pm Mon-Fri; per hr $3) in the Bicentennial Gardens on Prince St.

Sights

There's a small **museum** (admission free; ⏰ 10am-4pm Tue-Sun) in the Wool & Craft Centre with displays on the town's pioneer history.

Some of the district's many **orchards**, growing nuts, cherries, blueberries and apples, welcome visitors. Ask at the Wool & Craft Centre for opening times and directions. Viticulture is also taking off in the region and there are several **wineries** nearby. The closest is the **Tumbarumba Wine Cellars** (☎ 6948 3055) on Albury Close next to the Tumbarumba Motel. The cellar is open for sales and tastings from noon to 4.30pm on weekends.

Festivals & Events

Held on New Year's Day is the **Tumbarumba Rodeo**, while **Tumbafest** is a weekend of food, wine and entertainment, celebrated in early February.

Eating & Sleeping

Red (34 The Parade; ☎ 6948 3228; s/d $65/85) Cosy timber rooms in the centre of town. Prices include cooked breakfast.

Tumbarumba Motel (☎ 6948 2494; tumbarumba motelelms@bigpond.com; cnr Albury Close & Mate St; s/d $77/92) Spacious, modern rooms and a good restaurant (mains $8 to $24).

Tumbarumba Hotel (☎ 6948 2562; 20 The Parade; s/d $30/45) Fairly ordinary pub rooms. Rates include a light self-serve breakfast.

Tumbarumba Creek Caravan Park (☎ 6948 3330; Lauder St; camp sites $11, bunkhouse $13, cabins from $36) Just off The Parade near the showground, this place is small but tidy.

Red Coffee Shop (☎ 6948 3228; 34 The Parade; ⏰ breakfast & lunch) This is definitely the hippest café in the region, serving imaginative food and great coffee.

Old Times Coffee Shop (☎ 6948 3300; 38 The parade; ⏰ lunch) Offers simple country fare at rock-bottom prices.

Bowling Club (☎ 6948 2016; Winton St; mains $10-15; ⏰ lunch Thu-Sun, dinner daily) Has Chinese meals.

SOUTHEAST

DETOUR: THE ELLIOTT WAY

Ignoring the superstar Alpine Way for a minute, one of the best drives in the Snowy Mountains region is the back road from Tumbarumba to Adaminaby. Take Tooma Rd south out of Tumba for about 18km until you reach a T-junction. Turn left onto the **Elliott Way**, which will take you through rolling farmland, with Pilot Reef Mountain on your right. You'll know you're in the Kosciuszko National Park when the landscape changes from grassy paddocks to soaring eucalypt forest. The road cuts around and follows the Tumut River, which it crosses at the site of the Tumut 2 power station. From there you climb up and out of the forest. Take a left and you're onto the eerily vacant highlands, a unique and rugged landscape. The road joins the Snowy Mountains Hwy at Kiandra, and from there it's another 40km to Adaminaby.

Getting There & Away

Countrylink (☎ 13 22 32) buses stop in town. From Tumbarumba, roads run west to the Hume Hwy, north to Tumut, east to the Snowy Mountains Hwy, and south to Khancoban, the Alpine Way and Corryong (in Victoria). The ski slopes at Mt Selwyn are about an hour away on the Elliott Way. You'll need chains in winter.

KHANCOBAN

☎ 02 / pop 310

Khancoban is a small town built by the Snowy Mountains Authority to house construction workers. Towns built by public authorities are often bureaucratic monstrosities, but Khancoban is a beautiful exception.

If you're heading along the Alpine Way, there's a **NPWS office** (☎ 6076 9373; ☽ 8:30amnoon & 1-4pm) where you must buy your park visitor's permit. It has a good range of information, publications and a free film. **Khancoban Roadhouse** (☎ 6076 9400) has some tourist information and sells permits when the NPWS office is closed.

Activities

There's good **fishing** in the Khancoban Pondage and the Swampy Plains River that runs off it. Hire boats (half-/full-day $55/85) from the Lakeside Caravan Resort (below).

Rapid Descents (☎ 1800 637 486; www.rapiddescents .com.au) has white-water rafting trips on the upper Murray River. The one-day trip costs $120 and the two-day camping trip, covering 24km of rapids, is $280.

Upper Murray Adventures (☎ 6076 9222; umaat@ corryong.albury.net.au) can book and organise a wide range of activities including rafting, mountain-biking, skiing and hang-gliding.

Sleeping & Eating

Alpine Hideaway Village (☎ 6076 9498; alpine hideaway@bigpond.com; s/d $40/70) Across the valley from the town, this has great views of the Snowies. Accommodation is in fully equipped, self-catering lodges. There's a variety of packages, a licensed restaurant and canoe hire is available.

Lyrebird Lodge (☎ /fax 6076 9455; s/d $35/66) Up the hill from Hideaway, this is a smaller place with the same great views.

Khancoban Backpackers & Fisherman's Lodge (☎ 6076 9471; Scott St; dm $14, s/d $19/28) Reasonable share accommodation; you need to supply your own bedding. Book and check in at the nearby Alpine Inn Hotel.

Lakeside Caravan Resort (☎ 6076 9488; www .klcr.com.au; camp sites $13, vans $25, cabins $40) By the Khancoban Dam, Lakeside is a wellequipped place with some shared accommodation for $15, and good cabins.

Alpine Inn Hotel (Scott St; mains around $10; ☽ lunch & dinner) Has counter meals and a daily $6 special.

Pickled Parrot Restaurant (☽ breakfast, lunch & dinner) At the Alpine Inn Hotel's motel section, this is good for a more upmarket meal.

JJ's Café (snacks $5, mains $10) Next to the roadhouse, JJ's has simple, well-prepared food.

Getting There & Away

Autopia Tours (☎ 03-9326 5536; 78 Howard St, North Melbourne, Victoria) stops here on its regular Sydney–Melbourne run. To Melbourne costs $50, to Sydney $100. If you're heading towards Albury, you can grab a ride in the mail truck, which leaves the post office at 12.30pm weekdays.

THE HUME HIGHWAY

The Hume Hwy is the busiest road in Australia, running nearly 900km from Sydney to Melbourne. It is named after Hamilton

Hume, who followed roughly this route when he walked from Parramatta to Port Phillip, later the site of Melbourne, with William Hovell in 1824. Hume was a native-born Australian, while Hovell was an upper-crust Englishman, and their association was not entirely happy. Their return journey became a race to be the first in Sydney with news of new lands. Despite chicanery on Hovell's part, they both arrived at the same time.

GOULBURN & AROUND

Goulburn is a medium sized country town (population 20,880) with a lazy Sunday feel on most days. The Hume Hwy bypassed Goulburn in 1992 so the old town centre is now relatively peaceful and worth a stroll.

Orientation & Information

Goulburn's main shopping street is Auburn St.

The new **Goulburn visitors centre** (☎ 02-4823 4492; 221 Sloane St; ☀ 9am-5pm), opposite Belmore Park, has an interpretive display, plenty of regional information and free Internet access.

Festivals & Events

The **Australian Blues Music Festival** (www.australian bluesfestival.com.au) comes to town in February.

Sights

Of all the impressive country courthouses in NSW, Goulburn's **courthouse** (Montague St), built in 1887, must be the most imposing. Around the corner, the **old courthouse** (Sloane St), did a lot of business in sentencing the bushrangers who plagued the highlands. The visitors centre has a good heritage walking-tour map of town (free).

The three-storey-high **Big Merino** (Cowper St; admission free; ☀ 8am-8pm) is a continuation of Australia's fascination with all attractions big. Climb the stairs inside, past displays on the history of the wool industry, to a **lookout** affording spectacular views of nothing in particular. There's local arts and crafts on sale at the Agrodome next door.

The **Old Goulburn Brewery** (☎ 02-4821 6071; 23 Bungonia Rd; adult/child $8/free; ☀ tours 11am & 3pm) dates from 1836. As well as the brewery and museum, you can see the cooperage, the maltings, a tobacco-curing kiln and a steam-powered flour mill. Try the traditional ale in the rustic bar.

About 40km southeast of Goulburn and abutting Morton National Park, **Bungonia State Recreation Area** (SRA; ☎ 02-4844 4277; Lookdown Rd) has a dramatic forested gorge and some deep caves. Bushwalking and canoeing are popular. There's a camping ground near the main entrance with showers, but no powered sites.

Just off the highway between Goulburn and Yass, **Gunning** is a small town with restored buildings, a number of antique and craft shops and several B&Bs.

Sleeping

Mandelson's (☎ 02-4821 0707; www.mandelsons.com .au; 160 Sloane St; s/d with breakfast from $120/130) A charming and luxurious B&B in a restored heritage building.

Yurt Farm (☎ 02-4829 2114; www.yurtworks.com .au; Grabben Gullen Rd; s/d/t private tents $12/24/36) Twenty kilometres north of Goulburn (follow Clinton St), this environmentally friendly place includes an activities camp for students, with the emphasis on learning to live simply. Travellers are welcome to stay in the Yurt village (a group of basic huts around a small lake), but should bring their own bedding. The farm is involved in the Willing Workers on Organic Farms (WWOOF) program, so quite a few backpackers come out here. It's a good idea to phone first to see if there's room.

Tattersall's Hotel (☎ 02-4821 3088; 76 Auburn St; dm $20) The backpacker rooms upstairs here aren't bad – there are four bunks to a room, but most likely you'll have one to yourself.

Alpine Heritage Motel (☎ 02-4821 2930; 248 Sloane St; s/d $45/70) There are good-value rooms in the main building and slightly cheaper motel-style rooms out back.

Governor's Hill Carapark (☎ 02-4821 7373; gover norshillcp@bigpond.com.au; 77-83 Sydney Rd; powered/ unpowered sites $21/18, d cabins from $59) Well-shaded place on the old highway 3.5km north of town. Facilities include camp kitchen and games room.

Ask at the visitors centre (above) about farmstays in the area.

Eating

Coffee Bean (210 Auburn St; meals from $8; ☀ breakfast & lunch) The best place in town for breakfast, with fresh-cooked food and sunny outdoor seating.

Paragon Café (174 Auburn St; mains from $9; ☺ lunch & dinner) The most impressive of several cafés along Auburn St, this is licensed and has an extensive menu, including huge pasta dishes ($9) and seafood meals.

Goulburn Worker's Club (☎ 02-4821 3355; 236 Auburn St; mains around $12; ☺ lunch & dinner) Big serves of reliable and tasty food; this place lacks atmosphere, but where else are you going to get 400g of rump steak for $13?

Kinaree (☎ 02-4821 2289; 120 Auburn St; mains from $11) A good Thai restaurant with a Bring Your Own (BYO) alcohol licence.

Getting There & Away

McCafferty's/Greyhound (☎ 13 20 30) buses between Sydney and Adelaide (via Canberra) stop outside the Goulburn train station. **Murrays** (☎ 13 22 51) also run buses three times a week to Canberra and Wollongong, and **Fearnes** (www.fearnes.com.au) has daily services to Wagga Wagga and Sydney (stopping outside the courthouse). The visitors centre makes bookings.

Trains between Sydney and Melbourne stop here daily. The **Countrylink Travel Centre** (☎ 02-4827 1485; ☺ 7.15am-5pm Mon-Fri, 6.15-11am & 12.10-3.15pm Sat & Sun) is at the train station. The one-way fare to Canberra is $14 and to Sydney $35.

YASS

☎ 02 / pop 4900

The Ngunawal people were in this area when Europeans arrived in the 1820s. Among the first to pass through were the explorers Hume and Hovell. Graziers soon followed and, by the time the Hume returned to settle in the area in 1830, a town was growing on the banks of the Yass River. These days Yass is a pretty place. Having been bypassed by the highway, it's quiet but atmospheric. There's a good compromise between old-style character and the new café and food scene.

Orientation & Information

The Yass Valley Way (the old highway) becomes Comur St, then Laidlaw St as it passes through town. **Yass visitors centre** (☎ 6226 2557; tourism@yass.nsw.gov.au; Comur St; ☺ 9am-4.30pm Mon-Fri, to 4pm Sat & Sun) is in Coronation Park on the Sydney side of town.

Red's Net Café (198 Comur St; ☺ 10am-7pm Mon-Fri, 10am-5pm Sat) provides Internet access for $5 per hour.

Sights

The **Yass Railway Museum** (☎ 6226 2169; Lead St; adult/child $3/2; ☺ noon-4pm Fri-Sun) tells the story of Yass' trains and trams and is said to have Australia's shortest platform.

Next to the visitors centre, the **Hamilton Hume Museum** (☎ 6226 2700; adult/child $2/1; ☺ 10am-4pm Sat & Sun) has a model reconstruction of the town in the 1890s. Hume's house, **Cooma Cottage** (☎ 6226 1470; adult/child $4/2; 10am-4pm Wed-Mon), is on the Yass Valley Way on the Sydney side of town. The original timber cottage was built in 1835 and restored by the National Trust. **Riverbank Park** is a great place for a picnic or a quiet sit by the river. Check out the Aboriginal murals on the toilet blocks and underneath the bridge.

Sleeping

There are a couple of fine old B&Bs to choose from in Yass.

Globe B&B (☎ 6226 3680; theglobe@interact.net.au; 70 Rossi St; s/d $100/120) A lovely old National Trust–classified guesthouse in a restored Victorian hotel in the middle of town.

Kerrowgair (☎ 6226 4932; www.kerrowgair.com.au; 24 Grampian St; s/d with breakfast from $110/130) Another National Trust–listed building set in ample gardens on a hill overlooking town.

Australian Hotel (☎ 6226 1744; pub r $20/40, motel $40/50) Decent pub rooms and quieter motel-style rooms out the back.

Yass Caravan Park (☎ 6226 1173; powered/unpowered sites $16/14, s/d cabins from $35/38) In one corner of pretty Victoria Park, on the Gundagai side of town.

Eating

Galutzi (☎ 6226 5261; Meehan St; sandwiches $5-8; ☺ 9am-5pm Mon-Fri, to 3pm Sat & Sun) Probably Yass's hippest café – there's a plethora of gourmet sandwich ingredients to choose from and the coffee is excellent.

Pampered Palate (Comur St; meals $10; ☺ breakfast, lunch & afternoon tea) Cheap, fresh sandwiches and good home-cooked meals. There are sunny tables out front.

Royal Hotel (Comur St; meals $12-16, specials from $6; ☺ lunch & dinner) Has a pleasant beer garden out the back, and does breakfast on weekends.

Getting There & Away

McCafferty's (☎ 13 20 30) and **V/Line** (☎ 13 61 96) buses heading to Melbourne stop at the visitors centre; heading to Sydney they stop at the NRMA garage across the road. Firefly services to Sydney and Melbourne stop at the Ampol petrol station. **Transborder Buses** (☎ 6241 0033) has services between Yass and Canberra ($13, daily). They leave from Rossi St.

Trains between Sydney and Melbourne stop at Yass Junction, 2km north of town.

AROUND YASS

About 57km southwest of Yass, the **Burrinjuck Dam** supplies water to the Murrumbidgee Irrigation Area, and its long arms wind among steep valleys. It's popular for water sports, including water-skiing and fishing, and there's wildlife in the surrounding bush. **Burrinjuck Waters State Recreation Area** (☎ 02-6227 8114) is about 30km from the highway and costs $5 per car to enter (for day use). There are cruises from here on the **Lady BJ** (☎ 02-6227 7270). There's camping ($12) and cabins, as well as boat hire.

HUME & HOVELL WALKING TRACK

This 370km walking track between Yass and Albury closely follows the historic route taken by explorers Hamilton Hume and William Hovell in their successful expedition to Port Phillip Bay (the site of present-day Melbourne) in 1824.

The party, which included another six men, took only four months to complete the return journey to Port Phillip, passing to the west of the Snowy Mountains before dropping down to the relatively flat plains through Victoria.

The walk, if you are dedicated enough to complete the entire route, takes about 21 days, winding its way through numerous state forests, along the shores of Lake Burrinjuck and Blowering Reservoir, and close to Wee Jasper, Tumut, Tumbarumba, Lankeys Creek and Woomargama. It's divided into 12 stages with six major trackheads, and there are various side trips and day walks off the main track.

The route is well signposted and there are at least 16 camp sites along the way. A good resource is H Hill's *The Hume & Hovell Walking Track Guidebook* (1993), published by Crawford House Press.

Lake Burrinjuck Leisure Resort (☎ 02-6227 7271; powered/unpowered sites $15/13, cabins $66) is closer to the highway and offers boat hire.

Wee Jasper

☎ 02 / pop 80

About 55km southwest of Yass, Wee Jasper is a small village in a beautiful valley near the southern end of Burrinjuck Dam. It's a favourite getaway for the Canberra weekender set, but during the week you may have the valley to yourself (and the 80 or so locals).

The **Wee Jasper Festival** is on the long weekend in October. Check www.weejasper.org for more details on the area. You can join the **Hume and Hovell Walking Track** here, and visit the limestone **Careys Cave** (☎ 6227 9622; www.weejaspercaves.com; adults/child $10/5) which is open Friday to Monday afternoons, but call first to confirm. There's a store and a pub, and fuel is available.

The **Stables** (☎ 6227 9619; cabins $50) has good-sized cabins, some with open fireplace and kitchens. More accommodation options (mostly self-catering) are available – ask at the **General Store** (☎ 6227 9640).

There's camping at five bush reserves in the area (some with river frontage), including the Fitzpatrick Trackhead of the Hume and Hovell Walking Track and at Carey's Reserve on the shores of Burrinjuck Dam. Contact the **ranger** (☎ 6227 9626) for more information.

The road from Yass has an 8km unsealed section but it's usually pretty good. Continuing southwest to Tumut, the road deteriorates for the climb out of the valley. Another unsealed road cuts across to Canberra. Both these roads are OK when dry, but check conditions after rain.

Wineries

Around **Murrumbateman**, on the Barton Hwy southeast toward Canberra, are a number of cool-climate wineries. Most are open for sales and tastings on weekends and some during the week. The Yass (opposite) and Canberra (p336) visitors centres have information.

GUNDAGAI

☎ 02 / pop 2000

Gundagai, on the Murrumbidgee River 398km from Sydney, is one of the more interesting small towns along (or bypassed by) the Hume Hwy.

The **visitors centre** (☎ 6944 0250; gundagcl@tpgi.com.au; 249 Sheridan St; ☺ 8am-5pm Mon-Fri, from 9am Sat & Sun) is on the grand main street and has plenty of info on B&Bs and farmstays in the area.

Sights

The long, wooden **Prince Alfred Bridge** (closed to traffic, but you can walk it) crosses the flood plain of the Murrumbidgee River. It's a reminder that in 1852 Gundagai suffered Australia's worst flood disaster; 78 deaths were recorded, but probably over 100 people drowned. There's a disused railway bridge (built in 1901) here, too.

Gold rushes and bushrangers were part of Gundagai's colourful early history, and the notorious Captain Moonlight was tried in Gundagai's 1860 **courthouse** and buried in the cemetery in William St.

Gundagai Historical Museum (☎ 6944 1995; Homer St; adult/child $3/1; ☺ 9am-3pm), is in a modern building with an impressive old sandstone portico. It's cluttered with old photographs, household items and farm machinery from the town's past. At the visitors centre, **Rusconi's Marble Masterpiece** is a 21,000-piece cathedral model that took 28 years to build. Is it art? Is it lunacy? Is it worth the $1 entry fee? Probably. You even get to hear a snatch of 'Along the Road to Gundagai'. It was Frank Rusconi who made the Dog on the Tuckerbox memorial (below).

The **Gabriel Gallery** (☎ 6944 1722; ☺ 8.30am-5.30pm Mon-Fri, 9am-noon Sat), above the Mitre 10 store on Sheridan St, has a free display of historic photos. The **Mt Parnassus lookout** has good views over the town and picnic facilities. It's reached by a steep walk (or drive) up Hanley St.

Festivals & Events

Held in mid-November, the **Snake Gully Cup** is Gundagai's annual race day and it coincides with the **Dog on the Tuckerbox** festival featuring a street parade and music. It's a great country event worth catching.

Sleeping

Poet's Recall (☎ 6944 1777; poets.recall@bigpond.com; cnr West & Punch Sts; s/d $70/90; ⚇) Touches like slate bathrooms and comfy furniture make this the best motel in town.

Sheridan Motel (☎ 6944 1311; cnr Sheridan & Otway Sts; s/d $45/55) An older motel that must have got a bulk deal on their carpet – it's on the ceilings and walls as well as the floors.

Blue Heeler Guesthouse (☎ 6944 2286; blueheel@ozemail.com.au; 145 Sheridan St; dm $20, d with breakfast $40) This refurbished backpackers lodge is in what used to be the Hotel Gresham. It has good kitchen and lounge areas, a balcony overlooking the street, Internet access and free bikes. The owners can help find seasonal work in the surrounding orchards and farms.

Criterion Hotel (☎ 6944 1048; 172 Sheridan St; s/d with breakfast $35/55) Reasonable pub rooms and a lively public bar.

Gundagai Caravan Village (☎ 6944 1057; Junee Rd; camp sites $14, cabins $48) Near the swimming pool, this place has well-presented vans and cabins.

Eating

Niagara Café (☎ 6944 1109; 124 Sheridan St; ☺ breakfast, lunch & dinner) Has an illustrious history (former Prime Minister John Curtin once visited), and is a gem among country town cafés, although the menu doesn't differ much from standard snacks and grills. Steak meals cost $13.50 and it's licensed.

Terra Verde Café Lounge (Otway St; ☺ 10am-6.30pm; lunch $8-12) This tidy little organic-food specialist does good lunches, fresh juices, home-made desserts and excellent coffee.

There's also a **bakery** (Sheridan St), supposedly the oldest still operating in Australia.

THE DOG ON THE TUCKERBOX

Gundagai features in a number of famous songs, including 'Along the Road to Gundagai', 'My Mabel Waits for Me' and 'When a Boy from Alabama Meets a Girl from Gundagai'. Its most famous monument is 8km east of town just off the Hume Hwy: the Dog on the Tuckerbox memorial (made by Frank Rusconi). It's a sculpture of the dog that in a 19th-century bush ballad (and a more recent, perhaps even better-known, poem by Jack Moses), sat by and watched as its master tried to get his bullock team out of a bog. A popular tale claims that the dog was even less helpful because in the original version it apparently shat, rather than sat, on the tuckerbox!

Getting There & Away

The tourist office sells bus tickets for the services that stop outside. **McCafferty's/Greyhound** (☎ 13 20 30) buses go to Melbourne and Sydney via Canberra, and **V/Line** (☎ 13 61 96) buses also stop here between Melbourne and Canberra. **Countrylink** (☎ 13 22 32) runs buses north to Cootamundra and south to Tumut and Tumbarumba.

HOLBROOK & AROUND

The Hume runs right through this small town (population 1300) and it's worth a look around – it's unlikely that you'll fail to see the submarine as you pass through!

Holbrook's good **Woolpack Inn Museum** (☎ 02-6036 2131; 83 Albury St; www.geocities.com /woolpackinn; adult/child $4/1; ☻ 9.30am-4.30pm) is packed full of more Australiana than most amateurs can probably cope with. The museum also has tourist information. Near the museum is a short walking track, the **Ian Geddes Bushwalk**, along the banks of Ten Mile Creek.

This is also the best place to turn off the highway for a drive through Morgan Country to the west (see p267). A road runs east through pretty Wontagong Valley and past the **Hume and Hovell Walking Track** at Lankeys Creek (a nice picnic spot) to Jingellic and then on to Tumbarumba or Khancoban.

HOLBROOK & SUBMARINES

Holbrook, founded in 1858, was called Germanton until WWI, when the town decided to display some patriotism and opt for a name change in honour of British naval commander, Douglas Holbrook. He and his crew earned the first Victoria Crosses (VCs) of the war when their submarine sank a Turkish ship near the Dardanelles.

Today, a 9m model of the vessel is on display in the town park. The town has enduring links with the Australian navy's submarine corps, which donated to the town a decommissioned submarine (the top part of which is on display near the model). Holbrook's wife has been over from Britain a number of times, maintaining another link. Occasional visits by official parties of sailors have seen some riotous times in the pubs.

All this in a town more than 250km from the sea!

ALBURY

☎ 02 / pop 42,150

Albury is a major regional centre on the Murray River, just below the big Hume Weir. The city makes a convenient stopover between Melbourne and Sydney and is a good base for trips to the Riverina, the Victorian wineries around Rutherglen, the Snowy Mountains and the Victorian high country.

Orientation & Information

The long Lincoln Causeway over the Murray River's flood plain links Albury with Wodonga, on the Victorian side of the river. Central Albury is a reasonably compact grid, but the city sprawls northwards into the residential suburb of Laverton. Dean St is the main shopping strip.

The **Gateway visitors centre** (☎ 1300 796 222; ☻ 9am-5pm) is part of a large 'island' complex, which includes cafés, craft shops and a brewery/restaurant. It's on the Lincoln Causeway on the Victorian side of the river and stocks loads of information on NSW and Victoria, and books accommodation.

Cyber Heaven (☎ 6023 4320; Kiewa St; per hr $9; ☻ 10am-6pm Mon-Fri, 10am-2pm Sat) has Internet access.

Sights

The **Albury Regional Museum** (☎ 6021 4550; Wodonga Place; admission free; ☻ 10.30am-4.30pm) in Noreuil Park has material on Aboriginal culture and early European settlement and the Bonegilla collection, covering postwar migration.

The **Albury Regional Art Centre** (☎ 6023 8187; 546 Dean St; admission free; ☻ 10.30am-5pm Mon-Fri, to 4pm Sat & Sun) has a good collection of Australian paintings, including works by Russell Drysdale and Fred Williams, and displays contemporary photography.

The paddle steamer **Cumberoona** (☎ 6041 5558), moored on the river behind Noreuil Park, isn't the original boat (which lies at the bottom of the Darling River). It's a replica built as a community project to celebrate Australia's bicentenary of European settlement. One-hour trips run on Saturdays (adult/child $14/5).

The **Botanic Gardens**, at the northern end of Wodonga Place, are old, formal and beautiful. The **Nail Can Hill Walking Track** rambles over the steep, bush-covered ridges on the western side of town. You can start from Noreuil Park or head up Dean St to

SOUTHEAST

the war memorial and pick up the trail there. The visitors centre has a map. The **Wiradjuri Walkabout** is an easy interpretive trail around Gateway Island starting from the information centre.

Tours

Albury Backpackers (☎ 6041 1822) Popular canoe trips on the Murray River (half-/full-/two-day trips $20/26/ 55). See also review opposite.
Mylon Motorways (☎ 6056 3100; 153 High St, Wodonga) Tours to the Rutherglen wineries on weekends ($28).

Festivals & Events

There's a two-day gastronomic affair, the **Albury-Wodonga Food & Wine Festival**, in early October. The **Ngan Girra Festival** celebrates the traditional Aboriginal gathering to feast on the bogong moths that swarm into the area on their annual migration from Queensland to the cool caves of the Victorian Alps. There's traditional music and dancing, workshops and a bushcraft display. It's held at the Mungabareena Reserve in late November.

Sleeping

Gundowring (☎ 6041 4437; thudson@albury.net.au; 621 Stanley St; s/d with breakfast $110/130; P) The best B&B near the centre, in a gorgeous Federation house a short walk from the botanical gardens.

   Quality Resort Siesta (☎ 6025 4555; www.siesta .com.au; 416 Wagga Rd; r from $110; P ⚭) Possibly

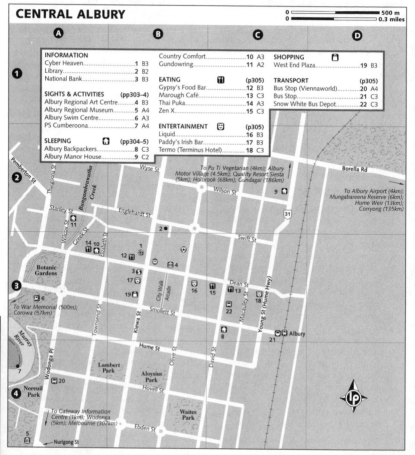

CENTRAL ALBURY

0 — 500 m
0 — 0.3 miles

INFORMATION	
Cyber Heaven	1 B3
Library	2 B2
National Bank	3 B3

SIGHTS & ACTIVITIES	(pp303–4)
Albury Regional Art Centre	4 B3
Albury Regional Museum	5 A4
Albury Swim Centre	6 A3
PS Cumberoona	7 A4

SLEEPING	(pp304–5)
Albury Backpackers	8 C3
Albury Manor House	9 C2

Country Comfort	10 A3
Gundowring	11 A2

EATING	(p305)
Gypsy's Food Bar	12 B3
Marough Café	13 C3
Thai Puka	14 A3
Zen X	15 C3

ENTERTAINMENT	(p305)
Liquid	16 B3
Paddy's Irish Bar	17 B3
Termo (Terminus Hotel)	18 C3

SHOPPING	
West End Plaza	19 B3

TRANSPORT	(p305)
Bus Stop (Viennaworld)	20 A4
Bus Stop	21 C3
Snow White Bus Depot	22 C3

To Pu Ti Vegetarian (4km); Albury Motor Village (4.5km); Quality Resort Siesta (5km); Holbrook (68km); Gundagai (186km)

To Albury Airport (4km); Mungabareena Reserve (6km); Hume Weir (13km); Corryong (135km)

Borella Rd

Wyse St
Wilson St
Englehardt St
Swift St
Dean St
Smollett St
Hume St
Hovell St
Ebden St
Nurigong St

Botanic Gardens

To War Memorial (500m); Corowa (57km)

Murray River

Lambert Park
Aloysius Park
Waites Park
Noreuil Park

To Gateway Information Centre (1km); Wodonga (5km); Melbourne (307km)

Pemberton St
Thurgoona St
Bungambrawatha Creek
Stanley St
Wilson St
Creek St
Elizabeth St
City Walk Arcade
Kiewa St
Townsend St
Olive St
David St
Macauley St
Young St (Hume Hwy)
Woodonga Pl

the most luxurious option – a vaguely Mexican-themed 4½-star resort with a bewildering array of options – spa, sauna, steam room, solarium, gym, a couple of decent restaurants and the Cantina Bar.

Country Comfort (☎ 6021 5366; www.countrycom forthotels.com; cnr Dean & Elizabeth Sts; r with breakfast from $140; P 🔊) Travelling salespeople head straight for this tall semicircular landmark at the western end of Dean St. There's a decent cocktail bar here and live music on weekends.

Albury Manor House (☎ 1800 641 774; alburymanor house@bigpond.com; 593 Young St; r from $110; P 🔊) A mock-Tudor motel with spacious rooms, a licensed restaurant and free in-house movies.

Albury Backpackers (☎ 6041 1822; thecanoeguy@ hotmail.com; 452 David St; dm/d $20/40) A well-run, central hostel with a good lounge area and a well-equipped kitchen. As well as Internet access and free bikes, the management organises adventure activities and can help you find farm work in the area.

Albury Motor Village (☎ 6040 2999; www.motor village.com.au/albury.htm; 372 Wagga Rd; powered sites & dm $20; d cabins $62; P 🔊) About 4.5km north of the centre, this is a tidy park with a range of cabins, vans and backpacker beds in clean dorms

Eating

The Albury eating scene has really picked up in the last few years – Dean St is a long strip of takeaways, cafés and restaurants.

Marough Café (Dean St; mains from $11; 🕒 lunch & dinner) A real find – excellent Lebanese food, belly dancing on weekends and a BYO (wine only) licence.

Thai Puka (☎ 6021 2504; 652 Dean St; mains from $13; 🕒 lunch & dinner) Next to the Country Comfort, this upmarket Thai restaurant has an innovative menu.

Zen X (☎ 6023 6455; 467 Dean St; mains from $15; 🕒 lunch & dinner) A Japanese restaurant which does excellent sushi and *teppanyaki*.

Pu Ti Vegetarian (☎ 6025 0086; 1083 Mate St, North Albury; mains around $10; 🕒 dinner Tue-Sat) Asian food with imaginative bean-curd concoctions such as vegetarian 'chicken', 'fish' and 'venison'.

Gypsy's Food Bar (582 Dean St; meals $8-12; 🕒 breakfast & lunch) Gypsy's famous breakfast ($9) is a mountain of sausages, eggs, bacon, tomatoes and toast.

Entertainment

Albury's nightlife is mainly in pubs and clubs.

Paddy's Irish Bar (491 Kiewa St) In the New Albury Hotel, it's the latest hot spot and has your typical Irish theme–bar ambience.

Termo (cnr Young & Dean Sts) Has bands on weekends.

Liquid (491 Dean St; 🕒 9pm-late Wed-Sat) Albury's most happening nightclub – there's a young crowd, a decent dance floor and mainstream disco music. Cheap drinks night is Wednesday. The place stays open until the crowds leave.

Getting There & Away

Rex airlines (☎ 13 17 13) flies to Sydney ($140) and Melbourne ($110). **Brindabella** (☎ 6248 8711) flies to Canberra ($213).

Long-distance buses running on the Hume Hwy between Sydney and Melbourne stop at the train station. Most also stop at Viennaworld (a petrol station/diner) across from Noreuil Park. Greyhound Pioneer stops only at Viennaworld and north of town at Laverton. You can book buses at the **Countrylink Travel Centre** (☎ 6041 9555; 🕒 8.30am-5pm Mon-Fri, 9.30am-4.30pm Sat & Sun) at the train station.

McCafferty's/Greyhound (☎ 13 20 30) has coaches to Melbourne ($40, 4½ hours), Wagga Wagga ($30, two hours) and Sydney ($43, 10 hours). **Countrylink** (☎ 13 22 32) runs to Echuca in Victoria via several towns in the southern Riverina three times a week. **V/Line** (☎ 13 61 96) coaches run to Mildura ($120).

XPTs (express trains) running between Sydney and Melbourne stop here. If you're travelling between the two capital cities, it's much cheaper to stop over in Albury on a through ticket than to buy two separate tickets. From Albury the one-way fare to Melbourne is $60 and to Sydney it's $90.

Getting Around

If you need a lift to some of the outlying areas, **Snow White Bus Depot** (☎ 6021 4368; 474 David St) is the pick-up point for mail, freight and passenger buses that run just about everywhere (eventually).

AROUND ALBURY

Oz E Wildlife (☎ 6040 3677; adult/child $10/5; 🕒 9am-5pm), 11km north on the Hume Hwy has a collection of Aussie fauna including plenty of inquisitive grey kangaroos that you can feed. Most animals arrive sick or injured, so this is a genuine sanctuary. About 4km north, the lopsided **Ettamogah Pub** looms up near the highway. It's a real-life re-creation of a famous Aussie cartoon pub that featured in the *Australasian Post* comic strip by Albury-born Ken Maynard.

About 15km farther north is **Bowna**, a town that has shrunk to a couple of build-ings, including **Jeff Leury's boomerang factory** (☎ 6020 3240). At Bowna there's a turn-off to the **Great Aussie Camping Resort** (☎ 6020 3236; sites from $20, cabins from $56) on the banks of the Hume Weir. This is a well-equipped place – you can hire boats and there's horse riding and other activities. This road leads to **Wymah** (22km on), where you can cross by vehicle ferry to the Murray Valley Hwy on the other side of the river.

South Coast

CONTENTS

The rugged and often wild South Coast has a good balance between development and natural beauty. Small(ish) coastal towns and villages nestle between spectacular national parks, while back from the coast wineries and charming historic towns sprawl at the feet of the Great Dividing Range.

The further you get from Sydney, the more laid-back these coastal hamlets become. Kiama is hip and highly polished, Jervis Bay is cosmopolitan, but with rough edges. By the time you get to Eden – a working port town which has made the transition from being a centre for whale hunting to a centre for whale- watching – the gloss has all but worn off.

During school holidays and Christmas time you'll probably find the more popular locations packed out, and even weekends can be problematic in places like Batemans Bay and Kiama (favourite getaways for Canberrans and Sydneysiders, respectively), but any other time, and in most other places, you'll find the pace leisurely and the options plentiful.

The ocean is definitely the focus in this part of the world, and people with strong constitutions (or a good wetsuit) won't let chilly temperatures deter them from the myriad of swimming, surfing and diving opportunities, particularly in the crystal waters around Merimbula and Jervis Bay.

Drier (and warmer) options include fishing, whale-watching and, of course, exploring the staggering biodiversity of the region's national parks.

HIGHLIGHTS

- Taking a boat tour to see the wildlife on Montague Island near **Narooma** (p321)
- Snacking away on a bush tucker tour in **Booderee National Park** (p314)
- Diving or snorkelling in the coastal waters off **Jervis Bay** (p313) and **Merimbula** (p326)
- Munching on fresh oysters at **Greenwell Point** (p313)
- Pottering around in a houseboat from **Batemans Bay** (p319)
- Whale-watching at Twofold Bay in **Eden** (p328) during October and November
- Taking a Koori cultural tour of **Wallaga Lake** (p322)
- Sleeping in a reconstructed pioneer village at **Old Mogo Town** (p320)

SOUTH COAST

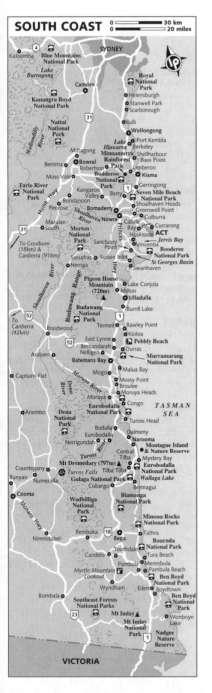

| 0 | 30 km |
| 0 | 20 miles |

Getting There & Around
BUS
Nowra-based **Premier Motor Service** (☎ 13 34 10; www.premierms.com.au) offers the most comprehensive services from Sydney to Eden (and on to Melbourne), and the cheapest sector fares. From Sydney fares include Batemans Bay ($35), Narooma ($40), Bega ($44) and Eden ($49). Two buses a day go as far as Eden.

Greyhound Pioneer (☎ 13 20 30, 13 14 99; www .greyhound.com.au) also travels along the Princes Hwy daily between Sydney and Melbourne. **Sapphire Coast Express** (☎ 1800 812 135) runs from Batemans Bay through to Melbourne on Monday and Thursday only; and **Murrays** (☎ 13 22 51; www.murrays.com.au) has daily services between Nowra and Narooma, and inland to Canberra.

CAR & MOTORCYCLE
The Princes Hwy starts at Sydney's George St and continues all the way to Adelaide via Melbourne. It's known as the coastal route, but don't expect too many ocean views (although there are some beauties). Most of the way the highway runs a little way inland. All along this route there are turn-offs to interesting places, both on the coast and up in the Great Dividing Range, where there's an almost unbroken chain of superb national parks and state forests. It's a longer, slower route between Sydney and Melbourne than the Hume Hwy, but it's infinitely more interesting.

KIAMA TO ULLADULLA

Shoalhaven is a large municipality stretching from north of Nowra almost as far south as Batemans Bay. It takes in some great beaches, state forests and, in the ranges to the west, the big Morton National Park (see Around Sydney, p122, for more information).

This area is a popular family holiday destination, but it isn't yet as crowded as parts of the north coast and much of the tourism is confined to weekenders from Sydney.

There are regional tourist information centres in Nowra and Ulladulla, and you'll also find information at www.shoalhaven .nsw.gov.au.

KIAMA & AROUND

Kiama (pop 12,300) is a pretty town with some fine old buildings, good beaches and a sense of community. The **Kiama Area visitors centre** (☎ 02-4232 3322; www.southcoast.com.au/kiama; ◷ 9am-5pm) is on Blowhole Point. Nearby is the town's major attraction, the **blowhole**, which has drawn visitors for a century and is now floodlit at night. Beside the visitors centre is the **Pilot's Cottage Museum** (adult/child $2/1; ◷ 11am-3pm Fri-Mon).

The **Terrace** (Collins St) is a neat strip of restored houses that date back to 1886 and are now mostly occupied by craft shops and restaurants.

There's a good **lookout** from the top of Saddleback Mountain, just behind the town. From Manning St, turn right onto Saddleback Mountain Rd. There's a small enclosed **surf beach** right in town and the broad **Werri Beach**, 10km south in Gerringong.

Minnamurra Rainforest Park is in **Budderoo National Park** (☎ 02-4423 9800; car/motorcycle $10/3.30). It's on the eastern edge of the park, about 14km inland from Kiama. There's a National Parks & Wildlife Service (NPWS) **visitor centre** (☎ 02-4236 0469) from where you can take a 1.6km loop walk on a boardwalk through the rainforest. There's a secondary 2.6km walk to the Minnamurra Falls. The visitors centre sells NPWS national park passes.

On the way to Minnamurra you'll pass through the old village of **Jamberoo**, which has a nice pub.

Sleeping

Elli's B&B (☎ 02-4232 2879; www.kiama.com.au/ellis; cnr Manning & Farmer Sts; s/d with breakfast $120/140; ⬛) A homely place with modern, spacious rooms and a family atmosphere.

Grand Hotel (☎ 02-4232 1037; 49 Manning St; r per person $30) This is one of several pubs with accommodation. It's on the corner of Bong Bong St, with featureless but tidy rooms.

Kiama Backpackers (☎ /fax 02-4233 1881; 31 Bong Bong St; dm $20, d $49) In the nondescript brown-brick building next to the Grand Hotel, this place has the usual facilities, including Internet access ($5 per hour) and free use of bikes.

Blowhole Point Caravan Park (☎ 02-4232 2707; 2-person camp sites from $19, vans from $42) Next to the visitors centre, this caravan park is in a terrific location if it's not too windy.

Eating

Terralong St (the main street) and nearby Collins St have the concentration of eating places.

Chachi's (☎ 02-4233 1144; 32 Collins St; mains $18-25; ◷ lunch Sat & Sun, dinner Wed-Mon) Does good nouveau Italian and has a BYO license.

Ritzy Gritz (☎ 02-4232 1853; 40 Collins St; mains $18-22; ◷ lunch Fri-Sun, dinner daily) A few interesting variations on the Mexican theme can be sampled here, like the shrimp *fajitas* (a sizzling hotplate with meat, capsicum and onion) with smoked *chorizo* ($22).

Getting There & Away

Long-distance buses stop in Kiama (but only if there's a booking) outside the Leagues Club on Terralong St. **Kiama Coachlines** (☎ 02-4232 3466) runs out to Gerringong and Minnamurra (via Jamberoo).

Frequent **CityRail** (☎ 13 15 00) trains run north to Wollongong and Sydney ($12.80), and south to Gerringong and Bomaderry/Nowra ($2.20).

BERRY

☎ 02 / pop 1600

Inland and about 20km north of Nowra is the pretty little town of Berry. Founded in the 1820s, it remained a private town on the Coolangatta Estate (see Around Nowra, p313, for more information) until 1912. **Queen St**, Berry's short main street, is worth a stroll for its National Trust–classified buildings and interesting shops and cafés.

Pottering Around (☎ 4464 2177), in the Berry Stores complex on Queen St, has some tourist information or try www.berry.net.au.

The **museum** (Queen St; admission free; ◷ 11am-2pm Sat, to 3pm Sun), near the post office, is in an interesting old building and the curators are more than happy to talk you through every exhibit in the place. Among the several antique shops, **Berry Antiques** (☎ 4464 1552; 83 Queen Street; ◷ 9am-5pm) stands out.

A recommended tour operator is **Mild to Wild** (☎ 4464 2211; www.m2w.com.au; 84 Queen St), which organises adventure trips (rock-climbing, kayaking, abseiling etc) of varying adventurousness from $25 for a half-day trip to $250 for two-day expeditions.

The popular **Berry Country Fair** is held on the first Sunday of the month at the showgrounds. There are several **wineries** in the area and the **Hotel Berry** (☎ 4464 1011; tour $14;

11am Sat) runs a short but exceptionally good-value wine tour.

Jasper Valley Winery (☎ 4464 1596) is only 5km south of Berry, and is open for tastings and lunches.

Sleeping

For a small town Berry has some wonderful accommodation options, and wandering weekenders take full advantage. Prices are between 10% and 50% higher on weekends and you'll almost certainly have to book ahead.

Bunyip Inn Guesthouse (☎ 4464 2064; 122 Queen St; s/d with breakfast $60/120; 🔊) Next to the Hotel Berry, this is an excellent place in one of the town's more impressive buildings: an old bank. There's a variety of spacious, beautiful rooms, some with spa.

Hotel Berry (☎ 4464 1011; 120 Queen St; s/d $55/75) This country pub is a rarity – it caters to weekending city slickers without totally losing its status as a local watering hole. The rooms are standard pub bedrooms, but large and well presented. Why can't more pubs be like this?

Great Southern Hotel (☎ 4464 1009; s/d $60/80) A newer place built in an old style, this is something different again, with some eccentric embellishments such as the hub-cap collection. The motel-style rooms are not quite that exotic, though.

Eating

Postman's Ghost Coffee Lounge (☎ 4464 2349; www.gabbys.com.au; Prince Alfred St; mains $17-25; 🍴 breakfast, lunch & dinner) This café, next to the museum, has an outdoor seating area and good solid meals like lamb and rosemary sausages with homemade gravy ($18).

Hungry House Café (☎ 4464 3813; 125 Queen St; meals $9; 🍴 breakfast & lunch) The best-value breakfasts in town. There's also an excellent Indian curry for lunch.

Hotel Berry (☎ 4464 1011; 120 Queen St; meals $10-18) A nice courtyard dining area and meals above the usual pub standard.

Peppercorns (☎ 4464 2035; cnr Alexander & Queen Sts; mains $12-15; 🍴 breakfast & lunch) Good value, healthy food and all-day breakfast.

Getting There & Away

Premier Motor Service (☎ 13 34 10) buses between Kiama and Nowra stop here on request. The main road to Kangaroo Valley

and Mittagong leaves the Princes Hwy south of Berry, but there's also a scenic route to Kangaroo Valley from Berry via Woodhill and Wattamolla.

NOWRA
☎ 02 / pop 24,800

The largest town in the Shoalhaven area, Nowra is a centre for the area's dairy farms, and for increasing tourism and retirement development. It's a fairly dull town and is not, as many people expect, on the coast – the nearest beach is at Shoalhaven Heads, about 17km east. It is, however, a handy base for excursions to beaches and villages around Jervis Bay, north to Berry and inland to Kangaroo Valley and Morton National Park.

Information

The **Shoalhaven visitors centre** (☎ 1300 662 808) is just south of the bridge over the Shoalhaven River and has copious amounts of information on the district. The **post office** (cnr Junction & Berry Sts) is in central Nowra.

There's also an **NPWS office** (☎ 4423 2170; 55 Graham St).

Sights & Activities

The 6.5 hectare **Nowra Animal Park** (☎ 4421 3949; 🕐 9am-5pm; adult/child $10/5), on the north bank of the Shoalhaven River, is a pleasant place to meet some native animals. Head north from Nowra, cross the bridge and immediately turn left, then branch left onto McMahons Rd at the roundabout; turn left again at Rockhill Rd.

Nowra Museum (☎ 4421 2021; cnr Kinghorne & Plunkett Sts; admission $1; 🕐 1-4pm Sat & Sun) has heaps of local history, tools and other old stuff. **Meroogal** (☎ 4421 8150; cnr West & Worrigee Sts; adult/child $7/3; 🕐 1-5pm Sat & 10am-5pm Sun Feb-Dec, 10am-5pm Thu-Sun Jan) is a historic house containing the artefacts accumulated by its generations of owners.

If you're at all interested in planes and helicopters, **Australia's Museum of Flight** (☎ 4421 1920; www.museum-of-flight.org.au; 489A Albatross Rd; admission $10; 🕐 10am-4pm), 10km south of Nowra at an operational airfield, has an excellent display, including a Sopwith Camel WWI biplane and a Douglas Dakota, which you can climb aboard. Also here is **Nowra Skydive** (☎ 0500-885 556), where you can make a tandem jump from over 3000m for $380.

SOUTH COAST

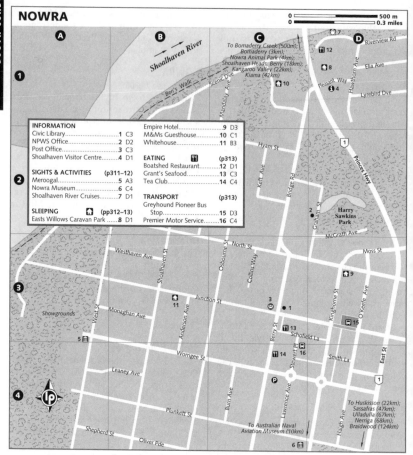

NOWRA

0 — 500 m
0 — 0.3 miles

Shoalhaven River

To Bomaderry Creek (500m);
Bomaderry (3km);
Nowra Animal Park (4km);
Shoalhaven Heads; Berry (18km);
Kangaroo Valley (22km);
Kiama (42km)

Ben's Walk

INFORMATION		
Civic Library	.1	C3
NPWS Office	.2	D2
Post Office	.3	C3
Shoalhaven Visitor Centre	.4	D1

SIGHTS & ACTIVITIES	(p311–12)	
Meroogal	.5	A3
Nowra Museum	.6	C4
Shoalhaven River Cruises	.7	D1

SLEEPING	(pp312–13)	
Easts Willows Caravan Park	.8	D1

Empire Hotel	.9	D3
M&Ms Guesthouse	.10	C1
Whitehouse	.11	B3

EATING	(p313)	
Boatshed Restaurant	.12	D1
Grant's Seafood	.13	C3
Tea Club	.14	C4

TRANSPORT	(p313)	
Greyhound Pioneer Bus		
Stop	.15	D3
Premier Motor Service	.16	C4

Harry Sawkins Park

Showgrounds

To Huskisson (22km);
Sassafras (47km);
Ulladulla (67km);
Nerriga (68km);
Braidwood (124km)

To Australian Naval
Aviation Museum (10km)

The visitors centre produces a handy compilation of walks in the area. The pleasant **Ben's Walk** starts at the bridge near Scenic Dr and follows the south bank of the Shoalhaven River (6km return). North of the river, the 5.5km **Bomaderry Creek Walking Track** runs through sandstone gorges from a trailhead at the end of Narang Rd.

Shoalhaven River Cruises (☎ 4447 1978; ☼ 1.30pm Wed & Sun) has tours up the beautiful river, leaving from the wharf just east of the bridge near the visitor centre.

Sleeping

Whitehouse (☎ 4421 2084; www.whitehouseguesthouse.com; 30 Junction St; s/d from $55/75) A friendly family operates this beautifully restored

guesthouse. The light breakfast out on the wide veranda is a great way to start the day.

M&Ms Guesthouse (☎ 4422 8006; www.nowrabackpackers.com; 1a Scenic Dr; dm $25, s/d $55/75) This is a wonderfully rustic place in a good location near the river. There are common rooms, including a games room with jukebox and pool table, and an outdoor barbecue area. Management has a discount car hire deal with Avis.

Empire Hotel (☎ 4421 2433; pfrazer@shoal.net.au; cnr Kinghorne & North Sts; s/d $30/60) An unusual building with very ordinary pub rooms.

East's Van Park the Willows (☎ 4421 2977; Pleasant Way; camp sites $14, cabins $41) This place is off the highway close to the bridge (and thus noisy), but also right on the river.

Nowra Animal Park (☎ 4421 3949; camp sites per person $5) This animal park has camp sites in riverside bushland. Prices rise to $9 at peak times.

Eating

Grant's Seafood (☎ 4421 2742; off Stewart Place; mains $10-15; ☺ lunch daily, dinner Thu-Sun) This casual indoor/outdoor eatery serves good-value fish and chips and juicy ribs. The Cajun chicken kebabs ($14) are worth a shot.

Tea Club (☎ 4422 0900; 46 Berry St; mains $10; ☺ lunch & dinner Tue-Sat) Nowra's Bohemian set hangs out at this comfortable little café. There are informal jam sessions here on Friday nights.

Boatshed Restaurant (☎ 4421 2419; 10 Wharf Rd; mains $28-30; ☺ lunch Sat & Sun, dinner Tue-Sun) This is the place to go for an upmarket meal with a view – it overlooks the river just next to the bridge. Try some local delicacies, like the venison pie with garlic mash ($29).

Getting There & Away

Premier Motor Service (☎ 13 34 10; Stewart Place) runs bus services north to Sydney ($19, three hours) and goes down south to Melbourne, while **Greyhound Pioneer** (☎ 13 20 30) runs daily to Sydney and Melbourne, stopping at the Nowra Mall.

The **train station** (☎ 4421 2022) is at Bomaderry. Frequent **CityRail** (☎ 13 15 00) trains go to Sydney ($15, 2½ hours).

The Princes Hwy runs north to Kiama (42km) and south to Ulladulla (67km), with several turn-offs to Jervis Bay.

An interesting and mainly unsealed road runs from Nowra to Braidwood, through Morton National Park and the hamlets of Sassafras and Nerriga. At the south end of Kinghorne St take Albatross Rd, which veers off to the right.

AROUND NOWRA

East of Nowra, the Shoalhaven River meanders through dairy country in a system of estuaries and wetlands, finally reaching the sea at Crookhaven Heads.

Greenwell Point, on the estuary about 15km east of Nowra, is a quiet, pretty, fishing village specialising in fresh oysters. **DJ's**, near the wharf, and **Backgate Seafood** sell oysters (and will also open them) and fish and chips. On the way there from Nowra you'll pass the **Jindyandy Mill** (☺ 10.30am-5pm Thu-Mon)

a convict-built flour mill that is now a craft centre. Further around the inlet at **Crookhaven Heads** there's a beach and walking tracks leading to a lighthouse.

On the north side of the estuary is **Shoalhaven Heads**, where the river once reached the sea but is now blocked by sandbars. Just north of the beach here is the **Seven Mile Beach National Park** (admission free) stretching up to Gerroa.

Just before Shoalhaven Heads you pass through **Coolangatta**, the site of the earliest European settlement on the South Coast. **Coolangatta Estate** (☎ 02-4448 7131; www.coolangattaestate.com.au; s/d Mon-Fri from $90/100) is a slick winery with a golf course, a good restaurant and accommodation in convict-built buildings. You can sample the wines from 10am to 5pm daily. The wine is made from grapes grown here but vintaged at Tyrrells in the Hunter Valley.

JERVIS BAY

Despite extensive housing development, this large, sheltered bay retains its clean, white beaches and crystal-clear water (no large rivers flow into it). Dolphins are regularly seen, and whales sometimes drop in when swimming past on their annual migrations from June to October.

In 1995 the Aboriginal community won a land claim in the Wreck Bay area and now jointly administers the Booderee National Park (formerly Jervis Bay National Park – Booderee means 'plenty of fish') at the southern end of the bay.

Most development in Jervis Bay is on the southwestern shore, around the towns of Huskisson and Vincentia. The northern shore is much less developed and state forest backs onto the beaches at **Callala Bay**. There are caravan parks near here.

Despite the close proximity of Callala Beach, south of Callala Bay, to Huskisson, there's no way of crossing Currambene Creek – you have to drive back to the highway and head south (which is just the way the locals like it).

Beecroft Peninsula forms the northeastern side of Jervis Bay. Most of the peninsula is navy land, which is off limits to civilians, but **Currarong**, near Beecroft Head, is a small town with camping at **Currarong Tourist Park** (☎ 02-4448 3027; powered/unpowered sites $20/16, cabins from $70).

Huskisson

☎ 02 / pop 3300

With much of this area turning into a sprawl of holiday homes, it's surprising that Huskisson, the oldest town on Jervis Bay, still has the feel of a small fishing port and a sense of community.

The **Lady Denman Heritage Complex** (☎ 4441 5675; Dent St; adult/child $8/4; 🕑 10am-4pm), by the bay on the Nowra side of Huskisson, includes an interesting maritime museum and the *Lady Denman*, a ferry dating from 1912. Also here is **Timbey's Aboriginal Arts & Crafts**, which displays and sells work produced on site by the local Koori community; and a boardwalk through wetlands.

South of Huskisson, **Hyams Beach** is a spectacularly white stretch of reasonably secluded sand.

Dolphin Watch Cruises (☎ 1800 246 010; Owen St) has several whale and dolphin-watching trips, starting at adult/child $25/12 for 2½ hours. June to November is prime whale time.

DIVING

Jervis Bay is popular with divers and at least two places in Huskisson offer diving and courses. **Pro Dive** (☎ 4441 5255; 64 Owen St) charges $90 for two boat dives, plus equipment hire (about $35 for a full set). You can do a Professional Association of Diving Instructors (PADI) open-water dive course for $420. **Sea Sports** (☎ 4441 5012; Owen St) has similar rates and also runs cruises. There are some good wreck dives in the bay.

SLEEPING & EATING

There's quite a lot of guesthouse and motel accommodation in Huskisson and Vincentia (which more or less merge into one), but book ahead on weekends. Prices can be quite reasonable during the week and at off-peak times, but prices rocket on weekends and holidays.

Jervis Bay Guesthouse (☎ 4441 7658; www.jervis bayguesthouse.com.au; 1 Beach St, Huskisson; r with breakfast $130-430) This beautifully restored wooden guesthouse is opposite the beach. Most rooms have a beach view and wide verandas.

Jervis Bay House (☎ 4441 8431; www.jervisbay house.com.au; 1 Caroline St, Vincentia; r from $125; 🖳) A Mediterranean-style villa right on the (rocky) beachfront. The swimming beach is a short walk away.

Husky Pub (☎ 4441 5001; Owen St; s/d $40/60) There are reasonable pub rooms here, some with fantastic bay views.

Huskisson Beach Tourist Resort (☎ 4441 5142; Beach St; powered/unpowered sites from $26/24, cabins from $68; 🖳) Run by the Shoalhaven Council, this camping ground has a great location right on the beach. It's a little way out of Huskisson on the road to Vincentia. There are several other caravan parks in the area.

Seagrass Café (☎ 4441 6124; 13 Currumbene St; mains $14-18; 🕑 lunch Fri-Sun, dinner Tue-Sun) Fresh, carefully prepared food is served in modern surrounds. The front deck is a great place to while away a balmy evening, munching on wild mushroom risotto with prawns ($17). It's fully licensed and reservations are often necessary.

Booderee National Park

This interesting national park occupies Jervis Bay's southeastern spit. There's good swimming, surfing and diving on bay and ocean beaches. Much of the park is heathland, with some forest, including small pockets of rain forest. It's administered jointly by the federal government and the Wreck Bay Aboriginal Community. It's home to the naval training base **HMAS Creswell** (☎ 02-4429 7845). The base is open to visitors for a short 'drive through' on weekends and you may be able to visit its museum. There's a good **visitors centre** (☎ 02-4443 0977) at the park entrance with walking trail maps and information on camping. Inside the park is the **Booderee Botanic Gardens** (🕑 8.30am-5pm), with a number of walks in varying environments.

There are many walking trails around the park and some good secluded beaches. Be careful on the cliff tops as apparently people occasionally fall off. After walking in the park check for ticks, which are common. Although Wreck Bay is a closed community, you can experience some Aboriginal culture with a local guide on **Barry's Bush Tucker Tours** (☎ 02-4442 1168). The programme of tours varies, so call first.

Entry to the park costs $10 per car or motorcycle and is valid for a week (NPWS passes are not valid). There are **camping grounds** (camp sites $14-17) at Green Patch and Bristol Point, and a more basic **camping area** (camp sites $8-10) at Caves Beach. You have to book at the visitors centre and sites might not be available at peak times.

JERVIS BAY TO ULLADULLA

The southern peninsula of Jervis Bay encircles **St Georges Basin**, a large body of water that has access to the sea through narrow Sussex Inlet. The north shore of the basin has succumbed to housing developments reminiscent of the suburban sprawl on the Central Coast.

Further south is pretty **Lake Conjola**, with a quiet town of holiday shacks and a couple of caravan parks; the **Lake Conjola Entrance Tourist Park** (☎ 02-4456 1141; powered/unpowered sites from $23/19, cabins from $65) is the closest to the ocean.

Milton, on the highway 6km north of Ulladulla, is this area's original town, built to serve the nearby farming communities. Like so many early towns in this coastal region, Milton was built several kilometres inland – how tastes have changed! There are several cafés and a few antique shops on the main street (the Princes Hwy) and it gets pretty busy here on weekends. **Pilgrim's Café** (meals $8-11; ☯ breakfast & lunch Mon-Sat) has healthy lunches and coffee.

ULLADULLA

☎ 02 / pop 9600

Ulladulla is not an especially attractive town but it does have excellent beaches and is close to Pigeon House Mountain and to Budawang National Park. It is also the largest town on the highway between Nowra and Batemans Bay.

Orientation & Information

Ulladulla is on rocky Warden Head, but a short walk north of Ulladulla harbour is Mollymook, a suburb on a lovely surf beach.

Burrill Lake, a few kilometres south of Ulladulla, is a small town on the inlet to the lake of the same name.

Ulladulla's **visitors centre** (☎ 4455 1269; www .ulladulla.info; ☯ 10am-5pm Mon-Fri, 9am-5pm Sat & Sun) is in the Civic Centre opposite the harbour. The **library** (☯ 10am-7pm Mon-Fri, 9am-noon Sat), in the same building, has Internet access for $1 per hour.

Sights & Activities

The **Coomee Nulunga Cultural Trail** is a walking trail in town, established by the local Aboriginal Land Council. It begins near the Lighthouse Oval (take Deering St east of the highway) and follows the headland through native bush to the beach.

Climbing **Pigeon House Mountain** (720m) in the far south of Morton National Park is an enjoyable challenge. A road runs close to the summit, from where it's a walk of four hours to the top and back. The first hour's walk from the car park is a steady climb, but after that it levels out a little. The main access road to Pigeon House Mountain leaves the highway about 8km south of Ulladulla, then it's 26km to the car park.

Ulladulla Divers Supplies (☎ 4455 5303; Wason St) runs dive courses and offers single boat dives for $30 ($70 if you need gear).

Festivals & Events

At Easter there is a **Blessing of the Fleet** ceremony and local celebrations. In late August there's a **Food & Wine Fair**. In nearby Milton, the **Settlers Fair** is held on the first holiday Monday in early October.

Sleeping

Ulladulla has plenty of motels.

Top View Motel (☎ 4455 1514; 72 South St; s/d $60/70) Possibly one of the friendliest motels on the South Coast, and in a good location overlooking the town.

Ulladulla Guest House (☎ 4455 1796; www.guest house.com.au; 39 Burrill St; r from $180; ☐P ☒ ☒) This is an award-winning, five-star, luxury guesthouse, set in beautiful gardens. The on-site gallery features work by local and international artists and the French restaurant (see below) serves the best food in town by far.

Hotel Marlin (☎ 4455 1999; cnr Princes Hwy & Wason St; s/d $30/50) A central, loud place with standard pub rooms.

South Coast Backpackers (☎ /fax 4454 0500; 63 Princes Hwy; dm $20, d $45) A small, clean place with spacious four- and six-bed dorms. It's north of the shopping centre.

Ulladulla Tourist Park (☎ 4455 2457; South St; camp sites from $16, cabins from $45) This park is on the headland a few blocks from the town centre (at the end of South St), but it's a bit of a walk to the beach.

Eating

There are plenty of coffee shops and pasta places on Ulladulla's main street and in the arcades running off it.

Ulladulla Guest House (mains $26-30; ☯ breakfast daily, dinner Mon & Thu-Sat) The fully licensed restaurant at this guesthouse (see above) serves fine French food and has a classy ambience. On chilly nights you can warm your bones next to the open fire as classical music tinkles in the background.

Just Good Food (Bellbrook Arcade; ⏱ breakfast & lunch Mon-Fri) You'll get excellent coffee, sandwiches and fresh juices from $3 here.

Milton-Ulladulla Bowling Club (lunch from $4) You can't beat this place near the tourist office for good-value meals.

Plaza Deli (⏱ lunch Mon-Sat) This deli sells good, cheap and healthy burgers and sandwiches with lots of vegetarian options. The mega-felafel ($5) is a real meal.

Ulladulla Palace (☎ 4455 2340; 107 Princes Hwy; mains $11-15; ⏱ lunch Mon-Sat, dinner daily) The menu here features mostly Chinese and Asian dishes, and the lunch specials ($6) are reasonable value. It's opposite Hotel Marlin.

Getting There & Away

Buses stop on the highway outside the Marlin Hotel (northbound) or Traveland (southbound). Ticket agents are **Traveland** (☎ 4455 1588; Shop 3, The Plaza, 107 Princes Hwy) and **Harvey World Travel** (☎ 4455 5122; Powers Arcade).

Priors Scenic Express (☎ 1800 816 234) is a good bus to catch if you want to get off at the smaller places such as Milton, Burrill Lake, Tabourie Lake or Termeil. It continues on to Narooma.

Getting Around

Ulladulla Bus Lines (☎ 4455 1674) services the local area, mainly between Milton, Mollymook, Ulladulla and Burrill Lake. There are two services each weekday.

FAR SOUTH COAST

The Far South Coast is the least-developed stretch of coast in the state and it has some of the best beaches and forests. The population triples during holiday times, especially in the Eurobodalla area (from Batemans Bay to Narooma), and prices rise accordingly. As well as the beaches and inlets, with swimming, surfing and fishing, there are good walks in the national parks and whale-watching during the migration season (June and July and September to November). The Sapphire Coast, stretching from Bermagui to Eden, is a popular holiday area centred on Merimbula.

The visitors centres in Batemans Bay and Narooma sell topographic maps and copies of Graham Barrow's book *Walking on the South Coast*, which details mainly short walks between Nowra and Eden. Information on national parks is available from **NPWS offices** (Narooma ☎ 02-4476 2888; Merimbula ☎ 02-6495 5000).

MURRAMARANG NATIONAL PARK

This beautiful coastal park begins about 20km south of Ulladulla and extends almost all the way south to Batemans Bay.

Merry, **Pebbly** and **Depot Beaches** are all popular with surfers, as is **Wasp Head** south of Durras. There are numerous walking trails snaking off from these beach areas and a steep but enjoyable walk up **Durras Mountain** (283m). This is also a great place to meet kangaroos. There's a park entry fee of $6 per car plus camping fees if you stay overnight (around $5 per person).

Sleeping

IN THE PARK

Pebbly Beach Holiday Cabins (☎ 02-4478 6023; cabins from $88) There's a minimum stay of two nights here and weekly rates are reasonable.

Pebbly Beach camping ground (☎ 02-4478 6006; camp sites $10) This camping ground, run by the NPWS, is in a lovely spot. Sites are scarce during school holidays, so you should book.

To get to Pebbly Beach, turn off the highway onto North Durras Rd south of East Lynne – avoid Pebbly Beach Rd, which is very rough. Caravans can't be taken on the last section of the road to Pebbly Beach.

Depot Beach camping area (☎ 02-4478 6582; camp sites per person $5) This is another NPWS camping ground, with basic amenities.

There's a very basic **bush camping site** (free) in the far south of the park at North Head Beach; turn off the highway at Benandarah and follow North Head Rd.

NEARBY SETTLEMENTS

There are small towns on the borders of the park and one or two on old leases within the park itself. If camp sites in the park are booked out you could try these places.

Turn off the highway at Termeil to get to **Bawley Point** and **Kioloa**, near the north end of the park. There are caravan parks in these small towns, and just south of Kioloa are caravan parks at **Merry Beach** and **Pretty**

Beach, both privately run. They're reasonable places and the beaches are excellent, but they lack the steep and forested slopes behind the beaches that you'll find further south.

Take the East Lynne turn-off from the highway to get to **North Durras**, on the inlet to Durras Lake. There's not much here except a lovely beach and six million caravans squeezed into three abutting caravan parks.

Durras Lake North Caravan Park (☎ 02-4478 6072; camp sites from $14, cabins from $45) usually has a cabin or an on-site van set aside for backpackers and charges $12 a bed.

In the south of the park (turn off the highway at Benandarah), **Durras** is a quiet village of substantial holiday houses. At the south end of the town is **Murramarang Resort** (☎ 02-4478 6355; www.murramarangresort.com.au; camp sites $13-15, cabins from $59). It's a big, modern place with lots of activities and even 'floorshow' entertainment! Prices rise considerably during holidays.

Getting There & Away

The Princes Hwy runs parallel to Murramarang, but it's about 10km from the highway to the beaches or the small settlements in and near the park. There's no public transport into the park but **Priors Scenic Express** (☎ 1800 816 234) buses stop on the highway at Termeil, East Lynne and Benandarah.

BATEMANS BAY

☎ 02 / pop 10,200

Batemans Bay is a fishing port that has boomed to become one of the South Coast's largest holiday centres, partly because of its good beaches and beautiful estuary, and partly because it's the closest coastal town to land-locked Canberra.

Information

The large **visitors centre** (☎ 1800 802 528; Princes Hwy; ⏱ 9am-5pm) is opposite McDonald's. **Total Computer Care** (10 Citi Centre Arcade, Orient St) offers Internet access for $3/4 per half/full hour.

Sights & Activities

The **Old Courthouse Museum** (☎ 4472 8993; Museum Place; adult/child $5/1; ⏱ 1-4pm Tue-Thu) just off Orient St, has displays relating to local history. Behind the museum is the small **Water Garden Town Park** and a boardwalk through wetlands.

On the north side of the Clyde River estuary just across the bridge (if you're driving you'll have to keep going to the Canberra

---

BUSH CAMPING

Got a car? Get a tent, and some of the best accommodation options on the coast open up to you. The national parks that line the South Coast are a camper's dream: uncrowded for most of the year, wild (often without being primitive) and easily accessed in any type of car. Listed below are a few of the best national parks where you can camp. Most of the camping areas in these parks have flush toilets, gas barbecues and hot showers. For more detail, pick up a copy of the NSW National Parks and Wildlife Service (NPWS) *Guide to National Parks*, free from any NPWS office.

- **Ben Boyd National Park** (see p329) Surreal, multicoloured rock formations, historic wood mills and whaling stations, and some of the best coastal walks in the state.
- **Bournda National Park** (see p327) Plenty of water-based fun in freshwater lagoons and saltwater lakes.
- **Eurobodalla National Park** (see p320) Indigenous heritage and the captivating beauty of the rock formations at Bingie Bingie Point.
- **Mimosa Rocks National Park** (see p323) Secluded beachside camping surrounded by native forests, caves and pounding surf.
- **Murramarang National Park** (see p316) Good surf beaches, stunning views from atop Durras Mountain (283m) and almost overly-friendly kangaroos.
- **Wadbilliga National Park** (see p322) Dramatic subalpine woodlands, waterfalls and the 5km Tuross River Gorge. Much of this park is in near-pristine condition and can be accessed in any type of car.

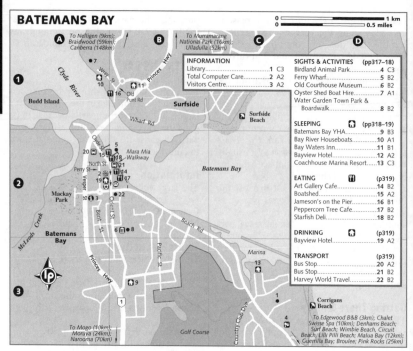

BATEMANS BAY

0 ——————— 1 km
0 ——————— 0.5 miles

To Nelligen (9km);
Braidwood (59km);
Canberra (148km)

To Murramarang
National Park (16km);
Ulladulla (52km)

INFORMATION		SIGHTS & ACTIVITIES (pp317–18)
Library....................1 C3		Birdland Animal Park...........4 B2
Total Computer Care.....2 A2		Ferry Wharf......................5 B2
Visitors Centre............3 A2		Old Courthouse Museum......6 B2
		Oyster Shed Boat Hire........7 A1
		Water Garden Town Park &
		Boardwalk.....................8 B2

SLEEPING (pp318–19)
Batemans Bay YHA...........9 B3
Bay River Houseboats.......10 A1
Bay Waters Inn..............11 B1
Bayview Hotel...............12 A2
Coachhouse Marina Resort...13 C3

EATING (p319)
Art Gallery Cafe.............14 B2
Boatshed...................15 A2
Jameson's on the Pier......16 B1
Peppercorn Tree Cafe.......17 B2
Starfish Deli...............18 B2

DRINKING (p319)
Bayview Hotel..............19 A2

TRANSPORT (p319)
Bus Stop...................20 A2
Bus Stop...................21 B2
Harvey World Travel........22 B2

Surfside
Surfside Beach

Budd Island
Old Punt Rd
Wharf Rd

Mara Mia Walkway
North St
Perry St
Vesper St
Mackay Park
Batemans Bay

Batemans Bay

Beach Rd
Marina
Orient St
Bent St
Pacific St

McLeods Creek

Princes Hwy

To Mogo (10km);
Moruya (24km);
Narooma (70km)

Golf Course

Country Club Dr

Corrigans Beach

To Edgewood B&B (3km); Chalet
Swisse Spa (10km); Denhams Beach;
Surf Beach; Wimbie Beach; Circuit
Beach; Lilli Pilli Beach; Malua Bay (12km);
Guerrilla Bay; Broulee; Pink Rocks (25km)

turn-off and take the first left) there are a couple of boat hire places. **Oyster Shed Boat Hire** (☎ 4472 6771) hires out runabouts from $50 for two hours.

Several boats offer **cruises** up the estuary from the ferry wharf just east of the bridge. The standard three-hour cruise stops at Nelligen (adult/child $24/12) and you can have lunch on board (usually fish and chips). There are also sea cruises, during which you might see penguins at the Tollgate Islands Nature Reserve in the bay.

Birdland Animal Park (☎ 4472 5364; 55 Beach Rd, near Batehaven; adult/child $10/5; 9.30am-4pm) has snake and wombat displays and koala feeding.

BEACHES

Corrigans Beach is the closest beach to the town centre. South of Corrigans Beach is a series of small beaches nibbled into the rocky shore. There are longer beaches along the coast north of the bridge, leading into Murramarang National Park.

Surfers flock to Surf Beach, Malua Bay, the small McKenzies Beach (just south of

Malua Bay) and Broulee, which has a small wave when everywhere else is flat. For the experienced, the best surfing in the area is at Pink Rocks (near Broulee) when a north swell is running. Locals say the waves are sometimes 6m high. Broulee itself has a wide crescent of sand, but there's a strong rip at the northern end.

Festivals & Events

The **Clyde River Carnival** is held in November, and there are **game-fishing tournaments** in February and May. Up in Nelligen, a **Country Music Festival** twangs along during the first weekend in January.

Sleeping

There are many holiday apartments that do good business in summer. Out of season you might be able to rent one for less than a week. Letting agents are the **Professionals** (☎ 1800 808 054; www.bayproperty.com.au) and **Ray White Real Estate** (☎ 4472 4799).

Chalet Swisse Spa (☎ 4471 1671; info@chaletswisse spa.com.au; 676 The Ridge Rd, Surf Beach; d with breakfast from $105) This quirky, Swiss-flavoured health retreat is up in the hills, 10km south of town. Various health treatments are available.

Bayview Hotel (☎ 4472 4522; 20 Orient St; s/d $20/35) Although it's central, this place has very ordinary pub rooms.

Bay Waters Inn (☎ 4472 6344; cnr Princes & Kings Hwys; r from $90) This is one of many motels in town. It overlooks the river and has a decent restaurant.

Batemans Bay YHA (☎ 4472 4972; Old Princes Hwy; dm $26, d $55) The youth hostel is in the Shady Willows Holiday Park just south of the centre. The backpacker section has a TV room and kitchen. There are also bikes and canoes for hire.

There are several caravan parks along the coast road south of town.

Coachhouse Marina Resort (☎ 4472 4392; www .coachhouse.com.au; 49 Beach Rd; powered/unpowered sites $25/20, cabins from $40; ☑) A well-equipped park at the beginning of Corrigans Beach. There's a good bar/restaurant on the grounds.

HOUSEBOATS
Bay River Houseboats (☎ 4471 2253; www.bayriver houseboats.com.au; Wray St) You can hire eight- and 10-berth houseboats from this operation on the north side of the river. From May to August (low season) an eight-berth boat costs $510 for four nights (Monday to Friday) or a weekend, or $820 for a full week. Prices more than double in December and January. Shared between a few people this is good value in the shoulder season, and a great way to get around.

Eating
The main shopping area around Orient St and the riverfront has some good cafés and restaurants.

Boatshed (☎ 4421 2419; Clyde St fishing wharf) You can buy seafood straight off the boats here, and fish and chips.

Starfish Deli (☎ 4472 4880; Promenade Plaza, Clyde St; mains $13-19; ☑ dinner) This buzzing place has a great outdoor dining area right on the waterfront serving gourmet wood-fired pizzas and pasta.

If you wander around the corner and along the Mara Mia walkway you'll find interesting waterfront places (also accessible from Orient St).

Art Gallery Café (Orient St) This place has a good early breakfast (from 7am) for $8.90 with bottomless coffee.

Peppercorn Tree Café (Orient St; mains $17-21; ☑ breakfast & lunch daily, dinner Wed-Sat) This café, further along from the Art Gallery, serves some good food, including a lamb rack with plum sauce ($20).

Jameson's on the Pier (☎ 4472 6405; Old Punt Rd; mains $18-24; ☑ lunch & dinner) This is one of Batemans Bay's finest restaurants, and a superb place for lunch, or dinner on a balmy evening. The emphasis is on fish, but they have other interesting dishes, like the marinated spatchcock on couscous ($24).

Drinking
Bayview Hotel (☎ 4472 4522; 20 Orient St) Gets going on weekends. It should do since it's the only real pub in town.

The **Soldiers Club** (☎ 4472 4847; www.baysoldiers .com.au; 2 Beach Rd) and the **Catalina Country Club** (☎ 4472 4022; www.catalinacountryclub.com.au; 154 Beach Rd) have music of some sort on weekends.

Getting There & Away
Harvey World Travel (☎ 4472 5086; Orient St) handles bus bookings and has timetables in the window. The bus stop is outside the newsagent on Clyde St.

Premier Motor Service (☎ 13 34 10) runs south to Eden ($30) and north to Sydney ($35) twice a day. **Murrays** (☎ 13 22 51) runs to Narooma ($19) and Canberra ($24) at least daily. **The Sapphire Coast Express** (☎ 1800 812 135) runs between Batemans Bay and Melbourne ($72) twice a week.

As an alternative to the Princes Hwy, you can follow the beachfront road south as far as the north shore of the Deua River (also called the Moruya River) and rejoin the highway at Moruya. A scenic road runs inland to Nelligen, Braidwood and Canberra from the highway just north of Batemans Bay.

DEUA NATIONAL PARK
Inland from Moruya, Deua National Park is a mountainous wilderness area (82,926 hectares) with swift-running rivers (good for **canoeing**) and some challenging walking. There are also many caves.

There are simple camping areas off the scenic road between Araluen and Moruya and off the road between Braidwood and Numeralla, plus a couple more within the park. On the eastern side of the park, near the Berlang camping area, the Big Hole and Marble Arch are excellent **short walks**.

Admission to the park is free. Contact the **Narooma NPWS** (☎ 02-4476 2888) for more information.

BATEMANS BAY TO NAROOMA

This stretch of coast features the **Eurobodalla National Park** (admission free), an area of many lakes, bays and inlets backed by spotted-gum forests. Eurobodalla is an Aboriginal word meaning 'place of many waters' and there are Aboriginal middens (the remains of shellfish feasts) here, as well as native wildlife such as potoroos, hooded plovers and white-footed dunnarts. Don't miss the incredible rock formations at **Bingie Bingie Point**.

Mogo

Mogo is a quaint strip of old wooden shops and houses almost entirely devoted to Devonshire teas, crafts and antiques. Just off the highway is **Old Mogo Town** (☎ 02-4474 2123; www.oldmogotown.com.au; James St; adult/child $14/6; cabins per person $22-105; ☯ 10am-5pm), a rambling re-creation of a pioneer village. You can stay in cabins inside the complex, giving you a good opportunity to wander around once all the day trippers have gone home. **Mogo Zoo** (☎ 02-4474 4930; adult/child $16/8; ☯ 9am-5pm), 2km east off the highway, is a small but interesting zoo with exotic wildlife such as Bengal and Sumatran tigers, a Himalayan red panda, snow leopards and jaguars. Feeding time for the tigers is 11am and 2pm.

Moruya

Moruya, 25km south of Batemans Bay and about 5km inland, is on the estuary of the Deua (Moruya) River. The river's banks turn into wetlands as it sprawls down to the sea at **Moruya Heads**, the hamlet on the south head, where there's a good **surf beach** and views from Taragy Point.

The **Bush Orchestra** (☎ 02-4474 3554; cnr Cheet ham St & Ted Hunt Tce; adult/family $4/8; ☯ 8am-6pm), about 2km west of the highway is a guided forest walk with the 'music' provided by the abundant birdlife – bellbirds, lorikeets, bowerbirds and cockatoos. There's a popular country **market** every Saturday, on the south side of Moruya Bridge.

The best place to stay in town is the **Post & Telegraph B&B** (☎ 02-4474 5475; www.southcoast .com.au/postandtel; cnr Page & Campbell Sts; s/d from $90/110), the beautifully restored old post office, which features polished floorboards,

iron beds and lots of period charm. Rooms come with supper and full breakfast.

Priors Scenic Express (☎ 1800 816 234) buses run from Batemans Bay to Moruya and you might be able to get a lift to Moruya Heads on a school bus.

Congo

South of Moruya Heads Congo, in the national park, is a small cluster of houses on an estuary and a long surf beach. It's very pretty and peaceful. Volunteers are helping to repair damage to the dunes here and they welcome assistance. There's a basic **camping area** (2-person camp sites $5). You'll need to bring in all your food and bring or boil drinking water.

A dirt road to Congo runs off the road between Moruya and Moruya Heads; another partly sealed road leaves the highway about 10km south of Moruya.

NAROOMA
☎ 02 / pop 3400

Narooma is a seaside holiday town that isn't as developed as Batemans Bay to the north or Merimbula to the south, yet it's one of the more attractive spots on the South Coast.

The good **visitors centre** (☎ 4476 2881; Princes Hwy; ☯ 9am-5pm) is just south of the bridge. Narooma is an access point for both Deua and Wadbilliga National Parks, and there's a **NPWS information office** (☎ 4476 2888; cnr Princes Hwy & Field St).

There's free Internet access at the **library** (☎ 4476 1164) behind the Narooma Cinema.

Sights & Activities

You can cruise inland up the Wagonga River on the **Wagonga Princess** (☎ 4476 2665). A three-hour cruise, including a stop for a walk through the bush and some billy tea, costs $20/14 for adults/children. Book directly or through the visitors centre.

There are several **boat-hire** places along Riverside Dr, so you can go boating on Wagonga Inlet under your own steam. There's a nice **walk** along the inlet and around to the ocean, and safe swimming just inside the heads.

A good rainy-day weekend activity is to see a film at the **Narooma Cinema** (☎ 4476 2352; 94 Campbell St), a picture palace that began showing flicks in 1926 and hasn't changed much since.

For **surfing**, Mystery Bay, between Cape Dromedary and Corunna Point, is rocky but good, as is Handkerchief Beach, especially at the north end. Narooma's Bar Beach is best when a southeasterly is blowing. Potato Point is another popular hang-out for surfers.

Fishing charters are popular and cost around $80 for four hours including all equipment. The visitors centre has a list of operators.

The small **Lighthouse Museum** (☎ 4476 2881; ⊙ 10am-4pm) is near the visitors centre.

Montague Island

About 10km offshore from Narooma, this small island was once an important source of food for local Aborigines (who called it Barunguba) and is now a nature reserve. **Fairy penguins** nest here and although you'll see some all year round, there are many thousands in late winter and spring. Many other seabirds and hundreds of sea-lions make their homes on the island. There's also a historic **lighthouse**. A 30-minute **boat trip** to Montague Island and a tour conducted by a NPWS ranger costs $60/45 for adults/children. Take the afternoon trip if you want to see the fairy penguins. Trips should leave daily in summer but are dependent on numbers and weather conditions at other times, so book ahead through the visitors centre.

The clear waters around the island are good for **diving**, especially from February to June; you can snorkel with the sea-lions. **Island Charters Narooma** (☎ 4476 1047; www.island chartersnarooma.com; 16 Old Princes Hwy) offers diving (from $70 per person), snorkelling (from $60 per person) and whale-watching (from $55 per person). Attractions in the area include grey nurse sharks, sea-lions and the wreck of the SS *Lady Darling*.

Festivals & Events

The **Narooma Festival** is held in February and the **Surfboat Marathon** is in November.

Sleeping

Narooma Real Estate (☎ 4476 2169), across the road from the visitors centre, deals in holiday accommodation.

Bay St B&B (☎ 4476 3336; 5 Bay St; d with breakfast $120) A central place, with modern rooms and wide sunny verandas.

Whale Motor Inn (☎ 4476 2411; Wagonga St; s/d $95/105) This motel offers large, clean rooms and a restaurant.

YHA Bluewater Lodge (☎ 4476 4440; 11-13 Riverside Dr; dm $18, d $40; ▣) This is a well-run, recommended hostel.

Narooma Houseboats (☎ 4476 4654; 6 Lakeside Dr, Kianga) You can hire an eight-berth houseboat from $275 a night ($440 over Christmas) or $880 a week ($1320 at Christmas).

Surf Beach Resort (☎ 4476 2275; camp sites from $16, d cabins from $44). This small place is one of several caravan parks.

Eating

Quarterdeck Marina (☎ 4476 2763; 13 Riverside Dr; mains $15-18; ⊙ lunch daily, dinner Sat & Sun) Pull up a chair on the great deck overhanging the river and tuck into the good portions of fresh seafood served here. There's usually live music in the evening on weekends.

Casey's Café (☎ 4476 1241; 120 Wagonga St) Casey has the best coffee in town and serves well-presented meals and great smoothies.

Bowling Club (☎ 4476 2433; Princes Hwy) You can get an almost unbeatable $5.50 lunch buffet here.

Raw Prawn (☎ 4476 3691; breakfast $7-12, mains $15; ⊙ breakfast, lunch & dinner) This bistro, inside O'Brien's Hotel, serves good solid pub meals with an awesome view off the rear deck.

Rockwall Restaurant (☎ 4476 2040; mains $18-22; ⊙ dinner Tue-Sun) Just up from O'Brien's, this is a highly rated licensed restaurant featuring a wide variety of seafood dishes and local wines.

Getting There & Away

Bus bookings are handled by **Traveland** (☎ 4476 2688), near the post office on the hill. Buses stop nearby.

Premier Motor Service (☎ 13 34 10) buses stop in Narooma on the run between Sydney and Melbourne. **Murrays** (☎ 13 22 51) stops on its daily run between Narooma and Canberra via Batemans Bay.

AROUND NAROOMA
Mystery Bay

Near Cape Dromedary, about 12km south of Narooma, this little settlement of new houses has a fine rocky beach (there are sandy beaches nearby) and a big but basic **camping area** (☎ 02-4473 7242; unpowered sites $8) in a forest of spotted gums.

Central Tilba & Around

Central Tilba is a tiny town that's remained almost unchanged since the 19th century – but now the main street is jammed with visitors' cars, especially on summer weekends. There's information, including a town guide, at the **Tilba store** at the start of the main street. You can visit several working craft shops and the **ABC Cheese Factory** (☎ 02-4473 7387; ☼ 9am-5pm), producer of some fine cheeses.

Not far from Central Tilba towards Batemans Bay are **Tilba Valley Wines** (☎ 02-4473 7308) and **Brooklands Deer Farm** (☎ 4473 7330).

The **Tilba Festival**, with lots of music and entertainment, is held at Easter; it's hard to imagine how this small town can cope with the 8000-plus visitors.

Central Tilba perches on the side of **Mt Dromedary** (797m), one of the highest mountains on the South Coast. There's lush forest on the mountain, which forms the **Gulaga Flora Reserve**, and great views from the top. Beginning at Pam's Store in **Tilba Tilba** you can walk up along an old **pack-horse trail**. The return walk of 11km takes about five hours, but don't miss the loop walk at the summit. There is often rain and mist on the mountain, so come prepared.

From Tilba Tilba the highway swings inland to **Cobargo**, another small town that has changed little since it was built, and where there are craft shops, a pub and motels.

SLEEPING & EATING

Two Storey B&B (☎ 02-4473 7290; s/d with breakfast $85/105) This place, next to the Tilba store, has plenty of atmosphere and charm with great views and a cosy log fire.

Wirrina (☎ 02-4473 7279; goodnite@acr.net.au; Blacksmiths Lane; s/d with breakfast $80/105) A charming B&B set up in little cottages just off the main street.

Dromedary Hotel (☎ 02-4473 7223; d with breakfast $30) This is a nice old pub in Central Tilba with basic rooms.

There are plenty of good cafés and teashops on Bate St in Central Tilba. **Tilba Teapot** (☼ 10am-4pm) offers good home-style bakery items, and the **Rose & Sparrow** (lunch $10; ☼ breakfast & lunch) serves generous portions of healthy food, like vegie burgers ($10).

GETTING THERE & AWAY

Premier Motor Service (☎ 13 34 10) buses come through both Central Tilba and Tilba Tilba on their daily run between Sydney and Melbourne.

If you're heading for Bermagui or if you just want an interesting drive, leave the highway at Tilba Tilba and take the sealed road that follows the coast through Wallaga Lake National Park to Bermagui.

WADBILLIGA NATIONAL PARK

A rugged, subalpine wilderness area which covers around 79,000 hectares, Wadbilliga offers good walking for experienced bushwalkers. One popular trail is along the 5km **Tuross River Gorge** to the **Tuross Falls**. There's a camping area on the northwestern side of the park, near the walk to the falls. Access is off the road running from Countegany south to Tuross. Another camping area, in the centre of the park on the Wadbilliga River, is reached via Bourkes Rd from the east. If you don't have 4WD, you can only enter the park as far as the picnic area. Similarly, access to the Cascades camping area and the centre of the park is by 4WD only.

For more information, contact the **Narooma NPWS** (☎ 02-4476 2888).

Brogo Wilderness Canoes (☎ 02-6492 7328) offers canoe hire in the park for $20 per person for four hours. The hire office is at the boat ramp, but call ahead so someone can meet you.

WALLAGA LAKE NATIONAL PARK

This small park takes in most of the western shore of Wallaga Lake, a beautiful tidal lake at the mouth of several creeks, and has prolific birdlife. There's another chunk of the park off the highway west of here.

There's no road access into the park (and no camping allowed), but the little settlements of **Beauty Point** and **Regatta Point** are on the lake and you can hire boats there. **Merriman Island**, in the lake off Regatta Point, is off limits because of its significance to the Aboriginal community. Similarly, sites such as middens and relics you might come across in the park are protected.

Umbarra Cultural Centre (☎ 02-4473 7232; ☼ 9am-5pm Mon-Fri, to 4pm Sat & Sun), run by the Yuin people from Wallaga Lake Koori community, runs tours of the lake and other places of historical and cultural importance (from $30). The centre, 3km from the highway on the road to Wallaga Lake, also has a display of local Aboriginal art and culture.

Sleeping

There are several caravan parks in and near Regatta Point and Beauty Point.

Ocean Lake Caravan Park (☎ 02-6493 4055; unpowered sites from $16, cabins from $66) This big park is one of the nicest and best equipped.

Wallaga Lake Park (☎ 02-6493 4655; camp sites from $16, cabins from $52; 🐾) This park is the closest one to the ocean. It's off the main road between Narooma and Bermagui, just south of Beauty Point.

BERMAGUI

☎ 02 / pop 1300

Bermagui is a small fishing community centred on pretty Horseshoe Bay. Many visitors come here, mainly to fish, and there are six big-game tournaments a year. April to May is the busiest season. It's also a handy base for visits to Wallaga Lake, Mimosa Rocks and Wadbilliga National Parks.

US novelist Zane Grey (1872–1939), author of more than 80 books and considered the father of the American West literary genre, was a renowned game-fishing enthusiast. He once visited Bermagui and included his experiences in *An American Angler in Australia*.

The **information centre** (☎ 6493 3054; info@ bermagui.auz.net; Lamont St; 🕙 10am-4pm) is on the main street.

There are several **walks** around Bermagui. You can wander 6km along the coast north to **Camel Rock Beach** (a good surfing spot) and a further 2km around to Wallaga Lake. The route follows **Haywards Beach**.

Sleeping & Eating

There are many holiday houses and apartments. Letting agents include **Bermagui First National** (☎ 6493 4255; www.fisknagle.com.au /framebermagui.htm; 14 LaMont St).

Bimbimbi House (☎ 6493 4456; bimbimbihouse@ bigfoot.com.au; Nutleys Creek Rd; r with breakfast $100-170) This is a gorgeous homestead set in tranquil gardens about 2km out of town. The 3-hectare property slopes down to the Bermagui River.

Horseshoe Bay Hotel/Motel (☎ 6493 4206; 10 Lamont St; motel r $49, pub r $60) This place has fairly ordinary motel rooms and recently renovated pub rooms. Prices nearly double in peak times.

Zane Grey Park (☎ 6493 4382; Lamont St; camp sites from $17, cabins from $57) Located so it overlooks Horseshoe Bay, this park is central and close to the beach. Prices rise considerably at peak times.

Saltwater (☎ 6493 4328; mains $20; 🕙 lunch daily Dec-Feb, dinner Wed-Sun year-round) Down by the marina, Saltwater is probably the best restaurant in town and specializes in superfresh seafood: the seafood platter ($23) puts many a fisherman's basket to shame.

That Italian Mob (☎ 6493 3165; mains $13-16; 🕙 dinner Mon-Sat) The Mob serves authentic Italian cuisine, including excellent *calzones* (pastries with savoury stuffing) and dessert pizzas.

Getting There & Away

Bermagui is off the highway, so not all buses call in here. **Bega Valley Coaches** (☎ 6492 2418) has a weekday service between Bermagui and Bega, and **Premier Motor Service** (☎ 13 34 10) stops here once a day on its Sydney–Melbourne run.

Driving north, the quickest way back to the highway is to go past Wallaga Lake National Park, and this is also a pretty drive. Heading south, the quickest way is to go west and join the highway at Cobargo, but if you have time you could drive south on the unsealed road that runs alongside Mimosa Rocks National Park to Tathra, from where you can rejoin the highway at Bega. Look out for lyrebirds.

MIMOSA ROCKS NATIONAL PARK

Running along 17km of beautiful coastline, Mimosa Rocks (5624 hectares) is a wonderful coastal park with dense and varied bush, caves and great beaches. Admission is free and there are basic **camp sites** (per person $5) at **Aragunnu Beach, Picnic Point** and **Middle Beach**, and a camping area with no facilities at **Gillards Beach**. These camping areas and the picnic areas are accessible from the road running between Bermagui and Tathra.

Contact the **NPWS** (Narooma ☎ 02-6476 2888; Merimbula ☎ 02-6495 5000) for more information.

BEGA

☎ 02 / pop 4400

Bega is a centre for the rich dairy and cattle country of the southern Monaro Tableland. Most of Canberra's milk and some fine cheddar cheese comes from the valleys around here. After the tourist bustle of the coastal or mountain resorts, you'll find

Bega very much a working country town; it's worth a stopover perhaps for that reason alone and it makes a good base for a number of excursions.

Information

The **visitors centre** (☎ 6492 2045; Gipps St; ☉ 9am-5pm Mon-Fri) is near the corner of Carp St. It also usually opens on Saturday morning in summer. The **library** (☎ 6499 2127; Zingel Pl) has Internet access for $3 per half hour.

Sights & Activities

There are a number of mildly interesting old buildings; the visitors centre has a walking-tour map.

The **Bega Pioneers Museum** (☎ 6492 1453; 87 Bega St; adult/child $2.50/1; ☉ 10.30am-4pm Mon-Fri) focuses on local heritage, with particular emphasis on farming and forest machinery. There's an **art gallery** (Zingel Pl; admission free; ☉ 10am-4pm Mon-Sat, to 2pm Sun) with changing exhibitions next to the library.

At the **Bega Cheese Factory & Heritage Centre** (☎ 6492 1714; Lagoon St; admission free; ☉ 9am-5pm Mon-Fri, 10am-4pm Sat & Sun), north across the river, you can look down on the factory operations from a viewing area, taste cheese samples until you've made a nice little pile of cocktail sticks, and visit an interesting dairy museum. **Grevillea Estate Winery** (☎ 6492 3006; ☉ 9am-5pm) is open to visitors for tastings and sales. They also have a decent outdoor **eatery** (☉ lunch) featuring big bits of barbecued beef ($12). It's about 2km from the town centre – follow the highway across the river and take the first left after the bridge.

Sleeping

Pickled Pear (☎ 6492 1393; 60 Carp St; s/d with breakfast from $80/95) This lovely 1870s house near the centre of town has beautiful rooms.

Girraween B&B (☎ 6492 1761; 2 Girraween Cr; r/apt with breakfast from $50/65) Girraween offers an excellent (if somewhat plain) deal in a quiet location. The apartment has a full kitchen.

Central Hotel (☎ 6492 1263; 90 Gipps St; s/d pub r $40/50, motel r $50/60) This big, converted pub has a bit of character and some permanent residents. The large pub rooms are clean and light, and the motel rooms are set in a leafy garden out back.

Bega Valley Backpackers (☎ 6492 3103; Kirkland Cres; dm $15, d $34) A clean, friendly, family-run (and owned) hostel in a quiet area just west

of town. The owners offer a free tour of the cheese factory and Grevillea Winery, and have inexpensive 4WD trips to Tathra and Bournda and Mimosa Rocks National Parks, a horse stud, Tilba and Mumballa Falls.

Bega Caravan Park (☎ 6492 2303; camp sites from $16, cabins from $36) This park is on the highway south of the centre. Prices almost double in summer.

Eating

There are a couple of good cafés in town.

Goose is Out Café (Church St; mains from $6; ☉ breakfast & lunch Mon-Fri) You can get healthy wholefood meals and snacks here. The fresh juices are a winner as are sandwiches and falafel ($6).

Khai's (☎ 6492 3999; 248 Carp St; mains $10-15; ☉ dinner) A recommended Asian restaurant with Chinese, Thai and Vietnamese on the menu.

Getting There & Away

Traveland (☎ 6492 3599; 163 Carp St) handles bus bookings. Buses leave from near the tourist office.

Greyhound Pioneer (☎ 13 20 30) buses stop here on the run between Sydney and Melbourne, and will also drop off near the Bega YHA if requested. **Premier Motor Service** (☎ 13 34 10) also stops here. **Countrylink** (☎ 13 22 32) has an Eden to Canberra service that passes through Bega.

A local service, **Edwards** (☎ 6496 1422), runs between Bega and Eden (via Merimbula) daily (the Sunday service is Countrylink). **Bega Valley Coaches** (☎ 6492 2418) has a weekday service between Bermagui and Bega. On weekdays, **Tathra Bus Service** (☎ 6492 1991) leaves for Tathra from the post office at 9.30am (7.45am during school holidays), and from Church St at 2pm and 3.30pm.

AROUND BEGA

Off the highway about 5km north of Bega is **Mumballa Falls**, where there's a picnic area.

Candelo is a pleasant old village 26km southwest of Bega (see p325). It straggles along both sides of a steep valley and is split by the large, sandy Candelo Creek. The nearby country is cleared but pretty. There are several **craft galleries** and a great craft **market** on the first Sunday of each month.

About 6km from Candelo, **Tantawanglo Trail Rides** (☎ 02-6493 2350) has horse rides into

DETOUR: CANDELO & BEMBOKA

If all this magnificent coastal scenery is getting a bit dull, maybe you should head for the hills. About 8km south of Bega and 15km north of Pambula on the Princes Hwy (1) is the turn-off for **Candelo**, a tiny village that packs out on the first Sunday of the month for market day. The drive there is on a beautiful sealed road, which swoops through undulating country past quaint homesteads and tranquil cows.

Candelo itself is cute, built on both sides of a steep valley, and if it's not market day you could spend an hour or so wandering the streets checking out the ramshackle houses before stopping in at the pub to marvel at its memorabilia collection. From Candelo it's another 20km on a similarly gorgeous road to **Bemboka**, a town perched on the crest in a valley and famed for its pie shop. Otherwise you can complete the loop and head back to the coast.

the beautiful surrounding national parks and state forests. Two-hour rides must be booked and cost $40 per person.

From Candelo you can drive back to the Princes Hwy via **Toothdale**, or continue south to the Bombala road. This route takes you over **Myrtle Mountain** where there's a picnic area with good views, and drives in the state forest. The Bombala road leads west to **Wyndham**, a small village just after the intersection with the Candelo road, or east to Pambula and Merimbula.

TATHRA
☎ 02 / pop 1650
This small town is popular with people from the Bega area in summer. It starts on a headland, where you'll find the post office and the pub as well as access to the historic wharf. Down a steep road and to the north, Tathra follows a long beach towards Mimosa Rocks National Park.

Tathra wharf (☎ 6494 4062) is the last remaining coastal steamship wharf in the state and a popular place for fishing. The wharf storehouse now houses a small **Maritime Museum** (adult/child $1.50/50c; ☺ 9am-5pm); as well as a tackle shop and small café.

Cliff Place, a narrow street that runs off the headland road next to the road down to

the wharf, has great views. You can take a path that begins near the surf club.

Sleeping
Prices for accommodation in Tathra rise considerably in summer. **Tathra Beach Accommodation Service** (☎ 6494 1306) is one of the agents handling holiday letting.

Fennerty's at Tathra (☎ 6494 1792; 6 Wheeler's Ave; s/d with breakfast from $75/110) Head 2km out of town, to a bluff overlooking the bay, to find this place, which boasts incredible views. Rooms are spacious and modern.

Tathra Hotel-Motel (☎ 6494 1101; s/d $50/80) This is a popular eating, drinking and dancing place on the headland. Some of the decent motel-style rooms have excellent sea views. The pub has entertainment on weekends and in summer it hosts big touring acts.

Tathra Beach Tourist Park (☎ 6494 1302; camp sites from $17, cabins from $50) This caravan park in the centre of town is a bit run down, but you can't beat the seaside location.

Eating
Harbourmaster Restaurant (☎ 6494 1344; 15 Bega St; mains $14-18; ☺ dinner) This pleasant place is on the headland next to the road going down to the beach, in an old house. Specials include the warm Thai seafood salad ($15) and a healthy cocktail list.

Mimosa Rocks Pizza (☎ 6494 1483; mains $14; ☺ dinner Wed-Sun) Excellent wood-fired pizza, steaks, ribs and seafood are on the menu at this place on the main street.

Tathra Hotel (☎ 6494 1101; Bega St) Come here for counter meals or the bistro with good views over the ocean.

Tathra Bakehaus Swiss (☎ 6494 1822; ☺ 8am-5pm) Passing Europeans give this place the thumbs up for their delicious fresh-baked pastries and savouries.

Getting There & Away
Buses to Bega depart at 8.20am, 10.30am and 2.30pm on weekdays. See the Bega Getting There & Away section (opposite) for more information. Tathra is 18km from the Princes Hwy at Bega. If you're heading north, consider the unsealed road to Bermagui, which runs through forest and alongside Mimosa Rocks National Park. South to Merimbula, you can turn off the Bega road 5km out of Tathra onto Sapphire Coast Dr, which runs past Bournda National Park.

SOUTH COAST

MERIMBULA

☎ 02 / pop 4900

Merimbula's a holiday and retirement mecca, and motels and apartments have mushroomed on the hillsides surrounding the impressive lake (which is actually an inlet). If this sounds to you like a recipe for tackiness and claustrophobia you're partly right, but there is still some charm about the town's setting, and the lake is big enough to dwarf the development.

Nearby Pambula Beach is a much quieter option.

Information

The **tourist information centre** (☎ 1800 670 080; ◷ 9am-5pm Mon-Sat, to 4pm Sun) is on the waterfront at the bottom of Market St, the main shopping street. Next door (in the same building) is a handy **booking office** (☎ 1800 150 457) for accommodation, tours and activities. You can access the Internet at the library ($3 for half an hour).

There's a useful NPWS office and **Discovery Centre** (☎ 6495 5000; cnr Merimbula & Sapphire Coast Drs; ◷ 9am-5pm).

Sights & Activities

At the wharf on the eastern point is the small **Merimbula Aquarium** (☎ 6495 4446; adult/child $9/5; ◷ 10am-5pm). There are good views across the lake from near here and the jetty is a popular little fishing spot. The **Old School Museum** (☎ 6495 2114; Main St; adult/child $2/free; ◷ 2-4pm Tue, Thu & Sun) isn't dedicated to ageing rappers, but it *is* one of those delightful volunteer-run museums featuring knick-knackery from over the years and displays on local history.

Diving is popular, with plenty of fish and several wrecks in the area, including two tugs sunk in 1987. **Merimbula Divers Lodge** (☎ 1800 651 861) offers basic instruction and one shallow dive for $40. Four-day PADI-certificate courses cost $400. It also does snorkelling trips.

There are cruises from the Merimbula marina, opposite the Lakeview Hotel, including a dolphin cruise run by **Sapphire Coast Fishing Charters** (☎ 6495 1686; adult/child $30/20).

There are two **boat-hire** places – at the Merimbula Marina jetty and at Top Lake, on the north shore west of the bridge (follow

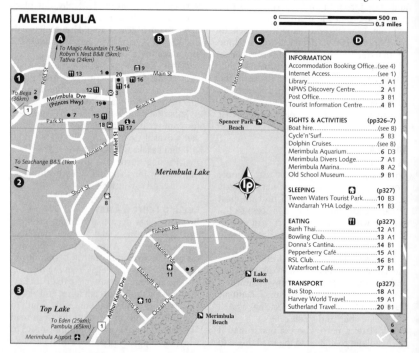

MERIMBULA

0 _____ 500 m
0 _____ 0.3 miles

To Magic Mountain (1.5km);
Robyn's Nest B&B (5km);
Tathra (24km)

Main St

Henwood St

To Bega
(36km)

Merimbula Dve
(Princes Hwy)

Reid St

Beach St

Park St

Monaro St

Market St

Spencer Park
Beach

To Seachange B&B (1km)

Merimbula Lake

Short St

Fishpen Rd

Marine Pde

Elizabeth St

Lake
Beach

Top Lake

Arthur Kaine Dve

Dunna Rd

Ocean Dve

*Merimbula
Beach*

To Eden (25km);
Pambula (65km)

Merimbula Airport

INFORMATION	
Accommodation Booking Office..(see 4)	
Internet Access.........................(see 1)	
Library...**1** A1	
NPWS Discovery Centre.............**2** A1	
Post Office...................................**3** B1	
Tourist Information Centre..........**4** B1	

SIGHTS & ACTIVITIES	(pp326-7)
Boat hire.....................................(see 8)	
Cycle'n'Surf..................................**5** B3	
Dolphin Cruises...........................(see 8)	
Merimbula Aquarium...................**6** D3	
Merimbula Divers Lodge..............**7** A1	
Merimbula Marina........................**8** A2	
Old School Museum.....................**9** B1	

SLEEPING	(p327)
Tween Waters Tourist Park........**10** B3	
Wandarrah YHA Lodge..............**11** B3	

EATING	(p327)
Banh Thai...................................**12** A1	
Bowling Club..............................**13** A1	
Donna's Cantina.........................**14** B1	
Pepperberry Café.......................**15** A1	
RSL Club....................................**16** B1	
Waterfront Café.........................**17** B1	

TRANSPORT	(p327)
Bus Stop.....................................**18** A1	
Harvey World Travel...................**19** A1	
Sutherland Travel......................**20** B1	

Lakewood Dr). They have power boats, small yachts, canoes and rowing boats. **Cycle 'n' Surf** (☎ 6495 2171; Marine Pde), south of the lake, hires out bikes, boogie boards and surf-skis, as well as fishing tackle.

Sleeping

There are hundreds of motels and holiday apartments scattered all around Merimbula. Self-contained apartments are usually let on a weekly basis, particularly in summer. Letting agents for the area include **Fisk & Nagle** (☎ 6495 1301; Centrepoint Mall) and **LJ Hooker** (☎ 6495 1026; 35 Market St)

Seachange B&B (☎ 6495 3133; www.sapphire coast.com.au/seachange; 49 Imlay St; s/d with breakfast from $110/135) This comfortable and modern B&B is 2km out of town. It has fantastic water views.

Robyn's Nest B&B (☎ 6495 4956; www.robyns nest.com.au; 188 Merimbula Dr; s/d with breakfast $150/ 165) This place is 5km out of town. The setting is idyllic and tranquil, the furnishings less so.

Wandarrah YHA Lodge (☎ 6495 3503; wanlodge@ asitis.com.au; 8 Marine Pde; dm $22-27, d $48-58) This is a clean place, with a good kitchen and hanging out areas, near the surf beach. It hires out bikes and canoes and offers tours.

Tween Waters Tourist Park (☎ /fax 6495 1530; Dunns Rd; powered sites from $21, cabins from $60), located south of the bridge, has access to surf and lake beaches. Prices multiply exponentially over Christmas.

Eating

Merimbula offers quite a wide range of eateries, most of them concentrated in the busy shopping area.

Waterfront Café (☎ 6495 2211; cnr Beach St & Market St; mains $12-16; ☺ breakfast, lunch & dinner) Try this place for coffee or a snack while looking out over Merimbula Lake. It's next to the information centre.

Pepperberry Café (☎ 6492 0361; Ayres Walkway; sandwiches $6-8; ☺ breakfast & lunch Mon-Fri) Good lunches and cheap breakfasts.

Bahn Thai (☎ 6495 3800; 17 Merimbula Dr; mains $15; ☺ dinner) This Thai restaurant serves good food in semi-authentic surrounds.

Donna's Cantina (☎ 6495 1085; 56 Market St; mains $14-18; ☺ lunch & dinner) Donna's is one of the best restaurants in town. The menu features imaginative seafood dishes and Spanish-styled entrées.

Licensed clubs, including the **Bowling Club** (☎ 6495 1306) and the **RSL Club** (☎ 6495 1724), both on Main St, have bistros and restaurants.

Getting There & Away

Travel bookings can be made at **Harvey World Travel** (☎ 6495 1205; Merimbula Dr), or **Summerland Travel** (☎ 6495 1008; 16 Market St).

There are daily flights to Melbourne ($97) and to Sydney ($100) with **Regional Express Airlines** (Rex; ☎ 13 17 13). The airport is 1km out of town on the road to Pambula.

Buses stop outside the Centrepoint Mall on Market St. **Greyhound Pioneer** (☎ 13 20 30) and **Premier Motor Service** (☎ 13 34 10) buses stop in Merimbula on their Sydney–Melbourne service. **Countrylink** (☎ 13 22 32) stops here on the Eden to Canberra run.

Edwards (☎ 6496 1422) is a local bus company that runs between Bega and Eden.

AROUND MERIMBULA
Bournda National Park

Taking in most of the coast from Merimbula north to Tathra, **Bournda National Park** (admission per car $6) is a 2378-hectare park with some good beaches and several walking trails, as well as tea-tree forests, abundant birdlife and the chance to swim in freshwater lagoons and saltwater lakes. All this means it can get pretty crowded at peak times. **Camping** (per person $7.50) is permitted at Hobart Beach, on the southern shore of the big **Wallagoot Lagoon**, where there are toilets and hot showers. During the Christmas and Easter holidays, sites are usually booked out. Contact the **Merimbula NPWS** (☎ 02-6495 5000) for more information.

Woodbine Park (☎ 02-6495 9333; low season cabins per day/week $100/300, high season $120/450) borders Bournda and is 1km from the beach. It's a friendly place with six-person self-contained cabins. Head north from Merimbula on Sapphire Coast Dr and take the signposted turn-off after about 7km.

Pambula
☎ 02 / pop 1100

Just south of Merimbula, Pambula is a small town that has largely avoided the development of its glitzy neighbour.

Between Pambula and Merimbula, **Wheeler's Kiosk** (☎ 6495 6089; adult/child $7/3) is run by one of the local oyster farmers (there are many oyster leases on the inlets around Merimbula). There are tours of the small processing factory daily (except Sunday) at 11am, as well as a video screening and oyster tasting. You can also buy fresh oysters and other seafood here.

Holiday Hub Tourist Park (☎ 6495 6363; powered/ unpowered sites $26/23, cabins from $60) This caravan park is at Pambula Beach, which is 4km east and right on the beach. It hosts some very friendly marsupials. Keep your food hidden!

EDEN
☎ 02 / pop 3150

Eden is still very much a fishing port, with one of the largest fleets in the state and a busy enclosed harbour. It's also a timber town. The local population doubled when a woodchip mill opened in the 1970s, so you won't meet many people voicing anti-woodchipping sentiments. It's a good place to base yourself, with easy access to the surrounding national parks and a more laid-back feel than Merimbula. In summer, Eden's flies can drive you to distraction.

The **Eden visitor centre** (☎ 6496 1953; Mitchell St; ☽ 9am-5pm Mon-Fri, to 4pm Sat & Sun) is well stocked with brochures about the area. The **library** (☽ 9am-5pm Mon-Fri, to noon Sat) in the same building has Internet access for $3 per half hour.

Sights & Activities

The interesting **Killer Whale Museum** (☎ 6496 2094; 94 Imlay St; adult/child $6/2; ☽ 9.15am-3.45pm Mon-Sat, 11.15am-3.45pm Sun) was established in 1931, mainly to preserve the skeleton of Old Tom, a killer whale and local legend (see the boxed text below). If you've ever read Moby Dick, this is your chance to see a real whale boat with all those arcane pieces of equipment described by Melville.

Cat Balou Cruises (☎ 6496 2027) has whale-spotting cruises (adult/child $60/30) in October and November. At other times of the year, dolphins, sea-lions and seabirds can usually be seen during the shorter bay cruise ($22.50).

Boydtown, off the highway 10km south of Eden, has relics of Ben Boyd's stillborn empire (see the boxed text The Rise & Fall of Benjamin Boyd, opposite). The ruins of a church can be seen and the impressive Seahorse Inn still operates (see Sleeping, opposite).

Festivals & Events

Eden comes alive in mid-October for the **Whale Festival**, with the typical carnival, street parade and stalls plus some innovative local events. The winning toss in the 2003 Slimy Mackerel Throw was a whopping 38m.

FROM WHALING TO WHALE-WATCHING

Migrating humpback and southern right whales pass so close to the coast near the fishing port of Eden that whale-watching experts consider this one of the best places in Australia to observe these magnificent creatures. Often they can be seen feeding or resting in Twofold Bay during their southern migration back to Antarctic waters.

Around 170 years ago, the whales attracted interest for very different reasons. Australia's first shore-based whaling station was set up here in 1828, starting a prosperous and lucrative whaling industry that continued until 1929. When a pod of whales was spotted, crews (many of them Aborigines recruited from the area) would race out in open whaling boats, but it was a remarkable alliance between the whalers and the wild killer whales (orcas) that made Eden so unique.

The killer whales would gather, locate the migrating whales, then herd them into Twofold Bay for the waiting whalers. They would then assist the whalers in making the kill, preventing the hapless whales from escaping or diving. Why? It was a matter of convenience. Once the whales had been killed, the orcas would feast on the huge lips and tongue – the only bits they wanted – and the whalers would later take the rest of the carcass for the valuable whale oil.

'Old Tom' was the leader of the most successful killer whale pack, assisting the whalers in their slaughter for many years until his death in 1930 (around the same time that whaling ceased in Eden). Discovering Old Tom's carcass in the bay, locals decided to save the skeleton and exhibit it for future generations. You can see it at the Killer Whale Museum in Eden (above). You can also see the ruins of the Davidson Whaling Station on Kiah Inlet in Ben Boyd National Park (p329).

Sleeping

Crown & Anchor Inn (☎ 6496 1017; www.crownand anchoreden.com.au; 239 Imlay St; s/d with breakfast from $120/140) This is the place to stay if you really want to spoil yourself. The historic house (1845) has been beautifully restored and has a lovely view over Twofold Bay from the back patio. Each room is different but all have stylish period furniture (such as four-post beds and claw-foot baths).

Gibsons by the Beach (☎ 6496 1414; www.babs .com.au/gibsons; 10 Bay St; s/d with breakfast from $130/150) Gibsons has modern and spacious rooms. The beach is five minutes' walk away, through lush bushland.

Hotel Australasia (☎ 6496 1600; Imlay St; s/d $40/60) Unexciting pub rooms are on offer here. Try to get one at the back as the front ones are noisy.

Seahorse Inn (☎ 6496 1361) Down at Boyd-town, this place overlooks Twofold Bay and is a solid old building, built by Ben Boyd as a guesthouse in 1843. It was being renovated at the time of research, and looks like being converted into a luxury resort. There's also a camping ground (powered/unpowered sites $18/12).

Eden Tourist Park (☎ 6496 1139; Aslings Beach Rd; powered/unpowered sites $18/15, cabins from $50) This park is serenely situated on a spit separating Aslings Beach from Lake Curalo.

Eating

Fare n Square Café (☎ 6496 3007; 126 Imlay St; ☺ breakfast & lunch) Come here for decent breakfasts and excellent coffee. The outdoor terrace area is a fine place to watch the world go by.

Wharfside (☎ 6496 1855; meals $12-18; ☺ break-fast & lunch) Down at Snug Cove, Eden's fishing harbour, this place serves good breakfasts and imaginative seafood dishes.

Oyster Bar (☎ 6496 1304; mains $15; ☺ breakfast & lunch daily, dinner Fri & Sat) An atmospheric, tiny seafood café specialising in Italian and Asian cuisine.

Getting There & Away

Bus bookings can be made at **Traveland** (☎ 6496 1314; cnr Bass & Imlay Sts).

BEN BOYD NATIONAL PARK

Protecting some relics of Ben Boyd's opera-tions, this national park (9450 hectares) has

---

THE RISE & FALL OF BENJAMIN BOYD

Benjamin Boyd was a strange person, part empire builder, part capitalist and part adventurer, mixed with a large dash of incompetence. He never really completed anything he set out to do and he was unsuccessful in a big way.

Boyd was a stockbroker in London who decided that the colony of New South Wales (NSW) offered scope for the large amounts of money he could raise. His plans were vague and included a half-baked idea for a private colony in the South Pacific.

He founded the Royal Bank, which quickly attracted £1,000,000 in investments, then set out for Sydney in his racing yacht *Wanderer*, arriving in 1842. Boyd, who so far had accomplished nothing except the acquisition of a great deal of other people's money, was greeted with much official and public enthusiasm in Sydney.

He began a coastal steamship service, but the boat was damaged and withdrawn in its first year of operation. Boyd nevertheless convinced the governor that he was a fit person to be granted vast landholdings, second only in size to the Crown's.

Boyd decided to set up headquarters at Twofold Bay and an extensive building programme began. Money ran short, although the investors were assured that their golden reward was just around the corner, and Boyd issued his own banknotes.

Things went from bad to worse and the Royal Bank (nominally the owner of Boyd's empire) sacked him. By 1849 the bank decided that it was easier simply to collapse than to untangle Boyd's complex financial wheelings and dealings.

The entrepreneur smiled amid the ruins of his speculations, decided NSW wasn't really the right place for his ventures after all and set sail in *Wanderer* for the Californian goldfields.

Things didn't quite work out there either, and in 1851 Boyd sailed back into the Pacific. One morning, while moored at Guadalcanal in the Solomon Islands, he left his yacht to go shooting and disappeared without trace.

dramatic coastline, bush and some walks. The main access road to the park is the sealed Edrom Rd, which leaves the Princes Hwy about 25km south of Eden. Edrom Rd ends at the big woodchip mill on the south shore of Twofold Bay.

Before the mill there's a turn-off to the left that leads to the old **Davidson Whaling Station** on Twofold Bay, now a historic site. There's not much left of the try works, which turned whale blubber into oil from the late 19th century, but interpretive signs tell the story. Further along Edrom Rd is the turn-off for **Boyd's Tower**, an impressive structure built with sandstone brought from Sydney. It was intended to be a lighthouse but the government wouldn't give Boyd permission to operate it. From the lookout at Redstone Point you can see the forces of nature in the folded rock on the coastline.

Off Edrom Rd closer to the highway is Green Cape Rd, which runs right down to Green Cape, from where there are some good views and a **lighthouse**. Running off Green Cape Rd are smaller roads which lead to **Saltwater Creek** and **Bittangabee Bay**. There are **camp sites** at both places and a 9km walk between the two. You should book sites for Christmas and Easter at the **Merimbula NPWS** (☎ 02-6495 5000).

The northern section of Ben Boyd National Park runs up the coast from Eden; access is from the Princes Hwy north of the town. From Haycock Point, where there are good views, a walking trail leads to a headland overlooking the Pambula River. Another good walk is to the **Pinnacles**, an eroded formation of layered rock; access is from the car park not too far in from the Princes Hwy.

NADGEE NATURE RESERVE

Nadgee Nature Reserve continues down the coast from Ben Boyd National Park, but it's much less accessible. Much of it is official Wilderness Area, but vehicle access is allowed as far as the ranger station near the Merrica River, 7km from Newton's Beach. Admission is free.

On Wonboyn Lake at the north end of the reserve, the small settlement of **Wonboyn** has a store selling petrol and basic supplies. Wonboyn is near access roads into Nadgee, including one down to Wonboyn Beach.

Wonboyn Cabins & Caravan Park (☎ 02-6496 9131; d camp sites $22, cabins from $70) is spacious and has some friendly rainbow lorikeets.

MT IMLAY NATIONAL PARK

This small national park (3808 hectares), 32km southwest of Eden, surrounds **Mt Imlay** (886m). The tough 3km **Mt Imlay Walking Track**, from the car park to the summit, is steep, and the last 500m follows an extremely narrow ridge. Admission is free but there are no facilities in the park.

The road to the start of the track runs westwards from the Princes Hwy just south of the turn-off to Ben Boyd National Park.

Australian
Capital Territory

The Australian Capital Territory (ACT) occupies a bushy inland plot totalling 2366 sq km, with rugged, blue-grey ranges to the south and to the west. Within these smallish territorial boundaries – 88km from north to south and 30km from east to west – are the spread-out environs of the national capital, Canberra, an ultra-clean metropolis with an externally serious aesthetic but a lively interior life. Only a few gear-shifts from the city are some relaxing old towns and an abundance of camera-friendly natural sights, including the splendid ridges and rivers of Namadgi National Park, which covers 40% of the territory and adjoins Kosciuszko National Park in New South Wales (NSW). Bushwalkers, bird-watchers, cyclists and connoisseurs of leisure will all find plenty to occupy them here.

When Australia's separate colonies were federated in 1901 and became states, a decision to build a national capital was written into the constitution. In 1908 the site was selected, diplomatically situated between the arch-rival cities of Sydney and Melbourne, and in 1911 the Commonwealth government formally established the land-holdings of the ACT. But although it's the nexus of Australian political power and home to many government institutions, the territory maintains a relatively low-key, family-nurturing profile where ostentatious man-made landmarks form a minority when compared to Canberra's predominantly low-rise skyline, and an abundance of typically Australian vegetation softens the capital's concrete and bitumen core.

HIGHLIGHTS

- Ogling the view from the lawn atop **Parliament House** (p337)
- Unravelling the startling tangle of Australiana in the **National Museum of Australia** (p338)
- Getting an eyeful of beguiling artistry in the **National Gallery of Australia** (p338)
- Walking, cycling or skating around **Lake Burley Griffin** (p336)
- Taking a guided tour at the **Australian War Memorial** (p339)
- Sipping a martini at the welcoming **Trinity Bar** (p349)
- Losing your sense of direction on a track in **Namadgi National Park** (p355)
- Taking a deep urban breath without having a coughing fit

| ■ TELEPHONE CODE: 02 | ■ POPULATION: 321,700 | ■ AREA: 2366 SQ KM |

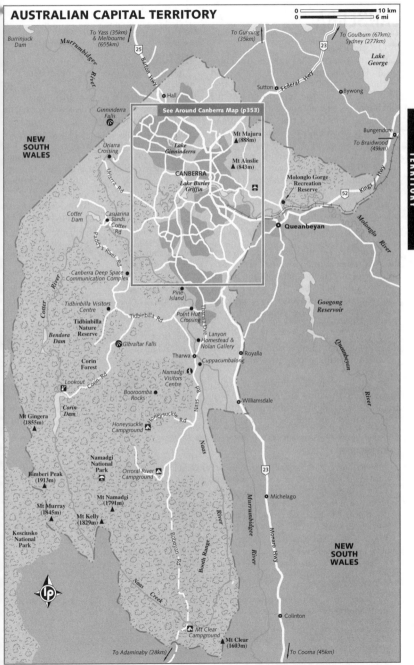

AUSTRALIAN CAPITAL TERRITORY

0 —————— 10 km
0 —————— 6 mi

CANBERRA

☎ 02 / pop 309,800

Canberra is a city that thrives outdoors, amid lakeside parks, green hills and patches of naturally ragged bushland that lie in and around the suburbs. When the inhabitants aren't admiring the autumnal dressage of millions of trees, the crisp and often clear-skied days of winter (when the city experiences an average of six sunny hours each day), the blooming colours of spring or the depths of a waterhole during a hot summer's day, they can take a cultural dip in Canberra's museums or work up an appetite in one of the many restaurants and cafés. This is also one of the few Australian cities in which kangaroos do occasionally jump into view.

The relative serenity and orderliness of the Australian capital isn't to everybody's taste, especially the unapologetically homogenous suburbia. But the days when Canberra was an incubator for a uniform public service are long gone, with more than half the workforce now employed in the private sector. And the thriving arts scene means that theatres and galleries are full of thoughtful, provocative and nicely designed fare.

An exploration of Canberra will also expose you to some intriguing modern architecture, a highly visible collective of distraction-seeking university students and the political enclave on and around Capital Hill. So pack an open mind and investigate the possibilities.

HISTORY

After the Commonwealth government sold itself a chunk of land in 1911 on which to build the nation's capital, an international competition was held to design the city. The winning entry out of a field of 137 submissions was a spacious urban plan drawn up by American architect Walter Burley Griffin. On 12 March 1913, when the foundation stones of the new capital were being laid, the city was officially baptised 'Canberra', believed to be an Aboriginal term for 'meeting place'.

Canberra took over from Melbourne as the seat of national government in 1927, but development of the site was slow and virtually stopped during the Depression – real expansion of the city only got under way after WWII.

ORIENTATION

The city is arranged around the damp centrepiece of Lake Burley Griffin. From the north side the main arterial road, Northbourne Ave, intersects compact Canberra City (aka Civic). The pedestrian malls to the east comprise Canberra's main shopping areas.

South of the city, Northbourne Ave becomes Commonwealth Ave and spans Lake Burley Griffin to Capital Circle. This road encircles Parliament House on Capital Hill, the apex of Walter Burley Griffin's

---

BUSHFIRES

In mid-January 2003, several massive bushfires combined to strike the western and southern outskirts of Canberra. Over a single weekend, the fires claimed four lives, 530 homes, 30 farms and the historic Mt Stromlo Observatory, and decimated large swathes of Namadgi National Park. Almost all of the 5500 hectares of the Tidbinbilla Nature Reserve, including most of the wildlife, was destroyed – the sole survivor of the reserve's 20 koalas was christened 'Lucky' and had a public recuperation at the city's zoo. Looking out from the observation deck of Telstra Tower after the blaze had passed, you could clearly see the expanses of burnt-out land, including a black arc that had been extinguished almost at the foot of Black Mountain.

The aftermath of the fires heard an impassioned public debate over the competency of emergency services and the need for the 'bush capital' to address the natural kindling overgrowing in some residential areas. Meanwhile, in the national park, an amazing process of regeneration was taking place, with greenery beginning to sprout from blackened tree trunks and the charred earth, and the surviving wildlife starting to reappear. It wasn't clear how long it would take for the Australian bush and its inhabitants to re-establish themselves, or how much flora would now be allowed to run wild in proximity to the suburbs, but the display of nature's resilience was a welcome sign of ongoing life.

parliamentary triangle. Located within and near the parliamentary triangle are a number of important buildings, including the National Library of Australia, the High Court of Australia, the National Gallery of Australia and Old Parliament House.

The rest of the city is made up of suburban clusters, including Belconnen (to the northwest), Gungahlin (north), Tuggeranong (southwest) and Woden Valley (south), each with their own 'town centres'.

Maps

The **NRMA** (Map pp340-1; ☎ 13 21 32; 92 Northbourne Ave, Braddon) has a *Canberra & Southeast New South Wales* map ($7), good for tours of the countryside. The Canberra visitors centre (p336) stocks detailed city maps and cartography for lookouts and bushwalks.

INFORMATION
Bookshops

Electric Shadows Cinema & Bookshop (Map pp340-1; ☎ 6248 8352; City Walk, Civic) This bookshop, part of a well-established cinema (see p350), specialises in books on theatre and film, plus gay and lesbian books and rentable arthouse videos.

Gilbert's (Map pp340-1; ☎ 6247 2032; 102 Alinga St) Great selection of eclectic second-hand books.

Map World (Map pp340-1; ☎ 6230 4097; Jolimont Centre, 65 Northbourne Ave, Civic) Numerous maps and travel guides.

National Library Bookshop (Map pp340-1; ☎ 6262 1424; Parkes Pl, Parkes) Stocks exclusively Australian books, including a superb range of fiction.

Paperchain Bookstore (Map pp340-1; ☎ 6295 6723; 2/14 Furneaux St, Manuka) Has an all-purpose book list.

Smiths Alternative Bookshop (Map pp340-1; ☎ 6247 4459; 76 Alinga St, Civic) Sells everything from New Age 'science' to gay and lesbian literature.

Cultural Centres

Alliance Française (Map p354; ☎ 6247 5027; 66 McCaughey St, Turner)

Das Zentrum (Map pp340-1; ☎ 6230 0441; Griffin Centre, 19 Bunda St, Civic) German-Australian cultural centre.

Spanish-Australia Club (Map p354; ☎ 6295 6506; Jerrabomberra Ave, Narrabundah)

Emergency

Ambulance (☎ 000, TTY 106)

Canberra Rape Crisis Centre (☎ 6247 2525, TTY 6247 1657) 24-hour help.

Fire (☎ 000, TTY 106)

Lifeline (☎ 13 11 14) 24-hour crisis counselling.

Police (☎ 000, TTY 106)

CANBERRA IN...

Two days

Have a hearty breakfast in a **Kingston** (p348) or **Manuka** (p348) café, then disappear into the parliamentary triangle, the slice of Parkes that includes **Parliament House** (p337) on the crest of Capital Hill, the once-busy corridors of **Old Parliament House** (p337) and the well-hung **National Gallery** (p338). After a breather on the foreshore of **Lake Burley Griffin** (p336), head into the city to grab a restaurant table in **Garema Place** (p347), followed by a tumbler of Bombay Sapphire at **Hippo** (p349). After an educated sleep at **University House** (p346), dive headlong into the iconic chaos of the **National Museum** (p338) and stroll through the **Botanic Gardens** (p338). Finish the evening with a feast at **Dickson Asian Noodle House** (p348) and either a martini at **Trinity** (p349) or a home-brew at **Wig & Pen** (p349).

Four days

Follow the 'Two days' itinerary, then start the third day with a munch at **Tilley's** (p350) and spend the rest of it talking to animals at the **zoo** (p338) and getting a sombre history lesson at the **War Memorial** (p339). Celebrate the day with a meal at **Green Herring** (p348) or **Aubergine** (p349), then chill at **Toast** (p350). Put aside at least one whole leisurely day to have a **picnic**, a **walk** and perhaps a **swim** somewhere around Canberra (p353).

Internet Access

Public libraries, the Canberra YHA Hostel (p345), Victor Lodge (p345), the Canberra Centre (p351; near the information desk) and the Jolimont Centre (pp340-1) all have public Internet access.

Medical Services

Canberra Hospital (Map p354; ☎ 6244 2222, emergency dept 6244 2611; Yamba Dr, Garran)

Capital Chemist (Map p354; ☎ 6248 7050; Sargood St, O'Connor; ⏰ 9am-11pm)

Travellers' Medical & Vaccination Centre (Map pp340-1; ☎ 6257 7156; 5th fl, 8-10 Hobart Pl, Civic; ⏰ 8.30am-4.30pm Mon-Fri, to 7pm Thu) Appointment essential.

Money

Branches of major banks are scattered around the city. Foreign-exchange bureaux include the following:

American Express (Map pp340-1; ☎ 6247 2333; 1st fl, Centrepoint, City Walk, Civic)

Thomas Cook (Map pp340-1; ☎ 6247 9984; Canberra Centre, Bunda St, Civic)

Post

Pick up poste restante at the **GPO** (Map pp340-1; ☎ 13 13 18; 53-73 Alinga St, Civic). Mail can be addressed: Poste restante Canberra GPO, Canberra City, ACT 2601.

Tourist Information

Canberra visitors centre (Map p354; ☎ 1300 554 114, 6205 0044; www.canberratourism.com.au; 330 Northbourne Ave, Dickson; ☒ 9am-5.30pm Mon-Fri, to 4pm Sat & Sun) Operated by the ACT's peak tourist information body, the Canberra Tourism & Events Corporation.

Community Information & Referral Service (Map pp340-1; ☎ 6248 7988; www.cirsact.org.au; Griffin Centre, 19 Bunda St, Civic; ☒ 10am-4pm Mon-Fri, to 1pm Wed) An excellent source of community information.

Government Info Shop (Map pp340-1; ☎ 6247 7211; 10 Mort St, Civic; ☒ 9.30am-5pm Mon-Fri) Information on federal government matters, plus some wildlife publications.

SIGHTS

Canberra's many significant buildings, museums and galleries are splayed out on either side of Lake Burley Griffin, while most appealing natural features lie in the territory's west and southwest. Wheelchair-bound visitors will find that most sights are fully accessible. Nearly all attractions close on Christmas Day.

Those keen on visiting Questacon (p339), the Australian Institute of Sport (p341) and Cockington Green (p355) should get a **3-in-1 Ticket** (family/adult/concession/child $85/30/21/15) giving access to all three attractions; you can buy it at any of the three sites or at the visitors centre.

Bus No 34 from the Civic bus interchange is handy for many of the following sights. For more detailed information on bus services, see p352.

Lookouts

Great views of Canberra can be had from the surrounding hills and their approach roads. **Black Mountain** (812m) is topped by the 195m-high **Telstra Tower** (Map p354; ☎ 6219 6111; Black Mountain Dr; adult/child $3.30/1.10; ☒ 9am-10pm), which has a unappealing concrete exterior but the best windblown vista around, plus a display on the history of local telecommunications and the revolving **Tower Restaurant** (☎ 6248 6162; mains $30-35; ☒ lunch & dinner). A 2km bush-lined walking track to the top starts on nearby Frith Rd, while other tracks wander northwest around the other side of the mountain from Belconnen Way and Caswell Drive; you can get a basic walking-tracks map from the tower.

Mt Ainslie, just northeast of the city, stands at 843m and has particularly fine views day and night. Walking tracks to the mountain start behind the Australian War Memorial and end 4km further on at 888m-high **Mt Majura**.

Lake Burley Griffin

Named after Canberra's architect and consisting of three water basins, **Lake Burley Griffin** was created by damming the Molonglo River in 1963. Swimming is not recommended, but the lake is conducive to boating (beware of sudden strong winds, some of it courtesy of the politicians on Capital Hill) and is also great to cycle or walk around. Boats, bikes and in-line skates are available for hire at Acton Park ferry terminal on the northern shore; see p342.

Around the lake's 35km shore are many places of interest. The most visible, built in 1970 for the bicentenary of Cook's landfall, is the **Captain Cook Memorial Water Jet** (Map pp340-1; admission free; ☒ 10am-noon & 2-4pm, also 7-9pm during daylight saving), which flings a 6 tonne column of water up to 147m into the air – and sometimes gives free showers, despite its automatic switch-off in strong winds. At nearby **Regatta Point** there's a skeleton globe on which Cook's three great voyages are traced. Also here is the **National Capital Exhibition** (Map pp340-1; ☎ 6257 1068; www.nationalcapital.gov.au/exhibition/index.htm; admission free; ☒ 9am-5pm), where the city's interesting history is on display. Just north of here is beautiful **Commonwealth Park** (Map pp340-1), where a series of paths leads you through flower gardens and alongside Nerang Pool.

Further east around the lake is the simple stone-and-slab **Blundells' Cottage** (Map pp340-1; ☎ 6257 1068; adult/child/family $2/1/5; ☒ 11am-4pm), built in 1860 to house workers on the surrounding estate and now a reminder of the area's early farming history.

On Aspen Island, at the far end of Commonwealth Park, is the 50m-high **National Carillon** (Map pp340-1; ☎ 6257 1068; recitals 12.45-1.35pm Tue & Thu, 2.45-3.35pm Sat & Sun), a gift from Britain on Canberra's 50th anniversary in 1963 and opened seven years later. The tower's 53 bronze bells weigh from 7kg to six tonnes. Bookings are required for Carillon **tours** (adult/child/family $8/4/20; ⊙ 12.45pm Mon, Wed & Fri).

Parliament House

The striking **Parliament House** (Map pp340-1; ☎ 6277 5399; www.aph.gov.au; admission free; ⊙ 9am-5pm) is worth a few hours' exploration (see the boxed text below).

There are free 45-minute guided tours on nonsitting days and 20-minute tours on sitting days (every half-hour from 9am to 4pm daily), but you're welcome to self-navigate and watch parliamentary proceedings from the public galleries. Tickets for question time (2pm on sitting days) in the **House of Representatives** are free but must be booked through the **Sergeant at Arms** (☎ 6277 4889); tickets aren't required for the **Senate Chamber**. Visitors can also explore 23 hectares of landscaped gardens.

Old Parliament House

The low-slung **Old Parliament House** (Map pp340-1; ☎ 6270 8222; www.oph.gov.au; King George Tce, Parkes; adult/concession/family $2/1/5; ⊙ 9am-5pm) was the seat of government from 1927 to 1988 and is a great place to get a whiff of bygone parliamentary activity, be it by wandering through the prime minister's suite, silently addressing the House of Representatives, or buying your own Hansard bookend from the gift shop. There's a free guided tour (40 minutes; 9.30am, 10.15am, 11am, 11.45am, 12.45pm, 1.30pm, 2.30pm and 3.15pm), or pick up the *Self-Guided Tour* brochure.

DESIGN FOR A NATION

Parliament House is another aspect of Walter Burley Griffin's vision to become reality. Opened in 1988, it took $1.1 billion and eight years to build and replaced the Old Parliament House, which served 11 years longer than its intended temporary 50 years. It was designed by Romaldo Giurgola of Mitchell, Giurgola & Thorp architects, winners of a design competition that attracted 329 entries from 28 countries.

The structure was built into the hillside and covered by grass to preserve the site's original landscape. Its splendid interior incorporates different combinations of Australian timbers in each main section and more than 3000 original artworks.

The main axis of Parliament House runs northeast–southwest in a direct line with Old Parliament House, the Australian War Memorial and Mt Ainslie. Two high, granite-faced walls curve out from the axis to the corners of the building; the House of Representatives (east of the walls) and the Senate (to the west) are linked to the centre by covered walkways.

Enter the building across the 90,000-piece **forecourt mosaic** by Michael Nelson Tjakamarra – the theme of which is 'a meeting place' – representing possum and wallaby Dreaming, and through the white marble **Great Verandah** at the northeastern end of the main axis. In the **foyer**, the grey-green marble columns symbolise a forest, and marquetry wall panels are inlaid with designs of Australian flora.

The first floor overlooks the **Great Hall** and its 20m-long **tapestry**, inspired by the original Arthur Boyd painting of eucalypt forest hanging outside the hall. Beyond it is the **Members' Hall**. In the public gallery above the Great Hall is the 16m-long **embroidery**, created by more than 500 members of the Embroiders Guild of Australia. Both works make subtle references to European settlement.

The Great Hall is the centre of the building, with the flagpole above it and passages to chambers on each side. One of only four known copies of the 1297 **Magna Carta** is on display here. South of the Members' Hall are the committee rooms and ministers' offices; visitors are welcome to view committee rooms and attend some of the proceedings.

On the building's grassy rooftop are 360-degree views and a four-legged, 81m-high flagpole carrying a flag the size of a double-decker bus.

The building incorporates the **National Portrait Gallery** (☎ 6270 8210; www.portrait.gov.au), which exhibits painting, photography and new-media portraiture. It has a lakeside annexe at **Commonwealth Pl** (Map pp340-1).

Opposite the main entrance to Old Parliament House is the culturally significant **Aboriginal Tent Embassy** (Map pp340-1), established in 1972 in response to governmental refusal to recognise land rights. It's where the Aboriginal flag first gained prominence.

National Gallery of Australia

The stunning **National Gallery** (Map pp340-1; ☎ 6240 6502; www.nga.gov.au; Parkes Pl, Parkes; permanent collection admission free; 10am-5pm) has an Australian collection ranging from traditional Aboriginal art (*pukumani* burial poles from the Tiwi people of Melville and Bathurst islands alongside printed fabrics by the women of Utopia and Ernabella in central Australia) to 20th-century works by Arthur Boyd and Albert Tucker. There are also works from the early decades of European settlement and examples of the early nationalistic statements of Charles Conder and Tom Roberts.

Sharing gallery space with paintings are sculptures (visit the Sculpture Garden), drawings, photographs, furniture, ceramics, fashion, textiles and silverware. Visiting exhibitions (an admission fee is charged) have included 'Jackson Pollock & the Big Americans' and 'Three Centuries of Italian Art'. In addition to regular all-inclusive guided tours (11am and 2pm), there's also a tour (11am Thursday and Sunday) focusing on Aboriginal and Torres Strait Islander art.

High Court of Australia

The grandiose **High Court** (Map pp340-1; ☎ 6270 6811; www.hcourt.gov.au; Parkes Pl, Parkes; admission free; 9.45am-4.30pm Mon-Fri, closed public holidays) was dubbed 'Gar's Mahal' when it opened in 1980, a reference to Sir Garfield Barwick, chief justice during the building's construction.

The rarefied heights of the foyer and main courtroom are in keeping with the building's name, while the mishmash of thick concrete blocks, pillars and beams possibly represents the full weight of the law. Have a chat to a knowledgeable attendant about judicial life, and check out the photos in the foyer of men trying to

look dignified in nice long wigs. High Court sittings, which usually occur for two weeks each month (except January and July), are open to the public; call for times.

National Museum of Australia

This wonderfully engaging **museum** (Map pp340-1; ☎ 1800 026 132, 6208 5000; www.nma.gov.au; Lawson Cres, Acton Peninsula; admission free; 9am-5pm) is one big abstract Australian storybook. Using creativity, controversy, humour and fearless self-contradiction, the National Museum dismantles national identity rather than upholding one single notion of it, and in the process provokes visitors to come up with some ideas of their own. From the outside Garden of Australian Dreams to the use of interactive technology, it's a collision of aesthetics, and all the more inspiring for it. Don't miss the introductory 'Circa' show. While general admission is free, a fee is usually charged to access visiting exhibitions.

Bus No 34 runs here. There's also a free bus on weekends and public holidays, departing regularly from 10.30am from platform 7 in the Civic bus interchange.

Australian National Botanic Gardens

Spread over 90 invigorating hectares on Black Mountain's lower slopes are these beautiful **gardens** (Map p354; ☎ 6250 9450; www.anbg.gov.au/anbg; Clunies Ross St, Acton; admission free; 9am-5pm Mar-Dec, to 8pm Jan & Feb), devoted to the growth, study and promotion of Australian floral diversity. While enjoying the gardens' tranquillity, take the **Aboriginal Plant Use Walk** (1km, 45 minutes), which passes through the cool **Rainforest Gully** and has signs explaining how Aborigines related to indigenous plants. The **Eucalypt Lawn** is peppered with 600 species of this ubiquitous tree.

The **visitors centre** (9.30am-4.30pm) is the departure point for free guided walks (11am and 2pm, also 10am summer). Nearby is **Hudsons in the Gardens** (☎ 6248 9680; mains $8-12; breakfast & lunch), a café with a pleasant patio that's popular with stroller-pushing parents in the afternoon.

National Zoo & Aquarium

Nestled behind Scrivener Dam is this engaging **zoo and aquarium** (Map p354; ☎ 6287 8400; www.zooquarium.com.au; Lady Denman Dr, Yarralumla; adult/child/concession/family $19/10.50/16/55; 9am-5pm), which you should definitely devote a few hours to. It has a roll call of fascinating animals, including capuchins, newly hatched sharks, long-necked tortoises, diminutive sun (Malay) bears, alpine dingoes and creatures in the lobster tank that resemble living hacky-sacks. Also competing for attention are otters, a tigon (the unnatural result of breeding tiger-lion crosses in captivity, a practice thankfully discontinued), a disconcerting snow-leopard lair, and much more.

Australian War Memorial

Opened in 1941, the massive **war memorial** (Map pp340-1; ☎ 6243 4211; www.awm.gov.au; Treloar Cres, Campbell; admission free; ☺ 10am-5pm) looks along Anzac Pde to Old Parliament House across the lake. The building houses an enormous collection of pictures, dioramas, relics and exhibitions detailing the events, weapons and human toll of wartime; most of the heavy machinery is arrayed within **Anzac Hall**. Entombed among the mosaics of the Hall of Memory is the **Unknown Australian Soldier**, whose remains were returned from a WWI battlefield in 1993 and who symbolises all Australian war casualties.

There are free guided tours (90 minutes; 10am, 10.30am, 11am, 1pm, 1.30pm and 2pm) and a *Self-Guided Tour* leaflet ($3).

Along **Anzac Pde**, which is Canberra's broad commemorative way, are 11 memorials to various campaigns.

Questacon

The hands-on **National Science & Technology Centre** (Map pp340-1; ☎ 1800 020 603, 6270 2800; www .questacon.edu.au; adult/child/concession/family $11/6/7/32; ☺ 9am-5pm) is a child magnet, with its lively, educational and just-plain-fun interactive exhibits on the merits of everyday science and technology. Within the spiral arrangement of galleries, kids can learn indigenous bushcraft from the Burarra people, explore the physics of fun parks, cause tsunamis and take shelter from cyclones and earthquakes. There are also science shows; tickets cost a few dollars extra.

Canberra Museum & Gallery

This stylish **museum and gallery** (Map pp340-1; ☎ 6207 3968; www.museumsandgalleries.act.gov.au/museum/index.asp; Civic Sq, London Circuit, Civic; admission free; ☺ 10am-5pm Tue-Thu, to 7pm Fri, noon-5pm Sat & Sun) is ostensibly devoted to Canberra's social history and visual arts. The interesting

permanent exhibition, 'Reflecting Canberra', includes a charred dishwasher salvaged from a house destroyed in the January 2003 bushfires, while visiting collections have run the aesthetic gamut from traditional Palestinian crafts to Korean sculptors. The museum also holds talks and craft-oriented workshops.

ScreenSound Australia

The **National Screen & Sound Archive** (Map pp340-1; ☎ 6248 2000; www.screensound.gov.au; McCoy Circuit, Acton; admission free; ☺ 9am-5pm Mon-Fri, 10am-5pm Sat & Sun) preserves Australian moving-picture and sound recordings for posterity. Highlights of the absorbing permanent exhibition 'Sights + Sounds of a Nation' include Norman Gunston's priceless interview with a vapid Zsa Zsa Gabor, and the 1943 Oscar awarded to high-voltage propaganda flick *Kokoda Front Line*. Temporary exhibitions (there's usually an admission fee) have included a history of locally prominent Festival Records. Films are also screened here; see p350.

National Library of Australia

This enormous, symmetrical **library** (Map pp340-1; ☎ 6262 1111; www.nla.gov.au; Parkes Pl, Parkes; admission free; ☺ main reading room 9am-9pm Mon-Thu, to 5pm Fri & Sat, 1.30-5pm Sun) was established in 1901 and has since accumulated over six million items, most of which can be accessed in one of eight reading rooms – the main room is rather characterless, which is possibly the intention as it definitely won't distract you during your reading. Bookings are required for the free one-hour **guided tour** (☎ 6262 1271). The **exhibition gallery** (admission free; ☺ 9am-5pm) offers some terrific visual treats, most recently the famous antipodean Gothic designs of Augustus Pugin and the flowery paintings daubed over 50 years by Ellis Rowan.

National Archives of Australia

Canberra's original post office now houses the **National Archives** (Map pp340-1; ☎ 6212 3600; www.naa.gov.au; Queen Victoria Tce, Parkes; admission free; ☺ 9am-5pm), a repository for Commonwealth government records in the form of personal papers, photographs, posters, films, maps and paintings. There are short special exhibits, such as the recent display of Matthew Flinders' personal paraphernalia, including his chess set, dress sword and scabbard. But the centrepiece exhibit is the **Federation Gallery** and its original charters, including Australia's

AUSTRALIAN CAPITAL TERRITORY

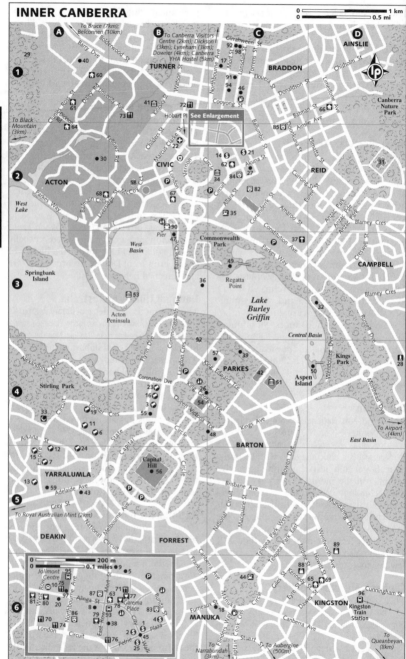

INNER CANBERRA

0 _____ 1 km
0 _____ 0.5 mi

To Bruce (7km);
Belconnen (10km)

To Canberra Visitors
Centre (2km); Dickson
(3km); Lyneham (3km);
Downer (4km); Canberra
YHA Hostel (5km)

A **B** **C** **D**

29

40

60

Bolkenwood St

Barry Dve

University Ave

Daley Rd

Clianthus Rd

Watson St

TURNER

Girrahween St

92
98
17
91
46
94

Mort St
Lonsdale St
Torrens St

BRADDON

Cooyong St

Elouera St

Donaldson St

Limestone Ave

Chisholm St

AINSLIE

Canberra
Nature
Park

Batman St
66

Doonkuna St

Ainslie Ave

Currong St

REID

31

Euree St

Antill St

**To Black
Mountain
(3km)**

61
64

Fellows Rd

Childers St

Marcus Clarke St

41
72
73
22

Hobart Pl

See Enlargement

14
62
34

21
84
27

Akuna St

82

35

Alinga St

Elimatta St

Blamey Cres

Anzac Park
Anzac Ave

CAMPBELL

Blamey Cres

ACTON

30

58
68
67

McCoy Cct

Balmain Cres

Lennox Cres

CIVIC

Vernon Cct

London Cct

City Hill

Constitution Ave

Commerce St

Amaroo St

Parkes Way

37

**West
Lake**

Parkes Way

**West
Basin**

90
47

Pier

Barrine Dve

**Commonwealth
Park**

49

**Springbank
Island**

36

53

**Acton
Peninsula**

Regatta
Point

**Lake
Burley
Griffin**

Central Basin

32

Commonwealth Ave

Kings
Park

50

Aspen
Island

28

92

57
39

PARKES

42
51

Wendouree Dve

Moorhead Dve

Stirling Park

Alexandrine Dve

Flynn Dve

Langton Cres

Coronation Dve

King Edward Tce

26
54

Yarra Glen

To Airport
(4km)

East Basin

33
19
11
6
12
24
15
7

Forster Cres

State Circle

Queen Victoria Tce

55

48

Kings Ave

BARTON

Bowen Dve

13
59
43

Adelaide Ave

Capital Circle

YARRALUMLA

**Capital
Hill**
56

Circle

Brisbane Ave

Mundaring Dve

Grey St

To Royal Australian Mint (2km)

National Circuit

Melbourne Ave

DEAKIN

FORREST

Canberra Ave

National Circuit

Macquarie St

Telopea Park West
Telopea Park East

Jardine St

Wentworth Ave

89

Enlargement

0 _____ 200 m
0 _____ 0.1 miles

95
9
5

Jolimont
Centre

71
75
10

Mort St

77
63
87
8
79
93
78
97
38

Alinga St

Garema
Place

81
80
20
86
70
74

Northbourne Ave

East Row

London Circuit

76

18

45
25

2
4

Bunda St

83

City
Walk

Petrie
Plaza

44

88
65
69

Giles St

Kennedy St

Eyre St

Dawes St

Howitt St

96

Cunningham St

KINGSTON

Kingston
Train
Station

MANUKA

Furneaux St

Flinders Way

Captain Cook Cres

Manuka Circle

To
Narrabundah
(3km)

To Aubergine
(500m)

To
Queanbeyan
(8km)

AUSTRALIAN CAPITAL TERRITORY

1900 Constitution Act and the 1967 amendment ending constitutional discrimination against Aboriginal people. Public research facilities include a reading room.

Royal Australian Mint

To see the country's biggest money-making operation, visit the **Mint** (Map p354; ☎ 6202 6800; www.ramint.gov.au; Denison St, Deakin; admission free; ◷ 9am-4pm Mon-Fri, 10am-4pm Sat & Sun). It has a gallery showcasing the history of Australian coinage, where you can learn about the 'holey dollar' and its enigmatic companion, the 'dump'. Also on show are Mint-produced official insignia and Sydney Olympics medals. Plate-glass windows give a view to the production of proof (collectable) coins and circulating coins; note that production ceases over the weekend.

As a souvenir, you can mint your own brand-new $1 coin, complete with a special

'c' mark. And to emphasise that you're in the cradle of capitalism, it'll cost you $2.

Australian National University (ANU)

The attractive, busy grounds of the **ANU** (Map pp340-1; ☎ 6125 5111; www.anu.edu.au) have taken up most of the area between Civic and Black Mountain since 1946 and make for a pleasant wander. Drop into the **Drill Hall Gallery** (Map pp340-1; ☎ 6125 5832; Kingsley St; admission free; ◷ noon-5pm Wed-Sun) to see special exhibitions and paintings from the university's art collection; a permanent fixture is the near-phosphorescent hue of Sidney Nolan's *Riverbend*. While you're here, collect the ANU *Sculpture Walk* brochure to get a fine-arts appreciation of the university grounds.

Australian Institute of Sport (AIS)

The country's elite and aspiring-elite athletes hone their sporting prowess at the

AIS (Map p354; ☎ 6214 1444; www.aisport.com.au; Leverrier Cres, Bruce). Institute **tours** (adult/child/ concession/family $12/6/9/33; ☯ 10am, 11.30am, 1pm & 2.30pm) are led by resident sportspeople, with information on training routines and diets, displays on Australian champions and the Sydney Olympics, and interactive exhibits where you can publicly humble yourself at basketball, rowing and skiing.

Other Attractions

You can only peek through the gates of the prime minister's official residence, the **Lodge** (Map pp340-1; Adelaide Ave, Deakin), and the governor general's official residence, **Government House** (Map p354; Dunrossil Dr, Yarralumla). **Scrivener Dam lookout** gives a good view of both.

Canberra's 80-odd diplomatic missions are mostly nondescript houses in Yarralumla, but some are architecturally worthwhile and periodically open to the public. The **Thai embassy** (Map pp340-1; Empire Circuit, Yarralumla), with its pointy orange-tiled roof, is reminiscent of Bangkok temples. The **Papua New Guinea high commission** (Map pp340-1; ☎ 6273 3322; Forster Cres, Yarralumla) resembles a *haus tamberan* (spirit house) from the Sepik region and has a **cultural display** (☯ 9am-1pm & 2-4pm Mon-Fri).

At the eastern end of Kings Ave is the 79m-tall **Australian-American Memorial** (Map pp340-1; Kings Ave, Russell), a pillar topped by an eagle that, from a distance, looks like Bugs Bunny's ears. It recognises US support for Australia during WWII.

The **Church of St John the Baptist** (Map pp340-1; Constitution Ave, Reid) was finished in 1845, its stained-glass windows donated by pioneer families. The **St John's Schoolhouse Museum** (Map pp340-1; ☎ 6249 6839; Constitution Ave, Reid; admission $2.20; ☯ 10am-noon Wed, 2-4pm Sat & Sun), adjoining the church, houses memorabilia from Canberra's first school.

The enterprising **Canberra Tradesmen's Union Club** (Tradies; Map p354; ☎ 6248 0999; 2 Badham St, Dickson; ☯ 8-5am) has garnished its endless rows of poker machines with a **bicycle museum** (admission free), which includes a penny farthing and the aptly named Boneshaker Tricycle. The Tradies also operates the Downer Club, where you can make planetary observations at the **Canberra Space Dome & Observatory** (Map p354; ☎ 6248 5333; www.ctuc.asn.au/planetarium; 72 Hawdon Pl, Dickson; adult/child/family $8.50/6/24; ☯ observatory 7.30, 8.30 & 9.30pm Tue-Sat, planetarium 7 & 8.30pm Tue-Sat); bookings essential.

ACTIVITIES

Thanks to Canberra's bushland locale, artificial lakes and nearby ranges, not to mention a pretty good climate and a local appreciation of the outdoors, there are plenty of vitalising activities on offer here. Bushwalking is plentiful, swimming in river-fed waterholes is a must, and you can hire bikes and skates to explore the inner-city greenery.

Boating

Lake Burley Griffin Boat Hire (Map pp340-1; ☎ 6249 6861; Acton Jetty, Civic) has canoe, kayak, surf-ski and paddleboat hire (from $12 per hour).

Bushwalking

Tidbinbilla Nature Reserve (p353), southwest of the city, has marked tracks. Another great area for walking is **Namadgi National Park** (p353), which is one end of the difficult 655km-long Australian Alps Walking Track; the other end is Walhalla in Victoria.

Local bushwalking maps are available at **Mountain Designs** (Map pp340-1; ☎ 6247 7488; 6 Lonsdale St, Braddon). The *Namadgi National Park* map ($4.40), available from the Canberra and Namadgi visitors centres, details 23 walks in the area.

Cycling

Canberra has one of the most extensive cycle-path networks of any Australian city, with dedicated routes making it almost possible to tour the city without touching a road. One popular track circles the lake while others shadow the Murrumbidgee River. The visitors centre sells the *Canberra Cycleways* map ($6.50) and *Cycle Canberra* ($15), the latter published by **Pedal Power ACT** (www.pedalpower.org.au) for super-keen recreational cyclists.

Mr Spokes Bike Hire (Map pp340-1; ☎ 6257 1188; Barrine Dr, Civic; ☯ 9am-5pm Wed-Sun, daily during school holidays) is near the Acton Park ferry terminal. Bike hire per hour/half-/full-day cost's $12, 30/40. **Canberra YHA Hostel** (p345), **Canberra City Accommodation** (p345) and **Victor Lodge** (p345) also rent bikes. **Row'n'Ride** (☎ 6254 7838, 0410 547 838) delivers bikes (hired per day/week $40/90) to your door.

In-Line Skating

Mr Spokes Bike Hire (Map pp340-1; ☎ 6257 1188; Barrine Dr, Civic) rents skates for $11 for the first hour, then $5.50 for each subsequent hour.

Also hiring out skatewear is **Adrenalin Sports** (Map pp340-1; ☎ 6257 7233; Shop 7, 38 Allara St, Civic), which charges $17 per two hours.

Swimming

Canberra's swimming pools include the **Canberra Olympic Pool** (Map pp340-1; ☎ 6248 6799; Allara St, Civic), the pool at the **AIS** (Map p354; ☎ 6214 1281; Leverrier Cres, Bruce) and the wonderful, heritage-listed **Manuka Swimming Pool** (Map pp340-1; ☎ 6295 1349; Manuka Circle, Manuka). Swimming in Lake Burley Griffin is not recommended because of occasional high pollution levels, algal blooms and changeable weather conditions.

See Around Canberra (p353) for more on some inviting waterholes around the city.

WALKING TOUR
Parliamentary Triangle Walk

Canberra is widely spread, but many of its major attractions are in or near the parliamentary triangle defined by Lake Burley Griffin, Commonwealth Ave and Kings Ave.

The focus of the triangle is **Parliament House** (**1**; p337) on Capital Hill. Heading north from here along Commonwealth Ave towards the lake, you'll pass the Canadian,

---

WALK FACTS

Start/Finish: Parliament House
Distance: 12km
Duration: 3 hours

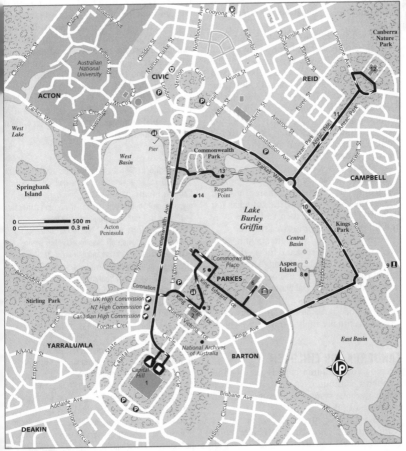

New Zealand and UK **high commissions** on your left. Turn right (east) at Coronation Dr to King George Tce and **Old Parliament House** (**2**; p337), which houses the **National Portrait Gallery** (p338). Opposite the main entrance to Old Parliament House is the **Aboriginal Tent Embassy** (**3**; p338).

Crossing diagonally (northwest) across the lawn in front of Old Parliament House to King Edward Tce, you arrive at the **National Library of Australia** (**4**; p339). Beside it is **Questacon** (**5**; p339), Canberra's interactive science museum.

Towards Kings Ave along King Edward Terrace is the grand **High Court of Australia** (**6**; p338), with its ornamental watercourse burbling alongside the path to the entrance. Next door, across Parkes Pl, is the wonderful **National Gallery of Australia** (**7**; p338).

Follow King Edward Tce to Kings Ave, turn left (northeast) and follow the avenue across the lake. As you cross you'll see the **National Carillon** (**8**; p337) on Aspen Island to your left. Before reaching the **Australian-American Memorial** (**9**; p342), at the end of Kings Ave, turn left (northwest) at the roundabout onto Parkes Way, which follows the lake's northern shore. After 1km turn left (south) again off Parkes Way to the historic **Blundells' Cottage** (**10**; p336).

Continue along Parkes Way to the next roundabout. **Anzac Pde** (**11**), leading northeast from here, is lined with memorials and ends at the largest of them, the **Australian War Memorial** (**12**; p339). Return to Parkes Way and follow it to Commonwealth Ave.

Turn left (south) and, after 500m, turn left (east) onto Albert St and follow the path to the **National Capital Exhibition** (**13**; p336) at Regatta Point. Linger a moment to gaze at the **Captain Cook Memorial Water Jet** (**14**; p336) on the lake.

Continue south along Commonwealth Ave to eventually make your way back to Parliament House.

CANBERRA FOR CHILDREN

Keeping your children happily occupied in Canberra without overloading your own fragile nervous system, or even your wallet, is a piece of cake.

The visitors centre has two factsheets (*Children's Activities* and *Parks & Playgrounds*) to get you started.

For fresh air and exercise, stroll through the lovely (and free) **Australian National Botanic Gardens** (p338), the wild and wonderful **National Zoo & Aquarium** (p338), and/or one of the ACT's naturally overgrown reserves. Energy levels can be further accommodated by a swim at one of the city's **pools** (p343) or **waterholes** (p353), or by hiring **bikes** (p342).

For some hands-on fun, visit **Questacon** (p339). Another place with a scientific bent is **CSIRO Discovery** (Map pp340-1; ☎ 6246 4646; Clunies Ross St, Acton; adult/concession/family $6/3/15; ☼ 9am-5pm Mon-Fri), where you can come to grips with virtual reality.

Playgrounds and miniature steam train rides can be found at **Gold Creek Village** (p355). There's also a plethora of museums custom-built for curiosity and active imaginations, among them the **National Dinosaur Museum** (p355) and the brilliant **National Museum of Australia** (p338). The littlest littlies will appreciate a spin on Civic's landmark **merry-go-round** (Map pp340-1).

For professional short-term childcare, look up 'Baby Sitters' and 'Child Care Centres' in the *Yellow Pages* telephone directory. **Dial An Angel** (☎ 6282 7733) has been locally recommended.

TOURS

Balloon Aloft (☎ 6285 1540; tours per adult/child from $180/120) For aerial views, take a one-hour ride.

Canberra Tours (☎ 6298 3344; canberradaytours@ bigpond.com) Shuttles you around various capital sites for $40/65 per half-/full-day, including entry fees.

City Sightseeing (☎ 6257 3423; adult/child $30/15) Operates a hop-on, hop-off double-decker bus service. Tickets are valid for 24 hours and give access to 14 places of interest, including Parliament House and Questacon. The first departure is at 9am from the block immediately south of the Jolimont Centre; services run every 40 minutes after that, up to and including 5pm.

Go Bush Tours (☎ 6231 3023; www.gobushtours.com.au; tours per adult/concession from $35/30) Reputable tailored excursions around Canberra, including a circuit of city lookouts. They have a wheelchair-accessible vehicle.

Heli Air (☎ 6257 0777; Canberra Airport; flights per person from $200) For a noisier flight.

SS Maid Marion (☎ 0418-828 357; adult/child $10/5) Operates one-hour cruises that pick-up/drop-off at lakeside locales such as Acton Park ferry terminal, the National Library and the National Museum. There are up to five cruises daily, depending on whether the boat has been chartered for a function.

FESTIVALS & EVENTS

January
Summernats Car Festival (www.summernats.com.au)
Hot rods and custom cars rev up in January at Exhibition Park.

February
National Multicultural Festival (www.multicultural
festival.com.au) Celebrated over 10 days in February, with
most events in Commonwealth Park.
Royal Canberra Show (www.rncas.org.au/showwebsite
/main.html) End of February.

March
Celebrate Canberra (www.celebratecanberra.com) The
city's extended birthday party in mid-March, which kicks
off with a day-long food, drinks and arts feast called Taste
(adult/concession/child $10/5/admission free).

March/April
National Folk Festival (www.folkfestival.asn.au) One of
the country's largest, held every March/April.

September/October
Floriade (www.floriadeaustralia.com) Held in September/
October and dedicated to Canberra's spectacular spring flowers.

SLEEPING

There is only a handful of accommodation
choices in the centre of Canberra. Most
hotels and motels are either strung out
along Northbourne Ave or hidden in well-
established northern suburbs like Ainslie,
Braddon, O'Connor and Downer. The other
main accommodation area lies south around
Capital Hill, particularly in the politician and
diplomat-favoured domains of Kingston
and Barton. Mid-range lodgings in Canberra
are becoming rarer, with a number of places
either recently closed or upgraded.

Most places can supply kids cots and a
room or two suitable for a family-sized stay.
Travellers with limited mobility will find that
few places outside top-end accommodation
have true barrier-free rooms, though most
will claim to have something that's accessible
by wheelchair.

Budget
HALLS OF RESIDENCE
Some of the ANU's pleasant halls of residence rent out rooms from late November
to late February during university holidays.
Most offer similar facilities and room
prices start from around $50 (up to $15
more for B&B).

Bruce Hall (Map pp340-1; ☎ 6267 4000) and **Burton & Garran Hall** (Map pp340-1; ☎ 6267 4333) are at
the northern end of Daley Rd. The affiliated
Ursula College (Map pp340-1; ☎ 6279 4303) and **John
XXIII College** (Map pp340-1; ☎ 6279 4905) lie to the
south, opposite Sullivans Creek. Civic is a
brisk 15-minute walk across campus.

HOSTELS
Victor Lodge (Map pp340-1; ☎ 6295 7777; www.vic
torlodge.com.au; 29 Dawes St, Kingston; dm/s $25/55, d & tw
$65; P) This thoroughly welcoming place
is a great budget accommodation option, offering compact rooms with linen provided,
use of a commercial kitchen (cleaned by the
staff), a BBQ area, filling breakfasts, bicycle
hire ($15) and Internet access, plus a helping
hand if you need info on local attractions.
They'll pick you up from Jolimont or the
train station if need be; otherwise catch bus
No 38, 39 or 80 from Civic.

Canberra City Accommodation (Map pp340-1;
☎ 6257 3999; www.canberrabackpackers.net.au; 7 Akuna
St, Civic; dm $24-26, s/d $55/70;) This bright,
well-run 300-room hostel has an impressive
list of services including a pool, 24-hour reception, a bar, cable TV, continental breakfasts ($4.50) and bicycle hire ($16 per day).
It remains fond of backpackers, but has all
the facilities to attract other individuals and
families seeking central, reasonably priced
rooms.

Canberra YHA Hostel (Map p354; ☎ 6248 9155;
canberra@yhansw.org.au; 191 Dryandra St, O'Connor; dm/d/f
from $20/55/85; P) This excellent, purpose-
built hostel is in a peace-inducing clump of
bushland 6km northwest of the centre,
where you'll find bicycles for hire, well-
equipped kitchen space and lots of places
to just sit. Bus No 35 takes you there.

City Walk Hotel (Map pp340-1; ☎ 1800 600 124,
6257 0124; 2 Mort St, Civic; dm $22-25, s $45-70, d $60-
80) This five-storey budget hotel is smack
in the middle of Civic and is in pretty
good shape besides a slight mustiness. The
interior climate is assisted by the fact that
you can't smoke or drink alcohol on the
premises.

CAMPING & CARAVAN PARKS
Canberra Motor Village (Map p354; ☎ 6247 5466;
canmotorvillage@ozemail.com.au; Kunzea St, O'Connor;
camp site $15-22, caravan site $30, d $60-125; P) Doz-
ing in a peaceful bush setting 6km northwest of Civic, this place has an abundance

of amenities, motel rooms and self-contained cabins in various sizes, and a laid-back ignore-your-watch feel.

Also see the listing for Eaglehawk Holiday Park (below).

Mid-Range

The **Canberra visitors centre** (Map p354; ☎ 1300 554 114, 6205 0044; www.canberratourism.com.au; 330 Northbourne Ave, Dickson; ☿ 9am-5.30pm Mon-Fri, 9am-4pm Sat & Sun) organises accommodation-events packages that are worth checking out. Note that slightly cheaper motel accommodation can be found in Queanbeyan, 12km southeast of Canberra.

Eagle Hawk Rydges Resort (☎ 6241 6033; www.rydges.com.au; Federal Hwy, Sutton; s & d from $100, f $145; P ※) It's well outside the centre on its own expansive block of non-urban land, but that's one of the things that attracts families to this recreational, facility-laden resort. Users of good-standard motels will already be familiar with the rooms.

Motel Monaro (Map pp340-1; ☎ 6295 2111; www.bestwestern.com.au/motelmonaro; 27 Dawes St, Kingston; s/d from $95/110; P ※ ▣) This well-maintained motel, on a quiet street near the coffee-scented Kingston shopping centre, is run by the same efficient, convivial folk who manage Victor Lodge (p345) next door. It has a couple of large, multibed rooms that are ideal for groups. Book ahead when parliament is sitting.

Olims Canberra Hotel (Map pp340-1; ☎ 1800 020 016, 6248 5511; www.olimshotel.com; cnr Ainslie & Limestone Aves, Braddon; s & d $105-150; P ※) This 1927 National Trust heritage-listed building and its later refurbishments surround a nice, terraced courtyard garden. The façade's concrete stubble looks a little worn from close-up, but the rooms are well appointed and the facilities, including several bars and restaurants, are very good.

Tall Trees Motel (Map p354; ☎ 6247 9200; www.bestwestern.com.au/talltrees; 21 Stephen St, Ainslie; d $120-170; P ※) The green, fountain-decorated grounds of this accommodating motel and its location in a quiet part of leafy Ainslie lend it a very relaxed air. It's a good place to base yourself if you want to be relatively near the centre but outside any hubbub.

Miranda Lodge (Map p354; ☎ 6249 8038; book@parkviewcanberra.com.au; 534 Northbourne Ave, Downer; s/d $100/120; P ※) This motel-style lodge has clean-cut rooms in a variety of sizes (some with spa) and puts a full cooked breakfast under your bleary morning eyes.

Parkview Lodge (Map p354; 526 Northbourne Ave, Downer; P ※) The owners of Miranda Lodge also run this nearby, equally priced lodge, though the 'view' is primarily of the netball centre across the road, with some greenery beyond it; direct all inquiries to Miranda Lodge.

Blue & White Lodge (Map p354; ☎ 6248 0498; blueandwhitelodge@bigpond.com; 524 Northbourne Ave, Downer; s $80-85, d $90-95, f $110-130; P ※) The pillared façade of this lodge does a good impression of a Masonic temple, though the exterior colour scheme is pure Mediterranean. The prim and comfortable rooms come with cooked breakfasts.

Canberran Lodge (Map p354; 528 Northbourne Ave, Downer; P ※) The owners of Blue & White Lodge also manage this similarly styled place two doors down; direct inquiries to Blue & White Lodge.

Northbourne Lodge (Map p354; ☎ 6257 2599; 522 Northbourne Ave, Downer; s/d $65/80; P ※) The adobe-washed bricks aren't altogether convincing, but this lodge has a fairly stylish interior and does breakfast for an extra $10. All rooms have bathrooms.

Eaglehawk Holiday Park (☎ 6241 6411; www.eaglehawk.contact.com.au; Federal Hwy, Sutton; camp/caravan site $17/22, s & d $70-125, f $90-145; P) This friendly highwayside complex is 12km north of the centre, just over the NSW border. It has plenty of sheltered mid-range accommodation (campers have to settle for the edge of a field) and meals are available at the pub next door – avoid the adjacent cabins as the pub can be noisy.

THE AUTHOR'S CHOICE   *Paul Smitz*

University House (Map pp340-1; ☎ 6125 5211; www.anu.edu.au/unihouse; 1 Balmain Cres, Acton; s $75-130, d $125-180; P) This 1950s-era building, with furniture to match, is soothingly positioned in the midst of the rambling university grounds. The spacious rooms can be hired with or without breakfast and come with a small balcony from where you can watch attendees of academic conferences come and go. There's also a pleasant courtyard in which to let your thoughts wander, and a good selection of wine in the cellar bottle shop.

Top End

Old Stone House (☎ 6238 1888; stnhsebb@tpg.com.au; 41 Molonglo St, Bungendore; s/d $125/180; ℗ 🔀) For a bit of well-catered country living, wander out to Bungendore, 35km east of Canberra. Minding its own private business here is a charismatic 1867 stone house offering B&B in four antique-furnished rooms. There's also a nice garden and you can arrange set dinners ($40 to $50 per person).

Novotel (Map pp340-1; ☎ 1300 656 565, 6245 5000; www.novotel.com.au; 65 Northbourne Ave, Civic; s & d $140-260; ℗ 🔀 🖳 🖘) The 200-room Novotel occupies prime central real estate, adjacent to the Jolimont Centre and just a few minutes' stroll from a satisfying selection of restaurants and shops. The four-star mod-cons include in-room data points, a business centre and a pool. They've thought of pretty much everything, down to the daily weather reports posted in the lifts.

Pacific International Apartments – Capital Tower (Map pp340-1; ☎ 1800 676 241, 6276 3444; www.pacificinthotels.com.au; 2 Marcus Clarke St, Civic; apt from $195; ℗ 🔀 🖘) Rooms on the southern side of this apartment complex's curving façade face the soporific waters of Lake Burley Griffin; alternatively, fix your gaze on the courtyard pool. The majority of apartments are very comfortable two- and three-bedroom joints that can fit up to six people.

EATING

Canberra's diverse grouping of eateries include plenty of lip-smacking long-stayers. Other places open in a blaze of publicity and die of customer starvation, but even this adds to the dynamism of local restaurant scene. Most eateries are in Civic, which has raised its menu standards to compete with the upmarket selections in Kingston, Manuka and Griffith. There's also a fantastic, inexpensive Asian strip in Dickson and many other possibilities scattered throughout the suburbs. Most of the city's major sights have a decent cafe or restaurant attached, many with lake views.

Civic   Map pp340–1

Garema Pl has changed a lot since the days when it served mainly as a nocturnal skateboarding rink, and is now replete with eateries and outdoor seating. West Row restaurants are lively at lunch time.

Caffe della Piazza (☎ 6248 9711; 19 Garema Pl; mains $14-20; ☽ lunch & dinner) It's stretching credibility to compare Garema Pl to a fully-fledged piazza, but it's no exaggeration to say that this decade-old restaurant offers excellent, hearty Italian fare, prime outdoor seating and a heady wine list. Plunge your fork into a mound of *pappardelle con salmone*.

Lemon Grass (☎ 6247 2779; 65 London Circuit; mains $8-16; ☽ lunch Mon-Fri, dinner Mon-Sat) A favourite of local Thai connoisseurs, this informal place cooks up a long list of tasty vegetarian, stir-fry, curry and seafood dishes. If you're a fan of king prawns and garlic, order the *goong gratiam*.

Fringe Benefits avec Jean-Pierre (☎ 6247 4042; 54 Marcus Clarke St; mains $30; ☽ lunch Mon-Fri, dinner Mon-Sat) Sample lambs brains, barramundi and other meat-dominated mains in this elegantly simple, award-winning restaurant, where the chef gets top billing. The seductive desserts are along the lines of *bavarois à la mandarine* (honey-mandarin mousse with chocolate sauce and lemon *tuille*). The restaurant is often booked out for functions on Saturday nights.

Gods Café & Bar (☎ 6248 5538; Arts Centre, University Ave, Acton; mains $8-15; ☽ breakfast & lunch Mon-Fri) Though yet to open a Mt Olympus branch, this café in the university district of Acton makes a refreshing pit stop after wandering the university campus. Offerings range from toasted focaccias and chargrilled vegetarian snacks to grilled veal kidney. Eat in the main low-lit den or the light-filled side hall.

Asian Café (☎ 6262 6233; 32 West Row; mains $9-19; ☽ lunch & dinner) Chinese and Malaysian standards such as roast duck and laksa are professionally dished out in this brightly coloured café, along with non-Asian stowaways such as King Island black-pepper steak. Takeaway is available if you just can't sit still.

Tosolini's (☎ 6247 4317; cnr London Circuit & East Row; mains $13-20; lunch & dinner Mon-Fri, dinner Sat) Fancy pork and veal terrine or three-cheese lasagne? Tosolini's has predominantly rich, meaty meals, though there are also some good meatless salads and a shitake mushroom omelette. The roadside tables are less appealing when the traffic cranks up.

Little Saigon (☎ 6230 5003; Alinga St; mains $9-15; ☽ lunch & dinner) There are plenty of Vietnamese meals to get stuck into in this simple eatery. Early afternoon sees a roaring trade in 'lunch boxes': cheap takeaway chicken, beef, pork or vegetarian ($5) accompanied by rice or noodles. To substitute squid or prawns costs a little extra ($7.50).

Fast food is on the menu at the Canberra Centre's **food hall** (Bunda St; meals $5-12; ☒ breakfast, lunch & dinner), including sushi, kebabs, burgers, laksa, gourmet rolls and smoothies.

Manuka   Map pp340–1
Southeast of Capital Hill is the well-groomed café culture of Manuka shopping centre, which considers itself an upmarket hub for diplomats and businesspeople. Try French, Spanish, Turkish, Italian, Lebanese, Vietnamese, Indonesian cuisines, and more, in the local eateries.

Alanya (☎ 6295 9678; Style Arcade, Franklin St; mains $16-21; ☒ lunch Mon-Fri, dinner Mon-Sat) This long-standing, authentic Turkish restaurant has plenty of banquet options (including vegetarian) and stand-alone mains like the excellent *hünkâr beğendi* (eggplant, cream and diced lamb).

Atlantic (☎ 6232 7888; 20 Palmerston La; mains $25-30; ☒ lunch Mon-Fri, dinner Mon-Sat) In a small laneway, this is the place to dine formally on a select seafood menu of snapper, kingfish and Western Australian lobster. The rooftop terrace is ideal for sunny liaisons.

My Café (☎ 6295 6632; Franklin St; mains $8-15; ☒ breakfast, lunch & dinner) This self-possessed café has cheerful meringue walls and sidewalk tables that are inevitably claimed at lunch time. It's popular for its breakfasts and gourmet bagels and focaccias; try the 'Kakadu' version for a taste of kangaroo.

Legends (☎ 6295 3966; Franklin St; mains $20; ☒ lunch Mon-Fri, dinner Mon-Sat) Spanish fare is served here, upstairs in the Capital Cinema Centre. House specialties include paella (a vegetarian version is available) and *bacalao* (salted cod), and there are lots of delicious tapas dishes ($7 to $8.50) to nibble. There's also the odd bit of live flamenco guitar.

Kingston   Map pp340–1
Kingston has enough gleaming cafés and outdoor seating to give Manuka a run for its latte.

Silo (☎ 6260 6060; 36 Giles St; lunches $10-13; ☒ breakfast & lunch Tue-Sat) This accomplished bakery can be soothingly subdued outside the breakfast and lunch rushes. Besides a fine range of breads and breakfast standards

like eggs Florentine, it offers unexpected fare like potato, anchovy and chilli-jam pizzas. And just try walking out without buying a passionfruit and mascarpone or mixed berry and almond tartlet.

Santa Lucia (☎ 6295 1813; 21 Kennedy St; mains $12-20; ☒ lunch Mon-Fri, dinner Mon-Sat) Canberra's first Italian restaurant is three decades old and still going strong. The patent red-and-white-checked tablecloths get smeared with pizza, pasta and meat dishes, and the rustic Italian music is played with gusto.

First Floor (☎ 6260 6311; Green Sq; mains $18-25; ☒ lunch Mon-Fri, dinner Mon-Sat) Occupying a higher culinary plane above Green Sq is this fine-dining, minimalist-décor establishment, where the seasonal Mod-Oz menus have included lime and chilli-marinated spatchcock, Morocco-spiced eggplant and wok-seared field mushrooms. Sip wines from around Australia.

Dickson
Dickson's consumer precinct is an Asian smorgasbord where Chinese, Thai, Laotian, Vietnamese, Korean, Japanese, Turkish and Malaysian restaurants compete with other gastronomic treats like Granny's Bakery.

Dickson Asian Noodle House (Map p354; ☎ 6247 6380; 29 Woolley St; mains $9-14; ☒ lunch & dinner) This perennially popular Laotian and Thai café is usually booked up towards the end of the week, though thankfully there's always takeaway. Within minutes of ordering, eat your fill of wok-fried, Hokkien-style or soup-laden noodles. Pick of the menu is the addictive combination laksa.

Äu Lac (Map p354; ☎ 6262 8922; 39 Woolley St; mains $8-10; ☒ lunch Tue-Sun, dinner daily) This simple Vietnamese vegetarian restaurant employs soya bean as a culinary chameleon, making it pretend to be a beef curry, fried fish or honey-roast chicken. The meals are tasty and the service quick, which is a hallmark of restaurants in the area.

Also recommended:
Green Herring Restaurant (Map p354; ☎ 6230 2657; Ginninderra Village, O'Hanlon Pl, Nicholls; mains $23-26; ☒ lunch Fri-Sun, dinner Tue-Sat)
Bernadette's Café & Restaurant (Map p354; ☎ 6248 5018; Wakefield Gardens, Ainslie; mains $8-17; ☒ lunch & dinner Tue-Sat)
Kingsland Vegetarian Restaurant (Map p354; ☎ 6262 9350; Shop 5, Dickson Plaza, off Woolley St, Dickson; mains $7.50-13; ☒ lunch Sun-Fri, dinner daily)

Aubergine (☎ 6260 8666; 18 Barker St, Griffith; mains $30, degustation with/without wine $110/80; ☺ lunch Mon-Fri, dinner daily)

DRINKING

Canberra's liberal licensing laws have nourished a vigorous drinking scene, though local government recently decided it was time to 'regulate' drinking and gambling hours; even the formerly 24-hour Tradies (p342) had to close for three hours a day. Pubs and bars are concentrated in Civic, but some good establishments have also set themselves up in northern suburbs like Dickson and O'Connor, and across the lake in Kingston.

Phoenix (Map pp340-1; ☎ 6247 1606; 21 East Row, Civic) Walking into the cosy Phoenix is like walking into a mellow share-house party, albeit one with a penchant for incense sticks and antique decorations like old jugs. It's a great place for slurred conversation and is unpretentious enough to get away with playing Led Zeppelin on a Friday night.

Toast (Map pp340-1; ☎ 6230 0003; City Walk, Civic) Located upstairs behind the Electric Shadows cinema (p350) is this great little bar, decked out with a pair of pool tables, antique computer games and a relaxed young crowd who come here to lift their spirits (literally) and watch the odd gig (see p350).

Hippo (Map pp340-1; ☎ 6257 9090; 17 Garema Pl, Civic) Chilled-out Hippo is indeed hip and, appropriately for a lounge-bar, its dimensions are small. The polished floorboards and red poufs are accosted by a young crowd of cocktail slurpers, who also file in for Wednesday night jazz; see under Live Music (p350).

Wig & Pen (Map pp340-1; ☎ 6248 0171; cnr Alinga St & West Row, Civic) This jovial little brewery pub has its two-room interior packed out on Friday nights by thirsty office workers,

and the rest of the time is frequented by a youthful, down-to-earth beer-tasting crowd. It tries to produce a few different styles of beer each year, including real English ale, served without gas and at a higher temperature than chilled Australian beers. Popular brews include Bulldog Best Bitter, an amber *hefe-weizen* and the delicious Pass Porter dark ale.

All Bar Nun (Map p354; ☎ 6257 9191; MacPherson St, O'Connor) This popular suburban bar has a diminutive interior tailor-made for crowded carousing, and tables appealingly sprawled all over the sidewalk. It also has a decent selection of snacks and light meals, and despite its name would undoubtedly serve a nun if one ventured in.

King O'Malley's (Map pp340-1; ☎ 6257 0111; 131 City Walk, Civic) More Irish theme park than pub, this derivative liver-disposal centre is notable for its labyrinthine interior, a boisterous end-of-week crowd of office escapees, and the fact that its name literally takes the piss out of the teetotalling bureaucrat who kept Canberra 'dry' from its foundation until 1928.

For more of the same, head across Northbourne Ave to **PJ O'Reilly's** (Map pp340-1; ☎ 6230 4752; cnr Alinga St & West Row, Civic), which is endearingly referred to by the locals as Plastic McPaddy's.

The **Durham Castle Arms** (Map pp340-1; ☎ 6295 1769; Green Sq, Kingston) is known in pint-size shorthand as the Durham. This cosy village pub wannabe might seem anachronistic in the middle of café-filled Kingston, but those who prefer Guinness to an espresso don't mind. Next door is **Filthy McFadden's** (Map pp340-1; ☎ 6239 5303; 62 Jardine St, Kingston), another of Canberra's whisky-drenched Irish drinking dens.

ENTERTAINMENT

Canberra is livelier than its reputation suggests, with the Friday night wind-down being the week's biggest social event. Mainstream music is as big here as anywhere else, but the city has always been curiously good at nurturing alternative-music malcontents and they pop up around town. You'll find entertainment listings in the Times Out section of Thursday's *Canberra Times* and in the free monthly street mag *bma*. For arts news, check out the free monthly magazine *Muse*.

THE AUTHOR'S CHOICE *Paul Smitz*

Trinity Bar (Map p354; ☎ 6262 5010; 28 Challis St, Dickson) Sleek, DJ-equipped Trinity has fine vodkas, martinis and cocktails to sample, plus beer pulled from ceiling-hanging taps. Start your evening standing at the space-engulfing bar or loitering on the patio at the front entrance, then marvel at how quickly you slouch on a bar stool and end up slumped incoherently on a couch.

AUSTRALIAN CAPITAL TERRITORY

Casino

Sheltering behind the Crowne Plaza hotel is **Casino Canberra** (Map pp340–1; ☎ 6257 7074; www.casinocanberra.com.au; 21 Binara St, Civic; ☺ noon-6am) where you can 'play to win', though there's no money-back guarantee if you lose. The only dress requirement is that you look 'neat and tidy'.

Cinemas

Multiplex cinemas can be found on Mort St, Civic, and within Canberra's various suburban shopping malls.

Electric Shadows (Map pp340–1; ☎ 6247 5060; City Walk, Civic; adult/child/concession $14/7/8.50) A well-established cinema that prefers the artful approach to a blockbuster rampage. Films like *Adaptation* feel right at home here. Matinee sessions (pre-5pm) cost adults only $8.50 and all Wednesday sessions are $7.

ScreenSound Australia (Map pp340–1; ☎ 6248 2000; McCoy Circuit, Acton; adult/concession $9/7; ☺ 7pm) Weekly, the National Screen and Sound Archive fires up a projector to screen Australian and international films, be it the eerie *Ghosts of the Civil Dead* (with Nick Cave) or the chaotic *Dogs in Space*. Check out the programme online (www.screensound.gov.au/ScreenSound/screenso.nsf).

Live Music

Many pubs have free live music. Those belonging to the pro-forma Irish collective usually have bands three or four nights a week (free).

ANU Union Bar (Map pp340–1; ☎ 6125 2446; www.anuunion.com.au; Union Court, Acton; admission $5-15; ☺ gigs usually 8pm) The Uni Bar is the mainstay of Canberra's live-music scene, with the sounds of bands reverberating around its walls up to three times a week during semester. When there are no gigs, it's a good place for a game of pool or a drink; 'happy hour' starts at 5pm weekdays. Big touring acts often play in the high-ceilinged Refectory.

Tilley's Devine Café Gallery (Map p354; ☎ 6249 1543; cnr Wattle & Brigalow Sts, Lyneham; usually $30) People of all ages breeze in and out of Tilley's cool, smoke-free interior, with its scuffed furniture, dark booths and eclectic menu of local and international musicians and comedians. It also does poetry nights, writers sessions and great cooked breakfasts.

Toast (Map pp340–1; ☎ 6230 0003; City Walk, Civic; admission $2-5; ☺ gigs Fri & Sat) This highly likable bar (see p349) has live music (solo acoustic bands, CD launches) at week's end. It also likes going retro; think Dead Kennedys and Sex Pistols, not ABBA.

Hippo (Map pp340–1; ☎ 6257 9090; 17 Garema Pl; usually $5; ☺ gigs from 9pm Wed) This is another good place for emerging live music, where you can hear jazz and turntable sounds.

Nightclubs

In Blue (Map pp340–1; ☎ 6248 7405; cnr Mort & Alinga Sts, Civic; disco $5 on Sat; ☺ disco Thu-Sat from 7pm) Formerly known as Pandora's, the decibel-ignorant In Blue has a downstairs space that's more sports bar than nightclub, and an upstairs disco that goes for glam over groove – come here if you feel like raucous, centrally located predictability.

icbm & Insomnia (Map pp340–1; ☎ 6248 0102; 50 Northbourne Ave, Civic; Insomnia on Sat $5; ☺ icbm 7pm-late daily, Insomnia 9pm-late Wed-Sat) Young drinking crowds similar to those at In Blue also attend this clubbing complex, with the music-blasted bar icbm downstairs and the dancehall Insomnia upstairs, but it arguably plays better clubbing music, hosts the odd international DJ, and diversifies with weekly comedy nights.

Club Mombasa (Map pp340–1; ☎ 0419-609 106; www.clubmombasa.com.au; 128 Bunda St, Civic; events $5-7; ☺ 8pm-late Wed-Sun) The energetic patrons of Club Mombasa spend their evenings counting the beat to African and Latin rhythms, reggae, hip-hop, funk and drum 'n' bass.

Performing Arts

Canberra Theatre Centre (Map pp340–1; ☎ box office 1800 802 025, 6275 2700; www.canberratheatre.org.au; Civic Sq, London Circuit, Civic; ☺ box office 9am-5.30pm Mon-Sat) There are many dramatic goings-on within this highly cultured centre, from Shakespeare to David Williamson plays, Circus Oz and indigenous dance troupes. Information and tickets are supplied by Canberra Ticketing, in the adjacent North Building (Eftpos is not available here).

Gorman House Arts Centre (Map pp340–1; ☎ 6249 7377; Ainslie Ave, Braddon) Gorman House hosts various theatre and dance companies that stage their own self-hatched productions, including the innovative moves of the **Australian Choreographic Centre** (☎ 6247 3103).

Spectator Sports

The Canberra Raiders are the home-town rugby league side and during the league season (March to September) they play regularly at **Canberra Stadium** (Map p354; ☎ 6256 5700; www.canberrastadium.com; Battye St, Bruce). Also laying tackles at Canberra Stadium are the ACT Brumbies rugby union team, who play in the international Super 12 competition (February to May). You can catch the highly rated women's basketball team, the Canberra Capitals, in action (October to February) at **Southern Cross Stadium** (Map pp340-1; tickets ☎ 6253 3066; cnr Cowlishaw St & Athllon Dr, Greenway), while their compatriots the AIS play at the **AIS Training Hall** (Map p354; ☎ 6214 1201; Leverrier Cres, Bruce).

SHOPPING

The Australian capital is a crafty place where you can pick up a variety of creative gifts and souvenirs from galleries, museum shops or markets.

Canberra Centre (Map pp340-1; ☎ 6247 5611; Bunda St, Civic) The city's biggest and best shopping centre admits customers to dozens of speciality stores, including fashion boutiques, food emporiums, jewellery shops and several chain stores. The ground-floor information desk can help with wheelchair and stroller hire. More well-browsed shops line adjacent stretches of the pedestrianised City Walk.

Craft ACT (Map pp340-1; ☎ 6262 9333; www.craft act.org.au; 1st fl, North Bldg, Civic Sq, Civic) There are some wonderful exhibitions of contemporary work here, with cutting-edge designs in the form of bags, bowls, pendants and prints. It's worth visiting just to see the latest imaginative efforts of local and interstate artists.

Old Bus Depot Markets (Map pp340-1; ☎ 6292 8391; Wentworth Ave, Kingston; ☽ 10am-4pm Sun) This popular indoor market specialises in handcrafted goods and regional edibles, including the output of the Canberra district's 20-plus wineries.

HOW VERY SPORTING

The national capital's highly active and seriously competitive nature is embodied in the local love of sport, be it when Canberrans cheer on a rugby-match-winning try or stage an impromptu Frisbee tournament (complete with opposing teams and a spontaneous set of rules) on an unoccupied slice of parkland. So strong is the ACT's conviction that it boasts the nation's sportiest people that even the territory's tourism authority feels compelled to quote the Australian Bureau of Statistics (from 1997 to boot) in claiming that Canberra has the 'highest rate of participation in sport and recreation in Australia', whatever that means.

Mind you, the last few years haven't comprised the best sporting era for the city. Late in 2001, Canberra's sole representative in the National Soccer League (NSL), the Canberra Cosmos, was unceremoniously dumped from the competition due to ongoing financial problems. And more recently, the capital's once highly competitive men's basketball team, the Canberra Cannons, was replaced in the National Basketball League (NBL) by a Newcastle-based outfit after a similar economic crisis.

In contrast, women's basketball is dribbling along nicely in the form of the super-successful Canberra Capitals, who won back-to-back Women's National Basketball League (WNBL) championships in 2002 and 2003. The team's best-known player is Lauren Jackson, who was voted MVP (most valuable player) during her stint in the elite US women's basketball league in 2003.

The sport which attracts the loudest fervour is rugby league. Canberra's first-grade representative in the National Rugby League (NRL) competition is the Raiders, which had a strong season in 2003 after years of meagre success, only to be defeated by a solitary point by the New Zealand Warriors in a semi-final match. Raiders players sport some intriguing nicknames, like Jason 'Toots' Croker and Michael 'Get Out Of My' Weyman, but the biggest name in the team's history is Mal Meninga, who captained the Raiders to three premierships (1989, 1990 and 1994), has a grandstand named after him at Canberra Stadium, and also represented Australia in a record 45 international rugby league tests.

Rugby union fans also have plenty to cheer about in Canberra. The city fields a team called the ACT Brumbies in the international 'Super 12' competition, where they play against sides from elsewhere in Australia, New Zealand, South Africa and the UK. In 2001, the Brumbies became the first team from outside New Zealand to win the Super 12.

Gold Creek Village (see p355) has numerous shops selling good-quality leatherwork, woodwork, jewellery and other crafts.

Aboriginal Dreamings Gallery (Map p354; ☎ 6230 2922; 19 O'Hanlon Pl, Nicholls) Visit this gallery for an excellent selection of Aboriginal artworks that includes didgeridoos and bark paintings, with certificates of authenticity provided where possible.

Hall Market (Hall Showground; 10am-3pm first Sun each month Feb-Dec) The township of Hall, to the northwest of Canberra just past Gold Creek Village, has an authentically rural market where you can get fresh organic produce, plants and great home-made ice cream.

GETTING THERE & AWAY
Air
Canberra airport (☎ 6275 2236) is chiefly serviced by **Qantas** (Map pp340-1; ☎ 13 13 13, TTY 1800 652 660; www.qantas.com.au; Jolimont Centre, Northbourne Ave, Civic), **Virgin Blue** (☎ 13 67 89; www.virginblue.com.au) and **Regional Express** (Rex; ☎ 13 17 13; www.regionalexpress.com.au), with flights to Sydney (from $75 one way, 45 minutes) and Melbourne (from $90 one way, one hour). There are also direct flights to Adelaide (from $160 one way) and Brisbane (from $140 one way).

Smaller airlines fly to other NSW destinations. **Brindabella Airlines** (☎ 6248 8711; www.brindabella-airlines.com.au) flies between Albury-Wodonga, Canberra and Newcastle.

Bus
The interstate bus terminal is at the **Jolimont Centre** (Map pp340-1; Northbourne Ave, Civic), which has left-luggage lockers, showers, public Internet access and free phone lines to the visitors centre and some budget accommodation. Inside, the **Travellers Booking Centre** (Map pp340-1; ☎ 1300 733 323, 6249 6006; ☺ 6am-11.45pm) and **CountryLink travel centre** (Map pp340-1; ☎ 13 22 32, 6257 1576; ☺ 7.15am-5pm Mon-Fri) book seats on most bus services.

McCafferty's/Greyhound (☎ 13 14 99; www.mccaffertys.com.au) has frequent services to Sydney (adult/concession $35/24, 3½ to 4½ hours) and also runs to and from Adelaide (adult/concession $130/105, 20 hours) and Melbourne (adult/concession $60/50, nine hours). There are regular services to Cooma (adult/concession $37/30, 1½ hours) and Thredbo (adult/concession $54/43, three hours) in winter.

Murrays (☎ 13 22 51; ☺ counter 7am-7pm) has daily express services to Sydney (adult/concession $35/24, 3¼ hours) and also runs to Batemans Bay (adult/concession $24/22, 2½ hours), Narooma (adult/concession $36/32, 4½ hours) and Wollongong (adult/concession $31/24, 3½ hours).

Transborder Express (☎ 6241 0033) runs daily to Yass (adult/concession $13/9, 50 minutes), while **Summit Coaches** (☎ 6297 2588) runs to Thredbo (adult/concession $50/45, three hours) via Jindabyne on Monday, Wednesday, Friday and Saturday.

Car & Motorcycle
The Hume Hwy links Sydney and Melbourne, passing about 50km north of Canberra. The Federal Hwy runs north to connect with the Hume near Goulburn (for Sydney) and the Barton Hwy meets the Hume near Yass (for Melbourne). To the south, the Monaro Hwy connects Canberra with Cooma.

Rental car prices start at around $45 a day. Major companies with Canberra city offices (and desks at the airport):

Avis (Map pp340-1; ☎ 13 63 33, 6249 6088; 17 Lonsdale St, Braddon)

Budget (Map pp340-1; ☎ 1300 362 848, 6257 2200; cnr Mort & Girrahween Sts, Braddon)

Hertz (Map pp340-1; ☎ 13 30 39, 6257 4877; 32 Mort St, Braddon)

Thrifty (Map pp340-1; ☎ 13 61 39, 6247 7422; 29 Lonsdale St, Braddon)

Another option is **Rumbles** (Map p354; ☎ 6280 7444; 11 Paragon Mall, Gladstone St, Fyshwick).

Train
Kingston train station (Map pp340-1; Wentworth Ave) is the city's rail terminus. You can book trains and connecting buses inside the station at the **CountryLink travel centre** (Map pp340-1; ☎ 13 22 32, 6295 1198; ☺ 6.15am-5.30pm Mon-Sat, 10.30am-5.30pm Sun).

CountryLink trains run to/from Sydney (adult/child $50/24, four hours, three daily). There's no direct train to Melbourne, but a CountryLink coach to Cootamundra links with the train to Melbourne ($90, nine hours, one daily); the service leaves Jolimont at 10am. A daily V/Line Canberra Link service involves a train between Melbourne and Albury-Wodonga, then a connecting bus to Canberra ($60, 8½ hours, one daily). A longer but more scenic bus/

train service to Melbourne is the V/Line Capital Link ($60, 10½ hours) running every Tuesday and Friday via Cooma and the East Gippsland forests to Sale, where you board the Melbourne-bound train.

GETTING AROUND
To/From the Airport
Canberra airport is 8km southeast of the city. Taxi fares to the city average $18.

Deane's Buslines (☎ 6299 3722) operates the AirLiner bus ($5, 20 minutes, 11 times daily weekdays) which runs between the airport and the Civic bus interchange (bay 6).

Bus
Canberra's public transport provider is the **ACT Internal Omnibus Network** (Action; ☎ 13 17 10, 6207 7611; www.action.act.gov.au). The main Civic bus interchange is along Alinga St, East Row and Mort St in Civic. Visit the **information kiosk** (Map pp340-1; East Row, Civic; ☉ 7.15am-4pm Mon-Fri) for free route maps and timetables, or buy the all-routes *Canberra Bus Map* ($2) from newsagents.

You can purchase single-trip tickets (adult/concession $2.40/1.30), but a better bet for most visitors is a daily ticket (adult/concession $6/3). Tickets can be purchased in advance from Action agents (including the visitors centre and some newsagents), or buy them direct from the driver.

DETOUR: QUEANBEYAN TO BRAIDWOOD

Embark on one of the region's most popular day trips by driving east along Canberra Ave until it becomes the Kings Hwy, which stretches over the NSW border into the historic environs of **Queanbeyan** – nowadays it's virtually a suburb of Canberra, but has a clutch of attractive buildings dating from the town's establishment in 1838. Continue down the Kings Hwy to Bungendore, a few kilometres south of expansive Lake George and populated by numerous craft galleries and restored heritage buildings. Follow the highway as it wanders around the Great Dividing Range and into the pretty town of **Braidwood**, which has an abundance of antique and craft shops, plus some tempting rustic restaurants.

For details on the hop-on, hop-off double-decker bus service operated by City Sightseeing see p344.

Car & Motorcycle
Canberra's road system is as circuitous as a politician's answer to a straight question. That said, there are no inner-city one-way streets to further tax the navigation skills of visiting motorists, and the wide and relatively uncluttered main roads make driving easy, even at so-called 'peak-hour' times. A map is essential.

There's plenty of well-signposted parking in Civic. The visitors centre has a *Motorbike Parking in Canberra* pamphlet.

Taxi
Call **Canberra Cabs** (☎ 13 22 27). One of the main taxi ranks is on Bunda St, outside the cinemas.

AROUND CANBERRA

For information and maps on attractions around Canberra, including the unspoiled bushland just outside the outer urban limits and the network of roads that leads into it, ransack the visitors centre.

SIGHTS & ACTIVITIES
Picnic, Swimming & Walking Areas
Picnic and barbecue spots, many with gas-powered facilities, are scattered throughout the ACT, though they're rarely accessible by public transport. See the main ACT map (p333) to get your bearings on these sights.

Black Mountain is handy for picnics, and there are good swimming spots along the **Murrumbidgee** and **Cotter Rivers**. Other popular riverside areas include **Uriarra Crossing**, 24km northwest of the city, on the Murrumbidgee near its meeting with the Molonglo River; **Casuarina Sands**, 19km west of the city at the meeting of the Cotter and Murrumbidgee Rivers; **Kambah Pool Reserve**, another 14km upstream on the Murrumbidgee; **Cotter Dam**, 23km west of the city on the Cotter River and with a camping ground; **Pine Island** and **Point Hut Crossing**, upstream of Kambah Pool Reserve on the Murrumbidgee; and **Gibraltar Falls**, roughly 45km southwest of the city.

AROUND CANBERRA

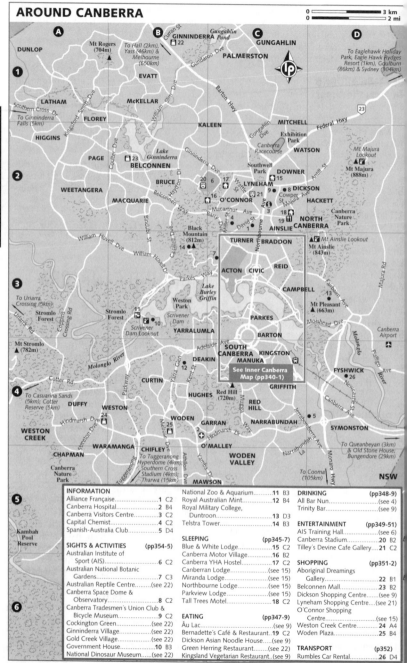

0 — 3 km
0 — 2 mi

AUSTRALIAN CAPITAL TERRITORY

INFORMATION
Alliance Française.....................1 C2
Canberra Hospital....................2 B4
Canberra Visitors Centre..........3 C2
Capital Chemist.......................4 C2
Spanish-Australia Club............5 D4

SIGHTS & ACTIVITIES (pp354–5)
Australian Institute of
  Sport (AIS)..........................6 C2
Australian National Botanic
  Gardens..............................7 C3
Australian Reptile Centre......(see 22)
Canberra Space Dome &
  Observatory..........................8 C2
Canberra Tradesmen's Union Club &
  Bicycle Museum......................9 C2
Cockington Green..................(see 22)
Ginninderra Village...............(see 22)
Gold Creek Village................(see 22)
Government House...................10 B3
National Dinosaur Museum......(see 22)

National Zoo & Aquarium........11 B3
Royal Australian Mint.............12 B4
Royal Military College,
  Duntroon...........................13 D3
Telstra Tower.........................14 B3

SLEEPING (pp345–7)
Blue & White Lodge...............15 C2
Canberra Motor Village..........16 B2
Canberra YHA Hostel.............17 C2
Canberran Lodge..................(see 15)
Miranda Lodge.....................(see 15)
Northbourne Lodge...............(see 15)
Parkview Lodge....................(see 15)
Tall Trees Motel.....................18 C2

EATING (pp347–9)
Âu Lac................................(see 9)
Bernadette's Café & Restaurant..19 C2
Dickson Asian Noodle House....(see 9)
Green Herring Restaurant.......(see 22)
Kingsland Vegetarian Restaurant..(see 9)

DRINKING (pp348–9)
All Bar Nun..........................(see 4)
Trinity Bar...........................(see 9)

ENTERTAINMENT (pp349–51)
AIS Training Hall...................(see 6)
Canberra Stadium..................20 B2
Tilley's Devine Cafe Gallery.....21 C2

SHOPPING (pp351–2)
Aboriginal Dreamings
  Gallery.............................22 B1
Belconnen Mall.....................23 B2
Dickson Shopping Centre......(see 9)
Lyneham Shopping Centre....(see 21)
O'Connor Shopping
  Centre.............................(see 15)
Weston Creek Centre.............24 A4
Woden Plaza........................25 B4

TRANSPORT (p352)
Rumbles Car Rental...............26 D4

Across the NSW border in the northwest is **Ginninderra Falls** (☎ 6278 4222; Parkwood Rd; adult/child/family $4.50/2.50/10; ☺ 10am-6pm summer, to 4pm winter); admire it from Pulpit Lookout or swim to it in the fantastic Upper Gorge Pool.

Tidbinbilla Nature Reserve (☎ 6205 1233; off Paddy's River Rd), 45km southwest of the city, is threaded with bushwalking tracks, though recovery from the January 2003 fires will take a long time. The facilities at **Corin Forest** (☎ 6235 7333; www.corin.com.au; Corin Rd), roughly 50km southwest of the city, which included a flying fox and an alpine slide, were destroyed in the 2003 fires but were expected to re-open at Easter 2004.

Other good walking areas include **Mt Ainslie**, to the northeast of the city; **Mt Majura** behind it (the combined area forms part of Canberra Nature Park); and **Molonglo Gorge** near Queanbeyan.

Namadgi National Park (camp sites per person $2.60-3.40) has eight peaks higher than 1700m and offers bushwalking and camping. For information visit the Namadgi **visitors centre** (☎ 6207 2900; Naas Rd; ☺ 9am-4pm Mon-Fri, to 4.30pm Sat & Sun), 2km south of Tharwa.

Canberra Space Centre

Within the Canberra Deep Space Communication Complex, 40km southwest of the city, is the **Canberra Space Centre** (☎ 6201 7800; www.cdscc.nasa.gov; off Paddy's River Rd; admission free; ☺ 9am-5pm), where there are interesting displays of spacecraft and deep-space tracking technology, plus a piece of lunar basalt scooped up by Apollo XI in 1969.

Gold Creek Village   Map p354

The attractions at **Gold Creek Village** (☎ 6253 9780; Gold Creek Rd, Barton Hwy, Nicholls; admission free; ☺ 10am-5pm) are a combination of colonial kitsch and genuinely interesting exhibits.

Kids can get in touch with their prehistoric selves at the attention-getting **National Dinosaur Museum** (☎ 6230 2655; www.nationaldinosaurmuseum.com.au; adult/child/concession/family $9.50/6.50/7.50/30; ☺ 10am-5pm), where some giant, chronologically arranged bones and fossil workshops await.

The **Australian Reptile Centre** (☎ 6253 8533; adult/child/concession/family $7.50/5/6/26; ☺ 10am-5pm) is a fascinating showcase of reptilian life. Behind glass are tree skinks and scrub pythons, plus the world's three deadliest (yet surprisingly nonaggressive) land snakes; *numero uno* is the inland taipan. The prehistory gallery will bring you up to speed on trilobites and has an impressive skeleton of a 70-million-year-old carnivorous fish, the *Xiphactinus*.

Ginninderra Village (admission free; ☺ 10am-5pm) was sporting a few 'For Lease' signs when we visited, but the place still had a couple of worthwhile galleries and a striking 1860s schoolhouse.

Nearby is **Cockington Green** (☎ 6230 2273; www.cockington-green.com.au; adult/child/concession/family $12/6/9/33; ☺ 9.30am-5pm), an immaculately manicured, too-quaint-for-its-own-good English village in miniature.

Other Attractions

Beside the Murrumbidgee River, 20km south of Canberra, is the beautiful National Trust property **Lanyon Homestead** (☎ 6237 5136; Tharwa Dr; adult/concession/family $7/4/15; ☺ 10am-4pm Tue-Sun), explorable via a guided tour. Also on-site but in a separate building is the **Nolan Gallery** (☎ 6237 5192; adult/concession/family $3/2/6; ☺ 10am-4pm Tue-Sun), containing paintings by celebrated Australian artist Sidney Nolan, including famous Ned Kelly art and spray-canned caricatures. You can buy a **combined ticket** (adult/concession/family $8/5/18.50) to both homestead and gallery.

Near Tharwa is **Cuppacumbalong** (☎ 6237 5116; Naas Rd; ☺ 11am-5pm Wed-Sun & public holidays), a 1922 homestead and heritage garden reincarnated as a quality Australian craftware studio and gallery.

AUSTRALIAN CAPITAL TERRITORY

Directory

CONTENTS

PRACTICALITIES

- Plugs have angled pins; the electricity supply is 220–240V AC, 50Hz.

- The *Sydney Morning Herald*, *Daily Telegraph* and the national *Australian* are newspapers available throughout NSW.

- On TV, find the government-sponsored ABC, the multicultural SBS, or one of three commercial TV stations: Seven, Nine and Ten.

- Videos use the PAL system.

- For weights and measures, the metric system is used.

---

paying up to $100 per double and 'midrange' places can end up costing you in the vicinity of $160 for a double.

In most areas you'll find seasonal price variations. Over summer (December to February) and at other peak times, particularly school and public holidays, prices are usually at their highest, whereas outside these times useful discounts and lower walk-in rates can be found.

The weekend escape is a notion that figures prominently in the Australian psyche, meaning accommodation from Friday night through Sunday can be in greater demand (and pricier) in major holiday areas. Highseason prices are quoted in this guidebook unless otherwise indicated. For more information on climatic seasons, see p360, and for holiday periods, see p366.

B&Bs

The local bed & breakfast (or guesthouse) birth rate is climbing rapidly, with new places opening all the time; options include everything from restored miners' cottages, converted barns, rambling old houses, upmarket country manors and beachside bungalows to a simple bedroom in a family home.

In areas that attract weekenders – quaint historic towns, wine regions, accessible forest regions such as the Blue Mountains – B&Bs are often upmarket and will charge premium rates if you want to stay between Friday and Sunday in high season (assuming you could

ACCOMMODATION

It's not difficult to get a good night's sleep in New South Wales (NSW), which offers everything from the tent-pegged confines of camping grounds and the communal space of hostels to gourmet breakfasts in guesthouses and at-your-fingertip resorts, plus the gamut of hotel and motel lodgings.

The accommodation listings in this book are in order of author preference. In larger towns and cities, the listings are arranged in budget, mid-range and top-end categories. We generally treat any place that charges up to $40 per single or $80 per double as budget accommodation. Mid-range facilities are usually in the range of $80 to $130 per double, while the top-end tag is applied to places charging more than $130 per double. Of course, in more-expensive areas like metropolitan Sydney, 'budget' can mean

even get in). Tariffs are typically in the $70 to $150 (per double) bracket, but can be much higher.

Local tourist offices can usually give you a list of places.

Camping & Caravan Parks

The cheapest accommodation lies outdoors, where the nightly cost of camping for two people is usually somewhere between $13 and $23, slightly more for a powered site. Whether you're packing a tent, driving a campervan or towing a caravan (house trailer in North American–speak), camping in the bush is a highlight of travelling in Australia. In places like the outback you often won't even need a tent, and the nights spent around a camp fire under the stars are unforgettable. Stays at designated camp sites in national parks normally cost between $3 and $8 per person. When it comes to urban camping, remember that most city camping grounds are miles away from the centre of town, especially in Sydney.

Most caravan parks are good value, with almost all equipped with hot showers, flushing toilets and laundry facilities, and, occasionally a pool. Many have old on-site caravans for rent, but these are largely being replaced by on-site cabins. Cabin sizes and facilities vary, but expect to pay $50 to $90 for a cabin with a kitchenette for two people.

Hostels

Hostels are a highly social but low-cost fixture of the Australian accommodation scene. In some areas, travellers may find hostels are reinventing themselves as 'inns' or 'guesthouses', partly to broaden their appeal beyond backpackers.

HOSTEL ORGANISATIONS

Two useful international hostel organisations, both with numerous hostels in NSW:

Nomads Backpackers (☎ 1800 819 883, 08-8363 7633; www.nomadsworld.com; 43 The Parade, Kent Town, SA 5067) Membership ($29 for 12 months) entitles you to numerous discounts.

VIP Backpacker Resorts (☎ 07-3395 6111; www.back packers.com; 3/41 Steele Pl, Morningside, Qld 4170) For $39 you'll receive a 12-month membership, entitling you to a $1 discount on accommodation and a 5% to 15% discount on other products such as air and bus transport, tours and activities.

INDEPENDENT HOSTELS

Australia has numerous independent hostels, with the fierce competition for the backpacker dollar prompting fairly high standards and plenty of enticements, such as free breakfasts, courtesy buses and discount meal vouchers. But some places are run-down hotels trying to fill empty rooms, while others are converted motels where each four- to six-bed unit has a fridge, TV and bathroom, but communal areas and cooking facilities may be lacking. The best places tend to be the smaller, more intimate hostels where the owner is also the manager.

Independent backpacker establishments typically charge $19 to $26 for a dorm bed and $40 to $60 for a twin or double room (usually without bathroom).

YHA HOSTELS

NSW has over 40 hostels that are part of the Youth Hostels Association (YHA). The **YHA NSW** (☎ 02-9261 1111; www.yha.com.au) is part of the **International Youth Hostel Federation** (IYHF; www.hihostels.com), also known as Hostelling International (HI). Nightly charges are between $10 and $30 for members; most hostels also take non-YHA members for an extra $3.50. Visitors to Australia should purchase a HI card, preferably in their country of residence, but also available at major local YHA hostels at a cost of $35 for 12 months; see the HI website for further details (www.hihostels.com). Australian residents can become full YHA members for $52/85 for one/two years.

YHA hostels provide basic accommodation, usually in small dormitories (bunk rooms), although many provide twin rooms and even doubles. They have 24-hour access, cooking facilities, a communal area with a TV, laundry facilities and, in larger hostels, travel offices. There's often a maximum-stay period (usually five to seven days). Bed linen is provided (sleeping bags are not allowed) in all hostels except those in wilderness areas, where you'll need your own sleeping sheet.

Hotels & Motels

Except for pubs (p358), hotels in cities or places visited by lots of tourists are generally of the business or luxury variety (insert the name of your favourite chain here) where you get a comfortable, anonymous and mod con–filled room in a multistorey block. These places tend to have a pool, restaurant/café, room service and various other facilities. We quote 'rack rates' (official advertised rates) throughout this book; often hotels/motels will offer regular discounts and special deals.

For comfortable mid-range accommodation that's available all over NSW, motels (or motor inns) are the places to stay in. Most motels are modern, low-rise and have similar facilities (tea- and coffee-making, fridge, TV, air-con, bathroom) but the price will indicate the standard. You'll mostly pay between $50 and $120 for a room.

Pubs

For the budget traveller, hotels in Australia are the ones that serve beer – commonly known as pubs (from the term 'public house'). In country towns, pubs are invariably found in the town centre. Many pubs were built during boom times, so they're often among the largest and most extravagant buildings in town. In tourist areas some of these pubs have been restored as heritage buildings, but generally the rooms remain small and old-fashioned, with a long amble down the hall to the bathroom. You can sometimes rent a single room at a country pub for not too much more than a hostel dorm, and you'll be in the social heart of the town to boot. But if you're a light sleeper, never (ever) book a room above the bar.

Standard pubs have singles/doubles with shared facilities starting from around $30/45, obviously more if you want a private bathroom. Few have a separate reception area – just ask in the bar if there are rooms available.

Rental Accommodation

The ubiquitous holiday flat resembles a motel unit but has a kitchen or cooking facilities. It can come with two or more bedrooms and is often rented on a weekly basis – higher prices are often reserved for shorter stays. For a two-bedroom flat, you're looking at anywhere from $60 to $95 per night. The other alternative in major cities is to take a serviced apartment.

If you're interested in a shared flat or house for a long-term stay, delve into the classified advertisements sections of the daily newspapers; Wednesday and Saturday are usually the best days. Notice boards in universities, hostels, bookshops and cafés are also good to check out.

Other Accommodation

Scattered throughout NSW are lots of less-conventional accommodation possibilities.

A decent number of the country's farms offer a bed for a night. At some you sit back and watch other people raise a sweat, while others like to get you involved in day-to-day activities. At a couple of remote outback stations, you can stay in homestead rooms or shearers' quarters and try activities such as horse riding. Check out the options on these websites:

Australian Farmhost Holidays (www.australiafarm host.com)

Tourism New South Wales (☎ 1800 803 007; www .visitnsw.com.au) Has detailed listings.

ACTIVITIES

See the NSW Outdoors chapter (p34).

BUSINESS HOURS

Most shops and businesses open around 9am and close at 5pm or 6pm Monday to Friday, and at either noon or 5pm on Saturday. Sunday trading is becoming increasingly common, but it's currently limited to the major towns and Sydney. In most towns there are usually one or two late shopping nights each week, normally Thursday and/or Friday, when doors stay open until 9pm or 9.30pm. Supermarkets are generally open from 7am until at least 8pm and sometimes 24 hours. You'll also find milk bars (general stores) and convenience stores often open until late.

Banks are normally open from 9.30am to 4pm Monday to Thursday, and until 5pm on Friday. Some large city branches are open from 8am to 6pm weekdays, and a few are also open to 9pm on Friday. Post offices are open from 9am to 5pm Monday to Friday, but you can also buy stamps on Saturday morning at post office agencies (operated from newsagencies) and from Australia Post shops in the major cities.

Restaurants typically open at noon for lunch and between 6pm and 7pm for dinner; most dinner bookings are made for 7.30pm or 8pm. Restaurants stay open until at least 9pm, but tend to serve food until later in the evening on Friday and Saturday. That said, the main restaurant strips in large cities keep longer hours throughout the week. Cafés tend to be all-day affairs that either close around 5pm or continue their business into the night. Pubs usually serve food from noon to 2pm and from 6pm to 8pm. Pubs and bars often open for drinking at lunchtime and continue well into the evening, particularly from Thursday to Saturday. For more dining information, see p39.

Keep in mind that nearly all attractions are closed on Christmas Day.

CHILDREN
Practicalities

All cities and most major towns have centrally located public rooms where mothers (and sometimes fathers) can go to nurse their baby or change its nappy; check with the local tourist office or city council for details. While many Australians have a relaxed attitude about breast-feeding or nappy changing in public, others frown on it.

Many motels and the better-equipped caravan parks have playgrounds and swimming pools, and can supply cots and baby baths – motels may also have in-house children's videos and childminding services. Top-end hotels and many (but not all) mid-range hotels are well versed in the needs of guests who have children. B&Bs, on the other hand, often market themselves as sanctuaries from all things child-related. Some cafés and restaurants make it difficult to dine with small children, lacking a specialised children's menu, but many others do have kids meals, or will provide small serves from the main menu. Some also supply highchairs.

If you want to leave Junior behind for a few hours, some of Australia's numerous licensed child-care agencies have places set aside for casual care. To find them, check under Baby Sitters and Child Care Centres in the *Yellow Pages* telephone book, or phone the local council for a list. Licensed centres are subject to government regulation and usually adhere to high standards; to be on the safe side, avoid unlicensed ones.

Child concessions (and family rates) often apply for such things as accommodation, tours, admission fees, and air, bus and train transport, with some discounts as high as 50% of the adult rate. However, the definition of 'child' can vary from under 12 to under 18

years. Accommodation concessions generally apply to children under 12 years sharing the same room as adults. On the major airlines, infants travel free provided they don't occupy a seat – child fares usually apply between the ages of two and 11 years.

Medical services and facilities in NSW are of a high standard, and items such as baby-food formula and disposable nappies are widely available in urban centres. Major hire-car companies will supply and fit booster seats for you, for which you'll be charged around $16 for up to three days' use, with an additional daily fee for longer periods. Lonely Planet's *Travel with Children* contains plenty of useful information.

Sights & Activities

There's no shortage of active, interesting or amusing things for children to focus on in NSW. Every town or city has at least some parkland, or you could head into the countryside for wide-open spaces, bushland, rainforests or beaches. Not all museums will hold the interest of kids, but there are still plenty of historical, natural or science-based exhibits to get them thinking – these range from zoos and aquariums to pioneer villages and interactive technology centres.

CLIMATE

Australia's seasons are the antithesis of those in Europe and the USA. Summer starts in December, autumn in March, winter in June and spring in September.

The climate in NSW varies depending on the location, but the rule of thumb is that the further north you go, the warmer and more humid it'll be. It's also hotter and drier the further west you go.

Sydney is blessed with a temperate climate. The temperature rarely falls below 10°C except overnight in winter and, although temperatures can hit 40°C during summer, the average summer maximum is a pleasant 25°C. Average monthly rainfall ranges from 75mm to 130mm.

Canberra is freezing in winter and baking in summer, so spring and autumn are the best times to visit the national capital.

Bourke, in the state's far west, claims NSW's highest recorded temperature, a blistering 51.7°C (125°F) in the shade.

See Getting Started (p9) for more information on NSW's seasons.

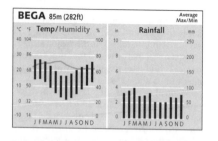

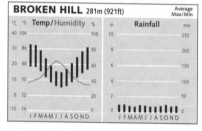

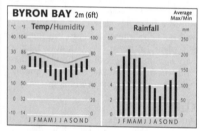

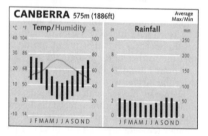

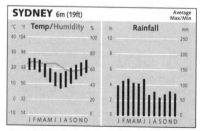

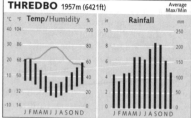

DIRECTORY

CUSTOMS & QUARANTINE

For comprehensive information on customs regulations, contact the **Australian Customs Service** (☎ 1300 363 263, 02-6275 6666; www.customs.gov.au).

When entering Australia you can bring most articles in free of duty provided that customs is satisfied they are for personal use and that you'll be taking them with you when you leave. There's a duty-free quota per person of 1125mL of alcohol, 250 cigarettes and dutiable goods up to the value of A$400.

Sydney has duty-free stores at the airport and in the city centre. Treat them with healthy suspicion: 'duty-free' is one of the world's most overworked catchphrases and it's often just an excuse to sell things at prices you can easily beat with a little shopping around. Alcohol and cigarettes are certainly cheaper duty free though, as they are heavily taxed in Australia.

When it comes to prohibited goods, there are a few things you should be particularly conscientious about. The first is drugs, which customs authorities are adept at sniffing out – unless you want to make a first-hand investigation of conditions in Australian jails, don't bring illegal drugs in with you. And note that all medicines must be declared.

The second is all food, plant material and animal products. You'll be asked to declare on arrival all goods of animal, or plant origin (wooden spoons, straw hats, the lot) and show them to a quarantine officer. The authorities are naturally keen to protect Australia's unique environment and important agricultural industries by preventing weeds, pests or diseases getting into the country – Australia has so far managed to escape many of the pests and diseases prevalent elsewhere in the world. Food is also prohibited, particularly meat, cheese, fruit, vegetables and flowers; plus, there are restrictions on taking fruit and vegetables between states (see boxed text, p384).

Australia takes quarantine very seriously. All luggage is screened or X-rayed – if you fail to declare quarantine items on arrival and are caught, you risk an on-the-spot fine of $220, or prosecution which may result in fines over $60,000, as well as up to 10 years imprisonment. For more information on quarantine regulations contact the **Australian Quarantine & Inspection Service** (AQIS; www.aqis.gov.au).

DANGERS & ANNOYANCES

For emergencies, dial ☎ 000.

Animal Hazards

Judging by Australia's remarkable profusion of dangerous creatures, Mother Nature must have been really pissed off when she concocted the local wildlife. Apart from the presence of poisonous snakes and spiders, the country has also had its share of shark and crocodile attacks and, to top it off, is home to the world's deadliest creature, the box jellyfish. Travellers don't need to be in a constant state of alarm, however – you're unlikely to see many of these creatures in the wilds of NSW, much less be attacked by them, as they are found in the north.

Hospitals have antivenin on hand for all common snake and spider bites, but it helps to know what it was that bit you.

INSECTS

For four to six months of the year you'll have to cope with those two banes of the Australian outdoors: the fly and the mosquito (mozzie). Flies aren't too bad in the cities but they start getting out of hand in the outback, and the further into the outback you go, the more numerous and persistent they seem to be. In central Australia the flies emerge with the warmer spring weather (late August), particularly if there has been good winter rain, and last until the next frosts kill them off. Flies also tend to be bad in various coastal areas.

Mozzies are a problem in summer, especially near wetlands in tropical areas, and some species are carriers of viral infections; see p388. Try to keep your arms and legs covered as soon as the sun goes down and make liberal use of insect repellent.

SHARKS

Shark attacks are extremely rare – you're more likely to be involved in a car accident (if that's any comfort). Some major beaches, especially around Sydney, have shark nets to deter sharks from cruising along the beaches and checking out the menu.

SNAKES

There are many venomous snakes in the Australian bush, the most common being the brown and tiger snakes, but few are aggressive – unless you're interfering with one, or have the misfortune to stand on one, it's extremely unlikely that you'll be bitten. The golden rule if you see a snake is to do a Beatles and *let it be*.

For information on treating snake bites, see p389.

SPIDERS

The deadly funnel-web spider is found in NSW (including Sydney) and its bite is treated in the same way as a snake bite. It has an especially nasty set of fangs. Another eight-legged critter to stay away from is the black one with a distinctive red stripe on its body, called the redback spider; for bites, apply ice and seek medical attention. For more on spider bites, see p389.

Bushfires & Blizzards

As has been dramatically illustrated in recent times, bushfires are a regular occurrence in NSW. Don't be the mug who starts one. In hot, dry and windy weather, be extremely careful with any naked flame – cigarette butts thrown out of car windows have started many a fire. On a total-fire-ban day it's forbidden even to use a camping stove in the open. Locals will not be amused if they catch you breaking this law; they'll happily dob you in, and the penalties are severe.

Bushwalkers should seek local advice before setting out. When a total fire ban is in place, delay your trip until the weather improves. If you're out in the bush and you see smoke, even a long way away, take it seriously – bushfires move very quickly and change direction with the wind. Go to the nearest open space, downhill if possible. A forested ridge, on the other hand, is the most dangerous place to be.

More bushwalkers actually die of cold than in bushfires. Even in summer, temperatures can drop below freezing at night in the mountains and the weather can change very quickly. Blizzards in the mountains of NSW can occur at almost any time of the year, even January. Exposure in even moderately cool temperatures can sometimes result in hypothermia – for more information on hypothermia and how to minimise its risks, see p389.

Crime

Australia is a relatively safe place to visit but you should still take reasonable precautions. Don't leave hotel rooms or cars unlocked, and don't leave your valuables unattended or visible through a car window. Sydney and Byron Bay get a dishonourable mention when it comes to theft, so keep an extra-militant eye on your belongings.

On the Road

Australian drivers are generally a courteous bunch, but risks can be posed by rural petrol heads, inner-city speedsters and, particularly, drunk drivers. Potential dangers on the open road include animals, such as kangaroos, which can leap out in front of your vehicle (mainly at dusk); fatigue, caused by travelling long distances without the necessary breaks; and excessive speed. Driving on dirt roads can also be tricky if you're not used to them. For more information on these and other potential dangers see p382 and p382.

Swimming

Popular beaches are patrolled by surf lifesavers, and patrolled areas are marked by flags (for details see the boxed text below). Even so, surf beaches can be dangerous places to swim if you aren't used to the conditions. Undertows (or 'rips') are the main problem. If you find yourself being carried out by a rip, the important thing to do is just keep afloat; don't panic or try to swim against the rip, which will exhaust you. In most cases the current stops within a couple of hundred metres of the shore and you can then swim parallel to the shore for a short way to get out of the rip and make your way back to land.

DISABLED TRAVELLERS

Disability awareness in Australia is pretty high and getting higher. Legislation requires that new accommodation meet accessibility standards, and discrimination by tourism operators is illegal. Many of Australia's key attractions provide access for those with limited mobility, and a number of sites have also begun addressing the needs of visitors with visual or aural impairments; contact attractions in advance to confirm the facilities available for disabled people. Tour operators with accessible vehicles operate from most capital cities.

DISCOUNT CARDS

The **International Student Travel Confederation** (ISTC; www.istc.org) is an international collective of specialist student travel organisations. It's also the body behind the internationally recognised International Student Identity Card (ISIC), which is only issued to full-time students aged 12 years and over, and gives the bearer discounts on accommodation, transport and admission to various attractions. The ISTC also produces the International Youth Travel Card (IYTC or Go25), which is issued to people who are between 12 and 26 years of age and not full-time students, and has benefits equivalent

---

BETWEEN THE FLAGS

On any popular ocean beach in Australia during summer you'll probably find a pair of poles stuck in the sand about 200m apart, each with a red-and-yellow flag on them. They signify that the area of the beach between the flags is patrolled by surf lifeguards. It also means that the area outside the flags may not be safe for swimming because of undertows and currents. If you swim between the flags, help should arrive quickly if you get into trouble; raise your arm (and yell!) if you need help. Outside the flags and on unpatrolled beaches you are, more or less, on your own.

Australia has a strong tradition of surf life-saving, with regular carnivals in which super-fit athletes compete in a series of events such as swimming, surf kayaking and running. The most well-known competition is the Iron Man series. There are surf life-saving clubs all along the east coast and most of the lifeguards are volunteer members.

NSW FOR THE TRAVELLER WITH A DISABILITY

Information

Reliable information is the key ingredient for travellers with a disability and the best source is the **National Information Communication & Awareness Network** (Nican; ☎ /TTY 02-6285 3713, TTY 1800 806 769; www.nican.com.au; 4/2 Phipps Close, Deakin, ACT 2600). It's an Australia-wide directory providing information on access issues, accessible accommodation, sporting and recreational activities, transport and specialist tour operators.

The website of the **Australian Tourist Commission** (www.australia.com) publishes detailed, downloadable information for people with disabilities, including travel and transport tips and contact addresses of organisations in each state. For more on the commission, see p370.

The publication **Easy Access Australia** (www.easyaccessaustralia.com.au) is available from various bookstores and provides details on easily accessible transport, accommodation and attraction options.

A comprehensive website covering public toilets nationwide lists every one that has disability access. For more information, visit www.toiletmap.gov.au.

The **Paraplegic & Quadriplegic Association of NSW** (☎ 02-8741 5600; www.paraquad-nsw.asn.au), provides some information about accommodation and care.

Air

Accepted only by Qantas, the **Carers Concession Card** (☎ 13 13 13, TTY 1800 652 660; www.qantas .com.au), entitles a disabled person and the carer travelling with them to a 50% discount on full economy fares; call Nican (see earlier in this box) for eligibility and an application form. All of Australia's major airports have dedicated parking spaces, wheelchair access to terminals, accessible toilets, and skychairs to convey passengers onto planes via airbridges.

Car Hire

Avis and Hertz offer hire cars with hand controls at no extra charge for pick-up at capital cities and the major airports, but advance notice is required.

The international wheelchair symbol (blue on a white background) for parking in allocated bays is recognised.

Taxi

Most taxi companies in major cities and towns have modified vehicles that will take wheelchairs.

Train

In NSW, **CountryLink** (☎ 13 22 32; www.countrylink.info) has XPT trains that have at least one carriage (usually the buffet car) with a seat removed for a wheelchair and an accessible toilet. In Sydney some, but not all, rail stations are accessible. **CityRail** (☎ 13 15 00; www.cityrail.info) has details.

to the ISIC. A similar ISTC brainchild is the International Teacher Identity Card (ITIC), available to teaching professionals. All three cards are chiefly available from student travel companies.

Senior travellers, and travellers with disabilities, with some form of identification are often eligible for concession prices.

Travellers over 60 years of age (both Australian residents and visitors) will simply need to present current age-proving identification to be eligible for discounts of up to 70% off regular air fares.

EMBASSIES & CONSULATES
Australian Embassies & Consulates

The website of the **Department of Foreign Affairs & Trade** (www.dfat.gov.au) provides a full listing of all Australian diplomatic missions overseas.

Canada Ottawa (☎ 613-236 0841; www.ahc-ottawa.org; Suite 710, 50 O'Connor St, Ottawa, Ontario K1P 6L2) Also in Vancouver and Toronto.

France Paris (☎ 01-40 59 33 00; www.austgov.fr; 4 Rue Jean Rey, 75724 Paris Cedex 15)

Germany Berlin (☎ 030-880 0880; www.australian -embassy.de; Friedrichstrasse 200, 10117 Berlin) Also in Frankfurt.

Ireland Dublin (☎ 01-664 5300; www.australianembassy
.ie; 2nd fl, Fitzwilton House, Wilton Terrace, Dublin 2)
Japan Tokyo (☎ 03-5232 4111; www.australia.or.jp;
2-1-14 Mita, Minato-Ku, Tokyo 108-8361) Also in Osaka,
Nagoya and Fukuoka City.
Netherlands The Hague (☎ 070-310 82 00; www.australian
-embassy.nl; Carnegielaan 4, The Hague 2517 KH)
New Zealand Wellington (☎ 04-473 6411; www.australia
.org.nz; 72-78 Hobson St, Thorndon, Wellington); Auckland
(☎ 09-921 8800; Level 7, Price Waterhouse Coopers Bldg,
186-194 Quay St, Auckland)
Singapore Singapore (☎ 6836 4100; www.singapore
.embassy.gov.au; 25 Napier Rd, Singapore 258507)
South Africa Pretoria (☎ 27 12 342 3781; www.australia
.co.za; 292 Orient Street, Arcadia, Pretoria 0083)
UK London (☎ 020-7379 4334; www.australia.org.uk;
Australia House, The Strand, London WC2B 4LA) Also in
Edinburgh and Manchester.
USA Washington DC (☎ 202-797 3000; www.austemb.org;
1601 Massachusetts Ave NW, Washington DC 20036) Also
in Los Angeles, New York and other major cities.

Embassies & Consulates in Australia

The principal diplomatic representations
to Australia are in Canberra. There are
also representatives in other major cities,
particularly from countries with a strong
connection with Australia such as the USA,
the UK or New Zealand.

Addresses of major offices include the
following.

Canada Canberra (Map p340-1; ☎ 02-6270 4000;
www.dfait-maeci.gc.ca/australia; Commonwealth Ave,
Canberra, ACT 2600); Sydney (☎ 02-9364 3000; Level
5/111 Harrington St, Sydney, NSW 2000)
France Canberra (Map p340-1; ☎ 02-6216 0100; www
.ambafrance-au.org; 6 Perth Ave, Yarralumla, ACT 2600);
Sydney (☎ 02-9261 5779; www.consulfrance-sydney.org;
Level 26, St Martins Tower, 31 Market St, Sydney, NSW 2000)
Germany Canberra (Map p340-1; ☎ 02-6270 1911;
www.germanembassy.org.au; 119 Empire Circuit, Yarra-
lumla, ACT 2600); Sydney (☎ 02-9328 7733; 13 Trelawney
St, Woollahra, NSW 2025)
Ireland Canberra (Map p340-1; ☎ 02-6273 3022;
irishemb@cyberone.com.au; 20 Arkana St, Yarralumla, ACT
2600); Sydney (☎ 02-9231 6999; Level 30, 400 George St,
Sydney, NSW 2000)
Japan Canberra (Map p340-1; ☎ 02-6273 3244; www
.japan.org.au; 112 Empire Circuit, Yarralumla, ACT 2600);
Sydney (☎ 02-9231 3455; Level 34, Colonial Centre, 52
Martin Pl, Sydney, NSW 2000)
Netherlands, The Canberra (Map p340-1; ☎ 02-6220
9400; www.netherlands.org.au; 120 Empire Circuit, Yarra
lumla, ACT 2600); Sydney (☎ 02-9387 6644; Level 23,
Plaza Tower II, 500 Oxford St, Bondi Junction, NSW 2022)

New Zealand Canberra (Map p340-1; ☎ 02-6270 4211;
nzhccba@austarmetro.com.au; Commonwealth Ave, Canberra, ACT 2600); Sydney (☎ 02-8256 2000; nzcgsydney@
bigpond.com; Level 10, 55 Hunter St, Sydney, NSW 2000)
Singapore Canberra (Map p340-1; ☎ 02-6273 3944;
17 Forster Cres, Yarralumla, ACT 2600)
South Africa Canberra (☎ 02-6273 2424; www.rsa.emb
.gov.au; Cnr Rhodes Place & State Circle, Yarralumla,
Canberra, ACT 2600)
UK Canberra (Map p340-1; ☎ 02-6270 6666; www.uk
.emb.gov.au; Commonwealth Ave, Yarralumla, ACT 2600);
Sydney (☎ 02-9247 7521; 16th fl, 1 Macquarie Pl, Sydney
Cove, NSW 2000)
USA Canberra (Map p340-1; ☎ 02-6214 5600; http:
//usembassy-australia.state.gov; 21 Moonah Pl, Yarra
lumla, ACT 2600); Sydney (☎ 02-9373 9200; Level 59,
19-29 Martin Pl, Sydney, NSW 2000)

It's important to realise what your own
embassy – the embassy of the country of
which you are a citizen – can and can't do
to help you if you get into trouble. Generally
speaking, it won't be much help in emergencies if the trouble you're in is even remotely
your own fault. Remember that while in
Australia you are bound by Australian laws.
Your embassy will not be sympathetic if you
end up in jail after committing an offence
locally, even if such actions are legal in your
own country.

In genuine emergencies you might get
some assistance, but only if other channels
have been exhausted. For example, if you
need to get home urgently, a free ticket is
exceedingly unlikely – the embassy would
expect you to have insurance. If you have all
your money and documents stolen, it might
assist with getting a new passport, but a loan
for onward travel is out of the question.

FESTIVALS & EVENTS

Some of the most enjoyable Australian festivals are also the most typically Australian –
like the surf life-saving competitions on
beaches all around the country during
summer; or outback race meetings, which
draw together isolated communities. There
are also some big city-based street festivals,
sporting events and arts festivals that showcase comedy, music and dance, and some
important commemorative get-togethers.

Details of festivals and events that are
grounded in a single place – be it a city, town,
valley or reserve – are provided throughout
the chapters of this book. But the following

events occur throughout a particular region, or the state, or even around the country.

January

Big Day Out (www.bigdayout.com) This huge open-air music concert tours Sydney and the Gold Coast, stopping over for one day in each city. It attracts big-name international acts and dozens of attention-seeking local bands and DJs.

Australia Day This national holiday, commemorating the arrival of the First Fleet in 1788, is observed on 26 January.

Survival Festival The Aboriginal version of Australia Day, also held on 26 January, is marked by Koori music, dance, and arts and crafts displays in Sydney.

Australasian Country Music Festival Tamworth is country music in Australia, and this festival, held on the Australia Day long weekend, is the showcase for the country's top country and western artists.

February/March

Gay & Lesbian Mardi Gras The most colourful event on the Sydney social calendar culminates in a spectacular parade along Oxford St.

Hunter Valley Harvest Festival Wine enthusiasts flock to the Hunter Valley for wine tasting, and grape-picking and -treading contests.

March

Surfest Australia's longest-running professional surf carnival is held at Newcastle Beach.

Canberra Festival This is a 10-day extravaganza in the national capital.

Royal Easter Show Livestock contests and rodeos are held in Sydney.

April

Blues Festival This huge event in Byron Bay attracts up to 10,000 visitors.

May

Sorry Day (www.journeyofhealing.com) On 26 May each year, the anniversary of the tabling in 1997 of the *Bringing Them Home* report, concerned Australians acknowledge the continuing pain and suffering of indigenous people affected by Australia's one-time child-removal practices and policies. Events are held in most cities countrywide.

July

Naidoc Week (www.atsic.gov.au) Communities across Australia celebrate the National Aboriginal and Islander Day of Celebration (inaugurated in 1957), from the annual Melbourne Naidoc Ball to local street festivals.

September

Mudgee Wine Festival Sample Mudgee's finest wine and welcome in the spring at this yearly festival.

October

Bathurst 1000 Motor-racing enthusiasts flock to Bathurst for the annual 1000km touring-car race on the superb Mt Panorama circuit.

Orange National Field Days Large agriculture show in Orange.

November

Melbourne Cup On the first Tuesday in November, Australia's premier horse race is run in Melbourne. Many country towns in NSW schedule racing events to coincide with it.

December & January

Sydney to Hobart Yacht Race (http://rolexsydneyhobart.com) Sydney Harbour is a fantastic sight as hundreds of boats farewell the competitors in the gruelling Sydney to Hobart Yacht Race.

FOOD

Visitors to NSW enjoy the range and wealth of food available in the state's restaurants, markets, delicatessens (delis) and cafés – especially in Sydney – but often in far less populated surrounds as well. The fine dining to be had is in large part due to the abundance of reasonably priced fresh produce, including seafood. Also, many people from different cultures have made their home here, bringing with them a huge range of ethnic cuisines that are now part of the country's culinary repertoire.

Diners who enjoy a pre- or post-digestive puff will need to go outside, as smoking has been made illegal in most enclosed public places in all Australian states and territories, including indoor cafés, restaurants and (sometimes only at mealtime) pub dining areas.

When it comes to major tourist centres, the eating recommendations provided in this book are usually broken down into the main food-infatuated areas or suburbs. The innovative food offered in top-quality eateries doesn't necessarily cost a fortune. Best value are the modern cafés, where you can get a good meal in casual surroundings for under $20. A full cooked breakfast at a café costs around $10. Some inner-city pubs offer upmarket restaurant-style fare, but most pubs serve standard (often large-portion) bistro meals, usually in the $10 to $19 range, and these are served in the dining room or lounge bar. Smart restaurants will start at $20 per person and go rapidly upwards from there. For general opening hours, breakfast is normally served between 6am and 11am, lunch starts around noon till about 3pm and dinner usually starts after 6pm. But note that in rural areas, the kitchen may close by 8pm.

It's customary to tip in restaurants and upmarket cafés if the service warrants it – a gratuity of between 5% to 10% of the bill is the norm.

See p39 for full details on NSW's specialities and modern Australian (Mod Oz) cuisine.

GAY & LESBIAN TRAVELLERS

Australia is a popular destination for gay and lesbian travellers, with the so-called 'pink tourism' appeal of Sydney especially big, thanks largely to the city's annual, high-profile and spectacular Sydney Gay & Lesbian Mardi Gras.

In Sydney and along the east coast, there are tour operators, travel agents, resorts and other accommodation places that are either exclusively gay and lesbian, or make a point of welcoming gays.

In NSW, certain areas are the focus of the gay and lesbian communities, among them Oxford St and King's Cross in Sydney, the Blue Mountains, Hunter Valley and the South Coast.

In terms of major gay and lesbian events, there's the aforementioned **Sydney Gay & Lesbian Mardi Gras** (www.mardigras.org.au) in February and March. Sydney also hosted the 6th international Gay Games in November 2002, further enhancing its reputation as the San Francisco of the southern hemisphere. See also the Gay & Lesbian Sydney boxed text, p61.

In general Australians are open-minded about homosexuality, but the further into the country you get, the more likely you are to run into overt homophobia. Homosexual acts are legal in all states but the age of consent between males varies – in the Australian Capital Territory (ACT) and NSW it's 16 years.

Publications & Contacts

All major cities have gay newspapers, which are available from gay and lesbian venues, and from newsagents in popular gay and lesbian residential areas.

The website of **Gay & Lesbian Tourism Australia** (GALTA; www.galta.com.au) is a good place to look

for general information, though you need to become a member to receive the full benefits. Other helpful websites:
Gay Australia (www.gayaustralia.com.au)
Pinkboard (www.pinkboard.com.au) Sydney-based.

Tour Operators

Tour operators in Sydney that cater exclusively or partly for gay and lesbian travellers:
Beyond the Blue (☎ 02-8399 0070; 685-687 South Dowling St, Surry Hills, NSW 2010)
Boyz Brick Road (☎ 02-9380 4115; 102 Oxford St, Darlinghurst, NSW 2010)

HOLIDAYS
Public Holidays

The following is a list of the main national and state public holidays. As the timing can vary from state to state, check locally for precise dates.

National
New Year's Day 1 January
Australia Day 26 January
Easter (Good Friday to Easter Monday inclusive) March/April
Anzac Day 25 April
Queen's Birthday (except WA) 2nd Monday in June
Queen's Birthday (WA) Last Monday in September
Christmas Day 25 December
Boxing Day 26 December

Australian Capital Territory
Canberra Day March
Bank Holiday 1st Monday in August
Labour Day 1st Monday in October

New South Wales
Bank Holiday 1st Monday in August
Labour Day 1st Monday in October

School Holidays

The Christmas holiday season, from mid-December to late January, is part of the summer school holidays – it's the time you are most likely to find transport and accommodation booked out, and long, restless queues at tourist attractions. There are three shorter school holiday periods during the year. They fall roughly from early to mid-April, late June to mid-July, and late September to early October.

INSURANCE

Don't underestimate the importance of a good travel-insurance policy that covers theft, loss and medical problems – nothing is guaranteed to ruin your holiday plans quicker than an accident or having that brand-new digital camera stolen. Most policies offer lower and higher medical-expense options; the higher ones are chiefly for countries that have extremely high medical costs, such as the USA. There is a wide variety of policies available, so compare the small print.

Some policies specifically exclude designated 'dangerous activities' such as scuba diving, skiing and even bushwalking. If you plan on doing any of these things, make sure the policy you choose fully covers you for your activity of choice.

You may prefer a policy that pays doctors or hospitals direct, rather than your having to pay on the spot and claim later. If you have to claim later make sure you keep all documentation. Some policies ask you to call back (reverse charges or collect) to a centre in your home country where an immediate assessment of your problem is made. Check that the policy covers ambulances and emergency medical evacuations by air.

See also Before You Go (p386) in the Health chapter. For information on insurance matters relating to cars that are bought or rented, see p380.

INTERNET ACCESS
Email and Internet access is fairly easy in Sydney and other popular destinations in NSW.

Access Points
Most public libraries have Internet access, but generally there are a limited number of terminals and these are provided for research needs, not for travellers to check their emails – so head for a cybercafé first. You'll find Internet cafés in cities, sizeable towns and pretty much anywhere that travellers congregate. The cost ranges from under $5 an hour in the cut-throat King's Cross places in Sydney to $10 an hour in more remote locations. The average is about $6 an hour, usually with a minimum of 10 minutes' access. Most youth hostels and backpacker places can hook you up, as can many hotels and caravan parks.

Throughout much of NSW look for **Community Technology Centres** (CTC; www.ctc.nsw

.gov.au), which provide Internet access for modest fees.

Hooking Up
If you're bringing your palmtop or notebook computer check with your Internet Service Provider (ISP) to find out if there are access numbers you can dial into in NSW. Most large international ISPs have numbers for Sydney.

Australia primarily uses the RJ-45 telephone plugs although you may see Telstra EXI-160 four-pin plugs – electronics shops such as Tandy and Dick Smith should be able to help.

LEGAL MATTERS
Most travellers to NSW will have no contact with the Australian police or any other part of the legal system. Those that do are most likely to experience it while driving.

There is a significant police presence on the country's roads, with the power to stop your car and ask to see your licence (you're required to carry it), check your vehicle for roadworthiness, and also to insist that you take a breath test to check your blood alcohol level – needless to say, drink-driving offences are taken very seriously here.

First offenders caught with small amounts of illegal drugs are likely to receive a fine rather than go to jail, but nonetheless the recording of a conviction against you may affect your visa status.

If you are arrested, it's your right to telephone a friend, relative or lawyer before any formal questioning begins. Legal aid is available only in serious cases and only to the truly needy (for links to Legal Aid offices see www.nla.aust.net.au). However, many solicitors do not charge for an initial consultation.

The legal driving age is 17 and the drinking age is 18.

MAPS
Good-quality road and topographical maps are plentiful in Australia. The NRMA (p379) is a dependable source of road maps especially for rural NSW. Local tourist offices usually supply free maps, though the quality varies.

Lonely Planet publishes the *Australia Road Atlas*, an easy-to-use, comprehensive book covering the entire country. Lonely Planet also produces a handy fold-out city map of Sydney.

For bushwalking and other outdoor activities for which large-scale maps are essential, browse the topographic sheets put out by **Geoscience Australia** (☎ 1800 800 173, 02-6201 4201; www.ga.gov.au; Scrivener Bldg, Dunlop Ct, Fern Hill Park, Bruce, ACT 2617), which is part of the Department of Industry, Tourism & Resources. Many of the more popular sheets are usually available over the counter at shops that sell specialist bushwalking gear and outdoor equipment.

MONEY

Changing foreign currency or travellers cheques is usually no problem at banks throughout NSW. Exchange rates are listed on the inside back cover.

In this book, unless otherwise stated, all prices given in dollars refer to Australian dollars. For an idea of the money required to travel in NSW, see p9.

ATMs

ATMs are common in NSW and are linked to international networks. They are an excellent way to procure local currency and avoid the hassle of carrying travellers cheques or large sums of cash.

Cash

Australia's currency is the Australian dollar, made up of 100 cents. There are 5c, 10c, 20c, 50c, $1 and $2 coins, and $5, $10, $20, $50 and $100 notes. Although the smallest coin in circulation is 5c, prices are often still marked in single cents and then rounded to the nearest 5c when you come to pay.

Credit Cards

MasterCard and Visa are widely accepted. American Express is limited more to major towns and destinations.

The most flexible option is to carry both a credit and an ATM or debit card.

Taxes & Refunds

The Goods & Services Tax (GST), is a flat 10% tax on all goods and services – accommodation, eating out, transport, electrical and other goods, books, furniture, clothing and so on. There are, however, some exceptions, such as basic foods (milk, bread, fruits and vege-

tables etc). By law the tax is included in the quoted or shelf prices, so all prices in this book are GST-inclusive. International air and sea travel to/from Australia is GST-free, as is domestic air travel when purchased outside Australia by nonresidents.

If you purchase new or second-hand goods with a total minimum value of $300 from any one supplier no more than 30 days before you leave Australia, you are entitled under the Tourist Refund Scheme (TRS) to a refund of any GST paid. The scheme only applies to goods you take with you as hand luggage, or wear, onto the plane or ship. Also note that the refund is valid for goods bought from more than one supplier, but only if at least $300 is spent in each. For more details, contact the **Australian Customs Service** (☎ 1300 363 263, 02-6275 6666; www.customs.gov.au).

Travellers Cheques

Amex, Thomas Cook and other well-known international brands of travellers cheques are easily exchanged. You need to present your passport for identification when cashing them.

Still, increasingly, international travellers simply withdraw cash from ATMs, enjoying the convenience and the usually good exchange rates.

POST
Letters

Australia's postal services are efficient and reasonably cheap. It costs 50c to send a standard letter or postcard within the country. **Australia Post** (www.auspost.com.au) has divided international destinations into two regions: Asia-Pacific and Rest of the World; airmail letters up to 50g cost $1.10/1.65, respectively. The cost of a postcard (up to 20g) is $1 and an aerogram to any country is 85c.

Parcels

There are five international parcel zones and rates vary by distance and class of service.

Sending & Receiving Mail

All post offices will hold mail for visitors, and some city GPOs (main or general post offices) have very busy poste restante sections. You need to provide some form of identification (such as a passport) to collect mail.

See p358 for post office opening times.

SOLO TRAVELLERS

People travelling alone in NSW face the unpredictability that is an inherent part of making contact with entire communities of strangers: sometimes you'll be completely ignored as if you didn't exist, and other times you'll be greeted with such enthusiasm it's as if you've been spontaneously adopted. Suffice to say that the latter moments will likely become highlights of your trip.

Solo travellers are a common sight throughout Australia and there is certainly no stigma attached to lone visitors. But in some places there can be an expectation that the visitor should engage in some way with the locals, particularly in rural pubs where keeping to yourself can prove harder than it sounds. Women travelling on their own should exercise caution when in less-populated areas, and will find that guys can get annoyingly attentive in drinking establishments (with mining-town pubs arguably the nadir); see also Women Travellers (p371).

TELEPHONE

There are a number of providers offering various services. The two main players are the mostly government-owned **Telstra** (www .telstra.com.au) and the fully private **Optus** (www.optus.com.au). Both are also major players in the mobile (cell) phone market, along with **Vodafone** (www.vodafone.com.au).

Information & Toll-Free Calls

Numbers starting with ☎ 190 are usually recorded information services, costing anything from 35c to $5 or more per minute (more from mobiles and payphones). To make a reverse-charge (collect) call from any public or private phone, just dial ☎ 1800-REVERSE (738 3773), or ☎ 12 550.

Toll-free numbers (prefix ☎ 1800) can be called free of charge from anywhere in the country, though they may not be accessible from certain areas or from mobile phones. Calls to numbers beginning with ☎ 13 or ☎ 1300 are charged at the rate of a local call; the numbers can usually be dialled Australia-wide, but may be applicable only to a specific state or STD district. Telephone numbers beginning with either ☎ 1800, ☎ 13 or ☎ 1300 cannot be dialled from outside Australia.

International Calls

Most pay phones allow ISD (International Subscriber Dialling) calls, the cost and international dialling code of which will vary depending on which provider you're using. International calls from Australia are very cheap and subject to specials that reduce the rates even more, so it's worth shopping around – look in the *Yellow Pages* for a list of providers.

The **Country Direct service** (☎ 1800 801 800) connects callers in Australia with operators in nearly 60 countries to make reverse-charge (collect) or credit-card calls.

When calling overseas you need to dial the international access code from Australia (☎ 0011 or ☎ 0018), the country code and the area code (without the initial 0). So for a London number you'd dial ☎ 0011-44-20, then the number. Also, certain operators will have you dial a special code to access their service.

Following is a list of some country codes:

Country	International country code
France	☎ 33
Germany	☎ 49
Japan	☎ 81
Netherlands	☎ 31
New Zealand	☎ 64
UK	☎ 44
USA & Canada	☎ 1

If dialling Australia from overseas, the country code is ☎ 61 and you need to drop the 0 (zero), such as 02 in NSW and ACT, in the state/territory area codes.

Local Calls

Calls from private phones cost 15c to 25c; local calls from public phones cost 40c – both with unlimited talk time. Calls to mobile phones cost more and are timed. Blue or gold phones that you sometimes find in hotel lobbies or other businesses usually cost a minimum of 50c for a local call.

Long-Distance Calls & Area Codes

For long-distance calls, Australia uses four STD (Subscriber Trunk Dialling) area codes. STD calls can be made from virtually any public phone and are cheaper during off-peak hours. Broadly, the main area codes are as follows:

State/territory	Area code
ACT	☎ 02
NSW	☎ 02
NT	☎ 08
QLD	☎ 07
SA	☎ 08
TAS	☎ 03
VIC	☎ 03
WA	☎ 08

In some border areas, NSW uses each of the four neighbouring codes.

Mobile (Cell) Phones

Local numbers with the prefixes ☎ 04xx or ☎ 04xxx belong to mobile phones. Australia's two mobile networks – digital GSM and digital CDMA – service more than 90% of the population but leave vast tracts of the country uncovered. Sydney, Canberra and the coast get good reception, but elsewhere (apart from major towns) it's haphazard or nonexistent.

Australia's digital network is compatible with GSM 900 and 1800 (used in Europe), but generally not with the systems used in the USA or Japan. It's easy and cheap enough to get connected short-term, though, as the main service providers (Telstra, Optus and Vodafone) all have prepaid mobile systems.

Phonecards

A wide range of phonecards is available from newsagents and post offices for a fixed dollar value (usually $10, $20, $30 etc), and can be used with any public or private phone by dialling a toll-free access number and then the PIN number on the card. Once again it's well worth shopping around, as call rates vary from company to company. Some public phones also accept credit cards.

TIME

Australia is divided into three time zones. NSW and the ACT are on Eastern Standard Time (GMT/UTC plus 10 hours) which also covers Tasmania, Victoria and Queensland. There are minor exceptions – for instance, Broken Hill is on Central time (plus 9½ hours). When it's noon in Sydney, the time in London is 3am (April to October) or 1am (November to March).

For more on international timing, see www.timeanddate.com/worldclock.

Daylight saving – for which clocks are put forward an hour – operates in NSW during the warmer months (October to March).

TOURIST INFORMATION

Australia's and NSW's highly self-conscious tourism infrastructure means that when looking for information you can easily end up being buried neck-deep in brochures, booklets, maps and leaflets, or get utterly swamped with detail during an online surf.

The **Australian Tourist Commission** (ATC; ☎ 1300 361 650, 02-9360 1111; www.australia.com; Level 4, 80 William St, Woolloomooloo, NSW 2011) is the national government body charged with improving foreign tourist relations. A good place for pre-trip research is the commission's website, which has information in nine languages (including French, German, Japanese and Spanish), quite a bit of it covering NSW.

Tourism New South Wales (☎ 02-9931 1111; www.visitnsw.com.au) is the state's tourism body and offers no end of information, touring ideas and contacts.

Local Tourist Offices

Within NSW, tourist information is disseminated by various local offices. Almost every decent-sized town in NSW seems to maintain a tourist office of some type and in many cases they are very good, with friendly staff (often volunteers) providing local information. If you're going to book accommodation or tours from local offices, bear in mind that they often only promote businesses that are paying members of the local tourist association. Details of local tourism offices are given in the relevant city and town sections throughout this book.

VISAS

All visitors to Australia need a visa – only New Zealand nationals are exempt, and even they receive a 'special category' visa on arrival. Visa application forms are available from Australian diplomatic missions overseas, travel agents or the website of the **Department of Immigration & Multicultural & Indigenous Affairs** (☎ 13 18 81; www.immi.gov.au). There are several types of visa, as follows.

Electronic Travel Authority (ETA)

Many visitors can get an ETA through any International Air Transport Association (IATA)–registered travel agent or overseas airline. They make the application direct when you buy a ticket and issue the ETA, which replaces the usual visa stamped in your passport – it's common practice for travel agents to charge a fee, in the vicinity of US$25, for issuing an ETA. This system is available to passport holders of some 33 countries, including the UK, USA and Canada, most European and Scandinavian countries, Malaysia, Singapore, Japan and Korea.

You can also make an online ETA application at www.eta.immi.gov.au, where no fees apply.

Tourist Visas

Short-term tourist visas have largely been replaced by the Electronic Travel Authority (ETA; see earlier). However, if you are from a country not covered by the ETA, or you want to stay longer than three months, you'll need to apply for a visa. Standard visas (which cost $65) allow one (in some cases multiple) entry, stays of up to three months, and are valid for use within 12 months of issue. A long-stay tourist visa (also $65) can allow a visit of up to a year.

Visa Extensions

Visitors are allowed a maximum stay of 12 months, including extensions. Visa extensions are made through the Department of Immigration & Multicultural & Indigenous Affairs and it's best to apply at least two or three weeks before your visa expires. The application fee is $160 – it's nonrefundable, even if your application is rejected.

Working Holiday-Maker (WHM) Visas

Young, single visitors from Canada, Cyprus, Denmark, Finland, Germany, Hong Kong, Ireland, Japan, Korea, Malta, the Netherlands, Norway, Sweden and the UK are eligible for a WHM visa, which allows you to visit for up to 12 months and gain casual employment. 'Young' is defined as between 18 and 30 years of age.

WOMEN TRAVELLERS

Australia, including NSW, is generally a safe place for women travellers, although the usual sensible precautions apply. It's best to avoid walking alone late at night in any of the major cities and towns. And if you're out on the town, always keep enough money aside for a taxi back to your accommodation. The same applies to outback and rural towns where there are often a lot of unlit, semideserted streets between you and your temporary home. When the pubs and bars close and there are inebriated people roaming around, it's not a great time to be out and about. Lone women should also be wary of staying in basic pub accommodation unless it looks safe and well managed.

Sexual harassment is an ongoing problem, be it via an aggressive cosmopolitan male or a rural bloke living a less-than-enlightened pro-forma bush existence. Stereotypically, the further you get from 'civilisation' (ie the big cities), the less enlightened your average Aussie male is probably going to be about women's issues. Having said that, many women travellers say that they have met the friendliest, most down-to-earth blokes in outback pubs and remote roadhouse stops. And cities still have to put up with their unfortunate share of 'ocker' males who regard a bit of sexual harassment as a right, and chauvinism as a desirable trait.

Lone female hitchers are tempting fate – hitching with a male companion is safer.

Transport

CONTENTS

GETTING THERE & AWAY

They don't call Australia the land 'down under' for nothing. It's a long way from just about everywhere, and getting here usually means a long-haul flight. That 'over the horizon' feeling doesn't stop once you're here either – even in just one state like New South Wales (NSW), the distances between key towns can be vast, requiring a minimum of a day or two of highway cruising or dirt-road jostling to traverse.

AIR

There are many competing airlines and a wide variety of air fares to choose from if you're flying in from Asia, Europe or North America, but you'll still pay a lot for a flight. Because of Australia's size and diverse climate, any time of the year can prove busy for inbound tourists – if you plan to fly at a particularly popular period (Christmas is a notoriously difficult time to get into Sydney) or on a particularly popular route (such as Hong Kong, Bangkok or Singapore to Sydney), make your arrangements well ahead.

Disembarking in Australia is generally a straightforward affair, with only the usual customs declarations and the fight to be first to the luggage carousel to endure. If you're flying in with Qantas, Air New Zealand,

> **THINGS CHANGE**
>
> The information in this chapter is particularly vulnerable to change: prices for international travel are volatile, routes are introduced and cancelled, schedules change, special deals come and go, and rules and visa requirements are amended.
>
> Airlines and governments seem to take a perverse pleasure in making price structures and regulations as complicated as possible. You should check directly with the airline or a travel agent to make sure you understand how a fare (and ticket) works. In addition, the travel industry is highly competitive and there are many lurks and perks.
>
> The upshot of this is that you should get opinions, quotes and advice from as many airlines and travel agents as possible before you part with your cash. The details given in this chapter should be regarded as pointers and are not a substitute for your own careful, up-to-date research.

British Airways, Cathay Pacific, Japan Airlines or Singapore Airlines, ask the carrier about the 'express' passenger card, which will speed your way through customs.

Recent global instability, thanks (or rather, no thanks) to terrorism and war-fever have meant conspicuously increased security in Australian airports, both in domestic and international terminals, and you may find customs procedures now more time-consuming. This is especially true in Sydney, where the immigration lines can seem endless.

For more information on customs and quarantine, see p360.

Airports & Airlines

Australia has a number of international gateways, with Sydney being the busiest. Sydney's **Kingsford Smith Airport** (code SYD; ☎ 02-9667 9111; www.sydneyairport.com.au) is 10km south of the city centre, in Mascot.

Australia's overseas carrier is Qantas. Viewed as one of the world's safest airlines, it flies chiefly to runways across Europe, North America, Asia and the Pacific. A low-fare subsidiary of Qantas, Australian

Airlines, has a growing list of nonstop flights to international destinations.

Airlines that visit Sydney include the following. (Note, all phone numbers mentioned here are for dialling from within Sydney.)

Air Canada (☎ 1300 655 757, 02-9286 8900; www .aircanada.ca; airline code AC; hub Pearson International Airport, Toronto)

Air New Zealand (☎ 13 24 76, 02-8258 8999; www.airnz .com.au; airline code NZ; hub Auckland International Airport)

Australian Airlines (☎ 1300 799 798; www.australian airlines.com.au; airline code AO; hub Kingsford Smith Airport, Sydney)

British Airways (☎ 1300 767 177, 02-9258 3200; www .britishairways.com.au; airline code BA; hub Heathrow Airport, London)

Cathay Pacific (☎ 13 17 47, 02-9667 3816; www .cathaypacific.com.au; airline code CX; hub Hong Kong International Airport)

Emirates (☎ 1300 303 777, 02-9290 9776; www.emirates .com; airline code EK; hub Dubai International Airport)

Garuda Indonesia (☎ 1300 365 330, 02-9334 9900; www.garuda-indonesia.com; airline code GA; hub Soekarno-Hatta International Airport, Jakarta)

Gulf Air (☎ 13 12 23, 02-9244 2199; www.gulfairco.com; airline code GF; hub Abu Dhabi International Airport)

Japan Airlines (☎ 02-9272 1100; www.jal.com; airline code JL; hub Narita Airport, Tokyo)

KLM (☎ 1300 303 747, 02-9231 6333; www.klm.com; airline code KL; hub Schiphol Airport, Amsterdam)

Lufthansa (☎ 1300 655 727; www.lufthansa.com; airline code LH; hub Frankfurt Airport)

Malaysia Airlines (☎ 13 26 27, 02-9364 3500; www .malaysiaairlines.com.au; airline code MH; hub Kuala Lumpur International Airport)

Qantas (☎ 13 13 13; www.qantas.com.au; airline code QF; hub Kingsford Smith Airport, Sydney)

Singapore Airlines (☎ 13 10 11, 02-9350 0100; www .singaporeair.com.au; airline code SQ; hub Changi International Airport)

South African Airways (☎ 1800 099 281, 02-9223 4402/4448; www.flysaa.com; airline code SA; hub Johannesburg International Airport)

Thai Airways International (☎ 1300 651 960, 02-9251 1922; www.thaiairways.com.au; airline code TG; hub Bangkok International Airport)

United Airlines (☎ 13 17 77, 02-9292 4111; www .unitedairlines.com.au; airline code UA; hub San Francisco International Airport)

Passports

There are no restrictions when it comes to citizens of foreign countries entering Australia. If you have a visa (p370), you should be fine.

ECONOMY-CLASS SYNDROME

Deep vein thrombosis (DVT) is a relatively rare but potentially serious condition that may develop when flying. DVT is the formation of a blood clot, usually in the legs, caused by sitting in cramped conditions for an extended period. It can be fatal if the clot moves to the heart or lungs.

The term 'Economy-Class Syndrome' is a bit of a misnomer since it can happen in any class, and indeed any situation. Awareness of the link between DVT and flying economy class heightened a few years ago when an Australian passenger died at Heathrow airport after a long-haul flight. Many passengers have since come forward to say they experienced blood clotting during or after flying.

You can't really avoid the flight to Australia, but you can get up and walk around during the flight, factor in stopovers rather than taking a direct flight, and see your doctor prior to flying if you feel you may be at risk. The elderly and overweight are most at risk of DVT complications.

Tickets

Be sure you research the options carefully to make sure you get the best deal. The Internet is a vital resource for checking airline prices. Note that many of the sites also have deals on business-class tickets.

Automated online ticket sales work well if you're doing a simple one-way or return trip on specified dates, but are no substitute for a travel agent with the lowdown on special deals, strategies for avoiding stopovers and other useful advice.

Paying by credit card offers some protection if you unwittingly end up dealing with a rogue fly-by-night agency in your search for the cheapest fare, as most card issuers provide refunds if you can prove you didn't get what you paid for.

For online bookings, start with the following websites.

Cheap Flights (www.cheapflight.com) Very informative site with specials, airline information and flight searches covering the USA and other regions.

Cheapest Flights (www.cheapestflights.co.uk) Cheap worldwide flights from the UK; get in early for the bargains.

Expedia (www.expedia.msn.com) A vast travel site; mainly US-related.

Flight Centre International (www.flightcentre.com) Respected operator handling direct flights, with sites for Australia, New Zealand, the UK, the USA and Canada.

Orbitz (www.orbitz.com) Excellent site for web-only fares for US airlines.

STA (www.statravel.com) Prominent in international student travel, but you don't necessarily have to be a student; site linked to worldwide STA sites.

Travel Online (www.travelonline.co.nz) Good place to check worldwide flights from New Zealand.

Travel.com (www.travel.com.au) Good Australian site; look up fares and flights into and out of the country.

Travelocity (www.travelocity.com) US site that allows you to search fares (in US$) to and from practically anywhere.

Roundtheworld.com (www.roundtheworldflights.com) This excellent site allows you to build your own trips from the UK, with up to six stops. A four-stop trip including Asia, Australia and the USA costs from £800.

DEPARTURE TAX

There is a $38 departure tax when leaving Australia. This is included in the price of airline tickets.

INTERCONTINENTAL (RTW) TICKETS

If you're flying to Australia from the other side of the world, round-the-world (RTW) tickets can be real bargains. They are generally put together by the two biggest airline alliances, **Star Alliance** (www.staralliance.com) and **Oneworld** (www.oneworldalliance.com), and give you a limited period (usually a year) in which to circumnavigate the globe. You can go anywhere the carrying airlines go, as long as you stay within the set mileage or number of stops and don't backtrack. An alternative type of RTW ticket is one put together by a travel agent. These are usually more expensive than airline RTW fares but allow you to devise your own itinerary. RTW tickets start from around UK£800 from the UK or around US$1800 from the USA.

CIRCLE PACIFIC TICKETS

A Circle Pacific ticket is similar to a RTW ticket but covers a more limited region, using a combination of airlines to connect Australia, New Zealand, North America and Asia with stopover options in the Pacific Islands. As with RTW tickets, there are restrictions and limits as to how many stopovers you can take. Star Alliance offers a good one with various prices for all classes of service.

From Asia

Most Asian countries offer fairly competitive air-fare deals, with Bangkok, Singapore and Hong Kong being the best places to shop around for discount tickets.

Flights between Hong Kong and Australia are notoriously heavily booked. Flights to/from Bangkok and Singapore are often part of the longer Europe-to-Australia route so they are also sometimes full. The motto of the story is to plan your preferred itinerary well in advance.

Hong Kong's travel market can be unpredictable, but excellent bargains are sometimes available. Some local agents:

Phoenix Services (☎ 2722 7378)

STA Travel Bangkok (☎ 02-236 0262; www.statravel.co.th); Singapore (☎ 65-6737 7188; www.statravel.com.sg); Tokyo (☎ 03-5391 3205; www.statravel.co.jp)

From Canada

The air routes from Canada are similar to those from mainland USA, with most Toronto and Vancouver flights stopping in one US city such as Los Angeles or Honolulu before heading on to Australia. Air Canada flies from Vancouver to Sydney via Honolulu.

Canadian discount air-ticket sellers are known as consolidators (although you won't see a sign on the door saying 'Consolidator') and their air fares tend to be about 10% higher than those sold in the USA.

Travel Cuts (☎ 800-667 2887; www.travelcuts.com) is Canada's national student travel agency and has offices in all major cities.

From Continental Europe

From the major destinations in Europe, most flights travel via one of the Asian capitals. Some flights are also routed through London before arriving in Australia via Singapore, Bangkok, Hong Kong or Kuala Lumpur.

Fares from Paris in the low/high season cost from €1000/1200. Some agents in Paris:

Nouvelles Frontières (☎ 08-2500 0825; www.nouvelles-frontieres.fr) Also has branches outside of Paris.

OTU Voyages (☎ 01-4029 1212; www.otu.fr) Student-/youth-oriented, with offices in many cities.

Usit Connect Voyages (☎ 01-4329 6950; www.usitconnections.fr) Student/youth specialists, with offices in many cities.

Voyageurs du Monde (☎ 01-4286 1600; www.vdm.com/vdm) Has branches throughout France.

A good option in the Dutch travel industry is **Holland International** (☎ 070-307 6307; www .hollandinternational.nl).

In Germany, good travel agencies include the Berlin branch of **STA Travel** (☎ 030-311 0950; www.statravel.de).

From New Zealand

Air New Zealand and Qantas operate a network of flights linking Auckland, Wellington and Christchurch in New Zealand with Sydney. Also look for foreign carriers like Emirates, which offers some reasonable fares.

Other trans-Tasman options:

Flight Centre (☎ 0800 243 544; www.flightcentre.co.nz) Has a large central office in Auckland and many branches throughout the country.

Freedom Air (☎ 0800 600 500; www.freedomair.com) An Air New Zealand subsidiary that operates direct flights and offers excellent rates year-round.

STA Travel (☎ 09-309 0458; www.statravel.co.nz) Has offices in various cities.

From the UK & Ireland

There are two routes from the UK: the western route via the USA and the Pacific, and the eastern route via the Middle East and Asia; flights are usually cheaper and more frequent on the latter. Some of the best deals around are with Emirates, Gulf Air, Malaysia Airlines, Japan Airlines and Thai Airways International. Unless there are special deals on offer, British Airways, Singapore Airlines and Qantas generally have higher fares but may offer a more direct route.

Discount air travel is big business in London. Advertisements for many travel agencies appear in the travel sections of the weekend broadsheet newspapers, in *Time Out*, the *Evening Standard* and in *TNT*, a free magazine .

A popular agent in the UK is the ubiquitous **STA Travel** (☎ 0870-160 0599; www.statravel.co.uk).

From the USA

Airlines directly connecting Australia nonstop across the Pacific with Los Angeles or San Francisco include Qantas, Air New Zealand and United Airlines. There are also numerous airlines offering flights via Asia, with stopover possibilities including Tokyo, Kuala Lumpur, Bangkok, Hong Kong and Singapore; and via the Pacific

with stopover possibilities like Nadi (Fiji), Rarotonga (Cook Islands), Tahiti (French Polynesia) and Auckland (NZ).

As in Canada, discount travel agents in the USA are known as consolidators. San Francisco is the ticket-consolidator capital of America, although some good deals can be found in Los Angeles, New York and other big cities.

The largest student travel organisation in America is **STA Travel** (☎ 800-777 0112; www .statravel.com).

LAND

See the Getting Around section for bus (p377) and train (p384) services between NSW and other parts of Australia.

Border Crossings

There are three main road routes to/from NSW and the rest of Australia.

East Coast North The Pacific Hwy follows the East Coast north into Queensland and on to Brisbane.

East Coast South The Princes Hwy (Hwy 1) follows the East Coast south into Victoria and on to Melbourne.

Inland The Hume Fwy/Hwy (Hwy 31) is the shortest route to Melbourne from Sydney and links with Wagga and Canberra.

As well, there are numerous other options, including remote tracks right across the outback.

See the Getting Around section (p376) for road rules and other considerations such as quarantine rules for driving to NSW.

SEA

International cruise lines are increasingly serving Sydney. **Princess Cruises** (www.princess.com) operates a variety of routes around Australia and New Zealand. However these voyages are mainly geared for travellers starting and ending their trip in the same city, such as Sydney. You'll have to look around for options that let you go one way.

Another option is travel by freighter. These huge container ships circumnavigate the globe and it is possible to book trips from both the US and UK to Sydney. However, note that ports of call may be remote container ports lacking in charm, and life aboard ship will be the exact opposite of the boozy excesses promised by cruise lines.

For details, try www.freighterworld.com and www.strandtravel.co.uk.

GETTING AROUND

AIR

Australia is so vast that flying is common between the far-flung cities. Within NSW however, the main route is really just Sydney to Canberra.

All domestic flights are nonsmoking.

Airlines in Australia

Qantas is the chief domestic airline, with able competition provided by Virgin Blue. Small towns in NSW are often served by subsidiaries and affiliates of Qantas, flying under the QantasLink moniker.

Regional airlines:

Jetstar (☎ 13 15 38; http://jetstar.com) At the time of writing, this Qantas-owned newcomer on the low-fare scene was due to start domestic flights in late May.

Qantas (☎ 13 13 13; www.qantas.com.au) Qantas is the chief domestic airline.

QantasLink (☎ 13 13 13; www.qantas.com.au)

Regional Express (Rex; ☎ 13 17 13, 02-6393 5550; www.regionalexpress.com.au) Flies to Sydney, Melbourne, Adelaide, Canberra and Devonport, as well as 12 other destinations in NSW, Victoria, South Australia and Tasmania.

Virgin Blue (☎ 13 67 89; www.virginblue.com.au) Highly competitive, Virgin Blue flies all over Australia – Virgin fares are cheaper if booked online ($10/20 less per one-way/return ticket).

Air Passes

With discounting being the norm these days, air passes are not great value. Qantas' **Boomerang Pass** (☎ 13 13 13) can only be purchased overseas and involves buying coupons for either short-haul flights (eg Sydney to Canberra) at $260 one way, or multizone sectors (including New Zealand and the Pacific) for $330. You must purchase a minimum of two coupons before you arrive in Australia, and once here you can buy up to eight more.

Regional Express has a **Rex Backpacker** (☎ 13 17 13) scheme, where international visitors (Australian residents aren't eligible) pay $500 for one month's worth of unlimited travel on the airline – standby fares only.

BICYCLE

Australia has much to offer cyclists, from leisurely bike paths winding through most major cities (Canberra has one of the most extensive networks) to thousands of kilometres of good country roads where you can wear out your chain wheels. Mountainous is not an adjective that applies to this country; instead, there's lots of flat countryside and gently rolling hills.

Australia's national cycling body is the **Bicycle Federation of Australia** (☎ 02-6249 6761; www.bfa.asn.au). Each state and territory (except the Northern Territory; NT) has a touring organisation that can also help with cycling information and put you in touch with touring clubs.

Bicycle New South Wales (☎ 02-9283 5200; www.bicyclensw.org.au; 822 George St, Sydney; ☻ 9am-5.30pm Mon-Fri) Excellent organisation; a stop by the office for advice, maps and books is worthwhile.

Pedal Power ACT (☎ 02-6248 7995; www.pedalpower.org.au)

Bicycle helmets are compulsory in NSW, as are white front lights and red rear lights for riding at night.

If bringing your own bike, check with your airline for costs and the degree of dismantling and packing required. Within Australia, bus companies require that you dismantle your bike, and some don't guarantee that the bike will travel on the same bus as you. On trains, supervise the loading and, if possible, tie your bike upright. Check for possible restrictions: most intercity trains will only carry two to three boxed bikes per service.

Much of NSW was settled on the principle of not having more than a day's horse ride between pubs, so it's possible to plan even ultralong routes and still get a shower at the end of each day. Most riders carry camping equipment but, on the east coast at least, it's feasible to travel from town to town staying in hostels, hotels or caravan parks.

You can get by with standard road maps but, as you'll probably want to avoid both the highways and the low-grade unsealed roads, the government series is best. The 1:250,000 scale is the most suitable, though you'll need a lot of maps if you're going far. The next scale up, 1:1,000,000, is adequate and is widely available in speciality map shops.

Carry plenty of water to avoid becoming dehydrated. Cycling in the summer heat can be made more endurable by wearing a helmet with a peak (or a cap under your helmet), using plenty of sunscreen, not cycling in the middle of the day, and drinking lots of water (not soft drinks). It can get very cold in the mountains, so pack appropriate clothing.

Outback travel needs to be properly planned, with the availability of drinking water the main concern – those isolated water sources (bores, tanks, creeks and the like) shown on your map may be dry or the water may be undrinkable, so you can't depend entirely on them. Also make sure you've got the necessary spare parts and bike-repair knowledge. Check with locals if you're heading into remote areas, and let someone know where you're headed before setting off.

Hire

The rates charged by most outfits for renting road or mountain bikes (not including the discounted fees offered by budget accommodation places to their guests) are anywhere between $8 to $12 per hour and $18 to $40 per day. Security deposits can range from $50 to $200, depending on the rental period.

Purchase

If you arrive in Australia without a set of wheels and want to buy a new road cycle or mountain bike that won't leave a trail of worn-out or busted metal parts once it leaves the city limits, your starting point (and we mean your absolute bottom-level starting point) is $400 to $500. To set yourself up with a new bike, plus all the requisite on-the-road equipment such as panniers, helmet etc, your starting point becomes $1500 to $2000. Second-hand bikes are worth checking out in the cities, as are the post-Christmas sales and mid-year stocktakes, which is when newish bicycles can be heavily discounted.

Your best bet for re-selling your bike is the **Trading Post** (☎ 1300 138 016; www.trading post.com.au), which is distributed in newspaper form in urban centres around Australia, and which also has a busy online trading site.

BOAT

There's a hell of a lot of water around Australia but unless you're fortunate enough to hook up with a yacht, it's not a feasible way of getting around.

BUS

Australia's extensive bus network is a relatively cheap and reliable way to get around, though it can be a tedious form of transport at times and requires planning if you intend to do more than straightforward city-to-city trips. Most buses are equipped with air-con, toilets and videos, and all are smoke-free zones. The smallest towns eschew formal bus terminals for a single drop-off/pick-up point, usually outside a post office, newsagent or shop.

It may look like there are two national bus networks, **McCafferty's** (☎ 13 14 99; www.mc caffertys.com.au) and **Greyhound Pioneer** (☎ 13 20 30; www.greyhound.com.au), but McCafferty's took over Greyhound a few years ago and consequently the tickets, terminals and passes of both companies are interchangeable. Despite this, both brand names continue to be used, which is why we refer to 'McCafferty's/ Greyhound' throughout this guidebook. Fares purchased online are roughly 5% cheaper than over-the-counter tickets.

Smaller regional operators running key routes or covering a lot of ground are listed as follows:

Countrylink (☎ 13 22 32; www.countrylink.info) Runs a rail and coach network in NSW.
Fearnes Coaches (☎ 02-6921 2316; www.fearnes.com.au) Runs between Sydney, Canberra and Wagga Wagga.
Firefly Express (☎ 1300 730 740; www.fireflyexpress .com.au) Runs between Sydney, Melbourne and Adelaide.
Murrays Coaches (☎ 13 22 51; www.murrays.com.au) Runs between Sydney and Canberra.
Port Stephens Coaches (☎ 02-4982 2940) Runs between Sydney and Port Stephens and Newcastle.
Premier Motor Service (☎ 13 34 10) Runs between Sydney and Melbourne along the east coast.

Bus Passes

The following McCafferty's and Greyhound passes can be used on either bus service. There's a 10% discount for members of YHA, VIP, Nomads and other approved organisations, as well as card-carrying seniors/pensioners.

AUSSIE EXPLORER PASS

This popular pass gives you from one to 12 months to cover a set route – there are 24 in all and the validity period depends on distance. You haven't got the go-anywhere flexibility of the Kilometre Pass (you can't backtrack), but if you can find a route that suits you it generally works out cheaper.

The Central Coaster Pass covers the east coast north of Sydney to Brisbane and costs $163.

AUSSIE KILOMETRE PASS

This is the simplest pass and gives you a specified amount of travel, starting at 2000km ($321) and going up in increments of 1000km to a maximum of 20,000km ($2258). The pass is valid for 12 months and you can travel where and in what direction you like, and stop as many times as you like.

Backpacker Buses

While the companies offering transport options for budget travellers in various parts of Australia are pretty much organised-tour operators, they do also get you from A to B (sometimes with hop-on, hop-off services) and so can be a cost-effective alternative to the big bus companies. The buses are usually smaller, you'll meet lots of other travellers, and the drivers sometimes double as tour guides; conversely, some travellers find the tour-group mentality and inherent limitations don't suit them. Discounts for card-carrying students and members of hostel organisations are regularly available.

Autopia Tours (☎ 1800 000 507, 03-9326 5536; www.autopiatours.com.au) has a three-day Melbourne to Sydney tour goes via the Snowy Mountains, Canberra and the Blue Mountains ($180).

Oz Experience (☎ 1300 300 028, 02-8356 1766; www.ozexperience.com) is a hop-on hop-off service you'll either love or hate. Many travellers complain they can't get a seat on the bus of their choice and are left on stand-by lists for days, or summarise it as a party bus for younger travellers, while others rave about it as a highly social experience. The country's biggest backpacker bus network, it covers central and eastern Australia. Travel is one-directional and passes are valid for six months with unlimited stops. A Sydney–Darwin pass via Melbourne, Adelaide and Alice Springs is $1030; Sydney–Cairns is $390.

Classes

There are no separate classes on buses, and the vehicles of the different companies all look pretty similar and are equipped with air-con, toilets and videos. Smoking isn't permitted on Australian buses.

Costs

Following are the average, non-discounted, one-way bus fares on some well-travelled routes through NSW.

Destination	Adult/child/concession
Sydney–Brisbane	$90/75/85
Sydney–Canberra	$35/30/30
Sydney–Melbourne	$65/55/60

Reservations

Over summer, school holidays and public holidays, you should book well ahead on the more popular routes, including inter-city and east-coast services. At other times you should have few problems getting on to your preferred service. But if your long-term travel plans rely on catching a particular bus, book at least a day or two ahead just to be safe.

You should make a reservation at least a day in advance if you're using a McCafferty's/Greyhound pass.

CAR & MOTORCYCLE

NSW ranges from the built-up east coast to the sparsely populated interior where public transport is often neither comprehensive nor convenient, and sometimes nonexistent. Many travellers find that the best way to see the place is to buy a car, and it's certainly the only way to get to those interesting out-of-the-way places without taking a tour.

Motorcycles are another popular way of getting around. The climate is good for bikes for much of the year, and the many small trails from the road into the bush lead to perfect spots to spend the night. Bringing your own motorcycle into Australia will entail an expensive shipping exercise, valid registration in the country of origin and a *Carnet De Passages en Douanes*. This is an internationally recognised customs document that allows the holder to import their vehicle without paying customs duty or taxes. To get one, apply to a motoring organisation/association in your home country. You'll also need a rider's licence and a helmet. The long, open roads are really made for large-capacity machines above 750cc, which Australians prefer once they outgrow their 250cc learner restrictions.

The **Roads & Traffic Authority** (RTA; ☎ 13 22 13; www.rta.nsw.gov.au) is NSW's government body in charge of roads. It provides a wealth of information on road rules and conditions. It has a downloadable brochure in several languages that summarises Australian road rules for foreigners.

SYDNEY TO MELBOURNE VIA THE PRINCES HWY

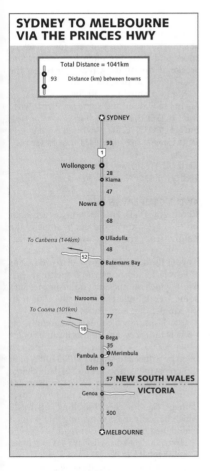

Total Distance = 1041km

93   Distance (km) between towns

SYDNEY

93

1

Wollongong
28
Kiama

47

Nowra

68

To Canberra (144km)   Ulladulla
48
52   Batemans Bay

69

Narooma
To Cooma (101km)
77

18   Bega
35
Pambula   Merimbula
19
Eden

57 **NEW SOUTH WALES**
Genoa   **VICTORIA**

500

MELBOURNE

Automobile Associations

In NSW and ACT, the **National Roads & Motorists Association** (NRMA; ☎ 13 11 22; www.nrma .com.au) provides emergency services when breakdowns occur, literature, excellent touring maps and detailed guides to accommodation and camping grounds.

NRMA has reciprocal arrangements with other states in Australia and with similar organisations overseas. So if you're a member of the AAA in the USA, or the RAC or AA in the UK, you can use any of the NRMA's facilities. Bring proof of membership.

Driving Licence

You can generally use your own home-country's driving licence in Australia, as long as it's in English (if it's not, you'll need a certified translation) and has your photograph for identification. Confusingly, some states prefer that you have an **International Driving Permit** (IDP), which must be supported by your home licence. It's easy enough to get an IDP – just go to your home country's automobile association and they issue it on the spot. The permits are valid for 12 months.

Fuel & Spare Parts

Fuel (super, diesel and unleaded) is available from service stations sporting the well-known international brand names. LPG (gas) is not always stocked at more remote roadhouses – if you're on gas, it's safer to have dual fuel capacity. Prices vary from place to place and from price war to price war, but basically fuel is heavily taxed and prices continue to climb. Unleaded petrol is now hovering around 90c to $1. Once you get out into the country, prices soar to $1.40 or more. Note that in rural NSW petrol stations may be 150km or more apart.

The further you get from the cities, the better it is to be in a Holden or a Ford – if you're in an older vehicle that's likely to require a replacement part, life is much simpler if it's a make for which spare parts are more readily available. See also Road Conditions, p382.

Hire

Competition between car-rental companies in Australia is pretty fierce, so rates tend to be variable and lots of special deals come and go. The main thing to remember when assessing your options is distance – if you want to travel far, you need unlimited kilometres.

As well as the big firms, there are a vast number of local firms, or firms with outlets in a limited number of locations. These are almost always cheaper than the big operators – sometimes half the price – but cheap car hire can often come with serious restrictions.

The major companies offer a choice: either unlimited kilometres, or 100km or so a day free, plus so many cents per kilometre over this. Daily rates in cities or on the east coast are typically about $55 to $60 a day for a small car, about $65 to $80 a day for a medium car, or $85 to $100 a day for a big car, all including insurance. You must be at least 21 years old to hire from most firms –

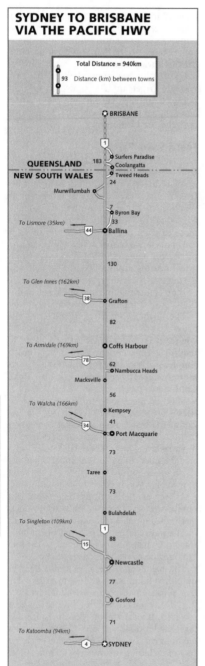

SYDNEY TO BRISBANE VIA THE PACIFIC HWY

Total Distance = 940km

93 | Distance (km) between towns

BRISBANE

1

Surfers Paradise
183 | Coolangatta
Tweed Heads
QUEENSLAND
NEW SOUTH WALES
24

Murwillumbah

7
Byron Bay
33
To Lismore (35km)
44 | Ballina

130

To Glen Innes (162km)
38 | Grafton

82

To Armidale (169km)
Coffs Harbour
78 | 62
Nambucca Heads
Macksville

56
To Walcha (166km)
Kempsey
34 | 41
Port Macquarie

73

Taree

73

Bulahdelah
To Singleton (109km)
1
15 | 88

Newcastle

77

Gosford

71
To Katoomba (94km)
4 | SYDNEY

if you're under 25 you may only be able to hire a small car or have to pay a surcharge. It's much cheaper if you rent for a week or more and there are often low-season and weekend discounts. Credit cards are the usual payment method.

Major companies all have offices or agents in Sydney and some smaller towns.

Avis (☎ 13 63 33; www.avis.com.au)
Budget (☎ 1300 362 848; www.budget.com.au)
Delta Europcar (☎ 1800 030 118; www.deltaeuropcar .com.au)
Hertz (☎ 13 30 39; www.hertz.com.au)
Thrifty (☎ 13 61 39; www.thrifty.com.au)

4WD & CAMPERVAN HIRE

Renting a 4WD enables you to get right off the beaten track and out to some of the natural wonders that most travellers miss. Something small like a Suzuki Vitara or Toyota Rav4 costs $85 to $100 per day. For a Toyota Landcruiser you'll spend at least $150, which should include insurance and some free kilometres (typically 100km to 200km per day, sometimes unlimited).

Check insurance conditions carefully, especially the excess amount, as it can be onerous – $5000 is common, although this can often be reduced to around $1000 (or even to nil) on payment of an additional daily charge (around $50). Even for a 4WD, the insurance offered by most companies does not cover damage caused when travelling 'off-road', which basically means anything that is not a maintained bitumen or dirt road.

Hertz, Budget and Avis have 4WD rentals.

Britz Rentals (☎ 1800 331 454, 03-8379 8890; www .britz.com) hires fully equipped 4WDs fitted out as campervans. The high-season costs start from around $120 (two-berth) or $215 (four-berth) per day for a minimum hire of five days (with unlimited kilometres), but the price climbs from there; to reduce the insurance excess from $5000 to zero costs an extra $50 per day. Britz has an office in Sydney.

Insurance

In Australia, third-party personal injury insurance is always included in the vehicle registration cost, ensuring that every registered vehicle carries at least the minimum insurance. You'd be wise to extend that minimum to at least third-party property insurance as well – minor collisions with other vehicles can be amazingly expensive.

When it comes to hire cars, know exactly what your liability is in the event of an accident. Rather than risk paying out thousands of dollars if you do have an accident, you can take out your own comprehensive insurance on the car, or (the usual option) pay an additional daily amount to the rental company for an 'insurance excess reduction' policy. This brings the amount of excess you must pay in the event of an accident down from between $2000 and $5000 to a few hundred dollars.

Be aware that if you're travelling on dirt roads you will not be covered by insurance even if you have a 4WD – in other words, if you have an accident you'll be liable for all the costs involved. Also, most companies' insurance won't cover the cost of damage to glass (including the windscreen) or tyres. Always read the small print.

Outback Travel

In western NSW there are plenty of roads and trails that bring new meaning to the phrase 'off the beaten track'.

While you may not need 4WD or fancy expedition equipment to tackle most of these roads, you do need to be carefully prepared for the loneliness and lack of facilities. Vehicles should be in good condition and have reasonable ground clearance. Always carry a tow rope so that some passing good Samaritan can pull your broken-down car to the next garage.

When travelling to very remote areas, such as the central deserts, it's advisable to carry a high-frequency (HF) radio transceiver equipped to pick up the relevant Royal Flying Doctor Service bases. A satellite phone and Global Positioning System (GPS) finder can also be handy. Of course, all this equipment comes at a cost, but travellers have perished in the Australian desert after breaking down.

Always carry plenty of water. In warm weather allow 5L per person per day and an extra amount for the radiator, carried in several containers.

It's wise not to attempt the tougher routes during the hottest part of the year (October to April inclusive) – apart from the risk of heat exhaustion, simple mishaps can easily lead to tragedy at this time. Conversely, there's no point going anywhere on dirt roads in the outback if there has been

> **OUTBACK ROAD SHOW**
>
> On many outback highways you'll see thundering road trains – huge trucks (a prime mover, plus two or three trailers) up to 50m long. These things don't move over for anyone and it's like something out of a *Mad Max* movie to have one bearing down on you at 120km/h. When you see a road train approaching on a narrow bitumen road, slow down and pull over – if it has to put its wheels off the road to pass you, the resulting shower of stones will almost certainly smash your windscreen. When trying to overtake one, make sure you have plenty of room to complete the manoeuvre (allow about a kilometre). Road trains throw up a lot of dust on dirt roads, so if you see one coming it's best to pull over and stop until it's gone past.
>
> And while you're on outback roads, don't forget the standard bush wave to oncoming drivers – it's simply a matter of lifting the index finger off the steering wheel to acknowledge your fellow motorist.

recent flooding. Get local advice before heading off into the middle of nowhere. For more information regarding NSW's climate see p359.

If you do run into trouble in the back of beyond, don't wander off – stay with your car. From the air, it's easier to spot a car than a human being, and you wouldn't be able to carry a heavy load of water very far anyway. Police suggest that you carry two spare tyres (for added safety) and, if stranded, try to set fire to one of them (let the air out first) – the pall of smoke will be seen for miles.

Of course, before you set out, let family, friends or your car-hire company know where you're going and when you intend to be back.

Purchase

When it comes to buying or selling a car, every state has its own regulations, particularly in regard to registration (rego). In NSW safety checks are compulsory every year when you renew the registration. Stamp duty has to be paid when you buy a car and, as this is based on the purchase price, it's not unknown for buyer and seller to agree privately to understate the price.

Note that it's much easier to sell a car in the same state that it's registered in, otherwise you (or the buyer) must re-register it in the new state, and that's a hassle.

BUY-BACK DEALS
One way of getting around the hassles of buying and selling a vehicle privately is to enter into a buy-back arrangement with a car or motorcycle dealer. However, dealers may find ways of knocking down the price when you return the vehicle (even if the price was agreed to in writing), often by pointing out expensive repairs that allegedly will be required to gain the dreaded roadworthiness certificate needed to transfer the registration.

A company that specialises in buy-back arrangements on cars and campervans is **Travellers Auto Barn** (☎ 02-9360 1500; www.travellers-autobarn.com.au), which has offices in Sydney and offers a range of vehicles. The buy-back arrangement is guaranteed in writing before you depart and the basic deal is 50% of the purchase price if you have the vehicle for eight weeks, 40% for up to six months, or 30% for up to 12 months.

Buy-back arrangements are also possible with large motorcycle dealers in major cities. They're usually keen to do business, and basic negotiating skills allied with a wad of cash (say, $8000) should secure an excellent second-hand road bike with a written guarantee that they'll buy it back in good condition minus around $2000. **Better Bikes** (☎ 02-9718 6668; www.betterbikes.com.au; 605 Canterbury Rd, Belmore) is a Sydney dealer that offers buy-back deals.

Road Conditions
NSW has few multilane highways, although there are stretches of divided road (four or six lanes) in some particularly busy areas of Sydney, although even here you will find yourself on coagulated local streets more often than you would like. Elsewhere the major roads are sealed two-laners.

You don't have to get far off the beaten track to find dirt roads. In fact, anybody who sets out to see the country in reasonable detail should expect some dirt-road travelling. And if you seriously want to explore more remote parts, you'd better plan on having a 4WD and a winch. A few basic spare parts, such as fan belts and radiator hoses, are worth carrying if you're travelling to places where traffic is light and garages are few and far between.

Motorcyclists should beware of dehydration in the dry, hot air – carry at least 5L of water on remote roads in central Australia and drink plenty of it, even if you don't feel thirsty. It's worth carrying some spares and tools even if you don't know how to use them, because someone else often does. Carry a workshop manual for your bike and spare elastic (octopus) straps for securing your gear.

The RTA (p378) can provide up-to-date road condition information.

Road Hazards
The roadkill that you unfortunately see a lot of in the outback is mostly the result of cars and trucks hitting animals during the night. Many Australians avoid travelling altogether once the sun drops because of the risks posed by animals on the roads.

Kangaroos are common hazards on country roads, as are cows and sheep in the unfenced outback – hitting an animal of this size can make a real mess of your car. Kangaroos are most active around dawn and dusk. They often travel in groups, so if you see one hopping across the road in front of you, slow right down, as its friends may be just behind it.

If you're travelling at night and a large animal appears in front of you, hit the brakes, dip your lights (so you don't continue to dazzle and confuse it) and only swerve if it's safe to do so – numerous travellers have been killed in accidents caused by swerving to miss animals.

A not-so-obvious hazard is driver fatigue. Driving long distances (particularly in hot weather) can be so tiring that you might fall asleep at the wheel – it's not uncommon and the consequences can be unthinkable. So on a long haul, stop and rest every two hours or so – do some exercise, change drivers or have a coffee.

Road Rules
Driving in NSW holds few real surprises, other than the odd animal caught in your headlights. Australians drive on the left-hand side of the road and all cars are right-hand drive. An important road rule is 'give way to the right' – if an intersection is unmarked

ROAD DISTANCES (KM)

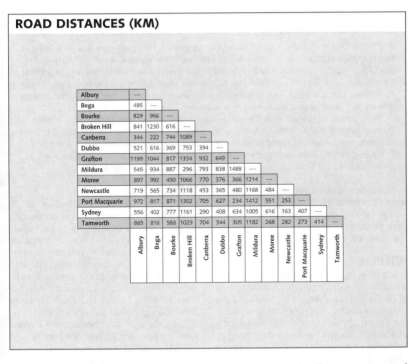

	Albury	Bega	Bourke	Broken Hill	Canberra	Dubbo	Grafton	Mildura	Moree	Newcastle	Port Macquarie	Sydney	Tamworth
Albury	---												
Bega	485	---											
Bourke	829	966	---										
Broken Hill	841	1230	616	---									
Canberra	344	222	744	1089	---								
Dubbo	521	616	369	753	394	---							
Grafton	1199	1044	817	1334	932	649	---						
Mildura	545	934	887	296	793	838	1488	---					
Moree	897	992	450	1066	770	376	366	1214	---				
Newcastle	719	565	734	1118	453	365	480	1168	484	---			
Port Macquarie	972	817	871	1302	705	627	234	1412	551	253	---		
Sydney	556	402	777	1161	290	408	634	1005	616	163	407	---	
Tamworth	865	816	588	1029	704	344	305	1182	268	282	273	414	---

(unusual), you must give way to vehicles entering the intersection from your right.

The general speed limit in built-up areas is 60km/h, although this has been reduced to 50km/h on residential streets in most states – keep an eye out for signs. Near schools, the limit is 40km/h in the morning and afternoon. On the open highway it's usually 100km/h or 110km/h. The police have speed radar guns and cameras and are fond of using them in strategically concealed locations.

Oncoming drivers who flash their lights at you may be giving you a friendly warning of a speed camera ahead – or they may be telling you that your headlights are not on. Whatever, it's polite to wave back if someone does this. Try not to get caught doing it yourself, since it's illegal.

All new cars in Australia have seat belts back and front and it's the law to wear yours – you're likely to get a fine if you don't. Small children must be belted into an approved safety seat.

Drink-driving is a real problem, especially in country areas. Serious attempts to reduce the resulting road toll are ongoing and random breath-tests are not uncommon in built-up areas. If you're caught with a blood-alcohol level of over 0.05% be prepared for a big fine and the loss of your licence.

The RTA (p378) provides a downloadable brochure in several languages that summarises Australian road rules for foreigners.

PARKING
One of the big problems with driving around Sydney (or popular tourist towns like Byron Bay) is finding somewhere to park. Even if you do find a spot, there's likely to be a time restriction, meter (or ticket machine) or both. It's one of the great rorts in Australia that by overstaying your welcome (even by five minutes) in a space that may cost only a few dollars to park in, local councils are prepared to fine you anywhere from $50 to $120. Also note that if you park in a 'clearway' your car will be towed away or clamped – look for signs. In the cities there are large multistorey car parks where you can park all day for between $10 and $25.

INTERSTATE QUARANTINE

When travelling in Australia, whether by land or air, you'll come across signs (mainly in airports, interstate train stations and at state borders) warning of the possible dangers of carrying fruit, plants and vegetables (which may be infected with a disease or pest) from one area to another. Certain pests and diseases – such as fruit fly, cucurbit thrips, grape phylloxera and potato cyst nematodes, to name a few – are prevalent in some areas but not in others and so, for obvious reasons, authorities would like to limit their spread.

There are quarantine inspection posts on some state borders and, occasionally, elsewhere. Quarantine control often relies on honesty, but many posts are staffed and officers are entitled to search your car for undeclared items. Generally they'll confiscate all fresh fruit and vegetables, so it's best to leave shopping for these items until the first town past the inspection point.

Many towns in NSW have a peculiar form of reverse-angle parking, a recipe for disaster if ever there was one. If in doubt, park your car in the same direction and at the same angle as other cars.

HITCHING

Hitching is never entirely safe in any country in the world, and we don't recommend it. Travellers who decide to hitch should understand that they are taking a small but potentially serious risk. People who do choose to hitch will be safer if they travel in pairs and let someone know where they are planning to go.

In Australia, the hitching signal can be a thumbs up, but a downward-pointed finger is more widely understood.

LOCAL TRANSPORT
Bus & Train

Sydney has a good public transport network. The **Transport Infoline** (☎ 131 500; www .131500.com.au) provides schedule and service information. In Canberra, Wollongong and Newcastle, it's also possible to get around by public transport. Anywhere else, it becomes a bit problematic. There are buses in cities such as Wagga Wagga, Nowra and Dubbo, but they're fairly infrequent.

Taxi

Sydney has a lot of taxis, but you won't see many plying for trade on the streets of country towns. That doesn't mean they aren't there – even small towns often have at least one taxi and you can find the number in a local phone book or at the tourist office.

Taxi fares vary through the state, but shouldn't differ much from Sydney.

TRAIN

Rail travel in Australia is something you do because you really want to – not because it's cheaper or more convenient, and certainly not because it's fast. That said, trains are more comfortable than buses, and on some of Australia's long-distance train journeys the romance of the rails is alive and kicking. The *Indian Pacific* across the Nullarbor Plain between Sydney and Perth is one of Australia's great rail journeys.

Long-distance interstate services in Australia are operated by **Great Southern Railways** (☎ 13 21 47, 08-8213 4592; www.gsr.com.au).

Rail services in NSW are run by the government's **Countrylink** (☎ 13 22 32; www.country link.info) which serves a variety of destinations with trains and connecting buses. Some services include destinations in Victoria and Queensland. Fairly fast trains known as XPTs serve Canberra (four hours), Wagga Wagga (six hours), Melbourne (10 hours) and Brisbane (14 hours).

Many other routes are served such as those to Byron Bay (13 hours), Broken Hill (13 hours) and Moree (seven hours) but these trains can run quite slow, and often only once a day or less.

Countrylink trains are air-conditioned and comfortable. There are usually two classes of service – first and economy – with the former offering more room and nicer seats. Food and drink are available for purchase. There are Sydney to Brisbane and Melbourne night trains, which include sleepers with twin compartments.

CityRail (☎ 13 15 00; www.cityrail.info), the Sydney metropolitan service, runs frequent commuter-style trains south through Wollongong to Bomaderry; west through the Blue Mountains to Katoomba and Lithgow;

north to Newcastle; and southwest through the Southern Highlands to Goulburn. Some services duplicate the near-Sydney portions of Countrylink services, but they're slower and much cheaper, especially if you buy a day-return ticket. Off-peak return fares are available after 9am on weekdays and all day on weekends.

Costs

Children can travel for reduced fares; advance purchase fares will save you 30% to 50%. First class costs about 40% more than economy.

Some standard one-way adult economy fares on Countrylink trains:

Destination	Fare
Sydney–Brisbane	$116
Sydney–Broken Hill	$123
Sydney–Byron Bay	$103
Sydney–Canberra	$50
Sydney–Melbourne	$116
Sydney–Moree	$90
Sydney–Wagga Wagga	$79

Reservations

As the Countrylink booking system is computerised, most stations can make a booking for most journeys. For reservations telephone ☎ 13 22 32 during office hours; this will connect you to the nearest main-line station.

You can't book seats on CityRail trains.

Train Passes

The **Great Southern Railways Pass** (☎ 13 22 32), which is only available to passport-equipped non-Australian residents, allows unlimited travel on the national rail network for a period of six months. The pass costs a meagre $590/450 per adult/concession (meagre when you consider the amount of ground you could cover over the life of the pass), but note that you'll be travelling in a 'Daynighter' reclining seat, and not a cabin. You need to pre-book all seats at least 24 hours in advance.

Countrylink (☎ 13 22 32; www.countrylink.info) offers two types of pass to foreign nationals with valid passports. The **East Coast Discovery Pass** allows one-way economy travel from Melbourne through NSW and Sydney and on to Brisbane and Cairns (in either direction) with unlimited stopovers, and is valid for six months – the full trip costs $394, while segments from Sydney to Brisbane and Sydney to Melbourne cost $94. The **Backtracker Rail Pass** allows travel on the entire Countrylink network and comes in four versions: a 14-day/1-/3-/6-month pass costing $218/250/273/383 respectively.

CityRail (☎ 13 15 00; www.cityrail.info) offers the **DayTripper Pass** (adult/child $15/7.50) good on trains buses and ferries throughout Sydney and its suburbs. The **Blue Mountains Explorer-Link** (adult/child $36/14.50) includes a day-return ticket to Katoomba and all-day access to the Explorer Bus that visits 27 attractions in the Blue Mountains.

Health Dr David Millar

Australia is a remarkably healthy country in which to travel, considering that such a large portion of it lies in the tropics. Tropical diseases such as malaria and yellow fever are unknown, diseases of insanitation such as cholera and typhoid are unheard of, and, thanks to Australia's isolation and quarantine standards, even some animal diseases such as rabies and foot-and-mouth disease have yet to be recorded.

Few travellers to NSW should experience anything worse than an upset stomach or a bad hangover, and if you do fall ill, the standard of hospitals and health care is high.

BEFORE YOU GO

Since most vaccines don't produce immunity until at least two weeks after they're given, visit a physician four to eight weeks before departure. Ask your doctor for an International Certificate of Vaccination (otherwise known as the yellow booklet), which will list all the vaccinations you've received. This is mandatory for countries that require proof of yellow-fever vaccination upon entry (sometimes required in Australia, see this page), but it's a good idea to carry it wherever you travel.

Bring medications in their original, clearly labelled containers. A signed and dated letter from your physician describing your medical conditions and medications, including generic names, is also a good idea. If carrying syringes or needles, be sure to have a physician's letter documenting their medical necessity.

If your health insurance doesn't cover you for medical expenses abroad, consider getting extra insurance; check Subwwway on www.lonelyplanet.com for more information. Find out in advance if your insurance plan will make payments directly to providers or reimburse you later for overseas health expenditures. See opposite for details of health care in NSW.

INSURANCE

Health insurance is essential for all travellers. While health care in NSW is of a high standard and not overly expensive by international standards, considerable costs can build up and repatriation is extremely expensive. If you are unsure whether your existing insurance will cover you check Subwwway on www.lonelyplanet.com for more information.

RECOMMENDED VACCINATIONS

Proof of yellow-fever vaccination is required only from travellers entering Australia within six days of having stayed overnight or longer in a yellow-fever-infected country. For a full list of these countries visit the website of the **World Health Organization** (WHO; www.who.int/wer/) or that of the **Centers for Disease Control and Prevention** (www.cdc.gov /travel/blusheet.htm).

If you're really worried about your health when travelling there are a few vaccinations you could consider for NSW. The WHO recommends that all travellers should be covered for diphtheria, tetanus, measles, mumps, rubella, chickenpox and polio, as well as hepatitis B, regardless of their destination. Planning to travel is a great time to ensure that all routine vaccination cover is complete. The consequences of these diseases can be severe and while Australia has high levels of childhood vaccination coverage, outbreaks of these diseases do occur.

HEALTH

MEDICAL CHECKLIST

- antibiotics
- antidiarrhoeal drugs (eg loperamide)
- acetaminophen/paracetamol or aspirin
- anti-inflammatory drugs (eg ibuprofen)
- antihistamines (for hay fever and allergic reactions)
- antibacterial ointment for cuts and abrasions
- steroid cream or cortisone (for poison ivy and other allergic rashes)
- bandages, gauze, gauze rolls
- adhesive or paper tape
- scissors, safety pins, tweezers
- thermometer
- pocketknife
- DEET-containing insect repellent for the skin
- permethrin-containing insect spray for clothing, tents and bed nets
- sun block
- oral rehydration salts
- iodine tablets or water filter (for water purification)

INTERNET RESOURCES

There is a wealth of travel health advice on the Internet. For further information, the **Lonely Planet website** (www.lonelyplanet.com) is a good place to start. The **WHO** (www.who.int/ith/) publishes a superb book called *International Travel & Health*, which is revised annually and is available online at no cost. Another website of general interest is **MD Travel Health** (www.mdtravelhealth.com), which provides complete travel health recommendations for every country and is updated daily.

FURTHER READING

Lonely Planet's *Healthy Travel Australia, New Zealand & the Pacific* is a handy, pocket-sized guide packed with useful information including pretrip planning, emergency first aid, immunisation and disease information

---

TRAVEL-HEALTH WEBSITES

It's usually a good idea to consult your government's travel-health website before departure, if one is available:
Australia www.dfat.gov.au/travel/
Canada www.travelhealth.gc.ca
United Kingdom www.doh.gov.uk/traveladvice/
United States www.cdc.gov/travel/

---

and what to do if you get sick on the road. *Travel with Children* from Lonely Planet also includes advice on travel health for younger children.

IN TRANSIT

DEEP VEIN THROMBOSIS (DVT)

Blood clots may form in the legs (deep vein thrombosis) during plane flights, chiefly because of prolonged immobility. The longer the flight, the greater the risk. Though most blood clots are reabsorbed uneventfully, some may break off and travel through the blood vessels to the lungs, where they could cause life-threatening complications.

The chief symptom of deep vein thrombosis is swelling or pain of the foot, ankle or calf, usually – but not always – on just one side. When a blood clot travels to the lungs, it may cause chest pain and breathing difficulties. Travellers with any of these symptoms should immediately seek medical attention.

To prevent the development of deep vein thrombosis on long flights, you should walk about the cabin, perform isometric compressions of the leg muscles (ie flex the leg muscles while sitting), drink plenty of fluids and avoid alcohol and tobacco.

JET LAG & MOTION SICKNESS

Jet lag is common when crossing more than five time zones, resulting in insomnia, fatigue, malaise or nausea. To avoid jet lag try drinking plenty of (nonalcoholic) fluids and eating light meals. Upon arrival, get exposure to natural sunlight and readjust your schedule (for meals, sleep etc) as soon as possible. Antihistamines such as dimenhydrinate and meclizine are usually the first choice for treating motion sickness. Their main side-effect is drowsiness. A herbal alternative is ginger, which works like a charm for some people.

IN NEW SOUTH WALES

AVAILABILITY & COST OF HEALTH CARE

Australia has an excellent health-care system. It is a mixture of privately run medical clinics and hospitals, and a system of public hospitals funded by the government. The Medicare system covers Australian residents for some health-care costs. Visitors from countries with which Australia has a reciprocal health-care agreement (New Zealand, the United Kingdom, the Netherlands, Sweden, Finland, Italy, Malta and Ireland) are eligible for benefits to the extent specified under the Medicare program. If you are from one of these countries, check the details before departure. In general, the agreements provide for any episode of ill-health that requires prompt medical attention. For further details visit www.health.gov.au/pubs/mbs/mbs3/medicare.htm.

There are excellent, specialised public-health facilities for women and children in Sydney.

Over-the-counter medications are available at privately owned chemists throughout NSW. These include painkillers, antihistamines for allergies and skin-care products.

You may find that medications readily available over the counter in some countries are only available in Australia by prescription. These include the oral contraceptive pill, most medications for asthma and all antibiotics. If you take medication on a regular basis bring an adequate supply and ensure you have details of the generic name as brand names may differ between countries.

In NSW it is possible to get into remote locations where there may well be a significant delay in emergency services reaching you in the event of serious accident or illness – do not underestimate the vastness between most major outback towns. An increased level of self-reliance and preparation is essential; consider taking a wilderness first-aid course, such as those offered at the **Wilderness Medicine Institute** (www.wmi.net.au); take a comprehensive first-aid kit that is appropriate for the activities planned; and ensure that you have adequate means of communication. NSW has extensive mobile phone coverage, but additional radio communications are important for remote areas. The Royal Flying Doctor Service provides an important backup for remote communities.

INFECTIOUS DISEASES
Bat lyssavirus
Related to rabies and has caused some deaths. The risk is greatest for animal handlers and vets. Rabies vaccine is effective, but the risk to travellers is very low.

Giardiasis
Widespread in the waterways around Australia. Drinking untreated water from streams and lakes is not recommended. Water filters and boiling or treating water with iodine are effective in preventing the disease. Symptoms consist of intermittent bad-smelling diarrhoea, abdominal bloating and wind. Effective treatment is available (tinidazole or metronidazole).

Meningococcal Disease
Occurs worldwide and is a risk with prolonged, dormitory-style accommodation. A vaccine exists for some types of this disease, namely meningococcal A, C, Y and W. No vaccine is presently available for the viral type of meningitis.

Ross River Fever
Widespread throughout Australia. The virus is spread by mosquitoes living in marshy areas. In addition to fever the disease causes headache, joint and muscular pains and a rash, before resolving after five to seven days.

Sexually Transmitted Diseases
Occurs at rates similar to most other Western countries. The most common symptoms are pain while passing urine and a discharge. Infection can be present without symptoms so seek medical screening after any unprotected sex with a new partner. Throughout the country, you'll find sexual health clinics in all of the major hospitals. Always use a condom with any new sexual partner. Condoms are readily available in chemists and through vending machines in many public places, including toilets.

ENVIRONMENTAL HAZARDS
Bites & Stings
MARINE ANIMALS
Marine spikes, such as those found on sea urchins, stonefish, scorpion fish, catfish and stingrays, can cause severe local pain. If this occurs, immediately immerse the affected area in hot water (as hot as can be tolerated). Keep topping up with hot water until the pain subsides and medical care can be reached. Marine stings from jellyfish such as box jellyfish also occur in Australia's tropical waters, particularly during the wet season (October to April). The box jellyfish

has an incredibly potent sting and has been known to cause fatalities. Warning signs exist at affected beaches, and stinger nets are in place at the more popular beaches. Never dive into water you have not first checked is safe with local beach life-saving representatives. 'Stinger suits' (full-body Lycra swimsuits) prevent stinging, as do wetsuits. If you are stung, first aid consists of washing the skin with vinegar to prevent further discharge of any remaining stinging cells, followed by rapid transfer to a hospital; antivenom is widely available.

SHARKS

Despite extensive media coverage, the risk of shark attack in Australian waters is no greater than in other countries with extensive coastlines. The risk of an attack from sharks on scuba divers in NSW is low. Check with local surf life-saving groups about local risks.

SNAKES

Australian snakes have a fearful reputation that is justified in terms of the potency of their venom, but unjustified in terms of the actual risk to travellers and locals. Snakes are usually quite timid in nature and in most instances will move away if disturbed. They are endowed with only small fangs, making it easy to prevent bites to the lower limbs (where 80% of bites occur) by wearing protective clothing (such as gaiters) around the ankles when bushwalking. The bite marks are small and preventing the spread of toxic venom can be achieved by applying pressure to the wound and immobilising the area with a splint or sling before seeking medical attention. Application of an elastic bandage (you can improvise with a T-shirt) wrapped firmly – but not tight enough to cut off the circulation – around the entire limb, along with immobilisation, is a life-saving first-aid measure.

SPIDERS

Australia has a number of poisonous spiders although the Sydney funnel-web is the only one to have caused a single death in the last 50 years. Redback spiders are found throughout NSW. Bites cause increasing pain at the site followed by profuse sweating and generalised symptoms. First aid includes application of ice or cold packs to the bite and transfer to hospital.

White-tailed (brown recluse) spider bites may cause an ulcer that is very difficult to heal. Clean the wound thoroughly and seek medical assistance.

Heat Illness

Very hot weather is experienced year-round in some parts of NSW. When arriving from a temperate or cold climate, remember that it takes two weeks for acclimatisation to occur. Before the body is acclimatised an excessive amount of salt is lost by perspiring, so increasing the salt in your diet is essential.

Heat exhaustion occurs when fluid intake does not keep up with fluid loss. Symptoms include dizziness, fainting, fatigue, nausea or vomiting. On observation the skin is usually pale, cool and clammy. Treatment consists of rest in a cool, shady place and fluid replacement with water or diluted sports drinks.

Heatstroke is a severe form of heat illness that occurs after fluid depletion or extreme heat challenge from heavy exercise. This is a true medical emergency with heating of the brain leading to disorientation, hallucinations and seizures. Prevention is by maintaining an adequate fluid intake to ensure the continued passage of clear and copious urine, especially during physical exertion.

A number of unprepared travellers die from dehydration each year in outback Australia. This can be prevented by following these simple rules:

- Carry sufficient water for any trip, including extra in case of breakdown.
- Always let someone, such as the local police, know where you are going and when you expect to arrive.
- Carry communications equipment of some form.
- In nearly all cases it is better to stay with the vehicle rather than walking for help.

Hypothermia

Hypothermia is a significant risk, especially during the winter months in the southern alpine region of NSW. Despite the absence of high mountain ranges, strong winds produce a high chill factor that can result in hypothermia in even moderately cool temperatures. Early signs include the inability to perform fine movements (such as doing

HEALTH

up buttons), shivering and a bad case of the 'umbles' (fumbles, mumbles, grumbles, stumbles). The key elements of treatment include changing the environment to one where heat loss is minimised, changing out of any wet clothing, adding dry clothes with wind- and waterproof layers, adding insulation and providing fuel (water and carbohydrate) to allow shivering, which builds the internal temperature. In severe hypothermia, shivering actually stops – this is a medical emergency requiring rapid evacuation in addition to the above measures.

Insect-Borne Illness

Various insects can be a source of irritation. Protection from mosquitoes, sandflies, ticks and leeches can be achieved by a combination of the following strategies:

- Wearing loose, long-sleeved clothing.
- Application of 30% DEET on all exposed skin, repeating application every three to four hours.
- Impregnation of clothing with permethrin (an insecticide that kills insects but is completely safe for humans).

Surf Beaches & Drowning

NSW has some exceptional surf beaches. Beaches vary enormously in the slope of the underlying bottom, resulting in varying power of the surf. Check with local surf lifesaving organisations before entering the surf, and be aware of your own limitations and expertise before entering the water.

Ultraviolet Light Exposure

Australia has one of the highest rates of skin cancer in the world. Monitor exposure to direct sunlight closely. UV exposure is greatest between 10am and 4pm so avoid skin exposure during these times. Always use 30+ sunscreen, applied 30 minutes before exposure, and repeat regularly to minimise sun damage.

Water-Borne Illness

Tap water is universally safe in NSW. Increasing numbers of streams and rivers and lakes, however, are being contaminated by bugs that cause diarrhoea, making water purification essential. The simplest way of purifying water is to boil it thoroughly. Consider purchasing a water filter. It's very important when buying a filter to read the specifications, so that you know exactly what it removes from the water and what it doesn't. Simple filtering will not remove all dangerous organisms, so if you cannot boil water it should be treated chemically. Chlorine tablets will kill many pathogens, but not some parasites such as giardia and amoebic cysts. Iodine is more effective in purifying water and is available in tablet form. Follow the directions carefully and remember that too much iodine can be harmful.

David Millar is a travel medicine specialist, diving doctor and lecturer in wilderness medicine who graduated in Hobart, Tasmania. He has worked in all states of Australia (except the Northern Territory) and as an expedition doctor with the Maritime Museum of Western Australia, accompanying a variety of expeditions around Australia, including the Pandora wreck in Far North Queensland and Rowley Shoals off the northwest coast. David is currently a Medical Director with The Travel Doctor in Auckland.

Glossary

ACT – Australian Capital Territory
arvo – afternoon

back o' Bourke – back of beyond; middle of nowhere
barbie – barbecue
beaut, beauty – great; fantastic
bikies – motorcyclists
billabong – waterhole in a riverbed formed by waters receding in the dry season
billy – tin container used to boil water in the *bush*
bitumen – surfaced road
black stump – where the *back o' Bourke* begins
bloke – man
blokey – exhibiting characteristics considered typically masculine
blow flies – large flies
blowies – see *blow flies*
blue – argument or fight ('have a blue')
body board – half-sized surfboard
bogan – young, unsophisticated person
boogie board – see *body board*
booze bus – police van used for breath-testing for alcohol
bottle shop – liquor shop; off-licence
brekky – breakfast
bush, the – country; anywhere away from the city
bush tucker – native foods
bushie – a person who lives in the bush
bushwalking – hiking
BYO – bring your own; a restaurant license that permits customers to drink alcohol they have purchased elsewhere

cask wine – wine packaged in a plastic bladder surrounded by a cardboard box (a great Australian invention)
chocka – completely full; from 'chock-a-block'
chook – chicken
chuck a U-ey – make a U-turn; turn a car around within a road
corroboree – Aboriginal festival or gathering for ceremonial or spiritual reasons
cozzie – swimming costume
crook – ill or substandard
cuppa – as in cuppa tea, an outback institution, especially when combined with a yarn

dag – dirty lump of wool at back end of a sheep; also an affectionate or mildly abusive term for a socially inept person
didgeridoo – wind instrument made from a hollow piece of wood, traditionally played by Aboriginal men
dinkum – honest or genuine; *true blue*
dob in – to inform on someone

donga – small, transportable building widely used in the *outback*
Dreamtime – complex concept that forms the basis of Aboriginal spirituality, incorporating the creation of the world and the spiritual energies operating around us; 'Dreaming' is often the preferred term as it avoids the association with time
drongo – worthless or stupid person
dunny – outdoor lavatory

earbash – to talk nonstop
Esky – large insulated box for keeping food and drinks cold

fair dinkum – see *dinkum*
flog – sell; steal
fossick – hunt for gems or semiprecious stones

galah – noisy parrot, thus noisy idiot
game – brave ('game as Ned Kelly')
g'day – good day; traditional Australian greeting
grazier – sheep or cattle farmer operating on a large scale
grouse – very good

homestead – residence of a *station* owner or manager
how are ya? – standard greeting (expected answer: 'Good, thanks, how are you?')

iffy – dodgy, questionable

jackaroo – male trainee on an *outback station*
jillaroo – female trainee on an *outback station*

kali – jumbo-sized boomerang
kick the bucket – to die
knackered – broken, tired
Kombi – a classic (hippies') type of van made by Volkswagon

lair – layabout; ruffian
larrikin – hooligan; mischievous youth
lay-by – to put a deposit on an article so the shop will hold it for you
lob in – drop in (to see someone)
lollies – sweets, candy
loo – toilet

mate – general term of familiarity, whether you know the person or not
milk bar – small shop selling milk and other basic provisions
Mod Oz – modern Australian cuisine influenced by a wide range of foreign cuisines, but with a definite local flavour
mozzies – mosquitoes

no worries! – no problems! That's OK!

ocker – uncultivated or boorish Australian; a derider
outback – remote part of the *bush, back o' Bourke*

PADI – Professional Association of Diving Instructors
piss – beer; see also *take the piss*
piss up – boozy party
pissed – drunk
pissed off – annoyed
plonk – cheap wine
pokies – poker machines
Pom – English person

reckon! – you bet! Absolutely!
rego – (car) registration
rellie – (family) relative
rip – a strong ocean current or undertow
road train – semitrailer truck towing several trailers
root – to have sexual intercourse
rubbish – to deride or tease

sanger – sandwich
schooner – large beer glass
sealed road – bitumen road
session – lengthy period of heavy drinking
shark biscuit – inexperienced surfer
sheila – woman

she'll be right – no problems; no worries
shellacking – comprehensive defeat
shout – to buy a round of drinks ('Your shout!')
sickie – day off work ill (or malingering)
station – large farm
stickybeak – nosy person
stroppy – bad-tempered
stubby – 375ml bottle of beer
swag – canvas-covered bed roll used in the *outback*; also a large amount

take the piss – deliberately tell someone an untruth, often as social sport; see also *piss*
tea – evening meal
true blue – honest or genuine; *dinkum*
tucker – food

unsealed road – dirt road
ute – utility; a pick-up truck

walkabout – lengthy walk away from it all
whinge – to complain or moan
wobbly – disturbing, unpredictable behaviour ('throw a wobbly')
woomera – stick used by Aborigines to propel spears

yabbie – small freshwater crayfish
yobbo – uncouth, aggressive person

Behind the Scenes

THIS BOOK

This is the 4th edition of *New South Wales*. The first edition was written way back in 1994, with a youthful Jon Murray covering the entire state on his own. Tom Smallman and David Willett updated the 2nd edition and a larger team (Paul Harding, Michelle Bennett, Andrew Draffen and Sally Webb) did the third. This edition we've increased the team size yet again, with Ryan Ver Berkmoes (coordinating author), Sally O'Brien, Miriam Raphael, Paul Smitz, Rick Starey, Justine Vaisutis and Lucas Vidgen doing the hard yards on the ground. Australia's leading environmental scientist, Tim Flannery, wrote the Environmental Challenges boxed text in the Environment chapter, and Dr David Millar wrote the Health chapter. For their work on the Food & Drink and The Culture chapters Ryan is indebted to the help of Matthew Evans and Verity Campbell.

THANKS from the Authors

Ryan Ver Berkmoes First, big thanks to the irreplaceable Virginia Maxwell for giving me the idea to do this book. Thanks also to Errol for sending me on my way and Kalya Ryan for closing the deal. My co-authors on this book were a delightful and (most importantly!) timely lot. Thanks to Sally O'Brien for her wicked wit, as well as Justine Vaisutis, Rick Starey, Lucas Vidgen and Paul Smitz. Miriam Raphael bought me coffee when I needed it most. In Sydney, thanks go to Jane Mathews for her voluminous tutoring on local wines. And big thanks to Erin Corrigan, who really knows what it means to get the sand out of your shorts.

Sally O'Brien Thank you to Astrid Friedrichs for a room of my own in Balmain; mum for mailing whatever it is I leave behind whenever I visit; dad for tipping me off about the Hollywood Hotel; Jen Strugar for swimming company at Andrew 'Boy' Charlton Pool, home-cooked meals and laughs; Annette Primero for eurostyle expeditions into deepest Double Bay; Helen Dunphy for all her great tips and advice; Gerard Walker for kindness and support as I worked far from home; all the old friends who were prepared to revisit past haunts and sample new ones; the staff at various visitor centres for reams of information; coordinating author Ryan Ver Berkmoes, and the hardworking folk at Lonely Planet (Errol Hunt, Maryanne Netto, Csanad Csutoros and Jackey Coyle).

Miriam Raphael Biggest, hugest, most massive thanks to dad, who was my editor and rock, right to the bitter end. Thanks also to mum, my co-driver and whip-cracker! *Grazie mille* Angela – Griffith should thank you! Cheers to Belle Rattigan for introducing me to Hilary Rogers who was the one who made me email Cathy Lanigan who subsequently handed me over to Errol Hunt! Thanks also to the crew at Martin Smith's Bookshop, Bondi. To Ian Perkins, Michelle Hush and all the people in the far west of NSW who are putting so much into their communities in such difficult times, your optimism and energy is inspiring – I wish you only the best. But most of all, big up to my niece, Tess Scarlet, whose birth means Wagga Wagga will always have a place in my heart!

THE LONELY PLANET STORY

The story begins with a classic travel adventure: Tony and Maureen Wheeler's 1972 journey across Europe and Asia to Australia. There was no useful information about the overland trail then, so Tony and Maureen published the first Lonely Planet guidebook to meet a growing need.

From a kitchen table, Lonely Planet has grown to become the largest independent travel publisher in the world, with offices in Melbourne (Australia), Oakland (USA), London (UK) and Paris (France).

Today Lonely Planet guidebooks cover the globe. There is an ever-growing list of books and information in a variety of media. Some things haven't changed. The main aim is still to make it possible for adventurous travellers to get out there – to explore and better understand the world.

At Lonely Planet we believe travellers can make a positive contribution to the countries they visit – if they respect their host communities and spend their money wisely.

Paul Smitz Thank you to all the people who helped me during the research and writing of the ACT chapter, including those who did Internet research and silly dances around the living room, let me play with their goldfish, argued with me in a restaurant, cooked meatballs, put a python over my shoulders, kicked my arse at *Grand Theft Auto*, discussed the evolution of morality, invited me into a circus tent, helped me rediscover *that* pub, bought me something vaguely orange in a glass, and crapped on about something to do with style. In other words, thanks Katie, Adrian & Lee, Judy, Josie & Carlos, Mandy & Michael, Stephen, Tom, Kathryn, Jane, Kalya, and Errol.

Rick Starey Cheers to beers Richard Plunkett, you're an inspiration and a true legend. Thanks to Cathy Lanigan and Errol Hunt for taking the punt. Madre, wouldn't have gone close without you, superb performance. Dad, you were critical, astute and great. Tia, you're tireless, fresh and sensational, *muchas gracias*. TezDOG and Kit, just the break I needed up *that* magnificent road, cheers. Jimmy, thanks for an indispensable insight into surfing NSW. Much appreciation to the staff of information centres who handled my questions with humour and enthusiasm. A massive cheers and much love to all the travellers who shared their experiences with me; Dave Wilson, for your time and a great story; Brian Cleary, a man of the road; Nicola Charles, you started this; and Boydy for having faith and advice.

Justine Vaisutis My biggest thank you for this project goes to my partner in crime – Alan Murphy, without whose driving, commentary, singing, companionship and overwhelming support, this job simply would not have been as much fun. Big thanks go to my mum and stepfather, Bill, for enabling me to exploit the beautiful NSW south coast every summer and all the times in between, and to Dame and Heidi for my initial taste of the Central Coast. Thank you also to Kaye for being so flexible for me, and to Amber and Rita, who put in plenty of hours at Amnesty International to cover for me in my absence.

Lucas Vidgen Special thanks to Emma and Nicolas Chavanne, Jo Hearnes, Kirsty Arnison, Andy C, Crazy Nick and Nath, Caramel Cam, Dr Crome and the anonymous guy who put me onto deep fried Mars Bars. I am forever in your debt, kind stranger.

CREDITS

New South Wales 4 was commissioned and developed in Lonely Planet's Melbourne office by Errol Hunt, with assistance from Susie Ashworth. Series publishing manager Susan Rimmerman and regional publishing managers Virginia Maxwell and Kate Cody oversaw the development of this guide. Cartography was developed by Corie Waddell, and the project was managed by Chris Love, with some timely help from Ray Thomson.

This book was coordinated by Maryanne Netto (editorial), Csanad Csutoros (cartography) and Adam Bextream (layout). Maryanne was assisted by Andrea Baster, Jackey Coyle, Melanie Dankel, Emily Coles, Thalia Kalkipsakis, Monique Choy, Brooke Lyons, Nancy Ianni, David Andrew, Emma Koch, Gina Tsarouhas and Kate McLeod. Many thanks to Darren O'Connell and Carolyn Boicos for eagle-eyed assistance throughout.

Csanad was assisted by Sarah Sloane, Laurie Mikkelsen, Hunor Csutoros, Karen Fry, Marion Byass, Kim McDonald, Tony Fanhauser, Celia Wood, Simon Tillema and Piotr Czajkowski. Helping Adam Bextream were Jacqui Saunders, Yvonne Bischofberger and Sonya Brooke. A big thanks to Kate McDonald and Sally Darmody, who oversaw layout; and to Carol Chandler and Graham Imeson from print production.

Daniel New designed the cover and Wendy Wright prepared the artwork.

THANKS from Lonely Planet
Many thanks to the travellers who used the last edition and contacted us with helpful hints, useful advice and interesting anecdotes:

A Anne Sissel Aaboen, Poppy Abbott, Joanna Abrahams, Adele Adair, Amir Aharon, Ellie Ahern, Julie Alexander, Caroline Alison, Rebecca Alsbury, Ricardo Costa Alves, Josie Amadon-Bedfond, Chritian Amon, Coral Anderson, Roderic Anderson, Betty Anido, Katie Armitage, Margaret Armour, Ian Arnold, Len Ashworth, John Atwood **B** Yvonne Backerra, Chris Bagley, Dave Baker, Andy Bakx, Sue Barnett, Elizabeth Basnight, Cris Bastianello, Elise Batchelor, Brett Baxter, Susie Beard, Sandra Beer, Sabrina Bekeschus, Maria & Tony Benfield, Julien Benney, Ilse Benthem, Auke Berenbroek, Theo & Marga van der Berg, Lisa Beringer, Bob & Jessica Berryman, Melanie Bettle, Lisa Bisgaard, Christian Blockhaus, Kerstin Blomqvist, Bev Blythe, Wendy Blythe, Matt Boddy, Marie Boisvert-Smithers, John & Karen Bolton, Jean Philippe Bombardier, Luca Borra, Dorothy Bremner, Stephen Brennan, David Brick, Katy Bridges, Samantha Briggs, Keith Brinkworth, Terri Bromley, Matt Buchan, Karen Buchanan, Stefan Burkart, Katherine Burnie, Kat Burns, Danny Byrne **C** Stuart Cadden, Danielle Caldow, Ruth Callan, Marco Camaiti, Hayley Cameron, Scott Cameron, Jann Capstick, Frances Cario, Sam Carter, Debbie Cashmore, Helen Chalmers, Ronald Charles, Nigel Chent, Lennert Christensen, Justin Clark, Pam Clarke, Danny Clayton, Henry Clifford, Jim & Elayne Coakes, Maurice

BEHIND THE SCENES

Coffey, Daniel Cole, Steve Cole, Dina Coll, Carolyn Corr, Ciara Coughlan, Natalie Cowin, Graham Craig, David Crossley, Alan & Stephanie Cunningham **D** Leila David, Sue Davidson, Anne Davis, Ray Davis, Marcel de Jong, Paul Delicata, Max della Torre e Tasso, David Dennis, Walter Denzel, Patrick D'Haese, Jerry & Lisa Diccox, Conor Dickson, Linda Dickson, Peter Dixon, Robert Dixon, Pia Dollmann, Emily Dommel, Katy Donnelly, John Michael Dovey, Nicola Downey, Brenda Drinkwater, N Duff, N & Jassie Duff, Jane Dunn, Derek Dupuis, Terence Durrant **E** Vicky Eaves, Jens Ebert, Roger Paul Edmonds, Chritian Egelseer, Sarina Eliyakim, Roz Elliot, Sarah Ellis, Bruce Evans **F** Chris Farber, Rowan Feldberg, Charles Fellowes, Julia Fiedler, Bethany Field, Simon Fielder, Wendy Firks, Serena Fischer, Peter Fiskerk-Skjolda, Scott Fitzjohn, Cassy Fleet, Rosie Fleming, Pam Foster, Claudia Fregiehn, Suzanne French, Kathy Friend, Lou Fyfe **G** Sarah Gallagher, Marie-France Gara, Jason Garman, Aiden Garrison, Ed Gee, Mark Geijsel, Markus Geissler, Suzanne Genever, Terry George, Trish George, Dave Gerrish, Arne C Gerson, Anna Gigante, Angelene Gill, Stephen Gilligan, Selina Gladstone-Thompson, Anne Glazier, Linda Goenen, Andrew Goffe, Nadine Golding, Jan Christoph Goldschmidt, Mark Gomm, Nick Goold, Ross Graeme, Sarah Gratton, Kerry Gray, Debbie Green, Natalie Greenway, Philipp Grefer, Nicola Grint, Andrea Grossmann, Annette Grossschmidt, Jim Grubb, Megan Grudem **H** Edward Haig, Tim Haldenby, Burton & Garran Hall, Tanja Hallich, Peter Hamblett, Kim Hamblin, Andrea Haniger, Rhian Harding, Liz Hardy, Joe Hartshorn, Cherise Haslam, Claudia Hauser, J Hawke, John Hedges, Gen Hemmer, T Henderson, Lisa Hepplewhite, Nicole Hermanns, Allison Herriott, L Hertog, Anne Hillie, Harry Hirschowitz, Rob Hocking, Sean Hocking, Geoff & Carol Hodgson, Dirk van der Hoek, Jane Holden, Lorna Holden, Margaret Hollis, Yaron Horing, Emily Horles, Gwyneth Horles, Dawn Horridge, Allison Horsfell, Pia Hotstad, Maren Hubbard, Alexandra Hubl, Nick Humble, Jan Hyde **I** Peter Iblher, Susan Irwin **J** Sally Jackson, Anette Faye Jacobsen, Jennifer Jamie, Dany Janssens, Ebban Jenkins, Nancy Jenkins, Melissa Jensen, Kristina Johansen, Sabine Johnen, Brook Johnson, Michele Johnson, Sharon Johnson, David Jones, Leanne Jones, Marion Juenger, Tim Julou, Tamara Jungwirth **K** Joy Kanz, Ute Kardinahl, Kaja Karlsen, Alistair Kelly, Irene Kelly, Kristel & Filip Kennis-Verbeek, Anthony Keogh, Silke Kerwick, Nabeel KHuweis, Tom Kleijwegt, Maureen Klijn, Silke Kluge, Oli Kneer, Deborah Koch, Lindsay Koehler, Jasper Kok, Silke Korbl, Frank Koslowski, Hannes Krall, Sandra Kruizenga, Kim Kuijltjes, Ingrid Kuipers, Sebastian Kvist **L** Lisa Laird, Garry & Carol Larkin, Julie Larkin, Rebecca Larratt, Carl Lauren, June Laux, John Lawlor, Thomas J LeCompte, Sue Lee, Victoria Lee, Peerapong Lekrungruangkit, Birgit Lenne, Clare Lennon, Joerg Lenz, Oeghan Lewis, R Lewis, Steven Lim, Derrick Little, Chris Lloyd, Tom Lloyd, Pete Long, Sonya Longfield, William Longland, Karine Louis-Jacques, Jane Lovell, Joanne Lowe, Laurel Lowe, Jonathan Ludgate, Robyn Ludwig, Francis Lyons **M** Gary MacDonald, Lorna macgougan, Julie Macklin, Susanne Macys, Annelies & Karolien Maes, Norm and Mary Mainland, Mary Male, Mary Maley, Dave Malleson, Norman & Vera Mangold, Vincent Mans, Peter Mansell, Celine

Marchbank, Anita Marchesani, Pam Martin, Studley Martin, Valerie Marx, Lisa Masters, Michaela Matross, A W Matthews, Peter Matthews, Susi Mattis, Richard Mayo, Kerry McArthur, Roy McCammont, Tony McCann, Melodee McCoy-James, Nathan McDonnell, Zina McIlraith, Gill and Neil McKay, Denni McKenzie, Doug McKenzie, Kat Mclean, Tony McLeod, Colleen McMahon, Andy McNiven, James McPhee, Maxine McTavish, Lisa Meingassner, Jody Metcalfe, Alexandra & Beverly Meyer, Tom Miller, Gillian Millett, Kelly Mitchell, Monique Moll, Silje Molvaer, Julie Morissete, Alan Morrison, Jo Mulholland, Thomas Munday, Natalie & Shane Mundy, Fiona Murphy, Lyn Murphy **N** Steve Nagle, Rani Nandan, Roderick Neilsen, Sue & Steve Neilson, Collette Neville, Jennifer Nevius, Janet Newman, Linden News, Helen Newton, Mark Nibbles, Per Nilsson, James Norman **O** Sarah O`Rourke, Elizabeth O'Brien, Christine O'Connell, Mark Oleniuk, Lesley Oliver, Sara Olliff, Suzanne Owen **P** Richard Palk, Gary Palmer, J D K Park, James Parry, Fiona Paterson, Christian Patteson, Pam Payne, Simon Payne, Toni Payne, Vivienne Payne, R N Peachey, Tamsyn Pearson, Fiona Peck, Brad Pedersen, Camilla Kragh Pedersen, Lena Pedersen, John Penlington, Scott Phillips, Nicholas Phoon, Chris Pickles, Esther Poelwijk, Bill Poiry, Nina Pool, Jackie Poole, Jeanette Pope, Joe Potter, Wendy Powell, Irena Predalic, Fiona K Priestley, Erin Prior, Helen Proud, Paul Prowting, Claire Pulker, Michael Pulman **Q** Caroline Quirk **R** David Rand, Terry Reading, Karen Redman, Bob Reed, Jennifer Regan, Mark Regan, Ian Reid, Anne Reilly, Marianne Reimann, Michael Reuter, Nick Rhodes, Anne Richardson, Paul Richardson, K Richmond, Sandra Richmond, Dennis Rijnbeek, Zoe Rimmer,

SEND US YOUR FEEDBACK

We love to hear from travellers – your comments keep us on our toes and help make our books better. Our well-travelled team reads every word on what you loved or loathed about this book. Although we cannot reply individually to postal submissions, we always guarantee that your feedback goes straight to the appropriate authors, in time for the next edition. Each person who sends us information is thanked in the next edition – and the most useful submissions are rewarded with a free book.

To send us your updates – and find out about LP events, newsletters and travel news – visit our award-winning website: **www.lonelyplanet.com**.

We may edit, reproduce and incorporate your comments in Lonely Planet products such as guidebooks, websites and digital products, so let us know if you don't want your comments reproduced or your name acknowledged. For a copy of our privacy policy visit www.lonelyplanet.com/privacy.

Libbie Ripper, Eva Riquelme, Angus Roberts, Edel Robinson, Michelle Rostant, Arianna Rotem, Xanthe Roxburgh, Peter Roy, Vicky Rushton **S** Nancy Sader, Mike & Fiona Saint, Rob & Gail Sanders, Leif Sandqvist, Andrew & Pippa Sargent, Peter Saundry, R Sayers, Odeke Schade van Westrum, Johanna Schafer, Ed Schenk, Gwen Scherer, Lori Schimenti, Ditte Schlüntz, Ute Scholl, Brad Scholz, Rene Schoute, Susanne Schroeder, Frank Schulte, Arthur Schultz, Jonas Schwartz, B J Scott, Eric Scott, Rob Scott, Matthew Scully, Maurice Sebok, Katie Sekah, Claudine Senn, Ira Sherak, Hans P Shomsaus, Michal Silber, Phil Simpson, Dag Sjoberg, Julie Slater, Anze Slosar, T & T Smallwood, Cameron Smith, Dale Smith, James Smith, Gaël Smits, Pepi Smyth, Warren Smythe, Tonia Sohns, Mavis Solomon, Emmanuelle Spadone, Gary Spinks, Nick Spokes, Saskia Sprengers, Dominique Staehli, Clare Staines, Barbara Stander, Barbara & Ivan Stander, Mark & Pamela Starnes, Simon Steele, Phil Stiffwick, Luke Stoltenberg, Neil Stopforth, Phill Stubbs, Martin Sullivan, Ken Sutherland, Peter Swan, Paul Sweet **T** Ximena Tapia, Hannah Taylor, Hanna Tettenborn, Jessica Thom, G Thompson, Jane Thompson, Scott Thompson, Sarah Thorne, Andy & Annette Tiefenbach, Cornelie Tijsseling, Helen Tingay, Iddo Toeg, Margaret Toohey, Simon Trippett, E G Trowbridge, Adrian Tschaeppeler, Karen Tsui, Theresa Tuke, Liz Turner, Barbara Tyler **U** Stuart Uren **V** Mike van de Water, Caroline & Herman van den Wall Bake, Rob van der Heijden, Bertrand Vanhees, Mara Vannes, Josine Vendrik, Chris & Judith Viney, Moi Vogel, Anja Voigtlander, Herbert Volk **W** Ida Wainschel, John Wakefield, Charlton Walker, Christoph D Walser, Jane Ward, John Ward, Adrian Warren, Carolyn Watson, Joanna Watson, Tessa Watson, Michael Weatherhead, Andrea Webb, Torsten Weickert, Sue Wells, Stephanie Wendel, Laura West, Annabel Westney, Clare White, Steve White, Helen Whitehead, Ann Whyte, Cajsa Wikstrom, Karin Wilde, Catherine Wiles, Trent Wilkes, Caroline Wilkinson, Alison Williams, Christopher Williams, David Williams, Katie Williams, Jo Wills, Bill Wills-Moren, Fiona Wilmot, Andy Wilson, Jon Wilson, M E Wilson, Stu Wilson, Markus Wirsing, Peter Wise, Jenny Wiseman, Fred Wohlers, Aileen Wolterink, Aileen & Frank Wolterink, Catherine Wood **Y** Lisa Yeates, Ian Young **Z** Yvonne Zuidam

ACKNOWLEDGMENTS

Many thanks to RailCorp for permission to use CityRail's Sydney suburban network map.

Index

INDEX

MAP LEGEND

ROUTES

Tollway	One-Way Street
Freeway	Unsealed Road
Primary Road	Street Mall/Steps
Secondary Road	Tunnel
Tertiary Road	Walking Tour
Lane	Walking Trail
Under Construction	Walking Path

TRANSPORT

Ferry	Rail
Monorail	Rail (Underground)
Bus Route	Tram

HYDROGRAPHY

River, Creek	Canal
Intermittent River	Water
Swamp	Lake (Dry)
Reef	Lake (Salt)

BOUNDARIES

State, Provincial	Regional, Suburb
Marine Park	Cliff

AREA FEATURES

Airport	Land
Area of Interest	Mall
Beach, Desert	Park
Building	Reservation
Campus	Sports
Cemetery, Christian	Urban

POPULATION

○ CAPITAL (NATIONAL)	◉ CAPITAL (STATE)
● Large City	● Medium City
○ Small City	○ Town, Village

SYMBOLS

Sights/Activities
- Beach
- Canoeing, Kayaking
- Castle, Fortress
- Christian
- Diving, Snorkeling
- Islamic
- Jewish
- Monument
- Museum, Gallery
- Picnic Area
- Point of Interest
- Pool
- Ruin
- Skiing
- Surfing, Surf Beach
- Windsurfing
- Winery, Vineyard
- Zoo, Bird Sanctuary

Eating
- Eating

Drinking
- Drinking
- Café

Entertainment
- Entertainment

Shopping
- Shopping

Sleeping
- Sleeping
- Camping

Transport
- Airport, Airfield
- Bus Station
- Cycling, Bicycle Path
- General Transport
- Taxi Rank
- Trail Head

Information
- Bank, ATM
- Embassy/Consulate
- Hospital, Medical
- Information
- Internet Facilities
- Parking Area
- Petrol Station
- Police Station
- Post Office, GPO
- Telephone
- Toilets

Geographic
- Lighthouse
- Lookout
- Mountain, Volcano
- National Park
- River Flow
- Waterfall

LONELY PLANET OFFICES

Australia
Head Office
Locked Bag 1, Footscray, Victoria 3011
☎ 03 8379 8000, fax 03 8379 8111
talk2us@lonelyplanet.com.au

USA
150 Linden St, Oakland, CA 94607
☎ 510 893 8555, toll free 800 275 8555
fax 510 893 8572, info@lonelyplanet.com

UK
72–82 Rosebery Ave,
Clerkenwell, London EC1R 4RW
☎ 020 7841 9000, fax 020 7841 9001
go@lonelyplanet.co.uk

France
1 rue du Dahomey, 75011 Paris
☎ 01 55 25 33 00, fax 01 55 25 33 01
bip@lonelyplanet.fr, www.lonelyplanet.fr

Published by Lonely Planet Publications Pty Ltd
ABN 36 005 607 983

© Lonely Planet 2004

© photographers as indicated 2004

Cover photographs: Surfers on beach, Stephen Simpson/Getty Images (front); Sydney, Chris Mellor/Lonely Planet Images (back). Many of the images in this guide are available for licensing from Lonely Planet Images: www.lonelyplanetimages.com.